WILLEM VAN KEMENADE

China, Hong Kong, Taiwan, Inc.

Willem van Kemenade was born in the Netherlands. He studied history at Nijmegen University and Chinese in Taiwan and at Leiden University. Since 1977 he has been a freelance journalist and correspondent in Beijing, Jakarta, Hong Kong, and Taiwan for the major Dutch newspaper *NRC Handelsblad*. He currently lives in Beijing.

CHINA, HONG KONG, TAIWAN, INC.

WILLEM VAN KEMENADE

Translated from the Dutch by Diane Webb

VINTAGE BOOKS

A Division of Random House, Inc.

New York

FIRST VINTAGE BOOKS EDITION, JULY 1998

Copyright © 1997 by Alfred A. Knopf, Inc.

The Afterword to the Vintage Edition was adapted from Willem van Kemenade's
article "China, Hong Kong, Taiwan: Dynamics of a New Empire," which was
written in English and published in *The Washington Quarterly* 21:2 (Spring
1998), pp. 107–122. © 1998 by the Center for Strategic and International
Studies (CSIS) and the Massachusetts Institute of Technology.

Publication has been made possible with financial support from the Foundation
for the Production and Translation of Dutch Literature.

Library of Congress Cataloging-in-Publication Data
Kemenade, Willem van.
China, Hong Kong, Taiwan, Inc. : the dynamics of a new empire /
Willem van Kemenade ; translated from the Dutch by Diane Webb.
p. cm.
Originally published: New York : Knopf, 1997.
Includes bibliographical references and index.
ISBN 0-679-77756-3
1. China.   2. Hong Kong (China).   3. Taiwan.   4. Chinese reunification question,
1949–   I. Webb, Diane.   II. Title.
DS706.K464   1998
951—dc21   98-5349
CIP

Book design by Virginia Tan

Random House Web address: www.randomhouse.com

Printed in the United States of America
10 9 8 7 6 5 4 3 2

For Phoenix and Alexander

Contents

Preface

Some people with ulterior motives have been spreading the
idea that China poses a threat to the world, while it has to
export 25 million pairs of shoes to buy one Airbus.

PEOPLE'S DAILY,
December 1995

China, Hong Kong, Taiwan, Inc. is an updated and expanded version of its
Dutch precursor, published in Amsterdam in early 1996. It contains substantial new sections on the major external events of 1996, such as the crisis
in the Taiwan Strait, Beijing's rapidly advancing preparations for the imminent takeover of Hong Kong, and the unexpected détente in U.S.-China relations resulting from the Clinton administration's shift in China policy
from inconsistent zigzagging to comprehensive engagement.

Important domestic developments, such as the further slowdown in
state enterprise reform, and the resurgence of Marxist ideology, socialist
spiritual civilization, and nationalism, have also been addressed. Less attention has been paid to the succession to the late paramount leader, Deng
Xiaoping, and the consequences of his recent death at the age of ninety-two.
The current formal party and state hierarchies have been in power since
1989, more or less guided, at least in the years immediately following the
Tiananmen crackdown, by the "invisible hand" of Deng Xiaoping. After his
last public appearance in 1994, however, Deng's influence receded into mere
symbolism. President and party leader Jiang Zemin has assumed Deng's ill-
fitting mantle of power, and the important issue now is who will replace Li
Peng, whose second constitutional term as premier of the State Council will
end in March 1998.

This book portrays and analyzes China's search for a new system, dealing with its transformation from a revolutionary Communist state obsessed
with ideology and political struggle to a more conventional developing
country, one that is trying to balance the key objectives of economic reform, social stability, and rapid growth. The Chinese people—one-fifth of
all mankind—have undeniably made great strides toward eliminating

poverty and backwardness and modernizing their economy. The implementation of measures designed to bring about this transition, however, has caused many contradictions to surface, leading to temporary reversals and undesirable phenomena, particularly all-pervasive corruption.

Since the early 1980s, extensive trade with and investment from Hong Kong—and, since the late 1980s, also Taiwan—as well as the contaminating influence of the social systems and lifestyles of these two "peripheral" Chinese territories, have played a major role in this transformation. In just twenty years, the Chinese people have evolved from "Mao-worshiping blue ants" to "nihilistic, ultra-individualistic, money-worshiping hedonists," perhaps the newest breed of "economic animals," as the Japanese were labeled at the peak of their industrial rise in the 1970s.

The relocation to the Chinese mainland of Hong Kong's and Taiwan's labor-intensive manufacturing bases, including their management skills and export know-how, has had a synergistic effect on the inexhaustible pool of cheap labor and emerging entrepreneurial talent in those areas. This has enabled the People's Republic, in less than a decade, to relinquish its impoverished autarky and join the league of major trading powers.

China is now well on its way to becoming the latest "East Asian miracle," as exemplified by Japan and the "four tigers" (South Korea, Taiwan, Hong Kong, and Singapore). One day, perhaps, it will assume the role of "mother of all tigers."

On 1 July 1997 China will resume sovereignty over Hong Kong on the basis of the "one country–two systems" formula. Although in economic and financial terms the merger can hardly fail, it is nevertheless beset with political pitfalls. During their final years of colonial rule, the British felt compelled to introduce formal democratic structures that would bolster the rule of law in Hong Kong after the Communist takeover in 1997. China wanted to maintain the status quo and keep Hong Kong a plutocracy ruled primarily by bureaucrats, bankers, and businessmen and only marginally by elected politicians. Beijing successfully mobilized the big-business community to oppose both the British and the Hong Kong Chinese democratic forces. Chinese leaders have stressed repeatedly that Hong Kong should be an "economic city," a subsidiary of "China, Inc.," and not a political city from which democracy might spread to the mainland.

The question of reunification with Taiwan is far more complex. Taiwan is a rival, alternative Chinese (sub)nation with a fully elected political system and a strong independence movement. Moreover, unlike the expiring ninety-nine-year lease of Hong Kong, there is no deadline for the return of Taiwan, and the island enjoys the (conditional) support of the United States in opposing Chinese coercion. Nonetheless, with the impending takeover of

Hong Kong, the resolution of the "Taiwan question" is moving to the top of China's national agenda.

As in Hong Kong, Beijing has managed to sow discord between the government of Taiwan and the country's capitalists. China's strategy is to lure the Taiwanese business community into making ever-larger investments, at the same time undermining what remains of Taiwan's international position with a policy of pressure and isolation. This policy has its ups and downs but is likely to become increasingly effective. China's threat of military force, aimed at intimidating the independence movement and influencing Taiwan's presidential elections in March 1996, backfired after the United States sent a naval task force to shield Taiwan from possible invasion from the mainland. Political reunification between China and Taiwan remains a long shot, but economically Taiwan is already part of "China, Inc.," with approximately $20 billion in investment and $18 billion in indirect trade through Hong Kong, according to 1995 figures.

After the Hong Kong takeover, China's leverage over Taiwan will increase substantially and Taipei may soon have to make major concessions to Beijing and agree to establish direct trade, shipping, and air links.

Following in the footsteps of "Japan, Inc." and the "four tigers," China has become a predominantly "economic" state and is perhaps on its way to becoming a "corporatist" state, in which state conglomerates run by central government bureaucrats will be the pillars of society. "China, Inc." is also highly mercantilistic, building up its industries behind high protective trade barriers. Government officials and businessmen connive in stealing foreign intellectual property and pirating foreign trademarks. At the same time, China is piling up trade surpluses that may soon exceed those of Japan.

"China, Inc." is far from cohesive and homogeneous, however. Economic reform has been incremental and piecemeal; its so-called "socialist market economy" is still a fragile halfway house. There has been no significant privatization yet, as has occurred in the former Soviet Union and Eastern Europe. The essence of Chinese reform has been in conserving the state sector and public ownership as the mainstay of the economy, while encouraging the emergence of other economic sectors, such as the collective sector with mixed ownership, the foreign investment sector including joint ventures, and the small private sector. The last three are the most dynamic and represent the lion's share of China's high economic growth, whereas the state sector is ailing beyond recovery. More than half of all state enterprises suffer losses, and many are beyond recovery. Declaring bankruptcy is out of the question, however, since massive layoffs and the absence of an adequate social safety net could lead to major social unrest.

Economic decision-making has been radically decentralized and delegated to local governments, although this devolution has been based on ad hoc experimentation and not on structured political or legislative reform. China exhibits some of the characteristics of a federation, yet constitutionally it remains a highly centralized state. The power of the central government to balance national and regional interests is limited indeed. Tax collection is extremely ineffective: fiscal revenue as a share of GNP is one of the lowest in the world. The big question is whether China can continue to exist as a unitary state with a strong central government that, in addition to dealing with matters of defense and foreign affairs, also conducts an effective monetary and fiscal policy.

China's own liberal scholars, overseas Chinese, and Western sinologists have written extensively about concepts of governance based on democracy and human rights, as well as expounding more enlightened views of sovereignty based on interdependence, (con)federalism, and transnationalism. The application of these concepts to China's stagnant polity could dramatically improve the prospects both for a solution to the Taiwan question and for long-term stability in the ethnic border regions. China's current leadership forcefully rejects these views, however, blaming the failure of progress in reunification with Taiwan on U.S. "hegemonism" and conspiracies, not on its own inability and unwillingness to reform its archaic, repressive political system.

Successful deepening of economic reforms, along with preservation of political and social stability, depends on reform of the political system. The attempts at political reform made during the 1980s were repulsed by aged, orthodox Marxists with whom paramount leader and arbiter Deng Xiaoping reluctantly sided at critical moments. After the student rebellion in 1989 and the ensuing crackdown, political reform was postponed indefinitely. The current (transitional) regime is more concerned with recentralization, strengthening traditional ideological dictatorship, fostering xenophobic neonationalism and so-called "Asian values," and curbing advocates of political change. The prospects for increased political freedom and some degree of democratization are uncertain, although individual freedom, especially in the economic sphere, has grown considerably in recent years. As prosperity increases, with per capita income predicted to reach $4,000 in major parts of the country by the year 2010, a new middle class may become the vanguard of democratic change, as was the case in Taiwan and South Korea in the late 1980s.

For the foreseeable future, however, Chinese politics seem to be fixed in their Marxist-Leninist ways, which are largely irrelevant to the great majority of the people. At the same time, leading academics are reinventing and reformulating China's own pre-Communist and premodern Confucian uniqueness and "superiority." China refuses to be lectured to by the United States, an "upstart" country still in its infancy, whose own internal social problems disqualify it from pontification. The (Soviet) Russian empire is gone, England, in China's view, is in irreversible decline, France is only a "mini-superpower," and Germany and Japan are just now reemerging. China, therefore, claims to have all the necessary ingredients to make it at least an equal of the United States and, in the long term, perhaps even "number one."

Willem van Kemenade
Beijing, March 1997

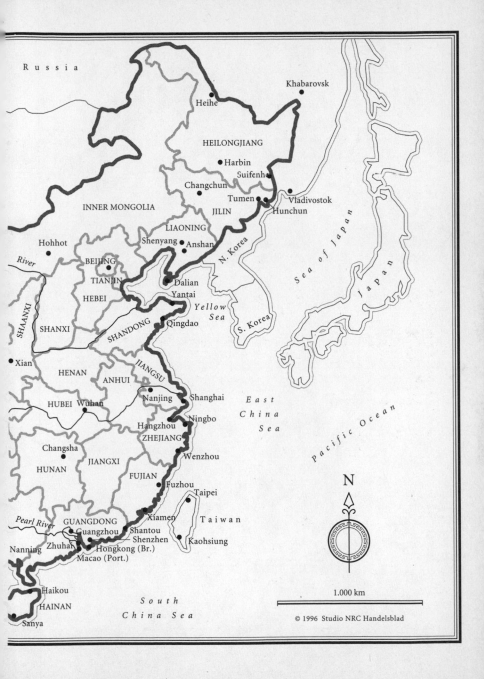

PART ONE

Anatomy of the Three Systems

CHAPTER 1

China: From Maoist Stalinism to "Market Socialism"

I favor a gradualist approach rather than shock therapy.
China is like an aircraft carrier rather than a sports car and
one has to work carefully to bring it along.

JAMES WOLFENSOHN,
president of the World Bank, September 1995

ON A SATURDAY morning in the fall of 1975, I was strolling with a fellow student from the Chinese Language Institute along Sun Yat-sen Boulevard in the center of Taipei, the "temporary capital" of the Nationalist Republic of China in Taiwan. Brian was a decommissioned officer of the recently "defeated" American army in Vietnam. Like me a graduate student of the University of Amsterdam, he had decided to stay in Asia, perhaps for the rest of his life, despite vague fears that Taiwan might eventually become the next Communist domino. We were supposed to have lunch at the officers' mess of the MAAG, the American Military Assistance and Advisory Group.

On our way there, we ran into a man we had met the night before at a party given by foreign businessmen living in Taiwan. He recognized us and struck up a conversation. His name was Luke and he was a shoe manufacturer from the southern Netherlands, home of the once-flourishing Dutch shoe industry. Luke seemed completely bewildered. He lamented, "They told me I was going to China and I thought everything here was Communist and Russian, but now I see American soldiers and girlie bars. It's beyond me." Our host of the previous evening was the son of another European shoe manufacturer who had decided, like his American competitors a few years before, that the only way to survive was to move production to Taiwan, which was then well on its way to becoming the largest shoe manufacturer in the world. It was difficult to make it clear to Luke that there were two Chinas, a big one and a small one, and that the big one lay across the sea, 150 kilometers to the west, and that things were not very Russian there anymore.

Since 1976 lots of remarkable things have happened. American troops left Taiwan in the spring of 1979, after the termination of the U.S.-Taiwan defense treaty and the severing of diplomatic relations by President Jimmy Carter. The American military did not move to the Chinese mainland, but the Taiwanese shoe manufacturers did, taking their Western business relations with them. Girlie bars still exist in Taiwan, but there are notably fewer than there used to be, while South China is now teeming with them. The world center of shoe production is now located in the southeastern Chinese coastal provinces, largely owing to Taiwanese investments. At the beginning of 1994, Frank Kung, chairman of the Taiwan Footwear Manufacturers Association, reported that its 665 members had built more than 500 shoe factories in China.

It is astonishing to see how fast the international economic cycle has moved, and how drastically this has affected the Chinese Communist system, making China the newest low-wage country with the highest economic growth in the world. The growth rates speak for themselves: 12.8 percent in 1992, 13.5 percent in 1993, 11.8 percent in 1994, and 10.2 percent in 1995.

China's brand of Communism now bears the hybrid name of "socialist market economy." Owing to the continuous flow of investments since 1979—at first from Hong Kong, Japan, and the West, and in recent years especially from Taiwan and overseas Chinese communities worldwide— China has become a mosaic of variant systems. In many areas capitalism is already dominant and in others socialism still has the upper hand, but nearly everywhere the two are mixed.

The idea of the coexistence of two different social systems—socialism and capitalism—was tailored to fit China's needs at the beginning of the 1980s by Deng Xiaoping, the "chief engineer of China's reform," to pave the way for China's reunification with Taiwan. Since the date set for this continued to recede into the distance, however, just as the horizon does when one moves toward it, the "one country–two systems" concept was adopted instead as the standard formula for the reintegration of the British crown colony of Hong Kong in 1997. The formula was originally intended to emphasize the strict separation of socialism and capitalism and was meant in particular to protect socialism from capitalist contamination. Capitalists from Hong Kong and Taiwan have indeed transmitted the Midas touch to once-orthodox Communists, who now worship wealth just as fervently as they used to idolize Chairman Mao.

MAO'S "NEW CHINA" was a utopia in which a biblical egalitarianism—not of shared wealth but of shared poverty—was elevated, by means of extreme struggle and coercion, to the position of a pseudoreligion with Mao as the supreme deity. The basis of Mao's legitimacy was his armed seizure of state power from the Japanese occupying forces and from the corrupt, bankrupt "dynasty" of Chiang Kai-shek's Kuomintang (1928–49). In doing so, he acquired, just as the emperors of old had, the "mandate of heaven," the divine right to govern the country until his death.

After "liberation" in 1949, China went through a period of peaceful reconstruction along Stalinist lines (1949–58) with Russian aid, but this did not agree with the conqueror's tempestuous disposition. He thought that China could be propelled more quickly and effectively down the stream of human progress in a state of "permanent revolution." This culminated in the destructive Great Leap Forward (1958–60) and the Cultural Revolution (1966–77), experiments aimed at whipping up hundreds of millions of Chinese into a frenzied mood of self-sacrifice that would lead to heroic economic achievements and to "new and greater victories." Instead, the whole of China dissolved into ideological bedlam. The overwhelming majority of urban Chinese played along with the game of self-destruction. For some it was a matter of "feigned compliance" (*kou-shi, xin-fei*—yes with the mouth, no with the heart). A Chinese with a degree in international law from Columbia University once told me that for months he had run with the masses every morning to Tiananmen Square in the heart of Beijing to roar at the top of his lungs with the rest of the crowd, "Long live Chairman Mao! Long live Vice-Chairman Lin Biao!" "I said my prayers every day, but I kept my independence of mind," he whispered to me with uncertain pride. Historians may in time refer to these episodes as the darkest moments in Chinese history.

At the time of Mao's death in 1976, China was at an economic impasse, socially torn apart, and morally adrift. The arrest in October 1976 of Mao's radical camarilla, the so-called Gang of Four, led by his maniacal widow, Jiang Qing, was the second "liberation," delivering the Chinese from the most extreme forms of ideological conditioning. Chinese intellectuals have an uncanny, dialectical way of looking at the excesses of the Mao era as a blessing in disguise: if they had been less extreme, there would have been no need after Mao's death to change course so radically. This about-face made Chinese

Communism more heterodox and flexible even in the late 1970s, which is one of the reasons why it was immune to the Eastern European domino effect in 1989–91.

AFTER AN INTERVAL of more than two years, during which China was led by the Mao loyalist Hua Guofeng, Deng Xiaoping, the ultimate pragmatist twice purged by Mao for revisionism and right-wing deviationism, became the new leader of a reformist coalition. He redefined the basis of the regime's legitimacy in practical terms as the transformation of China into a "rich and powerful" (*fu-qiang*) country. Reformers had pursued this objective since the middle of the nineteenth century but had been thwarted by a succession of foreign invasions, rebellions, revolutions, cultural despair, civil war, and twenty-seven years of dogmatic Communism. During the Deng era, China became a much richer and more powerful country. Hundreds of millions of Chinese rose above abject poverty and saw their standard of living triple in fifteen years, making up somewhat for the lost years under Mao.

From 1979 to 1995 the Chinese economy grew by an average of 9.9 percent annually, with the exception of a mere 4 percent in the catastrophic year of 1989. Economic freedom, pluralism, and efficiency have increased substantially. The share of the state sector in industrial production decreased in those years from 80 to approximately 40 percent. Rural industries with mixed ownership, joint ventures with foreign firms, and the private sector accounted for 60 percent. These enterprises, called "other than state-owned," experienced a rate of growth of 15.8 percent in 1995 (27.9 percent in 1994), as opposed to only 9.5 percent in 1995 for state-owned enterprises (5.5 percent in 1994). Approximately 80 percent of all goods are now traded at market prices.*

Foreign investments climbed from $51 million in 1979 to a cumulative total of approximately $200 billion by the end of 1995, of which $161 billion has been utilized, making China the second-largest recipient of foreign investments in the world, after the United States, although utilized foreign

---

* Chinese statistics often reflect the wishes and plans of regional and sometimes even central authorities instead of economic realities. Voluntaristic and futurological "roundings off" to the higher figure and projections on the high side are very common. Nevertheless, there is no doubt as to the robust upward trend in the Chinese economy. Chinese authorities at all levels regularly launch offensives against the fraudulent use of statistics by companies, as well as by regional and local government agencies.

investments amount to only $105 per capita, less than one-third that of Mexico and less than one-tenth that of Malaysia. Two-thirds of all investments come from Hong Kong* and Taiwan, 13 percent from Japan, and 13 percent from Europe and North America. There are currently around 260,000 foreign investment projects. China's foreign trade grew from approximately $20.7 billion in 1978 to $280.9 billion in 1995 (with a trade surplus of $16.7 billion), making it the tenth-largest trading power in the world. In short, since the end of the Mao era China has been transformed from an impoverished, isolated, revolutionary country into a "conventional" developing country, playing an ever-increasing role in the world economy and international financial markets.

Although the per capita income of its immense population is still very low—$530 in 1994—owing in part to the repeated devaluations of the currency, the renminbi, according to the World Bank calculation method of "purchasing power parity" (PPP), China rose in 1993 to the position of third-largest economic power in the world, after the United States and Japan. According to the *World Bank Atlas 1996*, China's per capita PPP income over the year 1994 amounted to $2,510. In the fall of 1996, however, the World Bank published a new report called *Poverty in China: What Do the Figures Mean?*, in which it substantially lowered the PPP figure to $1,800 and revised its calculation of the number of people living below the poverty line to 350 million, or one-third of the total population, rather than the 80 million, or 7 percent, that was the figure commonly used until then. All the euphoria about China as the next economic superpower, which had been uncritically accepted by part of the media and business sector since 1993, was now due for a fundamental reappraisal. Grand predictions that the Chinese economy would exceed the U.S. economy in size by the beginning of the next century have now been rejected, and according to new projections it will take about forty years for China to rival the United States, and then only in terms of the raw quantitative size of the economy.[1]

CHINA'S UNPRECEDENTED economic growth, its opening up, and its integration into the world economy contrast sharply with the situation in the former Soviet Union and some other centrally planned economies in Eastern Europe, where premature democratization has resulted in a political

---

* Part of the capital coming from Hong Kong originates in mainland China and is sent through dubious channels to the British crown colony to be "recycled," thereby taking advantage of the tax concessions enjoyed by foreign capital.

and sociopolitical implosion, as well as economic stagnation and decline. Nothing has been more responsible for China's relative success than the controversial Chinese developmental model of "economic reforms without parallel reforms in the political system." The chief architect of this strategy was Deng Xiaoping, a classic Leninist, or, if you will, an "enlightened despot," who wanted to clear away the havoc wreaked by the Mao era as quickly as possible, but was averse to wild experimentation and great risk-taking in the style of Mao.

Deng, born in 1904, had never been party chairman, head of state, or premier, owing his authority instead to his seniority in the three branches of power: party, state, and army. The Chinese political pendulum swung back and forth in cycles, from ultraliberal to orthodox left, both undesirable extremes as far as Deng was concerned. He settled scores with them both again and again, sometimes heavy-handedly, sometimes more subtly. When there was room for experimentation, Deng was usually liberal, but when experiments backfired, he closed ranks with the conservatives. If the pace of reform accelerated out of control, he applied the brakes; if it stagnated, he shifted into high gear. China's political spectrum was Deng's FM-band, requiring constant and frequent modulation, with him turning the knobs.

Deng's main objective was to maintain a broad coalition of interest groups in the state, party, army, security services, and provinces, which supported the main elements of his program of economic reform. No one was his equal in the art of political struggle (*dou-zheng yi-shu*). Mao had been a surrealist artist, dialectician, and polarizer; Deng was a superbureaucrat and tightrope walker. He occasionally had a firm grip on events, but more often than not just managed to maintain a delicate balance between opposing forces: economic and political, left and right, central and regional, civilian and military. He dismissed the personality cult, which he thought had been the main cause of Mao's derailment, and in the mystical, traditional style of Chinese rulers, he operated chiefly behind the scenes.

Deng's political blueprint, formulated already in 1975 when he replaced Premier Zhou Enlai, who was suffering from cancer, was called the "four modernizations": agriculture, industry, science and technology, and defense. Deng vaguely promised modernization of the political system, i.e., some form of democratization, though this was opposed by aged hardline conservatives. Wei Jingsheng, the main figure in the Democracy Wall movement in the fall of 1978, criticized Deng Xiaoping for ignoring the need for a fifth modernization: democracy. He was sentenced to fifteen years. Deng acquired international prestige—just as the Soviet leader Mikhail

Gorbachev did seven years later—through rapprochement with the West, culminating in the normalization of Sino-American relations under Jimmy Carter late in 1978 and the severing of diplomatic ties between Washington and Taipei.

In a historic plenum of 18–22 December 1978, the Party Central Committee resolved to shift the main task of the party from political struggle to economic development. After successful experiments in his home province of Sichuan under the leadership of one of his two "crown princes," Zhao Ziyang, Deng liberated the peasants across the country from the serfdom imposed on them by the people's communes of Mao. The subsequent burst of energy became the basis for the creation of new wealth. Although the land remained formally in the possession of the state, the new system of renting the land to families by means of renewable leases of fifteen years (meanwhile extended to thirty) amounted to de facto ownership. "On collective land we're as sluggish as snails, on our own land as energetic as tigers" was a popular aphorism.

Starting in 1979, the Maoist-Stalinist economic model was drastically overhauled, resulting in a policy of "readjustment, restructuring, and decentralization." The program was supervised by Chen Yun—an aging party stalwart who, like Deng, had been relegated to the sidelines for years by Mao's capriciousness—who later became Deng's chief rival. Agriculture became the top priority, followed by light industry, with heavy industry in last place. This definitive casting aside of the Soviet model gave China much better prospects for economic development than Russia, where the planned economy with its heavy (military) industry remained dominant and agriculture and the provision of consumer goods were of secondary importance. Foreign investments were welcomed with two objectives in mind: raising the level of exports and foreign currency revenues, and producing higher-quality goods for domestic consumption. To enable it to become more efficient and competitive, industry would have to be radically reformed.

On 20 October 1984 the Party Central Committee decided to "debureaucratize" state enterprises, in other words, to release them from the bureaucratic tyranny of central government ministries with their command economy orientation. Central planning would no longer be mandatory but would become "general and flexible." Party secretaries and cells were henceforth to limit themselves to ideological work and to leave the management side to engineers and economists. The enterprises themselves were supposed to choose new, flexible, diversified forms of organization, to be self-supporting, and to hand over only a percentage of their profits to the state in the form of taxes. The transition to a new system of industrial organization was supposed to take five years.

Parallel to these developments was to be the emergence of a "planned commodity economy," with state-controlled prices for strategic goods such as steel, raw materials, and grain, and market-determined prices for nearly all daily necessities. The new series of urban industrial reforms proved to be much more problematic than the simple agricultural reforms of the first phase. Restoring to the peasants the freedom to resume family farming on privately "owned" plots of land resulted in a revival of the work ethic and the creation of new wealth. Granting party bureaucrats the freedom to deviate from the plan during an uncertain transition, taking place in the context of a weak and still-evolving legal system, opened up the (back)door to all kinds of corruption—the theft of state funds, the proliferation of investments in nonessential "prestige projects," and a boom in the import of luxury goods—ultimately resulting in dwindling reserves of foreign currency and growing budget deficits. This was followed by drastic cutbacks and a two-year moratorium on further economic reforms.

THE LIBERAL WING of the party, with General Secretary Hu Yaobang and Premier Zhao Ziyang as its patrons, concluded that political reforms were necessary to clear the path of obstacles to further economic reforms. The first plan for political reforms instigated by Deng Xiaoping had run aground already in 1980 (see Chapter 9). It was Deng himself who reopened the debate on political reforms in the summer of 1986. For several months the corridors of power reverberated with proposals for reform: investing the rubber-stamp parliament, the National People's Congress, with real power; changing the "democratic parties,"* relics of the Kuo-

* The eight "democratic parties" that form the system of multiparty consultation under the leadership of the Communist party are the following:

1. the Democratic League;
2. the Revolutionary Committee of the Kuomintang, a postwar splinter faction of Chiang Kai-shek's Kuomintang;
3. the Chinese National Construction Association;
4. Jiusan (the Third of September) Society;
5. the Association for the Promotion of Democracy;
6. the Peasant and Workers Democratic party;
7. Zhi Gong Dang (the Party for Public Well-being);
8. the Taiwan Democratic Self-Government League, an organization of pro-Communist Taiwanese who already lived on or had fled to the mainland before 1949 and who advocate an autonomous Taiwan under Chinese sovereignty.

mintang era, from Communist satellites into real participants; transforming their umbrella organization, the Chinese People's Political Consultative Conference, into a kind of senate; and allowing some freedom of the press.

China's most liberal newspaper, the *World Economic Herald* of Shanghai, reintroduced Wei Jingsheng's theme of the "fifth modernization"—democracy—and many speculated that Wei, who had by then served seven years of his fifteen-year sentence, would soon be released.

The Central Committee was expected to tackle the problem of political reform at a plenary session in September of that year, but it limited itself to issuing "guiding principles for the furthering of a socialist society with advanced culture and ideology." These were aimed at combating the "spiritual pollution and bourgeois decadence" resulting from increasing prosperity and Western influence. Political reforms would not be dealt with until the Thirteenth Party Congress in 1987. Frustrated because political reforms were not forthcoming, and inspired by the first free elections, which took place in Taiwan at the beginning of December, students participated in the first great wave of demonstrations for democracy sweeping across China.

The driving force behind these demonstrations was the astrophysicist Fang Lizhi, the "Chinese Sakharov," who, in a series of lectures, had called upon China's traditionally docile intellectuals to form an independent class pressing for social innovation. A coalition of elderly orthodox Marxist ideologues, Stalinists, and generals seized the opportunity presented by this bold challenge to stem the tide of political reform from the outset. The liberal party leader Hu Yaobang was accused of lenience toward the advancing wave of "bourgeois liberalism" and was promptly deposed. Deng Xiaoping himself took charge of a purge of prominent, rightist bourgeois-liberal intellectuals, but after three months he considered the threat from the right negligible and called again for vigilance in the face of danger from the left.

The political struggle continued off and on until a cease-fire was called at the Thirteenth Party Congress in October 1987. Hu's successor as party leader, Zhao Ziyang, managed to stem the antibourgeois tide in the political-ideological realm; Zhao's successor as premier, Li Peng, forcefully put the brakes on further economic reforms. Even after formally relinquishing the premiership to Li in April 1988, Zhao, as general secretary of the party, continued to take a strong interest in the economy. With Deng Xiaoping's blessing, Zhao resolved on a new series of price reforms, which miscarried during Beijing's hot summer of 1988, leading to galloping inflation, hoarding, a run on the banks, demonstrations, and price riots.

The same coalition that had brought down Hu Yaobang a year and a half earlier now plotted an all-out assault on Zhao. Deng Xiaoping, who was actually at a loss as to how to handle the country's economic predicament and had no clear-cut economic philosophy other than his determination to make China rich and powerful, abandoned Zhao to his fate. The conservatives upbraided Zhao for not having a systematic, coherent plan for price reform and for leaving everything to haphazard experimentation. Supported by the conservative elders, Li Peng announced a drastic austerity program, ruling that there should be no more significant price reforms and postponing general price liberalization for five years. This in fact sealed the fate of Zhao, who was still party leader only in name. Deng Xiaoping was swept along once again by the conservative tide, admitting to foreign visitors that "rash action was an invitation to the left [conservative Marxists] to attack." A new and much more ominous trial of strength was in the making, however, between the "leftist" orthodox Marxists on the one hand and the "rightist" liberal reformists on the other.

IN 1989 all of these crisis factors—internal and external, political and economic—combined to bring about a catastrophe. The year began with a rebellion of intellectuals under the leadership of the astrophysicist Fang Lizhi, who, in tune with American pressure for the improvement of human rights, launched a movement to grant amnesty to political prisoners in general and to Wei Jingsheng in particular. The continued shrinking of the economy—owing to the austerity program, inflation (approximately 30 percent), and corruption—further contributed to the nationwide malaise. The biggest problem in the half-reformed Chinese economy was the inevitable conflict between the two systems: the stagnating state sector with its central planning as contrasted with the dynamic, pluralistic market sector consisting of township and village enterprises, joint ventures with foreign firms, and newly emerging private enterprises. The most pernicious aspect of the two parallel economies was the so-called "two-track price structure," which was abused by party officials on an ever-increasing scale to buy goods at low state prices and sell them at high market prices.

Public indignation at this was the catalyst of the protests that erupted in April. The large-scale demonstrations were triggered by the untimely death of Hu Yaobang, whom Deng Xiaoping had blamed for the earlier student protests in late 1986. The regime, driven into a corner, was not in the mood for dialogue, and the rebels could not be persuaded to back down. They made a grave error, however, in occupying the capital's main square and disrupting the historic Sino-Soviet summit between Mikhail Gorbachev and Deng Xiaoping in mid-May 1989. The enraged, humiliated regime resolved to teach the agitators a lesson. Armageddon was approaching.

Zhao Ziyang, who resisted using military means to solve the crisis, was suddenly dismissed—just as his predecessor Hu Yaobang had been—and on the night of 3–4 June hundreds of tanks and heavily armed soldiers spread death and destruction in the main streets of Beijing. The actual number of dead will probably never be known, as the Chinese government has never honored its promise to publish a list of casualties, under the pretext of wanting to spare the feelings of the next of kin (see Chapter 11 for a detailed treatment of this episode).

WHEREAS AT THE BEGINNING of the Deng era the focus of Chinese politics shifted from class struggle to economic development, after the turning point of 1989 it shifted from economic development to repressive stability. This time China lapsed for approximately two years into an ideological Ice Age of repression, stagnation, and paranoia over the prospect of a possible domino effect following the collapse of the Eastern European Communist regimes and the death throes of the Soviet Union. For nearly two years ultraorthodox octogenarians maneuvered tirelessly to recondition an unruly populace, spouting Stalinist-Maoist drivel on such subjects as political study, "ideological meditation" and self-criticism, flag-waving ceremonies and weekly visits to the graves of revolutionary veterans, and worn-out hardship slogans from the 1950s. It seemed to be the last stand of Chinese conservatism. Systematic attempts were made to curtail the collective sector and to eliminate the private sector altogether by denying them bank loans and raw materials. Deng's rival gerontocrats even launched an offensive against the "special economic zones" (SEZs) in the south, which they labeled "colonial enclaves."

The specter of a "leftist restoration" persisted until the dissolution of the Soviet Union and the fall of Gorbachev late in 1991. Shortly thereafter Deng Xiaoping rose from his perpetually rumored deathbed and issued his ultimate decree as ideological chief justice: his verdict blamed the fall of the Soviet Union not on the inherent flaws of Communism but on Gorbachev's failure to reform the economy. The best guarantee for the survival of the Communist regime in China was to redefine the role of the party in stimulating strong economic growth and in preserving order and stability, which meant a new wave of economic reforms combined with tight maintenance of the political status quo.

As the national media in Beijing had been firmly in the hands of leftist ideologues since 1989, Deng was unable to promulgate his "political testament" in the capital. The situation was similar to that in 1965, when Mao was plotting the Cultural Revolution. At that time, Beijing, including the media, was in the hands of "liberal" revisionists and Mao had no power base there. He turned to Shanghai, then the headquarters of the radical wing of the party, as the point from which to launch his appeals for ultraleft agitation. In 1992 the tables were turned, however. Beijing was the bulwark of the orthodox left and Shanghai was just beginning to recover its prewar status as the most cosmopolitan and innovative city in China.

IN THE MAOIST STYLE of a "direct appeal to the people," Deng traveled in January 1992 to Shanghai and the special economic zones in the deep south, armed with the slogan "Be More Bold in Reform." He now made a new contribution to the theory behind the convergence and mutual osmosis of socialism and capitalism which went beyond the "one country–two systems" model, in which the two systems were intended to remain separate. From now on, the two systems would be permitted to mingle and borrow from each other. Deng decreed that the planned economy was not necessarily the monopoly of socialism, because capitalist economies also practiced planning. Neither was the market an exclusively capitalist phenomenon, because socialism could also permit the existence of markets. All economic methods that furthered the productive forces and national and individual wealth—"the three benefits"—would be permitted from now on. More experimentation was encouraged, as well as the creative implementation of decrees from the central government. Deng's pronouncements in 1992 were a sequel to his earlier "imperial antiegalitarian edict" of 1985, in which he proclaimed that some individuals would be allowed to get rich more quickly than others, as would some parts of the country before the nation as a whole.[2]

Later on, party leader Hu Yaobang, Deng's liberal protégé, reportedly paraphrased this concept in the ideologically controversial slogan "To Get Rich Is Glorious." This became the motto of the Deng reforms and was often attributed to Deng Xiaoping himself, although Chinese sources have never quoted him as saying it or endorsing it. During the mid-1980s this get-rich-quick philosophy had already led to the emergence of the first Chinese nouveaux riches, who were advertised for a time as "role models for

Dengism." At that time, *wan-hu*—the family of ten thousand yuan—meant rich. In 1992–93 a new jingle came into fashion which stated the new "norms" of prosperity:

Ten thousand yuan now won't get you anywhere,
With one hundred thousand you'll have nothing to spare,
One million's no riches but your worries are past,
When you've made your ten million real wealth comes at last!

After Deng's "southern" whirlwind tour, "getting rich quick" became the national rage, taking on epidemic proportions. *Xiahai,* which means plunging into the sea of moneymaking by whatever means possible, was the catchword of 1992. Street peddling had been rampant in Chinese cities since the late 1980s, but now most of the main streets have become door-to-door bazaars.

Wheeler-dealers who make a lavish display of their newly acquired wealth, regardless of the methods used to amass it, have become the new winners in China. Honest officials and intellectuals—a shrinking minority—who have to subsist on 500 yuan ($60) a month, are again the losers. During the Mao era, they made up the "stinking ninth" category (the lowest class in that "classless" society) for ideological reasons. Now they are at the bottom again because of their lack of wealth.

Government agencies and research institutes have been deserted by their staff, who have plunged into that sea of irregular commerce in increasing numbers. The official media have campaigned intensively against "mammonism" (the cult of Mammon, the god of money), nihilism, hedonism, and ultraindividualism, which are the new social evils (one of the old social evils is ordinary corruption). The behavior of party and government officials is anything but exemplary, however. If there is one good indicator of top-ranking leaders' expectations for the future, it is surely the advice they give to their own children. Nearly all of these "red princes" have become entrepreneurs who use their fathers' political clout to fill their own purses.

One of the worst aspects of mammonism (*bai-jin zhu-yi*) is *luan shou-fei,* the random imposition of levies by local government bodies. Low-ranking officials demand money for routine services such as stamping forms, which used to be free of charge. Maintenance and repairs of water pipes or telephones are no longer carried out without the payment of a bribe in addition to the service fee. In some of the smaller cities, the Public Utilities Company turns off the gas and electricity if "special levies" are not paid on time. A train ticket is not to be had without a bribe or a tip, as well as a service fee. A booking and service fee is added to the price of airplane tickets, even if you go to the airport to book it yourself. Airports charge an airport tax, an airport maintenance tax, and a service fee for no service. Foreigners are charged 50 to 100 percent more than the Chinese for the same "services." In the city of Yichang on the Yangtze River, near the place where the huge Three Gorges Dam will be built, I was once presented with a bill for an airport tax amounting to 20 yuan ($2.40), even though I was traveling by train to Wuhan. The official in charge remarked casually, "Didn't you know that we're building an airport?" A senior official of the World Bank later called my attention to the fact that the Yichang airport was opened in 1996. He explained that special levies for airport construction are common throughout China. Without such levies, much of the infrastructure could not have been developed because the tax base is too narrow and tax collection inadequate.

Pulling the wool over people's eyes, or, as the Chinese say, "The butcher hangs a sheep's head in the window but he sells dog meat," is another variation on the Mammon theme. Every year thousands of people die from taking "fake" medicine and drinking "counterfeit" hard liquor (in French cognac bottles). In 1994, in a district in the province of Hubei, 20 percent of the cotton harvest was lost because the district government had issued a decree that required everyone to buy a certain brand of substandard pesticide, which was produced by a company owned by the local party secretary. An unexpected upshot of this was a surrealistic tragicomedy. A peasant sent a letter of thanks to the party secretary because his wife, after a violent quarrel, had tried to commit suicide by drinking the stuff, but had survived because it was a harmless imitation. A milkman in a village near Beijing went from door to door with his cow, calling out, "I milk while you watch so you can see it's real milk, and I don't water it down like my competitors do!"

The counterfeiting of Western brand-name products—Philips laser discs, Gucci bags, Benetton shirts, and so on—by state and military enterprises, as well as by small, private, pirate companies, is a large source of domestic and export income.

There are many reasons for the overwhelming preoccupation of the present-day Chinese with money, an obsession that was already obvious in the pre-Communist culture and is also conspicuous in Taiwan and even more so in Hong Kong. One explanation is that the Chinese lack the restraining influence of highly organized religion, which Muslims and Christians have to varying degrees. Evidence of a more pronounced materialism among the Chinese is only empirical and subjective, but is nevertheless highly illustrative of the situation in contemporary China and East Asia. As Western students at the Chinese Language Institute in Taiwan during the

1970s, we joked about it, saying, "Where other races have a heart, the Chinese have an abacus."

The Chinese character for wealth (*Fu*) is omnipresent on doors and walls. Instead of "Happy New Year," the Chinese wish one another "wealth" (*kung-hsi fa-tsai/gongxi facai*), and at receptions they present one another with red envelopes containing money (*hung-pao/hongbao*). During the Mao era, this was all bourgeois heresy, but during the 1980s this practice was revived and now thrives as never before. The well-publicized motto of the Deng era is "To Get Rich Is Glorious." In 1982, when China and Great Britain entered into negotiations concerning the future of Hong Kong, the Chinese insisted that discussions be limited to "maintaining the stability and prosperity of Hong Kong"—not its freedom or international status. One of the most popular puns in China nowadays is *wang qian kan*, which can mean either "looking ahead" or "looking for money" (the pronunciation and the tones are the same; only the middle character is different).

I once asked a government official to give me a detailed list of the historical causes of mammonism. He obliged me with the following:

- It could be seen as a reaction to the extreme poverty of the prewar and war periods and the excessive egalitarianism of the Mao era.
- The government's sudden change in attitude is also to blame. Before, nothing was permitted, and now—economically speaking— anything goes, so you just mess around until you get into trouble or until laws and rules are enforced.
- There is uncertainty about what the post-Deng era holds in store: a reversal of economic freedoms, chaos, or worse.
- The state no longer offers any protection and is no longer concerned about the underprivileged. Pensions and social security benefits are still in their infancy. If you lose your job or become ill, or if your child enters university, you have to shoulder the expenses yourself, drawing on your own limited resources. So grab what you can while it's there for the taking.
- Although China is on its way to becoming a market economy, it is still weak and unstructured. Neither a market ethic nor a market culture exists yet. There is a serious shortage of modern businessmen, economists, notaries, accountants, and lawyers. Management consultants and headhunters are still nonexistent.
- It is nearly impossible to curb corrupt party cadres who will be made idle by the transformation to a market economy. Political reforms have not yet begun, and there is a lack of direction. The party rejects the Western model but has no alternative of its

own. The reformist wing of the party is serious about introducing new methods of modern governance and the rule of law, but the party and the government consider themselves above the law.

"LAW-BLINDNESS" (*fa-mang*) is a typically Chinese trait, rooted in a moralistic culture lacking a strong legalistic tradition. Because of the absence of Western colonialism—with the exception of a couple of coastal enclaves—the Western concept of the rule of law has taken root to a lesser extent in China than in the former European colonies of Asia. The result is that most Chinese live not according to a fixed set of rules but according to the improvised demands of their struggle for a better life. Modern civic spirit, public morals, and identification with the public interest and the good of society are scarce.[3] China rejects the Western doctrine of "separation of powers" (executive, legislative, and judiciary) as a "bourgeois concept," preferring instead its own separation of powers—state, party, army, police, and regional power centers—which, in a way, are all states within the state.

During the last decade, much has been done by means of new legislation to introduce (yet again) the rule of law. During the late imperial era and the first decade of the Kuomintang (1928–37), there was growing legal security, but this was completely done away with by Mao. The legal profession was abolished in 1957, and it was reinstated only in 1980, at which time China was left with a mere thousand lawyers. In the meantime, their numbers have increased to eighty-two thousand (still far too few), but the legal profession remains sorely in need of rules and discipline.[4] During a recent visit to the southwestern city of Chongqing, I met the assistant director of an investment zone, who had eight titles on his business card, including "part-time lawyer." When I asked him about this, he said, "Yes, I studied a little bit of law."

The police force is grossly understaffed and woefully underpaid. In the interest of keeping the peace, the police fraternize with the underworld, whose bosses they consult about who will be prosecuted for which crimes. To generate some extra income for themselves, traffic policemen engage in automobile trading, repairs, car-washing, smuggling, and even theft. The vice squad runs nightclubs and brothels, arguing that this way the permits remain in the "trustworthy" hands of their own people, who keep prostitution discreet and unobtrusive.

Collusion between the government and secret societies, a historical phenomenon in China, is rearing its ugly head again, especially in South China.

The minister of public security, Tao Siju, shocked the population of Hong Kong in 1993 with the remark that some "triads" (criminal brotherhoods) are patriotic and therefore welcome to work for national causes. In the city of Wenzhou in the coastal province of Zhejiang, where many of the overseas Chinese in Europe come from, secret societies run underground factories that forge passports and other identification papers.[5] Their activities extend all the way to Holland, France, and Italy. Late in 1993 in the city of Jiamusi, not far from the border with the Russian Far East, 136 prosecutors, judges, and senior policemen—59.4 percent of all employees in this sector—were purged, reprimanded, or transferred [!] because of their connections with organized crime. Crime has not yet contaminated all of society, as it has in Russia, but many Chinese fear that it will come to this.

In parts of southern Hunan Province, the judicial apparatus was found in 1996 to be almost completely corrupt. In five cities and districts in the prefecture of Huaihua, 270 of the 515 hotels, restaurants, and dance halls were owned and run by party and government officials, many of them judges, prosecutors, and police chiefs. They compete with each other by providing a variety of sex services. Some officials, the head of the Land Registry Office in particular, make approval for land deals contingent on all members of the relevant departments wining, dining, and whoring in their hotels at public expense. Everyone seems to be corrupt and to have a lot to hide. The threat "If you turn me in, I'll turn you in" is their best protection. Since many of the merrymakers are high-ranking law enforcement officials, the establishments in question are protected from China's recurring anti-vice and anticrime campaigns. Other hotel owners without official positions take the poetic view "If monks [law enforcement officers] are allowed to indulge [in vices of the flesh], why aren't we?" In this way, the sex industry—with its endless supply of wandering teenage girls from the rural areas—proliferates.

The public is outraged not only by the corruption of social morals but particularly by the sanctimonious profiteering of these once-puritanical Communists. Prostitution, officially illegal, is the permanent target of widely publicized, though hypocritical, extermination campaigns, but the sex dens owned by well-connected officials remain above the law.

The state has for many years taken an ambivalent attitude toward the proliferation of dance halls, karaoke bars, saunas, and nightclubs. Because of their vulnerability to police harassment, these are one of the few categories of businesses that usually pay their taxes faithfully. The nightlife establishments owned by officials, however, use their power—including threats and blackmail—to scare away the tax collectors. As a result, the private bosses in the amusement sector tell the tax collector, "If you don't collect the taxes of this or that (corrupt) police chief or judge, I won't pay you either." Tax collection is in a state of chaos; the falsification of tax receipts is rampant. These tax-evading senior officials spend their lives running their hotels and restaurants, securing supplies, and scheming day and night to make more money. They continue to receive their salaries and bonuses every month, while completely neglecting their public duties, and no one criticizes them or does anything about it. All this was reported, not in an anti-China tabloid published in Hong Kong, but in the *China Discipline Inspection and Supervision Daily*, the official limited-circulation newspaper of the powerful Central Commission for Discipline Inspection of the Communist party, set up in 1987 to fight corruption.[6]

NATIONWIDE CAMPAIGNS against endemic corruption have been waged since 1983, when President Li Xiannian used caricatures of Santa Claus–like figures at the beginning of the first anticorruption campaign. He warned the Chinese people that "some bigwigs among us have been hit by the sugarcoated bullets [*tang-yi bao-dan*] of the bourgeoisie."[*]

In the summer of 1993, however, president and party leader Jiang Zemin used remarkably ominous language when he "declared war" on corruption, which he described as a virus threatening the survival of both party and state.

National anticorruption campaigns are generally conducted by means of moralistic slogans, ritualistic self-criticism, threats, and, to a lesser extent, legal and institutional sanctions. Petty and middling swindlers at the provincial and municipal levels are regularly rounded up and given heavy sentences—sometimes even the death sentence—as a deterrent measure, but the upper echelons are generally above the law. One of the reasons for the downfall in early 1987 of Hu Yaobang, liberal leader of the Communist party, was his demand that the children of various doddering top leaders be charged with corruption.[7] At last, in 1995 President Jiang Zemin spectacularly extended the target of the anticorruption campaign to include the very top of the party and its commercial princes. During the spring of 1995, several major corruption scandals dramatically confirmed the impression among most Chinese that large portions of their government and the Communist party are in the hands of an all-powerful syndicate of freebooting racketeers.

The most shocking case at the top provincial level occurred in the impoverished southeastern province of Guizhou, where the wife of the governor held the post of "vice-chair of the Discipline Inspection Commission," the very organ in charge of fighting corruption. In 1992 she set up the Guizhou International Trust and Investment Corporation and installed herself as chief executive. She attracted Hong Kong investors for her "development projects," but the money was used by her son in real estate and securities speculation in Shanghai and Shenzhen. Approximately 300 million yuan in state funds was lost. In January 1995 the "first lady" was convicted and executed.

In the realm of national politics, the offensive was launched in February 1995 with the arrest of Zhou Beifang, one of the most extravagant wastrels among the so-called "red princes"—the scions of the Communist aristocracy who have inherited power, privilege, and "supralegal" status from their fathers. Zhou Beifang was the son of Zhou Guanwu, chairman of Shougang (Capital Steel), a giant diversified steel and financial conglomerate in Beijing. Upon the young Zhou's arrest, the old Zhou, Deng Xiaoping's personal friend, was immediately forced into "early" retirement, early because he was only seventy-seven years old at the time. Shougang had a history of rampant corruption for which its party secretary had already been executed in 1992. The young Zhou—head of Shougang Holdings in Hong Kong, the international investment arm of the conglomerate—engaged in Nick Leeson–style futures speculation, but unlike the rogue trader at Barings who used fiduciary resources, Zhou utilized "extrabudgetary" state funds held by senior officials and their relatives. One of Zhou's senior business associates was Deng Zhifang—the son of Deng Xiaoping—who headed Shougang Concord in Shanghai. Shougang Holdings was intimately linked with Hong Kong–backed real estate projects in Beijing, for which top-level officials in the city government had received substantial kickbacks.

Shougang also had links with the largest Ponzi scheme* in the country, involving the Xinxing Industrial Corporation in Wuxi in the coastal province of Jiangsu. Xinxing was headed by Deng Bin, a femme fatale who used powerful political and judicial connections, bribes, and sex to persuade local bosses all over the country to turn over their slush funds to her for record dividends. She badly overextended herself, however, and in mid-1994 the scam was exposed. Deng Bin was sentenced to death and executed. Zhou had also run up heavy losses on the Hong Kong stock exchange, which by the end of 1994 could no longer be covered up. Both scandals were intimately connected with the Beijing city government, whose top leaders had

---

* A fraudulent investment scheme in which funds paid in by later investors are used to pay artificially high returns to the original investors, thus attracting more funds.

invested tens of millions of yuan of embezzled money in a number of schemes. On 4 April Vice-mayor Wang Baosen of Beijing shot himself, shortly after authorities had begun investigating him for the embezzlement of $37 million. Wang's case was only the tip of the iceberg with respect to financial irregularities and abuse of power for which the municipal authorities were notorious.

Zhou Beifang was married to the daughter of another vice-mayor, Zhang Baifa, who had long been accused of corrupt practices in connection with construction projects. The mayor at that time, Li Qiyan, who has since been demoted to the position of party secretary to the ministry of labor, was also an accomplice in the Xinxing scam. But president and general secretary Jiang Zemin chose to make his bold move only against "Big Number One," the first secretary of Beijing's municipal party apparatus, Chen Xitong. Only weeks after the suicide (or gang murder?) of his deputy, Chen was forced to resign as party secretary. In September he was also dismissed from the Politburo and the Central Committee and accused of "serious mistakes," including failing to restrain the criminal Wang Baosen, pursuing a "dissolute and extravagant" lifestyle, abusing power, and seeking illegal interests on behalf of his friends and relatives. In the end, no criminal charges were filed against Chen and most of his accomplices returned to work. One of his mistresses reportedly fled to Hong Kong with a portion of Chen's ill-gotten wealth.[8] The case against Chen was obviously political. The suicide of Vice-mayor Wang presented President Jiang with a golden opportunity to single out Chen and to use his corruption as an excuse to get rid of a headstrong "local" rival who had challenged the national leadership more than once. The ouster of Chen had stretched Jiang's power to the limit, and he was forced to back off from a full-scale purge of the "Beijing mafia" in order to prevent rivalry among the elite from degenerating into open warfare, which would have jeopardized stability in the capital and possibly in the whole of the country.

Another allegedly corrupt senior official, Jiang Chunyun, was nevertheless promoted to vice-premier in March 1995, though with an unprecedented number of votes against him—more than one-third of the 2,752 votes in the National People's Congress. Jiang's wife was one of the key figures in the big "Tai-an Scandal" in the province of Shandong, where he had been governor and party secretary. The psychological process by which the Chinese have become oblivious to the moral aspects of corruption cannot be expressed in a more down-to-earth way than in this wry remark made by Jiang himself during an anticorruption conference: "Corruption is like manure: the longer you smell it, the less it seems to stink." It is chiefly the olfactory organs of Communist officials, however, that no longer work. Ordinary people are overwhelmed by the stench but usually don't dare to report it for fear of retribution. The Chinese have so little faith in the social justice of the current regime and the fairness of the present-day society that, according to an opinion poll, 64.3 percent of the people questioned believed that an honest person would always be the loser.[9]

The newspaper for intellectuals, *Guangming Ribao* (Radiant Daily), once pinpointed the reason for the endemic corruption in government as the exceptionally low salaries of party and government officials: "This results in a serious loss of mental balance. When they look at the nouveaux riches, who radiate self-confidence and luxuriate in their custom-made Western suits and leather shoes, spending money as if it grew on trees, they feel their empty purses and are overcome by a feeling of humiliation and depression. Many cadres begin to idolize money because of this shocking loss of self-respect."[10]

"The only effective way of dealing with corruption is supervision of the governing apparatus by an independent People's Congress (parliament) and a free(r) press," said Professor Yuan Hongbing, an activist fighting for improvement of the legal system who was arrested again in March 1994. According to one political-risk report, China now vies with Indonesia for first place as the most corrupt country in Asia.[11] On a scale of one to ten, in which ten corresponds to a very serious corruption problem exerting an extremely negative influence on the business climate, China scored over eight. There are, however, no families like those of Ferdinand Marcos in the Philippines or Suharto in Indonesia, who openly defy the public by handing out licenses and granting monopolies to their relatives. This can be attributed in part to the Chinese tradition of secluding themselves behind walls. The privileged life of the Communist elite takes place "discreetly" behind the high walls of Zhongnanhai, the Chinese Kremlin, and many other walled compounds, where no outsider is permitted, with the exception of foreign VIPs and some journalists. This discretion and reluctance to show off wealth is also the result of decades of Communist restraint under the motto "Hard Work and Plain Living" (*jianku pusu*) during the guerrilla war.

During his last visit to China in late 1993, Milton Friedman described corruption as "manifestations of the market in a decaying planned economy."[12] Another popular view is that corruption cannot be all bad because it lubricates a machine that has become rusty and rickety after so many years of central planning. It can be—and often is—carried to extremes, however. The overriding factor here is best expressed by Lord Acton's pronouncement "Power tends to corrupt, and absolute power corrupts absolutely."

IN SPITE of the negative aspects, as amply reported in China's own official media, the positive balance of the "turning point of 1992" is incontestable. It was the third "liberation" from the remaining bureaucratic shackles that state and party control still had on the enterprising Chinese. The new surge of economic growth generated a mood of euphoria during the years 1992–93, both inside and outside China. Stimulated by optimistic reports from the World Bank, the International Monetary Fund (IMF), and the *Economist,* the worldwide "China Gold Rush" reached fabulous proportions. The boardrooms of multinational corporations and banks, government offices, the media, universities, and publishing houses all switched to "high China alert." The time was right for opening that legendary Chinese market, of which the Western business world had dreamed for more than a hundred years and which had now reached 1.2 billion in number. But behind that growth rate of 12 to 13 percent lurked immense problems that threatened to disturb, delay, and possibly derail China's transformation into an open market.

The lingering crisis in the state sector is chronic and, like cancer, incurable, though not necessarily fatal in the short run. Since the first important party conference on industrial reform, the third plenum of 1984, piecemeal reform has been introduced in state-owned enterprises: production based on quotas and contracts (instead of government orders based on the current Five-Year Plan), the recruitment of foreign managers, the issuing of bonds and (since 1990) shares, the formation of conglomerates in which the strong "adopt" the weak, and so on. However, reforms have fallen far short of their stated goal of "industrial Darwinism," whereby the strong survive and the weak perish. Fear of massive unemployment and social unrest has kept the weak alive through subsidies, loans, and other stopgap measures. The Bankruptcy Law was enacted in November 1988, but actual implementation of this "weed killer" among the loss-taking state enterprises had to await the introduction of basic social legislation, and this was not attempted until 1992.

At the Fourteenth Party Congress in late 1992, the new hybrid economy was redefined as a "socialist market economy," an oxymoron that can be bent to suit one's purpose. If the breakthrough to the market economy gets bogged down in endless, ambivalent bungling, then the emphasis will remain on the adjective "socialist," whereas if the breakthrough becomes a reality, it will simply be shortened to "market economy." In that case, however, it will continue for a long time to be a market based on networks of "special relations" instead of on supply and demand.

In November 1993 a historic third plenum—this time of the Fourteenth

Central Party Committee—was held which issued a systematic but still incomplete blueprint for the recovery of the state sector. Privatization of large state enterprises was still anathema, as these industries form the economic basis of the party's monopoly on political power. "Corporatization" became the catchword, meaning the transformation of large state enterprises into limited-liability companies with the state acting only as owner and largest shareholder, and no longer as operational manager. A change in ownership and property rights would have led to the emergence of a new bourgeoisie.[13] "This would constitute a fundamental threat to the socialist system," the *People's Daily* commented on the blueprint. However, things were not permitted to go beyond issuing additional shares on China's two stock exchanges in Shenzhen and the born-again national financial center of Shanghai, over-the-counter share-trading in an increasing number of large cities, and, for the chosen few, a listing on Hong Kong's international stock exchange. Initially, the state was meant to keep approximately 60 percent of the shares in its own hands. Flexibility is increasing, though, and this sometimes allows for state holdings as low as 30 percent.

The euphoria over this flagship of capitalism—issues of shares—was short-lived, however. In 1994 China's stock market sank into such a malaise that the issue of new stock was suspended for an indefinite period. In one year the index on the stock exchanges in Shenzhen and Shanghai plummeted by 60 to 70 percent, partly because of oversupply and weak regulation and partly because of the frequent issue of government bonds and treasury bills, a less risky form of investment for China's small-time investors. Even the shares issued on the Hong Kong stock exchange by Chinese state enterprises—in 1993 still the object of wild profiteering—had lost their luster by 1994 and were not even fully subscribed.

In 1994–95 the reform process faced a tremendous dilemma. If the state sector did not reform itself radically, it could not become competitive. If it did succeed in reforming itself radically, bankruptcies and social upheavals would ensue, and it would not be competitive for a long time to come. How could a chaotic, high-growth economy catering to quantity be turned into a modern and efficient economy based on quality?

As the minister in charge of the State Planning Commission, Chen Jinhua, said at the annual session of the National People's Congress in March 1996, the quality of economic growth and the economic returns achieved in the country are not satisfactory because of low technology and the high consumption of energy and raw materials. "Rapid development will not be sustainable if it relies solely on high consumption of resources when the scale of the Chinese economy keeps growing," the minister added.

If the state sector embarks on large-scale privatization, a period of high unemployment and social instability will be unavoidable and a growing middle class of entrepreneurs, stockbrokers, accountants, consultants, corporate lawyers, and headhunters will make the Communist party even more irrelevant than it is today. The golden mean is piecemeal experimentation based on local conditions, and if the repercussions cannot be dealt with, then backtracking is called for. This is in fact the most apt description of the Chinese model of economic reform.

Reliable figures on the number of loss-taking state enterprises are hard to come by, but in 1996 the official figure was slightly over 40 percent. According to a multitude of unofficial figures, though, large numbers of enterprises that were actually in the red reported profits. Under capitalism, companies face "hard-budget" constraints. If they stay in the red for too long, they are mercilessly declared bankrupt. Under socialism, the practice of a "soft budget" still applies, though it is rapidly losing favor, which means that loss-taking companies can no longer count on limitless borrowing. The government lurches forward on its unsteady course, weaving back and forth: its priority is stability, but because of all its zigzagging, it inadvertently relinquishes control over the monetary instruments at its disposal to fight inflation.

The companies in the worst difficulty produce goods for which there is no longer any market, continuing to churn out their outdated and unwanted products because it would be too risky to fire their workers, whom they pay with subsidies, bank loans, or so-called "triangular" loans from other companies, entangling themselves in "chain debts." Many of these enterprises no longer receive raw materials and have had their power supplies cut off, forcing them in many cases to stop production. Yet they are not legally bankrupt because they continue to obtain money from one source or another to pay at least partial wages to their workers, who no longer work but are nevertheless not "unemployed." Some enterprises pay their workers in goods—socks or bicycle bells, for example—which they then sell on the street, providing them with substitute wages.

According to Chinese economists, approximately one-third of all the 100 million workers employed in the state sector are superfluous. Other state enterprises suffer losses not because they are hopelessly antiquated and useless, but because the government can no longer afford to pay for the old Communist practice of the "iron rice bowl," or cradle-to-grave care, including housing, schools, health care, and so on. Enterprises of this sort can still save themselves if they manage to turn over their dormitories, schools, and clinics to local governments, but their fate depends largely on so-called "stability and unity" loans.

The flow of money stops and starts again depending on the political barometer. If the bank turns off the tap, money is borrowed from other companies. Triangular loans that lead to chain debts are on the increase and, according to the State Bureau of Statistics, amounted at the end of 1995 to 800 billion yuan, or more than one-fifth of all the bank assets in the country. According to unofficial estimates, however, the real total was 2.8 trillion yuan.[14]

A large proportion of these enterprises will never be able to repay their debts, and the banking sector cannot be reformed as long as this problem persists—another Catch-22 situation. If all the companies that find themselves in financial difficulty were to be declared bankrupt, one-fifth of all bank assets would have to be written off.

On 1 July 1994 the new Company Law (*Gongsi Fa*), a piece of legislation that was long overdue, finally became effective. The law's first priority was comprehensive registration of all firms in a "Registry of Companies." The number of companies had multiplied, but reliable statistics were hard to come by. Many of the new firms were government agencies that simply hung commercial nameplates on their doors without bothering to privatize. One famous example is PolyTechnologies Inc., formerly the Foreign Affairs Office of the General Staff and now one of China's largest arms dealers.

The new law distinguishes between private limited-liability companies and public limited-liability companies. Since the law went into effect, economic newspapers and periodicals have introduced models for the transformation of state enterprises into corporations, such as stock flotation, selling small- and medium-sized businesses at auction, slimming down firms, and hiving off one or more divisions to a foreign investor ("one factory–two systems"), as well as leasing. Everything is still in the experimental stage, however. In 1994 the State Council designated one hundred enterprises to serve as "national models for the modern enterprise system," in which state ownership must be reconciled with the market economy. Under the supervision of Zhu Rongji, eighteen cities were selected to conduct radical experiments in bankruptcy procedures.

Drastic amendments to the Bankruptcy Law were also announced to meet the demands of the market economy and to put an end to bureaucratic interference in the "rescue" of hopelessly failing enterprises. The original Bankruptcy Law of 1986 (put into force officially in 1988) had seen only sporadic enforcement because government and party officials continually exercised their de facto veto over court rulings. The most notorious case of this was the intervention of president and party leader Jiang Zemin in blocking the bankruptcy of Yi Min Foodstuffs Company, the largest producer of foodstuffs in Shanghai. In the early 1950s Jiang had been a manager of this company. In 1994 the party secretary of Shanghai, Wu Bangguo, wanted to end the agony of the company and initiate bankruptcy proceedings, but Jiang, who in the past had also been party secretary and mayor of Shanghai, ordered Wu to do all that he could to save it.[15]

It seemed that 1995 would be a critical year for reform of the state sector, but it turned out to be a year of backtracking rather than a year of progress. Wu Bangguo, a new member of the Politburo from Shanghai and a protégé of President Jiang Zemin's, became the new vice-premier in March 1995 and took over Zhu Rongji's responsibilities in connection with reforming state enterprises. Wu—perhaps more under the sway of Jiang Zemin than his predecessor—has taken a much more conservative approach, no longer mentioning the words "corporatization" and "bankruptcy" in his speeches. All efforts were redirected at experiments designed to save state enterprises. The plan announced earlier by Zhu Rongji to experiment in eighteen cities was reformulated by Wu Bangguo as "optimization of the capital structure of urban enterprises." In 1996 the number of pilot cities was raised to fifty.

Wu Jinglian, the leading reformist economist, has underscored one of the biggest problems: historical burdens. Chinese workers have worked for extremely low wages for the greater part of their lives, in exchange for social security—the "iron rice bowl"—for which the factory was directly responsible. Wu equates this with implicit payment of social insurance premiums, contributing to the accumulation of state assets. He argues that the state must now reimburse all these camouflaged social premiums. The new social security system is still in an embryonic stage, however, and Chinese workers in the state sector, who for decades have been fed the myth that they were the "masters of the state," now face the sad prospect of unemployment without compensation.

An experience in the South China city of Guangzhou (Canton) illustrates just how little room there is to maneuver in tackling the problems surrounding the state enterprises. Professor Chen Chi, deputy director of the Commission for Restructuring the Economic System of the Province of Guangdong, said that even in his province, where the state sector is proportionately smaller than in any other province in China, the bankruptcy of large state corporations is politically and socially impossible. After all, he said, the workers are the staunchest supporters of the Communist party. Their mottoes are "Follow the Communist Party! No Bankruptcy! Iron Rice Bowl! Socialism Is Superior!" Catch-22!

Another reason for the lack of progress in enforcing the Bankruptcy Law is the unsettled issue of property rights and the impossibility of ignoring them in bankruptcy cases. For instance, if a state-owned enterprise becomes a public limited-liability company with the state owning 30 percent of the stock, who can properly be said to have the rights of ownership? Communist leaders are not ready to tackle the question of ownership because it bears too much on the essence of the socialist system. Furthermore, in the volatile, transitional period just after the death of Deng Xiaoping, no one dares to make a decision on a question of this magnitude. Li Yining, senior professor of economics at Beijing University and a leading member of the National People's Congress, said during a meeting of its Standing Committee in August 1996, "Whenever reform of the property rights system is mentioned, they will link it with 'privatization' and turn it into a political issue." He called on state and party leaders to change their way of thinking and to free their minds of old concepts. Liu Suinian, a former minister in charge of materials and now chairman of the Economics and Finance Committee of the National People's Congress, described the debate on the reform of state enterprises as "hearing monks saying their prayers every day without seeing them carrying water."[16]

During 1996 there was another dramatic increase in the losses made by state enterprises. In mid-1996 the State Commission for Restructuring the Economy decided to extend the length of the "trial period" for the formation of the modern enterprise system by one year, from the end of 1996 to the end of 1997. China's semiofficial news service for Hong Kong and the overseas Chinese, Zhongguo Xinwen She (China News Agency, or CNA), which is always more informative than the orthodox state news agency, Xinhua (XNA), sharply criticized this backsliding. The agency reported that more than 80 percent of the enterprises selected to test the modern enterprise system preferred the old system of state ownership. This seriously thwarts the goal of the trial, which is to induce as many enterprises as possible to adopt the form of a limited-liability company characterized by holdings of shares by shareholders from various sectors: state, collective, and private. "There is a danger that reform of the form of asset organization of state-owned enterprises will degenerate into a mere formality." During the trial reforms, 70 percent of the pilot enterprises opted to have the chairman of the board of directors double as the general manager.[17]

Most factory managers in China are Soviet-style engineers without any schooling or expertise in financial management, and this explains their reluctance to have a board and shareholders above them. Under the old system, they could use their connections to plug the leaks: guaranteeing their supply of energy, raw materials, and credit; covering up fraud and theft;

using state funds to pay for luxurious meals, travel, and entertainment; and manipulating financial reports and falsifying statistics to ensure their promotion. Many if not most of them would prefer to keep it that way.

The Hong Kong newspaper *Ming Pao* threw an interesting sidelight on the severe constraints put on Vice-premier Wu Bangguo, the man in overall charge of the industrial transformation. Wu opposed the proposal put forward by some experts simply to freeze the debts of state enterprises after mergers and to allow them not to pay interest. "Merger must assume all liabilities and involves both taking over assets and paying debts. The method of asking the state to lay aside the debts of loss-taking enterprises and to allow them not to pay interest on loans is tantamount to shifting the burden to society and the country. This method is not advisable," said Wu. He reportedly felt sad about the harsh way common people were dealt with by the police whenever they tried to present petitions to leaders during inspections of crisis areas. Wu reiterated that the many difficulties handed down to them by history could not be solved by one method only. He adamantly opposed privatization as a panacea. Wu went on to say that a "breakthrough in property rights means privatization. . . . It does not work at all."[18]

The reassertion of orthodox Marxist principles was highlighted in a landmark page-long article in the *People's Daily* by the ultraleft economist Wu Shuqing, who replaced the popular liberal Ding Shisun as president of Beijing University immediately after the Tiananmen crackdown in 1989 and who retired from this position in July 1996. Wu serves as an adviser to the central leadership and is well connected with the leftist-dominated propaganda apparatus in Beijing. His writing probably reflects the thinking of Premier Li Peng, who feels that the erosion of the role of the state in the economy must be stopped and, if possible, reversed. Wu's dogmatic ranting cannot have much long-term impact on the fast-changing economic realities across the country, but since it is published by the top organ of the party it will go on causing much confusion and many delays in the implementation of further reforms.

Wu emphasizes the overall superiority of public ownership in the national economy and its broadening role in the socialist market economy. Other sectors, such as the private sector and those relying on foreign investment, may coexist but they are not equal to the state sector. He offers four main explanations for the existence of those who continually try to move China away from the socialist road:

1. Hostile forces in the West have tried by all possible means to infiltrate China by propagating privatization in the economic sector,

democratization in the political field, and pluralism in the ideological realm.

2. Domestically, China is still in the primary stage of socialism, whose innate superiority has not yet fully manifested itself. More time is needed to overcome the doubts of those who think that capitalism is superior.

3. Owing to the incomplete transition from orthodox socialism to the socialist market economy, state enterprises face numerous complications, such as the problem of "historical burdens," which have been building up over the years and cannot be solved in the near future. Nonstate enterprises are not burdened with these problems, and this leads to the erroneous conclusion that privatization is the answer.

4. As reforms "deepen," the proportion of state enterprises in the national economy has decreased while the proportion of nonstate enterprises has increased—a process that will continue for some time. The underlying cause of this process is twofold: population growth and the lack of employment and capital. The state sector cannot provide a solution to either of these problems. The nonstate economy is in a more favorable position to absorb the surplus of labor and to attract foreign investment to compensate for lack of funds. The nonstate economy has advantages of its own, and this of course produces its own *self-serving* [the italics are mine] ideology, resulting in demands that the nonstate economy become dominant, thereby publicizing its own superiority. Some people, either consciously or unconsciously, will take this viewpoint and suggest that privatization replace public ownership. "Drawing a line"—that is, putting a stop to further erosion of the state sector and blocking the constant growth of the private sector—is therefore a necessary and long-term process.

Wu Shuqing proceeds to quote at length from Marx to underpin his reactionary views, but refuses to admit that the flaws and shortcomings of the socialist system are the fundamental cause of the serious crisis in the state sector. Wu redefined the meaning of the speech given by Deng Xiaoping in 1992, in which Deng reinterpreted socialism and purposefully blurred the distinction between it and capitalism. Deng said that many economic concepts—the stock market, for example—were not exclusive to capitalism, and therefore socialism could use them as well, as long as they promoted the growth of the productive forces, increased the overall strength of the socialist state, and raised the standard of living—the three benefits. Deng's statement led many Chinese to the conclusion that one no longer had to insist on socialism. The essence of Wu's peroration was that in building "socialism with Chinese characteristics" it was necessary to ensure that the system remain socialist.[19]

Wu Shuqing is widely regarded as "the Deng Liqun of the economic realm." Deng Liqun, nicknamed the "leftist king," is China's leading orthodox Marxist, who for some time has been preparing an all-out assault on Deng Xiaoping and his legacy. The article by Wu Shuqing quoted earlier is seen by Chinese intellectuals as the pacesetter for the economic assault on the Deng Xiaoping legacy, to be followed by a host of similar diatribes during the next one or two years.

A prominent liberal economist, Fan Gang, takes a relaxed view of all this ideological bickering. "Whatever is decreed from above, things are already moving from the bottom up," he said. He thinks that the problems surrounding the state enterprises will go away by themselves in about ten years. Almost all of the small state enterprises have been put up for auction or opened up to shareholders. He estimates that in about five years larger enterprises will have taken the same path. Their debts will be partly repaid by the buyers and partly declared dead. "If the economy continues to grow at about 10 percent per year with annual inflation of 10 percent, the stock of bad loans will depreciate by 20 percent per year," he declared optimistically.[20]

In this way, Communism in China will slowly but steadily fade away, without a "big bang" of instant privatization such as occurred in the Soviet Union, but with the slow death, sale, and leasing of thousands of state enterprises.

NO MATTER what China looks like ten, fifteen, or twenty years from now—a permanently half-reformed state economy, a corporatist state, an incipient market economy, or on its way to becoming something else altogether—the implications for the rest of the world will be immense. In the year 2010 China will have close to 1.5 billion people, making it the largest homogeneous linguistic region in the world with the largest pool of talent and an increasingly well-trained supply of labor. In 1993 the combined trade of China, Hong Kong, and Taiwan—the Greater Chinese Trading Bloc—exceeded that of Japan for the first time. Greater China's trade amounted to 8.5 percent of all world trade, as opposed to Japan's, which was slightly over 8 percent. Until 1995 Chinese exports grew faster than those of Japan, but during 1996 they fell by 7 percent, owing to the Chinese government's lowering of its tax refund rate. In 1996 the combined reserves of China and Hong

Kong amounted to slightly more than $150 billion—almost as high as Japan's national reserves, which are the highest in the world—while those of Taiwan amounted to another $85 billion.

The big question is whether a powerful China will be a cooperative partner in an interdependent world economy or whether it will be a mercantilistic giant operating on the maxi-mini principle: deriving a maximum of benefits while making minimal contributions. China's trade practices are dubious and hurt not only the countries belonging to the Organization of Economic Cooperation and Development (OECD), whose intellectual property rights (IPR) are violated on a massive scale and whose markets are a target of Chinese dumping. Third World countries are also the victims of this unfair competition. A report issued by the Japanese Nomura Research Institute concluded that the smaller competitors among the developing countries in Asia—such as the Philippines, Indonesia, Thailand, and India—have the most to fear from China. The newly industrialized economies of South Korea, Taiwan, Hong Kong, and Singapore, as well as those of Japan and the West, have the most to gain as investors and as the source of increasing Chinese imports, assuming that China plays according to international rules, and not according to its own.[21]

In 1978 China ranked thirty-second on the list of trading powers; by 1995 it had risen to number ten, in imports as well as exports. China's growing role in world trade has so far been mainly positive,[22] although it has the potential to become an enormous negative influence if it continues to be a crypto-state economy controlled by inscrutable bureaucrats who protect whole sectors of industry by means of high tariffs and other opaque barriers to trade. With its immense reservoir of cheap labor, China could flood the world with low-priced products and would soon have trade surpluses exceeding those of Japan many times over. In June 1996 the U.S. trade deficit with China surpassed that with Japan for the first time.

The question of the American trade deficit with China is a highly political issue. The U.S. figures for Chinese trade surpluses were approximately $22.8 billion in 1993, $29.5 billion in 1994, and $33.8 billion in 1995. Chinese statistics, however, show much lower figures: approximately $6.3 billion in 1993, $7.5 billion in 1994, and $8.6 billion in 1995. There are two main reasons for the discrepancies: one is that the U.S. figures include the entrepôt trade via Hong Kong and Singapore, and the other is the difficulty of determining which part of the processing was done where, and to whose trading balance it should be credited.

Sixty percent of China's exports travel through Hong Kong, and the average markup in the price of toys and garments—as a result of quality inspection and transportation fees, for example—is 40 percent. Hong Kong, Taiwan, Singapore, and South Korea have transferred their labor-intensive industries to the Chinese mainland and now have trade surpluses with China instead of with the United States. "Therefore," said Wu Yi, China's trade minister, "China's favorable balance of trade with the United States is just the result of regional readjustments in industrial patterns and is by no means a key element with an adverse impact on the U.S. trade balance. The main beneficiaries are businesses in Hong Kong and Taiwan and the foreign investors there, not China. China receives only the processing charges and the actual amount of foreign exchange from exports, earned through processing trade, is very limited."[23]

ACCORDING TO THE U.S. acting trade representative, Charlene Barshefsky, China is currently the worst pirate of copyrights and patents in the world. It owes part of its schooling in the art of counterfeiting to investors from Hong Kong, Taiwan, Singapore, and even Japan. Traditionally, Taiwan was one of the top producers of falsified brand-name products, but since the late 1980s policing there has been very strict—hence the great exodus of Taiwanese "pirates" who have moved their base of operations to the mainland where it is still fair game for those with friends in the right places.

The conflict with the United States and the West in general over the massive theft of intellectual property rights—rights relating to computer software, laser and compact discs, CD-ROMs and video games, book copyrights, trademarks and patents on an endless list of products, including toothpaste, shampoos, shoes, and so on—is a deep-seated one and cannot be settled by a few diplomatic agreements. The law-blind Chinese simply do not see anything wrong with it, and the Chinese government is not always able to enforce compliance with its recently adopted antipiracy legislation. The American demand to close down all the (state) factories producing millions of copycat CDs for export cannot be met in the short run, apparently because the driving force behind some of them, according to detectives quoted by the American media, are the children of top leaders and senior military officials who are above the law, even more so than nonhereditary and civilian Communists.

The instant closure of factories producing imitation quality textiles and brand-name shoes is socially problematic in a country that faces massive unemployment and where tens of millions of wandering peasants trek to the coastal areas "to join the industrial revolution." Chinese leaders therefore say that American demands disregard "the needs of developing countries." The Chinese are particularly sensitive about American threats to use economic sanctions, which are unacceptable because they "hurt the national feelings of the Chinese people." Foreign overreaction to a Chinese misdemeanor is, in the eyes of the Chinese, more offensive than the misdemeanor itself. According to their logic, the United States is the perpetrator and China the victim, and not the other way around.

The Chinese have vowed to honor agreements and to make concessions, but of their own free will, based on their own national interests, and not under foreign pressure, which it labels "power politics, a violation of sovereignty, and interference in domestic affairs." When the United States accused China in 1996 of not implementing an earlier accord on IPR enforcement which had been signed in February 1995, Beijing indignantly blamed U.S. electioneering politics for the new flare-up. The United States then invoked "Super 301" and issued a full list of impending trade sanctions, levying a 100 percent tariff on Chinese imports to the United States worth $2 billion. Never one to be deterred in a war of words, China lashed back at American "nitpicking and overbearing acts of a coercive nature," while stressing its own record of "comprehensive and conscientious fulfillment of all its obligations." One Chinese newspaper said that China was leading other countries, such as Russia, India, Indonesia, and Vietnam, in protecting IPR and that U.S. bullying of China was tantamount to "whipping a willing horse."

The two powers have had a long history of going to the brink and then, after nerve-racking marathon sessions of negotiation, backing off again. This time as well, sanctions and retaliations were called off at the last minute, and a new agreement was signed on 17 June 1996 by Acting U.S. Trade Representative Charlene Barshefsky, thus averting a major trade war. China had conceded stricter supervision of offending factories but had refused to ease the access of domestic movies to its domestic market, more for ideological than for commercial reasons. Only weeks after the agreement was signed, pirates were out again in droves, hawking their CDs, CD-ROMs, and other merchandise along the tourist strips in Beijing. Law enforcement in China is out of control in many areas. Perhaps the final solution lies in legalization of the pirate companies, combined with a radically discounted price regimen.

For all of these reasons—old-style protectionism, IPR violations, dumping—and many others, China's ten-year struggle to join the GATT, now the World Trade Organization, has so far not been successful. The main obstacle is the nature of China's economy, which is still largely state-controlled, as opposed to the market economies of the WTO membership. The United

States is leading a campaign to impose stiff conditions on China's entry, treating it as a developed country. In terms of per capita income, China certainly belongs to the lower crust of the Third World, but considering the size of its economy, the quantitative strength and relatively advanced state of certain industries, and its imminent takeover of the highly advanced export economy of Hong Kong, China is definitely in a class by itself. China demands the right to joint the WTO as a developing country, which would enable it to invoke its "poverty" and "industrial weakness" to shield its own market by means of high tariffs for a longer period of adjustment and to entitle it to temporary special treatment in areas such as subsidies, investment, and IPR.

Until 1993 imported cars were taxed at a rate of 200 to 300 percent. In recent years this has been lowered to 140 percent. The United States is determined to pry open China's market even further, and although its European allies do not agree with American tactics, they are working toward the same goal. Although tariffs were actually reduced by an average of 30 percent in April 1996, the trend in China is toward even more protectionism to prevent Chinese brands from losing ground against foreign brands produced by joint ventures with foreign companies. This has coincided with the rise of Chinese nationalism, culminating in the urge to say no to the United States and turning the issue of competition and fair trade into jingoistic calls to take drastic measures against the new "economic invaders."

During his visit to Paris in April 1996, Premier Li Peng summed up China's growing exasperation with America's attempt to block Chinese membership in the WTO. "If China cannot join the WTO, then we think that the WTO should change its name to Regional Trade Organization."

Final negotiations on China's admission will go into high gear in 1997 and are expected to end in an agreement to let China join the WTO in phases.

AFTER THE MILITARY CRACKDOWN on the protest movement in 1989, China's dissident community went underground, but it ventured out into the light again three or four years later, switching the focus of its struggle for political pluralism to "the improvement of existing economic pluralism." Several groups devoted themselves to the improvement of workers' rights and the establishment of free trade unions in an attempt to bring about political change indirectly. The regime's seemingly newfound tolerance proved to be a sham, however. Dozens of dissidents were arrested in 1994, many of them during the visit to China of the U.S. secretary of state, Warren Christopher. He had come—believe it or not—to see whether China had made enough progress in the field of human rights to qualify for unconditional renewal of its status as a "most favored nation" (MFN) in trade. This demonstrated the bankruptcy of American "evangelism," which assumed it could exact improvement in the area of human rights through public confrontations and ultimatums. The Chinese thumbed their noses at this, making it clear that China operates according to Chinese rules, and not according to American dictates. This was the Chinese version of "dollar diplomacy."

Their rapidly growing imports of capital goods had shown the Chinese where their strength lay. They needed dozens of Boeing jets, telecommunications and information highway systems, car factories, airports, highways, nuclear power stations, pipelines—the shopping list went on and on—and they knew how to cajole the Western industrial and banking elite, even behind the backs of their government leaders. In October 1994 the minister of finance, Liu Zhongli, said that during the next ten years China hoped to tap $500 billion from international capital markets for the construction of infrastructure projects alone. The chairman of CitiCorp, John Reed, said at the same time in Hong Kong that China would need $55 trillion in order to become a fully developed country. He based his estimate on the amount per capita that Germany spent on the reconstruction of the former East Germany—$55,000—multiplied by 1 billion, the population of China, and rounded off to the lower figure.[24]

During the fall of 1992, China seemed for a while to be heading for a serious foreign policy crisis. The United States, under the leadership of China's foremost American friend, George Bush, had decided to supply 150 F-16 fighter planes to Taiwan, and France had followed suit with 60 Mirages. Germany and Holland were wondering (yet again) whether to provide it with large numbers of warships. In anticipation of the transfer of Hong Kong's sovereignty to China in 1997 and against the militant opposition of Beijing, the new British governor, Chris Patten, announced political reforms in the crown colony. The Chinese media went so far as to call it a new, well-orchestrated Cold War between the West and China, with Hong Kong and Taiwan as pawns, or a new "Eight-Power Allied Army" (*Ba-guo Lian-jun*). The first "eight-power army" had suppressed the Boxer Rebellion against foreign control which had fatally undermined the last imperial regime of the notorious dowager empress Ci Xi (Tzu Hsi) in 1900.

China's deft diplomacy managed to fend off the challenges one by one. Discrimination against American companies was stepped up and China refused to participate any longer in arms control talks. France was disqualified from building a subway system and a nuclear power plant in the southern province of Guangdong and was forced to close its consulate in Guangzhou (Canton). Germany and Holland were rewarded for forgoing further arms deals with Taiwan. Chancellor Helmut Kohl was the first Western leader to visit China, taking home a long Chinese shopping list worth 7 billion German marks in contracts. Kohl had mentioned human rights only perfunctorily. France eyed the German success with envy, and immediately after the defeat of the Socialists at the polls began negotiations on normalizing relations with China. Just as Holland had done ten years earlier after its controversial submarine deal with Taiwan, France signed an agreement renouncing the future delivery of arms to Taiwan. The new premier, Edouard Balladur, made a "commercial pilgrimage" to China shortly after that of Warren Christopher, and he also personally witnessed the arrest of daring dissidents. And France managed to secure its contract for the subway system and nuclear power plant after all.

The Clinton administration tried to wriggle out of its predicament, pretending that enough progress had been made in the field of human rights to unlink this issue from China's MFN status. This paved the way for the visit to China by Secretary of Commerce Ron Brown, who outperformed both Kohl and Balladur and took home $6 billion in contracts. In the end, Canada broke all the records. During the fall of 1994, Premier Jean Chrétien netted more than $6.3 billion in contracts and letters of intent, including agreements to build two nuclear power plants. He also got a vivid picture of the state of freedom and human rights in post-Tiananmen China. As part of his official program, Chrétien delivered a speech at Beida University, after which he had intended to mingle with the students for an open discussion; this was promptly prevented by the authorities.

China's leading dissident, Wei Jingsheng, who had been released after serving fourteen and a half years of his fifteen-year sentence in September 1993 as a political maneuver in China's campaign to host the Olympics in the year 2000, was again detained during the political-commercial charade of 1994. Wei had entertained the notion that American pressure would offer him enough protection, but he was sadly disillusioned in this respect: it made him the prime target of assaults by China's anti-American hardliners. Just before his rearrest, he remarked bitterly that Western governments placed more value on commercial orders for their capitalists than on human rights for the Chinese people.[25]

In 1995 Germany was again rewarded for its discreet approach to human rights violations in China. During President Jiang Zemin's jaunt to Bonn, Daimler-Benz received a $3.1 billion contract to build a car factory which had been coveted by both Ford and General Motors.

Premier Li Peng raised the stakes even more during a trip to Paris in

April 1996, where, to the dismay of Boeing and McDonnell Douglas, he signed a $2 billion order for thirty-three Airbus jetliners, including an agreement on a joint project between Airbus and a Chinese company to build a one-hundred-seat jetliner. Strongly dissatisfied with the "political strings" attached to these contracts by the United States, Li criticized the Americans in a blunt interview with the *Financial Times*, in which he praised the Europeans for extending "more favorable terms" to China in business cooperation.[26] This led the U.S. secretary of state for East Asian and Pacific affairs, Winston Lord—the architect of the Clinton administration's well-intentioned but ineffectual China policy—to comment on European and Japanese exploitation of America's fight with China. Lord said, "One of our biggest problems in China is that our friends in Europe and Japan hold our coats while we take on the Chinese and they gobble up the contracts."

ON THE BASIS of its historical self-consciousness and growing economic and military power, China, during the post-Tiananmen era, has irreversibly consolidated its position as an assertive and independent great power that often plays by the rules of world politics as established during the postwar period under Western dominance. When its own national interests are at stake, however, it resorts to its own unilateral interpretation of these rules: for instance, its dubious claims to the South China Sea islands in violation of the Law of the Sea Convention, which China itself ratified. Much more blatant are its efforts in at least one field to take the lead in creating a rival, non-Western world order—the sensitive field of human rights.

In November 1991 the Information Office of the State Council published a fifty-seven-page report that has since served as the standard rejection of Western criticism and interference. In the report, the Chinese government had high praise for the Universal Declaration of Human Rights, hastening to add, however, that the evolution of human rights is circumscribed by a country's historical, social, economic, and cultural conditions. "Owing to tremendous differences in historical background, social systems, cultural tradition, and economic development, countries differ in their understanding and practice of human rights. From their different situations they have taken different attitudes toward the relevant UN conventions. Despite its international aspect, the issue of human rights falls by and large within the sovereignty of each country . . . and cannot be evaluated according to a preconceived model or the conditions of another country or region."[27] The document declared the right to subsistence, for which the Chinese people have fought for so long, as the "foremost human right."

Before the world conference on human rights in Vienna in June 1993,

China and other Asian countries such as Indonesia convened a preliminary conference in Bangkok which formulated an alternative Asian definition of human rights. The "Bangkok Declaration" stressed that all countries, large and small, have the right to determine their own political system, to "dispose" of their resources (natural and human) as they see fit, and to determine their own economic, social, and cultural development. They opposed the use of human rights by Western countries to exert pressure on them and objected to using human rights as a condition for receiving development aid. They further emphasized their national sovereignty and territorial integrity, as well as their opposition to interference in their domestic affairs. China's forceful rejection of the universality of human rights, embracing instead "cultural relativism" and a "materialistic redefinition," was the first manifestation of a new interpretation of international relations since the end of the Cold War, as eloquently expounded by the leading American political scientist Samuel Huntington in his trailblazing article "The Clash of Civilizations." The crux of his view is that the fundamental cause of conflict within the "new world order" is no longer primarily ideological or economic, but cultural. Hong Kong, Taiwan, Singapore, and the overseas Chinese communities worldwide all belong to "Confucian civilization." A common culture will increasingly facilitate economic integration, while remaining ideological differences, such as those between China and Taiwan, will fade into irrelevance.

Huntington cites China's growing links—particularly military client relations—with anti-Western Islamic states as the "Confucian-Islamic connection," which poses a threat to Western interests, values, and power.[28]

SINCE THE FIRST WAR IN THE GULF, between Iran and Iraq (1982–87), China has become a major supplier of weapons to the very lucrative arms bazaar in the Middle East, supplying 22 percent of Iran's weapons ($3.3 billion) and 9 percent of Iraq's ($4.2 billion). Both Iran and Iraq received "Silkworm" missiles with which they shelled each other continuously, enabling them both to prolong the war. China allegedly provided Syria with missiles as well, although the United States has never been able to produce evidence of this. In 1988 China made inroads for the first time in the arms market of an American client state, Saudi Arabia. After the pro-Israeli lobby in Congress blocked their supply of American F-15s, the Saudis turned to China for their weapons. Although China could not supply them with an adequate fighter plane, it did have missiles of the "Eastwind" type. Concerned that the deal might damage Sino-American relations, the pragmatic

Chinese foreign ministry opposed it. Hua Di, the Chinese missile specialist who defected to the United States after the Tiananmen incident, revealed that the deal was sealed by Deng Xiaoping himself when he heard that it would yield between $2 billion and $3 billion. Deng's son-in-law, He Ping, was at that time chairman of PolyTechnologies Inc., the arms manufacturer that is actually an offshoot of the General Staff.[29]

China has also supplied nuclear technology to North Korea, Iran, and Pakistan, not only for peaceful purposes but also possibly for the production of nuclear arms. An arms deal with Algeria was canceled before completion.

China is also the largest supplier of arms to other Third World countries, such as Myanmar (Burma) and the former American client state, Thailand—a natural ally against their common historical enemy, Vietnam. Western pressure and the de-escalation of other Third World conflicts (Cambodia, Iran-Iraq, Israel-Palestine) have caused China's arms exports to drop considerably since 1989. The superiority of American technology was dramatically demonstrated during the Gulf War of 1991, and this also caused potential buyers to lose interest in obsolete Chinese hardware. The war alerted the backward Chinese military to the need for speeding up its military modernization, essential not only to China's becoming a military superpower but also to its efforts to increase its share of the international arms market. Moreover, the suspension of military cooperation with the United States in the aftermath of Tiananmen drove China into the welcoming arms of Russia. China became the largest importer not only of advanced Russian military hardware but also of Russian military technicians. The Russian ambassador to China, Igor Rogachov, once told me that he had no idea how many Russian experts were working at Chinese military research institutes. The largely invisible Russian-Chinese military links are a growing source of concern for the West, but the Russians have a simple rationale for it: if NATO moves East, we also move East.

The West is even more worried about the current large-scale military cooperation between China and Israel. After years of denials, the late premier Yitzhak Rabin finally admitted during his visit to China in 1993 that his country had supplied arms to China. According to military journals, the supply of guidance systems, missile warheads, and tank guns started in 1980, amounting over the years to perhaps $3 billion. Israel also moved into the void that arose after the rupture of Sino-American military cooperation as a result of the Tiananmen episode. It has been helping the Chinese with the development of new types of missiles, avionics, and even a new fighter plane based on the Lavi, originally a joint Israeli-American project. As far as China is concerned, cooperation with Israel replaced the "Peace Pearl Project," which was broken off by Washington. In early 1992 Israel was accused by American sources of secretly transferring Patriot missile technology to China, although the accusation was later retracted.[30]

The Sino-Israeli military liaison increasingly continues to jeopardize China's good relations with Islamic client states, therefore invalidating at least in part Huntington's scenario of a "Confucian-Islamic connection" opposed to the West. Israel entered into this relationship in order to gain a bit of leverage on the "China factor" in the Middle East, in other words, so as to influence China's supply of arms and missiles to the Arabs. So far China has benefited most from this relationship, getting the best of both worlds—hard currency from the Arabs and high tech from Israel.

American military experts are satisfied that China shows no signs of harboring malicious export schemes aimed at destabilizing areas of tension. The one time that American intelligence services were able to gloat over catching the Chinese red-handed turned into a public relations debacle for the United States. During the summer of 1993, U.S. naval vessels pursued a Chinese freighter, the *Yinhe* (Milky Way), for almost a month, suspecting it of carrying to Iran containers of chemical precursors of mustard and nerve gas. Invoking sovereignty, the Chinese rejected American demands for an instant search, but they finally permitted a third-party inspection in Saudi Arabia. Nothing whatever was found, but the Americans refused to comply with the Chinese demand that the United States apologize and pay damages.

American pressure and sanctions in the field of arms proliferation are routinely ignored by Chinese spokesmen, or else are met with a broad smile and dismissed with the following admonition, not based entirely on fact: "The United States is the largest arms supplier [also to developing countries] in the world. China also exports a small quantity of arms."

Arms Supplies to the Third World
1985–1992 (IN BILLIONS OF U.S.$)[31]

Soviet Union/Russia	108.3
United States	44.9
United Kingdom	22.3
France	20.2
China	12.2

China signed the Nuclear Nonproliferation Treaty in March 1992 but continued its nuclear tests until July 1996. Its attitude toward the Missile Technology Control Regime (MTCR)—a multilateral consultation forum set up to prevent the proliferation of missiles capable of carrying warheads—has been aloof for a number of years, since the freezing of Sino-American military exchanges. After its last nuclear test in July 1996, China finally signed the Nuclear Test Ban Treaty.

ONE OF THE MOST controversial questions in political and academic debates is China's rapidly increasing defense budget, which in certain circles has revived the specter of "the Yellow Peril." Every March, during the annual session of the National People's Congress, military attachés of the large embassies anxiously wait for the finance minister to reveal the new figure for defense expenditure. Official defense spending has increased over the past eight years by between 12.6 and 20.4 percent annually, from 21.8 billion yuan in 1988 to 65.6 billion yuan in 1995 ($7.5 billion, according to the new exchange rate). With a troop strength of 2.9 million, this is a figure that cannot be taken seriously by any criteria. This amounts to $2,000 per head per year, whereas the United States, with a defense budget of $280 billion, spends $180,000 per head per year. The People's Liberation Army also receives indirectly a great deal of "extrabudgetary" income and benefits from the motley allocation of funds to other sectors, such as science and technology. Commercial enterprises—including converted arms factories, farms, aviation and shipping companies, hotels, bars, and nightclubs—are also a major source of revenue. One of the most prominent in this respect is the pharmaceutical multinational "999 Enterprise Group" with factories in Russia, Germany, Thailand, and the United States. The international media have conveniently portrayed this military-commercial complex, nicknamed PLA Inc., as a highly corrupt, money-grabbing racket run by China's generals and their offspring. This is probably true to a large extent, although the full picture is considerably more complex. In the first place, the emergence of PLA Inc. is a positive result of economic reform, in particular the conversion of the many superfluous, obsolete, loss-taking arms factories to civilian companies producing consumer goods.

Since the early 1980s inflation and budget cuts have seriously eroded military finances—including the standard of living of rank-and-file soldiers and the quality of materials—to such an extent that commercialization was the only answer to the problem. This has not been a great success, however. The machinery and funds necessary to manufacture products on a sufficiently advanced technological level are lacking. Rapid social changes have led to a demand for cheap, mass-produced goods and the quick construction of amusement facilities. What is the easiest and most obvious solution? Catering to market demands for cheap cosmetics, foodstuffs, textiles, fans, disco equipment, and karaoke facilities was the first step. The next step was karaoke bars and discos run by the army units themselves.

It has all gotten out of hand. Mismanagement and the creeping corruption inherent in the process have not only undermined the already low level of regard in which the armed forces are held, but have further damaged military professionalism and efficiency. The Central Military Commission is trying in the meantime to regulate commercial activities. If it moves too quickly, then these military enterprises—like other state enterprises—will go bankrupt and the state will have to provide substitute funds for defense modernization, an unrealistic expectation in the short term.

Paradoxically, the effects of conversion are not all that negative. One American general confirmed that conversion has taken some of the pressure off Chinese arms exports to the Third World and that even the United States has become a partner in joint efforts to slim down China's bloated military-industrial complex as well as its own.

The income of PLA Inc. is estimated at $6 billion, but it is a closed circuit, accountable to no one. And it is only one of the many alternative financial sources for defense spending outside the official defense budget. In July 1994 the International Institute for Strategic Studies (IISS)—NATO's think tank in London—and Taiwan's Chinese Council for Advanced Policy Studies (CAPS) devoted a conference in Hong Kong to the subject of China's defense budget. Paul Goodwin of the National War College in Washington, D.C., speculated that no one, not even the director of the General Logistics Department of the PLA, knows the exact amount of the extrabudgetary income of PLA Inc. He even doubts that it is a major moneymaker. Goodwin also thinks there is no reason to assume that Chinese generals and analysts are deliberately concealing a massive defense buildup with the aim of dominating Southeast Asia in the future.[32]

In his presentation at the Hong Kong conference, David Shambaugh, formerly of the School of Oriental and African Studies at the University of London, made a detailed estimate of the Chinese "military revenue base," which he put at $45 billion. In 1993 the official defense budget amounted to only $7.4 billion, according to the higher exchange rate. On top of that came $1.5 billion from arms sales; $14.3 billion from direct state allocations to military industries; $24.5 million in state subsidies for the conversion of military industries for civilian purposes; $5 billion in commercial income, including income from converted enterprises; $5 billion from investments in research and development; $3 billion for the People's Armed Police and Special Troops; and undoubtedly more. After deducting 20 percent for inflation and possibly 20 percent for assets not in use, his estimate is that

$27 billion is spent on purely military purposes. In 1993 this was 3.7 times the amount of the official defense budget.[33]

Whichever figures one accepts, China has, according to official exchange rates, only the eighth-highest defense budget in the world, after the United States, Russia, France, Germany, England, Japan, and Italy. (According to the PPP norm, China ranks seventh, before Italy.) The IISS concluded that China does indeed conceal the scale and nature of its military efforts, but does not offer unequivocal estimates. In its 1995 annual report, it retains Shambaugh's sliding estimate for 1994, which was between $28.5 billion and $45 billion.[34]

The IMF estimates are between $23 billion and $32 billion a year from 1990 to 1995. The World Bank believes it to be $37 billion to $52 billion for the same period. The U.S. Arms Control and Disarmament Agency puts the figure at $56 billion. One senior military attaché pointed out the futility of racking one's brains over all manner of computations and estimates, because they give only the vaguest clues as to the real magnitude of Chinese defense spending.

Sino-American military relations were at their most relaxed since 1989 during the onetime visit to China of Defense Secretary William Perry in October 1994. In a speech delivered to three hundred Chinese generals and colonels—with "America the Beautiful" played by a Chinese military band as background music—Perry asked for more openness regarding the defense budget. "Your power in all areas, including military, is growing by the day. It would be very useful if your defense budget and strategic planning would be more open and transparent to the outside world."

Half a year later, however, relations were back to their usual pattern of mutual recriminations and bitter retorts.

DURING THE SUMMER of 1995, relations between the United States and China—the most volatile of the important bilateral relationships of the post–Cold War period—seemed to regress for a while to pre-1972 levels. The Manichaean worldview of a dichotomy between the realms of good and evil had become a recurrent theme in the American media again. The United States has known very little enduring stability in its relations with China, which have always been based on hard-nosed realities and interests. For most of the twentieth century, America has had the irresistible urge to change China "for the better," molding it in the American image, rather than managing to deal with its differences and accept it on its own terms. At the beginning of this century, the picture that most Americans had of the Chinese was one of people similar to themselves, "puritanical, hard-working, and inherently disposed toward good." The only thing they were lacking was the Bible, which would have to be brought to China on a massive scale by American missionaries.

When China turned Communist in 1949, America could neither comprehend nor accept this, branding it a satellite of the Soviet Union, which, like its master, had to be "contained." After China broke with Moscow in 1960, it became a hotbed of Maoist world revolution, which was the rationale behind the United States' ill-conceived war in Vietnam. After Richard Nixon's historic trip to China in 1972, China became the strategic partner of the United States in blocking Soviet expansionism. With the collapse of the Soviet Union in 1991, the partnership no longer had such a visible strategic foundation. As long as the United States needed China to thwart the Russians, Washington maintained a double standard on human rights—a strict one for the Russians and a flexible one for the Chinese. Sino-American relations were therefore relatively relaxed during the 1980s. Since the wave of repression in 1989, the United States has meted out the same tough treatment to China that it once reserved for the Soviet Union. The Chinese simply shrug their shoulders, as the Russians did under Brezhnev, resulting in U.S.-China relations being as highly partisan and negative in the 1990s as they were before 1972. Influential right-wing ideologues, such as Jesse Helms and Patrick Buchanan, demonize China as a country were there is religious persecution and compulsory abortion, where trade in the organs of executed criminals is a form of state revenue—in short, the epitome of moral depravity.

In strategic, political, and diplomatic circles, China is seen as a potential aggressor in the South China Sea, particularly against Taiwan, a large-scale importer of cheap Russian military hardware and renegade military scientists, a supplier of nuclear technology and missiles to reprehensible (Islamic) regimes, the oppressor of Tibet, and the bogeyman of Hong Kong. Optimists are still to be found in business circles, but some of them are repelled by the violations of intellectual property rights, lawlessness, corruption, and the export of goods produced by forced labor.

In this atmosphere of strategic indifference to and moral revulsion against China, President Lee Teng-hui of Taiwan was seen by many Americans as an alternative "good" Chinese, who deserved a bit more respect. After protracted and expensive lobbying in Congress, Lee was permitted to pay an unofficial visit in June 1996 to his alma mater, Cornell University in Ithaca, New York, where he had received his Ph.D. in agronomy in 1968.[35]

On 20 May the State Department was still refusing to grant permission for Lee's visit, angering the House and Senate, which then adopted resolutions to admit Lee with overwhelming majorities of 396 to 0 and 97 to 1. On 22 May the State Department's "nay" became a "yea," and Lee was given the go-ahead to pack his bags for New York. China reacted by working itself up into a state of unmitigated fury. American "treason" and "double-dealing" were cursed endlessly and were blamed for fatally undermining the basis of relations between the two countries. Beijing labeled the vote in Congress a cunning farce and fumed about the American conspiracy to keep China divided and to use Taiwan to "contain" China, thus obstructing China's advance to the status of economic and eventually even political and military superpower. "By putting domestic politics above international law and intergovernmental agreements, the United States displays a completely anachronistic, hegemonistic mentality," the commentator for the Xinhua News Agency stated. In ominous tones, the *People's Daily* wrote: "The Taiwan question is a powder keg. It is extremely dangerous to keep heating it up, whether this is done by the United States or by Lee Teng-hui. If their activities lead to an explosion, the consequences will be unimaginable."[36]

In another act of retaliation, China canceled the upcoming talks of the Missile Technology Control Regime, aimed at preventing the proliferation of missiles, which China had supplied to Iraq, Iran, Saudi Arabia, and perhaps Pakistan. It also suspended other arms control talks and canceled the forthcoming visit to the United States of Defense Minister Chi Haotian. The Chinese ambassador in Washington was recalled for consultations, and the *agrément* of former senator Jim Sasser, designated to succeed the U.S. ambassador to China, Stapleton Roy, was delayed for several months.

An unwelcome side effect of the crisis was the acceleration of Sino-Russian rapprochement, culminating in a rapid succession of top-level exchanges and enhanced military cooperation. During the visit of Chinese premier Li Peng to Moscow in late June, the following warning was issued in a joint communiqué: "Both China and Russia are great powers and we will allow no one to lecture us on how we should behave and how we should live. We will decide these matters for ourselves."

At the climax of this war of nerves, China arrested the activist Harry Wu Hongda, a former prisoner of China's "gulag" who had emigrated to the United States after his release and had then reentered China as an American citizen on undercover missions for the Western media and human rights organizations. He was intercepted at the Xinjiang-Kazakhstan border on the point of beginning a new assignment. His arrest for espionage pushed the anti-China rage in the United States to new heights. Retaliatory action against Taiwan took shape more slowly, indicating that there were deep differences of opinion within the Chinese leadership on how to handle Taiwan. The SEF-ARATS talks already under way continued for several weeks until they were finally suspended on 16 June. China also launched two series of vicious attacks on Lee Teng-hui in the form of eight commentaries issued jointly by the Xinhua News Agency and the *People's Daily* (see Chapter 2), as well as carrying out two series of missile tests in the waters off Taiwan. At the end of the second round of missile intimidation, Harry Wu was sentenced to fifteen years, with the unexpected *postscriptum* of "immediate expulsion" from China. This was meant as a clear signal to Washington that Beijing did not want Sino-American relations to suffer long-term paralysis, as this would only result in the strengthening of ties between the United States and Taiwan.

The Chinese produced a long list of demands, the most pressing of which was a pledge by the United States to bar any further visits—even unofficial ones—by Taiwan's top officials. They also produced a list of implicit and explicit accusations against the United States. What had hurt China most was American maneuvering in 1993 to prevent them from hosting the Olympic Games in the year 2000. Furthermore, the United States was guilty of plotting to keep China out of the World Trade Organization (WTO), of trying to "contain" China, and of conducting a policy of selective harassment on the issue of human rights. Not only was it continuing to rearm Taiwan, but it was now the main abettor of its diplomatic resurrection.

China reportedly demanded a "fourth communiqué" after the first three of 1972, 1978, and 1982. In the "Shanghai Communiqué" issued at the conclusion of Nixon's visit in 1972, the United States "did not challenge the position that all Chinese on either side of the Taiwan Strait maintain there is but one China and that Taiwan is part of China." In the second, the United States recognized "the government of the People's Republic of China as the sole legal government of China" and acknowledged the Chinese view "that Taiwan is part of China." In 1982 the United States committed itself to the gradual reduction of arms sales and, after an indefinite period, their termination. In the fourth, America would have to agree to refrain from any action that would thwart China's "strangulation strategy" with regard to Taiwan, and to rule out the possibility of visits to the United States by Taiwan's leaders under any pretext whatsoever. Taiwan would be allowed to thrive economically, but politically and diplomatically, it would have to be eliminated completely.

To make its point clear, China lobbied very hard for a state visit by Jiang Zemin to the United States with all due military honor and pageantry, marking the reconciliation between the Chinese dictatorship and American democracy as a new era of peaceful coexistence between countries with different social systems. The Americans took the view that state visits can be conducted only between countries with common ideals and affinity for each other. They refused Jiang the honor. As an alternative, the Clinton administration proposed a visit to Washington without pomp and pageantry, but the Chinese firmly rejected this. The two countries finally settled for a working meeting in New York, to follow Jiang's attendance of the celebrations marking the fiftieth anniversary of the United Nations in October. The Clinton-Jiang meeting in New York was like a brief sunny spell after a long period of unstable and sometimes very stormy weather. It cleared the air between the two countries somewhat but yielded little in terms of real progress. The two heads of state agreed to make a new beginning, to enter into (in the words of the White House spokesman) "a process that would lead to a series of dialogues which could help to improve the chances for comprehensive engagement with China." Jiang did not receive a fourth communiqué, nor an embargo on future visits of Taiwanese leaders to the United States—only an oral pledge that these visits would be considered "on a case-by-case basis and would be rare and private."

The Americans wanted to put the Taiwan question on the back burner again, where it had been during the Nixon and Carter administrations, as well as during most of the Reagan and Bush era. In China the question of changing the status quo in the Taiwan Strait topped the national agenda. More than ever, Beijing was determined to force an end to Washington's policy of seventeen years of "deliberate ambiguity," if not by economic and commercial pressure, then by renewed military action. The *New York Times* attributed rash statements to senior Chinese officers who, during the fall of 1995, had conveyed their belief to Chas Freeman—former senior diplomat at the United States embassy in Beijing and more recently assistant secretary of defense for regional security—that the United States would not intervene in a Chinese attack on Taiwan because "it valued Los Angeles more than Taiwan." This was perceived by Freeman and the assistant secretary of state for East Asian affairs at that time, Winston Lord, as a veiled threat "to nuke L.A." Newspapers throughout East Asia, often quoting Chinese sources, speculated about the kind of military action China would take, and equally important, about how the United States would react.

The previous show of military force had failed to undermine Lee Teng-hui's position, and now a third round was being planned to prevent his reelection in March or to sabotage the election altogether. Would it be another political threat this time, or would it be a real attack? A luncheon speech in Hong Kong by Chas Freeman kept everyone guessing. He said, "There is a history of American decision-making which is very unpredictable and they [the Chinese] should seriously consider the possibility that we will intervene, or in the case of Taipei, that we will not."

In late January Hong Kong's *Oriental Daily* was the first to report that "a U.S. military source had disclosed that the U.S. Seventh Fleet would dispatch naval vessels to the Taiwan Strait during Taiwan's presidential elections." At the same time, a State Department spokesman pointed out that it is the policy of the United States to "consider any efforts to determine the future of Taiwan by [military means] . . . a threat to the peace and security of the Western Pacific area and of grave concern to the United States."

On 13 and 14 February Defense Secretary Perry twice called on the Chinese to refrain from provocative, menacing maneuvers designed to intimidate Taiwan. In response to this, the spokesman for the Chinese Foreign Ministry, Shen Guofang, gave a hair-raising demonstration of the arcane nature of the Chinese political code. "No comment! Because there is no way for me to have knowledge of military operations or else I would be suspected of being involved in spying for military information."[37] It was not until early-March that China announced its new round of surface-to-surface missile tests near the Taiwanese ports of Keelung and Kaohsiung, to be held from 8 to 15 March, partly coinciding with a new round of air-sea live-ammunition exercises, to be held from 12 to 20 March. From 18 to 25 March there would be a third "triphibious" exercise.

On 8 March Secretary of Defense Perry disclosed that the United States had sent the aircraft carrier *Independence* to the waters off Taiwan, followed a few days later by the *Nimitz,* "to monitor China's missile tests and maneuvers." It was the largest U.S. military force to be dispatched to East Asia since the end of the Vietnam War in 1975. The rationale behind the deployment was obviously strategic: to maintain regional stability and to ensure the safety of the shipping lanes. If support for Taiwan's budding democracy was a factor, it was never stated explicitly, but Taiwan's president Lee hailed the dispatch of the American armada as "an act of assistance by one democratic country to another."

China's maneuvers were aimed primarily at the United States, to show its determination never to let up its pressure on Taiwan, and to demonstrate that it could bring Taiwan under its control without actually invading it. At the height of the "psy-war," Liu Huaqiu, director of the Chinese State Council's Foreign Affairs Office (approximately the equivalent of the U.S. special assistant to the president for national security), was in Washington. From his remarks it became apparent that China would not attack Taiwan, at least not this time. Commenting on the U.S. naval presence near Taiwan, Foreign Minister Qian Qichen said, "Perhaps some people have forgotten that Taiwan is part of China's territory and is not a protectorate of the United States."

In the aftermath of the (mini-)crisis, Secretary Perry said that America's gunboat diplomacy had pushed Beijing back into a more cooperative posture, but that China would undoubtedly test the Clinton administration's resolve again and would have to be pushed back again and again.[38] Chinese spokesmen said that the maneuvers had been successful because they had delivered a blow to the independence forces on Taiwan. More important, China's actions had definitely underscored Taiwan's vulnerability. Nevertheless, the crisis had again confirmed the pattern of Sino-American interaction ever since the end of the Korean War. The two would confront each other regularly, coming close to the brink but never going over it.

Apparently fortified by the latest showdown and convinced of China's ultimate restraint, the United States decided, after three years of Clintonian zigzagging, to "nuance" its relationship with China, changing the focus from "a referendum on China's political system to a vote for American interests"—in other words, the expansion of economic and trade exchanges between the United States and China. In a major China policy speech in May 1996, Secretary of State Warren Christopher was more expansive, advocating talks on a more regular basis with senior Chinese officials in all fields and the total integration of China into the international community. "We reject the counsel of those who seek to contain or isolate China. . . . That course would harm our national interests, not protect them. Demonizing China is as dangerously misleading as romanticizing it would be."[39]

Chinese officials, including Foreign Minister Qian, openly praised President Clinton for correcting the earlier errors in his China policy, welcoming the recent positive momentum that had also been boosted by the new agreement on protection of intellectual property rights. The visit of National Security Adviser Anthony Lake in July was optimistically described as "putting relations back on track." A whole range of top-level visits were agreed upon, including a state visit by President Clinton to China. Lake concluded that it was no longer wise policy to let human rights dominate the priorities of bilateral relations and expressed the belief that "progress in this area would be possible in the long term."

Chinese and China-inspired commentaries in Hong Kong noted the fact that the United States had been forced to make adjustments to its China policy, both because its global strategy had met with obstruction and because China had become increasingly powerful. The United States was now willing to exchange confrontation for accommodation because, to benefit its own global interests, it needed China's cooperation on issues such as nuclear proliferation, the Korean peninsula, and relations between China and Iran and the Middle East in general. But, the commentaries went on to say, the United States would still continue to sell arms to Taiwan and to step up its ideological, religious, and cultural infiltration of China with the intention of changing its social system and Westernizing it. These sentiments gave rise to a wave of nationalism and contributed to the popularity of such anti-American books as *China Can Say No* (see Chapter 18).

By the end of Clinton's first term, Assistant Secretary Lord was bemoaning the fact that the Chinese Communists were "the most difficult regime" with whom the United States had had to deal in the past twenty-five years. America's troubles with this regime had been seriously aggravated, however, by the administration's own ill-conceived, inconsistent policies.

Proclaiming human rights the most public, high-profile issue and making improvements in human rights the condition for trade privileges—to be enforced by much-publicized hectoring—was bound to provoke the Communist hard-liners. Once Beijing had refused to play by America's rules, Washington climbed down and vacillated, thereby exposing itself—in Beijing's view—as a "paper tiger" that could be manipulated. Clinton's first-term China policy had achieved exactly the opposite of what it had intended, weakening the bargaining position of the United States and strengthening that of the Communists.

Since Clinton's reelection, all indications are that the second Clinton administration will shift to a new postideological pragmatism and put democratic evangelism and human rights on a back burner—or on a separate stove altogether. When Secretary of State Warren Christopher visited Beijing in November 1996 to draw up a road map for Sino-American relations during the second Clinton administration, he said that the sentencing of prominent dissident Wang Dan just a few days before would not be an impediment to U.S.-China summits. It was a far cry from his ill-fated trip in 1994, during which he said: "With respect to the meetings at the highest levels, I'd emphasize the importance of the overall relationship, the fact that we need to have a steady and comprehensive approach to the relationship, that's not rooted in a single issue." But he added that "the full potential of the relationship cannot be reached unless there is progress on human rights." There are signs that China is willing to resume the dialogue on human rights, but whether this will yield results satisfactory to the United States remains to be seen.

Recurrent crackdowns on dissent, possible restrictions on civil liberties in Hong Kong after the resumption of Chinese sovereignty in mid-1997, and the likelihood of a new wave of repression in Tibet will continue to complicate the relationship.

At present there seems to be no incentive for the leadership of either side to produce a new blueprint for a relationship that both sides can be comfortable with. For Mao Zedong and Nixon and the latter's three successors, containment of the Soviet Union was the strategic foundation for a stable relationship. For Deng Xiaoping, stable Sino-American relations were essential to China's economic modernization, especially to developing its export markets and importing high technology, and he was prepared to be flexible on critical issues. The current weak leadership seems to take these benefits for granted without much reciprocity. To realize their grand design of national reunification, they demand cessation of U.S. support for Taiwan, but are unwilling to show any new flexibility or magnanimity toward Taiwan. As a result, the United States will not yield much on this issue and arms sales will continue. China's desire to be treated as a great power, magnified by the obsession of its leadership with protocol and prestige, means that China wants to be bestowed with the highest honors of a state visit without, however, showing any allegiance to the values of the host country. The state visit should help President Jiang Zemin to consolidate his power, but it is not without risk. His grand reception at the White House is planned for late 1997. If the resumption of Chinese rule over Hong Kong does not proceed smoothly, this may add to the list of negative factors. He may be met by demonstrations, perhaps massive ones, a hostile Congress, and public animosity.

Whichever way the reciprocal state visits go, they will increase Jiang's prestige, paying off at least in that respect. Nevertheless, the prospects for U.S.-China relations are uncertain; it will most likely remain a limited, fragile relationship for a long time to come. Nothing has illustrated this better than an incident in Shanghai during Secretary of State Christopher's visit. He was expected to deliver a speech to a university audience. The title, "Building a Partnership for the Twenty-first Century," was painted on a big blue sign above the podium. American officials objected to the inappropriate use of the word "partnership" and insisted that it be changed. Overnight a new blue sign appeared, reading "The U.S. and China: Cooperation in the Twenty-first Century." In his speech, Christopher said: "Cooperation must not mean silence on important areas of divergence." He named human rights in particular, out of the American conviction that individual freedom and the rule of law "advance our common interest in stability and prosperity—history shows that nations with accountable governments and open societies make for better neighbors . . . as well as better places for foreign investment and economic growth."[40]

CHAPTER 2

Hong Kong: From British Crown Colony to Special Administrative Region of China

Over the next thirty years a new "Asianized" Asia will develop, whose basic building blocks are less nation-states and more city-regions evolving from links between growth triangles. Hong Kong's ultimate destination should and can be as an autonomous and even independent player in a new Asian community.

STEPHEN FITZGERALD,
Australian diplomat and sinologist

IN THE HIERARCHY of world-class cities, Hong Kong is number one in the show of extravagance and ostentatious luxury, and number two (after New York) in the possession of an imposing skyline. As a megalopolis spread out over a craggy, sprawling archipelago, Hong Kong has some of the most breathtaking views in the world. Whichever way one approaches Kaitak—that supersaturated airport with its runway in the sea—or on whichever hilltop one stands, the coastline of mini-fjords, the jagged line of skyscrapers, the numerous villas, bungalows, and here and there shanties against the background of green hills and rocky slopes provide fantastic panoramas from any angle.

As history-less as Hong Kong is, it will never be able to vie culturally with London or Paris. Neither is it the political center of an important country, and therefore it lacks the weight and presence of Tokyo. But all things considered—its dynamism, flamboyance, and "stage presence"—it is undoubtedly one of the world's top five cities.

The greatest irony of fate is that, for historical reasons, a city of this caliber remained a colony for so long, ruled by a British governor. More recently it has been called a "territory" that could never become independent. On 30 June 1997 England will relinquish its sovereignty of this precious piece of real estate to China—an act of historical atonement for the humiliation inflicted by British opium traders and gunboats on the shattered Chinese empire during the nineteenth century.*

Hong Kong is one of the most spectacularly successful city-states in world history. It owes its success, however, not to its own genius and vision, but to fate, chance, its colonial ruler, and the Communist revolution in China. The more than 6 million Hong Kong Chinese have nevertheless made excellent use of the opportunities offered them since 1949 by China's revolution and regional wars—not by design but by coincidence. Never, not even in Venice in the late Middle Ages or in Amsterdam in the seventeenth century, has such immense wealth been accumulated in such a short time. Hong Kong owes its success to the unique synergy of flamboyant Chinese opportunism and the rule of law and stability of British colonial "enlightened despotism." Its per capita income is already higher than that of its "stepmother country," England, and forty times that of its historical motherland, China.[1]

The big question is whether the British legacy, in particular the rule of law with all its Western freedoms, will long survive under Chinese rule. That will not alter the fact that the Hong Kong Chinese are and will remain for a long time a "class apart" from their relatives and fellow Chinese in the People's Republic. Professor Hugh Baker of the School of Oriental and African Studies (SOAS) at the University of London described "'Hong Kong man' as a unique social animal . . . neither Chinese, nor British . . . quick-thinking, flexible, tough for survival, excitement-craving, sophisticated in material tastes, and self-made in a strenuously competitive world. He operated in the context of a most uncertain future, control over which was in the hands of others and for this as well as for historical reasons he lived 'life in the short term.'"[2]

First-time visitors to Hong Kong are flabbergasted at the spectacle of all

---

* Hong Kong was ceded to Great Britain in three "unequal treaties": the island of Hong Kong was ceded after the first Opium War in 1842 "in perpetuity"; the Kowloon Peninsula after the second Opium War in 1860, also "in perpetuity"; and the New Territories in 1898 on lease for ninety-nine years.

that nouveau riche grandeur, dynamism, and efficiency. Even veterans like me get a charge upon each arrival which makes the mental clock tick faster. It is the exact opposite of the therapeutic Western European welfare state, where social workers instruct the postindustrial leisure class in the ins and outs of milking the system for all it is worth. The limited social welfare available in Hong Kong is only for the elderly and the genuinely needy. After forcefully introducing democratic reforms, Chris Patten, the assertive, controversial—and last—British governor of Hong Kong, also tried to institute a comprehensive system of pensions for the aged, but laissez-faire capitalists managed to nip this plan in the bud with the active support of China. Hong Kong Chinese, including housewives and taxi drivers, study the prices on the stock exchange during their lunch breaks. After finishing work, Hong Kong Chinese typically go to one of the many betting offices of the Hong Kong Jockey Club to bet on their favorite horses, and regularly go to watch the races as well. If they have managed to save enough money, then during the weekend they go to one of the countless new high-rise buildings to scout around for an apartment to buy—not necessarily to live in, but for purposes of speculation. Or they take the hovercraft to Macau, the Portuguese enclave seventy kilometers to the west, to gamble in earnest at one of its many casinos, which are forbidden in Hong Kong.

HONG KONG IS A CITY of superlatives and hyperbole. It holds an endless list of world records, such as the largest per capita number of Rolls-Royces, Mercedes-Benzes, and BMWs, the highest consumption rate of VSOP cognacs, the highest levels of stress, the highest prices for real estate and land (considerably higher than Tokyo's), and the greatest density of skyscrapers. Manhattan, at least, offers a variety of high and low, old and not so new. But as Barry Will, professor of architecture at the University of Hong Kong, put it, "In Hong Kong there was hardly anything old that had to be conserved. That's why everything has been knocked down since the early eighties and replaced by an uninterrupted jungle of high-rises of at least forty stories." Lack of space and overpopulation—in some parts of the city, more than 125,000 people per kilometer^3—is another reason for the rampant construction of high-rises, but the decisive factor is the financial pressure to reap the highest possible profits from a small piece of land. Developers have had to build higher and higher to recover the high cost of land, charging proportionately high rents, among the highest in the world.

The first explosion of high-rise construction produced a shapeless forest of unimaginative, square, concrete-and-glass towers in gold, silver, blue, and green. By the mid-1980s Hong Kong had, in the words of the architect Rocco

Yim, "too many buildings and not enough architecture." Skyscrapers were designed with complete disregard for what might be built next to them a year later. The Swiss architect Remo Riva opened a new era with friendlier-looking, elegant, and varied towers in beige and pastels. Then came the British architect Norman Foster, with his showpiece for the Hong Kong & Shanghai Banking Corporation, which combines a futuristic exterior—reminiscent of a giant oil rig or a spacecraft launching site—with a sleek, user-friendly interior. Another innovative addition to Hong Kong's wealth of new construction was the Bank of China Tower, a 315-meter-high glass-and-metal shaft with impossible corners and peaks, designed by the Chinese-American architect I. M. Pei. It was meant to underline Beijing's confidence in the future after 1997, at the same time holding up Hong Kong as a model for the modernization of China itself. The late 1980s marked the end of the era of mindless building. The new tower blocks, no longer forty or fifty stories high but now reaching seventy or eighty, are experiments in a more aesthetic, more humane way of building, the favorite style of which is referred to as neo–art deco.

The Hong Kong Chinese see in their skyline a reflection of their Faustian, Darwinist character, but for psychologists serious doubts about the future of the magic city lie behind that imposing façade. The *hardware,* the concrete-and-glass megastructures, will certainly survive beyond 1997, but the question is whether the *software,* the cosmopolitan culture behind it, can survive under the rule of a discredited, semi-Communist regime that is now drawing new strength from a crude form of neonationalism.

China's spokesmen are very eloquent in their reassurances that Hong Kong can look forward to a more glorious period under Chinese rule than it ever experienced under the British. They then point to Shanghai, the center of world capitalism in China before 1949. In that year, however, the triumphant Communists made Shanghai the target of a destructive, revolutionary class vendetta, which reduced the city to a gray, urban-proletarian mass where any form of entrepreneurial activity was doomed for the following thirty-five years. In the 1960s and 1970s Shanghai became the arena for the most extreme forms of class struggle and political infighting. It was not until 1977, a year after the death of Mao Zedong, that a certain degree of economic normalcy began to return, but it was another ten years before the advent of a real economic renaissance. Now, in the late 1990s, there is little doubt that Shanghai will eventually overtake Hong Kong in terms of sheer economic power, but it is difficult to imagine it ever acquiring the sophistication, the symbiosis of East and West, the civil order and legal security, and the freedom of information that Hong Kong now enjoys.

One irony of fate to which Hong Kong owes its unprecedented prosper-

ity is the settlement there of a large part of the Shanghainese entrepreneurial class, which, under the policy of "positive nonintervention" of the British
colonial regime, found the freedoms in Hong Kong of which the Communists had deprived them. When, in the spring of 1993, China's verbal warfare
against Patten's proposed reforms escalated in pitch, Chinese spokesmen
threatened repeatedly to punish Hong Kong for Patten's "transgressions."
The secretary of a member of the Politburo told me that Hong Kong's
wealth offered the prospect of substantial benefits to China, but that "Beijing could not respect Hong Kong because it had cleverly exploited historical loopholes, such as the influx of Shanghai capitalists in 1949, the Korean
War, and the Vietnam War. Especially during the last fourteen years, Hong
Kong has seized the opportunities presented by the opening up and reform
of the mainland to enrich itself. It has grabbed the chances offered by the
Communist party and profited from them at the party's expense. . . . Except
for a handful of patriots, Hong Kong has never shown any loyalty to the
Communist party. Its only goal was to make profits. It doesn't deserve our
love. . . . It is simply a concubine. . . ."

DURING THE HEIGHT of the Sino-British fight over the future of Hong
Kong in 1993, I asked an official of the Research and Development Center of
the State Council who had written his doctoral thesis on Hong Kong why
China could not bring itself to make a few token concessions. He replied
that the continuing existence at the end of the twentieth century of a British
crown colony on Chinese soil is a daily reminder of the historical humiliation of imperialism, and that tolerating this is already a monumental concession in itself. Why, then, did China not put an end to Hong Kong's
existence earlier? The full inside story of China's "hands-off" policy has never
been written, but the gist of it has been pieced together by several authors.[4]
    After the Second World War, the United States and the Soviet Union saw
to the dismantling of the European colonial empires in Asia and Africa.
Hong Kong—at that time a small, picturesque, exotic entrepôt port—was
not overlooked. In 1945 both President Roosevelt and President Truman exerted pressure repeatedly on the British prime minister, Winston Churchill,
to let the Nationalist Chinese government of Chiang Kai-shek accept the
surrender of the Japanese occupying forces in Hong Kong, but Chiang had
no troops on the spot. British troops arrived before Chiang's, and Churchill
was adamant in his refusal, as was the Labour government that soon succeeded him. Chiang was very angry with Britain but was pacified after the
British promised to use Hong Kong to help him in the civil war with the

Communists.[5] After India gained its independence in 1947, the Americans again put pressure on the British to return Hong Kong to Chiang Kai-shek, but it was already apparent at the time that Chiang's regime had no future. The British Parliament concluded that "the democratic forces in China" [!] would not tolerate Hong Kong being turned over to the Kuomintang. When the Communist armies began marching south in 1949, England was still enough of a world power to provide Hong Kong with the reinforcements necessary to prevent its being taken. The new Communist rulers also decided that it would be unwise to tackle the question of Hong Kong hastily and without adequate preparation.

In October 1949 the prelude to a Communist invasion of Taiwan was literally stranded on the beaches of the coastal island of Quemoy, and in January 1950 President Truman declared that the United States would no longer protect Taiwan. A second Communist invasion of Taiwan had to be called off several months later because of an epidemic of schistosomiasis, but Taiwan's (and also Hong Kong's) days nevertheless seemed to be numbered.

The man who unexpectedly saved Taiwan and Hong Kong was the North Korean Communist leader Kim Il Sung. After the massive North Korean invasion of the South in June 1950, President Truman revoked his policy of nonintervention and stationed the Seventh Fleet in the Taiwan Strait and the Thirteenth Air Force on Taiwan itself to prevent further Communist expansion. The entire Chinese coast from Korea to Vietnam was blockaded by the Americans, and Hong Kong was the only back door the Communists had for their supply of essential goods.

This was the beginning of the Sino-British modus vivendi. England did send troops to Korea but did not join the Americans in their much broader policy of "containment" of China. They were rewarded for this by the new Chinese leaders, Mao Zedong and Zhou Enlai, who respected the status quo in Hong Kong, which for China would become the proverbial "goose that laid the golden eggs." Five years later, the governor of Hong Kong, Sir Alexander Grantham, visited Beijing for a confidential meeting with Premier Zhou Enlai, who requested the stationing of an official Chinese representative, a "high commissioner," in Hong Kong. The British rejected this proposal. They did, however, agree on certain "rules of mercy" that were never officially made public but that included the following requirements: the British would spare China "inconvenience and loss of face," would not allow Hong Kong to be used as a military base by the United States, would keep the activities of the Kuomintang within strict bounds, and in particular would not introduce any democratization process that would inevitably lead to an independence movement.[6] The Chinese took a philosophical attitude: Hong

Kong was a problem that historical events had landed them with, and it would have to be solved sooner or later. Sooner, if extreme circumstances were to force China to take action, or at the latest in 1997, with the expiration of the ninety-nine-year lease on the New Territories, the northern part of Britain's crown colony.

The tacit pact between the Chinese Communists—besieged by the United States—and the British colonial government to virtually ignore each other paved the way for Hong Kong's success. The Hong Kong Chinese enjoyed the unique liberty of being able to abstain from politics, which fully accorded with Chinese tradition. The British ruled, and they—the Chinese—could devote all their energy to making money.

Two types of refugees from China streamed into Hong Kong, one an impoverished proletariat and the other the Shanghainese entrepreneurial elite. They welcomed each other with open arms. The colonial administration was undemocratic but efficient and operated on the principle of the rule of law with most of the paraphernalia of Western democracies. In the economic realm, the guiding principle was that the best government is the one that does the least. There was no opposition. During the 1950s and 1960s there were only two manifestations of unrest, the first instigated by the Kuomintang and the second in 1967 during the violent climax of the Cultural Revolution in China. At that time, the radical wing of the Communist party tried to incite "patriots" in Hong Kong to revolt against the "imperialists." At the same time, secret messages were sent by moderate circles in Beijing stating that the Chinese government did not support the terrorists. The supply of drinking water to Hong Kong, a very lucrative enterprise for which the Chinese were paid in hard currency, was never cut off.

Owing to the incessant flow of refugees from China, the population of Hong Kong had grown by the mid-1970s to 4.7 million people, half of whom were natives and the other half immigrants from mainland China. A small number of the former refugees, those who had fled much earlier from the mainland and who were no longer afraid of repercussions, returned regularly to the border areas and to Guangzhou (Canton) to visit relatives. Otherwise there was little interaction between Hong Kong and the rest of China. Foreigners could obtain visas to China only with great difficulty; until 1978 there was only one border crossing. After riding northward on the British slow train to the Bamboo Curtain, travelers then had to carry their own luggage across a wooden bridge over the Lowu River to reach a Chinese train bound for Canton.

· · ·

AT THE END of the 1970s, Hong Kong was still an international "British" city with a Chinese population of 98 percent. One percent was composed of other Asians, and Americans and Europeans made up the remainder. Psychologically and commercially, Hong Kong belonged to the non-Communist part of Southeast Asia and to the rest of the world. China, where the "deconditioning" of Mao's "new man" had only just started, was on another planet. The new reformist regime of Deng Xiaoping had just proclaimed its open-door policy, or economic opening up to the capitalist world, but was still fully absorbed in consolidating its position and was not yet ready to think about the future of Hong Kong. Deng was forced to think about it sooner than expected by a cartel of special interest groups: local real estate developers and foreign investors who could no longer live without knowing Hong Kong's fate after the expiration of Britain's ninety-nine-year lease in 1997.

Deng's "open door" ushered in an era of new glory for Hong Kong: it became the financial and logistical base for China's modernization. In this atmosphere of euphoria, the governor of Hong Kong at the time, Sir Murray (now Lord) MacLehose, traveled to Beijing in the spring of 1979 in order to sound out subtly and cautiously China's plans for the future. Deng Xiaoping was caught off guard. In a difficult conversation with MacLehose, Deng stated unequivocally that China would eventually take back the leased and ceded parts of Hong Kong, but he was not sure when—whether it would be before, after, or in 1997. But he added meaningfully that "investors could put their hearts at ease."

Upon his return to Hong Kong, however, MacLehose revealed only the last part of Deng's message, which led to a massive influx of banks, multi-nationals, contractors, and real estate developers, which in turn led to the most fantastic real estate boom in postwar history. Real estate prices—already insanely high—doubled in one year and continued to soar for two more, until the market burst like a bubble in 1982. Hong Kong, which had been China's most important source of foreign currency since the 1950s, now became the base par excellence from which to make the great leap toward the fabulous Chinese market of which the West had dreamed for more than a hundred years.

In both London and Beijing, experts in international law began to search for the means of legitimizing this "illegitimate child of Western adventurism, born in shame." The Chinese had never recognized the three "unequal treaties" but had in fact respected the status quo. It was a fundamental clash between two civilizations and two political cultures. The British, however, felt a moral obligation toward Hong Kong. Only a few years before, China had still been the most extreme tyranny in the whole of the Communist bloc, and it was very much a question whether the newfound apparent rationality of the Deng regime would last. Even though the way in which the British had acquired Hong Kong had been one of the blackest pages in the history of Western colonialism, Hong Kong was now one of the most advanced cities in the world and could not simply be returned against the will of its people to a regime that had caused those very people to flee their homes less than a generation ago. The British also thought, and rightly so, that Hong Kong would be able to continue to fulfill its role as an international center of finance and transport only if the survival of the British legal system could be guaranteed.

A magic formula was needed that would do justice to the complexity of the situation. The British hoped for a sort of trusteeship: they would transfer sovereignty to China in exchange for Chinese tolerance of continued British administrative authority. The Chinese Communists had long ago rejected British fantasies of this kind but had not yet said so publicly. They were interested only in erasing the national humiliation they had suffered. Territory and power was their concern, not people.

The moment of truth arrived during the fall of 1982, when Prime Minister Margaret Thatcher made a visit to Beijing. The day before her arrival, a series of Chinese-language newspapers published in Hong Kong printed the story, prompted by Beijing, that "the Chinese leaders would inform Mrs. Thatcher that the resumption of Chinese sovereignty and administration over all of Hong Kong would take place after the expiration of the lease in 1997. China hoped for British cooperation in maintaining the prosperity of Hong Kong." Just before the beginning of his talks with Mrs. Thatcher, Premier Zhao Ziyang said the same thing to a group of journalists from Hong Kong. In other words, there was nothing to negotiate. If England did not cooperate, China would take Hong Kong back unilaterally.

The next day, the same message was conveyed to the Iron Lady in a more authoritative and brusque manner by the then seventy-eight-year-old "strongman" of China, Deng Xiaoping. Deng and Thatcher had one thing in common: they both hated to be contradicted. Thatcher, steeled by her recent victory in the Falklands War, contradicted Deng nonetheless, insisting that "the three 'unequal treaties' could be varied" but were nevertheless valid and should serve now as the basis for further negotiations. At this point, Deng lost his patience and said that "that woman should be bombarded out of her obstinacy."[7] Undaunted, Thatcher proceeded to say that the Chinese proposals to let Hong Kong function as a "special" part of China were unacceptable as guarantees of stability and continued prosperity. She declared herself willing to make concessions on the question of sovereignty only if a satisfactory arrangement could be made for the continued British administration of Hong Kong. Deng was furious. He was determined that China should resume sovereignty, and this included the actual administration of Hong Kong. The British flag must go, the British administration must go, and only China should have the right to decide on the proper form of government for Hong Kong under Chinese rule. Deng added that if China did not take back Hong Kong lock, stock, and barrel, he would be no better than Li Hongzhang, the viceroy of the weak imperial Qing government who had signed the lease in 1898. If the British would not cooperate, China would come up with its own unilateral settlement within two years. The only role to be accorded to the British was "cooperation during the transition." The meager result of Thatcher's visit was a curt communiqué: agreement to enter into "talks through diplomatic channels with the common aim of maintaining the stability and prosperity of Hong Kong."

THE BRITISH WERE GOING for high stakes, not so much because they thought their chances of success so great, but because they wanted to cover themselves against accusations on the home front and also from Hong Kong that they were willing to hand over the crown colony so hastily to a Communist regime whose record did not inspire confidence. Even if they achieved nothing, they would have the consolation of going down in history as having been willing to stick their neck out for the people of Hong Kong.

For the first four or five months, the highly confidential negotiations were deadlocked because the British still refused to make the essential concession on the issue of sovereignty. In February 1983, when the Chinese let it leak out for the first time that the draft of a plan for unilateral action was in its final stages, Thatcher was persuaded to write a letter to her Chinese counterpart in which she declared her willingness to "consider making recommendations to the British Parliament on the sovereignty issue, once the negotiations yielded arrangements acceptable to the people of Hong Kong."[8] The question of sovereignty had now been "finessed," but Thatcher's letter created a new obstacle: that of "acceptability" to the people of Hong Kong. The Chinese were fiercely opposed to this because it implied a trilateral negotiating process involving China, Hong Kong, and Britain. As far as China was concerned, the "Hong Kong question" was a bilateral historical problem—the removal of a foreign government that ruled over ethnic Chinese on Chinese soil. China's standpoint was that the Hong Kong Chinese should

be the audience—not the actors—in this drama. The Chinese regularly mobilized their supporters in Hong Kong through leaks of "confidential" information to the Hong Kong media, which put the British under even more
pressure. They also recruited delegations of select "Hong Kong patriots" to
visit Beijing, where they were given assurances that after 1997 Hong Kong
would be governed by "Hong Kong Chinese" and not "Beijing Chinese"
(*Gang-ren zhi gang*).

The Chinese were adamant about barring Hong Kong from the negotiations. Any efforts made by the governor or members of the Legislative
Council to act as representatives of the people of Hong Kong were blocked
from the outset, as this might be viewed as a first step on the road to self-
determination or even independence. When the governor of Hong Kong, Sir
Edward Youde, who had become a conegotiator in mid-1983, told agitated
journalists that he was representing Hong Kong at the negotiating table, he
was sharply criticized by the Xinhua News Agency, who replied, "Mr. Youde
is a member of the British delegation. Only the Chinese government can
represent the people of Hong Kong."

During the next several rounds of negotiations, British diplomats tried
to persuade their Chinese counterparts that an efficient market economy required the free international flow of capital, the enforcement of anticorruption laws, freedom of information, and an independent judiciary, and that
only a British administration could guarantee this. The Chinese answer was
simple: "Sovereignty and administration are indivisible." They judged nothing on its merits and only repeated the same old clichés, driving the other
side of the negotiating table to despair, which was the main strength of the
Chinese negotiators. The pro-Communist *Ta Kung Pao* asked the following
rhetorical question: "Will it be possible, after the resumption of Chinese
sovereignty over Hong Kong, for the administration to remain in the hands
of a government which has been appointed by and pledges allegiance to
another sovereign state? Where in the world does this happen? This is
absolutely impossible!"

The confrontation over the separation of sovereignty and administration reached a climax during the summer of 1983 with a campaign of
intimidation by the pro-Communist media in Hong Kong against everyone
who expressed skepticism toward Beijing. In September it had escalated to
such an extent that confidence in the real estate and stock markets, as well
as in the Hong Kong dollar, was almost fatally undermined. The Hong Kong
dollar had begun its free fall from three to the U.S. dollar to nine and a half
to the dollar in only a few months' time. Beijing and London accused each
other of manipulation for political gain. For a while everyone thought that

doomsday was near—economic collapse and a unilateral decree by Beijing announcing an immediate takeover.

As a first rescue bid, the government of Hong Kong—after strong urging by the local economist John Greenwood and after consulting the world's most eminent monetary economists, such as Milton Friedman, Alan Walters, and Maxwell Fry—decided on 14 October to relinquish its policy of nonintervention and to peg the Hong Kong dollar to a fixed exchange rate of 7.80 to the U.S. dollar.[9]

British steadfastness had lasted long enough to convince the Chinese that Hong Kong would not be handed to them on a silver platter. The negotiating goal of continuation of British administration was not abandoned but "amended" to include the principle of "conditionality": that is, the British would agree to return Hong Kong to China in its entirety, but only under a detailed set of conditions that would guarantee the maintenance of the status quo. As part of their "United Front strategy," the Chinese themselves had already made promises to this effect to the public—in this case, a twelve-point proposal to a delegation of high school students, suggesting the maintenance of the status quo for fifty years. It was up to the British, however, to lend the proposal more detail and precision.

On the chief assumption that China would resume sovereignty and administration yet maintain the status quo, the negotiations entered their final phase in February. China set down the general principles in a "Twelve-Point Plan."

1. The "special region" of Hong Kong would be permitted to retain its capitalist system for fifty years.
2. It would remain a free port and financial center.
3. It would retain a convertible currency.
4. It would not be run by emissaries from Beijing.
5. It would elect a mayor [!] who is a "patriot."
6. It would run its own affairs without interference from the central government, except in matters of defense and foreign affairs.
7. The "special region" of Hong Kong would be guaranteed a high degree of freedom to take part in international activities.
8. It would issue its own travel documents.
9. It would retain its present legal system, so long as this does not conflict with Chinese sovereignty, and it would maintain its own Court of Appeal.
10. It would assume responsibility for its own law and order, to be maintained by its own police force.

11. It would be alllowed to tolerate political activities, even those of the Nationalists from Taiwan, so long as these do not constitute sabotage.

12. It would be permitted to introduce its own social reforms, without pressure from Beijing.

By this time, an extension of British administration beyond 30 June 1997 had been ruled out and was no longer a subject of discussion, although the public at large, including the business community, did not know it yet. The mood in Hong Kong was consequently one of suspicion and agitation. The climax of this was the announcement on 28 March that Jardine Matheson, that flagship of the colonial economy, would move its legal domicile to Bermuda, while continuing to be the biggest employer in Hong Kong. No move symbolized the end of "British Hong Kong" more than this one. Jardine and Matheson were the two Scottish opium traders who lobbied in 1840 for the first Opium War, subsequently laying the foundations of the crown colony that would become the basis of the British commercial empire along the coast of China. They had been the first gold diggers and now, fearing Chinese retribution, were the first to leave with bulging purses. "What came with a stench now leaves with a stench," someone wrote at the time in a letter to the editor of the *Asian Wall Street Journal.*

DURING THE FINAL PHASE of negotiations, many obstacles had to be overcome, first and foremost the form of the agreement and the mode of implementation and supervision. The Chinese first considered issuing two parallel declarations, in which the British would state their aims and the Chinese a "protocol" of theirs. The aims of the Chinese would be of overriding importance, however, considering their position as the future rulers. The main theme of the intended protocol was to be the establishment of a Sino-British Joint Commission, making the Chinese coregents and instantly transforming Hong Kong from a British crown colony to a British-Chinese condominium.

The British negotiators found this solution completely unacceptable, and an emergency visit by Foreign Secretary Sir Geoffrey Howe was deemed necessary. Howe's relaxed, unpretentious manner was the opposite of Thatcher's, and although this was not enough to elicit immediate concessions from the Chinese, it helped to create an atmosphere of flexibility and trust in which to face the final obstacles. On his way home, Howe made a stopover in Hong Kong on 20 April 1984, to deliver the fateful message: "It would not be realistic to think in terms of an agreement that provides for continued British administration in Hong Kong after 1997." More details were not forthcoming, owing to the confidential nature of the talks. Many dreams were shattered and floods of tears were shed in Hong Kong on that dramatic day, but there was no turning back the clock.

The drafting of the text of the agreement was scheduled to start in June, for which an extra team of experts was deemed necessary. Before they could begin their assignment, however, the Hong Kong Chinese members of the Executive Council decided to go to Beijing on a last, desperate "lobbying mission" that was long overdue. Three of their members—Sir S. Y. Chung, Lee Quo Wei, and Lydia Dunn, all prominent members of the business community and longtime appointees to the colonial power structure— requested a private audience with Deng Xiaoping to hand over a manifesto on behalf of the people of Hong Kong, in which they expressed their doubts about China's ability to make a success of the formula "one country–two systems." They were afraid that Hong Kong would be taken over completely by Communist bureaucrats who would soon undermine the city's social and economic freedoms. In front of television cameras, Deng showed undisguised contempt for the three dignitaries from Hong Kong, whom he reproached for having revealed their "colonial mentality" in expressing their distrust of the policies of the People's Republic of China. Their ill-timed mission came to nothing, and Deng suspected that London had urged them on as a last-ditch effort to block the proceedings, although the bureaucrats at Whitehall, close to a nervous breakdown by this time, were desperate for a quick conclusion to the negotiations. Howe was compelled to fly to Beijing again for the final round.

By this time, the Chinese were also in the mood to wind things up and accepted most of Britain's objections to the Joint Commission as an organ of power. It would become instead an organ of "consultation," receiving the much more modest name of Joint Liaison Group. It would not begin work until 1988 and would continue until the year 2000, thus giving the British a voice in posttransitional matters. The Chinese also agreed that "Great Britain alone would be responsible for the administration of Hong Kong until 30 June 1997" and that they "would give their cooperation in this connection." The Chinese also no longer insisted on two parallel declarations but accepted the idea of one Joint Declaration, which, after ratification, would have the status of a treaty and be registered at the United Nations. The "twelve points" would constitute the heart of the treaty, but they would be woven into a masterpiece of precision by a special team of legal experts.

Everyone was as euphoric as could be expected under the circumstances. Howe's Chinese counterpart, Wu Xueqian, hailed the agreement as a breakthrough and added that details "would be finalized according to schedule," in other words, in late September, exactly two years after Mrs. Thatcher's visit to Beijing. Deng Xiaoping returned from his summer vacation in the resort town of Beidaihe to pay tribute to Sir Geoffrey Howe and other "knights of the realm," including Sir Richard Evans and Mrs. Thatcher's adviser Sir Percy Cradock. Deng even praised Thatcher in his own ideological way, putting her on a par with General de Gaulle: "It was General de Gaulle who ended French colonial rule in Algeria. Mrs. Thatcher will end British colonial rule in Hong Kong."

After his meeting with Deng, Howe hurried back to Hong Kong to calm the edgy nerves of the populace with better news than they had been given a few months before. Everyone was most impressed, even the three members of the Executive Council who had been dubbed colonial lackeys by Deng Xiaoping only a month before. The essentials—preservation of Hong Kong's unique social and economic system; a legally binding, detailed agreement; and liaison and consultation until the year 2000—were unexpected gifts. The stock market soared and most editorial comment was jubilant.

ACCORDING TO THE Joint Declaration, Hong Kong would become a unique phenomenon in the world: a special administrative region (SAR) that would function as a normal country in everything but defense and diplomacy—at least on the surface. The legal system would remain basically unchanged, which meant that the designation "royal" would have to go and that the link with the Judicial Committee of the Privy Council (the British Supreme Court) would have to be severed, but Hong Kong would have its own independent Court of Final Appeal. The government would be run by local Hong Kong Chinese, and the head of government—the chief executive—would be appointed by Beijing "after local elections or consultations." Foreign nationals working in government departments and the police force would be allowed to stay. Hong Kong's social and economic systems, as well as its lifestyle and personal freedoms, would remain unchanged. Hong Kong would remain a free port, a separate customs territory, and an international financial center with its own convertible currency. The special administrative region of Hong Kong would issue its own travel documents, maintain and develop its own economic and cultural relations under the name "Hong Kong, China," and maintain separate membership in the GATT (now the WTO) and international financial and transport organizations. It would have its own aviation agreements and its own shipping register. In short, in 1997 China would accept a number of restrictions on its sovereignty over its regained territory, granting it a multitude of exemptions from the constraints of the socialist system. During the formal signing of the agreement on 19 December 1984, Deng Xiaoping congratulated himself and Mrs. Thatcher and said that "the Joint Declaration, embodying the formula 'one country–two systems' [his brainchild], was a product of dialectical Marxism and historical materialism." Mrs. Thatcher responded coolly that it was an "ingenious idea."

The British congratulated themselves on having kept the negotiations from turning into a debacle, although the result seemed better than it actually was. The accord was accepted by the population of Hong Kong and ratified by the British Parliament, not so much because it inspired confidence in the future as because of the alternative: a unilateral *Diktat* by China and the premature departure of the British. Reading through the nine-page introduction and thirty-five pages of text, appendixes, and memorandums, one stumbled across so many pitfalls and ambiguities that future problems, big and small, seemed inevitable. For example, Annex I, "Elaboration by the Government of the People's Republic of China of its basic policies regarding Hong Kong," quotes Article 31 of the constitution (specially introduced for this purpose in 1982), which stipulates that the state may establish special administrative regions (Hong Kong now, Macau and Taiwan later) with a different economic system. The system in those three areas is capitalism. Article 24 of the same constitution still prescribes the struggle against "capitalist, feudal, and other decadent ideas."

More than anything else, it was China's glaring lack of political continuity and stability that worried forward-looking people. In 1984 and 1985 China's optimism about economic reform, as well as political and cultural tolerance, was at its height. Since then, it has declined, slowly but steadily. The clauses in Annex I concerning election of both the chief executive and the Legislative Council were so elastic as to make future controversy, if not outright conflict, unavoidable. "Hong Kong has become fully subject to the political trials and tribulations of China. . . . If a new leftist upsurge erupts, Hong Kong will be as defenseless as a goldfish among sharks," I wrote in a commentary at the time.[10]

The ambiguities in the agreement had sown the seeds of new, permanent Sino-British discord, as well as political polarization in Hong Kong itself. "Hong Kong Chinese will rule Hong Kong" was the Chinese maxim, but what kind of Hong Kong Chinese? Fellow travelers, opportunists, businessmen with interests in China, Beijing Chinese with the status of residents of

Hong Kong? The Legislative Council would be chosen in elections, but what kind of elections? Direct, indirect, general, limited? Hong Kong had no leaders of its own: the British governors were advised by appointed dignitaries, who did not actually represent the people but "interpreted" their wishes.

After a short-lived attempt from 1945 to 1947 to introduce democratic reforms in Hong Kong, the British never tried again, for the following simple reasons: Hong Kong would never become independent anyway; the future was uncertain; China would resist in any case; during the 1950s and 1960s civil strife would have been triggered between Kuomintang and Communist elements; and, perhaps the most important reason, there was no popular demand for democracy. Half the population had fled from an extremely politicized, repressive, impoverished society and was happy to discover in Hong Kong an apolitical society with a minimalist, nonintrusive government and a wealth of opportunities for rapid material gain. Apart from a handful of intellectuals, no one cared to think about the far-reaching implications that the early introduction of representative government might eventually have had after 1997.

The British offered every excuse imaginable for not introducing any form of self-rule before 1984. The early 1970s would perhaps have been the best time to revive the idea of democratic reforms. China was weak and just recovering from the worst excesses of the Maoist era, it felt threatened and besieged by the Soviet Union, and it had just launched a large-scale diplomatic offensive to normalize relations with the United States and Western Europe. The governor of Hong Kong from 1971 to 1982, Sir Murray (now Lord) MacLehose, who in 1993 joined the critics of the last governor, Chris Patten, for hammering through reforms only at the eleventh hour, rejects any suggestion that he should have acted otherwise. In his view, any moves toward representative government in the 1970s would have polarized society and China would have blocked them. Retired British officials who worked under MacLehose question this, however, and maintain that the British colonial bureaucracy, with its appointed elite advisers, had everything firmly under control and wanted to keep their power and privileges. Polarization of society would not have been an insurmountable obstacle. The absence of representative government eventually caused polarization anyway after 1984, and at a much less favorable juncture. And as far as China's resistance to democratic reforms was concerned, the British would have been in a much stronger position to deal with it in the early 1970s than they were fifteen or twenty years later.

· · ·

THE FIRST BRITISH "green paper" for indirect partial elections of the Legislative Council was announced in July 1984, two months before the signing of the Joint Declaration. By then, China's say over the future had almost been made formal, and the pro-Beijing media instantly denounced the British plan as "a blueprint for grooming a puppet government, a British Hong Kong without the British." China appropriated the right to define the perimeters of Hong Kong's future autonomy. China would draft the Basic Law for the future political structure of the SAR, and in that process there was no role for the British. Invoking their responsibility for the administration of Hong Kong until 1997, the British nevertheless put forward their own modest program for the "further development of representative government." When the Chinese escalated their opposition late in 1986, however, the British government finally accepted the principle of "convergence" of the process of democratization in Hong Kong with the Basic Law that was being drafted under China's supervision. The erosion of British authority and the extension of China's direct power in Hong Kong had become unmistakably apparent.

The next thrust, which forced the British to retreat further, came from Deng Xiaoping himself. During the spring of 1987, just after the first wave of student unrest in mainland cities and the toppling of his liberal "crown prince," Hu Yaobang, Deng told the Basic Law Drafting Committee that direct elections would not be good for Hong Kong, thus attacking the first direct partial elections that the British had planned for 1988. The Hong Kong government had just published its second green paper, "The 1987 Review of Developments in Representative Government," which provided for a minireferendum to be held on the desirability of these elections. It was called a "survey to collect, collate and report on public response to the green paper." The questionnaire was so complex and confusing, with its multiple-choice questions, options, and alternatives, that very few of those polled actually understood what it was about. The BBC described the way in which the questions were formulated as "mind-boggling obfuscation." Furthermore, the system of counting the opinions, petitions, signatures, and letters was so arbitrary that the government could not escape the impression that the end justified the means. They had to play down the fact of their capitulation to the Chinese, and the result was, in the words of an elderly member of the Legislative Council, "base deception."

The conclusion of the deeply flawed government poll was that only just over 12 percent of the population was in favor of direct elections in 1988, whereas independent market research companies had found it to be between 41 and 62 percent. The leader of the democratic camp, Martin Lee, was so furious that he branded it a conspiracy devised to conceal the fact that the government did not have the courage to confront China.[11] The most eloquent leader of the antidemocratic camp was a man with a unique background: the Austrian Helmut Sohmen, a businessman whose prominence in Hong Kong was due to his marriage to a daughter of shipping and real estate magnate, the late Sir Y. K. Pao. Sohmen thought the government was largely to blame for the polarization in Hong Kong, because in their first white paper in 1984 they had promised too much and had subsequently been forced to retract it under pressure from China. He was opposed in principle to direct elections in Hong Kong, not for traditional, conservative reasons but purely from a pragmatic point of view: "Fighting for direct elections in Hong Kong means confrontation with China, and because the future of Hong Kong is dependent on big business with China, this would lead to self-destruction." He thought there were no convincing arguments for direct partial elections. "It is a stopgap measure that would only whet the appetite for more, and in the present, rapidly changing situation—the increasing influence of China—this demand could not be satisfied. Further polarization in Hong Kong will only increase that influence."

According to Martin Lee, Sohmen had it the wrong way around. Democracy was precisely the sort of dam that would keep back China's influence and prevent it from expanding further. It would have to be fought for, though, and as yet the cries for democracy were far too weak and infrequent. Lee sighed resignedly: "The Chinese don't fight. They always bend with the wind, and in the 1990s that wind will become a typhoon from the north!"[12]

THE TYPHOON MADE ITSELF felt as early as 1989, however, with the shock waves emanating from the military campaign against the unarmed protest movement. Millions of people marched through the streets of Hong Kong in support of the demonstrators in Tiananmen Square in Beijing, and millions of Hong Kong dollars, tents, medicine, communications equipment, and other supplies had been sent to Beijing. After the bloodbath during the night of 3–4 June 1989, no one dared to go out on the streets in the cities of mainland China anymore. Hong Kong was the only city where mourning processions and memorial services were held, where the Chinese regime was pilloried—by Chinese—and where the newspapers were full of uncensored news about the new wave of extreme repression in China. Hong Kong was also the nerve center of various escape routes out of China, by which student leaders and other dissidents fled to the West. In short, the drama in Tiananmen Square had transformed Hong Kong overnight from an economic, financial, and logistical service base for China into a highly politicized potential base for subversive activities aimed at undermining China's regime. It was treated accordingly.

Deng Xiaoping's outburst in May 1984—that in spite of differences of opinion with the Chinese government, Chinese troops would be stationed in Hong Kong in 1997 in any case—now took on a new, darker meaning. Deng had argued at the time that those troops would be the symbol of China's sovereignty, and the Joint Declaration had stated that the troops would not interfere in the internal affairs of the SAR. But the Basic Law, passed in 1990 by the National People's Congress, stipulated that "in times of need the SAR government may ask the central government for assistance from the garrison in the maintenance of public order." Under the British system, the power to declare a state of emergency resided not with the authorities in London but with the "governor in council," meaning the governor in conjunction with the Executive and Legislative Councils. The Basic Law vested that power in the Standing Committee of the National People's Congress, a club of 150 party functionaries, many of them elderly, including a number of retired ministers. After the declaration of a state of emergency, "relevant Chinese national laws would apply" to Hong Kong.

Only the hard core of China's "patriotic legion" in Hong Kong still pretended to have faith in "a high degree of autonomy" after 1997. The silent majority resigned itself to its fate; the superrich upper crust already had foreign passports and real estate in one or more foreign countries; and the middle classes in the thirty-to-forty-five age group prepared to leave in increasingly large numbers. For this class of departing "yuppies"—doctors, lawyers, economists, accountants, computer specialists, and other young professionals—a unique Hong Kong term was coined: "yompies," or young outwardly mobile people. They were not willing to entrust their children's future to the regime in Beijing and chose instead a less affluent existence in countries such as Canada, Australia, and the United States. Before 1989 there were on average thirty thousand émigrés per year; after 1989 their numbers rose to sixty thousand.

England was at the bottom of the list of favored countries, not so much because economic prospects there were less bright than elsewhere, or because London had surrendered to Beijing in the fight for the democratization of Hong Kong, but because the Hong Kong Chinese had long ago felt betrayed by the British policy of treating them as second-class citizens. The right of Hong Kong Chinese to emigrate to Great Britain and to live and work there had already been revoked in 1962 by the Commonwealth Immigration Act. The Nationality Act of 1981 lent further force to this discrimination with the introduction of the British Dependent Territory Citizen passport, which did not extend to its holders the right to reside in Britain. During the crisis of confidence in 1989, fear of the future was acute, and a promise of passports in the case of a new crisis would have gone far to put minds at rest. The average well-educated Hong Kong Chinese was interested not in emigration to England as such but in obtaining a sort of insurance policy, a recognized passport of any civilized country, enabling him to carry on normally with his work in Hong Kong, but with the knowledge that in the event of a new crisis, he had an emergency home elsewhere. International banks and multinationals had to contend with the exodus of the upper echelons of their local staff. France extended passports to non-French-speaking Hong Kong Chinese to keep them working for French companies. After half a year of bickering within the Conservative party, Margaret Thatcher finally came up with fifty thousand British passports. China labeled this a conspiracy to keep Hong Kong in the power of "Yellow Brits" after 1997, and threatened nonrecognition of the passports and exclusion of their holders from government and representative functions.

As public outrage in the aftermath of the Tiananmen Square incident began to fade and attention was again focused on the resumed high growth of China's economy, Hong Kong's brain drain began to slow down. After two years, more and more emigrants who in the meantime had acquired Canadian or Australian passports wanted to return to their "money paradise" on the south coast of China, where salaries were at least twice as high as in the West. The brain drain now became a "brain gain," and the "yompies" became "rumpies" (returning upwardly mobile people).

THE TWO MOST IMPORTANT questions frustrating Sino-British relations from 1989 to the present are, in chronological order, the construction of the new, avant-garde airport Chek Lap Kok and the reform of the political structure. Without the latter, the airport controversy would never have been allowed to escalate to such an extent, and without the airport controversy, the state of Anglo-Chinese relations would never have arrived at the critical level reached in 1992. That year heralded a break with tradition with the appointment of the last governor of Hong Kong—not a diplomat-sinologist, as was customary, but a political heavyweight—causing Hong Kong to become bogged down in a destructive constitutional deadlock during the finale of the British era.

During the severe crisis of confidence in the aftermath of the Tiananmen drama in 1989, the governor of Hong Kong, Sir David Wilson, announced, without previously consulting China, spectacular plans for the construction of a new $20 billion superairport and accompanying infrastructure, a new city, gigantic land-reclamation projects, a train line, a superhighway, two bridges, and a tunnel. On a scale with the rebuilding of Kuwait after the Gulf War, it was hailed as one of the largest construction projects in the world, designed to inject Hong Kong, during its last years of British rule, with new energy and optimism that would help it to overcome its doubts about the future after 1997. China, who had not been consulted beforehand, immediately raised strong objections. The airport became Beijing's cause célèbre, and China now insisted on having a say in all matters that would straddle the takeover in 1997. The immediate cause of China's xenophobic paranoia—exacerbated by the new bunker mentality prevailing since the Tiananmen drama—was its fear that the British wanted to build an extremely expensive airport benefiting British contractors, squander the funds in the treasury, and leave Hong Kong bankrupt. If the airport controversy and later Patten had not been the precipitating factors, China would almost certainly have found another reason to take offense. The British, in complete control until 30 June 1997, technically did not have to consult China about building the airport, although financing by the private sector would be problematic because companies would have no faith in a megaproject—not sanctioned by China—that would not be completed until long after 1997. The Chinese dragged their feet indefinitely and the "doyen of the Mandarins" in the British Foreign Office, Sir Percy Cradock, was sent to Beijing for secret talks. In July 1991 China gave its blessing to the airport construction project, but at a high political price: a summit conference between Prime Minister John Major and his Chinese counterpart, Li Peng, who had been treated as an outcast by the West since 1989. Major was compelled to travel to Beijing to sign the "airport memorandum," which meant in effect putting an end to the Western sanctions against China that had arisen from the Tiananmen Square incident. From now on, China took a positive attitude toward loans to finance construction of the airport and related infrastructure projects, in exchange for a say in all important, long-term affairs in Hong Kong.

On his way to Beijing, Major did not bother to hide his indignation at being the first leader of a major Western country to have to shake hands with Li Peng. He made it clear that he had humbled himself so as to enable Hong Kong to move forward. On his way back to London, Major made a stopover in Hong Kong, where he exhausted himself giving hearty assurances of Hong Kong's glowing future. He stressed his complete confidence in the governor of Hong Kong, Sir David Wilson, in spite of the fact that

Wilson had misjudged China's reactions to the airport project and was seen by both British business leaders and advocates of democratic reforms as too weak and too lenient toward China. Within months Major was forced to eat his words, give Wilson a life peerage, and recall him to London. A political heavyweight was sought as Wilson's successor, someone with easy access to No. 10 Downing Street who could therefore command more respect from the Chinese. After the Conservative victory in April, Major's friend and kindred spirit Conservative party chairman Chris Patten was chosen. Ironically, Patten had just lost his own seat in the elections and was therefore not eligible for appointment to a ministerial post. "If you speak to Chris Patten, you speak to me. He speaks with the full authority of the British government," Major said to Li Peng at the international environmental summit in Rio de Janeiro in June 1992. In other words, don't bother me anymore.

BECAUSE OF the still-palpable aftereffects of the Tiananmen upheaval, the collapse of Communist regimes elsewhere, and the end of the Cold War, the British government—with the implicit approval and perhaps even outright support of Washington—was no longer willing to let China block democratic developments in Hong Kong. Martin Lee—the liberal lawyer who in 1991 had received the greatest number of votes in the first direct partial elections for eighteen of the sixty seats in the Legislative Council—had the ear of both the British government and the new governor. The days of the pro-Chinese business elite receiving preferential treatment were over.

In his first important policy speech, Governor Chris Patten announced a series of sweeping political reforms that set both him and Britain on a collision course with Beijing. He widened the margins of the 1984 Joint Declaration and the 1990 Basic Law to such an extent that at the elections to be held in 1995, not twenty but thirty-nine of the members of the Legislative Council were to be elected directly. A "Decision of the National People's Congress on the Method for the Formation of the First Government and the First Legislative Council of the Hong Kong SAR," appended to the Basic Law as a supplementary proviso, stipulated that the sixty-member Legislative Council would in 1997 have twenty members chosen by geographical constituencies by direct election, ten members elected by an election committee, and thirty members elected by functional constituencies.

Patten maneuvered to prevent the electoral college from being handpicked; it would include all 346 members of the district boards. These would be chosen by means of a general election in 1994, and in 1995 would then elect the bloc of ten. Of the thirty functional constituencies, twenty-one had been established after consultation with China, including the medical and legal professions, banking and educational institutions, trade unions, and so on. Patten reserved the remaining nine seats for members of the working class, which amounted to a second vote for a large segment of the population. Hong Kong's lower and middle classes are much less comfortable with their proletarian "motherland" than are the city's multimillionaires with their commercial interests in China. This, combined with the lowering of the voting age from twenty-one to eighteen, would produce in 1995 a new Legislative Council, 63 percent of which would be chosen by direct and indirect general election. Furthermore, Patten had considered transferring the base of power from the Executive Council (governor plus cabinet) to the Legislative Council. After sovereignty reverts to China, the chief executive and the top officials will be appointed by Beijing, and if Patten's plan were to be implemented, the chief executive would have less power than the elected, and in China's eyes pro-British, Legislative Council.

Again China had not been consulted. The implications of the reforms were "a British Hong Kong without the British." This alone was enough to make the Chinese furious, but their patience was tried to the utmost with the completely new, open, populist style of government that Patten introduced in Hong Kong. He walked the streets and visited working-class neighborhoods, kissing babies and pressing the flesh, and answering questions put to him everywhere. His pleasant appearance, quick intellect, and ready sense of humor made him more popular within a couple of months than any Chinese ruler had ever been, with the exception of Mao Zedong at the height of the personality cult. But it didn't last. "Patten shifted the traditional basis of support for the colonial regime—the local elite who have been converted to China—to the masses, who are more distrustful of China. In doing so, he has strengthened anti-Chinese feelings and polarized Hong Kong," stated Hong Kong's leading sociologist, Professor S. L. Wong.[13] The domestic Chinese and pro-Communist media in Hong Kong let loose a volley of epithets for Patten: haughty god of democracy, dictator, demagogue, liar, old-style imperialist, prostitute, and pirate.

Divested of their passion and fury, the Chinese demands boiled down to "convergence with the Basic Law" and the "through train," meaning elections on China's terms and retention in office after 1997 of those elected in 1995, with the exception of those elements displeasing to China, who happened to be Hong Kong's most popular politicians. China had already declared most emphatically that Martin Lee and Szeto Wah, the leader of the teachers' union, would have to be "pushed off the train." Seen in the wider context of post-Tiananmen paranoia, the collapse of the Soviet Union, and the American-French rearmament of Taiwan, it was only natural that China regarded Patten's plans as part of a "transatlantic conspiracy" to set Hong Kong up as a base from which to undermine the world's last strong Communist regime by means of "peaceful evolution," or infiltration without armed struggle.

China's first concrete reprisal was to delay once again the construction of the airport by putting financial obstacles in its path, but each time Patten paid it back in its own coin. He countered by saying that on the basis of the accords signed by John Major in 1991, he would begin construction without renewed approval by China, and that, if necessary, he would tap the foreign exchange fund to finance it. China followed suit by threatening to annul in 1997 all government contracts with Hong Kong's business world which had not been given official sanction, especially if Jardine Matheson had been a party to them.[14] The Hang Seng stock index experienced the darkest days since Black Monday of 1987. China's aim was to coerce the business world into putting Patten and the British government under pressure. Patten in his turn accused the Chinese of manipulating the stock market to enable themselves to buy huge quantities of shares.

HONG KONG SLIPPED AGAIN into a deep depression. Democratic activists continued to support Patten, but the media and a large segment of the population that had enthusiastically applauded him just half a year before now began to ask themselves glumly if further democratization was worth the effort if it meant risking a lethal, no-win confrontation with their future sovereign. China again urged secret negotiations, but they fell through when Patten insisted that Hong Kong Chinese with equal status be included in the British delegation. In 1983 China had already rejected British attempts to turn the question of Hong Kong into a trilateral affair, on the principle that Hong Kong was historically Chinese, making it a matter to be settled between the original ruler and the usurper. Lu Ping, the director of China's Hong Kong and Macau Affairs Office, was beside himself with rage at Patten's public gibes, and during an emotional press conference called him the "criminal of the millennium" (qian-gu zui-ren). Lu announced unilateral preparations for the government of the future special administrative region. A second group of advisers was speedily appointed, including Sir David Akers-Jones, a former chief secretary and acting governor who was a fierce critic of Patten. This was followed by the installation in July of a Preliminary Working Committee responsible for setting up the Chinese government of Hong Kong after 1997, for which China used the metaphor of a "second stove."

Negotiations eventually followed, although in the form of the ritual "deaf and dumb" dialogue. Every two or three weeks there was another round of talks, and after every couple of rounds Patten threatened unilateral action if no accord was reached. "Please Stop Boring Us" was the title of an editorial in Hong Kong's leading Chinese-language newspaper, *Ming Pao*, after seventeen rounds of talks. "Patten has bared his teeth so often without biting. If he doesn't bite now, the Chinese will deride him as a paper tiger," wrote the commentator. Patten ignored Chinese threats to take extreme action and submitted the draft of the new election law to the Legislative Council. China immediately elaborated on what its extreme action would be: dismantling all organs that came into being through unilateral British action at midnight on 30 June 1997, the moment of the transfer of sovereignty to China. It was now up to the Hong Kong Chinese either to show courage and daring and continue on the path shown them by Patten or to vote down the legislation and try before it was too late to ingratiate itself with China. Practically no one believed that there was still a chance of resuming the British-Chinese dialogue, let alone a chance of convergence and continuity of the political system before and after 1997. Adopting a new election law and holding elections in 1994 and 1995 meant a risky battle to set up political institutions that would be wiped out on 30 June 1997 by a decree from Beijing.

But the unbelievable happened: the majority of Hong Kong Chinese in the Legislative Council refused to succumb to Beijing's ultimatums, letting themselves be persuaded instead by the British master politician Chris Patten. After intense lobbying and a marathon session of seventeen hours, the new legislation was passed by thirty-two votes to twenty-four on 30 June 1994, exactly three years before the transfer of sovereignty to China.

China refused to get worked up about it, declared the legislation irrelevant, and reiterated in all seriousness its earlier position: "As a result of the break-off of the Sino-British negotiations on arrangements for the elections of 1994 and 1995, caused by the British, the three-tiered political structure of the Legislative Council, Municipal Councils, and District Boards of Hong Kong, regardless of the way they came into being, will be liquidated on 30 June 1997." Governor Patten responded that in no way did he intend to ignore China's sovereignty after 1997, but that there were no grounds for dismantling the new institutions because they accorded with the Joint Declaration of 1984 and the Basic Law for the Hong Kong special administrative region after 1997. Patten wanted to put this conflict behind him and return to business as usual.

And to a certain extent it has been "business as usual" since 1994. The long-awaited accord to finance the airport became a reality, as did the formation of an Infrastructure Coordination Committee, charged with coordinating the construction of highways, bridges, tunnels, and harbor facilities between Hong Kong and its border areas. China refrained from further obstructing the development of infrastructure, although Container Terminal No. 9 was put on hold for more than a year until the role of Jardine Matheson, that flagship of British commercial interests in Hong Kong, could be scaled down.

IN THE POLITICAL and judicial fields, another important question was still unsettled which had been dealt with in a secret British-Chinese accord in 1991, implementation of which had been stymied. The maintenance after 1997 of an independent judiciary hung in the balance. According to the Joint Declaration of 1984, the British legal system would be retained except for the removal of royal symbols, and Hong Kong would have its own Court of Final Appeal, which would replace the Judicial Committee of the Privy Council in London. The accord of 1991 had been reached during John Major's tense visit for the signing of the airport memorandum but had been rejected by the Legislative Council and the entire legal profession in Hong Kong because only one foreign judge was to be allowed to sit in the new court. The Bar Association had fought for a long time to set up the court unilaterally in order to let it start trying cases before 1997, but China had continually threatened to dissolve all such institutions set up unilaterally. China stressed that "acts of state" would be outside the court's purview, implying that Beijing itself would rule in such cases. China was worried that the court in Hong Kong might do something similar to what the Supreme Court of Rhodesia did in 1965 when it legalized the unilateral declaration of independence of Prime Minister Ian Smith.

The boards of large companies, foreign governments, and especially the U.S. Senate urged China to take this matter seriously. Although the 1990 Basic Law stipulated that "judges from other common-law jurisdictions may sit on the court," China now demanded that this be restricted to one. This demand was widely rejected in Hong Kong. In mid-1995, however, the British finally yielded and accepted the restriction, to the dismay of those in legal circles, the Democrats, and even the conservative Liberals in the Legislative Council. In all fairness, there was no reasonable alternative. Unilateral action on the part of the British would undoubtedly have led to dissolution of the court on 30 June 1997, followed by the unilateral establishment by the Chinese of a court that would certainly be even less independent. The agreement specified that the court be set up on 1 July 1997, that only one foreign judge be allowed per case, and that it be subject to the Basic Law, which stipulated that the judiciary in Hong Kong have no jurisdiction over "acts of state, such as defense and foreign affairs." That defense and diplomacy would be the prerogative of Beijing had been known for a long time and was not a point of dispute, but what did "such as" mean? An unwelcome subject such as human rights might easily be included in the such-as category. The Standing Committee of the National People's Congress has appropriated the sole right to interpret the Basic Law. If a citizen, a company, or a newspaper wishes to bring a case against the state, be it the special administrative region or the People's Republic of China, the chief executive might decide that it was an "act of state," disqualifying the courts. The Standing Committee of the National People's Congress in Beijing would then have the last word. Martin Lee gave some real-life examples: "If the Bank of America sues the Bank of China in Hong Kong for $100 million, China can declare it an 'act of state,' disqualifying the courts. Or if I am arrested by the Chinese army and my wife goes to court and asks for habeas corpus and China says that any act by the Chinese army is an 'act of state' related to defense, the court cannot save me."[15]

The debate over the Court of Final Appeal led to a complete reordering of Hong Kong's political spectrum. The relationship between Patten and the Democratic camp, having been souring for some time already, now turned overtly hostile, and the tone of the discussions between Patten and Martin Lee became bitter and venomous. Martin Lee called the agreement a "British sell-out of the rule of law in Hong Kong."[16]

IN JULY 1995 Lee moved for an unprecedented "vote of no confidence" against Patten, the first in the 152-year existence of Hong Kong. Even if it had passed, it would not have had any influence on Patten's position, appointed as he had been by the British Crown. Lee's aim had been merely to hurt and humiliate the governor. The motion was defeated by a vote of thirty-five to seventeen, owing to support from the pro-Chinese and conservative Liberal camp. It was a graphic illustration of the change that had taken place in the political psychology of Hong Kong. Martin Lee wrote in a column: "The governor should take a good, long look at himself in the mirror and ask himself why it is that all his former enemies now support him."[17] Patten in his turn accused Lee of being a doomsayer in the international media, spouting "simplistic sound-bites about the destruction of the rule of law in Hong Kong."[18]

The accord on the Court of Final Appeal nevertheless paved the way for normalization in other areas, including discussions pertaining to the continuity of the civil service, a resolution of the nationality issue, and the resumption of infrastructure projects. China's boycott of Patten remained in full force, in spite of the fact that his new pragmatism was benefiting them. High-level visitors from Beijing continually ignored the governor, and it was finally the chief secretary, Ms. Anson Chan (Fang On-sang), who was invited to pay a secret, ice-breaking visit to Beijing in mid-1995. Shortly afterward vice-premier and foreign minister Qian Qichen, in his capacity as chairman of the SAR Preliminary Working Committee, announced that all top officials and the whole civil service would be allowed to stay after 1997, and that those who opted for early retirement would be given their pensions no matter where they decided to settle down. This was a great relief, especially considering the confrontation in early 1995 over China's demand to see all the files kept on Hong Kong's top officials, which Patten had resolutely refused to give in to.

Shortly after her visit to Beijing, Ms. Chan was invited to travel to the province where she was born, Anhui, to attend ceremonies honoring her grandfather General Fang Zhenwu, a hero of the war against Japan. Since then there has been growing speculation that she will be chosen to be the first chief executive of the SAR, in spite of her close relations with the current colonial regime and in particular with Chris Patten, who had appointed her chief secretary. Anson Chan is extraordinarily capable, efficient, and decisive, and is a supersonic debater in three languages: English, Mandarin Chinese, and Cantonese. She is firmly rooted in the tradition of the elite civil service and is therefore rather intolerant of legislators and the media, which is exactly what China wants. If she could be persuaded to stay on as chief secretary, it would be a great contribution to stability and continuity in Hong Kong.

THE CAMPAIGN FOR Hong Kong's first (and last), largely democratic elections in September 1995 was a unique illustration of the psychological brinkmanship—life in the short term on the frontier of a new world—practiced by the Hong Kong Chinese. The politicians, most of them novices, campaigned for election to a parliament that would have a life span of only twenty months.

There were three political camps: the Democratic party, the Liberal party, and the Democratic Alliance for the Betterment of Hong Kong (DAB). The Democratic party and its allies were labeled "dogmatic idealists" by cynics and members of the business community because they strove for full democracy, which would have been a lofty goal under normal circumstances but was of course completely unrealistic in the context of the imminent Chinese takeover. The Liberal party was in fact a conservative business lobby with a philosophy of pragmatic opportunism. Party leader Allen Lee summed it up succinctly: "We have either to learn to live with our new masters or vote with our feet." The DAB was the pro-China party, allied with the largest union, the Hong Kong Federation of Trade Unions. The main plank in their platform was "dialogue with China at any price."

The pro-Beijing camp was an ambivalent lot. On the one hand, the whole machinery necessary for setting up pro-China, parallel governmental organs was working around the clock; on the other hand, China was giving the elections the benefit of the doubt. Reliable sources in the Hong Kong media estimated that China had given HK$4.8 million (US$620,000) to the campaign funds of the pro-China candidates. During the final week of the campaign, the influential Chinese Chamber of Commerce spent HK$800,000 on advertisements in pro-China and middle-of-the-road newspapers, in which they called on the people to vote for "patriotic" candidates who love Hong Kong as well as China. Chinese banks and state businesses in Hong Kong also instructed their twenty-five thousand employees to vote for the "patriots." On the eve of election day, China's chief spokesman in Hong Kong, Zhang Junsheng, deputy director of the New China News Agency, called on the population of Hong Kong to vote for candidates who could "enter into a dialogue with China so as to ensure a smooth transition." Chinese officials were convinced that the confrontational stand of the Democratic party toward China would be unpopular with the voters, but as a hedge against excessive losses, an hour before polling booths opened, the New China News Agency repeated for the hundredth time that China would dismantle the newly elected Legislative Council and install a new council of its own, appointing only those kindly disposed toward China.

Whatever China's strategists had in the back of their minds, they misjudged the situation completely. Not only did the DAB win a mere six seats (as opposed to nineteen for the Democrats), but all three of the DAB bigwigs were trounced, in spite of their being moderate, well-respected individuals—one a high school principal and the other two union leaders. The three charismatic heavyweights of the Democratic camp—Martin Lee, Christine Loh, and Emily Lau—all won with overwhelming majorities. The Liberal party, which is pro-China for business reasons but nevertheless is distrusted by China, won ten seats. The remaining twenty-five seats went to splinter parties and independent technocrats representing functional constituencies. Together with their allies, the Democrats were able to form a bloc of between thirty and thirty-two seats.

The disappointing results of the DAB could not be blamed on a lack of grassroots support. The DAB maintained close ties with the 200,000-member federation of workers' unions, the HKFTU. Moreover, its candidates were capable men of integrity. What probably worked against party leader Tsang Yok-sing was an incident in his past: after the Tiananmen drama of 1989, he had applied to emigrate to Canada but had changed his mind later on. There was a consensus among analysts, and Tsang himself concurred, that the reason for the DAB's defeat was simply that they were seen as "agents of Beijing." The majority of those who had turned out to vote—a meager 35.8 percent—apparently wanted to register a simple protest against China, the one time it was possible to do so. It was a stern notice to Beijing: you will get Hong Kong because of the inexorable forces of history, but not with our consent.

Chinese commentators attributed the DAB's defeat to a variety of other causes, including the inexperience of their candidates, the low turnout, and the district system. Altogether the pro-China candidates received 34 percent of the popular vote but only 10 percent of the seats. The pro-China news agency CNS commented that "if the turnout in mature democracies is below 50 percent, an election cannot be considered a success." Hong Kong is certainly not a mature democracy, and unless a miracle occurs, the fragile democratic shoots that have been allowed to spring up will be mowed down by the "typhoon from the north."

AFTER THE ELECTIONS, British-Chinese relations came full circle. No. 10 Downing Street and Whitehall had finally reached the conclusion that the long-term interests of British-Chinese economic cooperation extended beyond the two years during which Britain would still be responsible for Hong Kong. The great turning point in British policy toward Hong Kong and China had begun several months before, when the deputy prime minister and secretary of state for trade and industry, Michael Heseltine, paid a visit to China, heading a delegation of 150 captains of industry. The delegation, the first to make such a visit in four years, grumbled that Patten had become an unaffordable luxury for England, considering the stagnation of British-Chinese economic and trade relations. Once again China triumphantly observed that Western countries always let trading interests prevail above all other considerations in their relations with China. *Wen Wei Po* commented: "Why has the British side, after protracted bickering with the Chinese side over the political structure and the transition, suddenly changed course? The answer is that the British side has finally understood that it can reap huge benefits from cooperation with the Chinese side. By acting in this way, Britain can withdraw without loss of face and gain long-term profits in both Hong Kong and China. Those who advocate confrontation can only lead Britain down a blind alley and inflict great damage on themselves as well as others."[19]

Patten was now attacked from all sides. In 1992 Martin Lee had pinned his last hopes for democracy in Hong Kong on Patten; by the end of 1995 he was calling him "a fly in the soup of Sino-British trade."

Lee was strongly convinced that the rule of law in Hong Kong was in great jeopardy, and he was determined to fight to the bitter end for its survival. Lee held that the only guarantee for the survival of the rule of law in Hong Kong was to expand it across the border into China. Otherwise China's relative lawlessness would spill over into Hong Kong. The legal subgroup of the China-appointed Preliminary Working Committee—Beijing's response in 1993 to Patten's reforms—had been put in charge of verifying whether all the laws adopted during the Patten era conformed to the Basic Law. During the fall of 1995, the group came to the conclusion that many stipulations in Hong Kong's Bill of Rights contravened the Basic Law. Hong Kong had adopted the Bill of Rights in 1991 as the local implementation of the universal "International Covenant on Civil and Political Rights." The Bill of Rights had invalidated many repressive colonial laws that the British had invoked to deal with radical leftists and other anticolonials before the 1970s. Beijing considered the abrogation of these laws a British conspiracy to weaken the powers of the SAR government—to deal with anti-China liberals and demonstrators, and transgressions of the free media, for example—and its advisers in the PWC have demanded that they be reinstated. China's spokesmen have accused Patten of using the Bill of Rights as the means of making Hong Kong a base from which worldwide anti-China forces, human rights organizations, Greenpeace, and China-watching research institutes and journals will be able to undermine socialism in China. The bill obliges the SAR government to report annually to the United Nations in Geneva on the state of human rights in Hong Kong. China will have none of this, because it is not a signatory to UN human rights conventions. The British argue that they belatedly introduced the Bill of Rights in 1991 not to incapacitate the SAR government in any way but to ease the anxiety of the people of Hong Kong in the wake of China's massacre of democratic activists in 1989. China's philosophy, however, is that social and legal developments in Hong Kong must be frozen in the interests of stability on the mainland.

. . .

WITH THE ESTABLISHMENT of the Preparatory Committee for the special administrative region in January 1996, resumption of Chinese sovereignty over Hong Kong entered the "phase of implementation." Unlike the Preliminary Working Committee, the PC was not an advisory group but an organ of power, consisting of 150 appointed members, 94 (63 percent) of whom were Hong Kong Chinese. The remainder were Chinese functionaries of various state and party organizations, such as the National People's Congress, the Hong Kong and Macau Affairs Office, and the United Front. Half of the 94 Hong Kong Chinese were tycoons whose considerable business interests in China made them "patriotic." According to the Hong Kong media, they controlled $12 billion in shares on the Hong Kong stock exchange. One of the elected Hong Kong politicians on the Preparatory Committee, Frederick Fung, the leader of a small political party called the Association for Democracy and People's Livelihood, said with regard to this, "I am afraid that businesspeople don't understand the values, ideals, and lifestyles of the common people. This will cause conflicts and confrontation." Although the Preparatory Committee was a legal organ, rooted in the Basic Law, its public image was as poor as that of its "illegal" (according to the British) predecessor, the Preliminary Working Committee. The Hong Kong public did not consider it representative, and its mode of operation was murky and secretive. It consisted of six panels: one panel responsible for forming the Selection Committee, one for electing the chief executive, a panel for appointing the Provisional Legislature, panels for legal and economic affairs, and one for organizing celebrations. The last panel would determine the nature and details of the ceremonies on 30 June 1997, which was a highly sensitive matter owing to initial Chinese adamancy that Patten be excluded. Later on, they relented on this point but nevertheless ruled that Patten would not be allowed to preside over the ceremony because it would be the British government that would hand Hong Kong back to the Chinese government, and not the governor of Hong Kong ceding power to the chief executive of the SAR.

On 24 March, the day after the democratic breakthrough in Taiwan—the presidential election—Hong Kong experienced, in the words of Patten, a "black day for democracy." On that day, the Preparatory Committee made its final decision to replace the elected Legislative Council with an appointed Provisional Legislature (PL) on 1 July 1997, dashing all hopes that China would relent and make a magnanimous gesture on this most divisive of issues. The only member of the PC who had the courage to vote against it, Frederick Fung, was instantly disqualified from membership in the Selection Committee and the Provisional Legislature by an emotional, finger-wagging Lu Ping. In the capacity of secretary-general of the Preparatory Committee, Lu made a visit to Hong Kong in April, his first in over a year, to preside over the consultations of the Preparatory Committee with the people of Hong Kong on the formation of the Selection Committee responsible for choosing the chief executive and for setting up the Provisional Legislature.

The Provisional Legislature became the central political issue for the short time remaining of British rule, fully determining the pattern of polarization: one side against the PL and ipso facto against China, the other side in favor of the PL and ipso facto pro-China. China cultivated anyone who accepted the PL and isolated anyone who rejected it. Lu was met with a hostile reception by those who opposed the PL. The demonstrations were limited in scale yet vehement and rich in imagery that highlighted the deep chasm between China's authoritarian, backward, secretive political culture and the Western ways of the Hong Kong Chinese. Chinese officials refused to face demonstrators or accept their petitions, instead slipping out of buildings through backdoors and hopping into taxis instead of waiting for their official Mercedes limousines. The more determined among the demonstrators carried live turtles in cages and shouted, "Chinese officials are shameless. They are turtles hiding in their shells." Others carried birdcages that they smashed in front of the New China News Agency, China's representative office, symbolizing their opposition to China's intentions to "cage" democracy in Hong Kong. The hearings on setting up the Selection Committee were anything but representative: except for two groups—the Bar Association and the Student Union—all three hundred participating organizations, including foreign chambers of commerce, had been selected because of their previous statement of support for the PL. Martin Lee's Democrats were excluded; the eloquent legal presentation by the chairman of the Bar Association, Gladys Li, was dismissed as irrelevant to the formation of the Selection Committee; and the representatives of the Student Union were instantly removed by security guards when they took off their jackets, revealing protest slogans on their T-shirts.

The conclusion of these "Chinese-style" consultations was entirely predictable. Zhou Nan, China's top official in Hong Kong, said at a cocktail party in honor of the PC members that the meetings were a "fine example of the PC's working methods, abiding by the principle of catering to the wishes of the people of Hong Kong and relying on them."[20]

The more orthodox of the two local Communist newspapers, *Wen Wei Po*, placed the entire blame for the unrest on Governor Chris Patten, particularly on his "black day" statement. "The troublemakers were acting out a farce according to Patten's script. . . . Like a grasshopper trying to obstruct a chariot, their efforts will certainly be of no avail."[21] Patten retorted that the Chinese were deaf to dissenting voices and that he would certainly never dodge demonstrators and slip out of buildings through backdoors.

Pending the formation of the Selection Committee, attention was now focused on how China would set up the Provisional Legislature and what powers it would be given. Patten continued to act as if China could still be persuaded or else compelled to change course, and Martin Lee was still determined to challenge its legality in court, but Qian Qichen was coolly dismissive. "It is all over, like cooked rice." Both Patten and he were forced to endure almost daily attacks by China's spokesmen and in the media for their "self-deception, and their trust in luck or illusion." At the same time, China tried to put the Provisional Legislature in a more moderate perspective, stressing that its formation before the takeover did not mean that there would be two legislative organs or rival centers of power. It would only fill the legal vacuum resulting from the dissolution of Patten's council, functioning for one year, until 30 June 1998. It would make only those laws urgently needed for the inauguration of the SAR government and prepare for new elections in 1998, which would produce a new Legislative Council, elected according to Chinese laws under Chinese sovereignty. An editorial in *Ta Kung Pao* compared Patten's "crazy" idea of having a Legislative Council of his design continue to function after 1997 to the negotiating strategy of the British in 1982–83 of exchanging sovereignty for administrative power: "The British side has always referred to Hong Kong's 1997 handover as a transfer of sovereignty and refused to mention the transfer of administrative power. . . . Hong Kong's return to Chinese rule is irrepressible, so Britain evolves an idea about administrative power, trying, among other things, to prolong its legislative power."[22]

ON AUGUST 10 the Preparatory Committee approved the document on the formation of the Selection Committee. The committee would be established in November and select the chief executive and the Provisional Legislature in December. It would be broadly representative and consist of four hundred members, aged eighteen or older, from four sectors: the industrial-commercial-financial sector; the professional sector; the labor, grassroots, and religious sector; and a sector comprising former political figures, Hong Kong deputies to the National People's Congress, and Hong Kong members of the National Committee of the Chinese People's Political Consultative Conference (CPPCC). Each sector would elect one hundred members. The fourth sector would consist of the Hong Kong delegates of China's national organs, sixty altogether, who would become members automatically, as well as another forty former political figures. The latter would all be former appointees of the British colonial system who, after 1984, had gradually moved over to the Chinese camp.

In his capacity as chairman of the Preparatory Committee, Qian Qichen called the formation of the Selection Committee a historic event and "the first time for the Hong Kong people truly and democratically to participate in government and political affairs." In a jab at the British, he said it was "unimaginable progress compared to the royal appointment of British governors, never consulting the people of Hong Kong."

In his efforts to make the Selection Committee truly "broadly representative," Qian had even invited China's main foe, the Democratic party, to take part. In his address, Qian first defined a patriot. "What is a patriot? A patriot is one who respects the Chinese nation, sincerely supports the motherland's resumption of sovereignty over Hong Kong, and wishes not to impair Hong Kong's prosperity and stability. Those who meet these requirements are patriots, whether they believe in capitalism, feudalism, or even slavery. We do not demand that they be in favor of China's socialist system; we only ask them to love the motherland and Hong Kong." Qian then pinpointed the Democrats as "some people in Hong Kong who favor Hong Kong's return to the motherland but who hold different views on the way to develop democracy and on the pace at which democracy should be developed there. As long as they proceed from the common basis of supporting the motherland's resumption of sovereignty over Hong Kong and of desiring a smooth transition, prosperity, and stability for Hong Kong, they should and can sit down to discuss Hong Kong's affairs and handle these affairs well."[23]

Martin Lee took a principled stand, however, and rejected compromise solely for the purpose of having a seat at the table. He observed that China's leaders were offering an olive branch to the Democrats after most of the important decisions on Hong Kong's future had been made, namely, abolition of the elected Legislative Council, appointment of a Provisional Legislature, and emasculation of the Bill of Rights. "If we as Democrats agree to participate in a process leading to the destruction of Hong Kong's elected institutions, it would be a betrayal not only of everything we believe, but also of the solemn trust we asked voters to place in us."[24] According to a poll, however, the public was more pragmatic: 71.5 percent of those questioned thought the Democratic party should change its mind, and only 15.1 percent thought that the party's principled stand was correct. Of the party's own supporters, only 48 percent had no confidence in the selection process, as opposed to 42.3 percent who did. The rest were undecided.[25]

By September, a year after Hong Kong's first British-style general elections, China's increasingly powerful shadow establishment in Hong Kong was preparing the colony for selections Chinese style. For two weeks Chinese officials preoccupied themselves with distributing application forms for seats on the Selection Committee. It was not unpopular among large segments of the public, even among senior government officials who wanted to apply but were forbidden to do so by the governor. A group of senior bureaucrats went to court to fight for their civil right to elect the first postcolonial government, but the court dismissed their case. Some members of Patten's Executive Council also wanted a seat, but they were blocked by the governor. By mid-September 5,751 people had applied for membership in the Selection Committee, which meant that only one in fourteen would make it. Bankers, tycoons, movie stars, Buddhist monks, soccer clubs, and hobby groups such as the Kite-Flyers Association all joined in the scramble for one of the four hundred seats. The Preparatory Committee would decide who qualified in the preselection and who eventually got in. Only the Democratic camp was out, not because the PC explicitly excluded it, but because the Democrats themselves found China's main condition for participation, acceptance of the Provisional Legislature, unpalatable.

BY LATE SUMMER only one local luminary had publicly declared his candidacy for the post of chief executive of the SAR: Lo Tak-shing—lawyer, publisher of a pro-Beijing weekly, and scion of a prominent Eurasian family—whose father, Sir Man-kam Lo, had served the British his whole life. Lo was a clever, elitist Machiavellian who calculated that a solid network of connections among the powers that be in Beijing would land him the job, regardless of local popularity or credibility. In 1984, after the signing of the Joint Declaration, he had resigned from his (appointed) posts in the Executive and Legislative Councils, denouncing the British for selling out the people of Hong Kong, and had started preparing for his "new life after the British," i.e., lobbying Beijing and pro-China organizations in Hong Kong. By the mid-1990s he was widely rumored to be Premier Li Peng's man for the job.

By early 1996, however, Beijing had indicated that it would not impose an unpopular choice on the people of Hong Kong and that there was going to be a real contest. The director of the Hong Kong and Macau Affairs

Office, Lu Ping, had already dropped hints about a dark-horse candidate. This mystery man was soon singled out but proved to be very reluctant. At the end of January, during the installation of the Preparatory Committee in Beijing, President Jiang Zemin demonstratively walked toward shipping magnate Tung Chee-hwa (C. H. Tung), one of the vice-chairmen of the Preparatory Committee, and gave him a long, cordial handshake. From that moment on, it was universally believed that Tung was preordained for the job and that all further procedures would be mere ritual. Ironically, Tung had served on Governor Patten's Executive Council from late 1992 until mid-1996, but this was a little-known fact because everything he did was so low-key. Whether he had opposed Patten's reforms at the outset or had put up token resistance was also unknown. By the end of September, Tung had still not declared his candidacy, and there had been occasional speculation that he was not really interested in the job. After his eventual selection, a source close to the Tung family revealed that intense bargaining with Beijing had been the main reason for his procrastination. First of all, he had reportedly asked for stronger guarantees from both the central and provincial governments that they would not infringe on Hong Kong's autonomy with all kinds of carpetbagging schemes. Second, he had asked for Beijing's blessing for Anson Chan, Patten's chief secretary, to stay on as his second-in-command. Third, he had implored Beijing to mend fences with the Democratic camp, and fourth, he had asked Beijing to refrain from handing out consolation prizes—such as high positions in the SAR—to its cronies. If these had been Tung's real conditions and Beijing had taken them seriously, it would have been too good to be true.

After performing abysmally in all opinion polls, Lo Tak-shing withdrew his name in September, and *Window*, his loss-taking pro-China magazine, folded at the same time. By early October new candidates had emerged, ahead of Tung Chee-hwa. The first was the chief justice, Sir Ti Liang Yang, who resigned from his judicial post and renounced his knighthood so as to fend off charges of being a "lackey of the British." At first he was not seen as a serious candidate, but rather as someone who was willing to lend his name to the selection process to give it more credibility. The other candidate was tycoon Peter Woo, son-in-law of the late Sir Y. K. Pao, who had recently resigned from his business empire, Wharf (Holding) Ltd. and Wheelock and Company, to become chairman of the Hospital Authority. Tung finally declared his candidacy during the formal application period, October 14–28. Remarkably, the three candidates were all Shanghainese by birth and refugees from Communism, making some observers wonder whether the Shanghai faction in Beijing, led by President Jiang Zemin, had ruled against entrusting the leadership of Hong Kong to a Cantonese, who would be too willing to consider local interests. Tung even spelled his name "Chee-hwa" in the Shanghai dialect. In Mandarin it would be Dong Jianhua and in Cantonese Tung Kin-wah. He was followed by a fourth candidate, Simon Li, a retired appeal court judge who was indeed a native Hong Kong Cantonese.

On the surface at least, it was now a real campaign, illustrating the East-West synthesis that is the essence of Hong Kong. The Western aspect was that, for cosmetic reasons as well as for purposes of legitimacy, the candidates had to vie with one another for public support and attention in the media. The Oriental aspect was that the outcome was not decided publicly by the electorate, but behind the scenes by the oligarchic Selection Committee; indeed, perhaps not even by the entire committee but by a handful of kingmakers and power brokers.

The three candidates now went to grassroots civic and social organizations to gain a better understanding of lower-class problems and to solicit ideas for their political programs, which had to be drafted from scratch in two weeks' time. All of them lived in luxurious houses or huge multi-million-dollar apartments in Hong Kong's exclusive midlevels or on the Peak and moved around in chauffeur-driven Mercedes or other luxury cars. None of them had ever been in a slum or taken a public bus or even the subway.

Initially, Tung lagged behind Yang in popularity, perhaps because of his very conservative political agenda. He advocated a return to Chinese values, emphasizing obligations to society over individual rights. He warned against confrontation with China, saying, "Consultation doesn't mean spinelessness; to stand up for the interests of Hong Kong doesn't mean confrontation [with China]." He said that the Tiananmen incident of 1989 had been unfortunate but that it should be left to history to judge whether it could have been handled better. He advocated strong, efficient, executive-led government that would not let civil servants get bogged down in the politics of the legislative process, a trend that had only accelerated under Patten's democratic reforms. He soon confirmed a longtime public secret: China had helped bail out his near-bankrupt shipping empire in the mid-1980s, making him susceptible to charges of being beholden to Beijing. Tung himself emphatically rejected this. His relationship with Chinese leaders does date from those troubled times, however. The family empire—Orient Overseas Container Line, inherited from his father, C. Y. Tung—numbered at its peak 150 cargo vessels and tankers, but owing to the worldwide shift in the shipping market, it was sinking under more than $2.6 billion of debt in 1985. C. H., as he was known to foreigners, frantically flew back and forth to London, Tokyo, and New York to persuade his bankers not to seize his ships.

At the crucial moment, Chinese interests, led by pro-China tycoon Henry Fok, made a strategic investment of $120 million that secured the banks' approval for a restructuring. Now renamed Orient Overseas (International) Holdings, the fleet has been scaled down to thirty-one ships, and the firm is once again profitable and in the process of expanding.[26]

Tung's maxims for all future dealings with China are to show prudence and restraint, and to think of your own long-term interests. One of the most sensitive issues in Hong Kong is whether annual commemorations of the Tiananmen incident of 4 June 1989 will be permitted to take place after 1997. Tung was noncommittal about it. He said he would abide by the law and would consider the long-term interests of the 6 million Hong Kong Chinese.[27]

On 2 November the Selection Committee was "elected" in the Great Hall of the People in Beijing. The 150 members of the Preparatory Committee appointed by Beijing—one of whom was Tung!—picked 340 names (400 minus the 60 automatic Hong Kong members of China's state organs) out of the 5,700-odd applicants. The PC chose 61 from its own midst, thereby confirming what everybody already knew: that it was a case of blatant "electoral insider trading." A large number of losers of the 1995 general election for the Legislative Council were chosen not because they had gained in popularity since, but because the northerly wind from Beijing was now blowing more strongly over Hong Kong, and they were simply being rewarded for their pro-China stance.

The maiden act of the Selection Committee was the first stage of balloting for the chief executive on 15 November. Tung took a commanding lead, polling 206 votes, more than twice as many as Yang, who won 82. Peter Woo came in third with 54 votes, and Simon Li was disqualified for not meeting the minimum of 50—not because he was Cantonese, but because his histrionics had provoked several controversies. On 27 November the three candidates presented their fundamentally similar platforms to the Selection Committee. They all stressed the importance of stability, the paramountcy of the rule of law, and the desirability of minimal change during the initial years of the SAR. The three differed mainly in their personalities and styles. Tung is a forceful personality and a calm and kind listener who never shows any sign of impatience. According to insiders, he would handle any sensitive issues with the Chinese leaders in such a low-key, confidential way that compromise would be reached behind closed doors without any pressure from the media or other outsiders.

Yang is a rather edgy man, more sensitive than Tung to the social needs of Hong Kong's polarized, elite-ruled society. During his campaign, however, he gave long, detailed answers to legal questions in superb Queen's

English, which perhaps damaged his chances, if he ever had any in the first place. He tried, for instance, to blunt the controversy over the Provisional Legislature by stressing that it should never meet in Hong Kong before the handover, so as to avoid lawsuits in Hong Kong's courts over its legality. He also suggested that the PL should not touch upon the very divisive issue of new legislation on "antisubversion," because, though it was important, it was not urgent and could be left to the first elected Legislative Council during the second half of 1998.

Peter Woo is a cool, dynamic, Westernized businessman. According to some, he is too perfect, and according to others too autocratic, for the job. And—at fifty—perhaps a bit too young.

While the Selection Committee conducted hearings on the three platforms which were broadcast live on local television, reports surfaced in the Hong Kong media that several members of the SC had traveled to Beijing to lodge complaints about the "Tung faction's monopolization of the seats in the Provisional Legislature." In other words, Tung's victory in the race for chief executive was already a foregone conclusion, but now he and his supporters were allegedly preparing to excercise absolute domination over the PL as well. "Some SC members say that they dare to criticize the Communist Party but not Tung Chee-hwa for fear that they will be excluded from the executive organs, which are going to be the highest decision-making bodies of the SAR," reported one leading newspaper.[28]

No one described the upcoming (s)election of Tung better than Sir David Akers-Jones, a retired chief secretary who had been acting governor for a brief time in 1986. He had spent a lifetime in Hong Kong and was fully familiar with the Chinese penchant for the politics of consensus. Himself one of the few non-Chinese members of the Selection Committee, he said: "It's going to be a difficult choice. It's not voting along party lines like the American presidential elections. Here we are voting on friendly lines. I'm a friend of all candidates." He had shown his affinity for Chinese politicking a few years before when, in the early stage of the Patten-Beijing war of words, he aptly said in an interview that the Chinese were not opposed to elections as such. "They only want to know the result in advance."

Tung's selection was clinched with an overwhelming majority of 320 out of 398 valid votes, over 80 percent. Unexpectedly, Yang received only 42 votes and Woo 36. This suggested that the kingmakers had gone to great lengths to reach a consensus before going to the plenary meeting for approval and applause. If a popular vote had been held, it would have looked very different indeed. Tung had gained in popularity quickly, but his rating in the polls was only 46.7 percent, as opposed to 28.8 percent for Yang and 5.2 percent for Woo. Outside Hong Kong's state-of-the-art Convention Centre, which had been converted into a copy of the Great Hall of the People with bright red curtains and other PRC symbols, noisy demonstrators denounced the selection as a "farce," but there were only twenty-nine of them. The Hong Kong Chinese were clearly suffering from demonstration fatigue.

Tung was quick to call on the people to unite and have confidence in themselves, adding that Hong Kong had been much too politicized in recent years. He went on to say that the 6 million people of Hong Kong should feel as though they had participated in the process even though they "[had] not had a chance to vote." The chief executive designate particularly stressed Hong Kong's interdependence with China: "Today's Hong Kong is successful. There are many factors contributing to our success. In particular, the amazing economic achievements of our country in recent years have brought us many new opportunities and prosperity as well."

China welcomed Tung's victory and said that "through this election, a type of democracy which is open, fair, and civilized is gradually being formed in Hong Kong in accordance with law."

Governor Chris Patten also welcomed Tung's selection and promised that the Hong Kong government would provide all necessary assistance to Tung to help him in his preparations for assuming the office of chief executive on 1 July 1997. Even Martin Lee expressed his willingness to cooperate with Tung and the hope that he would be better than the unrepresentative system that produced him. Lee called him "a good man by all accounts" and gave him a "honeymoon on probation."

In the days after his elevation, a consensus emerged that Tung did have the best qualifications for the job. Hong Kong television broadcast a documentary on Tung's life, portraying his little-known but impressive network of international friends. He was shown in a warm embrace with Barbara Bush, who explained that the families had been friends for two generations. Henry Kissinger also belongs to his circle of friends, as does Winston Lord, the assistant secretary of state in charge of East Asia, the latter more through his Shanghai-born wife, novelist Bette Bao Lord, whose family is close to Tung's. Tung was born in 1937 in Shanghai, fled to Hong Kong from the Communists in 1949, and went to England to study marine engineering in Liverpool. He lived in the United States for almost ten years, working for General Electric, and returned to Hong Kong in 1969 to join the family business. He has served on a large number of boards of educational, social, and management institutions, both in Hong Kong and abroad. At the moment of his selection, he was still chairman of the Hong Kong/United States Economic Cooperation Committee and a member of the Hong Kong/Japan

Business Cooperation Committee, an international counselor to the Center for Strategic and International Studies in Washington, D.C., and a member of the advisory bodies of both the Council on Foreign Relations in New York and the Hoover Institution on War, Revolution, and Peace in Stanford.

Another big asset of Tung's is that, in addition to his excellent China credentials, he has a network of high-level contacts in Taiwan through relatives and old friends of his father, who was once a confidant of Chiang Kai-shek's. This may very well help to reinvigorate the stagnant dialogue between Beijing and Taipei, as well as Taipei's problematic post-1997 Hong Kong links.

Before his trip to Beijing for his official inauguration by the Chinese government, Tung gave a statesmanlike speech before the Joint Chambers of Commerce, which served as a kind of political manifesto. First and foremost, Tung praised the tremendous progress that China had made during the last twenty years, describing it in the words of former United States deputy secretary of state John Whitehead as "more progress for more people in such a short period of time than any other nation in the whole history of mankind." He then proceeded to outdo even the xenophobic, chauvinistic Chinese officials who claim that Hong Kong owes its success solely to the hard work of the Chinese people, expounding, "Indeed, much of the success of Hong Kong today is attributable to the rule of law, Western systems of governance, and the freedoms we enjoy. . . . Most of us are Chinese and have been in Hong Kong all of our lives. . . . There are others in Hong Kong who are non-Chinese. Some were born here; others have come here to work. Even though their numbers are small, they contribute greatly to the success of Hong Kong's economy and the richness of our culture. They are an essential part of Hong Kong. They help make our outlook more international and cosmopolitan. . . . We have the benefit of understanding Western culture, but at the same time we have been brought up with the virtues of Chinese culture. We understand instinctively Chinese values such as humbleness, patience, persistence, and hard work. Yet we also appreciate those Western traits such as creativity, aggressiveness, and directness that often get things done. . . . Combining the best of the East and the West makes each and every one of us a better person and in turn makes our society that much stronger. . . ."

Tung reiterated his plea for a return to Chinese (family) values, a belief in order and stability, an emphasis on obligations to the community rather than on the rights of the individual, and a preference for consultation rather than open confrontation.[29]

Soon after, Tung was appointed by the central government in a ceremony attended by China's top leaders and was handed a gold-framed order of the State Council, signed by Premier Li Peng. Some Hong Kong newspapers reported that he would be given the rank of "state councilor," one rank below vice-premier but above the rank of minister, provincial governor, or mayor of the four largest cities. Beijing did not confirm this because it would only have stirred up controversy within China, where the privileges of Hong Kong were increasingly resented. But the honors given to Tung were clear evidence that he is in a class by himself. Tung himself dodged the issue by pointing to Hong Kong's different system—in other words, cautioning against comparing the two.

THE FINAL and most problematic phase in setting up the postcolonial political structure was the selection of the Provisional Legislature. The British government in London, Governor Patten, and the Democratic camp had waged a crusade against it, branding it illegal and in violation of the Joint Declaration and the Basic Law. They would do everything in their power to thwart and frustrate it.

The Joint Declaration clearly states that "the legislature of the Hong Kong SAR shall be constituted by elections," without elaborating, however, on the mode of elections, though this was certainly not meant to be by a Committee of Four Hundred, handpicked by Beijing. The Basic Law does not mention a Provisional Legislature but provides details on the method of formation of the first post-1997 Legislative Council, i.e., twenty members returned by geographical constituencies through direct elections, ten members returned by an election committee, and thirty members returned by functional constituencies. The 1995 elections should have been held on the basis of these stipulations, and this council would then have sat for two years before the transfer of sovereignty, subsequently riding the "through train" to the post-1997 era and sitting for another two years until 1999. In China's view, Patten's crafty reinterpretation of these criteria, his subsequent break-off of the Sino-British negotiations in 1993, and his decision to hold elections in 1995 without Chinese consent were tantamount to "destruction of the 'through train.'" For Beijing this was reason enough to take unilateral action. China stressed that the Provisional Legislature had a legal basis: two resolutions of the National People's Congress, one dated 4 April 1990, empowering the Preparatory Committee to set up the SAR, and the other dated 30 June 1994, stating that "the term of office of the 1995 Legislative Council ends on 30 June 1997."

In May, Maria Tam, former British-appointed member of the Executive and Legislative Councils and now coconvener of the subgroup for the Provisional Legislature in the Preparatory Committee, had been the first to call for a third decision of the National People's Congress explicitly to confirm the legality of the PL, for the purpose of reducing controversy.

But Martin Lee, one of Hong Kong's preeminent legal eagles, vowed to challenge the PL in court. Patten barred it from meeting in Hong Kong, denied it funding, forbade all government officials to have anything to do with it, and implored China not to let it operate before 1 July 1997. China also wanted to de-escalate the conflict and decided to let the PL meet across the border so as to preempt legal action. Beijing stressed that it would continue to exist for at most one year, until new elections could be held in mid-1998, but insisted that it would have to operate before the handover to prepare the legislation essential for the first year of the SAR, thereby preventing a legal vacuum.

After his selection as chief executive, Tung also said that he would try to persuade Chinese leaders that a clear decision of the National People's Congress was needed to underpin the legality of the Provisional Legislature. He did not mean to say that it was illegal now, only that another resolution was needed, just to clear the air.

Despite the unsettled legal questions, nothing could stop China's determination to go ahead with the selection of the PL. By mid-November the assorted pro-China camp, including the losers of the real elections in 1995 and the middle-of-the-roaders, were out scrambling frantically for seats. Thirty-four incumbents of the elected Legislative Council applied for a seat on the new temporary body as well. Several candidates who had been winners in 1995, such as the four legislators from the Association for Democracy and People's Livelihood, reversed their earlier decision not to seek seats, invoking their electorate's wish that they still join the process. The big losers of the real elections of 1995—the candidates of the pro-China party, the Democratic Alliance for the Betterment of Hong Kong—sought seats without any public explanation, revealing that they were just interested in power and influence without principle. At the last minute, Legislative Council president Andrew Wong also defected to the pro-China camp to join the race. He avoided the media, his anger flaring up only when they savaged his naked opportunism. Elsie Tu-Elliott—an eighty-three-year-old former British missionary and social activist, and a big (and bad) loser in the real elections of 1995—was among the first to apply for a seat, confirming that the penchant to cling to power until the last breath was not confined to ethnic Chinese. Peggy Lam, a sixty-eight-year-old social worker who had been ousted by a margin of over twelve thousand votes in a district of just over forty-one thousand by the independent democrat Christine Loh, also engineered her comeback in this way. Both said that the elections of 1995 had been unfair.

On "Selection Day," 21 December 1996, in Shenzhen (the special economic zone bordering Hong Kong), the 400 members of the Selection Committee had to pick 60 names from a list of 130 candidates, which had been finalized only ten days before. Of these 130, 91 were members of the Selection Committee itself and 35 were losers of the elections of 1995. So a great many voted for themselves and for one another. In his introductory remarks, Chinese vice-premier and foreign minister Qian Qichen, in his capacity as chairman of the Preparatory Committee, condemned the British for their lack of courage in facing the reality of the Provisional Legislature. He said that the "election" should have been held in Hong Kong, "but since the British refused to cooperate, we were forced to do it in Shenzhen." Qian also criticized the British suggestion to submit the question of the legality of the PL to the International Court in The Hague, adding that any attempt by the British to play an international card would be futile. Loudly applauded by the plenary meeting, Qian sarcastically described the British position with a metaphor from a Tang dynasty poem: "Watching the flowers withering and falling helplessly."

In Hong Kong, Patten lashed back with equal venom. He called the whole process "stomach-turning" and told China that the reality it should face was that 1 million people had voted in September 1995 to elect the existing Legislative Council. "Now four hundred people—four hundred—in a bizarre farce are voting for a so-called Provisional Legislature. . . . The other reality is that Hong Kong is a First-World economy which some mainland officials are trying to get to accept the sort of political institutions which Third World countries would find unacceptable."

Watching the procession of delegates carry their big red envelopes to the ballot box was rather unreal. One pole of the political spectrum had been truncated. All the prominent faces from the Democratic camp—Martin Lee, Szeto Wah, Christine Loh, and Emily Lau—were absent. Watching the parade of winners was even more curious. Ten of them were unprincipled losers of yesterday, who had now, thanks to their networking with Chinese officials and pro-China power brokers, become "winners without glory." It highlighted more than anything else that Hong Kong's return to China in the political sense was a great leap back to the past.

DURING THE FINAL DAYS of 1996, the structure of the future SAR has been put into place, but many important issues remain unsettled. The most vital one is how many years a society, long used to a high degree of freedom, can maintain its stability if the largest and most popular political group, the Democratic party and its allies, is excluded from the political structure.

Pro-China advocates will counter that the Democrats marginalized themselves, but this is as disingenuous as it is untrue. Since the Tiananmen crackdown of 1989, China has been determined to sideline Martin Lee and other Democratic leaders and push them off the "through-train." When the Democrats performed spectacularly strongly in the first partial direct elections in 1991, China wanted to revise the original through-train arrangement and allow only a token number of democratic passengers on board. Since then, Britain has no longer been willing to let China block democratic development in Hong Kong, and Patten has placed the initiative back in British hands. It did not last long, but it is too early to say whether this struggle has been lost for good or only temporarily.

The more they perceive Hong Kong's freedoms and their own survival to be threatened, the greater the chance that the Democrats and their allies—altogether about half of the seats in the current Legislative Council—will become a permanent, fragmented street opposition, mobilizing international media and other support and taking legal action in Hong Kong courts against legislative transgressions by the Provisional Legislature. The Democrats will likely concentrate their protests on three legislative measures that the PL is required to pass during the first half of 1997. One is the amendment of the Bill of Rights, limiting civil liberties by reinstating outdated, draconian colonial laws that the British had abolished earlier. The second is the antisubversion legislation required by Article 23 of the Basic Law.* The worst-case scenario predicts that the Provisional Legislature will take a very conservative view of these matters and, depending on the political mood in Beijing and in Hong Kong itself, will enact harsh laws during the first half of 1997. This repressive legislation would then go into effect at the zero hour on 1 July 1997, enabling the SAR government, under direct orders from Beijing, to settle accounts with the anti-Communist and anti-China forces in Hong Kong.

To preempt this kind of Communist-flavored legislation, the British Hong Kong government tabled its own liberal antisubversion bill, which would penalize subversion only if it involves violence. This provoked a new storm of protest from China, which vowed to amend it according to its own definitions of subversion and sedition.

---

* Article 23 stipulates the following: "The Hong Kong SAR shall enact laws on its own to prohibit any act of treason, secession, sedition, or subversion against the Central People's Government, or theft of state secrets, to prohibit foreign political organizations or bodies from conducting political activities in the Region, and to prohibit political organizations or bodies of the Region from establishing ties with foreign political organizations or bodies."

A third highly objectionable law concerns the framework for the forth-coming election in 1998. The Democrats suspect that the Provisional Legis-lature, with its appointees and its ten losers of the 1995 election, will arrange future elections in a way that will enable them to keep their seats indefi-nitely, never having to face the risk of defeat in a direct election again.

Other major uncertainties are how the SAR government will relate to the three powerful men who will be dispatched from Beijing: the secretary of the Communist party's Working Committee, the head of the Foreign Min-istry Office in the SAR, and the commander of the People's Liberation Army garrison. Their main responsibility is to ensure that the SAR does not be-come a base for subversion of the socialist system on the mainland. Chinese Communist functionaries, depending on their mood, may consider demon-strations and critical articles in the media to be subversion, whereas for the Hong Kong Chinese these freedoms are a routine part of daily life.

Now, in early 1997, it cannot be said that there is a crisis in Hong Kong, despite the many imponderables. The future has been mapped out since 1984 and people have had twelve years to prepare themselves psychologi-cally. Most economic indicators are positive, confirming a typical East Asian trend that politics move one way and economics another. Economic growth in 1997 is expected to increase to 5.4 percent, up from 4.7 percent in 1996. The Hang Seng Index rose 8.1 percent during the last quarter of 1996, and property prices, already outrageously high, rose 29 percent during 1996, re-flecting high investor confidence. The Heritage Foundation, the conserva-tive American think tank, ranked Hong Kong the freest economy in the world in 1996 for the third year running. China was number 125.

But as political negatives loom very large on the horizon, these positive economic factors do not justify the propaganda in the (pro-)Chinese media—echoed by Tung Chee-hwa—that the future is bright and that 1997 will be better than previous years.

If one applies the universal rule that the future is in the hands of the younger generation, in the medium to long term Hong Kong may very well be in for another set of surprises. A Hong Kong University opinion poll taken in late 1996 established that 62.5 percent of those between the ages of fifteen and twenty-four do not consider themselves Chinese, preferring to think of themselves as "Hong Kong people." Only 30 percent said they were Chinese and 6.6 percent said they were both. In the same poll, 40 percent in the same age group said they would emigrate if they had a chance, and about 30 percent expressed grave concerns about human rights and other free-doms. In all age groups, 30 percent said they felt happy and excited about the approaching end to colonial rule, but 15 percent said they felt "worried and anxious" and 55 percent said they either had no feelings on the subject, felt it was too complicated to make a decision about it, or simply did not want to talk about it.

This is the reflection of the ambivalent mood in Hong Kong on the eve of the Chinese takeover. It will take more than just a few years to prove either the disheartened doomsayers or the starry-eyed optimists wrong.

CHAPTER 3

Taiwan: From "Republic of China" to De Facto Island State

The expectation that Lee Teng-hui—who doesn't even know what China is—will improve relations between both sides of the Taiwan Strait is like climbing a tree to catch fish.

Comment from the People's Daily, *July 1995*

Lee Teng-hui pays lip service to reunification with independence in his heart.

WEN WEI PO,
Hong Kong, March 1996

TAIWAN IS THE RICHEST and most successful pariah in the world. Its population and economy are larger than those of the great majority of member states of the United Nations, and its political system is preferable as well. Its presence is nevertheless shunned at international conference tables. A fourth application in September 1996 for "representation" (not necessarily full membership) in the United Nations was not even put on the agenda owing to massive opposition from China, one of the five permanent members of the Security Council wielding veto power. A previous request made in September 1995, led by Nicaragua, had been supported by fifteen countries and was accompanied by a "bribe" of $1 billion in development aid.[1]

Taiwan, after all, is not a country but a province of China. Both the Communists in Beijing and the Nationalists in Taipei agree on this, although the latter less wholeheartedly than before. Beijing considers China to be the Communist People's Republic and contends that Taiwan must be brought back to the fold—by peaceful or, if necessary, by military means. For the old-style Nationalists in Taiwan, China meant the Nationalist Republic, temporarily based in Taiwan, which would sooner or later be restored to its rightful place on the mainland.[2] For the new democratic Taiwanese, however, China is at best a cultural universe that should be transformed into a loosely knit (con)federal polity made up of mainland China, Hong Kong and Macau, Taiwan, and perhaps even Singapore. As historical trends point to the further decline and even collapse of Communism, the prospects for a comprehensive rapprochement between China and Taiwan would seem at first glance to be gradually improving. Since the protracted military intimidation of Taiwan from the summer of 1995 through the spring of 1996, however, the obstacles to reunification on China's terms appear to have become permanent and insurmountable. As an economic system, Communism continues to crumble, while politically it has taken an increasingly hard line. Political power in Taiwan has slipped more and more from the old mainland-born Nationalists to the younger native-born Taiwanese, further complicating relations with Beijing.

WHEN THE TATTERED remnants of Generalissimo Chiang Kai-shek's Nationalist government and army—about 2 million people in all—fled to Taiwan in 1948–49, they established a government-in-exile, subjecting more than 7 million islanders to their rule. These were mostly rice farmers and fishermen who had been liberated from Japanese colonial rule four years earlier. The ancestors of these islanders were mainland Chinese who had moved to the island over the past three centuries from the province of Fujian across the Taiwan Strait. During the Korean War (1950–53), the American Seventh Fleet protected Taiwan against possible Communist invasion, and in 1954 Taiwan's security was formalized in a bilateral defense treaty with the United States which remained in force until one year after the closing of the American embassy in Taipei in 1979. Washington continued to recognize Chiang Kai-shek's "rump regime" as the official government of the whole of China and provided Chiang Kai-shek with guarantees that he could keep China's seat in the United Nations, as well as its permanent place on the Security Council. Mao Zedong's Communist regime in Beijing was treated as an outcast. Until 1965 Taiwan was given generous military and economic aid by the United States, enabling it to arm itself to the hilt against Communism and to build up a modern industrial export economy that would pave the way for integration into the capitalist world economy.

Taiwan's population has now grown to 21 million people, 85 percent of whom are native Taiwanese who speak the Minnan (Hokkien) and Hakka dialects. The remaining 15 percent are post-1949 arrivals from all parts of the mainland whose common language is Mandarin. Chiang Kai-shek ruled Taiwan with an iron hand until his death in 1975. Native islanders who zealously fought for a "Taiwan for the Taiwanese" were either executed, given lengthy jail sentences for treason, or forced to flee to foreign countries.

Taiwan was considered to be more than just the island itself. According to amendments to the constitution it was the "free territory of the Republic of China," with the exiled government of all of China residing in the temporary national capital of Taipci. All of the ministers, generals, ambassadors, and directors of state-owned industries were mainlanders and unwavering followers of the Kuomintang. All political and economic activity was dedicated to "the annihilation of Communism and the glorious recovery of the mainland." The Taiwanese were permitted to set up their figurehead provincial government under a Taiwanese governor in the provincial capital of Taichung.

At the end of his life, it finally dawned on the elderly Chiang Kai-shek that a military victory over Communism was no longer realistic, and he readjusted his estimate of the means necessary for a reconquest of the mainland to 70 percent political and 30 percent military. After a short interlude under a loyal puppet leader, Chiang was succeeded by his son, Ching-kuo, whose brand of autocracy was milder and who steered the government away from the mainlanders' monopoly of power toward "Taiwanization" of the regime. Ching-kuo received the same education as many Communist leaders. During the early period of cooperation between the Communist and Nationalist parties in the 1920s, Chiang sent his sixteen-year-old son to Moscow to study at the Sun Yat-sen University for the Toilers of the East, a Comintern-backed institute for the grooming of Chinese Communist leaders. One of his fellow students there was Deng Xiaoping. After the breakdown of the United Front between the Nationalists and the Communists, Ching-kuo was put under house arrest, and it was not until 1935, at the start of the second period of Kuomintang-Communist cooperation against Japan, that Stalin finally allowed the young Chiang to return to China, where he was reeducated in Confucianism and Nationalist orthodoxy by his father. In spite of this double dose of authoritarian training in his past, Chiang Ching-kuo devoted the last years of his life to the liberalization and democratization of Taiwan. In 1978 and again in 1984, he selected a Taiwanese as vice-president, paving the way for his succession by a Taiwanese after his untimely death in early 1988.

The first decisive step in Taiwan's transformation from a one-party dictatorship to political pluralism was taken in 1986 by "young Chiang," then seventy-five years old. He achieved this by tolerating the merging of still-illegal independent opposition groups to form the Democratic Progressive party (DPP), which then took part in the first free parliamentary elections in December 1986. In mid-1987 he lifted the ban on travel to the mainland and revoked martial law, by which the Kuomintang had ruled Taiwan since 1949, exercising extreme resourcefulness in legitimizing repressive methods, gerrymandering, and constitutional fantasies. The lifting of martial law ushered in a period of radical reconstruction of the Nationalist state, culminating in 1996 with the first direct presidential election.

The consitutional tentacles of the fictitious Nationalist polity on Taiwan stretched to all of China, including Tibet, Chinese Turkestan (Sinkiang, or Xinjiang), and Outer Mongolia, of all places, which had even been recognized by the government in Beijing as an independent state.[3] In the National Assembly—the presidential electoral college, also empowered to make amendments to the constitution—and the Legislative Yuan, the great majority of seats were reserved for representatives from all the provinces of the mainland. Owing to the "Communist rebellion" that had continued since 1947, no elections could be held there, and the Council of Grand Justices (the constitutional court) had therefore granted the delegates elected in 1947 lifelong terms of office. In more than three hundred cases in which delegates died, their places were filled by the candidates who had been second on the list in the elections on the mainland in 1947. The result was that Taiwan, at the end of the 1980s, still had a "self-perpetuating" parliament of mainlanders with an average age of eighty-two. Dozens of them arrived at the parliament every day in official limousines and shuffled into the building using their canes and walkers. Supported by valets, they signed the attendance roll, only to shuffle off again and disappear into one of the many "napping rooms." For their services they were given accommodation in an official residence, a free car, and a monthly stipend of $4,000. They were derisively called the "delegates for ten thousand years" and "old thieves" (lao tsei). The main objective of the new opposition party was to drive out the old thieves by means of an unrelenting campaign that included demonstrations and the distribution of pamphlets. Parliamentary procedures frequently deteriorated into violent clashes, with octogenarian Kuomintang stalwarts wielding their canes against young members of the opposition party, who in turn cracked the heads of the old men with chairs and microphones.

On 13 January 1988 President Chiang Ching-kuo died, just two weeks after being hissed out of parliament by the opposition, who had demanded that reforms be speeded up.

In the days before reform, all the streets in Taiwan's cities were named after provinces, cities, rivers, and mountains on the mainland. People would remark sarcastically that the old mainlander delegates could get in their cars in the morning in Taipei and travel around the entire mainland in one day. But now Taipei's new radical native-Taiwanese mayor, Chen Suibian, has "reclaimed" some enclaves on the city map for the native and aboriginal Taiwanese. The most outstanding example is the wide street that runs through the government district in central Taipei up to the presidential plaza. It used to be called Chieh-Shou Street, which means "Long Life to Chiang Kai-shek." In 1995 Mayor Chen rebaptized it "Kai-Da-Ge Lan Boulevard" after the tribe of aborigines that inhabited that area of the island before Chinese immigration to Taiwan started in the seventeenth century.

CHIANG CHING-KUO'S SUCCESSOR, Vice-President Lee Teng-hui, is a man of fundamentally different background and orientation. He was born in 1923, the son of a native-born Taiwanese tea and rice farmer, and after attending an elite colonial high school, he received a scholarship to continue his studies at Kyoto Imperial University. In 1951 he went to the United States as a graduate student in agronomy at Iowa State University. After his return to Taiwan, he worked for the United States–Taiwan Joint Commission on Agricultural Reform, and in 1968, at the age of forty-five, he went back to the United States to get his Ph.D. at Cornell University and wrote a dissertation entitled "Intersectoral Capital Flows in the Agricultural Development of Taiwan." He rose through the ranks, becoming mayor of Taipei, provincial governor, and in 1984 vice-president. Lee is a devout Presbyterian and has no historical or sentimental attachments to the mainland. He is a product of the Japanese empire on Formosa and sees the world through Japanese eyes, which do not regard China highly. He likes to stress his hybrid cultural identity, such as the fact that he speaks better Japanese than Mandarin, which he started to learn only at the age of twenty-one and still speaks with a heavy Taiwanese accent and occasional injections of Japanese grammar.

During his first two years in office, Lee still operated in the shadow of the old-guard Kuomintang from the mainland. The party congress held in the summer of 1988 was still in the thrall of nostalgia for the mainland, to which Lee paid only lip service. The conservative premier, Yu Kwo-hua, harped on the now completely anachronistic position that the Kuomintang had held for the past forty years, having their "base in Taiwan, their heart in mainland China, and their eyes directed at the rest of the world." The more liberal secretary-general of the party, Lee Huan, indulged in fantasies about setting up action groups behind enemy lines for the purpose of transplanting Taiwan's model of development to the mainland and forcing the regime there to give up Communism. This was the last party congress in Taiwan to focus more on the past than on the future. In the Kuomintang Central Standing Committee (the equivalent of the Communist party's Politburo), fifteen of the thirty-one seats remained occupied by elderly mainlanders, owing to their method of voting by standing ovation. For the first time, the Taiwanese had a slight majority, although by this time, thirty-nine years after its flight from the mainland, the party's membership was 75 percent Taiwanese. When asked if the Central Committee could be considered to have a mandate from the people, a party spokesman grinned and answered, "It doesn't need a mandate. Chinese politics work differently."

Thus far, the schemes concocted behind the scenes by an aged oligarchy had been quietly accepted by the hedonistic, materialistic, and largely apolitical population of Taiwan, but times were changing, and rapidly. Very unorthodox methods were required to get the silent majority interested in politics. Pandemonium and unparalleled violence in the streets was just the beginning. There was more to come. The opposition set up a three-ring circus starring a thirty-year-old striptease artist, a Taiwanese "Cicciolina" named Hsu Hsiao-tan, who vowed to fight the clenched fists of the Kuomintang with bared breasts on the floor of parliament. She was outshone by an old battle-ax of the Kuomintang, who, in her turn, used her spike-heeled shoes to attack the most formidable fighter in the opposition, "Rambo" Chu Kao-cheng, who had pioneered fistfighting in parliament.

The metamorphosis of President Lee Teng-hui himself began in 1990 at the party congress. In front of the National Assembly, a legion of octogenarians and nonagenarians in wheelchairs who would be electing the president in March 1990, Lee promised that Taiwan and the mainland would be reunified within six years, and on Taiwan's terms. As a reward, he was reelected by geriatrics of both sexes, large numbers of whom had to be carried to the ballot box. One of them, Ku Cheng-kang, honorary president of the World Anti-Communist League, ranted on about voting for Chiang Kai-shek, "as always." The oldest elector, retired general Hsueh Yueh, was 101 years old. After this "election," the most anachronistic electoral farce ever, Lee was his own man and immediately embarked on a subtle but revolutionary overhaul of the Nationalist political structure, pushing it in the direction of a new Taiwanese state. Lee dubbed his own tactics "creative ambiguity," and these led to new tensions between the mainlanders and the Taiwanese within his own party, as well as to recurring flare-ups in Taiwan's confrontation with Beijing. Lee appointed as premier Taiwan's senior mainlander general Hau Pei-tsun, a Chiang family stalwart. This unleashed a storm of protest from the radical DPP opposition, while skillfully unnerving the obstructive traditional right wing of the Kuomintang. The Council of Grand Justices came to Lee's aid, ruling that all members of the National Assembly who had been given lifelong posts must resign before the end of 1991. Lee himself then proceeded to revoke all of the repressive emergency legislation that had provided the constitutional basis for the existence of the "Republic of China" in Taiwan. This paved the way for a whole series of elections for new representative organs that would no longer claim to extend to all of China. From now on, the people of Taiwan would elect directly most of the members of the National Assembly (the presidential electoral college, which also performs functions carried out by the Supreme Court in the United States and the Privy Council in Great Britain), the Legislative Yuan (comparable to the United States House of Representatives or the British House of Commons), and the Control Yuan (the modern version of the Imperial Censorate, which supervises the proper exercise of power by the government).

The dawning of the new era gave former political prisoners and pro-independence activists who had fled the island during Chiang Kai-shek's rule and who were still living abroad the courage to return to Taiwan. This gave an added degree of inexorability to the movement for a completely new and independent Taiwanese state. In 1991 the Democratic Progressive party defied all warnings of the Kuomintang (and also those of the Communist rulers in Beijing) and included in its manifesto its commitment "to build an independent state." President Lee was tolerant of this standpoint but preferred the middle ground himself, believing that maintenance of the status quo—"no reunification and no independence"—was the best solution for the time being. The Kuomintang split in two: the Taiwanese mainstream (*chu-liu*) led by Lee was in the majority; the nonmainstream, or mainlander faction (*chih-liu*), led by Premier Hau was in the minority. China was alarmed to such an extent that President Yang Shangkun threatened at election time in December 1991 that "those who play with fire will perish in the flames." Taiwan would have to be reunified with China at any price, even that of conflagration.[4] The first elections for the new-style National Assembly, representing only the people actually in Taiwan, resulted in a resounding victory for the Kuomintang, who got 71 percent of the vote. The people had no desire to stake everything on the DPP and race at breakneck speed toward independence. According to opinion polls, China's threats to respond to a declaration of independence with military force were taken seriously by a majority of the population. The DPP had learned its lesson the hard way and toned down its independence rhetoric to "One China–One Taiwan," yet another motto for maintenance of the status quo.

DURING THE FIRST ELECTIONS in December 1992 for a Legislative Yuan with a membership representing only Taiwan, the Kuomintang vote dropped to 53 percent and the DPP vote rose to 31 percent. Independence had not been the only issue this time, but rather the perception on the part of the voters that the Kuomintang was a decadent party that had been in power too long and that identified too strongly with the interests of big business. Many Kuomintang candidates were either business tycoons themselves (so-called "golden oxen") or else they accepted financial backing from corrupt business interests. Buying votes was the order of the day, especially in the rural areas.

There was a striking resemblance to Japan, where the ruling Liberal Democratic party (LDP) had been discredited by several "money politics" scandals in quick succession. In 1993 the LDP was voted out of office for the first time, a seeming omen that has haunted the Kuomintang ever since. Another similarity with the LDP was the crumbling of the Kuomintang into more and more factions. Occasionally President Lee's Taiwanese mainstream in the Kuomintang openly ignored the mainlander faction and formed ad hoc coalitions with the DPP. In this way, Lee, with the support of the DPP, succeeded in firing the premier, the mainlander Hau Pei-tsun, and replacing him with a Taiwanese: Lien Chan, who was, ironically enough, born on the mainland. This heightened tensions between mainlanders and Taiwanese within the Kuomintang even further, and during the party congress in August 1993, the first to be held since 1988, the rift widened into an open schism. Young second- and third-generation mainlanders founded the New Party. They accused President Lee of letting the Kuomintang deteriorate into a party that bought votes and sold power, used dictatorial methods, and was drifting, rudderless, toward independence. The New Party was adamantly opposed to all of this but could not turn back the clock. At the party congress in August 1993, the historical objective of recovering the mainland was formally abandoned, ushering in the most critical phase in the polity's reform: the dilemma of whether to draft a completely new constitution for a "Republic of Taiwan" or whether to give the old Nationalist Chinese constitution a radical overhaul.

The most sensitive question was whether the governor of the province of Taiwan and particularly the president should be elected directly by the people. Under the old constitution, the governor was appointed by the president and the president was rubber-stamped by the National Assembly. If the governor, but not the president, were to be elected directly by the people, who would then have more power and legitimacy? If Taiwan's new political structure applied only to the island and no longer—at least in theory—to the whole of China, how could a meaningful role be given to both a governor and a president? If the president were to be elected directly by the people, but only those of Taiwan, could he still call himself "president of the Republic of China"? And if the Republic of China were abolished—whether implicitly or by even more ambiguous means—wouldn't the People's Republic of China interpret this as a new and radical step in the direction of independence, or even as a de facto declaration of independence? At the very least, it would lead to increased tension in the Taiwan Strait, armed clashes, or worse. In spite of these uncertainties, after a marathon session of constitutional redrafting it was decided to hold the first gubernatorial election in December 1994 and the historic first direct election for president in March 1996.

TAIWAN'S INTERNAL CONSTITUTIONAL dilemmas and political discord are reflected clearly in its ambivalent policy toward the Communist mainland. Until the historic opening of the People's Republic of China by President Richard Nixon, Taiwan was the "little yellow adopted brother of the U.S.," who didn't have to decide anything for himself and constantly clung to the hand of his big brother in Washington for protection. If Nixon had survived Watergate and if the Vietnam War had ended less abruptly and in a less humiliating manner for the United States, Taiwan would probably have been dealt the blow that it eventually received at the end of 1978 two or three years earlier: the rupture of diplomatic ties with Washington and the termination of the defense treaty. Although the Taiwan Relations Act offered a new, albeit less solid, form of protection, after 1979 Taiwan was forced to grow up and find its own way in the world, finally facing up to the burden inherited by "illegitimate children."[5]

China reckoned in 1979 that Taiwan, bereft of American protection, would sink within three years, and that it would then be able to hoist the precious booty on board its rusty Communist ship. In 1981 China's acting head of state, Marshal Ye Jianying, chairman of the National People's Congress, launched the "Nine-Point Proposal for Peaceful Reunification." (During the Cultural Revolution Mao Zedong had abolished the position of head of state and it was not reinstated until 1982.) The document proposed a third period of cooperation between the Communist party and the Kuomintang to complete the great task of reunification. After establishing postal, trade, air, and shipping links, as well as permitting travel for the purpose of family visits, academic exchanges, and competitive sports, Taiwan would retain a high degree of autonomy as a special administrative region, including the maintenance of its own armed forces. Its social and economic system would remain unchanged and Taiwan would be permitted to maintain its own foreign economic and cultural relations. Taiwanese could be appointed to leading positions on the mainland, and Taiwanese businesses would be welcome to invest in and trade on the mainland. In case of emergency, Taiwan would be able to count on financial aid from the central government.[6]

TAIWAN REJECTED the "Nine Points" with "Three No's": no contact, no negotiations, and no compromise—all of which were rigidly observed until well into the 1980s. The "Three No's" became "Three Maybe's" when President Chiang Ching-kuo revoked martial law and lifted the ban on travel in 1987. In 1991 the "Three No's" were officially replaced by the "Guidelines for National Unification," which contained the following condition for the rebuilding of a united China: "a consensus on democracy, freedom, and the equal distribution of wealth, which should be reached on the basis of peace, equality, and reciprocity after a reasonable period of exchange, cooperation, and consultation."

By the mid-1980s China's ideas on reunification had crystallized into the formula "one country–two systems," whose prerequisite was submission of the capitalist provincial government in Taipei to the Communist central government in Beijing. Taipei steadfastly rejected this as a recipe for annexation. Explanatory notes to the "Guidelines" advocated "one country–two governments," "one country–two territories," or "one country–two political entities," with the added proviso that separation be a temporary transitional phase leading to future reunification, as witnessed by the German precedent and the potential situation in Korea.[7] China still firmly rejects all of these variations as independence in disguise and the splitting up of the motherland.

China's strategy for the ultimate subjugation of Taiwan is threefold:

1. Encourage Taiwanese businesses to invest and trade on a large scale.
2. Undermine Taiwan's residual international position by exerting increased pressure to isolate Taiwan further.
3. Use the threat of military force to intimidate the proindependence faction.

As Taiwanese investment and trade on the mainland have expanded, the government in Taipei has tried to restrict and regulate it. It has attempted to keep the flight of capital to the mainland within limits and has banned investment in strategic high-tech sectors (see Chapters 4 and 8). Clearly, trade with the mainland has been to the advantage of Taiwan, which has a trade surplus with China of approximately 80 percent of the total two-way trade volume. Taiwanese companies have had to go overseas because of the deterioration of the investment climate at home, owing to the high cost of labor and land, crime, street politics, and growing pressure from environmentalists. The constant revaluations—under pressure from the United States—of the New Taiwan dollar have forced Taiwan to look for new markets. In the early years, labor costs on the mainland were only 5 to 10 percent of those in Taiwan, and the margin of profit was at least three times as high.

On the diplomatic front, Taiwan has attempted to break out of its isolation by every means possible, including its dollar diplomacy, vacation diplomacy, and golf diplomacy. Between 1990 and 1992 two of Taiwan's most important remaining diplomatic partners, Saudi Arabia and South Korea, closed their embassies in Taipei. Taiwan sought to compensate for this loss by buying, in exchange for foreign aid programs, new diplomatic recognition from a series of troubled, impoverished Third World countries, including Liberia, Belize, Guinea-Bissau, Lesotho, and Niger. With Western countries Taiwan has developed a new form of unofficial yet substantial relations, which are managed by offices that are embassies in all but name, based on the model of the American Institute in Taiwan, the private corporation that replaced the embassy after the severing of official diplomatic relations and that is staffed by diplomats "on temporary leave." In Taipei's shining office towers one now finds the Institut Français, the German Trade Office, and the British Trade and Cultural Office. These offices perform most of the consular functions of embassies, and their directors enjoy diplomatic privileges and the status of ambassador without having the title printed on their business cards.

Taiwan's answer to China's threats of military force is to purchase weapons wherever possible. Reacting to Taiwan's large military transactions with Holland (submarines) and France (frigates and Mirage jets), China took such strong retaliatory measures that both countries were forced either to forgo new arms deals or to risk exclusion from the huge Chinese market. Only the United States is in a position to ignore Chinese pressure effectively, and America therefore remains the only reliable supplier of arms to Taiwan.

· · ·

TAIWAN USED TO HAVE considerable room to maneuver in challenging China in various areas, but where the gap between them was at its widest—in the areas of ideology and propaganda—pragmatism and restraint were at their strongest. After the massacre of 4 June 1989, for example, Western countries took economic and other sanctions against China. Exactly one month later, however, a delegation of seventy-six Taiwanese business tycoons visited a trade fair in the northeastern city of Dalian and one of them made an instant investment of $5 million.[8] The vacuum created by Western sanctions against China between 1989 and 1992 was largely filled by its adversary Taiwan. During the second half of 1989, for example, Taiwanese investments doubled compared with the first half of the year.[9]

Immediately after the Tiananmen drama, Taiwan spent a lot of money financing Chinese dissidents in exile in France and the United States, but as soon as these exiles wanted to take more drastic action and attempted in the summer of 1990 to anchor their broadcasting ship, the *Goddess of Democracy,* in Chinese waters, "Free China" bowed to the threats of Communist China and kept the boat from its shores.

Democratic principles were fine as long as they did not endanger Taiwan's growing interests in the Chinese market. Trade had grown from $2.6 billion in 1988, the first year of Taiwan's new "mainland fever" (*dalu re*), to $4 billion in 1990. Investments had grown from $600 million in 1988 to $3 billion in 1991.

Taiwan was hoping that the complementarity of economic and other interests would make China more flexible politically and lead to the recognition of the "Taiwan authorities" as a de facto government with which China would consent to reach intergovernmental agreements, first and foremost a nonaggression pact, followed by the treaties essential to large-scale economic intercourse, such as consular and investment protection. China remained unrelenting, however, and continued to repeat the same clichés: only sovereign governments could negotiate treaties, and the central government in Beijing already guaranteed the protection of investments and the safety of Chinese citizens, including, in their irredentist vision, those of Taiwan. China even proved that it was willing to keep this promise when, during the prelude to the Gulf War in the fall of 1990, the Chinese embassy in Baghdad assisted in evacuating more than a hundred Taiwanese technicians from Iraq.

ON 1 MAY 1991 President Lee Teng-hui put an official end to the "period of national mobilization for the suppression of the Communist rebellion," which had maintained the state of civil war since 1947. Lee hoped that China would reciprocate with a pledge to use only peaceful means to solve the Taiwan question. China remained implacable, however. As the liberal leader of the Communist party, Hu Yaobang, had said already in 1985, such a promise on the part of China would cause the Taiwanese to "sit back and relax and never talk about reunification." Chinese leaders stress from time to time that threats of force are aimed not at the people of Taiwan but at a handful of agitators for independence and certain "third parties" with ulterior motives, meaning the United States Congress and ultranationalists in Japan.[10]

Political circles in Taipei have meanwhile become increasingly divided over the wisdom of growing economic involvement on the mainland. Optimistic ideologues have indulged in much wishful thinking, hoping that the enormous influx of Taiwanese capital would help to undermine the Communist regime, accelerating its "peaceful evolution" into a capitalist democracy. Cynics worry that the Communists are luring them into a giant trap, the Taiwanese tiger no longer being able to free itself from the grip of the Chinese dragon. Economists working in government ministries and at research institutes express their concern that Taiwan is already in the process of deindustrialization and that if prevailing trends are not curbed, more and more industries will move to the mainland. Radical restrictive measures have been urged by various groups, but opposition has been strong, arguing that any scaling down of Taiwanese operations on the mainland would be playing into the hands of competitors from South Korea, Japan, and the West.

South Korea cut off diplomatic relations with Taiwan in 1992, simultaneously extending recognition to China, in order to facilitate its full-scale "economic invasion" of the mainland. The countries of Western Europe had largely lifted their Tiananmen sanctions by 1990 so as not to give Japan free rein in the Chinese market. Taiwan's Great Leap to the mainland continued, therefore, albeit with more circumspection.

IN NOVEMBER 1990 the "Taiwan authorities" answered China's unrelenting refusal to treat them as a sovereign government with the establishment of a nongovernmental foundation that would handle regular contacts with the Chinese authorities. Taiwan invited Beijing to do the same. This "Straits Exchange Foundation" (SEF) was the institutionalization of the "private exchanges" that had proliferated since November 1987. It took more than a year for China to reciprocate, but in December 1991 the "Association for Relations Across the Taiwan Strait" (ARATS) was born.

In terms of achieving a dialogue of equals, Taiwan had scored a victory of sorts. During the first year of the SEF-ARATS exchange, Taiwan did not want to go beyond practical consular matters such as an agreement on the verification of legal documents like birth certificates and property deeds. China, on the other hand, tried to raise the dialogue to a more serious level, trying to maneuver itself into a more authoritative position while at the same time doing justice to Taiwan's demand for equality. Vice-premier Wu Xueqian suggested negotiations between two equal political parties—the Communist party and the Kuomintang—thereby revealing his complete lack of understanding of (or perhaps contempt for) the altered political situation in Taiwan, which now had a multiparty system. China also tried to put direct post, air, and shipping links on the agenda. Taiwan had already permitted indirect postal links in the past and was not prepared to budge an inch until China renounced its threat to use force.

In spite of the low-key agenda, both sides agreed to hold a nonpolitical summit between the heads of the two organizations in 1993. Regarding the meeting place Taiwan rejected the suggestion of Hong Kong as not being neutral enough, owing to the steady increase of Chinese influence there. Singapore was finally chosen, partly as a tribute to Singapore's former prime minister (now senior minister), Lee Kuan Yew, whose untiring efforts had played a major role in bringing the two traditional enemies together.

In April 1993 the time was ripe. Both sides were represented by the heads of the two unofficial foundations, both of whom were refined elderly gentlemen. Representing China was Wang Daohan, President Jiang Zemin's predecessor as mayor of Shanghai. Wang had been Jiang's mentor when the latter was called to take over as party leader after the dismissal of the disgraced Zhao Ziyang following the Beijing massacre in 1989. Koo Chen-fu, a native Taiwanese aristocrat and billionaire businessman, who had acted as Taiwan's ambassador-at-large for many years, was also a confidant of the president.

The meetings were in fact at the presidential level, but by proxy, and were characterized by the tactics of "evasive minimalism"—a classic example of the Chinese political proverb "sleeping in the same bed but dreaming different dreams" (tong chuang yi meng). Koo spoke in his opening statement of the "two countries" but was immediately chided by Wang. China was adamant about muzzling any allusion to Taiwan as a country; the issue was skirted by referring to "both sides of the Taiwan Strait." Taiwan was concerned at this stage only in protecting the safety of travelers and trading interests, to be followed by the upgrading of its status to a de facto official level. China's primary preoccupation was to promote political reunification. The Chinese said openly that they also wanted to discuss political issues, refusing to discuss an agreement on investment protection until Taiwan dropped its opposition to direct trade and communications. Accords were reached only on trivial matters: the verification of documents, compensation for lost registered mail, and the agreement to seek regular contact in the future. The minutes of the meeting kept by both sides were not even identical: those of Taiwan were in old-style Chinese characters, those of China in simplified Chinese characters. Nonetheless, the uniform Chinese media called it a complete success, whereas the free media in Taiwan were more restrained in their enthusiasm.

TWO YEARS of fruitless dialogue had meanwhile persuaded Taiwan to abandon all hope that China would one day accept it as a separate political entity. The prospect of reaping diplomatic gains from the termination of the Cold War, as well as the upheavals in Eastern Europe and the Soviet Union, also proved illusory. Latvia was the only former Soviet republic to extend diplomatic recognition to Taiwan, but it was put under such pressure by China that Taiwan was forced to close its consulate general in Riga.

By mid-1993 Taiwan had opted for a more aggressive strategy to put an end to its isolation, launching a campaign to regain its seat in the United Nations, from which it had been expelled in 1971 after the admission of the People's Republic of China. Since the DPP's formation in 1986, membership in the United Nations had been a key plank in the party's platform. The government, however, considered it a lost cause and had consequently taken no action. After years of struggling in vain for a higher degree of recognition, it now concluded that a "return to the United Nations" was a much more effective mobilization slogan than bilateral "dollar diplomacy." It would be able to count on broad support among the 21 million people of Taiwan; it would take the wind out of the sails of the DPP; and international support would certainly continue to grow yearly. An unspoken agreement existed between the Kuomintang and the DPP to spare no costs in their all-out efforts the achieve this lofty goal. By September 1993 politicians in both parties were actively lobbying in Washington, New York, Brussels, and Strasbourg.

Jason Hu, the astute director-general of Taiwan's Government Information Office, spoke in Washington of "participation in the United Nations," knowing full well that an attempt to gain full membership would be vociferously vetoed by China. Hu called Taiwan's exclusion "a violation of the human rights" of the 21 million Taiwanese and an infraction of the United Nations charter, as well as a denial of Taiwan's political and economic achievements as a new democracy, the fourteenth-largest trading power in the world, the second-largest foreign investor in Asia, and a promoter of development in the Third World. He quoted an editorial from the *New York*

Times, "Taiwan, Too Big to Ignore," and went on to refer to the active role played by the United Nations in the peaceful reunification of Germany and to its ongoing efforts on behalf of Korea, which still has dual representation. This could also be a solution to the problem of a "divided China." Hu was noncommittal about the name under which Taiwan would participate in the United Nations and left this open to discussions and consultations "with any country that is concerned about the issue," suggesting that it was now China's turn to be realistic and flexible."

Increasingly alarmed that the rapidly changing situation in Taiwan was becoming more unfavorable to reunification every day, China nipped Taiwan's campaign for readmission to the United Nations in the bud. A white paper called "The Taiwan Question and the Reunification of China," published on 31 August 1993, reiterated the old hard line, renewed the threat of using force, and left no doubt about who was supposed to be in charge. It placed all historical responsibility for the "national trauma" (the division of the motherland) with Chiang Kai-shek and the United States and firmly rejected Taiwan's favorite analogy with Germany and Korea. Unlike Taiwan's "secession," those two divisions had been the result of international agreements between the Great Powers."

Taiwan was not deterred and countered that it had taken China twenty-two years—from 1949 to 1971—to gain admission to the United Nations and that Taiwan was also bracing itself for a long struggle. The Mainland Affairs Council (MAC) issued a detailed statement, maintaining that there was no "Taiwan question" but rather a "China question," i.e., the Communist system on the mainland. "The prompt realization of democracy, freedom, and a system for equitable distribution of wealth on the Chinese mainland would solve the China question once and for all."

Taiwan continued to rub China's rigidity under its nose. According to several articles in the Hong Kong media, the "Chinese Taipei" Olympic Committee voted for Sydney in the race to hold the Olympics in the year 2000. Taiwanese officials have never denied this but nevertheless refrain from gloating over it in public.

The question of Taiwan's participation in the United Nations has flared up repeatedly. A number of its diplomatic partners in the Third World and various persevering individuals have spearheaded an attempt to reopen it each fall. The *People's Daily* of 17 September 1994 described Taiwan's campaign as "clamor to nullify UN resolution 2758 of 1971" (the admission of China to the UN). In January 1995 the chairman of the United Nations Commission on Science and Technology, Oscar Serrate, became the first UN official to visit Taiwan. He expressed deep sympathy with Taiwan's undeserved fate and suggested that it proceed in perfecting its democratization in order to obtain more support for its UN cause from the democratic countries of the world. For a while there was even support for a UN seat for Taiwan in the Republican party. The Speaker of the House, Newt Gingrich, openly advocated it in 1995 but was instantly censored by Henry Kissinger, who had just returned from a trip to China.[14]

DURING THE SUMMER and fall of 1993, the whole China-Taiwan relationship was dominated by a series of airplane hijackings, ten in total, including three in one week alone in November. Taiwan was so perplexed that its air force suggested it was a Machiavellian scheme on the part of the Chinese to undermine Taiwan's air defense. It was wryly noted that at last there were direct air links between China and Taiwan, without a bilateral agreement on air services. The hijackings, which highlighted the low safety standards of China's burgeoning civil aviation industry, as well as the malaise on the mainland, became the dominant theme in the SEF-ARATS talks. ARATS accused Taiwan of encouraging the hijackers, who were still under the illusion that they would be welcomed with open arms in Taiwan as anti-Communist heroes, although this had happened for the last time in 1983. Taiwan refused to extradite the hijackers, instead handing out prison sentences of ten to twelve years to express its disapproval of China's automatic death sentences and to demonstrate its powers of jurisdiction as a sovereign state. Taiwan was ready to accept the principle of extradition if China would enter into bilateral agreements on it, but this was rejected by Beijing as being tantamount to recognizing Taiwan as a state. The regular SEF-ARATS talks never rose above the level of petty arguing about hijackings, smuggling, crime, the stream of illegal immigrants to Taiwan, and the violent clashes between fishermen. China was much too worried that it might accidentally say something that would suggest implicit recognition of Taipei's jurisdiction over Taiwan. Essentially, the Chinese negotiators did little more than offer—sometimes courteously, sometimes curtly—unilateral decrees from the central government. The first example was the "Draft Agreement on Protection of Investment by Compatriots from Taiwan," which had been submitted to the National People's Congress. This trifling "law," consisting of only fifteen clauses, referred to Taiwanese investments as "special domestic investments."

FOR A WHILE it seemed as though 1994 would be the year of the big breakthrough. In November 1993 Taiwan attended for the first time an important international conference, the summit of the Asia Pacific Economic Confer-

ence (APEC) in Seattle, chaired by President Clinton himself. China had vetoed the presence of President Lee Teng-hui, but consented to the participation of two cabinet members in charge of the economy: the minister of
economic affairs, P. K. Chiang, and the chairman of the Council of Economic Planning and Development, Vincent Siew, who were the two politicians with the most pragmatic and daring attitude toward the mainland.
Siew had recently criticized a statement from his colleague the minister of
finance, who had warned against increasing dependence on exports to the
mainland—totaling approximately 8.8 percent in 1993—pronouncing it already in the danger zone. Siew was convinced that there was no danger zone,
even if exports to China should reach 10 percent. Restrictions, he said,
would only hurt Taiwan first and the mainland afterward. On New Year's
Day, P. K. Chiang called for direct shipping links between Taiwan and the
mainland, as this would drastically cut the costs of shipping raw materials
and semifinished products from the mainland. The indirect trade route
through Hong Kong was costing Taiwan about $1 billion a year in agents'
fees. Chiang proposed to circumvent the "national" governments and to entrust the negotiations to municipal and port authorities as a means of
avoiding political complications. The Mainland Affairs Council held to its
view that higher considerations of national security should prevail and
would be more than worth the extra cost.

The newest political nuisance was the Chinese campaign to pressure
France into stopping the sale of arms to Taiwan, which it finally pledged to
do on 17 January 1994. French companies had faced serious discrimination
on the Chinese market after the French sale of Mirages to Taiwan in 1992,
and after German chancellor Helmut Kohl's highly successful visit to China
in late 1993, France—led by a new premier—did an abrupt about-face. Just
as Holland had done ten years earlier, France now signed a communiqué
pledging to stop the supply of arms to Taiwan. Completion of the Mirage
deal already under way was nevertheless allowed.

Taiwan continued to search for new successes and found these in the
"vacation diplomacy" of President Lee Teng-hui. China's rigid policy of isolation had prevented Lee from paying official visits to other countries, but
that obstacle was now sidestepped by his meeting the presidents of the
Philippines and Indonesia not in their palaces but on the golf course. Lee
was also granted a private audience with the king of Thailand. Vacation
diplomacy was one of the main weapons in Taiwan's so-called "South
Strategy," which encouraged Taiwanese entrepreneurs to invest less in China and more in Vietnam and the other countries of the Association of
Southeast Asian Nations.[15] China's threats and pointed protests aimed at

Southeast Asian governments had had no effect. Taiwanese investments, totaling $15 billion, were too important to them. The "Taiwan issue" was, moreover, one of the few instruments these countries had with which to show their displeasure at the signs of hegemonism displayed by a hard-line, neonationalist China—increasingly strong, both economically and militarily—in particular regarding its claims to the disputed islands in the South China Sea.

The SEF-ARATS process had still not risen above the level of ineffectual dialogue falling on deaf ears. A new "Wang-Koo summit" was planned for the end of March, but the conciliatory climate suddenly deteriorated when Taiwanese troops killed seven mainland Chinese fishermen off the coastal island of Matsu, one of the remaining territories held by Taiwan. The low-level talks on the settlement of fishery disputes, the repatriation of hijackers, and the problem of illegal immigration to Taiwan were broken off. Taiwan persisted in refusing to extradite airplane hijackers if China would not relent and take back the growing numbers of mainlanders who slipped into Taiwan illegally each year. The Taiwanese media blamed the rupture on the "Deng Xiaoping factor," the lingering power struggle behind the scenes in Beijing in anticipation of the death of the then eighty-nine-year-old leader, during which time no one dared to take the initiative in breaking the deadlock.

ON THE SAME DAY, 31 March, a far more serious incident occurred which would do even more long-term damage to the reconciliation process. During a fire on a pleasure boat on Lake Qiandao near Hangzhou, twenty-four Taiwanese tourists died, as well as eight Chinese crew members and tour guides. After the Taiwanese had been reported missing, the local authorities first kept silent for two days and then claimed that it had been an accident. Taiwanese journalists were kept away from the scene of the incident, and a film of the area, shot by a Taiwanese television crew, was even confiscated. Fifty relatives of the victims arrived promptly but were not allowed to see either the charred bodies or the burned-out hulk. After talks broke down concerning what should happen to the remains of the victims, their relatives were put under house arrest in a hotel. Postmortem examinations had been performed without the consent of the surviving relatives, but they were given no reports of the findings and were furthermore forced to give their consent to immediate cremation. They were then allowed to return home with the ashes.

Mourning and grief culminated in frenzied rage. Since 1990 between one and one and a half million Taiwanese had visited China annually. Nearly two hundred had died in airplane crashes and other accidents, and there had been eighteen robberies and murders.[16] This was the first mass murder, however, and the authorities were trying to cover it up. In particular, the callous treatment of the victims' relatives had convinced the great majority of Taiwanese that the mainland Chinese, embittered and dehumanized by forty-five years of Communism, actually harbored a deep hatred of the prosperous Taiwanese, despite all their reunification propaganda proclaiming fraternal affection. The Taiwanese media went so far as to advise their readers not to show off expensive clothes and especially not to wear Rolex watches, even imitation ones, while visiting the mainland.

Not until 9 April did the New China News Agency admit the possibility of sabotage as the cause of the accident. A spokesman for the Bureau of Taiwan Affairs of the State Council expressed the hope that "Taiwan's relevant departments will view the accident in an objective and calm manner to prevent some people from exploiting it to influence public opinion and to create trouble unfavorable to the development of cross-Strait relations."

President Lee Teng-hui harshly condemned the "utter disregard for human life" of the Chinese Communist authorities, going on to say that "a large group of evil forces . . . have behaved like bandits with the support of the authorities. Look, they've killed a great number of our fellow countrymen, haven't they? How can such a regime be called a government? The people should have renounced it a long time ago."

Taiwan's Secret Service reported that a group of mutinous soldiers with flamethrowers had been responsible for the crime, but on 17 April three young gangsters were suddenly arrested.

Anti-China sentiment in Taiwan rose to unprecedented levels. Support for independence increased threefold to 27 percent, and the demand for retribution and a moratorium on all contacts with China was universal. Realities were different, though. Tempers cooled rapidly, and except for the cancellation until the end of May of Taiwanese group tours to the mainland, no further action was taken. China lost at least $50 million in tourist revenues, but Taiwan's travel agencies and airlines also sustained considerable losses, as did the airlines and hotels in Hong Kong. (The air route Taipei–Hong Kong is one of the busiest in the world.)

China repeatedly accused Taiwan of "politicizing the boat incident." During the rapid-fire exchange of words, China launched a counteroffensive: ARATS held SEF accountable for the frequent shooting incidents in the Taiwan Strait in which Taiwanese troops had killed mainland Chinese fishermen.

China wanted to put an end to the matter quickly, if only to deprive Taiwan of its propaganda advantage. The three young gangsters were put on trial acted out on 11 June and subjected to summary justice according to a prepared script. Key witnesses were not permitted to testify. Relatives of the victims were allowed to attend the proceedings but not to bring along their lawyers. Journalists could watch the trial only on a television screen in a nearby building, and, for $100, were offered a twenty-minute videotape—edited and censored—of the proceedings. The three suspects refrained from defending themselves and cooperated perfectly with the judge, consulting prepared notes while replying to the judge's questions. The fact that they would be dead men within hours after the sentence seemed not to faze them. After listening to the pronouncement of the death sentence, one of them even expressed the hope that after their execution relations between the two sides would improve. They made no use of their right to appeal and were summarily executed the following day.[17]

On 20 June China Youth Travel, the travel agency that had arranged the trip of the murdered group, awarded damages of $330,000, or $13,790 per person plus $345 for baggage claims.

The Taiwanese remained highly indignant, however. "It is an unsolved case in which the truth was not allowed to come to light," said government spokesman Jason Hu. The Qiandao incident demonstrated dramatically the extent to which social order had deteriorated in China, the primitiveness of the legal system, and the high risks taken by investors on the mainland. The most serious miscalculation made by the Chinese authorities, however, was their assumption that they could treat the Taiwanese as they did their own docile subjects: tremble and obey, or else! The aftereffects would be long-lasting indeed.

As tempers cooled, Taiwan decided not to delay resumption of the SEF-ARATS talks any longer. New talks were scheduled to take place at the end of July or the beginning of August, to be preceded by a systematic reappraisal of the situation, during which the traditional dilemma—long-term economic interests on the one hand versus strategic security on the other—was highlighted more strongly than ever before. An important Mainland Working Conference held in early July became a showdown between the Ministry of Economic Affairs, the Council for Economic Planning and Development, and the business community on the one hand and the politically oriented Mainland Affairs Council on the other. Leading economists, including President Lee's top economic adviser, concluded that if Taiwan wished to compete with Hong Kong and Singapore as a regional base for multinationals, it would have to seek direct links with the mainland in the areas of transport, finance, and investment. "Therefore, we propose that Taiwan gradually open direct transportation links with the mainland, provided that such opening does not jeopardize national security." This proposal by the economists, however, encroached upon the territory of the Mainland Affairs Council, which, in a newly published "White Paper on Cross-Strait Relations," had put strict limits on the further development of relations. It demanded China's acceptance of the concept of two equal political entities as the basis of interaction and stressed its rejection of the notion of "one country–two systems," in which China would be the country and Taiwan only a special administrative zone.

This white paper was also a belated response to China's hard-line policy statement of the year before. The chairman of the Mainland Affairs Council, Huang Kun-hui, denied that Taiwan was an advocate of "one China–two states," "because political entity can apply to a country, a government, or a political organization." Huang proposed this flexible definition of political entity to China as a positive alternative that could prevent China from drifting toward permanent separation, because the Kuomintang had gradually lost control over the separatist forces as the DPP and other opposition groups had gained in strength. The white paper elegantly shifted the historical blame for the division of China to the Communists, who, as a branch of the Comintern, had organized uprisings against the Chinese government starting in 1921, and who had even set up a Soviet republic in the province of Jiangxi in 1931.[18]

The next round of SEF-ARATS talks in August led to the initialing of agreements on the extradition of airplane hijackers and illegal immigrants. A preliminary agreement on procedures to end the fishery conflicts was also reached. Political harmony was still nonexistent, because the settlement of matters pending was frequently thwarted by incidents in which China displayed its unrelenting hard-line policy, such as its systematic obstruction of Taiwan's participation in international events. By the beginning of 1995, the agreements had still not been signed officially because of political antagonism across the board—from investment protection on the mainland to Taiwan's participation in the United Nations and, more specifically, China's refusal to accept an implicit definition of Taiwan's territorial waters. China maintained that a tacit agreement had already been reached. Taiwan, however, wanted an official accord establishing an "imaginary" line in the middle of the Taiwan Strait which could not be crossed by "official boats"— patrol boats and navy vessels—of either side.

. . .

DESPITE THE DEADLOCK in the SEF-ARATS talks, moves were made to establish direct communications between China and Taiwan. Toward the end of 1993, Vincent Siew (Hsiao Wan-chang), who for years had been a staunch supporter of pragmatism and had sought to minimize political obstacles, was appointed chairman of the Mainland Affairs Council (MAC). In his acceptance speech, Siew said that rapidly growing trade between China and Taiwan had created the ideal conditions for Taiwan to become an "Asia-Pacific Business Operations Hub" along the lines of Hong Kong, assuming that the first step—the establishment of direct shipping links with the mainland—was taken without delay. As chairman of the Council for Economic Planning and Development, Siew had himself hatched the plan, the execution of which now depended on him as MAC chairman. His appointment was a victory for the MAC elements who, for reasons of maximum security, would not open the Bamboo Curtain at the front window, preferring to enter China through the backdoor only.

Within months it was apparent that Siew had the upper hand. On 5 January 1995 his brainchild was born, an offshore shipping link in southern Taiwan for entrepôt trade to the mainland. The prefix "offshore" was used to avoid giving the impression that it was a direct link. Taiwanese ships with foreign registration would henceforth be allowed to ship goods from Kaohsiung, Taiwan's largest port, directly to China, provided they had a foreign port of origin, and, more important, provided China approved the scheme. Since the ships would enter only that part of the harbor that had been declared "offshore," they would not have crossed Taiwan's border and officially would not have been in Taiwan at all. Thus, there would be no direct links, but only indirect ones, theoretically and legally the same as the current transit trade through the "free port" of Hong Kong, which, after the resumption of Chinese sovereignty in 1997, will no longer be able to serve as a neutral transit point. Even if Hong Kong is able to continue as an international free port with its own shipping register, politically it will be part of China. Declaring part of Kaohsiung "extraterritorial" was an ingenious compromise that enabled Taiwan to pave the way for increased economic integration with China, as well as to hold on to the political principle of "separateness," which had to be kept as a trump card in further negotiations on some form of Chinese recognition of Taiwan's separate status.

INTERNAL POLITICAL DEVELOPMENTS in Taiwan had meanwhile reached a new stage with important implications for relations with the mainland. In December 1994 the first direct elections were held for the highest posts in the second and third echelons: the provincial governor of Tai-wan—under the president of the Republic of China—and the mayors of the two major cities of Taipei and Kaohsiung. The result suggested that a subtle automatic-feedback mechanism had crept into the new democratic psyche of Taiwan. Elected to the post of governor of the indigenous Taiwanese provincial political apparatus in Taichung was James Soong, a second-generation mainlander who had put down roots in Taiwan but who never-theless symbolized continuity of the Kuomintang tradition of national reunification. Elected to the post of mayor of Taipei was the DPP candidate, Chen Suibian, an ardent advocate of independence. Taipei's election result was a signal to China of the strength of the independence movement at the local level, warning China to take it seriously and to deal with it prudently in the future. The fact that a mainlander had been elected governor, how-ever, meant that on the island as a whole, the majority of people were against independence.

China's recurrent threats of force and a steady flow of rumors that mili-tary preparations were already under way had played a major role in weak-ening support for independence. In October 1994 the *United Daily News* (*Lien Ho Pao*) quoted a secret military document concerning a conference on military maneuvers attended by China's top brass, citing various scenar-ios for an invasion of Taiwan that would supposedly take place if the elec-tion results showed that more than 50 percent of the Taiwanese supported the "independence forces."[19]

ONE BEST-SELLING BOOK, *1995 Jun Pa-yue: Chung Kung Wu Li Fan Tai Shih Chi Ta Yu Yen* (August 1995: Great Prediction of the Communist Chi-nese Invasion of Taiwan; English subtitle: *T-Day, The Warning of Taiwan Strait War*) by Cheng Lang-ping, had an alarming impact on public opin-ion. It begins with a large dose of traditional Chinese superstition: "The year 1995 will be the last leap year of the lunar calendar of this century with two intercalary months of August. Such years are always cataclysmic, and the ex-pectation is that 1995 will be such a year." The book further describes the his-torical, nationalistic, and Chinese (domestic) political imperatives that necessitate a speedy reunification with Taiwan and goes on to sketch the psychological, political, and strategic context in which China's ambition to be an international superpower depends on its possession of Taiwan. Cheng states that the force of the historical tradition impelling China to remain a large, unitarist country is undiminished. If the current Chinese regime fails to bring Taiwan back to the fold, it will go down in history as the "perpetuator of the national disgrace," never to be forgiven. World Communism has collapsed. Deng and his successors have no more trump cards, and new, hard-line nationalism is the only answer. The subjugation of Taiwan would be the last great stratagem in unifying the country. The people would support the invasion and conquest of Taiwan because they know how rich it is. Many of the older generals still hope to play an epic role in armed reunification and to go down in history as marshal or generalissimo (*yuan-shuai, tong-shuai*).

Cheng also thinks that sooner or later in the twenty-first century China will have to wage war against Japan for domination of the sea routes, the South China Sea, and the markets of Southeast Asia. Without control of Taiwan it cannot win such a war, nor can it hope to become a major naval power in the Western Pacific. The author asserts that Japan is actively scheming behind the scenes for Taiwanese independence, but offers no evidence for this whatever. For all these reasons, an invasion is inevitable: the only question is when. If China were to let internal political developments in Taiwan just drift along, Taiwan would declare de facto independence in 1996. This would be followed by international recognition and the unlimited rearmament of Taiwan, making it far more difficult to attack. For this reason, the invasion would have to take place at a time when Taiwan was at its weakest: during the campaign for the presidential elections in the spring of 1996. "T-Day" must be a swift knockout, a blitz with missiles taking place between August 1995 and election day, 24 March 1996, with the ideal moment being in February 1996. According to the author, the world would refrain from involvement, as, technically speaking, it would be China's domestic problem. Even the Americans would let their trading interests take precedence over the vague security guarantees in the Taiwan Relations Act, in which Congress promised that the United States would oppose any attempt to determine the future of Taiwan by other than peaceful means.[20]

Professional military analysts initially regarded Cheng's book as pure sensationalism. The military situation in the Taiwan Strait was a topic of discussion during a conference of the International Institute of Strategic Studies (IISS) and the Chinese (Taiwanese) Council of Advanced Policy Studies (CAPS) in Hong Kong in July 1994. Michael Swaine, a specialist at the Rand Corporation in Santa Monica, California, observed that as yet there was no serious arms race and concluded that Taiwan's military deterrent is such that China could not win a war now, adding that this situation will probably not change before the year 2007. Taiwan has one of the best air forces in Asia and is currently adding 150 F-16 fighter planes and 60 Mirages to its arsenal. China's air force has only twenty-four planes of similar fighting power, the SU-27. Chinese pilots are also no match for the well-trained Taiwanese. China's navy is large in number but largely obsolete. Half of China's approximately one hundred submarines are no longer operational, and the other half are not capable of an effective blockade. Large-scale modernization of China's navy is under way but is not yet past the stage of frigates. Construction or purchase of aircraft carriers has been under deliberation for years, but as yet without result.

In spite of unyielding pressure from China, Taiwan managed throughout the 1980s to buy new warships: submarines from Holland, frigates from France and the United States, and minesweepers—in disguise—from Germany.

Chinese missiles would have a dramatic first-strike effect but would not incapacitate Taiwan. From the underground air defense complex on its east coast, the Taiwanese air force could launch formidable counterattacks that would escalate into a full-scale war that neither side could sustain. According to Swaine, such a war would fatally undermine China's successful, reform-based domestic and foreign policy strategy of the last twenty years, severely destabilize Hong Kong and the entire Asia Pacific, destroy Sino-American détente, perhaps precipitate armed conflict between China and the United States, and probably lead to political unrest within China.[21]

The paradox of Cheng Lang-ping's book is that it contributed unwittingly to a new, though short-lived, thaw between China and Taiwan. His alarmism touched a chord of deep distrust among the Taiwanese, stirring up their fear of the Chinese Communists in the extreme. The majority of the Taiwanese took seriously the Chinese leaders who threatened to use force "if Taiwan declared independence," electing instead a governor who was opposed to independence. Cheng's book certainly played no small role in this. In the aftermath of the elections, the DPP has also toned down its aim of unconditional independence, declaring itself willing to let the matter be decided by referendum.

THE OUTCOME of the elections in Taiwan, the announcement of the off-shore shipping link, and the soft-pedaling of the independence clause in the platform of the DPP were evidently signs to Beijing to seek an alternative to the sterile SEF-ARATS talks and to initiate discussions at a higher level that would not stoop to threats of force. Indeed, the Chinese leaders had little hope of success in their attempt to break out of the vicious circle of domestic problems—economic, social, and political. The "epigone" who discovered the magic formula for a solution to the "Taiwan question" could become the next "supreme leader" of China. President Jiang Zemin accepted the challenge during the celebrations of the most important traditional holiday in China, the Lunar New Year. Despite the fact that the latest round of SEF-ARATS negotiations had ended inconclusively the day before, Jiang delivered a speech on "national reunification" which for weeks was hailed as "historic."[22] Every prominent Chinese at home and abroad was invited to comment on and endorse it. The speech was historic in one sense, as in 1995 it had been one hundred years since Japan had forced imperial China to relinquish control of Taiwan by means of the Shimonoseki treaty. Since then, Taiwan has been ruled by the Chinese mainland for only four years, from 1945, the year the Japanese surrendered to Kuomintang China, until 1949, when the Kuomintang were expelled by the Communists from the mainland and fled to Taiwan. The eight-point speech reiterated Beijing's earlier, unshakable principles of reunification, but the tone and presentation were less imperious than previous "decrees." Taiwan would be given no room for maneuvering to strengthen its international position *politically.* "Only after peaceful reunification is accomplished can the Taiwan compatriots and other Chinese people of all ethnic groups truly and fully share in the dignity and honor attained by our great motherland internationally. . . ." Jiang also seemed to offer more flexibility on the formal venue of the talks: "As regards the name, place and form of these political talks, a solution acceptable to both sides can certainly be found so long as consultations *on an equal footing* can be held at an early date." One optimistic analyst interpreted this as implicit acceptance by Beijing of "one country–two equal governments," but Chinese spokesmen still go out of their way to reject this idea.[23] The most sensitive point, the threat of force, was formulated in a new way: "Our undertaking not to give up the use of force is not directed against our compatriots in Taiwan, but against the schemes of foreign forces to interfere with China's reunification and to bring about the independence of Taiwan." This gibe was of course aimed at the Americans and the Japanese. Jiang said that the Taiwanese authorities were welcome to pay a visit to the mainland "in the right capacity," and "we are also willing to accept invitations to go to Taiwan." This meant, of course, the "Taiwan authorities" as provincial officials and "we" as central rulers.

Here was a new blend of sweet and sour, and Taipei, for once, could taste the sweet more strongly. President Lee Teng-hui and his ministers called the speech "significant" and said "we have to pay attention to it." Lee called for the broad exchange of views among all sections of the population and ordered experts to formulate counterproposals, after giving the matter serious thought. In April, Lee gave his answer, requesting compliance with only one condition before beginning preliminary talks to end the hostilities. In 1991 the Republic of China had already renounced the use of force as a means of achieving reunification, but Beijing had not reciprocated. He now asked that the Communists publicly renounce the use of force. He no longer insisted on the preliminary recognition of Taiwan as a separate and sovereign entity. This newfound flexibility did not have time, however, to produce the desired effect in Beijing.

THE FIRST THREE YEARS of Lee's term in office (1991–94) had been devoted to reforming the old constitutional order in Taiwan. From 1995 on, priority would be given to strengthening Taiwan's international status, as only from a position of strength could relations with the mainland be further developed. Lee's diplomats and American lobbyists were still trying to devise a way for Taiwan to break out of its isolation, finally settling on the plan of an "unofficial" visit to the United States, which would not reap any formal diplomatic gains but would undoubtedly provide unprecedented publicity. On 22 May President Lee was given the the green light to attend a reunion at Cornell University in Ithaca, New York, where he had received his Ph.D. in agronomy in 1968 and was now to receive an honorary doctorate. In his speech at Cornell on 9 June 1995, Lee, to the intense irritation of China, spoke of "popular sovereignty" and the "reunification of China under a system of democracy, freedom, and equitable distribution of wealth." China was furious at Lee for using this unofficial visit to reject Jiang Zemin's recent proposal for reunification by playing the "democratic card," and that on American soil, of all places. According to the Chinese and the international media, Lee Teng-hui had spent millions of dollars on "bribes" for his visit: $4.5 million to the public relations firm of Cassidy & Associates to lobby in Congress, $5 million on President Clinton's reelection campaign, and $2.5 million to Cornell for the founding of the "Lee Teng-hui Chair."[24]

Although the Chinese media had savaged the United States incessantly since its decision to admit Lee, no immediate action was taken against Taiwan. Tang Shubei, the number two man at ARATS, flew to Taipei four days after the American decision to admit Lee to prepare for the second Koo-Wang summit. Even the criticism of Lee's speech at Cornell was mild at first. Then suddenly, in early June, at the very moment the Dutch premier, Wim Kok, was walking into Chinese premier Li Peng's office in Beijing, the Taiwan premier, Liën Chan, gate-crashed his way into Amsterdam, "to receive an award" at Leiden University, of which the university knew nothing.[25] He quickly moved on to Austria, where the University of Vienna did host him, and from there to the Czech Republic, where President Václav Havel gave him a sympathetic reception. In addition, a host of articles appeared in the press announcing President Lee's intention of visiting Japan for the upcoming APEC summit in November and hinting that various countries were on the verge of changing their attitude, if not their policy, toward Taiwan. China was now alarmed that a "diplomatic renaissance" of Taiwan might be gaining momentum and canceled the upcoming Koo-Wang summit, stepping up its attacks on Lee and announcing the possibility of unspecified retaliation.

The next round of invective consisted of four commentaries issued jointly by the highest state and party organs, the Xinhua News Agency and the *People's Daily*, which suggested that they were of historical significance. Lee was labeled the "criminal of the millennium" (*qian gu zui ren*), just as the British governor of Hong Kong, Chris Patten, had been three years before—also for playing the "democratic card." The first commentary stated that Lee's trip to the United States had been a conspiracy "to split the motherland." It branded Lee a "traitor" because as a young man he had been a member of the Communist party—for less than a year—and had allegedly betrayed his comrades before quitting it. The second condemned Taiwanese democracy, not without some justification, as "a mixture of power hunger, money interests, and mafia politics." The third commentary attacked Taiwan's practice of trying to buy diplomatic recognition from impoverished Third World countries and even membership in the United Nations. The fourth accused Lee of disingenuousness and of willfully creating new obstacles at every turn in the reunification process. It concluded: "Facts have proven that the expectation that someone like Lee Teng-hui—who doesn't even know what China is—will improve the relationship between both sides of the Taiwan Strait is like climbing a tree to catch fish. No Chinese should have any illusions about Lee Teng-hui."[26]

These commentaries set the tone for a tragi-comic strip of character assassination of Lee in the Chinese and Hong Kong media. In a second series of commentaries, the Xinhua News Agency reported that Lee, during his studies in the United States in the late 1960s, had been a sympathizer of the WUFI, the World United Formosans for Independence, and a personal friend of Peng Ming-min, the father of the Taiwanese independence movement.[27] Peng had spent twenty-two years in exile in Sweden and the United States as a professor of political science, but was personally invited by Lee in 1990 to return to Taiwan. According to Xinhua, this was further proof of the sinister motives of the two to conspire together to bring about Taiwanese independence. In an interview with the famous Japanese historical novelist

Ryotaro Shiba, Lee—a devout Presbyterian—had compared himself to Moses. He would lead the people of Taiwan (the new Israelites) out of China (Egypt) to a new promised land. This provoked *Wen Wei Po*, China's mouthpiece in Hong Kong, to comment, "He is not Moses but Judas."[28]

In mid-July, a month and a half after Lee's trip to the United States, the Chinese General Staff announced a series of missile tests 130 kilometers east of Taiwan, together with naval and air force maneuvers lasting one week. Six Dongfeng SRBMs (short-range ballistic missiles) and M-class short-range missiles were launched for five days from pads in the coastal provinces, landing in the target zone but falling short of their political goal, which was to cow Taiwan into submission and to undermine the position of Lee Teng-hui. The tests did cause turmoil on the Taipei stock exchange, but since high volatility was not unusual, the lesson was not brought home hard enough.

Perhaps because Taiwan—and the United States—showed no signs of repentance, in mid-August China held a second series of missile tests, combined with heavy artillery shelling, this time from shorter range. Although China's military jingoists had undoubtedly hoped in this way to turn public opinion against Lee Teng-hui, they achieved exactly the opposite result. As persistent as always, Lee said during a plenum of the Kuomintang that the time was ripe for Taiwan to fight for a greater international role for itself, since the new world order was still in the process of taking shape.[29]

On 23 August Lee proclaimed his candidacy and immediately stood at 44 percent in the opinion polls, while his two rivals, who were more conciliatory toward the mainland, stood at 15 and 9 percent. The Communist propaganda machine now stepped up its mudslinging with an attack on Lee's father, who had been a "traitor to the country in heart and soul" during the Japanese colonial rule of Formosa.

Vicious personal attacks with no holds barred were common practice in Chinese political struggles, but only against losers. Lee was not a loser and there was no credible alternative to him. Lee was unique in that he had his roots in the Kuomintang establishment, yet he was a Taiwanese. He had no fixed views about the future but was "creatively ambiguous," willing to maintain the status quo but not willing to exclude the possibility of reunification—when the time was ripe—with a reformed, prosperous, democratic China. And if the conditions for reunification did not improve, then he would support independence, if the international political climate would permit it.

. . .

AFTER THE TWO SERIES of missile tests, cross-strait relations went into hibernation, showing no progress, but also no further retrogression. In Taiwan election season started: a parliamentary election in December, followed by the historical presidential election in March 1996. The election in December for the 164-member Legislative Yuan was clearly a referendum on relations with the mainland, and the result was not at all unfavorable to China. The Kuomintang majority was reduced by eleven—from ninety-six to eighty-five—retaining a majority of only two. The big winner was the New Party, a splinter party of former Kuomintang malcontents who were more reunification-minded, which tripled its number of seats from seven to twenty-one. The DPP with its proindependence rhetoric was the big loser. The Kuomintang losses were caused in part by the people's abhorrence of "money politics," as well as by tensions between Taiwan and the mainland, which were blamed on both Lee Teng-hui and the DPP.

Even the Chinese government welcomed the outcome of the election as a vote against independence and in support of reunification, although the media continued to attack Lee.

A few days after the election, two senior vice-chairmen of the Kuomintang, former premier Hau Pei-tsun and veteran politician Lin Yang-kang, were expelled from the party for campaigning against it. Hau had gone so far as to call Lee "a traitor to the motherland," thereby echoing Chinese propaganda and feeding persistent rumors that he (Hau) was colluding with the Communists in Beijing and receiving financial support from them.[30]

The culmination of six years of constitutional reforms in Taiwan was its first direct presidential election, to be held in March 1996. This election was unanimously considered to be the penultimate step toward a new independent country, at least a de facto one. China's vice-premier and foreign minister, Qian Qichen, had already spoken to this effect in early November, describing the so-called democratic presidential election in Taiwan as a farce because only sovereign states can hold presidential elections. Taiwan is legally a province of China, he maintained, and therefore "a presidential election in Taiwan is a separatist act leading to two Chinas."

According to a number of leaks in the Hong Kong media, China was redefining the conditions under which it would use force to solve the Taiwan question. In recent years it had threatened to use force only if Taiwan were to declare independence. Now it reportedly redefined the situation as "independence in disguise, the premeditated perpetuation of the state of national division and an intentional refusal to start reunification talks with the mainland." Such a situation would also warrant military action. Chinese generals had also lighted on the idea that they would now have to protect Taiwan against "traitors to the motherland" like Lee Teng-hui and his American and Japanese backers. "We will not sacrifice political concerns to economic interests. Like Japan and Germany after World War II, it is better to have a devastated Chinese Taiwan, which we can quickly rebuild, than an independent Taiwan under American-Japanese domination." One Chinese irredentist treatise compared China's determination to go to war in the case of a declaration of independence by Taiwan with the situation leading to the American Civil War: "The people of the Southern states wanted to secede from the Union and to maintain slavery. Was Lincoln wrong to go to war?"

During the final months of 1995 and the first months of 1996, newspapers throughout East Asia were regularly filled with scenarios of the coming war between China and Taiwan. Several of these were apparently planted by Chinese sources who wanted to sow panic and confusion and to test the reactions of the region and of the world at large. According to one scenario, China would conduct daily missile attacks on military targets for thirty days after the election. According to another, it would attack and temporarily occupy minor islands in the Taiwan Strait, and a third maintained that China would conduct a full blockade of all sea and air routes to Taiwan's major cities. Whatever the source of these theories, they did contain an element of truth: the advent of new missile tests and large-scale military maneuvers aimed at disrupting the election. In this sense, the book published in 1994 by Cheng Lang-ping predicting a Taiwan Strait war had indeed been prophetic.

After much speculation and rumor, China finally announced on 5 March its new series of missile tests. The tests and maneuvers of the previous year had already caused considerable damage to Taiwan's economy. According to Taiwanese newspapers, $18 billion had been remitted overseas since July 1995, and Taiwan's huge reserves of foreign currency had plummeted from more than $100 billion to $85 billion. One-fifth of the companies listed on the stock exchange had had a liquidity crisis or had gone bankrupt, forcing the government to establish a rescue fund. The property market was down by 40 percent, and banks were giving loans with property as collateral only up to 40 percent of its value. Things calmed down considerably, however, with the arrival of the United States naval task force, led by the aircraft carrier *Independence*, followed a few days later by the *Nimitz*. I was told by several friends that they had packed their bags and made reservations to leave, only to cancel them after they heard that the U.S. Navy was coming to protect them. Between 6 and 23 March all flights to Australia, New Zealand, the

United States, Canada, and Europe were fully booked. The big "if" remains: If the American carrier forces had not stabilized the situation, would the Chinese "siege" have caused the morale of the people of Taiwan to sink? Would it have derailed the election? Would the situation have escalated into a serious crisis with a highly unpredictable outcome?

When I arrived in Taipei on 15 March, no one was talking about war games any longer. Everyone was fully absorbed by the antics of the election campaign. The thirty-six-thousand-square-kilometer island with its population of 21 million was as noisy as a war zone. Indeed, with all its parades and rallies, accompanied by the music of gongs, drums, and cymbals, it sounded a bit like war—the drums like mock artillery and a host of *suo-na,* the piercing Chinese oboe, like high-alert sirens. One pun aptly expressed the historical crossroads at which Taiwan found itself: "*Chuan-dan* [election leaflets], not *dao-dan* [missiles] will decide our future." In other words, "ballots, not bullets." Unfortunately, this was true only up to a point. The atmosphere of excitement masked a deeply polarized society. The Kuomintang did not really have to fight for reelection, as the power and privileges of incumbency had made its candidates, President Lee Teng-hui and Premier Liën Chan, unbeatable. Chinese saber rattling had given them an extra boost, as well as the goodwill of world opinion. This made the rhetoric of the other candidates sound all the more desperate and often excessive. DPP parades sported witty signs, such as "Thank You, President Clinton, for Sending Us [the] *Independence*" and "Two Countries–Two Systems!" One radical DPP group carried a flag of the People's Republic of China with a bilingual inscription: "F*** China." The DPP candidate was Peng Ming-min, the revered leader of the exiled independence movement, who had returned to Taiwan in 1992 but was sadly out of touch with new realities. Peng was still in favor of full independence, and the only compromise he was willing to make was to submit the question to a referendum.

The demonstrations of the New Party were equally excessive, their main target being President Lee. The New Party is basically a party of second- and third-generation mainlanders who are loyal to the old ideals of a mainlander Kuomintang that no longer exists. Their candidates, Lin Yang-kang and Hau Pei-tsun, attacked President Lee for provoking the crisis with China. They, of course, would handle relations with Beijing better, but how? They are not willing to make the concessions demanded by China. Lin admitted that reunification would be possible only in the distant future, with a post-Communist, (more) democratic China. What is the difference, then, between the Kuomintang and the New Party? Seemingly, the New Party's willingness to pay more lip service to reunification. The New Party's main parade, held a few days before election day, invoked a whole litany of outbursts against President Lee: "We hate President Lee! He has destroyed the old true Kuomintang! He is corrupt! He abuses democracy to bring about independence!"

Lee's rhetoric had bestowed grandiose, epochal meaning on the election with the oft-repeated slogan that he would be "the first national leader in five thousand years of Chinese history to be directly elected by the people," and that "there was no going back." In the final speech of his campaign, he spoke directly to Beijing: "We hold presidential elections, you hold war games to disrupt them, but you have failed." In other words, history will not treat you kindly.

Most pollsters and commentators assumed that if China had abstained from its war games, Lee would have received slightly more than 40 percent of the vote, making him a minority president with a dubious mandate. China's saber rattling and Lee's bold denunciation of it had made him a folk hero and he won hands down with 54 percent, more than two and a half times that of his closest rival, Peng Ming-min, who received 21 percent of the vote, the lowest ever scored by the DPP. The Lin-Hau ticket had drawn 15 percent, and the remaining 10 percent went to Chen Lu-an, an ex-Buddhist former minister, who advocated a moral and religious revival.

After his victory, Lee stressed two major priorities: the resumption of détente with the mainland and, at the same time, intensifying the struggle for recognition by the rest of the world of a separate identity for Taiwan. Since Lee had been denounced by China for months as the epitome of evil, the new vice-president (and still premier), Liën Chan, was assigned the role of spokesman for relations with the mainland. At their victory celebration, Liën said that channels of communication with the mainland must be reopened and preliminary talks held at various levels, but that "this cannot be accomplished in one fell swoop." President Lee summarized the nation's priorities for the twenty-first century, one of which was "pursuing national dignity and vigorously establishing our own place in the world." This sounded like a recipe containing incompatible ingredients destined to lead to recurring stomach upsets.

China used its own arithmetic to explain away the election results. The Xinhua News Agency reported: "Taiwan today concluded its activities of changing the way in which its leaders are chosen." The agency explained the blow suffered by proindependence forces as the result of the two tickets that opposed independence, the New Party and Chen Lu-an, having received together 25 percent of the vote, which exceeded the DPP's 21 percent. Although for months China had abused Lee Teng-hui as a splittist and a plotter for independence, it now saw the necessity of distinguishing between "advocating independence" and "maintaining the status quo." From now on, Lee was a status quo figure who would have to be cultivated. This would take a long time, however. Relations between China and Taiwan have moved from crisis to stalemate, and that is where they still stand today.

PART TWO

Integration of the Three Systems, the Creation of New Hong Kongs, and the Erosion of Communism

CHAPTER 4

Origin of the Formula
"One Country–Two Systems"

In Western terms the China of today is as if the Europe of the
Roman Empire and of Charlemagne had lasted until this
day and were now trying to function as a single nation-state.[1]

LUCIAN W. PYE,
American sinologist

UNITY, CENTRALIZATION, CONTROL, and—after long or short periods of division—reunification: these have been the dominant themes in Chinese history. China, like Europe, is a civilization, but while the various versions of Christianity and European languages and dialects gave rise to separate states, the borders of which were permanently in flux, China remained whole.

Like Europe in the Middle Ages, China also went through a feudal period during which it was divided into small principalities, although in China this took place a thousand years earlier, during the Warring States period (475–221 B.C.). At that time, a unifying, centralizing political system (*junxianzhi*) contrasted with a fragmented feudal system of enfeoffment (*fengjianzhi*). In 221 B.C. Qin Shihuang, the first emperor of China, nevertheless succeeded in unifying these rival states into one empire. This was the beginning of an uninterrupted tradition of one indivisible empire, in which dynasties of widely differing lifespans followed each other, the degree of centralization and unification varied, and borders were pushed back and forth. The fourteenth to the nineteenth century saw only territorial expansion. Since huge territories were ceded to tsarist Russia in the second half of the nineteenth century, followed by the secession of Outer Mongolia in 1911, there have been no further significant border changes.

If one compares historical atlases of Europe and China, China is a smooth piece of silk to which pieces have been sewn on or trimmed off at regular intervals. Europe, on the other hand, is a chaotic mosaic, whose pieces are cut, polished, and shuffled around every generation. The dominant tradition in China is *da-yi-tong*, big-and-one, uniformity, harmony, stability, and continuity. As more and more arable land was needed to feed the growing population, the country was forced to expand into the ethnic periphery, since trade and industry were practically nonexistent. The need for more land still exists, not for agriculture but for other forms of creating wealth. "We still need Tibet and the islands in the South China Sea for their resources underground, and Hong Kong and Taiwan because of their mountain of wealth aboveground. Once we have enough monetary wealth, we'll simply be able to buy all the things we need," a Chinese researcher said to me in plain capitalist-imperialist terms.

The European tradition is one of a constantly changing "system of empires and states." From the viewpoint of Western political logic and according to some modern Chinese political thinkers, it would have been perfectly normal and even desirable if China had been partitioned or split up into a pluralistic system of states, in which trade and competition in the market and in the world of ideas would have accelerated its progress.[2] "The British have created dozens of countries around the world, the Chinese only Chinatowns, because there can be only one China," joked Professor Byron Weng of the Chinese University of Hong Kong.

If Hong Kong and Taiwan, both already flourishing, stable de facto states, were to achieve formal independence, China would still have the chance to create a limited variation on the European state system, in which three Chinas would coexist in an optimum state of constructive symbiosis. Universal concepts such as the right to self-determination, popular sovereignty, the plebiscite, and the referendum are anathema in the "People's Republic," where nothing is decided by the people. The Communist oligarchy's concept of sovereignty is a mixture of premodern despotic thinking and twentieth-century class dictatorship. Popular sovereignty means the power of some classes to suppress others. Mao Zedong split the nation into "people"—the alliance of workers and peasants—and others, such as intellectuals, who did not even qualify as people. Splitting up the state, however, would mean backsliding into feudalism. One Chinese historian, Zhu Yong, of the Development and Research Center of the State Council, compared the violent implosion of Yugoslavia and parts of the former Soviet Union with a reversion to the Warring States period, which China experienced twenty-four centuries ago. The indivisibility of China is an axiom engraved in stone. The fate of Hong Kong has already been sealed, and Taiwan will also be compelled, sooner or later, to bow to the central authority in Beijing, whether its 21 million inhabitants like it or not. Any attempt to discuss this with Chinese functionaries or intellectuals in official positions is futile. Their talk is riddled with minimalist clichés and dogma, and they are unrivaled in their ability to obstruct a relaxed exchange of ideas. During a dinner I once said to a senior Chinese official that time would eventually force a flexible, creative approach to the Taiwan question, such as a modern, very loose form of constitutional (con)federalism combined with transitional, temporarily divided sovereignty. "Impossible," he said in agitation. "Only things that tally with Chinese tradition are acceptable in China!" As though Communism were in keeping with Chinese tradition! China's bottom line is "one country–two systems," but within the framework of a unitary state.

BESIDE A DOMINANT TREND toward unity, Chinese tradition has known long periods of national division. A standard work on Chinese history records that China, in the 3,097 years of its recorded history, has experienced 1,963 years of unity and 1,134 years of division.[3] This is no argument against the reunification of China and Taiwan, but it does plead against overly hasty reunification under the coercion of a Communist dictatorship that is not everlasting. Official Chinese Communist party documents, murals, engravings, and inscriptions repeat ad nauseam that "Taiwan has been an inalienable part of China since time immemorial." This is an assertion, common in non-Western historiography, that history is not what happened but what should have happened. The People's Republic of China has never exercised sovereignty over Taiwan, and the same can scarcely be said of previous regimes either. Before the short-lived colonization by the Dutch East India Company early in the seventeenth century, the island was populated by Austronesian aborigines. There was no indigenous Chinese population.[4] From 1624 to 1661 there was a Dutch colonial regime on "Tayouan," then better known by the Portuguese name of Formosa, after which it became a loose dependency of the Chinese empire. Only in 1885 did it become a Chinese province. From 1895 to 1945 Taiwan was a Japanese colony, and after the capitulation of Japan it was handed over to the Kuomintang state, the Republic of China, which has governed it uninterruptedly for the past fifty years.[5]

The Chinese Communist party had a rather cavalier attitude toward Taiwan before its victory over the Kuomintang in China's civil war. In 1936, in a lengthy interview on the war with Japan, Mao Zedong said to the American journalist Edgar Snow, "It is the immediate task of China to regain all our lost territories. . . . We do not, however, include Korea, formerly a Chinese colony, but when we have reestablished the independence of the lost territories of China, and if the Koreans want to break away from the chains of Japanese imperialism, we will extend them our enthusiastic help in their struggle for independence. The same thing applies for Formosa."[6]

The Nationalist leader Chiang Kai-shek, however, had already claimed Formosa (Taiwan) for China in 1941. At the Cairo Conference in 1943, one of the great conferences of Allied leaders during the Second World War, Roosevelt and Churchill concurred. Communist successor claims followed automatically, especially after Chiang Kai-shek fled to the island at the end of 1948 with the remains of his defeated regime and installed a rival government to carry on the civil war.

The Communist invasion of Quemoy, an islet half the size of Lanai (Hawaii) off the coast of China across from Taiwan, ended in October 1949 in a crushing defeat, which convinced the generals of the People's Liberation Army that more large-scale preparations were necessary for what they called the "liberation of Taiwan." A second invasion of Taiwan in the spring of 1950 under General Su Yu had to be called off owing to an epidemic of schistosomiasis among 300,000 troops on the coast of Fujian.[7]

In January 1950 President Truman had declared a "hands-off" policy with respect to the "resumed" Chinese civil war and wished to leave Chiang Kai-shek and the tattered remnants of his army to fend for themselves. National reunification seemed only a matter of time, until new preparations for invasion were completed. Ironically enough, it was the North Korean Communist leader Kim Il Sung who became the "savior" of Taiwan. The Communist invasion of South Korea prompted Truman to revoke his "hands-off Formosa" policy. He dispatched the Seventh Fleet to the Taiwan Strait to prevent a Chinese Communist invasion of Taiwan and the opening of a "second front" in the Korean War. The new Communist government of China instantly accused the United States of "armed aggression" and wanted to put the case before the United Nations Security Council. The new People's Republic was nevertheless barred from membership in the United Nations, and the Chinese seat remained in the hands of the Nationalist regime in Taiwan, which had occupied it since 1945. For Beijing this was yet another reason to deal a crushing military blow to Chiang Kai-shek's regime once and for all, but another attempt would have to wait until after the war in Korea.

After the Korean armistice in July 1953 and the Geneva accords on the partition of Vietnam in July 1954, the United States was not at all convinced that the "domino effect" was no longer a threat to the rest of Asia. Under the leadership of Secretary of State John Foster Dulles, the United States began to build a dual structure for the containment of Communism in the East, modeled on NATO in the West. This resulted in the Southeast Asia Treaty Organization and the Sino-American defense treaty with Taiwan. Five days before the signing of the SEATO pact, the Communist People's Liberation Army began prolonged shelling of Quemoy. No invasion followed, however, suggesting that China only intended the shelling as a token military protest against the strategy of containment.

In December 1954 the United States committed itself by treaty to defending Taiwan and adjacent islands against Communist aggression. By now the Cold War had been institutionalized in Asia on four fronts: the armistice in and partition of Korea, the defense treaty with Taiwan, which perpetuated the Chinese civil war, the Geneva agreements on the partition of Vietnam, and the Southeast Asia Treaty Organization, which was supposed to contain or even roll back Communism in the entire region.

Chiang Kai-shek used the protection afforded by the defense treaty for a large-scale military buildup on Quemoy for his sworn "counterattack to annihilate the Communist bandits and to reconquer the mainland."

China was forced for the time being to abandon its goal of liberating Taiwan, either by military means or by the diplomatic intervention of the United Nations. China's premier and master diplomat, Zhou Enlai, used the first conference of nonaligned nations in Bandung in April 1955 to propose negotiations with the United States on demilitarization of the Taiwan Strait, and with Chiang Kai-shek on the possibility of "peaceful liberation." In a series of speeches, Zhou changed the standard Communist epithet for Chiang Kai-shek and his followers from "reactionary traitors' clique" to "patriots . . . and the responsible local authorities on Taiwan."

In 1956 Hong Kong rumors made the rounds for months that exchanges between the two sides were already in full swing. Communist mouthpieces let it be known that Chiang Kai-shek could expect honorable retirement in China or elsewhere in the world, or could become governor of an autonomous Taiwan with his own armed forces. The only concession he would have to make would be to sever all ties with the United States. Chinese political scientists called this the first precursor of the later formula "one country–two systems." At a press conference in Calcutta late in 1956, Zhou Enlai said, "If Taiwan returns to the motherland of China, Chiang Kai-shek will have made a contribution and will be able to settle down anywhere he chooses in the motherland." When asked whether Chiang would be given a ministerial post, Zhou replied, "A ministerial post is too low."[8] It is highly unlikely that such an arrangement would have worked at the time, considering the climate of ruthless class and power struggle that pervaded China until Mao Zedong's death. Chiang Kai-shek dismissed Zhou's sweet-talking, because according to his ideology, it was the mainland, and not Taiwan, that was in need of liberation.

AT A TIME WHEN Communism in Asia was still on the upswing, the United States was wary of abandoning Taiwan to its fate; neither did it want Taiwan to obstruct a rational dialogue with China. In August 1955, after six years of military confrontations, the Americans and the Chinese finally began to sniff each other out directly during ambassadorial talks in Geneva. At the beginning of every session, the Chinese invariably made the same three demands: the severing of diplomatic relations with Taiwan, the withdrawal of American military personnel and installations from Taiwan, and the termination of the defense treaty. The Chinese had no intention whatever of making even partial concessions on any of these three major issues of principle. The Americans would agree to talk only if China renounced the use of force in any settlement of the Taiwan question. For the Chinese, however, this was an internal affair and a sovereign right that could not be compromised. China's negotiating strategy was very simple: accept our demands, otherwise we are prepared to wait—one year, five years, ten years, or in this case twenty-three years—until you are ready to give in.

In the meantime, in the fall of 1958, there had been a short but much more serious crisis around Quemoy, which brought the world to the brink of a Third World War and was the beginning of the rift between China and the Soviet Union. Owing to Chiang Kai-shek's military buildup on Quemoy, his continuous nuisance raids on Chinese coastal targets, the American military presence in Taiwan, and the escalating tension in China itself, Mao Zedong, in August 1958, ordered much heavier shelling of Quemoy than in 1954, threatened an invasion of Taiwan, and demanded the surrender of the Nationalist Chinese garrisons on the coastal islands. Mao displayed complete contempt for American nuclear bombs in the mistaken belief that the Russians, after the launching of *Sputnik* in 1957, were technologically more advanced than the Americans and would offer him their wholehearted support. During the crisis, which lasted until October, it became apparent that Mao did not intend to invade Taiwan, hoping instead to cripple Quemoy by means of a blockade. This would force the surrender of Chiang Kai-shek's 100,000-man garrison—one-third of his land forces—causing the regime in Taiwan itself to collapse.

Mao, however, completely misjudged the American reaction. Dulles received Eisenhower's consent to make an ambiguous statement that intimated at the use of atomic weapons to put an end to the Communist blockade of Quemoy. Mao casually dismissed the risk of American nuclear bombs, but the Soviet leader Nikita Khrushchev immediately sent his foreign minister, Andrei Gromyko, to Beijing to bring Mao to his senses. Mao demanded that Khrushchev counter with his own threat of nuclear retaliation, but Khrushchev refused, placing more value on his new relationship of "peaceful coexistence" with Washington. Mao was forced to back down.

The crisis lasted another month, during which Chiang Kai-shek's navy, protected by the American Seventh Fleet, broke through the blockade, while his air force, equipped with heat-seeking Sidewinder missiles, shot down dozens of Communist MIGs. Mao had suffered serious defeat and held the Kremlin responsible.

Moscow had managed to restrain Mao, and now America took similar action against its Nationalist Chinese ally. Dulles himself flew to Taipei to put Chiang Kai-shek back on the leash. Chiang was forced to reduce his troop strength on Quemoy and would no longer be allowed to conduct raids on Chinese coastal targets, since his only goal was to provoke a war between the United States and the Chinese Communists which would carry him back to the mainland. At the end of the battle for Quemoy, Chinese defense minister Peng Dehuai called on the Nationalist garrison to put an end to the Chinese civil war and to exclude the Americans from the peace process. "We are all Chinese. . . . The day will certainly come when the Americans will leave you in the lurch. You don't believe it? The first step has already been taken: Dulles's declaration [that the United States would not help to reconquer the mainland]. In the end, the Americans are our common enemy."

Three weeks later, Marshall Peng issued another statement: "To make things easier for you I have ordered our troops not to shell the air field and the wharf of Quemoy on the even days of the month, to enable you to re-supply and to dig yourselves in for a long time to come. . . . The Americans have given you the title of 'small China,' but this is a big China."

Foreign Minister Chen Yi added, in characteristic Chinese fashion, "Time is on our side, not on the side of the Americans. . . . The Americans will withdraw from Taiwan before my hair is completely white . . . within ten or twenty years." This was rather prophetic, as in December 1978, exactly twenty years after the battle, President Jimmy Carter finally met China's three demands: the severing of diplomatic ties with Taiwan, the withdrawal of American troops from the island, and the termination of the defense treaty. Since China still refused to renounce the use of force in regaining Taiwan, the United States announced that it would continue to supply arms to

Taiwan. China protested and reserved the right to raise the matter again.[9] It was a breakthrough, but one full of pitfalls.

THE CHINESE EXPECTED that Taiwan, stripped of American diplomatic and military protection, would succumb to pressure from the mainland in a matter of years and ask to open negotiations for reunification on China's terms. From this perceived position of strength, China called a stop on 1 January 1979 to the shelling—every other day—of Quemoy, and called for the "authorities in Taiwan" to begin talks "to create the necessary conditions and a secure situation for both sides to initiate contacts and exchanges." They specifically mentioned family visits, but "peaceful reunification" had not yet become standard terminology. Several years earlier, Chinese leaders had still spoken of "gradual socialist reforms" in Taiwan (Deng Xiaoping in 1975) and of the "purging of reactionaries by military means" (vice-premiers Li Xiannian and Ji Dengkui in 1977).

Shortly thereafter a pro-Communist espionage group was brought to trial in Taiwan. Its leader, Wu Tai-an, was condemned to death, two fellow agents were sentenced to life imprisonment, and twelve other defendants were given prison sentences of eight to twelve years. Proof (though of questionable authenticity) was furnished of a plan, sanctioned by the Maoist chairman of the Chinese Communist party, Hua Guofeng, to establish a Taiwanese Revolutionary High Command to instigate an uprising against the government. Acts of subversion were possible without the use of military force and, as such, could be regarded as "peaceful."

China again badly misjudged the situation in Taiwan, as well as the extent to which Taiwan could count on American support, especially in Congress. The government in Taipei reacted like an oyster that snaps shut and then peers through the crack once in a while to see whether things have changed. Congress amended the "Omnibus Bill" submitted by President Carter calling for the establishment of "unofficial" relations with Taiwan, creating the Taiwan Relations Act, which amounted to an alternative security treaty. The act states that it is the policy of the United States

- to make clear that the United States' decision to establish diplomatic relations with the People's Republic of China rests upon the expectation that the future of Taiwan will be determined by peaceful means;
- to consider any effort to determine the future of Taiwan by other than peaceful means, including by boycotts or embargoes, a threat

to the peace and security of the Western Pacific area and of grave concern to the United States;

- to provide Taiwan with arms of a defensive character;
- to maintain the capacity of the United States to resist any resort to force or other forms of coercion that would jeopardize the security, or the social or economic system, of the people on Taiwan.

The Taiwan Relations Act rebaptized the island, turning it from an official into an unofficial, somewhat dubious protectorate of the United States, with a guarantee to maintain the existing system. As such, it was unique in the world.

The new president, Ronald Reagan, planned to restore official ties with Taiwan and to supply it with the most advanced weapons, including the F-16 fighter. Confronted with massive threats from Beijing that this would cause relations to decline to their 1950s level, and overruled by his secretary of state, General Alexander Haig, who considered China indispensable in his new strategy to curb the Soviet Union, Reagan was forced to recant. But the atmosphere of crisis in the relations between the two countries continued unabated.

To forestall a further escalation in Reagan's support of the Kuomintang, China, at the end of September 1981, launched a detailed "Nine-Point Proposal for Peaceful Reunification," whereby Taiwan would become a special administrative region of the People's Republic. It would maintain a high degree of autonomy, its own armed forces, its existing social and economic systems, and its own cultural and economic relations with other countries (see Chapter 3). It boiled down to "one country–two systems," but this magic formula had not yet been given official sanction. Taiwan rejected the plan as a propaganda trap and answered with three stern no's—no contact, no negotiations, and no compromise. This situation continued for another two years.

In the summer of 1983, Premier Sun Yun-suan surprised Americans attending an academic conference when he made the innovative remark, during a tea reception, that "as the political, economic, social, and cultural gaps between the Chinese mainland and Free China narrow, the conditions for peaceful reunification can gradually mature." China's "Nine-Point Proposal" had been intended at least in part for Washington's ears, and Premier Sun's words even more so.

Ironically, the gap between the Chinese mainland and Taiwan was at its narrowest in the first half of the 1980s. The whole world felt general goodwill toward China at that time. Although it was still predominantly a totalitarian dictatorship, there was optimism about economic reforms and hope for political reforms and relative cultural freedom. The three top leaders— Deng Xiaoping, Premier Zhao Ziyang, and party leader Hu Yaobang—enjoyed a fair amount of prestige both at home and abroad. Admittedly, the state of human rights in China was deplorable, but it was subject to a double standard: a strict one for the Soviet bloc and a flexible one for China.

Taiwan at that time was still an authoritarian police state with many political prisoners and three recent, and sinister, political murders.[10] Taiwan's leaders were unknown abroad, as their diplomatic isolation barred them from traveling nearly everywhere except to Latin American banana republics and apartheid-ridden South Africa. Economically, it had not yet reached its peak; politically and diplomatically, it was a nuisance, the source of much arguing between Western governments and Chinese diplomats. In short, China was the winner in those days, even in public relations.

AT THE BEGINNING of the 1980s, the debate on the resumption of Chinese sovereignty over Hong Kong became part and parcel of the tug-of-war between China and Taiwan. Taiwan was assigned second place on Deng Xiaoping's list of priorities for the 1980s. In first place was the fight against Soviet hegemonism, and third place was given to accelerating economic development.[11] Any leader who could reunite the country and put an end to the civil war and American interference could become greater than Mao Zedong. At that time, China still considered the Hong Kong question to be simply "the removal of a foreign, colonial government," which would take place at the latest in 1997. It had not yet given any consideration whatever to the complexity of the problem.

During the annual session of the National People's Congress in 1982, Article 31 was added to the constitution, providing for the creation of special administrative regions in which other systems could be instituted, to be prescribed by law. This clearly referred to the capitalist system, but the constitution as a whole was inconsistent on this point: for example, Article 24 prescribed state education to "combat capitalist, feudal, and other decadent ideas."

After the historic visit to Beijing in the fall of 1982 by British prime minister Margaret Thatcher, the Chinese concluded that settlement of the Hong Kong question would be a matter of relatively short negotiations with the British and that such a settlement could then serve as a model for peaceful reunification with Taiwan. In a talk with the Chinese-American professor Winston Yang in June 1983, Deng Xiaoping offered additional details regarding the high degree of autonomy to be expected. In judicial matters, for example, final adjudication would be vested in the supreme court in Taipei and not in Beijing. It was generally accepted in those days that China's plan for peaceful reunification with Taiwan was a "guarantee" that it would act prudently and with the proper restraint in Hong Kong. In other words, Hong Kong would become the model for the solution to the Taiwan question.

The explicit purpose of the Chinese Communists was to make the capitalist economies of Hong Kong and Taiwan serve the process of China's socialist modernization without actually leading to "systemic interaction." In Hong Kong and Taiwan there was no noticeable demand for Chinese-style socialism, but for the liberal, well-educated Chinese on the mainland, Hong Kong and Taiwan were "models" (and for some even the "ideal type") of a reconstructed Chinese society of the future. Few Chinese dared then to hope for the total eclipse of Communism, but liberal intellectuals wrote often and at length about a reformed Communist party that would move in a more humane, tolerant, and social-democratic direction.

Hong Kong and Taiwan were anything but social democracies, but they had a great deal to offer nevertheless, culturally as well as economically. When, during the National People's Congress in May 1984, Premier Zhao Ziyang elevated the concept of "one country–two systems" to "fundamental state policy," and in December the British-Chinese Joint Declaration regarding the future of Hong Kong became official, the first wave of investments in Hong Kong and the neighboring Pearl River delta region was already in full swing, bringing with it the "capitalist colonization" of South China. Taiwanese businessmen still risked heavy prison sentences if they traveled to the mainland, but the cultural infiltration of Taiwanese pop culture was already a fact.

CHINA'S PICTURE of Taiwan during the Mao era was one of stunning ignorance. Until 1979 every important intersection and street corner in China was decorated with huge billboards that stated, "We Shall Certainly Liberate Taiwan." The philosophy behind this was that Taiwan was languishing under the barbaric tyranny of Chiang Kai-shek and American imperialist occupation, and that the people were starving. "In Taiwan the old society lingers on and this is an abyss of darkness [*an-wu tian-ri*]," observed a staff member of a government office in Shandong in 1979 when she saw my Chinese-born Taiwanese wife wearing some modest jewelry. One of the most extraordinary propaganda clichés was that the leaders of the Kuomintang ate bananas and gave the peels to the people.

While visiting Shanghai in 1977, I was subjected for hours to a "dialectic polemic" on Taiwan, where I had just spent a year and a half. My interlocutors were two cadres, my escorts from the Municipal Foreign Affairs Office. That morning, they had marched without knocking into my suite at the government hotel, striding across the parquet floor with steel taps on their shoes. My planned visits to a university and a newspaper had been canceled. We would go to a picturesque teahouse in the old Chinese city instead. They questioned me endlessly about Taiwan, and my answers were a subtle mixture of positive and negative elements: chaotic, ugly, polluted cities, but unprecedented dynamism and prosperity; a colorful, tolerant society full of friendly, civilized people—in Chinese *you jen-ch'ing-wei* (traditional human warmth)—which had been completely destroyed on the mainland by decades of class struggle and political campaigns. They refused to believe it. "That cannot be true. You failed to observe that correctly with your bourgeois view of the world. . . . You were only in the cities and not in the countryside." They stopped short of calling me an outright liar, however, and concluded by saying that China was still a superior society because it was free of prostitution. Taiwan, on the other hand, was an immoral place. Indeed, in China at that time there was no visible prostitution, because there was no money and half of the population was always spying on the other half. Nearly twenty years later, prostitution is a "declining" industry in Taiwan, but in China it is a new, booming, nationwide racket.

In 1979 China took off the ideological blinkers it wore when looking at Taiwan and swapped them for bad-quality sunglasses. Its new vision was still blurred and distorted, but at least it was based on facts. Wang Kun-lun, aging leader of the Revolutionary Committee of the Kuomintang, the splinter faction of Chiang Kai-shek's party that had stayed behind in 1949, told me at the time, "Taiwan has preserved the Chinese tradition of government by highly educated [modern] 'mandarins.'" China, on the other hand, was saddled with a party, the majority of whose leaders had barely had any formal education. "In China, politics has been in charge for thirty years, in Taiwan economics," said Wang. The fact that an alternative Chinese society, 21 million strong, had flourished under the discredited Kuomintang regime and emerged as a newly industrialized country was a source of inspiration and hope for many Chinese intellectuals. There were indications that Deng Xiaoping had a great deal of respect for Chiang Ching-kuo, the president of Taiwan at that time, and that he considered Taiwan to be a model for Chinese development. To admit this openly, however, would have been anathema. Professor Byron Weng, a Taiwanese political scientist at the Chinese University of Hong Kong, told me in the mid-1980s that academic visitors from China cherished the survival of Taiwan, which they considered "the archives, the treasury, where many good elements of traditional Chinese culture had been preserved."

Weng also commented on the fact that so many Taiwanese senior officials had received their doctorates at top American universities. "During the years of repression under Chiang Kai-shek and the first years of Chiang Ching-kuo's regime, many of them didn't dare return. They all stayed in America, and what better way to spend their time than by getting a Ph.D.?" The same thing is happening now to the many thousands of mainland students who didn't want to return even before the repression of 1989, and now face too many risks if they try to. There are now approximately 100,000 Chinese undergraduates and graduate students in the United States, and a large number of them are entitled to permanent residence there. Research carried out in 1994 by Zhao Xinshu, a Chinese student at the School of Journalism of the University of North Carolina, revealed that Chinese students in the United States are typically married couples between the ages of twenty-nine and thirty-three, both of whom are working on a doctorate in science. After finishing their dissertations, they hope to get jobs in the United States. For the time being, they do not wish to return to China, not trusting the government's promise to let them travel in and out freely. Most of them hope to return to China in the not-too-distant future, however, possibly as guest lecturers or advisers, or even as permanent residents.

Taiwanese students in the United States faced the same problem until the mid-1980s. Many who wanted to return could not do so as arrest warrants were awaiting them because of their activities in the Taiwanese independence movement. A small number of Kuomintang insiders had returned earlier, though, to become president, premier, and 60 percent of the ministers in what is perhaps the most highly educated cabinet in the world. The massive return of Taiwanese Ph.D.'s did not begin until the late 1980s, however, when the democratic transformation was well under way. Once liberalization and political reform have taken hold in China, the Ph.D.'s will probably flock back in large numbers to assume top academic and political posts. If Taiwan is a model in this respect, it is not unlikely that Ph.D.'s from top American universities will be governing China in the twenty-first century.[12]

TAIWAN HAS MADE the greatest impact on China with its pop culture. It all started with songs by the "crooner" Teresa Teng (Teng Li-chun). Teng has the same surname as Deng Xiaoping (formerly Teng Hsiao-ping, as written in Wade-Giles, the old romanization of Chinese still widely used in Taiwan). Teng owed her success to the bankruptcy of the revolutionary culture that had been dominant since the 1950s but had degenerated during the Cultural

Revolution into howling fanaticism. Most of the older generation didn't know any better, but the younger generation was sick of model operas, the Internationale, marches, and folk music. They yearned for cheerful light music, simple entertainment, and recreation.

Already during the Cultural Revolution pop cassettes had been smuggled into China from Hong Kong. When the chink in the Bamboo Curtain widened after the fall of the Gang of Four in 1976, Teng's music flowed in from Hong Kong and soon became the central element in a nationwide subculture. In the early 1980s Teng's cassettes were still banned, yet everyone had a few. No radio or television station was allowed to play her songs, yet everyone could sing or hum a couple of them. Her strength lay in the fact that she sang in Mandarin—unlike the *Cantopop* stars from Hong Kong— in a sweet, crystal-clear voice, accompanied by ripping guitar and saxophone glissandos with gasping and groaning that no one in China had ever heard before. A variation on the theme of "one country–two systems" appeared: one country–two Dengs or Tengs. The old Deng Xiaoping ruled during the day, but at night it was the young Teng Li-chun who reigned (in Pinyin: Deng Lijun).

Teng sang about love, sorrow, desire, loneliness, and regret—all bourgeois emotions in great demand in a society warped for decades by sermons on "patriotism and class love," which were meant to take precedence over everything. "Class love is as deep as the ocean" (*jie-ji ai, si da-hai shen*) had been the prosaic slogan of the Cultural Revolution. In the 1980s many taboos were broken. Vulgar, sensual, stirring, and provocative music and films from Hong Kong and Taiwan began to invade the country and were copied on a massive scale. In only a few years the cassette and hi-fi industry managed to supply the most remote parts of the country with copied tapes. Videos and pornography were the next step. Campaigns against "spiritual pollution" in 1983–84 and "bourgeois liberalization" in 1987 delayed social "normalization" somewhat but could not stop it. Ideologues who saw "the closing of the door" (to the rest of the world) as the only way to save orthodox socialism were told by Deng Xiaoping that slamming the door was no precaution against filthy vermin—one needed a flyswatter.

DURING THE LATE 1980s and early 1990s, dance halls, bars, karaoke lounges, discos, KTVs, and MTVs* sprang up like mushrooms, mostly with

---

* KTV (karaoke TV) and MTV (music TV) are more private versions of karaoke. They are private rooms that one can rent for sizable fees, furnished with a karaoke or hi-fi TV set, as well as one or more girls for company.

investment money from Hong Kong and Taiwan. Karaoke, which originated in Japan and means "missing voice," has become a national rage. It is music in which the vocal part is missing and has to be filled in with the help of a videotape and a microphone. It was first "sinified" in Taiwan and Hong Kong and rebaptized *ka-ra* in Chinese characters with a romanized OK tacked on (kara-OK), and has conquered the mainland to such an extent that there is now one on every street corner. They are bars, restaurants, or dance halls with video recorders and sound equipment, and one can't eat a meal or drink a beer anymore without being amused or annoyed by the squeaking and screeching of amateur vocalists. The Chinese do everything on a massive scale, and now there are perhaps just as many Chinese crooning tearjerkers in Hong Kong or Taiwanese style as there were singing songs of praise to Chairman Mao on the street during the Cultural Revolution. More and more indigenous songs compete with those from the mainland, but many Chinese say that the lyrics and melodies of the Taiwanese songs are much better. Concerts by Taiwanese pop stars drew huge crowds even in remote inland cities such as Chongqing until relations between both sides of the Taiwan Strait soured in 1994 after the Qiandao Lake incident.

Taiwanese writers such as Chong Yao and San Mao have also become immensely popular. Chong writes in a genre that is comparable to the dimestore romance, stories of adulterous relationships, broken marriages, and crimes of passion. They appeal perfectly to the emancipated taste of the Chinese, who are completely fed up with sanctimonious sermons on puritan values given by the notorious senior sybarites of the party.

San Mao was an international tramp whose travelogues broadcast the message that the way to find happiness is not by engaging in small-minded navel-gazing and sticking with stale relationships, but by getting out and exploring the world. Her Spanish husband died while deep-sea diving, and San herself committed suicide. This makes her stories even more appealing to the Chinese, who cherish as no others the notions of tragedy and fate. "Eating bitterness" (*chi-ku*), they call it, and they indulge in this national cult with masochistic grandeur.

Even the official media contributed selectively to the dissemination of Taiwanese pop culture. During the annual celebrations surrounding the Chinese New Year, which go on for days, variety shows from all of the provinces and by all of the country's minorities were presented. Spurred on by the unrelenting campaigns for national reunification, something of the culture of Hong Kong and Taiwan had to be shown on national television. It worked like a boomerang. Singers from Hong Kong and Taiwan became more popular than those from the mainland. It began with school and student songs and continued with folk and patriotic songs, not sung to march music but in the form of pop. The Taiwanese composer and singer Hou De-jian (Hou Teh-chien) became famous throughout China for his song "De-scendants of the Dragon" (*Long de Chuan-ren*). Fei Hsiang—half Taiwanese, half American—achieved renown for his "Come Back" (to China!). Hou had "defected" in 1983 to escape Taiwan's smallness and to unleash his na-tional songs on the vastness of China.

In 1989 Hou became caught up in the protest movement, playing a his-toric and heroic role in the dramatic final phase. Three days before the army marched on Tiananmen Square, Hou and three other dissidents went on a second hunger strike to protest against the threat of military force. During the night of 3–4 June, these four played a key role in preventing a bloody fi-nale in the central part of the square. Army units had rushed to the edge of the square where hundreds of die-hard students—armed with clubs, iron bars, and a handful of captured guns—had sworn to defend it to the last man. Hou and the other three persuaded the students to abandon their sui-cidal plan and negotiated with the army commander to open up a corridor for a "peaceful retreat" on the southern corner of the square.

Hou was the first to confirm that no one had died in the center of the square, thereby unintentionally helping the Chinese propaganda machine. But in the aftermath of Tiananmen, he turned out to be the regime's loud-est critic. Because of his reputation as a defector from Taiwan, he was again invited to perform at the official Lunar New Year celebrations in 1991, where he stunned everyone with an ode to the student rebels. His studio became a political salon and his red Mercedes a free taxi to enable fellow dissidents to dodge the police. On 30 May 1991 he was arrested just as he was about to cir-culate a petition for the release of political prisoners. Fearful of unrest dur-ing the anniversary on 4 June, the Chinese police put him on a boat in the South China coastal city of Xiamen and ferried him halfway across the Tai-wan Strait, where a Taiwanese patrol boat picked him up and took him back to Taiwan.

DENG XIAOPING'S TRIP to the south in the spring of 1992 led to a huge increase in investments from Hong Kong and Taiwan, which in their turn stimulated explosive growth in the number of hotels, fancy restaurants, and amusement centers. Now more than ever before, Hong Kong and Taiwan became the trendsetters, not only for the economy but for the whole of so-ciety. Modern Chinese looked to Taiwan for the latest fashions, trends in social life, the most up-to-date professional expertise, and for non-official, more reliable information on Chinese politics. Even in the most isolated corners of the country, Hong Kong and Taiwan became synonymous with "modern." In August 1994 I was in Ürümqi, the capital of China's remote Islamic "Wild West." I asked a taxi driver where it was the hottest and noisiest (*re-nau*) at night. "Taiwan City!" he replied. It was a kitschy dump with disco, kara-OK bar, dancing, the works. Was it a Taiwanese investment? "No, but if it's called Taiwan, everybody knows it's new and exciting," said the taxi driver.

Hong Kong and Taiwan have become the filters through which the whole world enters China. With their enormous commercial experience, the Chinese from Hong Kong and Taiwan have adapted things from all over the world to Chinese tastes. "If it's popular in Taiwan, it will be popular in China," say Taiwanese businessmen. "Most of Shanghai, the most advanced city in China, wears underwear from the Chung Shing Company of Taiwan, and soon all of China will wear our designs." The lifestyle of the young, well-educated, urban Chinese who works for a foreign firm or a bank and is not dependent on the state or the Communist party is scarcely different from that of his "ethnic brethren" in Hong Kong or Taiwan. The forward thrust of Hong Kong and Taiwan into China has shown them that there is "a better way of being Chinese": earning a high income, buying brand-name goods and clothing from Hong Kong and Taiwan, eating Cantonese food or other regional Chinese cuisine in joint-venture restaurants run by Hong Kong or Taiwanese chains with polite personnel—all in sharp contrast to the mess and incivility to be found in state restaurants. More and more Chinese now have their business cards printed in old-style Chinese characters, which have remained in general use in Hong Kong and Taiwan, rather than in the less complex and less elegant simplified characters of proletarian culture. They watch satellite television from Hong Kong, which can be received throughout the country, or Taiwanese television, which reaches only as far as the southern coastal provinces. They go to karaoke bars and discos where much of the music still comes from Hong Kong and Taiwan. Owing to these irrepressible developments, the "apartheid in reverse," which until a few years ago applied to the Chinese in their own country—no access to the best hotels, restaurants, and offices, which were reserved for foreigners and Chinese from Hong Kong and Taiwan—has been largely abolished. Security guards are not able to pick out the overseas Chinese from the locals at first sight anyway. The guards of the People's Liberation Army at diplomatic compounds can still be very nasty to the Hong Kong or Taiwanese wives of foreigners, assuming them to be locals unless proven otherwise.

.   .   .

IN SPITE OF MUCH sociocultural and economic-commercial interaction, the three areas of Greater China remained oblivious to one another politically. Owing to their own benign neglect and the uncertainty that persisted regarding the future, the British had failed to provide Hong Kong with democratic institutions before 1984. When they finally attempted after 1984 to do so, their efforts were met with massive resistance from Beijing.

In 1986 Taiwan had begun the transition from "neoauthoritarianism" to a multiparty system, which further encouraged democratic activists in Hong Kong to defy China's obstruction of the natural political evolution of the colony. In China the tide turned in the opposite direction. In 1986 political reforms were postponed, and in 1987 they failed (see Chapters 9 through 11). Economic reforms foundered slowly but surely, leading to a severe crisis in 1988. The golden years of the cultural thaw (1984–86) were also over.

With the end of martial law, the lifting of the ban on establishing new political parties in 1987, and the repeal of restrictions on travel to the mainland in 1988, large-scale interaction began between Taiwan and the mainland: family visits, tourism, trade, investments, and cultural cross-fertilization. Political interaction, however, was still out of the question.

The Tiananmen incident in 1989 hardened political rigidity on the Chinese side, but this was no obstacle to the rapid expansion of economic intercourse between China, Hong Kong, and Taiwan. Censorship was still practiced, however, even on letters exchanged between high school students. In 1990 four thousand pen-pal letters from Taiwan were confiscated, because during a random inspection of twenty letters, eighteen passages referring to the crackdown of 1989 were discovered.

By the beginning of the 1990s, interaction between the three components of the Greater Chinese Triangle had taken the form of progressive economic osmosis, cultural penetration, and political and diplomatic tension. In Hong Kong the new populist governor, Chris Patten, set out to broaden democracy through creative reinterpretation of the Joint Declaration and the Basic Law. Having sped up its breakthrough to complete democratization, Taiwan was enjoying an increase in international goodwill, and although this did not result in complete diplomatic recognition, it did receive more attention and respect from the international community, despite Beijing's fierce protests. To keep Hong Kong and Taiwan in the "Greater China straitjacket," Beijing stuck firmly to the formula devised in 1984, "one country–two systems," without reviewing its altered content. In 1984 it had been a question of state socialism versus laissez-faire capitalism, but what was left of socialism twelve or thirteen years later? "One country–two systems" in the year 1997 means Third World dictatorship with its inherent corruption and instability in China versus modern capitalism and expanding democracy in Hong Kong and Taiwan.

But because China is big and hardened and the (Western) world divided, opportunistic, and full of self-doubt, the West is not able to take a joint stand in supporting and strengthening the democratization process in Hong Kong and the consolidation of democracy in Taiwan. "One country–two systems" is a static dogma for China, where the voice of the people does not count, while in Hong Kong and especially in Taiwan this voice is becoming increasingly loud and counts more every day. China subscribes to the totalitarian, holistic axiom that the future of Hong Kong and Taiwan is the business of all 1.2 billion Chinese, although the will of the 1.174 billion mainland Chinese has never found expression in anything but the clichés of the Communist propaganda machine.

Since the early 1980s China has cherished the hope that rediscovery of the common Chinese cultural identity and economic self-interest will automatically create in Hong Kong and Taiwan a desire for political reunification. Hong Kong has no choice, but in Taiwan cultural and economic interaction with the mainland has only strengthened its awareness of being a separate subnation.

CHAPTER 5

The Special Economic Zones and the Reopening of the Old "Treaty Ports"

Before "liberation" Beihai was so prosperous that it was called a second [French] Hong Kong. There were regular services to Hong Kong, Guangzhou, Kunming, and Guiyang, but these ceased in 1950. Now, finally, the city is open again.

MENG GUOYAN,
mayor of Beihai, 1984

IN ONE OF THE MOST MOMENTOUS speeches of his career, dubbed the "Speech for the Ten Thousand Cadres" and delivered on 16 January 1980, Deng Xiaoping listed China's main strategic tasks for the 1980s:

1. the fight against hegemonism (the English term China commonly uses to refer to the policy of world domination as pursued by the superpowers, in particular the Soviet Union, but also the United States);
2. the return of Taiwan to the motherland;
3. the acceleration of economic construction.[1]

The struggle against Soviet hegemonism has meanwhile been won. The struggle against American hegemonism resembles a fight between husband and wife in a bad marriage: there is always discord but never a fistfight, and divorce is never a real option.

Deng said that "in the final analysis, the return of Taiwan also depends on our running our affairs at home well. We are superior to Taiwan politically and in terms of economic system, but we must surpass Taiwan at least to a certain extent in economic development as well. Nothing less will do. With the success of the four modernizations and more economic growth, we will be in a better position to accomplish reunification."

But the fact that Deng put the return of Taiwan ahead of the economy suggests that he attached more value to that than to economic construction and that he thought China should be prepared to sacrifice material progress to the higher national and historical goal of reunification. Sixteen years later, considerably more progress has been made in economic construction than in reunification with Taiwan. The two have become inseparable; the second was meant to pave the way for the third.

The return of Hong Kong to the motherland was not considered a major problem at that time. The eventual departure of the British was a foregone conclusion and arranging the details only a matter of time. When the Chinese door to the outside world was opened in 1979, Hong Kong, through its geographical position as the appendix on the soft underbelly of China, was already accustomed to its role as dynamo and service base for the new, modern sectors of China's economy. Taiwan would have to be coaxed into abandoning its orientation toward the United States and Japan and moving into orbit around the Chinese mainland as the next satellite.

To further China's dual goals of reintegration with Taiwan and Hong Kong and acceleration of outward economic development, four special economic zones (SEZs) were established in the southeastern coastal belt near Hong Kong and Taiwan. Three of them were situated in Guangdong Province: Shenzhen, north of Hong Kong; Zhuhai, north of the Portuguese enclave of Macau; and Shantou, opposite southern Taiwan. The fourth was Xiamen in the southern part of Fujian Province along the Taiwan Strait. Shenzhen and Zhuhai were unspoiled fishing and rice-growing regions. Shantou (Swatow in the local Chaozhou dialect) and Xiamen (Amoy in the Hokkien dialect) had been prewar treaty ports— Xiamen one of the original five major ports—and had a rich history of overseas trade, particularly with the European colonial empires in Southeast Asia. The majority of Thai overseas Chinese originally came from Swatow and the overseas Chinese in Malaysia, Singapore, and Indonesia from Amoy.

The creation of these zones was inspired partly by the pre-Communist experience of the old treaty ports, partly by the more recent worldwide experience of developing market economies, most of all Taiwan. Thanks to the establishment of three export processing zones during the 1960s, Taiwan had emerged by the early 1980s as a major trading power, whereas China was still at the starting line.

The treaty ports, about ninety of them altogether, were extraterritorial enclaves under Western, Russian, and Japanese jurisdiction, which had been set up as a result of "unequal treaties," often enforced by gunboat diplomacy. The treaties entitled consuls and traders to settle in special "concessions" where they were exempt from Chinese law. It was a form of colonialism that, in economic terms, had been both modernizing and highly profitable, for the Chinese as well as the foreigners. Politically and culturally, though, it had become an unacceptable anachronism that had to be stopped. The Kuomintang achieved this through negotiations that were almost completely successful. By 1945 the extraterritoriality in all Chinese coastal cities had been abolished, with the exception of the cities in Manchuria—in the sphere of influence of "socialist" Russia—and Hong Kong, whose status as a crown colony was maintained. The Communists, however, were determined in 1949 to eradicate the "colonial, imperialist, capitalist plunderers" rather than renegotiate their continued presence on Chinese terms for their mutual benefit. After thirty years of destructive class struggle and extreme political campaigns, the Communists once again saw the light and welcomed the capitalists back to China.

NONE OTHER THAN the future president Jiang Zemin played a role in the spadework preparatory to the establishment of the special zones. In 1980 he was vice-chairman of the State Commission for Import and Export Administration, and, in this capacity, was invited by the United Nations Industrial Development Organization (UNIDO) to lead a study mission to ten countries, including Sri Lanka, Singapore, Mexico, and Ireland. In an interview in 1990, he said that Jurong in Singapore and Shannon in Ireland had made the deepest impression on him.[2] The trip's special aim was to study legislation, the degree of autonomy of the zones, the system of management, and the training of staff. Jiang's role in establishing the SEZs is practically the only reformist exploit in his past record.

If they lived up to their high expectations, the SEZs were destined to become showplaces of high technology, modern management, and efficiency. Production was meant to serve the foreign market, with the aim of raking in foreign currency, in its turn to pay for the import of high technology. This experience would then seep out to the hinterland, leading to the proliferation of advanced industrial estates. The zones were exempt from administrative interference from local authorities, received sizable funding for infrastructure projects, and were allowed to extend special privileges to foreign investors, including exemption from taxes for a maximum of five years, and permanently lower taxes, depending on the type of technology. The rate of income tax was 15 percent, compared with 20 percent outside the zones.

The SEZs did not develop according to plan in two respects. The first disillusionment was the scarcity of Western investment in high technology. The investment that did come in was mostly in cheap processing and "compensation trade" (the supply of machines that then made the goods offered in payment) from Hong Kong. The British crown colony was bursting at the seams and sought to expand to the other side of what was then known as the Bamboo Curtain, where there was an abundance of cheap land, raw materials, and labor. The Shenzhen SEZ was not to become a dynamo of high-tech investment but, in terms of social geography, a new suburb of Hong Kong, a de facto extension of the New Territories, the part of Hong Kong that had been leased to the British for ninety-nine years in 1898. In 1983 $1.7 billion of foreign capital was invested in the SEZ—60 percent of all foreign investment in the whole of China—and most of it came from Hong Kong: toy and textile factories, and especially speculative investment in the unprecedented building boom in Shenzhen, which at that time was perhaps the biggest construction site in the world. In 1985 investment contracts were signed to the tune of $2.6 billion, of which only $700 million was realized.

Another headache was the zones' ideological nature, which was highly controversial. Orthodox Marxists saw them as new treaty ports or worse: capitalist bases from which to undermine socialism. For this reason, the SEZ was hermetically sealed off from the rest of the municipality of Shenzhen by a new "Iron Curtain"—an electric fence fifty kilometers long made up of steel poles and fortified wire netting with barbed wire on top—to bar smuggling and the free flow of people to and from the new "horn of plenty." In just five years Shenzhen had grown from a muddy backwater of fishing villages with thirty thousand people into a sprawling, chaotic, industrial city of half a million. Gold diggers and frustrated intellectuals from the whole country had flocked there by the thousands to escape the suffocating bureaucracy in the interior, setting up a Chinese version of a late-nineteenth-century American frontier boom town. Local farmers and fishermen quickly built three- and four-story houses on land that had been leased to them after the disbandment of the communes and rented them to the newcomers, thus becoming new "landlords," whose newfound squandermania went to their heads. In a few years' time, Shenzhen had turned into a dynamic melting pot of pioneers from all the provinces of China: investors from Hong Kong, adventurers, swindlers, and prostitutes from near and far.

In 1985 a delegation of elderly veterans visited Shenzhen. According to the Hong Kong journal *Cheng Ming*, they were overcome by heartrending nostalgia. "We've fought against capitalism our whole lives. Chairman Mao taught us how to build up socialism, and now a few people want to amputate parts of our motherland and abandon them to capitalist colonization," they lamented. Deng Xiaoping himself had to go on the defensive. During an "imperial" inspection of Shenzhen in 1984, he had written that the experience of Shenzhen had proved that the decision to establish SEZs had been correct. In 1985 he corrected this statement, however, saying that Shenzhen was "an experiment that still had to prove itself." It was widely assumed that the only reason the government still supported the further development of the SEZs was because it had already invested so much in their infrastructure and that the reformers, especially Deng Xiaoping himself, could not permit themselves to make an abrupt about-face. In internal ideological treatises, the policy was defended using Lenin's rationalization of the New Economic Policy (NEP) of the 1920s that capitalists were "useful idiots whom you later hang with the rope they themselves first handed you."

While things in Shenzhen were going relatively well, little had happened in the other three zones. In Zhubai the building boom did not begin until 1984, and in Shantou the first pile still had to be driven into the ground. In early 1984 Xiamen was also honored with a visit and a calligraphy from Deng Xiaoping, although the supreme leader could not force himself to write more than a warning that they should work faster and harder. The original 2.5-square-kilometer zone in Xiamen was enlarged to 131 square kilometers. This was a clear message to Taiwan to remove all political obstacles and cross the bridge (i.e., the Taiwan Strait) to invest in China. Xiamen had only one major American investment in 1984: R. J. Reynolds, which produced its Camel cigarettes there for export. This brought in foreign currency but did not contribute to China's technological progress.

Officials in Xiamen at that time openly displayed their contempt for Shenzhen, which they considered a rice paddy and quagmire of swampy fishing ponds and chicken farms, a place where all the brainpower had to be imported. During my first visit in April 1984, the director of the Chamber of Commerce, Chen Mingge, expounded with pride on Xiamen's glorious trading tradition and prestigious university. Xiamen hoped to become a center of computer technology, precision mechanics, fine chemicals, and new types of building materials. The city fathers of Xiamen talked eagerly about the scientific industrial park in Hsinchu in Taiwan, which they considered a model for Xiamen. At that time, the business cultures in Taiwan and Xiamen were a century apart. In Taiwan businessmen take visiting journalists out to eat at their exclusive clubs. I invited my host to have lunch with me at my hotel, but he was obliged to take his own mess tin to the zone's soup kitchen.

AS AN ALTERNATIVE to adding to the number of SEZs, of which only one—Xiamen—had any trading tradition to speak of, the leadership contemplated the idea of reopening the most important of the former treaty ports, giving them the same privileges as the SEZs. The Chinese *Journal for the World Economy* wrote in the spring of 1984 that China's eastern seaboard should become the central part of the "Gold Coast" that would extend from Korea to Singapore. At the same time, visions of the twenty-first century becoming the "Pacific Century," with the focus of the world's economy shifting from the Atlantic to the Pacific Ocean, became popular. China, with its outward-looking premier Zhao Ziyang, did not want to miss the boat because of its Communist system. "If China seizes this opportunity to establish more SEZs and gears itself to the new technological revolution in the Western countries and Japan, it could become an economic superpower," the economist Chen Qiaozhi wrote in 1984.

In April 1984 fourteen coastal cities were opened for preferential treatment of foreign investors. Most of them had been treaty ports, including China's largest multi-million-inhabitant cities of Shanghai, Tianjin (Tientsin), Guangzhou (Canton), and Dalian (Dairen). Shanghai was the "mother of all treaty ports" and the premier prewar trading and financial metropolis in East Asia. Before the Second World War, Tianjin had been China's number two "international" city, with nine "concessions," including Italian, Austro-Hungarian, and Belgian. Dalian, also known as Dairen or Port Arthur (the naval port on the southern tip of the city), began the twentieth century as a "Russian Hong Kong" but was taken over by Japan after its epochal defeat of the Russian navy in the Tsushima Strait in 1905.

The Fourteen Open Coastal Cities

Dalian (Dairen)	Shanghai
Qinhuangdao	Ningbo
Tianjin (Tientsin)	Wenzhou
Yantai (Chefoo)	Fuzhou
Qingdao (Tsingtao)	Guangzhou (Canton)
Lianyungang	Zhanjiang
Nantong	Beihai (Pakhoi)[3]

From 1889 until 1914 Qingdao had been a German naval base with a medium-sized, newly built, German model city. It would have become a "German Hong Kong" had the Japanese not dislodged the Germans at the beginning of the First World War. Japanese control over the former German sphere of influence was recognized by the Allied powers in the Treaty of Versailles, which provoked the first outbreak of modern Chinese patriotism, the famous May Fourth Movement. Ningbo and Guangzhou had been China's most historic trading ports, which the Portuguese had descended upon in the sixteenth century, to be followed by all Westerners. Wenzhou was the birthplace of a large number of the French, Italian, and Dutch overseas Chinese. The rest were specialized port cities, each with its own specific hinterland rich in minerals, crops, and commodities.

Before the war, all of the treaty ports had a small, Westernized middle class that worked for the foreign trading houses as compradors (agents). Survivors of this era, who spoke foreign languages and knew all the tricks of the trade, were still in great supply after the "reopening" in 1984. Owing in part to this pool of talent and earlier industrialization under Communism, these new "open cities" had much better prospects of becoming centers of high technology than other cities. They were at a disadvantage compared with the SEZs, however, because they had to remain part of the planned state economy for ideological reasons. Whereas in the SEZs there was no investment ceiling, the two largest of the fourteen cities—Shanghai and Tianjin—could not attract investments above $30 million without approval from the central government. In Dalian the maximum was $10 million, and in the other cities $5 million.

Hong Kong, the only treaty port that had remained intact, suddenly became a supermarket for investment acquisition. In November the first "Investment Symposium on China's Fourteen Open Cities" was held in the British crown colony. In his opening address, the leader of the Chinese delegation of mayors, the deputy minister of foreign trade, Wei Yuming, said that Hong Kong was the city with the most extensive international economic contacts. "It is an important channel through which China can conduct economic relations and trade with the rest of the world." All of the cities participating—even the smallest of the fourteen, Beihai, which is close to the border with Vietnam—issued glossy brochures, presenting themselves as "the new Hong Kongs of the future." Mayor Meng Guoyan candidly described his city's former glory as a treaty port and the decay that had followed "liberation." "Before 'liberation' Beihai was so prosperous that it was called a second [French] Hong Kong. There were regular services to Hong Kong, Guangzhou, Kunming and Guiyang, but these ceased in 1950. Now, finally, the city is open again."[4]

Dozens of deals were clinched for airport modernization, telecommunications systems, and electricity plants, but, remarkably enough, none for the construction of ports. The Chinese would build these themselves, which was distressing news to the world's construction firms, which had hoped that China would be the next Saudi Arabia.

Shanghai was kept on a conspicuously tight rein. It was, after all, the primus inter pares on the Chinese coast, and its industrial production amounted to half that of all the fourteen cities together, but it was granted no higher status and there was no question of its becoming a special super-zone, at least not yet. The media in Hong Kong reported at the time that China's top leaders were sharply divided over the role Shanghai was to play in the modernization process. Party leader Hu Yaobang would have liked to open up Shanghai to the same extent as Shenzhen, but Premier Zhao Ziyang reportedly made a strong case for keeping Shanghai distinct from Shenzhen and Hong Kong, and for making it a model of pure socialist economic development, so that in the future the whole world would be able to see the superiority of socialism. This is where the barometer stood in Orwell's year of 1984. Nine years later, Deng Xiaoping said in Volume 3 of his *Selected Works* that one of his biggest mistakes had been not declaring Shanghai a special economic zone in the early 1980s.

XIAMEN WANTED TO LEARN from the mistakes of Shenzhen and avoid becoming a haven for fast deals in labor-intensive processing and speculation in real estate. It would rather let its 340,000 square feet of factory space stand empty for a while and wait for the arrival of real high technology. In 1987, however, Xiamen had managed to attract only four substantial foreign investors: the Reynolds Camel cigarette factory; the Indonesian (overseas Chinese) Inhwa tile factory; Xoceco, a television factory operating with Hong Kong capital and French technology; and Wang Laboratories from the United States, with a total capital of $58 million.[5] Before the Taiwanese began arriving en masse in 1988, the number of investments had increased to 150 projects, but the great majority came from Hong Kong and overseas Chinese from Southeast Asia, whose ancestors had emigrated from Xiamen during the last century. The city government of Xiamen had adopted various measures designed to attract Westerners as well, but with mixed success. One such measure was doing away with the practice of requiring a Chinese to hold the sinecure of deputy to the firm's foreign director, as this Chinese was usually a party functionary who was only a millstone around the foreigner's neck. In the attempt to demonstrate to a group of visiting journalists how much this measure had improved management, the SEZ of Xiamen organized a rather unconvincing symposium of foreign managers of joint ventures. Most of the directors were Chinese—from Hong Kong, Southeast Asia, or the United States—and Japanese, all of whom were better able to adapt to conditions in China than were white Westerners. They spoke with a mixture of patriotism and Oriental caution, and the Japanese only with the latter. One note of discord was sounded by the only "big nose" (a Chinese nickname for Westerners) in the group, a Dane. "I've decided to speak my mind; otherwise I wouldn't have come," he said loudly. He had a small factory with twenty-two employees of Great Nordic Danavox, which produces high-quality electronic hearing aids. One million dollars was invested in this company, 50 percent Chinese and 50 percent Danish. The Chinese had provided only the building, the Danes the technology. The Dane wanted out because his expense package had skyrocketed and he was fed up with living in Xiamen. He wanted to designate his (Chinese) successor himself, but his candidate was not a member of the Communist party. As the general manager, the Dane had no Chinese deputy under him, but a chairman of the board above him. This chairman was an elderly orthodox Communist who had a chauffeur-driven company car but contributed nothing to running the company. To safeguard his privileges, the chairman wanted to appoint one of his own cronies as general manager. The Danish general manager and the Chinese chairman were locked in a grim battle that the Dane eventually lost. This is a typical conflict that has occurred in more than half of the tens of thousands of joint ventures in China and has already led to the failure of thousands of firms.

Xiamen was cut out to be an investment center, not so much for Westerners, however, as for overseas Chinese, especially the newcomers from Taiwan.[6]

CHAPTER 6

Shenzhen and "Greater Hong Kong"

Special economic zones ought not to be special. Their ultrahigh income is seven or eight times the national average. If regional inequalities continue to increase, it will cause social instability, which will turn out to be a political rather than an economic problem. But this has nothing to do with the future development of Hong Kong and Macau, because SEZs and SARs are two completely different things.

HU ANGANG,
economic adviser to the Chinese government, August 1995

"NOW THERE IS ONLY ONE Hong Kong, but we plan to build several more Hong Kongs in the interior," said Deng Xiaoping on 3 June 1988 in a talk with participants of the "International Conference on China and the World in the Nineties."[1] Earlier that year, the major theme in China's economic debates had been gearing the entire coastal belt to the "great international economic cycle and division of labor," i.e., taking over the labor-intensive industries from countries that were pricing themselves out of the market, such as South Korea, Taiwan, and Hong Kong itself. Since the early 1980s China has gradually taken over the role of mass producer of textiles, shoes, toys, and electronics for chain-store businesses in the West. The Shenzhen Special Economic Zone was originally meant to attract high-tech investments from the West but unintentionally emerged as a processing center for Hong Kong's light industries. From Shenzhen they spread to the fishing villages in the Pearl River delta, where many of Hong Kong's industrial tycoons were born. In no time at all, the villages and towns along the myriad muddy arms of the Pearl River became featherweight industrial satellites of Hong Kong.

Between 1950 and 1979 a large part of the delta population fled to Hong Kong. The newly rich refugees of yesteryear now brought employment to thousands of their fellow villagers in the delta, who were put to work making plastic flowers, Cabbage Patch dolls, and remote-controlled cars for wages that were one-tenth (or less) those in Hong Kong or Taiwan. By the late 1980s the wages in the areas bordering on Hong Kong had risen to such an extent that they were no longer competitive and work had to be contracted out to more remote inland areas. Standards of quality left much to be desired in China, but there were many remedies for that: designing and cutting took place in Hong Kong, after which the merchandise, along with zippers, ribbons, and buttons, was sent to China to be sewn together, accompanied by overseers to supervise the assembly process. The last step, quality inspection, again took place in Hong Kong.

One month after Deng uttered his memorable words about building more Hong Kongs, high inflation escalated into the worst economic crisis since the 1960s, obstructing the whole blueprint for reform for more than two years. In the draconian austerity program announced by Li Peng, the SEZs were the first target. Capitalist contamination was now seen as a threat to socialism in the interior and would have to be contained. The SEZs would be required to turn over more of their foreign exchange revenue to the empty central coffers and would not receive any more funds for improving the infrastructure. They would have to fend for themselves by doing more advanced assemblage for Hong Kong industries, and, since 1988, for Taiwanese firms as well, because their low-wage advantage had been lost to the nearby countryside with its much cheaper labor.

The economic crisis culminated in the historic protest movement in the spring of 1989 and the notorious debacle in Tiananmen Square. For many months South China lived with the threat of massive reprisals because of its Hong Kong connections. Hong Kong was a target because of the financial support it had given to the Tiananmen protest, and the southern provinces because they were considered the autonomous, disloyal stronghold of deposed party leader Zhao Ziyang. Zhao had been party secretary and governor of Guangdong before the Cultural Revolution and again after his rehabilitation in the 1970s. If he had a network of sympathizers anywhere, it was there, especially in Shenzhen and on the island of Hainan, where his friend Liang Xiang was governor and Zhao's two sons controversial (and corrupt) businessmen. The impending purge never materialized, but Guangdong's so-called "special rights" were revoked, whereby the province had been allowed to keep 60 percent of its foreign exchange revenues, 5 percent more than the other SEZs.

The SEZs also came under fire from the aged hard-liners who wanted to abolish them "in the interest of national unity [and equality]." Whether or not they were serious about this, they soon repented (see Chapter 12). In February 1990 a national conference was held on the fate of the SEZs. In his speech, Premier Li Peng said that the zones should continue to develop faster than the national average and that the market should be allowed to prevail over the plan. They would be expected to contribute more to the central government because of all the money it had invested in them. The conference rejected a proposal that Shenzhen institute its own currency. In March 1989 the National People's Congress had granted Shenzhen the legislative autonomy to make laws more closely resembling those of Hong Kong, but in the resurrected ideological Ice Age of neo-Stalinism, repression, and recentralization, this had to be put on hold. The SEZs were also called upon to observe the Four Cardinal Principles of orthodox socialism more strictly and to strengthen the building of advanced socialist ethics: in other words, to fight prostitution, crime, smuggling, and corruption more forcefully. This was continually professed but rarely implemented. It was again stressed that "Shenzhen was a special economic zone, not a special political zone, and had only economic and no political dispensation."

The continuing disquiet in Shenzhen was demonstrated during the tenth anniversary of the foundation of the zone. The celebration in August was extremely modest and no top party or government leader attended. General Secretary Jiang Zemin had paid Shenzhen an inspection visit in April, but only after visiting Jinggangshan in Jiangxi and Yanan in Shaanxi, Mao's revolutionary bases of the 1920s and 1930s. This was his way of showing that inward-looking ideological orthodoxy was an antidote for outward-looking capitalist reform. Jiang thus ingratiated himself with the aged conservatives, sowing as well a lot of confusion. No one could tell anymore which way the political wind was blowing.

Owing to the Euro-American Tiananmen sanctions, the chances of attracting Western high-tech investments were very slim for the time being. Seventy percent of all investments came from Hong Kong and most of the rest from Japan. Taiwan was the great, but discreet, newcomer. It was still anti-Communist, but unlike Hong Kong had not caused any commotion about the Tiananmen drama, instead instantly taking the opportunity to leap eagerly into the gap left in China's investment markets by Western sanctions.

A new category of investors were the *jia yang-guizi* (camouflaged Western devils), who were mostly mainland Chinese, usually children of highly placed Communists, who had surreptitiously channeled Chinese state funds to Hong Kong, using a Hong Kong Chinese figurehead to reinvest the money in Shenzhen, thereby enjoying the privileges of foreign investors. Many new projects were so-called "Sino-Sino-foreign joint ventures," i.e., one partner from Shenzhen, one from the Chinese interior, and one foreigner or Hong Kong Chinese.

In 1990 Shenzhen was already the largest source of exports from China after Shanghai, and number one in the export of bicycles, watches, cameras, and household appliances. Ninety percent of Shenzhen's goods left the country through Hong Kong, and 95 percent of its imports came in through Hong Kong, making the varying customs regimes increasingly bothersome. Proposals to set up "bonded warehouses" for the tax-free storage of goods had already been made in 1988 but were subsequently derailed by the hardline turning point of 1989. After 1990 this debate was renewed and broadened, this time to include the transformation of the whole SEZ into a free trading zone with a free flow of goods and people to and from Hong Kong.

INTEGRATING HONG KONG with the mainland in 1997 had been the watchword since 1984, but now the idea of integrating Shenzhen with Hong Kong came into vogue. Socioeconomically and logistically, Shenzhen was already an extension of Hong Kong, and the trend was to broaden this to the fiscal, customs, and even legislative realms. "Unless Shenzhen succeeds in creating special links with Hong Kong and the outside world, it will lose its position as economic atlas of China," Wong Pui-yee, head of the Research Center for SEZs at the Chinese University of Hong Kong, wrote in 1990.

The "guiding position" of Shenzhen was further threatened in 1990 with the establishment of a new and much larger zone in Shanghai—Pudong, the fallow eastern bank of the Huangpu River (see Chapter 14). The launching of Pudong was a reflection of two tendencies. The SEZs had been the brainchild of deposed former premier and party leader Zhao Ziyang and were situated in the recalcitrant south, which might become even more headstrong and untrustworthy after the merger with Hong Kong in 1997. Pudong was the home base of the new party leader Jiang Zemin, the former mayor of Shanghai. Foreign influence in China's most international city had been eradicated after 1949, and Shanghai had become the staunchly loyal industrial bastion of the Communist state economy. Pudong was meant to be a grandiose state project under the central government, and unlike Shenzhen, with its small fry from Hong Kong and Taiwan, was meant to attract the large multinationals. Shenzhen was supposed to continue to draw capital from Hong Kong and Taiwan so that in ten or twenty years Guangdong Province would be the "fifth tiger of Asia" and perhaps the largest light-industry belt in the world.

THE TERM "Greater Hong Kong" was introduced in 1992 in a report by the Japanese Nomura Research Institute to describe the phenomenon of the unique synergy produced by the combination of Hong Kong's industrial management and superior financial and other services with China's cheap land and labor market. The report, *Hong Kong: Entering a New Phase,* was meant to encourage Japanese industries—which thus far had paid too much attention to Northeast China (Manchuria) and the east coast—to concentrate their efforts on South China. Economists and businessmen had introduced yet another concept: the "South China Economic Zone" with the de facto capital of Hong Kong and consisting of Hong Kong plus Guangdong, Taiwan plus Fujian, and the island province of Hainan, which would serve as a bridge to Southeast Asia. The South China Economic Zone, with a combined population the size of Japan's, would develop much faster than the rest of China and would have more potential than the whole of the ASEAN area. The Japanese government therefore encouraged its industries to follow up the revolution in light industry orchestrated by Hong Kong with a revolution in heavy industry, in which South China was way behind, orchestrated by Japan. This strategy was part of a growing tendency on Japan's part to reorient its investment activities away from the United States and Europe and back to East Asia. Hong Kong was the ideal place from which to direct this reorientation.

The Nomura report described Hong Kong as a de facto advanced country with the highest income in Asia after Japan. "Greater Hong Kong" in the narrower sense meant the crown colony plus Shenzhen and the Pearl River delta. In the broader sense, it meant Hong Kong plus Guangdong Province, with which it formed a medium-sized "national economy" and South Chinese subnation of 70 million people with its own language, Cantonese.[2]

Family ties dominate everything in China. More than half the population of Hong Kong consists of Chinese who fled from Communism in Guangdong between 1949 and 1980 and have subsequently repenetrated first the delta region and then the whole province. According to Ezra Vogel's book *One Step Ahead in China: Guangdong Under Reform,* there is hardly a village in the province, no matter how remote, that is not connected by one family tie or another to the flow of money from Hong Kong, thereby boosting its head start.[3] Statistics published by the Hong Kong Trade Development Council show that more than 20,000 Hong Kong companies in Guangdong practice the system known as "outward processing" and "forward integration." There are another 10,000 joint ventures that altogether offer work to 4 million people, whereas Hong Kong itself has only 680,000 industrial workers left. In 1992 Harbour Ring, Hong Kong's largest toy manufacturer, had only 400 employees left in Hong Kong and 10,000 workers in six factories across the border. The Hong Kong dollar has become the regional currency of southern China, where one-fifth of the entire money supply circulates, most of it in Shenzhen. Specialists from Hong Kong influence nearly everything: management, the stock market, taxation, auditing and accountancy, the real estate market, the legal system, and even the training of civil servants.

In 1988 35 percent of Hong Kong's exports were still manufactured inside Hong Kong, but by 1995 this had shrunk to 10 percent. Hong Kong factories in China produced 35 percent of the territory's exports in 1988, but this had risen to 60 percent in 1995. During these years, Hong Kong transformed itself from a player in an economy of 6 million people into a participant in an economy of 1.2 billion people, thereby becoming the eighth-largest trading economy in the world, according to a 1996 Harvard Business School study.[4]

In 1995 there were 120,000 industrial projects undertaken by Hong Kong firms in all of China, 80.5 percent of which were located in the Pearl River delta. The amount of realized investment from Hong Kong was $63 billion, 62.5 percent of the total of all foreign investment. By the end of 1995, at least another 11,000 investment contracts were signed between parties from Hong Kong and China, with planned investments of $25 billion. A 1996 survey of Hong Kong's top sixty companies revealed plans for an additional $20 billion to be invested in China in the coming three years.[5]

DENG XIAOPING'S SPECTACULAR whirlwind tour of Shenzhen early in 1992 stifled the leftist antireform offensives, strengthening the position of the SEZs on the one hand but also containing a veiled threat. Deng proclaimed the takeoff of South China a model for the whole country and issued Document No. 4, which decreed the introduction of special zones and "open cities" extending deep into the interior. The whole Yangtze valley, with Shanghai as "the head of the dragon" was meant to become the "second Gold Coast." Document No. 4 was a new manifestation of Mao Zedong's metaphor: "A Single Spark Can Light a Prairie Fire."

Special zones multiplied faster than Mao statues during the Cultural

Revolution. By the end of 1991 there were 117 zones, and by the end of 1992 there were 1,700, according to the Special Zone Bureau of the State Council in Beijing. The ministry of agriculture, however, in charge of guarding over scarce arable land, reported the number to be 8,000. Vice-premier Zhu Rongji was put in charge of suppressing the "zone epidemic," which had led to a shocking waste of agricultural land, soil erosion, overextension of the construction sector, and an inflationary credit boom. Zhu complained that 9.7 million hectares of agricultural land had been leveled without any sign of development. More than 6,000 zones were simply lying fallow. Zhu said that the state would have to invest 100 million yuan in infrastructure for every square kilometer of zone, and developers would have to borrow 200 million yuan to put buildings on every square kilometer. If that were done, though, the country would be perpetually bankrupt.

NONETHELESS, enough zones survived to deprive Shenzhen and the other four original zones of their "specialness," and Shenzhen now sought a new way of distinguishing itself in the form of greater legislative autonomy. In 1981 the National People's Congress had already authorized the Provincial People's Congress of Guangdong to make special laws for Shenzhen, but in ten years' time it had passed only seventeen such laws. In the legislative sense, therefore, Shenzhen was hardly special yet. In the field of contract and mortgage law, however, Shenzhen was way ahead of the rest of China, but as an emerging market economy it was almost completely lawless. The national, orthodox socialist laws still applied in theory, but they served more as vague guidelines than as laws in the Western sense.

The campaign for legislative autonomy began at a conference in the fall of 1990. There was a consensus among the speakers, including the mayor and the party secretary, that the zone (Shenzhen) was in need of special laws and powers to enable integration into the world economy, thereby putting it in a better position to strengthen its ties with capitalist Hong Kong. Shenzhen hoped at first to have a Legislative Council modeled on that of Hong Kong, but this was considered unworkable under the "socialist system."

On 2 July 1992 Shenzhen was given its Municipal People's Congress, which was officially responsible for introducing the legal instruments necessary for the development of the socialist market economy, but had in fact to prepare the legal streamlining necessary for integration with capitalist Hong Kong. Professor Tong Likun, head of the law faculty at the newly founded University of Shenzhen, explained that "in order to become a 'socialist Hong Kong,' Shenzhen would have to follow Hong Kong's example and adopt a comprehensive corpus of laws that would guarantee the stability of society and would immunize it against political fluctuations": in other words, no interference from the provincial or central government in local administration, the economy, and social developments. In terms of legislation, Shenzhen is now the most advanced part of China, with laws in the fields of property and real estate, auctions, stock trading, and leasing, most of them based on Hong Kong precedents.

Hong Kong law is saturated with references to private property, and this is one area of incompatibility with Shenzhen law, although there are more. Professor Peng Baoluo, vice-chairman of the law faculty, explained in 1995 that Shenzhen was studying Hong Kong's exemplary anticorruption legislation but was having fundamental problems in copying it. Hong Kong is one of the few places in Asia, along with Singapore, where corruption is effectively combated by an "Independent Commission Against Corruption" (ICAC). Peng said that the very powerful ICAC was accountable only to the governor of Hong Kong and that it was unfeasible that a similar commission in Shenzhen would report only to the mayor. "Hong Kong has three prosecution agencies: the special branch of the police, the judiciary, and the ICAC. China has only the people's procuratorate [district attorney]," Peng added. Ingenious jurists will therefore have to invent something new before an organ to combat corruption can take shape.

Peng concluded that in the field of legislation, Shenzhen has become a model for other provinces and regions, and in this respect at least still remains special. Cities across the country regularly send study groups to Shenzhen to copy its laws, which in their turn are clones of Hong Kong laws. Although all regional laws must comply with the national constitution, China's legal profession and also the central government are aware of the disadvantages of increasing legislative diversity, which only intensifies the federal, centrifugal tendencies in the country without being balanced by a federal constitution.[6]

IN 1994 SHENZHEN FOUND a field in which it was a step ahead of the rest of the country and could call itself "special": the newest phase of market reforms, the conversion of state enterprises. An editorial in the SSEZ *Daily News* described it in the spring of 1994 as "the end of the nurse-ward relationship" between government organs and state enterprises. The municipal government was meant to set up an "independent organ" that would become the owner of all state enterprises. The "Management Committee for State Assets" would take over the administrative role that ministries had with respect to state enterprises, put an end to government interference, and appoint the management that would function like a company's board of directors. As owner, the Management Committee for State Assets would then farm out the management of companies to management firms. The management firm "Shenzhen Investment Management Company" was set up in November 1994 and manages the state's shares in all local state enterprises converted to public limited-liability companies. Li Heihu, the director of the management firm, said that he has a contract with every company which requires him to prevent state assets from depreciating further. If he doesn't succeed, he will lose his management contract. It is actually a Chinese version of a holding with aspects of the "interim management" typical of companies in crisis. Li Heihu's task is to prepare companies for the market and make them competitive. He has the power to "influence" the hiring and firing of managers and to order inspections of financial supervisors. Under the old system, the government financed itself simply by taking what it needed from healthy enterprises. The main element of successful company reform is a fiscal construction that generates enough income for the government, as well as compensation for workers who are laid off. This is relatively easy to implement in Shenzhen, with its low percentage of state enterprises. But again there is intense opposition from local and central bureaucrats, who warn that severing ties between enterprises and the state bureaucracy will lead to chaos and anarchy. Director Li Heihu says that Shenzhen has nevertheless become the trendsetter and is way ahead of other cities in this area.[7]

ANOTHER EXPRESSION of "specialness" in Shenzhen is the stock exchange, which opened without sanction from Beijing just before the official opening of the approved stock exchange in Shanghai in December 1990. The reopened stock exchange for large industrial funds of state enterprises and multinationals was supposed to flourish in the historic trading city of Shanghai, which had the largest stock exchange in Asia before the Second World War, while Shenzhen's stock exchange was more of a study and experimental center in the shadow of Hong Kong. Shenzhen's stock exchange therefore became a small casino for light industry and real estate funds with low liquidity and without a broad, diversified base of shareholders. During the decades of spartan socialism, there had been nothing to buy in China and so much savings had been amassed that people were desperately looking for ways to make money. The government offered only treasury bills, and the official banks offered only low-interest deposits on currency with approximately 20 percent inflation. The rare, new issue of shares, therefore, fell like manna from heaven.

For the first two years, the indexes of both stock exchanges rose sharply and the demand for shares was insatiable. During the summer of 1992, a large-scale "shares riot" broke out, which confirmed in a spectacular way Shenzhen's image as the "Wild South" of China. Thousands of prospective small-time shareholders who had traveled from near and far to subscribe to new share issues clashed with police for two days running in what was the first large-scale confrontation between the people and riot police since the Tiananmen bloodbath of 1989. The demand was so great and the supply so minuscule that 800,000 people were forced to stand in the hot sun in a line that stretched for miles just to get hold of a subscription form, with which one could participate in the lottery and become one of the chosen "punters." The 5 million subscription forms were sold out in one day, leaving two-thirds of the waiting masses with nothing to show for their efforts. They accused the authorities of keeping the forms for their own friends and relatives, at which point all hell broke loose. The police tackled the losers with electric cattle prods, bamboo canes, and leather belts, putting two hundred of them in the hospital. Battles continued throughout the night while subscription forms were sold on the black market for ten times the normal price. Those who had managed to lay their hands on a form still had only a one-in-ten chance in the lottery. Mayor Zheng Liangyu said that the chaos had seriously damaged Shenzhen's reputation. In any case, it hurt him enough to cost him his job.[8]

For a while a threatening rumor made the rounds that orthodox Communists in Beijing wanted to use this incident as an excuse to close Shenzhen's controversial stock exchange, which had only been tolerated by way of "experiment," although it never came to this. After the riot, a conference was convened which implemented drastic reforms in the procedures. Since then, it has only been possible to buy shares through computerized bank transactions, and with the exception of a few minor incidents caused by false rumors—designed to manipulate shares prices—Shenzhen's stock exchange has been rather peaceful.

Since 1994 the exchange has sought new legitimacy by issuing B-shares in foreign currency for foreign buyers in the large construction companies handling infrastructure projects in the Pearl River delta. International brokers have routinely declared that Shenzhen's stock exchange had no right to exist independently and would be merged with that of Hong Kong in 1997, although director Xiao Zhijia vehemently denied this, saying, "Shenzhen is a socialist and Hong Kong an international capitalist stock exchange, and the border between the Special Administrative Region of Hong Kong and the Special Economic Zone of Shenzhen will be strictly maintained."[9]

. . .

THE RISE OF CHINA as an export country during the past few years has largely been due to the combination of Hong Kong and Taiwanese investments and neo-Dickensian working conditions in the satellite territories of Hong Kong in the Pearl River delta. Indeed, this is one of the "moral" complaints of the West. The whole of the Pearl River delta north of Hong Kong, as well as the coastal areas of Guangdong and Fujian provinces, is an endless belt of textile, shoe, and toy factories—extremely polluted, ugly, unsanitary, and unsafe. Hundreds of thousands of teenagers from the poor, inland provinces work there ten to fifteen hours a day, six or seven days a week. They sleep thirty to a room on moldy beds, eat poorly, and are threatened with summary dismissal if they complain. Sick leave, breaks, and vacations are practically nonexistent. Workers are allowed to go to the toilet only once a day. Those who refuse to work after hours, often without pay, are often fired. For each worker fired there are a hundred destitute drifters from all the remote corners of the country waiting outside at the gate to take their place.

The shocking conditions prevailing in its factories have contributed to Shenzhen's reputation as the Wild South. The true extent of these sordid conditions has become known only in the past few years owing to a series of accidents. In 1992 in the district of Baoan, bordering on Shenzhen, 3,067 complaints were registered against companies with foreign investments for nonpayment of wages. But it was not until several large fires claimed the lives of dozens of workers in unsafe factories, and the party went on the defensive for fear of the workers founding free unions, that China's official media began to devote some attention to the frightening abuse to which workers were subjected.

The most tragic incident was a fire in the Zhili doll factory at the end of 1993, in which eighty-seven people died and fifty-one were injured, most of them young girls. All of the doors and windows were closed to prevent the workers from stealing the toys. One year later, the Hong Kong director of the factory, two managers, and the electrician were given prison sentences of between two and six years. The electrician was not properly qualified, the fire safety regulations had been willfully ignored, and the permit had been issued by the local authority in exchange for a bribe, all with an eye to boosting profits. In June 1993 three more accidents occurred in rapid succession in which a total of seventy-one people died, all of them in Shenzhen and its vicinity. On 7 June 1994 the *People's Daily* printed a long article with the title "Foreign Investors Seek Maximum Gains and Minimum Responsibilities," which recorded cases of abuse, especially in small- and medium-sized Japanese, Taiwanese, Hong Kong, and South Korean factories. It came to three depressing conclusions:

1. Some firms will go to any lengths to recruit workers, including children, will offer them no contracts, and will fire them again arbitrarily.
2. More than half of the companies with foreign investments in the three SEZs in Guangdong pay far less than the minimum wage.
3. Working hours are much too long, safety standards leave much to be desired, and there is a complete lack of insurance and social services.

President Jiang Zemin and Foreign Minister Qian Qichen both went on inspection tours to visit victims of the disasters. Their first response was a decree that within half a year all of the companies with "foreign" (i.e., Hong Kong and Taiwanese) investments would have to permit unions to guarantee workers' rights more effectively. Only 12 percent of the companies in that category had unions by then. They were not to be independent unions, however, but branches of the official Communist unions, which are too weak to take effective action. In the interest of "stability and unity," strikes would remain illegal. Control would also be tightened on monitoring the payment of the minimum wage. In 1993 this was 1.20 yuan, slightly less than fifteen cents an hour, but with working weeks of fifty to sixty hours, workers could nevertheless earn a monthly wage of about $35. Western investors have hardly been affected by the new decrees, because their workers' conditions are better than average and anyway superior to those in the state enterprises.

Charles Dickens wrote about the injustice of Victorian society 130 years ago. By the end of the nineteenth century, however, the condition of the working class had improved tremendously in Western industrialized societies thanks to the church, secular charitable institutions, the social-democratic parties, and Bismarck's social legislation. Churches play a negligible role in China. The Chinese do not engage in charitable activities outside their circle of friends and relatives, and the vanguard of the proletariat, the Communist party, colludes with rigorous laissez-faire capitalists from Hong Kong to exact a maximum of profit from young down-and-out peasants. The ironic result is that forty-seven years after the foundation of the socialist People's Republic, China's *Lumpenproletariat* is certainly no better off than its Western counterparts of a century ago.

. . .

IT IS DIFFICULT to present a balanced view of Shenzhen after fifteen years of spectacular development: it has grown from a town of thirty thousand inhabitants to a city of 3.4 million with an annual economic growth rate of 36 percent. Corruption, crime, and exploitation of a whole generation of young peasants in the sweatshops of the factory districts are a universal and inevitable complication of Third World development and should not be allowed to detract from the overwhelming success of the zone. Its success lies in the decisive role it has played in establishing China's position as an export power, its function in helping to bridge the socioeconomic gap between Hong Kong and China, and its role as a model for accelerated development in the entire country. The problem is that Shenzhen's identity and future course are not clear. Shenzhen was the brainchild of Deng Xiaoping, and the Deng era is over.

On the central square in Shenzhen stands the biggest billboard in China, with a saintly apparition of Deng Xiaoping in the clouds. Until mid-1993 it bore the slogan "The Development and Experience of Shenzhen Demonstrates That Our Policy of Setting Up Special Economic Zones Is Correct." In the summer of 1994, in the middle of a storm of rumors about Deng's approaching death, the slogan was changed to "Firmly Grasp the Party's Basic Line and Do Not Waver for 100 Years." From his "eternal hunting grounds" Deng will not be able to see if his successors are continuing in his path. The prospects of Shenzhen's continuing to fulfill its role as a special, reformist guiding center for socialist China without the patriarchal protection of Deng Xiaoping were very much in doubt for two years, but reassurances have recently been given by the top leadership.

The city government has set its mind on internationalization and a merger with Hong Kong. During a municipal conference on town planning in 1994, party secretary Li Youwei said that Shenzhen should become a "cosmopolis" (*guo-ji du-shi*). "We have to focus on integration, on convergence with the neighboring territories. . . . Strengthening ties will enable us to become the 'fifth tiger.'. . . We must establish a new urban concept in which the economies of Hong Kong and Shenzhen will become integrated." Convergence with Hong Kong would mean further divergence from the rest of China, however, with the big question being whether the law of economic gravity will cause Shenzhen to be swallowed up by the special administrative region after the resumption of Chinese sovereignty over Hong Kong, in spite of the continued existence of the border after 1997.

In recent years Shenzhen and the other SEZs have become an issue in the national debate on the growing disparity in regional development. Hu Angang, research fellow with the "Study Group of the National Situation" (under the auspices of the Chinese Academy of Social Sciences) and a pioneer of a new egalitarianism, first urged the government in early 1994 to abolish the tax exemptions and other preferential policies that have enabled the SEZs to prosper at the expense of others, leading to an increase in the interregional income gap.[10] He reiterated his demands in several interviews printed in Singapore and Hong Kong newspapers, until the Shenzhen city government became angry and went on the counteroffensive in the summer of 1995, calling Hu an "academic rascal" (*liu-mang*).[11] In Shenzhen's defense, party secretary Li Youwei invoked Deng Xiaoping's instructions that "some regions had to get rich first so as to benefit the whole country later." Shenzhen also had other structural problems, such as the exodus of enterprises that hope to escape the high cost of land, labor, utilities, and services.

After much debate, it was concluded that the essence of the SEZs was not to grant tax exemptions but to continue as laboratories for further experimentation in the market economy. A State Council Work Conference on Special Economic Zones held in Zhuhai in April 1996 decided that the basic state policies for the SEZs would remain unchanged, but as a gesture to poorer regions, the conference abolished the preferential tax treatment. Premier Li Peng called the zones "windows" for reform and opening up, experimental zones for reforming economic structure, which had to take the first steps in the establishment of the market economy and function as special bases for strengthening economic cooperation with Hong Kong, Macau, and Taiwan.[12]

Li went on to say that the SEZ of Shenzhen should be run as a "socialist Hong Kong": the two should "link up" (*xian jie*) but not "link the rail lines" (*jie gui*), as was advocated in the past. Linking the railways would mean connecting Shenzhen to Hong Kong's capitalist system, which is happening in any case but cannot be admitted to openly.

Four areas were selected for new experimentation:

1. Equal treatment of foreigners: China has a nationwide dual-track price system—one for foreigners and one for locals—for hotel accommodations, train and airplane tickets, and entrance fees. Pending nationwide abolition, Shenzhen must first experiment with offering foreigners domestic prices that could make a difference of between 20 and 75 percent.

2. Reform of port management: Shenzhen must be the pioneer in cutting red tape, such as reducing port management departments, simplifying clearance and inspection rules, and raising the professional level of frontier inspection personnel.

3. Improvement of financial services: Shenzhen already has the most

extensive network of banks and other financial services, but it must adopt international standards of service from Hong Kong in order to serve as a halfway house between Hong Kong and the rest of China. Until recently, however, foreign banks were not allowed to do business in local currency. The ban has now been lifted for the Pudong New Area of Shanghai but, alas, not for the Shenzhen SEZ.

4. Encouragement of high-tech development: As processing industries relocate to lower-wage locations, Shenzhen must introduce more advanced industries, such as bioengineering, new materials, and new categories of energy.

Shenzhen has thus acquired a new lease on life by being "neo-special." How long will it take to link up the rail lines with Hong Kong, or will Hong Kong's rail links to the rest of the world be "unlinked" after 30 June 1997?

CHAPTER 7

Hainan: China's "New Hong Kong Plus Taiwan"

> I thought that Africa was the most underdeveloped region in the world, but now I see that it's Hainan.
>
> ZHAO ZIYANG,
> *premier of China, 1983*

IN 1988—when Shenzhen was the unassailable trendsetter for accelerated economic development and its name synonymous with getting rich quick, Zhuhai and Shantou were just getting off the ground, and Xiamen was still waiting for the big influx of Taiwanese—a new breakthrough came in China's zoning. The backward tropical island of Hainan in the South China Sea, an appendix of Guangdong Province, was proclaimed China's thirtieth province and declared in its entirety to be a special economic zone. For generations this island, about half the size of West Virginia, and its 6.6 million inhabitants had been neglected, more recently because its location bordering on the Gulf of Tonkin had put it dangerously close to the smoking guns of the Indochinese wars.

"Immediately upon establishing the province, we started with a new political system which is characterized by the principles 'small government–big society,'" said the governor at the time, Liu Jianfeng, in an interview in July 1992. The fifty-six-year-old Liu was born in the northern port city of Tianjin and had been deputy minister of the Electronics Industry. This demonstrated that Beijing did want to grant freedoms to its deepest Wild South, but also wanted them to be safeguarded by "imperial" Mandarins from the north.

It was relatively easy to start with a small government in unspoiled, remote Hainan, because as yet there was none at all. Like Shenzhen, Hainan was given the legislative autonomy to enact its own flexible laws to further its market economy. When local laws were enacted in any particular area, the socialist laws from Beijing became ineffectual. According to Hainan's governor, "The economic policy of the SEZ of Hainan can be summed up as follows: three times low and three times free—low taxes, low real estate prices, low labor costs; personnel free to come and go, foreigners free to come and go, and a free stream of money and goods both in and out."¹ The latter was very easy because the Hong Kong dollar was the generally accepted currency along with the Chinese yuan. In the capital of Haikou, new high-rise developments sprang up like palm trees, including branches of Hong Kong banks and duty-free shopping malls where one could buy luxury goods with Hong Kong dollars. Architectural harmony and other aesthetic considerations were completely absent. Haikou's specialties were the blinding neon lights of the karaoke bars, nightclubs, hairdressers' establishments with backrooms, and countless "street chicks" under twenty. Hainan was the lawless Sicily of China, where crime, corruption, piracy, and prostitution were rampant.

Governor Liu did not deny this but said that these things should be viewed in perspective: "For historical reasons, the economy of Hainan was extremely underdeveloped, but this has improved a lot. Social services and pensions are the best in China. Crime-fighting is effective and violent crime has been greatly reduced. Prostitution has increased since we opened our doors to the outside world, but we tackle the problems in the order prescribed by Deng Xiaoping. First you take economic development in hand, and then you deal with the negative side effects. You just can't solve these problems in one fell swoop." When asked if Hainan's system could still be called socialism, Liu answered: "We have no 'isms' here. We apply flexible methods to accelerate development and modernization." Hainan thus openly admits to having entered the era of post-Communism, unlike Shenzhen, where the leaders still modify everything with the adjective "socialist."

HAINAN EVEN WENT a step too far in ignoring decrees from Beijing. The pivot of the skyrocketing economy was the real estate sector. Its showpiece was a stock exchange that had started up early in 1992 without permission from Beijing. The central government, however, had become afraid that it would turn into a casino for speculators in real estate and had ordered suspension of its operations. Governor Liu decided to wait and see, saying that he would shoulder all responsibility if things went wrong. And things did go wrong. In April Vice-premier Zhu Rongji, the unbending economic tsar, flew to Haikou. "He swatted us just like a fly," said one of the initiators of the stock exchange. In January 1993 Governor Liu was replaced because he was considered too tolerant of the tropical "catch-as-catch-can culture." Liu returned to his earlier job as deputy minister of the Electronics Industry in Beijing. He wasn't the first in Hainan's tumultuous history to try to make the island catch up with the world too quickly, only to be recalled prematurely.

In 1983 Premier Zhao Ziyang paid a visit to Hainan on his way back to Beijing from a trip through Africa. He was shocked, exclaiming, "I thought that Africa was the most underdeveloped region in the world, but now I see that it's Hainan."[2] Hainan was at that time a "special district" of Guangdong Province. The cities were still unbelievably primitive, and in the mountains lived non-Chinese, indigenous tribes—the Li and the Miao—who were no better off than the people in Somalia or Sudan: women in the frayed rags of their traditional dark blue costumes and naked children covered with sand and flies.

Beijing wanted to change things all at once but did not have the means to do so. Hainan would have to make the money required for modernization, through smuggling and extortion if necessary. It was granted special powers to import seventeen categories of goods duty-free, which normally would have required authorization from the central government. And what happened? Like the dyed-in-the-wool pirates they always have been, the Hainanese imported, duty-free and on the black market, 89,000 luxury cars, 3 million television sets, and countless video recorders and motorcycles with dollars obtained through official bank loans, and sold them for three to eight times their import price on the mainland, where high prices prevailed. Naval vessels lent a helping hand in shipping the stuff "gratis" to mainland ports. All import permits were signed by Lei Yu, who had been sent to the island as an administrative genius with the title "special executive district administrator."

At first Beijing looked the other way, but when Hainan became the flashy importer of Mercedes for the whole of China, it was forced to take action. In just two years' time, Hainan had earned more than half a billion dollars with this "mafia project." Lei Yu had personally signed all import permits and therefore became the scapegoat, although at the same time he was a folk hero who had brought the people of Hainan a life of luxury under the palm trees. Lei was removed from office but otherwise was not blamed for the situation. He had done it not to enrich himself but to further the development of Hainan. Two years later, he became deputy mayor of Canton and shortly thereafter vice-chairman of the neighboring Guangxi-Zhuang Autonomous Region, which was his birthplace.

The mayor of Shenzhen, Liang Xiang, was appointed the first governor of Hainan after it became a province in 1988. He launched the most controversial project ever in the history of China's opening to the outside world: leasing to foreigners (or a foreign consortium) a coastal zone of thirty square kilometers for seventy years—"a new Hong Kong," though on a smaller scale. Hainan's ambitions knew no bounds. In twenty years it hoped to rival Taiwan in industrial strength, Hong Kong in financial scope, and Hawaii in tourist attractions.

Then came the turning point of 1989. After the military suppression of the student revolt, the liberal party leader Zhao Ziyang, Hainan's patron in Beijing, was deposed. There followed a month later the firing "on account of corruption" of Zhao's friend, Governor Liang Xiang, whose biggest mistake was having the wrong friends. His predecessor Lei Yu, who had the right friends, was promoted on account of corruption. Liang was the first victim in the orthodox campaign to curb rampant capitalism in the south. Uncertainty lasted more than two years but was allayed by Deng Xiaoping's blitz in January 1992, in which the eighty-eight-year-old patriarch actually encouraged the freebooters not to be too choosy in the means they employed to stimulate economic growth to the maximum.

THE LEASING of the coastal zone near Yangpu had for more than two years been the most important target of the Stalinist "restorationists," who labeled it capitulation to imperialism and a return to the era of the colonial treaty ports. Deng's trip, however, gave the go-ahead for the resumption of radical reforms. After four years of squabbling, a plan was finally approved at the annual session of the National People's Congress in April 1992 to establish the most special zone within the SEZ of Hainan under conditions unheard of in a sovereign country. For the first time, "late communist China" was to lease a piece of land thirty square kilometers for seventy years to a capitalist consortium managed by the Hong Kong subsidiary of the Japanese construction giant Kumagai-Gumi.[3] The "Yangpu Economic Development Area" (YEDA) lies on a protected bay with a natural harbor 18 meters deep on the northwestern coast of Hainan, 140 kilometers west of Haikou. The project was originally the brainchild of ex-party leader Zhao Ziyang. After his fall in 1989, everything was up in the air for a time, but in August 1992 the lease was signed, in all secrecy so as not to stir up debate again.

China's usual practice until then had been first to open up territories itself, then to build the infrastructure, and finally to lease the land at high rates and for short periods—fifteen to thirty years—to foreign companies. In Yangpu the territory was leased to foreigners all at once at the rate of less than half a dollar per square kilometer for seventy years. The foreigners then had to build everything themselves but were virtually the masters within their own zone. "Yangpu is an SEZ within the SEZ and will have a separate administration and its own customs border. Inside the zone it's like a 'bonded warehouse.' The Chinese government will manage only the administrative sovereignty: in other words, public security, immigration, and customs. Companies will be completely independent in their business, commercial, financial, and technical decisions," said Ding Shilong, director of the zone.

A new city would be built with a population of 400,000, 85 percent of whom would be recruited from the whole of China. Approximately 15 percent would be foreigners. The new city would be fenced off from the rest of the island. Foreigners would also be allowed to work in the service sector, such as real estate, banking, transportation, and tourism. Banks would not be required to pay a preliminary tax on interbank transactions, and the tax on profits was only 15 percent. All goods and materials imported for the purpose of developing the zone, with the exception of consumer goods, would be exempt from import duty. No income tax would be payable on work on infrastructure projects for the first five years, after which the income tax would not exceed 15 percent.

The consortium was required to invest $1.28 billion in the infrastructure during the first five years, and another billion during the second five years. Investments in the infrastructure would eventually amount to $5.75 billion. Kumagai has the right to contract out large projects to subcontractors, the first of whom was Siemens, which contracted to build a power station. The Chinese government will play no further role in this. Chinese officials maintained that the Chinese government had to approve all contracts between Kumagai-Gumi and third parties. C. P. Yu, a Japanese-speaking Chinese from Manchuria who is now chairman of Kumagai-Gumi Hong Kong, showed me the document he signed in August 1992, which states that Kumagai must register all contracts and that no approval from the government is necessary (*dengji, wuxu pizhun*).[4]

This kind of skirmishing showed just how controversial the new project still was. China's aged leaders were especially touchy about Japanese domination of Yangpu and therefore stressed the international character of Kumagai-Gumi Hong Kong, only 29 percent of which was owned by its

Japanese parent company. C. P. Yu owned 13.6 percent of the shares; Li Ka-shing, Hong Kong's largest real estate magnate and one of the richest men in the world, owned 16 percent; and the rest of the shares were in the hands of institutional investors. Other infrastructure projects under construction included a sewage treatment plant, a petrochemical complex, a cement factory, a small airport, and a freeway to Haikou.

Kumagai-Gumi's managing director, Frederick Ma, emphasized the uniqueness of Yangpu, which had never before been recognized. "Many of the megaprojects go broke because of the extremely high cost of land. Here we have thirty square kilometers for a song." He had nothing good to say about the skeptics who see Yangpu merely as one of the many hundreds of new investment zones in China. "Yangpu is in a class by itself, the first zone free of Chinese government control. Numerous companies, domestic Chinese as well as international, want to come here to keep out of the way of Chinese bureaucracy. Even domestic companies prefer to conduct negotiations on a commercial basis with us than [to engage in] bureaucratic negotiations with the government," said Ma.

THAT WAS THE SITUATION in 1992. Three years later, this most revolutionary of projects was still little more than a real estate soap bubble. Siemens had installed two diesel turbines and two gas turbines and the wharf was ready, but other than that there was nothing. Nothing more is heard of Yangpu in the Chinese media because it remains controversial. The regime isn't sure if it should be proud of Yangpu or ashamed of it. The foreign media no longer mention Yangpu because almost nothing is happening there. Leasing the land was no problem, but the twelve hundred real estate companies signed their leases not so much in order to develop the land as for purposes of speculation and subleasing. In Hainan they call it stir-frying the land. "The point is not letting speculation turn it into a ghost town," sighed Frederick Ma in 1993.

Since the end of 1993, even land speculation has stopped because banks no longer extend loans for such activities. Foreign investors also lost their enthusiasm when they discovered that labor was grossly overpriced. There are no well-trained local workers, and importing workers from the mainland is too expensive. Investment in nearby Vietnam, 250 kilometers to the west, is much more profitable and labor is considerably less expensive. Since it will be three or four years before the basic infrastructure is ready, investors are still holding back. On the other hand, there are state enterprises that have started large projects just outside the YEDA under the same preferential conditions but are paying much less rent on the land.[5] They are also able to take advantage of the infrastructure paid for by Kumagai-Gumi, such as the power station. Yangpu's uniqueness—that firms can deal with private land management companies instead of having to wrestle with Chinese bureaucracy—has therefore become a farce. Chinese firms seem actually to prefer their bureaucratic networks for making opaque deals. In 1996 Frederick Ma said that Kumagai-Gumi had reaped profits of HK$1.2 billion from land sales in the zone but had stopped selling land because of the Chinese national austerity program. Only 8 percent of the land had been sold by 1996, and to inject new cash into the project, the company was to obtain a second, separate listing exclusively for the Yangpu project on the Hong Kong stock exchange by the end of 1996. The highway from Haikou to Yangpu is not even under construction yet, because Kumagai-Gumi does not want to take responsibility for it and the government is still trying to think of "creative" ways of financing it. Negotiations are still under way concerning the airport, and it is doubtful whether the project will ever get off the ground.

It is still too early to call Yangpu a complete failure, but since the "zone epidemic" of 1992–93, it has lost its pioneering value, now that there are so many places in China where seventy-year leases on land are available. The high-flown optimism of 1992 has given way to doubt and, at best, hope that Yangpu will one day amount to something after all.

With the adoption in 1994 of a national, uniform system of taxation, Hainan even seems in danger of losing its fiscal attraction. The only unique privilege that Hainan still offers is visa-free entry, to the benefit of business as well as tourism.

HAINAN'S BIGGEST GOLD MINE will have to be tourism, centered on the city of Sanya, which is the southernmost inhabited point of China and therefore in the traditional Chinese view the end of the (civilized) world. It is situated on the same line of latitude as Chiang Mai in northern Thailand. Chinese tourist officials boast that Sanya, once it has been developed, will have more to offer than Bali or Hawaii. Sanya—with its picturesque but dilapidated town center, located on a muddy bay full of stranded junks—is still anything but a Honolulu. Big attractions are near at hand, however: dozens of beautiful, winding beaches with silver-white sand, separated by lagoons and rugged hills.

"We are determined to transform Sanya into an international, tropical, top-class tourist center," said Mayor Wang Yongchun. Development companies from Hong Kong, Singapore, and the rest of the world have already invested hundreds of millions of dollars in building hotels, golf courses, country clubs, and beach attractions.

In 1993 the city drew almost 2.5 million tourists, 90 percent of whom were Chinese, however, who still consume little. In mid-1994 the Phoenix Airport in Sanya was finished, the first airport in China to be owned by a public limited-liability company. It has flights to twenty-four international and domestic destinations, and wide-bodied jets can land there. The optimistic planners think that the flood of international tourists on high budgets is about to materialize. In the spring of 1995 Sanya was the only place in all of China where you could rent a "Beijing Jeep" and discover the island for yourself.

The growth of tourism has nevertheless been far below expectations. The area around Sanya is too primitive, and services are far inferior to those of developed tourist centers in neighboring countries, such as Phuket in Thailand, Penang in Malaysia, and Bali in Indonesia. It will take years for the Chinese to acquire the beach and recreation culture that the middle classes of many other Asian countries long ago made their own. The beaches are magnificent, but the majority of Chinese only thrash about in the water in their underwear, with the grannies stuffing their hiked-up dresses into their underclothes. Remains of homemade picnics blow around on the silver beaches, which in some places look like garbage dumps.

In its next phase of development, Sanya will probably resemble a mini–Las Vegas. The city government has offered a small island of two square kilometers off the coast to businessmen from that American gambling paradise for the purpose of setting up a nightlife complex complete with casinos. The deputy mayor, He Longqin, said that gambling is illegal in China, but that the central government had exempted Sanya to allow for "special facilities," which will help to speed up economic development of the area.[6]

GEOGRAPHICALLY and economically, Hainan is part of commercial Southeast Asia and therein lies the key to its potential success. The waves of well-to-do visitors include descendants of Hainanese who emigrated in past centuries to Thailand, Indonesia, and Singapore and who are now prominent businessmen. Their affinity with the culture and knowledge of the dialect should be a big help in obtaining assistance from the authorities on Hainan to modernize completely.

A serious obstacle to Hainan's being embraced by the regional business community, however, lies in the secluded bays near Sanya, where the head-quarters of the South China Fleet are based. From this point Chinese naval vessels patrol the South China Sea, lending weight—by means of intimida-tion and shelling, sometimes symbolic and sometimes real—to China's du-bious claims to sovereignty over all the archipelagoes in the South China Sea. The most disputed are the Spratly Islands, which lie a thousand kilo-meters to the south of Hainan and only several hundred kilometers from the coasts of Vietnam, the Philippines, and Malaysia. China routinely reaffirms its claims but until recently has refused to found them in international mar-itime law.[7]

The rulers in Beijing have called time and again for the dispute to be set-tled by negotiations and, in anticipation thereof, want to develop the islands with capital from foreign investors. In 1992, China granted an oil franchise to the American company Crestone Energy Corporation, and when Viet-nam, together with an American consortium including Mobil, erected a drilling platform nearby, China sent warships to prevent supplies being brought to the island. In 1995 the Chinese navy built structures on Mischief Reef, a collection of rocks claimed by the Philippines lying two hundred kilometers off the Philippine island of Palawan.

Beijing's talk of peace and display of power are two tactics in the same dialectical game, but they have led to increased concern among the ASEAN countries. The smaller countries in Southeast Asia are fearful of condemn-ing China's claims and behavior openly, thereby taunting the dragon even more. But a Malaysian expert, B. A. Hamzah, chairman of the Malaysian In-stitute for Maritime Affairs, has warned against "Tibetization." "I want to warn the world about what is happening in the South China Sea. Otherwise people will forget about it and later it will become, just like Tibet, a part of China."[8] Beijing's contradictory policy in the South China Sea remains the largest unknown quantity in the long-delayed development of Hainan.

CHAPTER 8

Xiamen: Taiwan's Great Leap to the Mainland

Move all your obsolete machinery to the mainland and
keep the quotas and orders from the international market.

Motto of Taiwanese investors in China

IN 1987 THE XIAMEN SEZ had only twenty companies with Taiwanese
investments, the majority of them assembly plants doing work farmed out
to them. In November of that year, the government of Taiwan lifted the ban
on travel to the mainland, and within a year the number of companies with
Taiwanese investments quadrupled.[1] Of the $740 million of foreign money
invested in Xiamen by the end of 1989, $695 million came from Taiwan. The
Taiwanese had an aversion to joint ventures and wanted to keep their companies completely in their own hands, persuading their Chinese counterparts to accept this. Of the 242 investment projects, 177 were completely
owned by Taiwanese. This was a new tendency and something that the Hong
Kong Chinese had not been able to achieve in the Pearl River delta, where
only 235 of the 5,291 companies were entirely in Hong Kong hands.[2] By the
end of 1991, 369 of the 476 investment projects (77.5 percent) were completely owned by Taiwanese.[3] Most of the investments from Taiwan were in
so-called "sunset industries"—in other words, light industries both labor-
intensive and polluting, such as chemicals and plastic (nearly 48.8 percent),
shoes, paper, textiles, consumer electronics, and aquatic products. More
than 80 percent of the goods produced were destined for export. A popular
saying in Taiwan was "Move all your obsolete machinery to the mainland
and keep your quotas and orders from the international market." In 1991 real

estate became the fastest-growing and most important sector of the economy, after chemicals.

The reason for Hong Kong's thrust into the Pearl River delta six years earlier was nothing other than natural expansion from an urban area that was bursting at the seams. There were no political obstacles. Between China and Taiwan, however, the political obstacles were larger than life, but the price of letting them remain insurmountable had become too high. There were also structural changes in world trade which had forced Taiwanese investments to move to the mainland. In late 1985 Taiwanese economists had already concluded not only that their share of the world market for cheap, labor-intensive products had begun to suffer seriously from Chinese competition, but that a number of their more advanced products were becoming less competitive compared with those of the other three new industrial countries: South Korea, Hong Kong, and Singapore, all three of which buy cheap raw materials directly from China. In 1987, for example, bulk carriers transported coal directly from ports in North China over the Yellow Sea to South Korea, infuriating the North Korean government, while Taiwan was forced for political reasons to buy expensive coal in South Africa (still ruled at the time by President P. W. Botha), placing it in the "International League of Pariah States." The South African ambassador in Taipei said at the time that his country was happy to trade with them, but asked a Taiwanese industrialist why Taiwan didn't buy cheap coal on the Chinese mainland. The Taiwanese rebounded with the question "Why don't you buy oil in Nigeria?"[4]

TWO EVEN MORE formidable external factors compelling Taiwan to restructure its foreign trade were American protectionism and the fall of the U.S. dollar, combined with a parallel rise in the value of East Asia's hard currencies. The New Taiwan dollar had increased in value by 28 percent in two years: from forty New Taiwan dollars to one U.S. dollar in 1986 to twenty-nine to one dollar in 1988. This had seriously weakened Taiwan's competitiveness on the American market. Obviously, market diversification was necessary, and the natural place to expand was China. A former finance minister, Wang Chien-hsien, gave the best rationalization for the Taiwanese entry into the mainland market: "The mainland market is a market for Chinese, and the Chinese from Taiwan shouldn't trail behind the Japanese and Koreans."

Another important factor was of a sociopsychological nature. Taiwanese businessmen were fed up with the increase in crime in Taiwan. Kidnapping millionaires had become a national sport, and there were turbulent political and environmental demonstrations every day. The mainland was a natural escape route, but within a year they discovered that there as well, violent crime, endemic corruption, and political instability were the order of the day.

Xiamen was the first choice of Taiwanese businessmen with investment plans, owing to its geographic proximity, ethnic kinship, and similar dialect. Seventy percent of Taiwan's population of 21 million (then 19.7 million) had originally come from the southern part of Fujian Province, where Xiamen is the largest city. Starting in the middle of the seventeenth century, their ancestors had emigrated to the island, which at that time was still inhabited by non-Chinese aborigines, of whom there are still 350,000. Another 15 percent are Hakkas, originally a kind of Chinese gypsy, who also came from the mainland, and the remaining 15 percent are those who followed the defeated generalissimo Chiang Kai-shek, and they came from all the provinces of China. The Taiwanese businessmen in Xiamen are all indigenous islanders who speak the same dialect, Minnan, forming an exclusive regional subculture in South China and the Chinatowns of Southeast Asia.

At first the Taiwanese were euphoric about the rediscovery of 20 million "regional relatives" on the other side of the 125- to 160-kilometer-wide Taiwan Strait. The South Fujianese were also thrilled about the new opportunities promised by the heaps of money from Taiwan and delighted with the affinity they felt for the new "identical" batch of rich overseas Chinese. After all, they share a language with the Taiwanese, while in the north of their own province a different dialect (Hokcheou) is spoken, which is completely unintelligible to them. At the time, I asked a colleague at the *Xiamen Daily* what it is that binds the Taiwanese and the South Fujianese. "Our love of Zheng Chenggong and our common worship of the goddess Mazu," he replied. Zheng Chenggong, called Koxinga in Western history books, was the seventeenth-century corsair-prince who crossed the Strait from Xiamen to Taiwan in 1660 to drive out the Dutch colonizers. According to popular superstition, Mazu is the regional goddess who also crossed over to Taiwan in the seventeenth century. Her historical temple is situated in Meizhou on the coast, and it is visited every year by large groups of old people from Taiwan who make the roundabout trip via Hong Kong to Fujian solely for this purpose, traveling around with statues of Mazu strapped to their bodies like babies.[5]

THE TIANANMEN DRAMA of 1989 had no effect at all on the eagerness with which the Taiwanese business community threw itself on the Chinese market. On the contrary, in spite of the anti-Communism that was still their article of faith, the Taiwanese viewed the Western sanctions against China as a godsend, enabling them to fill the void that had opened. China welcomed them with open arms and promptly established special investment zones for Taiwan just outside the original SEZ of Huli: Mawei near the provincial capital of Fuzhou, and three in and around Xiamen—Haicang for heavy industry and chemicals, Xinglin for medium-sized companies, and Jimei for light industry.

The driving force behind the new phase in investments was Taiwan's biggest industrialist, Y. C. Wang (Wang Yung-ch'ing) of Formosa Plastics. He proposed a plan to build a complete petrochemical city, including a power station, a naphtha cracker, an oil refinery, a polyethylene plant, a sewage treatment plant, and auxiliary facilities on the coast of Fujian for a total of $7 billion. Formosa Plastics had reached the ceiling in Taiwan and could no longer expand there, owing to new, strict environmental legislation and the high cost of labor and land.

Wang's grandiose plan seemed to be a murky ménage à trois consisting of three ambivalent parties. The government of Taiwan wanted to prevent Wang from setting up such large-scale projects on the mainland. The central government in China and the provincial government in Fujian would rather not bring in so many environmentally unfriendly industries and open up the domestic market to them. Perhaps Wang played his China card in order to pressure the government in Taipei into being more flexible and letting him expand his business in Taiwan. If that was his aim, then he was successful. In early 1993, after seven years of negotiations, the government of Taiwan granted him extraordinarily favorable conditions to enable him to build a still larger project worth $9.5 billion, including a sixth naphtha cracker, on a series of new, still-to-be-reclaimed islands in the sea next to Yunlin on the west coast of Taiwan, where the distance to Xiamen is the shortest.[6] From that point he will be able to serve efficiently the hundreds of Taiwanese firms in Xiamen and the rest of Fujian that use his raw materials. By the time the project is completed, around the year 2000, there will undoubtedly be a complete network of direct shipping links. Staying in Taiwan will also facilitate his struggle against his Japanese and South Korean competitors in the world market.

In the expectation that Y. C. Wang would set up a complete upstream base for raw materials for the plastics industry, more and more small, downstream Taiwanese chemical producers had moved to Xiamen, so that Taiwanese investments there are dominated by the rubber and plastics industry: automobile tires, toys, artificial flowers, umbrellas, and so on. This conflicted with Xiamen's original master plan of becoming a center of computer technology and precision mechanics. Even the later, readjusted goal of attracting mainly Taiwanese electronics firms has not been reached. Y. C. Wang's playing for time has nevertheless turned Xiamen against its will into a center for the chemical industry. Although after ample deliberation Wang finally decided to build his mammoth project on the other side of the Strait, Formosa Plastics did start up several smaller-scale activities in Xiamen to the tune of $70 million.

Within the space of only a couple of years, Taiwanese investors contributed greatly to Xiamen's economy. They brought work with them, paying their workers more than twice as much as the local state enterprises, although working conditions in many companies, just as in those in the Pearl River delta, left much to be desired.[7] In the spring of 1995, 100,000 of the 400,000 industrial workers in the Xiamen region were working for Taiwanese companies.[8] Moreover, the investors played a decisive role in China's rise as an export power. In 1992 China's toy exports rose by 41 percent and its shoe exports by 44.3 percent.[9]

The changes that the Taiwanese industries wrought on the region of Xiamen, however, were less sweeping than those caused by Hong Kong on the Pearl River delta, where complete osmosis and integration of the two socioeconomic systems took place, with populations that also shared a common language, Cantonese. The Taiwanese brought "social dualism" to Xiamen, and there was no integration of the indigenous state sector and the Taiwanese private sector, so that one could speak of "one city–two systems." Many state enterprises lost their best-trained workers and foremen to Taiwanese factories, which exacerbated the serious breakdown and demoralization of the state sector.

IN THE LATE 1980s the differences in way of life on both sides of the Taiwan Strait were still very great, much greater than those between Hong Kong and the Pearl River delta. There was, moreover, Shenzhen, an artificial settlers' town of adventurers and gold diggers, built as a buffer zone and accustomed to quite a lot of excitement from outside. During the Mao era, Hong Kong television had already brought the people there into contact with the "normal" world. Xiamen, on the other hand, had remained an isolated, conservative city for much longer. The playboy-like lifestyle and wild wining and dining engaged in by many Taiwanese businessmen led in the early years to animosity and was denounced as hedonism (*xiang-le zhu-yi*) by ideologues. Doing business until late at night, accompanied by Chinese singers, hostesses, dancing girls, and masseuses, is the normal state of affairs for young, well-to-do Asian businessmen. Many Taiwanese immediately acquired mistresses in Xiamen, for whom they bought apartments equipped with fax machines, thereby setting themselves up with an extra office and a comfortable "parallel life." It was called "one family–two systems," and in 1991–92 the police in Xiamen launched an offensive against this practice. Typical action taken to punish offenders was stamping *piao-ke* (whoremonger) in the passports of those caught in the act. Taiwanese businessmen punished in this way would then report the loss or theft of their passports upon their arrival in Hong Kong. The Communist newspaper *Wen Wei Po* in Hong Kong held the government in Taiwan responsible for this evil practice on account of its refusal to establish direct air links with the mainland, which would have enabled businessmen to fly home in one hour. Using the indirect air link via Hong Kong meant traveling for two days.

In the early 1990s the number of "girlie clubs," luxury barbershops, and saunas (euphemisms for whorehouses) in Taiwan decreased considerably. According to an official in Taipei, there were two reasons for this: as prosperity rose, there were fewer and fewer girls in Taiwan who were willing to do this kind of work, and more and more of their clientele had a permanent address on the mainland. Sex had also become a "sunset industry" in Taiwan.

Tolerance and pragmatism have increased in China accordingly. Li Shuquan, head of the Bureau for Taiwanese Affairs of the municipal government in Xiamen, said in 1995 that the Taiwanese are good managers and that their companies are eight times as profitable and efficient as state enterprises. "The flip side of the coin is their high consumer needs, tax evasion, and hedonism, but we think they may decide for themselves how to spend their free time."

EVEN THOUGH the government of Hong Kong had let the law of comparative advantage have completely free rein, Hong Kong is now largely deindustrialized and the service sector makes up 80 percent of its economy. The scale of economic integration between Hong Kong and South China now knows no limits.

For reasons of political and national security, the government of Taiwan continues to play an admonitory and restrictive role in the Great Leap of its business community to the mainland. Businessmen have interpreted these restrictions creatively and, where possible, have dodged them as their only means of combating competition from Hong Kong, Singapore, and South Korea. The official policy of the government in Taipei has continually been adjusted depending on the pressure exerted by business circles and the activities of the competition in China. In 1992 investments were authorized in 3,764 labor-intensive, low-technology categories. In 1994 the number was increased to 4,196. Capital-intensive petrochemicals, cement, and industrial parks would be considered case by case. Investments in four hundred high-tech and defense projects were still completely prohibited. This actually meant that indirect investments in China were to be permitted in the future as long as the company concerned was willing to invest more in Taiwan and keep its "roots" there.

The government nevertheless prevented Acer, Taiwan's largest producer of PCs, from investing $10 million in a circuit-board factory in Guangzhou. Neither was Taiwan's largest shipping company, Evergreen, allowed to build a container terminal in Shanghai. Cheng Shin Rubber International, in early 1995 Taiwan's largest tire producer, received an injunction from the government prohibiting its setting up an automobile and bicycle tire factory in Shanghai worth $30 million. The reason given was that they already had a factory in Xiamen and that the two investments together would have amounted to 53 percent of Cheng Shin's total capital. This was seen as a dangerous development for the Taiwanese economy and a risk for Cheng Shin's customers in Taiwan itself.

Reliable and uniform figures for Taiwanese investments have always been difficult to find. According to the *Asian Wall Street Journal,* $3.8 billion was registered at the government in Taiwan, but according to the Chinese government, the cumulative total was $14.5 billion. Some officials in Taiwan think that if real estate were included, the amount would exceed $20 billion.[10] The SEZ of Xiamen, which was given the nickname "the Shenzhen of Taipei," was good for an estimated one-seventh of the total. According to the eighth Five-Year Plan for Xiamen, Taiwanese firms produced 55 percent, or 12 billion yuan, of the GNP, which amounted to 22 billion yuan in 1995. The investments' technological influence remained limited, however, because of high-tech restrictions imposed by the government in Taipei, which resulted in Y. C. Wang's decision to stay away.

THE POLITICAL BAROMETER measuring relations between China and Taiwan is aptly illustrated by the course of events in Haicang (literally, "dark blue sea"), the zone specially reserved in 1989 for large Taiwanese projects. In the hope that Y. C. Wang would clinch the deal, Xiamen had reserved 20 kilometers of the one-hundred-square-kilometer Haicang zone for the exclusive use of Formosa Plastics. When announcing this, Xiamen hastened to add that if Wang were to decide not to invest there after all, then the area would welcome other investors. In support of Wang's petro-city, Xiamen had invested 900 million yuan in the infrastructure, one-third of which had been paid for by the central government.

After Wang's decision to stay in Taiwan, Vice-premier Zhu Rongji, "the economic tsar," paid his third visit to Haicang in February 1994, accompanied by a hundred senior officials from various economic departments. He changed the original name given in 1989 from "Haicang Taiwan Investment Zone" to "Haicang Project Investment Zone." In doing so, he meant to convey the message that Taiwanese enthusiasm had cooled and that the zone had been opened up to investors from other regions and countries. In the meantime, the Swedish-Swiss heavy-industrial concern Asea–Brown Boveri has built a switch-gear factory and the Japanese firm Matsushita has established a video recorder factory completely in Japanese hands. The Rotterdam company Paktank, under the Chinese name of Bo Tan, is building an oil depot with twenty tanks (200,000 cubic meters), involving investments of $60 million, 40 percent of which comes from the parent company, Pakhoed. Negotiations have been under way for two years with large American chemical concerns regarding alternatives for Y. C. Wang's multi-billion-dollar project.

The deputy director of the Haicang zone, Zou Pinzhu, invoked the law of unintended results to rationalize the unsuccessful deal with Y. C. Wang: "Y. C. Wang put Haicang on the map of the international investment world and we thank him for it. He abandoned his big project and we criticize him for that. But we understand it. Why he abandoned it, only Y. C. Wang himself knows. We're still friends."[11] What turned the scales for Wang—whether it was the fact that China would not give him unlimited access to the domestic market or whether he succumbed to pressure and the kid-glove treatment from Taipei—no one in Taiwan knows for sure. Wang will one day carry through with large projects in China, but then in the area of Shanghai and Canton. He will be able to serve Fujian from his new offshore base in Taiwan itself.

Wang's decision to postpone his megaprojects in China for an indefinite period was and still is the most spectacular demonstration of the strength of Taiwan's trump card to avoid being "swallowed up" by China.

IN THE SPRING of 1995, I was in the Xinling district of Xiamen and visited Keentech, an ultramodern Taiwanese company that makes tennis rackets from carbon and fiberglass for worldwide export. The spotless factory has 950 employees and produces between 660,000 and 1 million rackets per year. It is a combination of high technology and labor-intensive work. The carbon-fiber paper is brought in from Taiwan, cut into strips in Xiamen, folded into molds, and then vulcanized. The final emergence of light-weight, elegant rackets in all the colors of the rainbow is a multistep process. Ten million dollars has been invested in the factory, but according to manager David Shiau, "That amount has to be recovered in four years." Why? "Because relations between the two sides of the Strait are too unstable," he said in the presence of an official from the district council. He didn't think a major crisis would erupt, but thought that sooner or later China's political views on attracting Taiwanese investments would end in a dramatic de-nouement in the form of force or a display of power.[12] Trade with and investments from Taiwan remain, after all, an instrument, a prelude to bringing about political reunification—if not willingly, then unwillingly.

The future of the model factory was not Shiau's only concern. He had enough daily problems as it was. There were eight Taiwanese managers among them. "There are enough Taiwanese who want to come here, but most of them only for a short time. The working hours are too long, four-teen hours a day. And the pressure is too much. The mainlanders' work ethic is so different. In Taiwan there is teamwork between managers and foremen. Not here. There's always something to worry about, even when you're lying in bed. They don't close the taps, don't clean anything, don't turn the ma-chines off, never give them proper maintenance. This morning I fired some-one on the spot because he was willfully damaging a machine. Why? Because he had to pay a fine for ignoring safety regulations. There's not one govern-ment organ that takes care of these things."

Shiau went on to say that legislation is satisfactory, but its implementa-tion inadequate. "The top officials in the city government and also the dis-trict council are all right, but the greed of the lower echelons knows no bounds." Other complaints are that the local schools are unsuitable for Tai-wanese children and that there are no proper banks. "There is only one country in the whole world where the banks always say that they have no money," said Shiau. The Taiwanese banks have all asked for permission to open branches, but the Taiwanese government will not let them come yet.[13] Considering the companies' mixed results, lack of investment protec-tion, corruption, constant changes in policy such as cooling-off programs with "tight money" politics, fear for personal safety, and the restrictive pol-icy of the government in Taipei, it is no wonder that the "mainland fever" of the Taiwanese business community is on the decline. Only small companies with obsolete machinery and technology, which could no longer survive in

Taiwan, have moved by the thousands to the mainland without giving it further thought. All the others make the move only on terms favorable to themselves.

THE ALTERNATIVE DESTINATION for investment is Southeast Asia, which has an assortment of rapidly growing economies from Indonesia to Thailand, including Vietnam. Language barriers exist here as well, but the countries are smaller, better organized, less lawless, and more inclined to give-and-take. Taiwanese investments in the Philippines amounted to approximately $1 billion by the end of 1993, in Vietnam $2 billion, in Indonesia $4.5 billion, in Thailand $5 billion, and in Malaysia $6 billion. During the first half of 1994, there were twenty-seven new projects under contract in Malaysia worth $329 million with another $971 million on the way, including a steel plant.

In the realm of trade as well, there was constant concern about Taiwan being in the danger zone. The government in Taipei had declared the ceiling to be 10 percent of total trade, otherwise trade dependence would reach an unacceptable risk level. At the end of 1993, it was 5.3 percent, but taking into consideration the large trade surplus, the export dependence was more than 8.8 percent. By the end of 1994, China and Hong Kong had become the biggest source of Taiwan's trade surplus by far, estimated at $20 billion. Much of that trade is with the twelve thousand Taiwanese firms on the mainland.

The Board of Foreign Trade in Taipei warned at the end of 1994 in alarming terms that China, owing to the starting up of various new industries, would soon no longer need entire categories of products from Taiwan. Taiwan should therefore invest much more in research and development and accelerate technological upgrading and diversification of export markets.

Casper Shih, director of the China Productivity Center in Taipei, which is in charge of the transformation of Taiwan's industry to higher technology, finds all these political and diplomatic concerns exaggerated and argues for far-reaching cooperation with China's scientific research institutes as soon as possible. According to him, they have an unparalleled wealth of basic research results but are lacking the R and D and the management necessary to commercialize them. "The mainland is rich in missile technology, microbiology, medicine, optics, and nuclear physics. Taiwan has first-class computer and information technology, aircraft construction, engines and electrical appliances. They could help each other in upgrading, but first must come trust and strategic, long-term vision," says Shih. Wen C. Ko, president of WK Technology Fund, who advises local companies and provides them with capital for their internationalization, including moving to the mainland, rejects Shih's ideas as those of someone walking with his head in the clouds and falling into a trap. "American libraries are full of inventions and research results on paper. That is not to say that they could quickly become profitable." He said that Taiwan must continue to integrate its economy up to 70 or 80 percent with those of Japan, Western Europe, and the United States, and not more than 20 to 25 percent with the mainland. "If we plunge in completely, then we'll regress," said Ko.[14]

DESPITE NUMEROUS RESERVATIONS in Taiwan on further trade and investment expansion on the mainland, there are overwhelming reasons, given by the government as well as by the business community, for doing it anyway. Taiwan's prospects for continued and relatively high economic growth are inextricably tied to the further opening up of the Chinese market. Considering the continued liquidation of labor-intensive industries in Taiwan and the necessity for industrial diversification, the service sector, especially transportation, has enormous potential to serve the whole East Asian region. This can only be taken advantage of to the fullest if there are direct transportation links to China. The first step is the plan devised by Vincent Siew, during his short tenure as chairman of the Mainland Affairs Council, to set up an offshore center as camouflage for direct shipping links. Furthermore, the likelihood of various industrial sectors in Taiwan being able to create multinationals depends on expansion of their production base on the mainland. President Enterprises, Taiwan's largest foodstuffs conglomerate, wants to play a major role in the world market, but if it does not drastically expand its activities on the mainland, it will lose its battle against the Charoen-Pokphand Group (*Jia-Tai*), a Thai-Chinese multinational. President Enterprises has nine factories in China, some as remote as Xinjiang, mainly for the production of instant noodles, but also of various other products such as ketchup.

Xiamen also has important reasons to intensify relations with Taiwan. During my fourth visit there in early 1995, the Taiwan Affairs Office explained that the zigzag development in trade and investments since 1993 has had a negative influence on Xiamen, not only on the industrial economy but also on tourism. Like Shenzhen, Xiamen also has an identity problem as a special economic zone, now that there are so many new zones all over the country. "The continued specialness of Xiamen lies in its acting as a base for national reunification [with Taiwan]," said Vice-mayor Zhu Yayan.[15] The weekly *Liaowang* (Outlook) gave more details and stated that Xiaman should exploit even further the proximity of Taiwan, move forward and step up the construction of the new system (the market economy), attract high technology as the main pillar of the economy, and build more harbors.[16] Existing harbors, hovercraft and ferry services, and airlines are all ready to start services to Taiwan, as soon as it becomes politically feasible. The distance from Xiamen to Taichung is 126 nautical miles, to Kaohsiung 167 nautical miles, and to Quemoy, the coastal island that is still governed by Taipei, 8 nautical miles. The Port Authority in Xiamen had hoped to establish direct links in 1995, but their hopes were dashed by the crisis over President Lee Teng-hui's trip to the United States. At the end of 1996, the outlook is still uncertain.

To speed things up, Xiamen introduced even more preferential measures for Taiwan businessmen, but response so far has been lukewarm. "The Taiwanese who want to live in Xiamen for a long time should be given the same rights as local citizens," said Vice-mayor Zhu. He presented me with a copy of Xiamen's recently ratified "Regulations for the Protection of Investments of Compatriots from Taiwan." The rules offer new guarantees against nationalization, increase the number of investment categories and tax exemptions, and grant Taiwanese the right to establish bank branches, a Chamber of Commerce, and special schools for their children. Taiwanese may be issued a passport of the People's Republic alongside their Taiwanese (Republic of China) passport, or a travel document that entitles them to enter and leave Xiamen without a visa. They may also obtain a "temporary residence permit" that gives them the right to vote in elections for local government organs, such as the district and municipal people's congress. The temporary residence permit also allows them to buy train and airplane tickets at domestic rates, and Taiwanese driver's licenses will be valid in Xiamen as well. Vice-mayor Zhu said that the Taiwanese are very enthusiastic about the new rights and that more than a thousand of them have applied for residence permits. Altogether eight hundred Taiwanese managers and businessmen live in Xiamen, many of them with their families. It is not to be expected, however, that the measures will attract a new wave of Taiwanese investments until the severe political chill of 1995–96 begins to thaw. And this will take a long time. By the end of 1996, China had further tightened the noose of diplomatic isolation around Taiwan's neck by pressuring South Africa into breaking off diplomatic ties, the biggest blow to Taiwan since the closure of the Saudi Arabian and South Korean embassies in the early 1990s. A new siege mentality is emerging in Taiwan, strengthening the government's resolve to block any major new investment in China.

But with or without restrictions, Taiwanese investments have been a decisive factor in the transformation of Xiamen from a small city of 442,000 inhabitants to one of the most dynamic, cosmopolitan cities in China. In terms of numbers of inhabitants, Xiamen is not even among the top fifty cities in China, but in terms of importance it is number ten, with the fourth-largest international airport and the sixth-largest harbor. In the coming years, consulates will be opened there by various Southeast Asian countries whose populations include large numbers of descendants of Xiamen immigrants. Xiamen will not really begin to take off, however, until relations between China and Taiwan have been normalized.

PART THREE

Economic Hypergrowth Versus Political Stagnation

CHAPTER 9

Political Reforms, 1981–86: Labyrinth Without Exit

Reforming communism is like baking snowballs.

LESZEK KOLAKOWSKI,
Polish Marxist philosopher

AS SEEN in the first two parts of this book, Hong Kong and Taiwan have made essential contributions to the metamorphosis of China from a predominantly state economy to economic pluralism and from a socialist monoculture to an eclectic pop culture. Going by the precedent in many other developing countries suggesting that economic modernization naturally leads to political modernization, the chance that Hong Kong and Taiwan might also contribute to the evolution of the Leninist political culture seemed greater before the crisis of 1989 than afterward.

Since the Tiananmen tragedy, the Chinese regime has rigorously staved off political-ideological interaction with the *free* parts of China. Hong Kong was punished for its exuberant support of the protest movement: China is blocking the process of democratization there, although since 1992 the British governor Chris Patten has paid little attention to it. China has also tried to influence the internal political evolution in Taiwan, but with little success. The recent elections in 1995 and 1996, which will make Hong Kong predominantly democratic and Taiwan completely so, are new challenges for the Communist regime, which has no electoral mandate with the exception of village and district councils. There is still the possibility that Hong Kong and Taiwan will become the future catalysts of democratization in China.

From the late 1970s until the crisis in 1989, the prospects for political reform seemed greater than they do in 1997. Only the most conservative elderly politicians and the most reactionary ideologues were obsessed during the 1980s with the fear that any political change would destabilize the country. After 1989, and especially after the upheavals in Eastern Europe and the Soviet Union, patriarch Deng Xiaoping began to share that fear, with the result that, until his death in February 1997, all movement had come to a standstill. Neither are his successors expected to launch any initiatives toward major political reform anytime soon.

Since the epic Democracy Wall Movement at the beginning of the Deng era (1978), the pendulum of tolerance and repression has swung back and forth continuously. Deng Xiaoping had permanent and varying opposition to contend with, first from the remaining Mao loyalists, then from the army—which was forced to surrender the high budgets and power it had amassed during the Cultural Revolution—and finally, opposition continuing to the present day from conservative, aged ideologues, who fear that Deng's legacy will ultimately lead to complete Westernization and subversion of the socialist system.

Slowly but surely, Deng worked to consolidate his power, and the first step necessary was eliminating the orthodox Maoists. Wall posters (*dazibao*) criticizing Mao's heir Hua Guofeng and the remaining followers of the Gang of Four suited Deng perfectly. They were tolerated with ill-concealed gloating, but "blasphemous" attacks on Mao himself and the Communist system—which still called itself infallible—were likewise attacks on all of the rehabilitated Mao opponents. Deng and his comrades had been servants of Mao for the greater part of their careers and had more to hide than they cared to admit.

New times had come, however. The Chinese thought the worst was over; now things could only get better. Many, including critical intellectuals, thought that in the dialectic, polar (under)world of the Chinese Communists, the bad guys of yesterday were now the good guys. It was generally thought that humiliation and exile, and especially the cruelty shown to Deng's son by the Red Guards, had brought about a catharsis, a moral cleansing, and that the old Deng was now more human. His speeches of that period, or in any case the edited versions produced by the massive ideological apparatus, show little sign of this, however. Deng's most important policy speeches were sometimes published years after the event. Through channels in Hong Kong, Taiwan, or the United States (the CIA), there were sometimes different versions in circulation that suggested an enlightened, liberal Deng.

Wall posters were banned during various waves of repression, but the eventual suppression of the whole movement did not take place until the spring of 1981, at which time the party leadership experienced another coughing fit in the aftermath of the trial against the Gang of Four. Unlike the amorous Mao, Deng was a real puritan and had already lashed out at libertine excesses, such as Chinese girls who had sold "body, soul, and country," "swinging their hips" and dancing with foreigners. It was the same speech in which he had decreed the fearsome Four Cardinal Principles, which would be used like a whip in the coming years to uphold the dictatorship of the party.[1] A telling illustration of Deng's view of the world is a passage from his diatribe against the Democracy Wall writers: "There is also a so-called 'Society Advocating a Thaw,' which has issued a manifesto that openly opposes the dictatorship of the proletariat for the reason that it divides mankind. How can we tolerate this kind of freedom of expression, which is a flagrant violation of our constitution?"[2] The kind of spontaneous freedom of expression that Mao had anchored in the constitution—the four great freedoms: hanging up wall posters, conducting debates, holding demonstrations, and the right to strike—were abolished on orders from Deng during a session of the Standing Committee of the National People's Congress in September 1980.[3]

BY THE SPRING of 1980 Deng's ideological about-face had been largely accomplished. The Cultural Revolution had been discredited as a "disgusting catastrophe which overwhelmed our entire nation,"[4] economic reform was solidly on its rails, and the most notorious Maoists, the so-called "Gang of Four Junior," had been expelled from the party in March. The most prominent victim of Mao's erratic, bloody tyranny—ex-president Liu Shaoqi—was solemnly rehabilitated in May under Deng's pontificate.

Deng now intended to institutionalize the new order by means of far-reaching "political reforms." He delivered his first important address on this subject in August 1980, but owing to opposition from orthodox left ideologues, it was not made public until 1982. Deng's ignorance and crass ideological blindness to Western democracy is amazing indeed. And the contrast between his ambitions and the minimum steps necessary to realize them is just as unbelievable. Deng pretended that it was China's goal to catch up with the developed capitalist countries—without setting a deadline[5]—to create a higher level of democracy with more substance than those of the West, and to train better experts. He observed that China's socialist system was imperfect, especially because it lacked the rule of law.

It was nevertheless "much better than the capitalist system, which is based on the law of the jungle and the principle of getting ahead at the expense of others." In his ideological need to paint the West black, Deng often contradicted himself: "Stalin undermined socialist legality to a serious extent and did things that Chairman Mao said were impossible in Western countries like England, France, and the United States. In spite of the fact that Chairman Mao was aware of this, he did not solve problems like these in our country."[6]

Deng's analysis of China's problems did not go beyond the organizational realm. He also closed his eyes to the cultural-philosophical dimensions of democracy and summed up China's problems as follows:

- bureaucracy, which leads to the abuse of power;
- overconcentration of power (in party committees), which obstructs democratic procedures;
- patriarchal methods;
- functionaries holding lifelong positions with all attending privileges.

Deng's solution consisted of five steps, the first being a constitutional overhaul that would regulate the people's right to manage state and enterprise organs and other institutions. He specifically mentioned improving the system of people's congresses on all levels. Fifteen years later, only the lowest level of people's congresses are elected, those at the village and district level, and elected members who fail to please party secretaries are prevented from taking office. Another step was instituting a Central Discipline Inspection Commission, mainly responsible for fighting corruption, which it does, though on a selective basis. At the same time, a host of methods would be necessary to curtail the power of party committees. This was especially aimed at companies in which aged party secretaries with no expertise were getting in the way of younger and better-trained managers. The main goal of these modest "reforms," which were called "Gengshen reforms" after the year 1980 in the Chinese calendar, was to improve the prospects for increasing productivity in the state enterprises.

Their desired effect politically was probably of secondary importance, but they are nevertheless recorded in the history of the Deng era as the first phase of political reforms. Deng's adviser at this time was Liao Gailong, one of the trendsetting party historians, whose conviction that the power of party committees had to be crushed at the base was inspired by his study of the situation in Poland, where workers had taken the law into their own hands and founded the trade union Solidarity. Liao believed that China faced the same problems, although they did not become acute until 1989 and again in 1994.

The big dilemma in 1981–82 was this: Who is the real Deng Xiaoping? He was undoubtedly a pragmatist par excellence and anyway preferable to the others in that clique of gerontocrats, whose lust for power remained undiminished till the day they died. Did he have only one "zero option": to renounce Mao's worst aberrations in order to put China without further zigzagging and delay on the track of accelerated economic development? Or did he have a more enlightened view of China's future: a somewhat more modern political structure in which a minimum of checks and balances would curb the worst excesses and abuses of power by Communist potentates. According to Liao Gailong and a new version of Deng's speech of 1980, Deng had supported far more radical proposals to restrict the party's power, including the institution of a two-house parliament, one house with regional representatives and the other with functional (party) representatives. Independent trade unions would not be permitted, but workers would be allowed to choose their own leaders. Liao also suggested having a free, independent press. If these later versions of Deng's intentions are authentic, then one must conclude that he concurred, or at least was prepared to experiment, but was not powerful enough to get his way. In the style of China's classical military philosopher Sun Zi, he tactically withdrew and declared himself the victor.

Only a part of the Gengshen reforms, even the minimal version, were ever carried out. There was more tolerance and flexibility in the cultural and literary realm, but it was bestowed as a favor from above, not granted as a codified right. The eight so-called "democratic fringe parties" (see Chapter 1) were once again encouraged to put forward opinions, although any opinions with more than symbolic content were ignored. The Deng regime had consolidated its power as an informal oligarchy full of contradictions, whereby Vice-premier Deng, later on only chairman of the Central Military Commission, arbitrated behind the scenes and usually, though not always, had the last word. The constitution was referred to only when convenient, though not in essentials. Real political reforms were put on a back burner for five years.

WHAT DID OCCUR in the years between 1981 and 1986 in the midst of the continuous "left-right swing of the pendulum between repression and tolerance" was a liberalization of cultural and intellectual life and of society as a whole. The driving force behind this was not Deng Xiaoping but the formal number one in the hierarchy, party general secretary Hu Yaobang. Hu, eleven years younger than Deng Xiaoping, was the odd man out in the gray, sinister, ruthless world of the Chinese Communists. The greatest tribute to Hu Yaobang was paid to him after his fall in 1987 by the prominent journalist Liu Binyan, who now lives in exile in the United States: "He was not mean." In other words, the others are. He was a party hack of high caliber, but with deep emotions. The son of a poor peasant, Hu was born in 1915 in Hunan Province, where Mao Zedong was born. He received little formal education but was an unusually well-read autodidact and spent a large part of his career working in the Communist Youth League, to which he owed his great affinity with the younger generation and the problems of intellectuals. Out of an inborn sense of justice, Hu, as director of the personnel and organization department of the party, had since 1977 rehabilitated all the victims of the Mao era and restored them to their senior posts. Ironically, this became one of the main causes of chronic instability and power struggles during the 1980s and after. These old men had admittedly opposed Mao, but most of them were not reformists and certainly not at all liberal, and it was they who now made it impossible for Hu Yaobang to be an effective, innovative leader.

Hu's main objectives as party leader were to clear away the havoc wreaked among intellectuals by Maoism and to restore the spirit of trust between intellectuals and the party which had existed at the beginning of the revolution. He hoped in this way to improve the prospects of building a scientific structure for China's advancement, to set up think tanks for political and social reforms, and to achieve a renaissance in art and literature. Only in his first goal did he receive wholehearted support from Deng Xiaoping, because this served his historical goal of making China rich and powerful. Deng was indifferent to Hu's other two aims. He let Hu get on with things, and when conflicts arose he kept his distance or else sided with Hu's aged opponents.

The first test of strength occurred in 1981, when the opportunistic party theoretician Hu Qiaomu (then seventy-two) opened fire on the writer Bai Hua, who had asked himself in his play *Unrequited Love* whether Communist China really deserved the love of its citizens. Hu Yaobang and his "network of liberal intellectuals" in top positions tried to check this character assassination of Bai Hua from the outset. His rehabilitated, elderly colleagues, however—with Deng Xiaoping's approval—thought that the play, and the film version, "reflected a mistaken ideological trend with a great deal of negative social influence which will unleash an epidemic, harming the mental health, stability, and unity of the masses."[7] Hu Yaobang was successful in averting the worst of the onslaught aimed at Bai Hua, but the affair established a precedent that still holds today: not only is the general secretary of the party's Central Committee—formally the highest policy maker and executive in the country—not the highest authority, but he has a board of aged guardians above him (the remaining veterans of the Long March of the 1930s), and he also has no power to prevent them from taking all kinds of initiatives that run counter to his political convictions. This precedent was institutionalized at the Party Congress in 1982. At the instigation of Deng Xiaoping, a Central Advisory Commission was formed, which he had originally intended as a political teahouse to which his elderly colleagues, himself excluded, could be relegated. Instead, it became a new organ of power that obstructed the freedom of movement of the younger reformists, even to the extent of sabotaging their efforts. There was in fact a certain amount of political reform, though not in the direction of democracy. It tended, rather, toward an institutionalized gerontocracy. Rejuvenation at the top, another strategic goal of Deng Xiaoping, was completely out of the question. At the National People's Congress in 1983, the seventy-four-year-old conservative Li Xiannian was chosen president. The newly chosen vice-president, the seventy-five-year-old Liao Chengzhi, died before he could take office, and the seventy-nine-year-old Mongolian Ulanhu was installed in his place.

Hu Qiaomu and his coinquisitor Deng Liqun (often called Little or Young Deng) subsequently launched a campaign against writers and prominent journalists who depicted the alienation and dehumanization of socialism. Both "supercommissars," as they were called, lobbied Deng Xiaoping during the whole of 1983 to initiate a much broader witch-hunt for all new "liberal" tendencies, collectively called "spiritual pollution." On 12 October 1983 Deng Xiaoping gave a comprehensive speech at a party plenum in which he defined this phenomenon as "all corrupt and decadent ideas of the bourgeoisie and other exploitative classes and the sowing of distrust of socialism and the leadership of the Communist party."

At the end of November, the commissars were given the go-ahead for an attack on members of Hu Yaobang's network of intellectuals, among whom were writers, legal philosophers, Euro-Marxists, political scientists, and others. For the overzealous work and inspection teams that were sent out across the country, there was no end of targets: Western literature, music, clothing (including spike heels), makeup, pornography, rock music, and even new domestic capitalist phenomena, such as bank accounts held by peasants, who had become rich since the decollectivization of agriculture and the disbandment of the people's communes.

Hu Yaobang and Premier Zhao Ziyang quickly took up the counter-offensive, warning Deng Xiaoping that if the leftist martinets were not restrained, a new Cultural Revolution might break out, and China might revert once again to a dreary mass of blue and gray ants, driving out foreign investors. When leftist ideological campaigns threatened to have negative repercussions for Deng's economic reforms, he immediately took action. The campaign against spiritual pollution was stopped.

THE NATIONAL DEBATE over the intended second round of political reforms began in the fall of 1984 with the historic resolution on urban industrial reforms. The program of agricultural reforms, which had begun in 1979, had been relatively uncomplicated: abolish the straitjacket of the communes, let the peasants take up family farming again, and allow them to sell their produce on the free market. Reforming the political structure was not strictly necessary to accomplish this. Transforming the colossal state enterprises, some with as many as 200,000 employees, into rational and efficient corporations was another thing altogether and meant breaking the domination of ministries and party committees. This did require political reform, including a complete redefinition of the role of the party in the state, the economy, and society.

The academic and political debate on this subject ran parallel to a new, unprecedented blossoming in literature and the arts. The starting signal was the great debate on Marxism in December 1984, which was like a boxing match. The first blow was a commentary on the front page of the *People's Daily,* personally inspired by Hu Yaobang and directed against the orthodox Marxist exegetes. Marx had written his works more than a hundred years earlier, and they were not all relevant to the social realities of the time. Since then, monumental changes had taken place in every realm. "We cannot expect that the works of Marx and Lenin of that time can still offer solutions to our present problems."

Ideologues issued a call to arms, and a rectification was printed the next day: Marx and Lenin were extremely relevant in finding solutions to present-day problems, though perhaps not all of them. The next round came a couple of weeks later, using forceful language to state that Marx was not only irrelevant but even harmful with his simple theory that trading goods and money would become superfluous in socialist society. Hu Yaobang's intellectuals had acquired a taste for debate, and the writers' conference at the end of December became the high point in the liberal tide. Hu Yaobang's lieutenant, Hu Qili, encouraged writers to choose their own subjects and modes of expression and to cast off the political-ideological strait-jacket of bygone days.

In the party, a new rectification campaign was held against cadres and senior military officers who opposed economic reforms. There were various indications that Deng Xiaoping now openly supported the liberals and that he was considering transferring his military authority to Hu Yaobang. Hu had reached the apex of an apparently independent position of power. He repeatedly called upon the aged "defenders of the true Marxist faith" to resign completely, something that Deng Xiaoping had not been able to accomplish in 1982. A special party conference—not an official Party Congress—at which Hu Yaobang presided was convened to discuss the historical goal of rejuvenation of the party. The average age of the members of the Politburo dropped from seventy-five to sixty-three. The youngest member was Hu Qili (fifty-six), Hu Yaobang's lieutenant. He was generally tipped to be the next party leader, the first with a college education who could speak English to boot. Remarkably, the elderly widow of Premier Zhou Enlai, Deng Yingchao, resigned, but her place was taken by her foster son, Li Peng (then fifty-seven), who later became premier.

In April 1986 Hu saw to it that the avant-garde writer Wang Meng became minister of culture, whereby the role of orthodox Marxists in this realm seemed to be over—at least for the time being. That same spring, a series of academic forums were held in memory of the commencement thirty years before of Mao's Hundred Flowers Campaign: "Let a hundred flowers bloom and a hundred schools of thought contend." At the time, Mao had called on intellectuals to criticize the socialist system, but when too many sarcastic thorns and nettles began to flourish among the flowers, they were crushed by a landslide of repression, the so-called "Anti-Rightist Movement." Prominent members of the Chinese Academy of Social Sciences, the think tank of the reformists, argued for expansion of the newly acquired academic and cultural freedoms into the political sphere. Only formal laws and institutions would be able to guarantee that the new freedoms would be firmly anchored in society and could not be swept away again by a sudden turn in the political wind, such as happened in 1957. Newspaper editors urged the foundation of independent newspapers alongside the official party newspapers and the removal of the commissars of the Central Propaganda Department, who could exercise vetoes over editors in chief. The political scientist Yan Jiaqi, adviser to Premier Zhao Ziyang, suggested in a long series of articles that Western political theories be used to prevent the derailment of rulers like Mao Zedong. In June, Hu Yaobang paid a visit to the four major Western European countries and returned with a much-repeated idea: "the right to do everything that is not forbidden by law." During his visit to London, Hu Yaobang pulled off a stunning feat of waywardness by demonstratively refusing to visit the grave of Karl Marx, going instead to see the library in the British Museum where Marx had worked. He would soon be made to see the error of his ways, and not just once.

Nowhere was the historical need for far-reaching political reforms expressed in more compelling terms than in China's pioneering newspaper of the late 1980s, the *Shijie Jingji Daobao* (World Economic Herald). This paper had been founded in 1980 at the instigation of the Chinese Academy of Social Sciences in Shanghai by Qin Benli, an indefatigable champion of his own ideals and a victim of every repressive campaign of the Mao era. The newspaper admittedly belonged to a state think tank but was nevertheless semi-independent. The *Herald* became the forum par excellence for reformist debates between prominent intellectuals. With tacit support from Hu Yaobang and Zhao Ziyang, it was actually used in their fight against the hard-liners. The main theme of the paper was that economic reforms would fail if the political status quo were stubbornly maintained. A comparison was made with the final years of the Qing dynasty, the low point of modern Chinese history, when all economic modernization was obstructed by the rotten political system. Furthermore, the Marxist argument was brought into play to affirm that the political superstructure must be in harmony with its economic base.

Only alarming arguments of this nature seemed to get a hold on Deng Xiaoping. He began to plead for political reform in all his speeches during internal conferences and meetings with foreign delegations.

DENG'S UTTERANCES during this crucial episode indicate either that he was indecisive or that he expected so much opposition that he became more and more reticent. During a session of the Politburo on 28 June, he again expanded on the traditional lack of a codified legal system in China. He stressed that the party's power would have to be curtailed if the people were ever to have a feeling of legal security. But he would brook no weakening of the party, none at all. The party should not interfere with every aspect of daily life, though, and should save its energy for effective political and ideological leadership. These were declarations of principle without any detailed instructions for practical implementation. Deng was more specific about matters to do with economic growth. During the organizational and administrative reforms of 1981–82, a number of central government bodies had been abolished and their authority delegated to local government agencies. The functionaries who had lost their jobs had founded new state firms, however, which had once again usurped power. "While we demand that authority be delegated to local organs, they take it back again. Reports have reached me that human error has also been responsible for lower economic growth in the first half of this year [1986] and that this tendency of government bodies to take power back is one of them. Our policy is devolution, but numerous institutions are opposed to it, resulting in enterprises deprived of power and their initiative seeping away. This is one of the reasons, therefore, for the drop in growth."[8]

Deng said to a Japanese delegation three months later that the scale of political structuring was not yet clear. "We will try one or two reforms at a time, not everything at once, because we don't want chaos. It is so difficult and complex that we have as yet no clear plan as to where to begin."[9] During a conference of financial and economic leaders on 13 September, he said that a plan should be ready for the Party Congress in 1987 in which the separation of party and state would be the first priority. He implied, however, that at most it would call for a redistribution of power between the current rulers without a system of checks and balances. "In reforming our political structure, we must not imitate the West and liberalization is quite unacceptable. Our present-day structure of leadership has advantages, of course, because we can make decisions quickly. If, on the other hand, we devote too much attention to creating checks and balances, we might find ourselves in difficulty."

The most prominent advocates of checks and balances were Deng's friend and bridge partner Vice-premier Wan Li, and Fei Xiaotong, China's leading sociologist and the best-known victim of the ill-conceived "Hundred Flowers Campaign" of 1956. At a scientific conference at the end of July, Wan had pleaded for "political decision-making on the basis of scientific and democratic procedures . . . and not based on the erratic, antiquated ideas of party leaders." Wan further suggested legal protection for policy researchers, so that they could no longer be attacked if their research papers were unpalatable to the leadership.

The most concrete suggestion for supervision came from Fei Xiaotong, who, after all the persecution and humiliation he had suffered, was again China's most influential academic at the age of seventy-six. He is still the leader of the Democratic League, the most vocal of the eight non-Communist intellectual elite parties. As a demonstration of "political pluralism," he had accompanied Hu Yaobang in June on his state visit to Western Europe. Fei proposed that the Chinese People's Political Consultative Conference (CPPCC), the powerless umbrella organization of the "democratic" parties, should play the role of watchdog, functioning as a sort of senate. "The people who dare to speak the truth are still in the minority in the CPPCC, although it's much better than several years ago. . . . The delegates should be able to speak directly on behalf of their constituency and be given more power, including the right of inquiry and impeachment of officials. There are too many officials in this country and it is too easy to be one. Officials get off scot-free when they make catastrophic blunders and cause losses of millions."[10]

AT THE END OF SEPTEMBER, a plenum of the Party Central Committee would convene to discuss the long-awaited political reforms—at least that was everyone's hope and expectation. A few weeks before the plenum, however, a counterattack was launched in the party's theoretical organ, the *Red Flag*. The elderly conservatives had been successful in persuading Deng Xiaoping that political reforms would be the beginning of the end of the whole Communist system and himself. At this point, Deng probably withdrew his support for Hu Yaobang, and Hu in turn left his academic vanguard in the lurch. Instead of a summit on reforms, the plenum became an ideological council, issuing an encyclical on "socialist ethics" entitled *Guiding Principles for the Construction of a Socialist Society with Advanced Culture and Ideology*. It was a direct counterattack on the great debate over Marx which had taken place in late 1984, and also a sarcastic reprimand of Hu Yaobang and his failure to visit Marx's grave on his visit to Europe. "It is wrong not to acknowledge the basic precepts [of Marxism], to view them as antiquated theories and to worship instead bourgeois philosophies and social doctrines. . . . The tremendous changes that have taken place in China and the rest of the world are proof of the immense vitality of Marxism, demonstrating at the same time that we should adopt the basic principles and methods of Marxism for creative solutions to new problems."[11]

INTELLECTUAL LEADERS, especially the three most fearless among them, would not let themselves be muzzled. The period of "guarded liberalization" was over. They now had to move ahead without the support of Hu Yaobang and thus appealed directly to the people, i.e., the students. It was the beginning of a new chapter in Chinese intellectual history. In dynastic times, there had been a tradition in China that the intellectuals, the learned Mandarins, were permitted to report abuse, although this was generally through the offices of a powerful court dignitary. The criticism was delivered indirectly in a highly literate code language, mostly in the form of historical allegories. A good emperor would then listen and take corrective measures. In the twentieth century, the whole imperial world lived on under a different name. A bad "emperor" like Mao unleashed on his critics his fanatical ideologues or the henchmen of his secret service.

In the early 1980s and again for a short time in 1986, China's most prominent intellectuals were under the illusion that Deng was a good emperor, who listened to tempered criticism. Owing to the lack of legal security, however, they only dared to express their tempered criticism through the offices of senior dignitaries, in this case Wan Li and Hu Yaobang. Their criticism was also offered in the same spirit as the criticism offered by a loyal opposition in the West, but within the ruling party. To this end, Yan Jiaqi had invented the variation "one party–more wings" (in political-science jargon: "a one-party multifaction system"), whereby one wing complemented and corrected the other. By now the leaders had reached the stage of making a mental break with the party. Their criticism became confrontational in nature, no longer remaining internal but finally becoming public. They actually achieved the exact opposite of what they had hoped for.

Liu Binyan, vice-chairman of the Writers' Union and social critic for the *People's Daily*, Wang Ruowang, a political satirist in Shanghai, and Fang Lizhi, internationally renowned astrophysicist and vice-rector of an important university for the sciences, became the independent conscience of the political reform movement. In the fall of 1986, they were much sought after as speakers at academic forums and student congresses. Their interviews were published in newspapers in the most remote parts of the country. The most flamboyant of these was an interview with Fang in the *World Economic Herald* (24 November 1986), in which he said that the biggest tragedy in China was that intellectuals had no independent status and no sense of self-worth. In advanced societies in the West, those who possess knowledge—not those who are most powerful—are held in the highest regard. According to world statistics on education expenditure, China was at the bottom, together with Cambodia and Haiti. Fang went on to explain that the Chinese Communist authorities, owing to their peasant tradition, were still not aware that intellectuals were the guiding influence in the modernization of society. He then criticized Chinese intellectuals themselves for their spinelessness and lack of courage, always bowing to the powers that be. "Science and politics are inextricably linked and intellectuals only dare utter things that agree with the leadership or that have already been written in the newspaper." Fang further emphasized that for its modernization

China must rely on foreign experience, especially in the realm of social ideas. According to Fang, the success of modernization depended largely on the younger generation of intellectuals. To what extent would they be prepared to stand up and not be shaken in their beliefs, to refuse to be the rulers' yes-men, to balk at waiting for instructions from above for every little thing, and especially to avoid linking their destiny to that of the present rulers? "As soon as the intellectual has shown his strength just once, it will immediately reflect his power, because knowledge is power," concluded Professor Fang.[12]

THE STUDENTS at Fang's university in Hefei took up the challenge and started a series of demonstrations that spread to twenty other cities in China. Student groups in Beijing were under the illusion that they could help Deng Xiaoping in his struggle against still more conservative party elders and sent him petitions to this end. Deng's answer was a police raid, firing and expelling Fang, Liu, and Wang from the party, and in particular removing his faithful liberal lieutenant Hu Yaobang from office. This occurred in flagrant violation of the party constitution, not after a vote in the Central Committee, but after a special session drummed up by the Politburo, supplemented with senior generals and fully retired elders. Deng held Hu chiefly responsible for the overly tolerant "bourgeois liberal" atmosphere on university campuses, in cultural circles, and among the media, which had been the hotbed of the demonstrations.

In the following weeks and months, it appeared that there was much more behind it. Among other things, Hu had ignored instructions given by Deng to use force to put an end to the demonstrations in early December, issuing his own orders not to make any arrests. Furthermore, Hu had taken seriously Deng's periodic and ritual declarations of intent to retire completely, and had publicly challenged him to suit his actions to his words and transfer power fully to him. No one can say for sure whether Deng really wanted to relinquish his power or whether he had only been putting out feelers to find out who his loyal followers were. According to one version of events, Deng was forced to sacrifice Hu because the military had refused to accept him as chairman of the Military Commission. The political-ideological gap between Deng and Hu had in any case become unbridgeable.[13] In principle, Deng Xiaoping was sympathetic to a minimum of democratization, but if he saw a conflict surfacing, he sacrificed everything for the sake of stability and economic growth. For Hu Yaobang democracy was just the ideology needed to ensure stability and economic growth in the long run. Hu and his intellectuals were the losers, because in China, it would appear, it is not knowledge but old age that means power. During the first few months of 1987, China returned to an ideological Ice Age, but after the first ice had melted, "bourgeois liberalism" immediately came out of hibernation again.

CHAPTER 10

Bourgeois Liberalization and a Neoauthoritarian Alternative

Political parties are class instruments, and considering that in a socialist society class differences no longer exist, one party is enough.

RED FLAG,
theoretical organ of the Chinese Communist party, 1987

IN THE CONTEXT of the permanent power struggle between the orthodox and the liberal wings of the Communist party, the years 1987 and 1988 were a period of cease-fire, temporary liberal advances, renewed deadlock, and regression. These fluctuations were closely linked to Deng Xiaoping's own political mood. At the high point in the student demonstrations, an agitated Deng declared that the fight against bourgeois liberalization would last at least twenty years. "Bourgeois liberalization would throw the land in chaos again. Bourgeois liberalization means rejection of the party leadership. There would be nothing more to unite our people, one billion strong, and the party would lose the will to fight." He praised the Polish general Wojciech Jaruzelski for suppressing Solidarity five years earlier and said that China could not exist without a dictatorship either.[1]

Orthodox ideologues and elderly conservatives took advantage of this forbidding climate to prepare a large-scale—and this time, crushing—counteroffensive against all the liberal forces. This time Deng Xiaoping would not block their retreat to the left—at least that's what they thought.

The main goal of the elderly conservatives was to dismantle the immense network of kindred spirits and friends that Hu Yaobang had installed in key positions across the whole of the country. The tree, Hu Yaobang, had been felled, but the monkeys had not let themselves be driven away.

It was, however, Hu Yaobang's acting successor, Zhao Ziyang, who immediately set about preventing the decimation of Hu's network and an about-face to the left. Zhao was a pragmatic leader, averse to all ideological drivel and, just like Deng, primarily interested in economic results. He promptly issued instructions to all provincial and municipal governments to keep the campaign against bourgeois liberalization within bounds, to immunize the economy, the countryside (rich farmers), and the science establishment, and especially not to fire any liberal university administrators and professors. Zhao's strategy, supported by Deng, was to let the elderly conservatives dominate the ideological front in exchange for noninterference in economic reforms.

The Red Old Men's Choir—conducted by the extreme, barbaric, retired general Wang Zhen (seventy-nine), vice-chairman of the Central Advisory Commission, and Peng Zhen (eighty-five), ultraorthodox chairman of the National People's Congress—refused to give up, croaking out daily at the top of their lungs revolutionary songs of the 1930s and 1940s. Wang called on students to stop demonstrating and urged them instead to hold daily "flag-waving ceremonies" and to make weekly visits to the graves of revolutionary heroes. Peng told writers to go back and study the "theses of Chairman Mao regarding the literature of peasants, workers, and soldiers," uttered in 1942 in Yanan. The reactionary president Li Xiannian, by then eighty-one years old, told foreign delegations in no uncertain terms that power was firmly in the hands of the octogenarians: "Waves that come later will not wash over previous waves." Li assured them that China had a collective leadership, in other words: Deng Xiaoping is at most a primus inter pares and certainly no supremo.

The leftist cyclops fought a grim battle against Western decadence but was not successful in outlawing discos and social dancing. For days on end, debates were conducted in the media on the reintroduction of the Mao uniform. The minister of textiles, Mrs. Wu Wenying, also had her say: "Embellishing the life of our people is the traditional duty of fashion designers. A pleasing appearance and bourgeois liberalization are two different things which should not be confused with each other." The campaign continued to go back and forth like a two-handed saw: a pull to the left and a pull to the right, with Deng Xiaoping standing in the middle as overseer.

The elderly conservatives were not satisfied, however, with the division of labor limiting them to ideological matters. In the newspaper for intellectuals, *Guangming Ribao* (Radiant Daily), they launched a campaign against Western economic theories and in support of the rehabilitation of orthodox Marxist economic ideas, mobilizing whole legions of dogmatic scribes and paying them to write defamatory pamphlets denouncing everything that was liberal.[2] Zhao was concerned that if the obsessed aged zealots were not curbed immediately, the whole process of economic reform would be derailed. He managed to convince Deng Xiaoping of the extent of this danger, at which Deng once again swerved to the right. Starting in April, he again told foreign visitors that "the danger from the left is now greater than the danger from the right." Within three months this Janus had turned again from antiright to antileft.

According to the Hong Kong media, heads had rolled behind the scenes. Deng himself supposedly dismissed the leftist "supercommissar" Deng Liqun (no relation). The old Deng (eighty-two) ordered the "young" Deng (seventy-two) to withdraw from the arena completely, just as he himself was planning to do. The young Deng grumbled that he belonged to the younger generation, at which Deng apparently roared with laughter: "Ha-ha, that's a good one. You're younger in age but your brain is more ossified than mine."[3]

In early August at the party conclave in the resort town of Beidaihe—China's equivalent of a summer capital—a new cease-fire was declared. Leftist agitation would have to stop, but the left was given the consolation prize of being allowed to punish a few more avant-garde intellectuals. The dramatist Wu Zuguang was expelled from the party, and the director of the Institute for Marxism, Leninism, and Mao Zedong Thought in the Chinese Academy of Social Sciences[4]—Su Shaozhi, China's best-known Euro-Marxist—was removed from his post.

THE THIRTEENTH PARTY CONGRESS now had to stabilize its shaky balance, and Zhao Ziyang did this with verve and resourcefulness. The political earthquake of the previous winter and its aftershocks had blocked any substantial political reforms. Rejuvenation took place only on the surface. Zhao's success lay in his ability to legitimize China's gradual advance toward becoming a market economy in terms of orthodox Marxist theoretical jargon. This gave him a perfectly designed shield with which to deflect all attacks by ideological snipers, who continually armed themselves with quotations from Marx. The new ideological concept, devised by Su Shaozhi, held that China was still in "the primary stage of socialism." This stage could last a long time because Chinese socialism had been born of a semicolonial, semifeudal society and had not known a capitalist basis, such as in the developed industrial countries for which Marx had intended his teachings. "Therefore," said Zhao, "we can follow blindly neither Marxist books nor the examples of other countries." At this primary stage, the main task of socialism, which Zhao estimated would take a hundred years to achieve, beginning in 1949, was overcoming poverty and underdevelopment. "All economic activity which increases the productive forces must therefore be permitted, and public ownership of the means of production does not have to be complete as long as it is dominant."

Zhao also had some criticism for the overconcentration of power in the party and said that party bodies that overlap government bodies should be abolished. Zhao thought the concept of "cadre" (party functionary) too broad, proposing that civil servants take their place. As to their selection, he had this to say: "Those who deal with personnel matters have too little professional know-how: their methods are antiquated and simplistic, which hinders the intellectual growth of talented people.... The idea of giving preference to old age and other worn-out methods that dampen people's initiative should be abandoned." They were sympathetic declarations of intent, but nothing concrete ever came of them.[5]

The top of the Politburo had admittedly been rejuvenated and the power of the super-Politburo, the Council of Elders, was curtailed, although in practice this did not mean much. The constitution, regulations, and statutes were used by the strong in a power struggle to legitimize their newly extended power all over again. A call from weaker elements for legislation to invoke the law in order to expose abuses of power by stronger elements always failed. The elderly conservatives continued to exercise power through their network of protégés. The two main supervisors of the witch-hunt for liberal forces, Hu Qiaomu and Deng Liqun, lost their seats in the Party Central Committee but were "elected" to the Central Advisory Commission, which they were to use as a forum for spinning new ideological webs.

On behalf of Deng, Zhao expressed his opposition to the Western democratic model of the separation of powers, and the practice of one party taking over the reins of government from another. This was a pet theme of Deng's, one that he repeated in the speech he made after the fall of Hu Yaobang. Deng said that the United States actually had three governments (legislative, executive, and judiciary) and that they often took different paths. This creates problems and would be unacceptable in China. The ideological objection to a multiparty system, as expressed earlier that year by orthodox ideologues, was that political parties were instruments of class struggle. As there were no longer fundamental conflicts of interest between classes in a socialist society, one party was enough. Deng Xiaoping subscribed to the goal but not to its wording. As a former revolutionary, he did not believe in a loyal opposition. Kill or be killed. Live and let live didn't work. According to Deng, an opposition party was always scheming to sabotage and destroy the ruling party (the Communists versus the Kuomintang), which undermined the unity and strength of the nation. In the end, the only political reform to be introduced by Zhao was "cooperation with the eight token democratic parties under the leadership of the Communist party."

Zhao already anticipated the next round in the deepening conflict over China's future political structure. He said that advancing economic reforms would be accompanied by more fundamental conflicts of interest in society and that channels would have to be designed through which to express them in an orderly fashion. Yielding to pressure from Deng, Zhao (then sixty-eight) was installed by the Party Congress as general secretary, against his own repeatedly declared wish. And considering that Li Peng was to succeed him as premier, the seeds were already sown for a new power struggle. Zhao was an administrator, who for eight years had formed think tanks of young economists trained in the United States. After much trial and error, they had finally formulated a coherent economic policy. Zhao had, moreover, built up his network in the state hierarchy and not in the party. As premier, he strove for economic results and acted as China's face to the outside world. As party leader, he would have to conduct ideological skirmishes with the rear guard of still-surviving troglodytes of Mao's revolutionary headquarters in Yanan. Zhao was Deng Xiaoping's protégé but benefited from his support only in economic matters.

Li Peng (then fifty-nine) was a foster son of Premier Zhou Enlai and one of the elite who was trained as an engineer in Moscow in the early 1950s. Li, a conservative, rigid, humorless model Communist, was unanimously supported by the elderly conservatives, who first of all wanted to use him to curb reforms drastically and if possible to bring about a Stalinist restoration.

SINCE THE FALL of 1987, a potentially tense situation had prevailed in Chinese cities as a result of rising prices and inflation. It was thought that the simmering social discontent might escalate, proving more serious than the student protests in late 1986. In losing the post of premier, Zhao had also lost his podium for presenting his solutions to these problems every year during his "State of the Union" address, the report of the premier to the annual session of the National People's Congress. This now became the domain of Li Peng. Acting as though he were still premier, Zhao called a meeting of the Party Central Committee just before the National People's Congress convened, where he again pleaded for the need to find the means to conduct a broad dialogue with the grass roots. He proposed a Chinese version of glasnost—*toumingdu* (transparency)—and said that the people must be told the truth about important matters regarding the stability of society. The great dilemma was whether to persevere with new hikes in the dual-track price structure (planned economy prices versus market prices) or to postpone these until inflation and social tension were better under control. Zhao's philosophy, supported by his think tank, maintained that it was better to pursue a high-risk policy for a short period and to break through to a new economic structure dominated by the market mechanism than to let the old system of central planning limp along for an indefinite period next to the emerging market economy.

The new premier, Li Peng, had on the other hand suggested in his annual report to the National People's Congress that a price freeze be implemented for a number of industrial goods and price subsidies instituted for daily necessities. Persuaded by Zhao and his think tank—the Research Center for Economic, Technological, and Social Development—Deng Xiaoping began in May to insist on further, immediate price liberalization, claiming that it was better to suffer a lot of pain for a short time than to suffer lingering pain for a long time. In June and August the Politburo approved two documents that held out the prospect of complete abolition of price controls for nearly all goods by around 1993.

Society reacted by panicking. In July the price index rose by 19.2 percent. For weeks there was a run on the banks, accompanied by unbridled hoarding. The People's Bank of China raised the interest rate twice, but the withdrawal of savings continued. On 30 August the State Council announced a price freeze for 1988 and only limited price reforms for 1989. During a plenum, the Party Central Committee decided that a drastic austerity program would have to be implemented in the coming two years.

The elderly gentlemen, who for months had been plotting an all-out attack on Zhao and the liberal wing of the party, decided to take advantage of the economic chaos to bring down Zhao, just as Hu had been brought down in the fall of 1986. During the summer conclave in the resort town of Beidaihe, Zhao was accused of not having pursued a coherent policy on price reforms during his eight years as premier, relying instead on haphazard experimentation. This was a widely accepted practice, which was described as "groping your way across the river by feeling the stones." No one had any ready-made answers anyway, but Zhao was by now an almost defenseless scapegoat. Deng Xiaoping, who had taken the initiative himself in the most recent breakthrough in price liberalization, left Zhao in the lurch, at which point the resentful Zhao left in a huff for an inspection tour of Manchuria. He submitted his resignation, anticipating that it would not be accepted, and during his trip he fired several merciless broadsides at "the old farts," as they were popularly called. "They never take a rest, abusing their power and privileges—at the country's expense—for the comfort and enjoyment of themselves and their children." A tug-of-war followed concerning the duration of the freeze on price reforms and Zhao was requested to stay on, although he was no longer to have a say in economic matters. Owing to Deng Xiaoping's umpteenth "tactical" withdrawal, Li Peng had won the first round. Zhao would have to trudge on by himself through the political minefield.[6]

ON THE CULTURAL-IDEOLOGICAL FRONT, a bloody battle had also taken place that summer over a six-part television series that pointed to traditional Chinese culture—symbolized by the Yellow River, the Great Wall, and the Dragon—as one of the main reasons for China's inability to modernize. The series, *He Shang* (River Elegy), was without doubt the most sensational and shocking program in the history of Chinese television. It was broadcast for the first time that June and caused just as much turmoil among China's thinking populace as the great debate on Marxism of 1984 and the fall of Hu Yaobang.

The main theme of the series was the question, which had been recurring for more than a hundred years and had never been satisfactorily answered, as to how China could rid itself of the millstone around its neck represented by an ancient, moribund culture. It was a brilliant new example of the Chinese literary technique of "pointing to the mulberry bush to disparage the ash tree." Traditional culture was the target, but in reality it was aimed as well at the equally worn-out Communist culture. The Yellow River is a silted-up pool of mud, the Great Wall a symbol of isolationism, and the dragon a sign of superstition. For all of these symbols the intelligent viewer could substitute contemporary symbols, such as the paralyzing hold of orthodox ideology, Communist xenophobia, and the hammer and sickle. "After its consolidation, each new dynasty adopts the evil practices of its predecessor. . . . The great Confucian network of Mandarins no longer exists, but the same spirit still haunts us: bureaucracy, the privileged class, corruption," went the script.

The writers were former Red Guards, some of whom had studied in the West in the 1980s and, since 1989, now lived in the West, in exile. The documentary featured spectacular cinematography showing the river, the wall, traditional festivals, and the madness of the Mao era, alternating with interviews with prominent intellectuals, including Zhao Ziyang's advisers. Never before had such a systematic and critical analysis of the whole of Chinese history and society been seen. Never before had so many taboos been broken in public. At least once in every installment, the makers of the series came to the dramatic conclusion that the old Chinese culture was over and done with. China found itself in a spiritual vacuum because of the complete bankruptcy of Communism. Attempts by ideologues paddling against the tide to fill that vacuum with selective aspects of the old culture would also, according to them, come to naught. The message behind the elegy was that only the instant construction of a "maritime-commercial-industrial democracy," in other words, (complete) Westernization, would be able to propel China down the path of human progress.

During the first broadcast, General Wang Zhen, who had become vice-president of China at the age of eighty,[7] phoned the television station and demanded that the program be stopped immediately. The climate at the time was such that everyone just laughed at the angry old crackpot. For a very short time it seemed that China was becoming a law-based state. An official at the television studio asked on what grounds the program should be stopped. Wang replied that the program was a plea for total Westernization and that the Thirteenth Party Congress had passed a resolution opposing that. Moreover, his orders were enough, since as one of China's eight major "immortals," he was above the law. The TV employee said that as far as he was concerned, the law applied, but if Wang found the sanction of the party more important, then he could report that they already had the party's authorization: General Secretary Zhao Ziyang supported the broadcast of the series.[8]

In the meantime, Wang Zhen had rallied the opposition. The television station was admonished and ordered to exercise self-criticism in a special broadcast. The series was so immensely popular, however, that seven newspapers published the entire script and there was a general call for a rerun. Zhao Ziyang nevertheless had the audacity to ignore the elderly opposition and decided in late July that in spite of the program's debatable aspects, the "River Elegy" was "essentially proreform" and could be broadcast again.[9]

The main target of the satire is the Yellow River, already for millennia the "scourge of China" not only because of its silt and sand but also because of its symbolic value as an emblem of the monotonous, stagnating, inward-looking agrarian civilization. The Yellow River is the cradle of that civilization, and the forefather of the Chinese race is the Yellow Emperor. The

Chinese peasant, the yellow man, is fettered to the yellow soil, the lifeblood of which is the yellow water of the river. The emperor was the tyrant of the human world and the dragon the tyrant of nature. "The emperors are no more, but the psychology of 'tremble and obey' is still very much with us. Of undiminished importance is the paradoxical cult of the dragon, that 'assembled' animal with the head of a horse, the antlers of a deer, the body of a snake, and the feet of a chicken."

The philosopher Xie Xuanjun says that the Chinese have a great tolerance for evil: "It is said that the Chinese are slippery characters and cunning as well, that they resign themselves easily to the will of heaven and submit meekly to oppression. This is no coincidence. The lifeblood of old agrarian societies is water and water is dominated by the dragon. The people love the dragon yet hate and curse him. . . . But at festivals they beat on gongs and produce drum rolls for him, have fun worshiping that old fetish and dispel their discontent by throwing themselves in the dust at his feet, burning incense. This is Chinese wisdom and humor."

The documentary recounts that other great river civilizations from antiquity, such as those that sprang up around the Nile, the Tigris and Euphrates, and the Indus, had all vanished. Through the protection of the Himalayas and, in a sense, the Great Wall, the Yellow River civilization managed to prolong its life until the present day. "It is a source of great pride for many Chinese that they represent the only old civilization that has survived till modern times, but what exactly is there to be proud of? At the end of the twentieth century, foreign pressure is no longer exerted by gunboats. Our four-thousand-year-old civilization is too weak to withstand cultural and economic pressure from abroad," say the writers of the series.

The fatal weakness of Chinese civilization, according to them, is the absence of a continuous maritime tradition of any significance. Already during the Han dynasty (206 B.C.–A.D. 220), a Chinese fleet made an expedition to the Indian Ocean. During the Tang dynasty (618–906), there was intense trading by land and sea with the Middle East, but Chinese seafaring collapsed after a defeat by Muslim armies in Central Asia. The Chinese discovered the compass, gunpowder, and the arts of making paper and publishing books, but none of these led to important changes in society. Their enduring, all-encompassing preoccupation was working the yellow soil and keeping the Yellow River within its banks. Later on, they turned their imagination to the building and maintenance of the Great Wall.

In the fourteenth century, the Chinese fleet again made systematic expeditions—a hundred years before the Portuguese voyages of discovery—to Java, India, Arabia, and Africa, but they had no expansionist or economic objectives. Admiral Zheng He only wanted to grant favors to the kings he visited, delivering the message that the Chinese emperor was their superior. The documentary also cited Hegel, "The great oceans invite people to conquest and to conduct trade," but then added sadly, "The Chinese who accepted this invitation were meek-spirited people who were not hunting for an advantage." When Vasco da Gama and Ferdinand Magellan undertook their voyages around the world, laying the foundations of colonial empires, there was no longer the ghost of a Chinese fleet to be seen.

The Ming emperor Jia Qing quickly decided to close the doors of the Middle Kingdom and forbade the building of oceangoing vessels, because they brought undesirable foreign influences home with them. This was occasioned by an argument at court with a Japanese envoy, who did not want to be put off as a minor tributary envoy. Japanese pirates were in future only to be driven from the Chinese coast and were not to be followed to their home port to see what things looked like there.

The prophet of laissez-faire capitalism, Adam Smith, was cited more often in the television program than Karl Marx. In his classic, *An Inquiry into the Nature and Causes of the Wealth of Nations,* Smith wrote in 1776: "The history and civilization of China are stagnant because this country does not attach any importance to overseas trade. . . . The closing of the door accelerates their suicide." The voice of the commentator then added somberly: "It is lamentable that no Chinese heard this warning in time."

It was not until a century after Adam Smith wrote his *Wealth of Nations* that the debate on reopening the door broke out with a vengeance. After the humiliating defeat of China in the Opium Wars, the traditional Confucian world order collapsed. A group of conservative, learned generals thought it could be rebuilt in all its purity by setting a good moral example. They also maintained that China would be able to hold its place in the modern world merely by importing Western military technology.

The scriptwriters saw nothing positive in this unsuccessful "restoration," choosing instead as their hero one of the Chinese students who was sent to the British Naval Academy in 1870. Yan Fu (1853–1921) quickly discovered that the West's strength lay not so much in better warships as in the prevailing social philosophy and social institutions. "During his intense observation of the West, Yan Fu concluded that individualism was the essential motivating factor in everything. The West's greatest gift to the world is its ability to let the individual flourish." He proposed a social contract in which competition and other functions of capitalism would bring about positive changes in society.

Yan Fu did not become an admiral, instead devoting the rest of his life to the translation of great writers like Adam Smith, Thomas Henry Huxley, John Stuart Mill, Herbert Spencer, and Charles Darwin. He was one of the leaders of the bourgeois reform movement of 1898, which was crushed by the feudal palace clique. The Meiji restoration in Japan, on the other hand, was successful, and Yan Fu's classmate at the British Naval Academy, Hirobumi Ito, became premier. Japan then quickly entered the league of world powers.

The last installment of the program ended with an ode to the azure waters of the Pacific Ocean and the sky above, the azure that will eventually have to replace the dominant yellow of the river. "But we still have a hundred years to go before we'll be able to see through the yellow mud to the transparent azure!"

The *River Elegy* aggravated the rebellious mood of China's intellectuals and students. It was now or never. With Zhao Ziyang in his eroded position hanging by a silk thread, the obvious course of action was a life-or-death struggle, pitting the natural alliance of the intellectuals and Zhao against Li Peng and the elderly reactionaries.

PRIOR TO THE THIRD all-out attempt to exact political reforms, this time with the help of organized opposition groups, another crucial debate now took shape. It centered on finding a middle-of-the-road solution, something other than Communism yet not democracy. The advocates of "neoauthoritarianism" rejected the total monopoly of the Communist party but realized that China was not ready for Western democracy. The goal was to find an institutional model to strengthen the position of Zhao Ziyang, making him a post-Communist, reformist "strongman" after the model of the former authoritarian rulers of South Korea and Taiwan. Zhao was meant to gain the power required to take the unpopular measures necessary to force the breakthrough to a market economy. This was, after all, a prerequisite to becoming a democracy.

There were vague indications that Deng Xiaoping supported the idea, although he had reservations about what it should be called. This academic debate had already begun in late 1988, but owing to the stamp of approval given by Deng Xiaoping, it became a dominant theme in the early stages of the protest movement in April 1989.

The most important advocate of a neoauthoritarian variant for China was the young political scientist Wu Jiaxiang, who had been a member of one of Zhao's think tanks, the Research Bureau of the party's Central Committee. Before anyone really had the chance to listen to Wu's arguments, a flood of criticism rained down upon him from the radical-democratic elite. They already found the term itself sinister and asked how the neoauthoritarian "strongman" was meant to gain the means of power. The debate also distracted them from their goal of fighting directly for democracy, not via a detour.

Inspired by the American political scientist Samuel P. Huntington and his standard work, *Political Order in Changing Societies* (1968), Wu Jiaxiang explained that there were three stages of development in the process of democratization: traditional autocratic authority, the beginning of the development of individual freedoms under the protection of neoauthoritarianism, and the third stage of integration of freedom and democracy. According to Wu, it was not possible to jump from the first stage to the third, the reason being that during the process of decentralization, the old centralized autocracy created all sorts of interest groups to serve as a transitional structure. These grab power arbitrarily and block the transition to freedom and democracy. This is precisely what happened in China during the Deng era: decentralization that destroyed not only centralism but also the democratic forces. Power was usurped halfway by the children of the top leaders—the red princes—corrupt bureaucrats, regional and local interest groups, army units, and the mafia. According to Wu Jiaxiang, a modern strongman is necessary in such a situation, someone willing to take draconian measures to avert a social crisis, in which vestiges of the old structure and the hybrid transitional structure are allowed to grow unchecked. There is no going back to the old autocracy, as that will only exacerbate the social crisis. The neoauthoritarian strongman, who rises to power by election, hereditary succession, appointment, or a coup, is needed to accelerate the transition to the new structure—first to more freedom, then to democracy.

First it is necessary that the market economy be consolidated, however, for without a market there are no equal chances in the economy. A market economy means economic democracy. In China there is economic elbow room and latitude to play around, but political power or connections are usually necessary for the creation of room to maneuver. For the realization of the market economy, the fragmented political power would again have to be centralized, and that would have to be the task of the neoauthoritarian strongman.

Some critics of neoauthoritarianism say that the market economy could be realized by extending political participation, but Wu Jiaxiang does not think this can be done quickly. And if it were to happen slowly, it would only lead to still more corruption and chaos. The number of interest groups that amass political connections in order to obtain economic advantages increases every day. Another problem is how to prevent neoauthoritarianism from backsliding into the old autocracy. Wu's answer is that neo-authoritarianism usually comes into being during a democratization move-ment, when the regime still has just enough power to stop it halfway. Once a neoauthoritarian regime has been formed, the democratic movement must continue to exert pressure, not by demonstrations but through politi-cal activities within the context of China's existing representative organs, such as the National People's Congress and the Chinese People's Political Consultative Conference. Since the mid-1980s these had evolved from mo-notonous rubber-stamp jamborees into somewhat effective critical forums. Wu did say that it would be necessary to reduce drastically the number of members of both bodies—each about three thousand—to facilitate sensible debate and consultations and to reduce costs. Wu said all this at an acade-mic forum on 10 April 1989, five days before the death of Hu Yaobang, which became the starting signal for an epic wave of demonstrations.[10]

CHAPTER 11

Tiananmen: Requiem for the Democratic Forces

I envy you that you're already in power at such a young age.

DENG XIAOPING *(then eighty-three),*
to the Dutch prime minister Ruud Lubbers (then forty-seven)

I envy you that you're still in power at such an old age.

RUUD LUBBERS,
to Deng Xiaoping in 1987

IN THE SPRING OF 1989, China was well and truly ready for Armageddon, the highest form of conflict between good and evil. For the elderly conservatives this was destined to be the year of the "Final Solution to Bourgeois Liberalization." They were obdurate in their vision of China's future. For them the "end of history" was a society in which an elusive Communist utopia and the worst aspects of traditional Chinese culture would walk hand in hand in a hereditary oligarchy of revolutionary veterans and their offspring.

For intellectuals and the youth of China, however, this year was destined to produce a breakthrough in political reforms. The first phase would be to establish independent academic, cultural, and student organizations. For them the end of history was to be part of the world of universal freedom and democracy. Since 1986 both parties had prepared themselves, dug themselves in, and lost all understanding of each other's position.

In Western society, this generational conflict would have solved itself by means of the legal retirement age. In China one had to wait for the octogenarians' natural death, and the twenty-to-fifty age group was no longer willing to do so.

IN EARLY JANUARY the malaise at the universities came to a climax during a riot against the African students in Beijing. The precipitating circumstance was the great irritation felt by Chinese students at the sight of the boisterous drinking bouts and dances held by the Africans with their Chinese girlfriends, although the underlying cause was the special privileges enjoyed by the Africans. They lived in comfortable, heated apartment buildings, two to a room, with tiled floors and furniture provided, where they were able to enjoy their privacy and take turns spending time alone with their girlfriends. The Chinese lived in barrack-like buildings with bare concrete walls and floors, six to eight of them sleeping on bunk beds in one room. Their laundry hung in the dark corridors that stank of urine and were strewn with garbage. Only cold water flowed in the raw concrete sinks; heating and lighting were kept to a minimum; and they had no privacy whatever. Their complaints were legion, and very little was necessary to spur them to action.

Fang Lizhi soon circulated a petition among intellectuals in support of a general amnesty for political prisoners on the occasion of the fortieth anniversary of the People's Republic. Their cause célèbre was Wei Jingsheng, the courageous pamphleteer who in 1979 had been sentenced at Deng Xiaoping's personal orders to fifteen years in prison and had meanwhile served ten years of his sentence.

At the end of February, the new American president, George Bush, was scheduled to pay a short visit to China after attending the funeral of the Japanese emperor Hirohito. Dissidents and intellectuals in general wanted to seize the opportunity offered by Bush and the entire media circus that accompanied him to step up pressure on the Chinese government with regard to human rights, and to do so with the whole world watching. It was a debacle. Bush wanted no direct altercation with Deng Xiaoping, whom he regarded as an old friend from the period 1974–75, when he was President Richard Nixon's special envoy to China. Bush did have a surprise for the media, however, which enabled him to say with a clear conscience after his return to the United States that human rights had been high on his agenda. He invited Fang Lizhi to a Texas barbecue that he offered as a farewell banquet to the Chinese leaders. The regime gave full priority to considerations of domestic power politics rather than the prospect of international scorn and scandal. Fang was physically prevented even from approaching the banquet hall by the Chinese police, thereby becoming a greater media hero outside the banquet hall than he would have been inside. The regime's domestic priority was a powerful condemnation of the American practice of "extending dialogue between countries from the intergovernmental to other circles," because that would strengthen the tendency toward political pluralism.

Nothing transcends the Leninist one-party state in China. During official contacts with other countries, even if they are not Leninist, no unofficial parties may be present, and certainly none that represent a nail in the coffin of intolerant old men. Fang was the nemesis of Deng Xiaoping, a renegade who had been expelled from the party. He cherished his new image as the "Chinese Sakharov," especially after the Soviet president Mikhail Gorbachev had demonstratively rehabilitated the nuclear physicist. For the elderly ruling clique in China, honoring Fang was tantamount to lèse-majesté. Together with other imprudent intellectuals, he would have to be intimidated and silenced. This justified the role of the police, and in one sense it was effective, because Fang kept quiet for months, did not take part in the demonstrations, and did not show himself at Tiananmen Square.

NOTHING MORE than the sudden death of Hu Yaobang on 15 April was responsible for unexpectedly turning Tiananmen Square (literally, Square of the Gate of Heavenly Peace) into the symbol of everything adrift in China. For the elderly conservatives Hu's death was the last and most emotional event in the "accumulation of negative factors."

"The one who should not have died is dead, while those who should have died remain alive" (*Gai-si mei-si, bu gai-si que si-le*) was the epitaph written for Hu by the aged female author Bing Xin (eighty-nine), one of the last survivors of the May Fourth Movement, the first wave of student activism in Chinese history in 1919. This death wish was posted two days later on the Monument to the People's Heroes on Tiananmen Square and was a startling warning to Deng Xiaoping and his aged cohorts of just how unpopular they were. If Hu had died at a less tense moment, he probably would never have been given the status of hero and received the honors paid to him now, in this explosive "proto-crisis." Hu had been a humane ruler and a man of integrity, and as such the odd man out among the gray, amoral autocrats, which assured him of a certain amount of popularity with the people. Intellectuals worshiped him because, in the words of the playwright Wu Zuguang, "Under his leadership the party had had the best relations with them and ideologically it had been China's most lively and liberal period since 1949." He had not been a forceful leader, however. He was boisterous, garrulous, too ready to enter into dialogues and to grant concessions, and wanted to change things too quickly, without taking account of China's archaic political culture and power structures.

Deng Xiaoping thought that Hu was ahead of his time. A Chinese leader should not be popular but feared, and at best respected. He should neither appear nor speak too often in public, but should maneuver behind the scenes with the help of such methods as "divide and conquer" and other classical techniques of power, borrowed from the Chinese Machiavelli, the military philosopher Sun Zi. What Hu had wanted in life had become a threat to Deng, a mass movement he had been able to repulse because it was still so weak in late 1986. Now the dead Hu suddenly became the symbol of a new mass movement that was growing breathtakingly fast and that seemed much stronger and more courageous than the previous one.

Deng Xiaoping knew only one solution: crush the movement as quickly as possible. It was obvious that it would be impossible to do this before Hu's funeral. To ban mourning, let alone prevent it with violence, was unthinkable. Any repressive action would therefore have to wait until after 22 April, the day of the official memorial service for Hu. The mourning processions by students and academics had, within just a few days, taken on a strong political character, not only in Beijing but also in Shanghai. Thousands of students demanded the following:

- abolition of censorship;
- posthumous rehabilitation of Hu Yaobang and active reimplementation of his ideas on political reform and democratization;
- denunciation of the campaign against bourgeois liberalization and rehabilitation of its victims, especially Fang Lizhi;
- serious measures taken against corrupt party functionaries and their children.

On the evening of 19 April, there was a chance to prevent the movement from escalating. A couple of hundred students, carrying a petition for Premier Li Peng, had staged a sit-in in front of the gate of Zhongnanhai, the Chinese Kremlin. The unpopular premier was not in any mood to show even the slightest sign of "weakness" by receiving a petition or even by sending a secretary or assistant to receive it. That night, violence erupted, directed especially at girls who could not get away fast enough, resulting in further escalation the next day.

To take the sting out of the protests, government newspapers began to print articles praising Hu's career, literally and figuratively extolling him to the skies. This was one way of "nationalizing" the spontaneous, unofficial mourning; another was threatening to hold manifestations of mourning only in work units and not in public. The government announced that on the day of the memorial service—Saturday, 22 April—to be held in the Great Hall of the People, Tiananmen Square would be hermetically sealed off. Tens of thousands of students had anticipated the actions of authorities and had started on Friday evening to occupy the square, bringing wreaths, banners, pamphlets, and provisions for that night and the following morning.

The funeral service itself was a macabre, hypocritical ritual. The same old men who more than two years earlier had plotted against Hu now stood there shedding crocodile tears for him. Zhao Ziyang, the man who had actively helped to undermine Hu Yaobang's position but who was now the flag bearer of liberalism, delivered the eulogy. This was full of praise in general, but Zhao did not dare to mention the conspiratorial way in which Hu's downfall had been brought about. An estimated hundred thousand students had installed themselves in the square, and a deputation tried unsuccessfully for hours to present a petition to Li Peng. When a staff member of the Great Hall finally agreed to speak to the students, he refused to pass the petition on to the premier's secretariat.

From this moment on, the movement was directed primarily at Li Peng. The next day, banners calling for his resignation began to appear. Li Peng embodied nearly everything that was wrong with China: the unbridled arrogance of power, intolerance, secretiveness, distrust, lack of culture, and a working style consisting of barking and intimidation. It was speculated that if Zhao Ziyang had still been premier, he would have accepted the students' petition in the early stages, and the movement could have been co-opted by the liberal wing of the party.

Immediately after Hu Yaobang's funeral, a new phase began in the escalation of the protests. Zhao left on 24 April for an official visit to North Korea. Deng and Li Peng thought they now had a free hand, and the students in turn wanted to forge the spontaneous masses of demonstrators of the previous week into a tightly knit organization. Beida, Beijing's leading university, was the nerve center of the movement. Mass meetings of students took place at which radical and moderate students screamed at each other at random. A new student organization, the Provisional Students' Federation of Capital Universities, was founded with Wu'er Kaixi (twenty-one), a flamboyant Uighur from the Islamic west of China who was studying education management, as the top man in a collective leadership.[1] Wang Dan (twenty-three), a calm, contemplative history student, and Chai Ling (twenty-three), a passionate psychology student who was given the nickname "La Pasionaria," were the other members of the triumvirate. Their first demand was the resignation of Li Peng. Their first specific action, besides demonstrating, was to call a strike at all Beijing universities.

IF THERE WAS STILL HOPE of averting a bloody confrontation, these hopes were dashed by the extreme tone used by Deng Xiaoping. Deng delivered a threatening speech, most of which was repeated the following day in an editorial in the *People's Daily*. In true patriarchal Chinese style, the students were dismissed as innocent children who did not know what they were doing. The real villains were "an extremely small group of people who spread rumors, attacked party and state leaders by name, and incited the masses to storm Zhongnanhai. . . . Nevertheless, after the memorial service [for Hu Yaobang] an extremely small number of people with ulterior motives exploited the feelings of mourning held by the young students. They spread all sorts of rumors to poison people's minds and confuse them. . . . Their goal is to sow discord . . . throw the whole country into chaos, and sabotage political stability and unity. This is a premeditated conspiracy. Its purpose is to undermine the rule of the Communist party and the socialist system once and for all. This is a serious political struggle confronting the whole party and people of all nationalities in the whole of the country. . . . A China with great prospects and a brilliant future will become a chaotic and unstable China with no future whatever," predicted the editorial in the *People's Daily*.

The editorial went on to threaten disbandment of illegal organizations and prosecution of those who spread rumors. Moreover, a ban on demonstrations was issued and students were forbidden to visit factories, rural areas, and high schools in order to gain support.[2]

It is doubtful whether the secret service had already identified the masterminds behind the movement. At the very end of June, three weeks after the bloodbath, Mayor Chen Xitong of Beijing told his version of the "inside story" of the activists behind the movement in a sixty-page report. The precursors of the "conspiracy" were academic seminars, magazines from Hong Kong that published their proceedings and that were distributed "illegally" in China, petitions for amnesty, and democratic salons on university campuses.

In Chen's report, Fang Lizhi was repeatedly cast in the role of conspirator, but only because of the row over the presidential dinner invitation at the end of February. The report dwelled on the influence his earlier writings and speeches had had. Fang had mostly kept to the background so as not to become both an easy target and the fuse of the powder keg. His wife, Li Shuxian, also a professor, had participated in the political salon of the student leader Wang Dan. Mayor Chen pointed out the fact that articles by prominent Chinese academics had been printed in foreign papers as proof of international complicity in the conspiracy. There were, however, no organizational ties between the sometimes unwitting conspirators and student organizations, at least not at that time.[3]

Of the two "black hands" who in 1991 were given the heaviest sentences—thirteen years—Mayor Chen named only one, Chen Ziming, who on 19 April had taken part in an unofficial memorial gathering for Hu Yaobang at which sympathy was expressed for the demonstrators. It was not until much later, when the exiled leaders of the movement began to give interviews in Paris and New York, that it became apparent that an action committee of prominent intellectuals and seasoned activists had been the brains behind the movement. They had, however, tried to exert a moderating rather than a radicalizing influence.[4]

Deng was in no way prepared to bend to pressure from outside the party. Concessions could only be made in a less tense situation, as though granted from above as a token of "imperial benevolence." In his eyes, rebellious students were a new version of the Red Guards, those even younger students who had been Mao's ideological storm troopers in 1966, and had in a very short time spread death, destruction, and anarchy across all of China.

Deng Xiaoping's stakes were so high that if everyone did not now immediately tremble and obey, it would be clear proof that he was no longer taken seriously. This is precisely what happened. After a day of feverish deliberation on the brink of the abyss, large numbers of students wrote farewell letters to their parents in their own blood, in which they declared their readiness to face police bullets rather than let themselves be intimidated and maligned by an eighty-five-year-old dictator.

The following morning, the unimaginable occurred. From all the university campuses in northwest Beijing, tens of thousands of well-organized students marched toward the city center. Dense cordons of policemen stood with loudspeakers at strategic intersections along the wide streets of Beijing's suburbs, calling out, "This demonstration is illegal. Disperse!" At this, student leaders came forward again and again, holding the editorial from the *People's Daily:* "We condemn this slander of the people by the *People's Daily. People's Daily*—People's Fraud!" In the course of the morning, there were an estimated hundred thousand students on the streets and at least half a million civilians, who brought with them sandwiches, soft drinks, wet towels, money, and whatnot, imploring the police not to commit any historic crimes. At first police cordons bent like rubber bands from the pressure of the crowds; then they burst forth like a corps de ballet in a V-formation. The sociopsychological motivation for the people's support was not only sympathy with the young students but shared indignation at corruption and inflation.

THE HUMILIATION of Deng Xiaoping was complete. No editorial had caused so much commotion since the climax of the Cultural Revolution. It had reportedly been written by Xu Weicheng, propaganda director of the city of Beijing, who had been the poison pen of Mao Zedong's wife, Jiang Qing, twenty years earlier. The Beijing city government has been a sinister, leftist stronghold ever since.

Many Chinese intellectuals thought that if the editorial had not been printed, there would have been a big demonstration on 4 May anyway—the seventieth anniversary of the May Fourth Movement of 1919—and then the movement would have fizzled out, owing to fatigue and the summer exams. The editorial steeled the will of the students to sacrifice themselves, persuading them not to give up just yet. Dictators who make such big miscalculations would, in a somewhat more normal political climate, resign or be forced to resign. But not in China. Deng Xiaoping decided then and there to shed blood. "We should not shy away from shedding some blood or losing face. This will not damage our image in the world," said Deng.

If it had been up to Deng, the army would probably have been called into action at the end of April instead of at the beginning of June. After returning from his visit to Pyongyang on 30 April, Zhao Ziyang, as general secretary of the party, wanted to take control of the situation. He wished to block Deng's plans for violent repression and hoped to reach a peaceful solution to the crisis. After his dismissal in June 1989, Zhao gave a long speech justifying his actions during the critical month of May. The contents of the speech surfaced in Hong Kong at the time of the fifth anniversary of the massacre in 1994, amid rumors that Zhao had made contacts with former sympathizers in the hope of again playing a role in the post-Deng era. Zhao said that immediately after his return from North Korea he had searched for ways to have the controversial editorial revoked. At the time the editorial was printed, it was claimed that Zhao had telegraphed his assent from the North Korean capital, but according to the transcript of his speech, this had not been the case. Only the gist of Deng Xiaoping's remarks and the minutes of the Politburo's meeting had been sent to him, not the text of the article. Zhao's standpoint was that "it was wrong to suppose that the actions of hundreds of thousands of people were manipulated by only a handful—this can be no explanation for what happened." Zhao said that in this way the students had been cast as "counterrevolutionaries," which had angered him intensely: "I think that if these words had not been written, the majority would not have become so agitated."[5]

An important domestic memorial celebration, that of the May Fourth Movement of 1919, and two important international events limited the hard-liners in their freedom of action: the annual meeting of the Asian Development Bank (ADB) on 3 and 4 May, and especially the upcoming Sino-Soviet summit between Deng and Gorbachev, which would be the crowning achievement of Deng Xiaoping's revolutionary career, which had spanned seven decades. It was Zhao, however, who was first successful in transforming the confrontational climate into one conducive to dialogue. This nevertheless led to a futile tug-of-war, as the government, represented by Li Peng's slippery spokesman Yuan Mu, did not intend to recognize the independent students' union, which would have made "Chinese Lech Walesas" of its leaders.

During a reception for the governors of the ADB, Zhao gave a strikingly conciliatory speech, in stark contrast to the government's rigid stance, after which the confusion and possibly complete paralysis in the upper echelons of government and party were exposed for all to see. Zhao pleaded "for the reasonable demands of the students to be met." He was confident that there would be no major outbreaks of violence and that the demonstrations would eventually calm down. He did not think that the demonstrations were an indication of China's instability. The students were not against socialism but wanted to see mistakes corrected that had been made in the workings of the government and party. In other words, they were a loyal opposition and not conspirators and saboteurs. Zhao maintained that "common sense, reasonableness, moderation, discipline, and dedication to the principles of democracy and the rule of law are the conditions essential for a solution to the problems."

Actively encouraged by Zhao, the media gave free and factual reports of the demonstrations for the first time the very next day. Zhao had openly criticized party secretary Jiang Zemin of Shanghai—his successor after the massacre—for his curbing and closing of China's freest newspaper, the *World Economic Herald.*

After a few days of calm, there was another demonstration on 9 May. This time it was not the students who were protesting, but over a thousand journalists from the official media. With Zhao's encouragement, they felt strong enough to protest the closing of the *Herald* and the dismissal of its editor in chief, Qin Benli. They also demanded a dialogue with the government on the subject of reforming China's "industry of lies," the media. The most hotly disputed lie had been Deng Xiaoping's editorial of 26 April. Calls for its revocation and an apology became the main theme of student demonstrations in the following days, some of which were attended on bicycles because the students were too tired to walk the long distances involved.

Days went by and the triumvirate of student leaders, Wu'er Kaixi, Wang Dan, and Chai Ling, began to realize that Zhao was powerless in his fight against the hard-liners. Party discipline, however, prevented him from coming to the square. The elderly conservatives were afraid that, once at the square, he would mobilize the people in his own struggle for political survival. Rumors circulated that Deng Xiaoping had already left the capital twice to visit regional army commanders to prepare for massive military repression.

The students' dilemma was now whether to end the movement without any appreciable results before the beginning of the Sino-Soviet summit. The other option was to let things escalate, trying to attract all the attention they could get from the world media amassed in Beijing to cover Gorbachev's visit and humiliating Deng Xiaoping for the second time. Chai Ling made a passionate plea for a hunger strike on the square, and on Saturday afternoon, a day and a half before Gorbachev's arrival, things finally reached that point. Two attempts by the mayor of Beijing, the education minister, and a senior party leader to clear the square on Sunday (14 May) failed utterly. The result was that Gorbachev was welcomed not by a guard of honor but by thousands of fasting students carrying banners with texts such as "The Soviet Union Has Gorbachev! What Does China Have?" and "Down with the Old Men and the Corrupt Government of Li Peng."

Only now did the establishment's intellectuals come into action, not "conspiratorially" but openly. The political scientist Yan Jiaqi, the Marxist humanist Su Shaozhi, the essayist Su Xiaokang, the prominent journalist Dai Qing, and many others all stood at the head of a march of more than a thousand professors, writers, and artists. They sent a petition to the government requesting a real and not a mock dialogue. Otherwise they would have no alternative but to support the students to the bitter end. Even more than the daring students, they recognized the seriousness of the situation and worriedly asked themselves what would happen after Gorbachev had left. They begged the students "to quit the square temporarily in the interest of long-term reforms." Wu'er Kaixi and Wang Dan let themselves be persuaded, but the militant majority of hunger strikers under the wing of "La Pasionaria Chai Ling" had now fixed their sights on a higher world of patriotic heroics and martyrdom. They wouldn't think of listening to these middle-aged ladies and gentlemen, whose priority was to save Zhao instead of letting the students win.

If the students had ever been the pawns of the "conspirators," that stage was now past. On 16 May there was a meeting of the Standing Committee of the Politburo. Zhao made a last-ditch attempt to unravel the knot created by the editorial without actually causing Deng Xiaoping to lose face, and to lay the blame at the feet of the Standing Committee. Deng Xiaoping had, after all, issued his rash instructions to print the editorial after a meeting of the Standing Committee on 24 April, where they had first heard a report by Li Peng. Zhao had not been present, as he was visiting Pyongyang at the time. Details of Li Peng's report have never been made public, but it was generally assumed that Li, together with Li Ximing, the party secretary of Beijing, and Mayor Chen Xitong, were determined to let things escalate until they spun out of control. This would serve as an excuse for getting rid of Zhao Ziyang. Numerous residents of Beijing have since confirmed that Li Peng and his cohorts did not shun one lie, one means of manipulation, or one agitprop scheme in their design to mislead and alarm Deng Xiaoping to such an extent that violent repression would be the only way out.

Zhao opened the May 16 meeting with the observation that the situation was critical: it was no longer possible simply to bandy about words concerning the editorial. Li Peng was unrelenting, however, and said that the words "premeditated conspiracy . . . the undermining of the party once and for all" had been uttered by Deng Xiaoping himself and could therefore not be changed. Zhao did not agree. "Comrade [Deng] Xiaoping uttered those words after hearing the report of the Standing Committee under the chairmanship of Li Peng. Considering Comrade Xiaoping always gave his complete support to the work of the Standing Committee as long as its decision was made collectively, he would certainly have supported this as well." Li Peng, supported by Yao Yilin and perhaps others, did not want deescalation, because this would strengthen the position of Zhao Ziyang. In other words, if the document containing Zhao's speech was authentic, there could be no doubt that Li Peng was the great conspirator behind the escalation of the unrest.[6]

· · ·

MEANWHILE, TIANANMEN SQUARE had been transformed into one big first-aid camp with the sound of screaming sirens as ambulances screeched to a halt and tore off again, bearing unconscious hunger strikers away to hospitals. Every organization that was not still under the thumb of the party, as well as universities throughout the country, sent support teams to the square. Sympathizers from Hong Kong sent thousands of colorful tents and umbrellas. The public-address system had been donated by China's newest entrepreneurs, especially Stone, the computer manufacturer, whose director, Wan Runnan, was a prospective new-style politician who ran his own socioeconomic research institute.

Immediately upon Gorbachev's departure for Shanghai, the Politburo called an emergency midnight meeting at Deng's home on 17 May and decided to declare martial law. An American writer has supplied interesting details of a conversation that took place between Deng and Zhao, without, however, mentioning his source.

"I have the army behind me," Deng supposedly said to Zhao.

"But I have the people behind me," retorted Zhao.

"In that case, you have nothing," Deng answered simply.[7]

Zhao voted against declaring martial law, refused to do it, and offered to resign. His resignation was not accepted, as this would have made him a free man and a martyr, just like Hu Yaobang, which at that moment would have had the same effect as a nuclear bomb.

The plan to declare martial law was leaked to the students via Zhao's secretary, Bao Tong, and became the starting signal for a broadly based resistance movement that immediately began to make preparations for "defending" the city against a military invasion.

The next morning, 18 May, Zhao visited hospitals and the square as a token of his sympathy, probably still hoping to avert a crisis. He could not make any concessions, however, as his every step was dogged by Li Peng. In spite of pouring rain, the first general mobilization of the people took place a few hours later. Between 3 million and 5 million people were milling around the streets of Beijing, accusing the government, in an unprecedented burst of anger, of cowardice and crassness in refusing to speak to the people earlier.

That afternoon, the government declared itself ready for a dialogue that would be broadcast directly on television. Failure was inevitable. The government wanted to use a display of empty gestures to influence public opinion; the students hoped to win unobtainable concessions. Wu'er Kaixi, the charismatic rebel, wandered theatrically into Li Peng's reception hall wearing pajamas, with an oxygen bottle under his arm and an intravenous drip in his nose. Apparently he was interested only in humiliating Li Peng, thereby winning the sympathy of millions of people but in fact achieving nothing. He made it clear to Li that he should not be talking about unimportant side issues but be offering an apology for the slanderous editorial in the *People's Daily* on 26 April. "If you print that tomorrow in the *People's Daily* and offer your apologies to the whole country, we will be able to persuade those students outside to stop their hunger strike."

Li Peng called Wu'er Kaixi rude and improper for wanting to dictate the agenda unilaterally. The dialogue never got beyond futile accusations. An apology was out of the question.

THE FINAL EPISODE began on Friday, 19 May. A tearful Zhao went to the square again that morning. It was his last farewell. More than seven years later, he has still not appeared again in public. Zhao said that finding solutions would take time and warned the students of approaching disaster: "After seven days of fasting you should not cling to the idea that you will not give up until you are given satisfactory answers. It will be too late and the loss will be irreparable."

The whole day long, there was nothing but total confusion, agitation, and aggressiveness on the square. In the early hours of the evening, the students' "security guards" closed off the innermost part of the square for a "very important meeting of very important people." The eloquent "great leader" Wu'er Kaixi had been brought from the hospital for the occasion, just as he had been before his trial of strength with Li Peng. There he stood, in the protected area that served as the "supreme command" post, with the intravenous drip in his nose, surrounded by five bodyguards. The new Politburo! The meeting was called to discuss the hunger strike and was held in the highest secrecy.

At nine o'clock the shrill voice of Chai Ling screeched over the students' loudspeaker. She said that the hunger strike had achieved its aim, because the government had been shaken to the core. "We have won a great victory, because the people support us." A group of militant protesters booed loudly. She continued: "No capitulation! If we stop now, it will all have been for nothing." A small minority declared the newly founded student federation dissolved and called a new meeting in a bus. Before they could reach a decision, the much louder public-address system of the government was suddenly put into operation. It was Li Peng, who declared martial law in a barking, bellicose tone of voice. When the crowd finally realized that the army would be called in, the students' mood immediately became militant and their spirit united. Thirty thousand young people decided to go on a hunger strike. It was generally assumed that it would only be a matter of hours before the army arrived.

Barricades were instantly erected to block the way of army vehicles. The Flying Tigers, Beijing's version of the Hell's Angels, raced back and forth to coordinate information on the whereabouts of the army columns. Ambulances, buses, and trucks were parked in the middle of intersections "for the protection of the people against the People's Liberation Army," the anachronistic name still borne by the Chinese armed forces. Rumors were rampant that the army was split and that various generals had refused to obey orders. If indeed the attack had been planned for that night, then it was a monumental failure.

The next day, resistance escalated. Elderly generals protested and whole army units deserted. Barricades had been set up everywhere using building materials, sewage pipes, and fences. In the suburbs, peasants in tractors punctured the tires of army vehicles. Li Peng had not been seen or heard from for days. Deng Xiaoping had allegedly gone to Wuhan to find troops that were more trustworthy.

During the last week of May, a coalition of students, workers' unions, and societies of intellectuals seemed to be taking shape. Once out on the street, Yan Jiaqi and his colleagues revealed themselves to be determined activists. On 25 May an autonomous federation of workers' unions was founded by Han Dongfang, a railway electrician. Various attempts were made to engineer the downfall of Li Peng by constitutional means, based on his "unconstitutional declaration of martial law," but this was a nonstarter in the current life-or-death struggle in which Mao's old dictum—"Political power comes from the barrel of a gun"—was the only solution.

In the meantime, the square had degenerated into a huge, stinking garbage dump with emergency latrines that could not possibly cope with the amount of human waste. Sanitation workers patrolled all day with cans of Lysol to prevent the outbreak of epidemics. In this situation, Chai Ling, the last survivor of the troika that had called itself "the supreme command of the United Action Headquarters on Tiananmen Square," judged it best to call an end to the occupation on 27 May. Three days later, however, students from eight art academies made a last spectacular and challenging gesture that fanned the flames of the nearly extinguished movement: they set up a ten-meter-high Chinese version of the American Statue of Liberty. The blocks were brought to the square on five large bicycle carts, and the police made no attempt whatever to stop them. To provide water for the cementing of the enormous plaster blocks, a full tank truck from the municipal waterworks stood at the ready. This proved yet again that almost no public organ was still in the government's firm control. Anarchy was almost complete. The sculpture was placed on the square's central axis, halfway between the Monument to the People's Heroes and Tiananmen Gate. It faced the most important icon of the Chinese revolution, the portrait of the forbidding Mao, staring it in the eyes as the symbol of a new age. A more sarcastic provocation was inconceivable.

THE RULERS' PATIENCE had run out. That same day, three workers from the new autonomous union and eleven motorcycle riders from the Flying Tigers were arrested. The next day, the government organized for the first time counterdemonstrations in the suburbs, where effigies of Fang Lizhi were burned, branding him "the most important instigator of the protest movement behind the scenes." "Conquer the square at all costs," ordered Deng Xiaoping after new troops from different parts of the country had taken up their positions around Beijing.

On Saturday, 3 June, at ten o'clock in the evening, the troops were ordered to clear the square before six o'clock on Sunday morning. Hundreds of tanks and armored vehicles broke through the barricades. After bloody battles in which hundreds were killed and 364 tanks and armored vehicles were set on fire and destroyed by frenzied civilians, the square was finally surrounded that night by 2:30 a.m.

Now began the great controversy of the whole drama, which the regime skillfully exploited to the dismay of the assembled world media. In the total chaos that ensued, the first reports, made after prompting by the Chinese Red Cross and the CIA, said that between 2,600 and 3,000 people had died in the "mass murder *in* the square." Days before, the Taiwanese pop singer Hou Dejian, together with three well-known Chinese intellectuals, had begun a last hunger strike at the Monument to the People's Heroes in the center of the square. Hou and his buddy, the eccentric philosopher Liu Xiaobo, were now able to persuade the military commander to negotiate and were successful in securing safe conduct for the remaining 5,000 students in the square. A Spanish television crew filmed the retreat from the southeast corner of the square at five a.m. This put the government in a position to vehemently refute the reports in the international media that there had been a massacre *in the square itself,* suggesting that the bloody battles that occurred during the army's march to the square could not have been so bad.

After two days of silence—time enough to doctor the videos and falsify the figures—Li Peng's spokesman Yuan Mu appeared with the story that 300 people had been killed, including 23 students, the rest being mostly soldiers. Four hundred soldiers were still reported missing; 5,000 soldiers and 2,000 civilians had been injured. The gist of the story was that the People's Liberation Army had wanted to protect the people from gangs of armed counterrevolutionary bandits and had suffered great losses in the attempt. The counterrevolutionaries were the aggressors, the soldiers the victims.

DENG XIAOPING, who had not been seen in public since the summit with Gorbachev, suddenly appeared on 9 June, first of all to offer his condolences to the generals because of all the dead in their midst, and also to give his apocalyptic "pastoral" vision of the recent turn of events: "This storm was bound to happen. It was determined by the international macro-climate and China's own micro-climate, and was independent of man's will. It was only a question of time and extent. We should consider ourselves lucky that it happened now . . . because we have a large group of veteran-comrades who are still alive. They have survived many storms and they know what is at stake. They support resolute action to suppress a rebellion. Although some comrades do not yet understand this, one day they will, and then they will support the decision of the Central Committee."[8]

Deng thought therefore that higher powers had been behind the conspiracy. It was a Greek tragedy with a Chinese twist. Independent of each other's will, both parties had thrown themselves into the abyss.

China was plunged into a new phase of Red Terror which lasted several months, with all the accompanying jargon of struggle, deception, and hatred of an incipient revolution. Within months all the leaders of the movement who had not fled abroad had been arrested and were waiting to be sentenced. Those who had committed acts of violence against the army were quickly sentenced to death and executed. Those who had rebelled only verbally were given sentences of four to thirteen years.

Who was the biggest loser? At the time, everyone thought it was Deng Xiaoping. He had wanted to go down in history as a strong but moderate leader who had set China firmly on the path of modernization after the tyranny of Mao Zedong, creating for the first time in history a structure for orderly succession. All that seemed to be lost now. The relatively liberal, internationally respected Zhao Ziyang was replaced by Jiang Zemin, a bombastic apparatchik from Shanghai, who seven years later has not yet managed fully to shake off his image as a colorless transitional figure.

During his first press conference as the new party leader, Jiang Zemin was asked the simple question "How could the Tiananmen tragedy have been avoided?"

Beaming, Jiang replied loudly, "That was no tragedy. That was counter-revolutionary turmoil!" Jiang left no doubt as to where he stood. He said that his two predecessors had lost their jobs because they had not fought hard enough against bourgeois liberalization. He would not make the same mistake.

PART FOUR

Regionalism Versus Centralism, Interdependence, and Transnationalism.

CHAPTER 12

The Central-Regional Swing of the Pendulum in Historical Perspective

China's economic miracle has taken place at the expense of the central government.

HU ANGANG,
economic adviser to the Chinese government

China needs a Robin Hood–like program of redistribution to prevent social instability from occurring. The state must rob the rich to help the poor.[1]

FAN GANG,
leading Chinese economist

CHINA IS A CONTINENTAL SUPERSTATE consisting of thirty administrative units, five autonomous regions, twenty-two provinces, and three self-governing megacities, each with an average of 40 million inhabitants. The most populous province, Sichuan, has 110 million inhabitants, and the least populous region, Tibet, has 2.2 million.[2]

The innovative trend in the world economy during the transition from the twentieth to the twenty-first century is the formation of economic region-states as the form of organization most efficient in promoting prosperity with the help of the four I's—investment, industry, information, and individual consumers. The world's best-known business strategist, Ken Ohmae, writes in his latest book that the power of the spendthrift nation-state has been usurped by "the four C's"—capital, corporations, consumers, and communications—and that regional economies with between 5 million and 20 million consumers, free or largely free from the control of central government bureaucracies, are increasingly taking their places as centers of economic power and prosperity.[3]

This phenomenon has also begun to take effect in China. One of the most typical region-states in the world is Hong Kong and the border areas of Guangdong Province in the Pearl River delta. Ultramodern infrastructure, financial services, and pampered consumers have forced this limited part of China to close ranks completely with the global economy. The Chinese coast, and at a later stage of development the border areas, can accommodate dozens of similar region-states, but only in the case of much more far-reaching economic and administrative decentralization than has so far taken place.

China tends to view such internationalization, globalization, multilateralism, and interdependence as encroachments on its sovereignty, which it automatically opposes. Regionalism and federalism are likewise anathema, being tantamount to warlordism, national disintegration, and a weakening of central authority. China is the only country of its size in the world that still has a unitary, highly centralized political structure, which is actually causing it to malfunction more and more.

The only recognized regions in the Chinese administrative establishment are the autonomous regions (*zizhiqu*) of national minorities. Here autonomy is not a reflection of federalism but an empty cliché. They are nominally ruled by indigenous governors, but above them is a Han Chinese party secretary.

In China, the term "region" also refers to groupings of provinces. These existed temporarily in the early years of the People's Republic and were reinstated in the mid-1980s. They are large (economic) regions, each with 100 million people or more. Some of the regions came into being without any conscious planning on the government's part, as the natural result of the decentralization and market transformation of the last fifteen years.

The ninth Five-Year Plan (1996–2000) and the long-term development program up to the year 2010 divided the country into seven economic regions or zones (I quote directly from the Chinese):

1. a zone in the Yangtze River valley and along the river—to take advantage of a solid agricultural and industrial foundation and high technological level, ride on the momentum of the Pudong New Area in Shanghai and the construction of the gigantic Three Gorges Dam project, and stand face-to-face with the large- and medium-

sized cities along the river, such as the steel and car manufacturing center of Wuhan and the defense industry center of Chongqing;

2. a zone around the Bohai Gulf including the Liaodong and Jiaodong peninsulas, Beijing, Tianjin, and Hebei Province—to take advantage of developed transportation, a concentration of large- and medium-sized cities and scientific and technological personnel, as well as abundant resources of coal, iron, and petroleum;

3. a zone in the southeastern coastal areas—to take advantage of the geographical location of neighboring Hong Kong, Macao, and Taiwan and of high-level openness. The zone will rely mainly on the Pearl River delta and the southeastern areas of Fujian Province and will focus on growth of export-oriented agriculture, capital- and technology-intensive foreign-funded enterprises, and high-value-added industries;

4. a zone covering parts of the southwest and south (Sichuan, Guizhou, Yunnan, Guangxi)—to take advantage of coastal, riverside, and boundary locations and abundant resources in agriculture, forestry, water, minerals, and tourist attractions. The zone will rely on the technological force of the defense industry and will become an important national base for energy, nonferrous metals, phosphorus, sulfur, and tropical and subtropical crops;

5. a zone in the northeast (Liaoning, Jilin, Heilongjiang, Inner Mongolia)—to take advantage of developed transportation, a complete heavy-industry system, and rich land and energy resources. The zone will be focused on revamping the old industrial base there, revitalizing enterprises, and increasing the technological level and comprehensive development of agricultural resources, thereby forming an important national base for heavy and chemical industries and farm produce;

6. a zone covering five provinces in central China (Gansu, Shaanxi, Shanxi, Henan, Anhui)—to give scope to the relatively developed agriculture and transportation and a relatively sound industrial foundation, in order to accelerate development along the rail routes of Lanzhou–Lianyungang, Beijing–Kowloon, and Beijing–Guangzhou and form important agricultural, raw-materials, and machinery bases;

7. a zone in the northwest (Xinjiang)—to bring into play the advantage of being a linkage between East and Central Asia, rich resources in agriculture, animal husbandry, energy, and minerals, as well as the advantage of military enterprises. The zone, with the Eurasian Continental Bridge from Lianyungang to Rotterdam as a

linkage, is designed to boost construction of infrastructure facilities and development of resources and become a leading national base for cotton, animal products, petrochemicals, energy, and non-ferrous metals.[4]

The upper northeast, the provinces of Jilin and Heilongjiang, together with the Russian Far East, a united Korea, and Hokkaido (the northernmost island of Japan) could in future become a transnational superregion and an important center of heavy industry. Although Tibet has been classified as part of the southwest, it is a world unto itself, immense in size and probably rich in minerals, but too isolated and economically still too insignificant. Xinjiang, the Islamic Far West, is just as isolated yet is economically important for three reasons: the transnational orientation toward the new Commonwealth of Independent States (CIS) in Central Asia, the flow of money and people to and from the Middle East, and the oil reserves expected to be found in the Taklimakan Desert.

CHINA IS SO HUGE, diverse, and complex that it is barely feasible to categorize its regional, ethnic, religious and cultural, geographical, climatological, political, and economic contrasts. The most important split is between the outward-oriented coastal belt and the inward-looking interior, and between the urban and the rural areas. This split is further complicated by the contrast between the conservative agrarian-bureaucratic-militaristic north and the freewheeling, commercial southern coast, which in recent years has become a gigantic export zone, transnationally integrated with the world economy but dependent on the rest of China for cheap "migrant labor."

The colors symbolizing these contrasts are yellow and blue, after the Yellow River and the blue ocean. Mao Zedong represented yellow, autarkic, isolationist peasant thinking. Deng Xiaoping stood for blue, the "open door," and the reform of China into a trading and naval power. The contrast of the 1990s is between the blue and yellow water provinces, which coincide in large part with the lines dividing east and west and rich and poor. Mao Zedong's policy of national egalitarian development brought the whole country down to the same level of impoverishment. Deng Xiaoping put an end to this impractical anomaly in 1978 and urged the regions with better prospects for rapid economic development to "get rich first, so that eventually everyone will get rich" by way of the "trickle-down effect."

The decentralization and preferential treatment of the coastal zones during the 1980s increased these contrasts considerably. Some economists and sociologists are now talking about "internal colonization." The poor western territories furnish raw materials to the developed eastern coastal areas and receive cheap but low-quality industrial products in return. Better-quality goods are always exported. The standard of living is rising faster in the east than in the west; the discrepancy in development between the two is the widest since 1949. In Guizhou Province the better-off parts are fully ten times richer than the poorer parts of the province. Hu Angang, a young, leading economist at the Chinese Academy of Social Sciences, who has been the most vocal opponent of growing regional inequality, presented shocking figures at the end of 1995: China may be divided into six income categories—extremely low, low, middle, upper middle, high, and extremely high. Extremely high incomes in the special economic zones are seven to eight times the national average, while extremely low incomes are less than 10 percent of the national per capita income. This means that the gap between the lowest and highest incomes is one to eighty or more.[5]

This wide gap does not exist only between coastal and remote inland areas. A glaring contrast also exists between the neighboring Guangdong and Guangxi provinces. In 1984 Guangxi's gross product was one-third that of Guangdong, and by 1991 it had dropped to one-fourth. Guangxi has a population of 43 million and Guangdong 65 million. The per capita income of Guangxi, which, by the way, is not in the interior but also has a coastline on the South China Sea, dropped between 1984 and 1991 from 61.5 percent to 59.6 percent of the national average.[6]

Seventy percent of all raw materials come from territories west of the rail line Canton–Beijing. The production of raw materials, however, is in some cases just as profitable as exporting goods produced by light industry. The front-runners are two cities situated four thousand kilometers apart: Zhuhai, a manufacturing center and special zone north of Macau, and Karamay, the oil town near the border of Kazakhstan. In 1995 the per capita income in both cities was 20,000 yuan ($2,375). Of the twenty richest cities in China, however, 80 percent are located on the southeast coast.

In Hu Angang's opinion, the escalating inequality of income is no longer a social problem but a political one, which could result in national disintegration.[7]

BESIDES GREAT DIFFERENCES in income among the regions, there also exist deep contradictions in the administrative structure of China which must once again be corrected. The goal of decentralization in the Deng era was to mobilize local initiative to spur economic growth. It had no structural or political implications but has nevertheless produced a budding form of federalism that Beijing constantly tries to curb. The "unitary, vertically integrated family state" still reigns. In spite of continual amendments to the constitution, decentralization still has no constitutional underpinnings, and this means that the central government, the head of the family, remains potentially omnipotent. The balance of power is informally determined by the personal relations between the Politburo and the regional military leaders, governors, mayors, and (provincial) party secretaries. "We want the rule of the individual, not the rule of law" (*Yao ren-zhi, bu-yao fa-zhi*) was the leitmotiv of Mao Zedong. That was also the changeless philosophy that had determined the whole of China's dynastic and pre-Communist twentieth-century history. The rise and fall of dynasties depended on the way in which relations between the central and local governments were regulated. Since the middle of the nineteenth century, there have been both the permanent erosion of central imperial power and the rise of regional centers of power. After 1949 the Communist's answer to this was overcentralization using three instruments of coercion: ideological orthodoxy, party discipline, and the central planning mechanism.

The new People's Republic was first divided into six "greater administration regions" (*da xing-zheng qu*) under the authority of a military party secretary. At that time, Deng Xiaoping, a former army political commissar, was secretary of the southwest in Chongqing. Below the GARs were the autonomous territories of national minorities, provinces, and cities with the rank of provinces (Beijing, Shanghai, Tianjin). Below the provinces (*sheng*) are the counties (*xian*) and the cities (*shi*). This vertical dictatorship, embodied in the State Planning Commission, was formed in 1952 and had a paralyzing effect on local initiative. "Ministerial autarky" reigned; horizontal coordination was out of the question. Planning of production, allocation of materials, and budgetary control of income and expenditures, even for small purchases of office supplies—everything took place in Beijing. The greater administrative regions were dissolved in 1954. One of the abuses they had led to was the formation of regional power blocks. The party secretary of Northeast China, Gao Gang, was accused in 1954 of "forming an independent—pro-Soviet—kingdom" in the northeast in order subsequently to make a bid for power over the whole country together with Rao Shushi, the secretary of East China. Both were purged, in the first top-level purge to take place in the new state.

The first systematic decentralization followed in 1957, with the goal of mobilizing provincial initiative in accelerating economic development. Chairman Mao Zedong said in his speech "On the Ten Major Relationships": "Our land is so vast, our population so large, and conditions so complex that it is much better to let initiative emanate from both the center and the local authorities." Mao hoped, through decentralization, to secure support from the provinces for the Great Leap Forward, which he launched a year later. The Great Leap was a campaign to accelerate industrialization under the motto "Surpass England in fifteen years in the production of iron and steel." The methods used were mass mobilization, regimentation, collectively melting down pots and pans to make steel, and other forms of economic construction in the style of guerrilla warfare. Agriculture was neglected, resulting in failed harvests, faulty distribution of foodstuffs, famine, and a catastrophe that cost China years of economic growth. Mao was shunted to the sidelines, and during the "rehabilitation program," led by president Liu Shaoqi and General Secretary Deng Xiaoping, the whole process of decentralization was reversed in the early 1960s. Although the Great Leap Forward had created localism at the lowest level, it was negative localism, based on autarky and a refusal to be patronized by higher levels of government. Since then, localism has lived on, forming the basis of the anarchy of the Cultural Revolution and the later, dynamic "market localism" of the 1980s and 1990s.[8]

A new wave of decentralization followed in 1964. Local government was given the freedom to invest in nineteen nonindustrial sectors, such as agriculture, cattle breeding, fishing, forestry, and transportation, and more authority over industries such as artificial fertilizers, cement, and coal. The orderly implementation of the new decentralization was upset in 1966, however, by Mao's launching of another extreme experiment: the Cultural Revolution. The central government organs no longer ruled, and Mao encouraged the spirit of "relying on one's own strength," which further strengthened local initiative and self-reliance. During the fourth Five-Year Plan (1970), most of the enterprises controlled by the central government were turned over to provincial and local governments. A system of distributing shared finances, materials, and investments was initiated, which gave provinces and municipalities considerable control over their own resources.

In 1976, at the end of the Mao era, there had been two cycles of decentralization and recentralization—"twice 'top down'—twice 'bottom up,'" in the Chinese idiom. The trend, however, was toward further decentralization, and in spite of routine attempts at recentralization, the central-local relationship has never returned to its old pattern. Ideology as a unifying tool had been discredited by ultraleft extremism, party discipline had been seriously weakened by power struggles and instability within the central leadership, and the central planning mechanism had also failed to bring about economic modernization. More and more local party secretaries, governors, and mayors in their regions of birth kept watch over local interests in their own way, and carried out instructions from the central government as they saw fit. In 1984 two-thirds of all appointments to the nomenklatura were delegated to lower levels. Only vice-ministers, vice-governors, and higher officials, as well as presidents of top universities, are still appointed by the central government. This policy has done much to promote the appointment of natives.

THE NEWEST, most radical decentralization of the 1980s concerned four main areas: the "household responsibility system" (HRS) for peasant families, the various forms of contract systems for state enterprises, taxation, and foreign trade.

After the death of Mao, HRS was the natural solution to rural poverty, which had been caused by the regimentation in people's communes and extreme-leftist political campaigns. Restoration of the freedom to engage in family farming—selling produce on a quota basis to the state and trading the surplus on the free market—was initiated by Deng Xiaoping to enlist popular support in his struggle for power with the remaining Mao loyalists led by Hua Guofeng, but it also arose spontaneously from the grass roots. Wan Li, kindred spirit and bridge partner to Deng Xiaoping, was the first to effect systematic implementation of this scheme in poor Anhui Province, which had been hit by a severe drought in 1978. Zhao Ziyang also carried out pioneering work in Sichuan, leading most of the provinces gradually to adopt the household responsibility system, not because of pressure from the central government but because of pressure from their own people. The more the HRS was given free rein, the more it swept away the people's communes, undermining the power of the party as well as that of the local government, and consequently weakening the central government's hold on the countryside.

The decollectivization of agriculture was immediately followed by commercialization and industrialization in the rural areas. Rural cadres and a new, upcoming class of peasant entrepreneurs formed coalitions that invested their profits from production and trading on the free market in so-called "township and village enterprises" (TVEs). These were to become the most important motivating force behind China's high economic growth.

The free markets created great demand for the TVEs' products in the cities and helped China to break out of the vicious circle that other socialist countries were unable to shake off. Attempts made in 1980 by Deng Xiaoping's rival Chen Yun to halt reforms and "to place the economy in a cage" failed because the dynamics of the market mechanism could no longer be stopped. Already by 1981 collectively organized investments made by farmers accounted for 37 percent of all state investment, and the number of employees in the TVEs had mounted to 30 million, also more than one-third of all workers in the state sector. Agricultural reforms in China were a success, at least in the beginning stages, because, owing to Mao's anarchic tendencies, the centrally planned economy was much less rigid and less developed in China than those in the Soviet Union and Eastern Europe. Also in contrast to the situation in those countries, agriculture had never been completely integrated into its economy. The agricultural sector was a passive, segregated barter economy, which was freed from state restrictions in 1979 and again monetarized. The flow of agricultural products to the cities broke the state monopoly on foodstuffs, laying the foundation for the decentralization of urban industry. The rapid growth of rural incomes created in turn a great demand for urban industrial goods, which further strengthened the urban economy's tendency toward decentralization and its ability to adapt to market conditions.

The rise of a new, moneyed elite in the rural areas did a lot to undermine the power base of both the central government and the Communist party. The politically subservient were naturally not permitted to be richer than their rulers, but owing to the dynamics of the HRS, village bosses were forced to stand by and watch shrewd, enterprising peasants grow richer than themselves. The next step was allowing low-level party cadres to engage in business so as not to be outdone by the peasants. In this way, village administrators grew wealthier than state functionaries: the lower the rank, the higher the income. In 1986 Luo Xiaoping discovered in the course of research in the Pearl River delta that the average salary of village cadres was just as high as the premier's, and three times that of ministers in the central government.[9] Newly rich farmers invested capital in the cities, and agrarian surpluses led to a drop in agricultural imports and a rise in exports of products from rural industries. This provided foreign currency for imports by the state sector, making central planning even more superfluous. The expansion of the rural market even led to the creation of jobs in the cities. The breakthrough in the countryside was the flywheel for further urban industrial reform, launched by the top leadership in 1984. More than twelve years later, they are still revolving, though in another kind of vicious circle.

THE DECOLLECTIVIZATION of agriculture unintentionally created the conditions that made China a nation of small-time entrepreneurs which could not in essence continue to be Communist. Parallel reforms in the state-industry sector, however, created big problems that would keep China semi-Communist for a long time to come. During the era of orthodox

Communism, profitable state enterprises were the state's most important source of income and the central government took from them whatever it needed. Their high social security premiums, their low productivity, and, since the reforms, the diminishing marketability of their products meant that an increasing number of state enterprises were becoming a burden to the central government, which kept them afloat by extending subsidies and bank credit. In 1984 the central government therefore decided—under the motto "Eating in Various Kitchens"—to hive off a large part of this burden to local governments. Large numbers of state enterprises were freed from the ministries of the central government and turned over to provincial and municipal governments. A new system—"tax payments replace profit deliveries" (*li gai shui*)—was introduced, whereby the relationship between the central government and locally run state enterprises was given a fiscal rather than a bureaucratic basis. State enterprises would no longer contribute their profits to the state; in future they would pay taxes instead, in the hope that this would lead to greater efficiency and an increase in state revenues. Besides shifting its burden to local governments, Beijing hoped that a greater degree of autonomy would completely mobilize the regions' potential and put an end to the passive cooperation they offered under the old system of central command.

The plan backfired. The new system hindered the patronage of local governments previously enjoyed by the enterprises, and their resistance led to a fall in both profits and taxes. Local authorities increased their own revenues wherever possible but refused to turn over more to the central government. The methods employed by provincial and local governments to pay as little as possible into the central coffers varied from endlessly drawing out negotiations and noncooperation to feigned compliance and confrontation. The Chinese say that "policy is made higher up and countermeasures lower down."

Concerned about the yearly rise in the budget deficit, the central government strove for a permanent solution for its fiscal distress, although it was not until 1993 that a remedy was found. An intermediate solution was the "fiscal contract responsibility system," which provided for tax revenues to be shared between the central government and the provinces. In 1988 detailed rules were established for sharing tax revenues, including progressive percentages per province, depending on their level of development. The system contributed to rapid economic growth in the provinces, but impeded further structural reforms. The provinces were skillful at exploiting loopholes in order to maximize their local revenues at the expense of the central government, which was confronted with a drop in income and the strengthening of regionalism.

Local governments also increased their revenues through *tanpai,* extra-budgetary funds (EBF), which were often arbitrary, exorbitant levies of which the central government received nothing. By the end of the 1980s, there were tens of thousands of forms of *tanpai,* which provided local governments with 20 billion yuan in annual revenues. In 1990 the financial-fiscal trial of strength between the central and provincial governments seemed to come to a climax, then fizzled out. Beijing was all for serious implementation of its fiscal reforms of 1988, but an ad hoc coalition of the most affected provinces, led by then governor of Guangdong Province Ye Xuanping, forced Li Peng to postpone his plans.

In the early 1990s the central government's rise in revenues lagged far behind the rate of national economic growth. The main reason for this was tax fraud at the provincial and local level. In most countries, taxes are collected by the central government and then distributed to lower authorities. In China they are collected by lower authorities and distributed upward, leaving a great deal of room for tax evasion and fraud. China's deputy finance minister, Xiang Huaicheng, estimated the total amount of tax evasion in 1991 to be 100 billion yuan. It was high time to introduce a new system of taxation.

The new wave of hypergrowth that followed on the heels of Deng Xiaoping's trip to the south in 1992 led to such an increase in regional incomes that in 1993 the central leaders went ahead and confronted provincial leaders with the complete facts.

In May 1993 two influential Chinese economists at Yale University had published an alarming report, commissioned by the Chinese government, on the sad state of China's finances, underlining the urgency of the situation. Hu Angang and Wang Shaoguang had calculated that China's state revenues had dropped from 32.1 percent of its GNP in 1978 to 14.2 percent in 1992, one-third or less than that of developed industrialized countries. "If there is no drastic reform of the current fiscal contract responsibility system, this percentage will drop even further." Using flexible methods of calculation, the authors estimated that in 1995 China's state revenues would amount to only 13.3 percent of its GNP and in the year 2000 only 11.3 percent. Hu and Wang then demonstrated that China has a weak central government and strong local authorities. In 1989 the income and expenditure of the central government were both 6.9 percent of its GNP, the second lowest in the world, just ahead of the federal government of Yugoslavia (with figures of 5.6 and 5.3 percent). According to the prevailing trend, China's state revenues in the year 2000 would drop further, to 4.9 percent, approximately the same level as that of Chiang Kai-shek's Kuomintang government in 1934 and that of the Yugoslav government shortly before that country's violent disintegration. The authors then sketched a "worst-case scenario": "When the political strong man—Deng Xiaoping—finally dies, it is possible that we will find ourselves in the same situation as Yugoslavia after Tito: while the conflicts of interest between central and lower authorities and between lower authorities among themselves escalate, upsetting the balance between them even more, and the extractive power of the state continues to go downhill, it will only be a question of a number of years, at most ten, before political rupture follows economic collapse and the country finally disintegrates."[10]

The government's long-awaited answer came swiftly. The so-called "blueprint for the transformation to a market economy" of November 1993 concluded that the financial and fiscal relations between the central government and the provinces should be drastically reformed, "changing from the current fiscal contract responsibility system for local authorities to a tax assignment system on the basis of a rational division of power between central and local authorities, and establishing separate central and local taxation systems."[11] The fiscal share of the central state revenues must be drastically increased, and a system implemented "wherein the central fiscal authority receives 55 percent of fiscal returns and transfers payments to local authorities. . . ." According to the *People's Daily*, the main goal was "redistribution of the fruits of economic growth."

THE NEW NATIONAL SYSTEM of taxation, the first in Chinese history, took effect on 1 January 1994. The most important points included the introduction of a modern value-added tax (VAT) and a reduction in taxes for state enterprises from 55 to 33 percent, the same percentage paid by joint ventures. Companies with low profits could ask for further reductions, down to 17 percent. There are centrally levied taxes such as customs duties, a consumers' tax, bank and income taxes for businesses, local taxes such as a business tax, users' rights for land, and an income tax for individuals with widely diverging tax-free deductions (800 yuan a month for the Chinese, $2,000 for foreigners), on a progressive scale from 5 to 45 percent. The VAT (*zengzhishui*) is shared between central and local authorities on the basis of a 7.5:2.5 ratio. The VAT has a single rate of 17 percent, but preferential rates of 13 and 6 percent are possible in certain categories. Tax holidays and tax exemption for foreign investors will be abolished in stages. To fight tax evasion and fraud, a two-stage system of tax collection, national and local, will be introduced. Local tax revenues will account for 45 percent, and central taxes and share taxes will account for 55 percent.

There is widespread doubt as to whether China will be able to educate tens of thousands of accountants, inspectors, and tax collectors within a reasonable time limit, and especially whether it can muster up the "fiscal culture" and discipline necessary to implement a modern taxation system. Until now the few who were required to pax taxes in China and actually did so negotiated the amount of their assessment in exchange for gifts, bribes, other favors, or pure intimidation. The numerous ad hoc concessions and variable rates have retained an element of "everything is negotiable," which undermines the feasibility of true reform.

A study by the World Bank showed that the rich provinces do not take tax collection seriously, as they just have to hand it over to the poor provinces, whereas the poor provinces collect taxes very effectively because they are allowed to keep it all themselves. The World Bank estimates that it will be seven to ten years before the tax system begins to function reasonably well. According to official reports, however, the first year of the new, national tax system was already a success. The income from industrial and commercial taxes rose in 1994 by 25.5 percent and in 1995 by 29.1 percent, but since it started from such a low base, the yield is still far from adequate. During the first half of 1995, there was twice as much tax fraud as in 1994. Ma Jiantang, director of the macroeconomic department of the Research and Development Center of the State Council, said that during that period 30 percent of state enterprises, 60 percent of joint ventures, 80 percent of all private firms, and 100 percent of all street vendors evaded taxes.[12]

In a new study, Hu Angang has verified that state revenues as a percentage of the GNP are still dropping, amounting to only 9.1 percent of the GNP, as opposed to 14.2 percent in 1992, when his first alarming report was published. He warned that the government was in fact bankrupt and had no money even for vitally important infrastructure projects. He concluded that the fiscal power of the state must be restored; otherwise the country would still face ruin.[13]

According to the official media, however, the year 1996 was a lucrative year in every respect. The State Administration on Taxation reported that the year-by-year increase in tax revenues exceeded 100 billion yuan ($12 billion). Vice-premier Zhu Rongji confirmed that tax revenues effectively supported China's reforms and "opening" policy as well as economic growth.[14]

BEFORE 1979 China conducted limited, balanced foreign trade that was the monopoly of state trading corporations under the auspices of the Ministry of Foreign Economic Relations and Trade (MOFERT). Starting in the early 1980s, Guangdong and Fujian provinces and a few firms unconnected to MOFERT were given the freedom to import and export directly. After 1984 the "foreign trade plan" was further simplified: the state corporations no longer acted as principals but as agents, thereby shifting responsibility to the businesses. These businesses were increasingly allowed to keep the foreign currency they received, enabling them to finance their imports of technology directly. To keep up with competition in the world market, the central government subsidized exports, simultaneously creating trade surpluses and budget deficits, or so-called trade-off deficits. Budget deficits increased further because domestic demand for many raw materials and raw-material-intensive products was greater than the international demand, and the central government made up the difference.

In 1988 China began the climb to the status of major trading power, with an annual growth in exports of approximately 20 percent. The decisive factor in this was the breakup of the MOFERT monopoly, which retained control over a limited number of products only (coal, oil, grain, steel). All other products could now be traded through thousands of new provincial, municipal, and collective firms, which were responsible for their own profits and losses, including their reserves of foreign currency. The crucial figure in the decentralization of foreign trade was Zhao Ziyang. His goal was not only to emulate the "four Asian tigers" and to make a breakthrough in export-led economic growth, but also to pacify the provinces and to secure their support for economic reforms in general: in other words, to use the freebooting provinces in the struggle against the antireform forces in Beijing. Within the framework of the austerity program initiated in the summer of 1988, energetic attempts were made to recentralize foreign trade. These failed because the local authorities had so much control over their own resources that they were powerful enough to stand up to the central government. Export subsidies decreased annually until they were abolished in 1991, although MOFERT firms retained all sorts of privileges, subsidies, and special credit facilities.

In 1988 permits were still required for 257 export products, but only 91 were granted by MOFERT and associated bodies and the remaining 166 by Provincial Economic and Trade Commissions. In 1993–94 import permits were abolished for nearly 400 products, and the trend points to more and more companies and institutions being given complete autonomy in the field of foreign trade.

IN A CONTINENTAL COUNTRY like China, with north–south distances of four thousand kilometers and east–west distances of five thousand kilometers, the greater part of goods transported are destined for domestic markets. For a number of Chinese provinces, domestic and even internal provincial trade is often more profitable than exporting to foreign markets, not only because of the distances involved but also because domestic prices are often higher than international market prices. Often there are fiscal advantages attached to not exporting, although provincial protectionism encourages export.

The decentralization of foreign trade was not always in the best interests of the provinces by any means, as witnessed by Henan Province, which refused to export tobacco because the tax on cigarettes was the provincial government's most lucrative source of income. It kept all its tobacco for the home market and built as many cigarette factories as possible. Interprovincial trade encountered more and more obstacles, and the Chinese constitution was not equipped to deal with them. China was absolutely centralized politically, but no longer economically.

The inequality between the developed and the underdeveloped provinces came to a climax in the late 1980s in the form of industrial protectionism and blockades of raw materials and agricultural products on various interprovincial borders. By means of road blockades and militias, the poorer provinces prevented both raw materials from leaving their territory and industrial products from the rich provinces from entering. By the late 1980s local protectionism had resulted in the "balkanization" of China's economic system. Economists and political scientists talked of "neofeudalism" and China's disintegration into a "ducal economy," the *zhuhou jingji* of thirty duchies (provinces) and two thousand mini-principalities (*xian*).[15] They also observed that there was considerably less economic integration between China's provinces than between the member states of the European Union.[16]

The most notorious example of "economic warlordism" was the so-called "rice war" between Guangdong and Hunan in 1988. Guangdong wanted to buy rice in adjoining Hunan Province for the official state price, but Hunan demanded more from its rich southern neighbor. Buyers from Guangdong then ignored the official, provincial selling channels and went directly to Hunan's rice farmers. The provincial government of Hunan subsequently called out the army to prevent rice convoys from crossing the provincial border. Guangdong then moved to import rice from Thailand.

Shanxi, the national center of the coal industry, demanded exorbitant coal prices from its neighboring provinces to increase its own profits and set up an arbitrary inspection station in the Niangzi Pass, the main port of entry to Hebei Province, for the purpose of levying "service fees" on all coal trucks going to other provinces. Hebei immediately hit back with an embargo on grain, oil, and vegetables and blocked the entry of all coal trucks. This caused a crisis in Shanxi and led to energy shortages in the surrounding provinces.

Because of the high tax on alcoholic beverages, authorities all over China have encouraged the building of breweries. Each town and county has its own beer brewery. Jilin refused to permit the import of beer from Heilongjiang and Liaoning provinces. Owing to the constant decline in the state price for wool, Xinjiang Province, the home of 80 percent of the nation's wool production, ignored official state channels and forbade the import of yet another forty-eight categories of goods, because this would damage the internal economy. Since 1991 regional trading conflicts have been arbitrated by interprovincial trading teams, stationed on provincial borders "to learn from each other" and to prevent further skirmishing. The problems on the border between Hunan and Guangdong were solved by bartering goods—grain for electronics. During an inspection trip in October 1993, Zhu Rongji issued a strong warning on the danger of trade barriers, and for a while much less was heard on the subject. But during 1996 the Chinese media reported that these practices were still rife. In April a ceremony was held in Sichuan to delineate the border between Xinjiang and Tibet, kicking off a nationwide campaign to fix internal borders so as to avoid violent disputes over valuable natural resources in poorly defined areas. Even Shanghai engages in thinly veiled protectionism, setting new standards for cars that can be used as taxis. The rules refer to engine capacity and luggage space, and their effect is to favor cars made by the local carmaker "Shanghai Volkswagen." "Some regions, the *People's Daily* wrote, have formed enclosed markets, set up blockades, limited trade and used some abnormal or even unreasonable means to interfere in normal trading and marketing activities."[17]

Another type of local protectionism was rampant by 1996, namely, legal corruption, and local interference and sabotage in legal cases across provincial and local borders. A first national conference was convened by the "Political and Legal Group" of the Party Central Committee to study ways to oppose these practices. It did not mention specific cases by name but revealed that local governments across the country were blocking judicial organs from other locations from investigating (economic) crimes in their territory without their permission. A certain locality might, for instance, enjoy great benefits from a counterfeiting, smuggling, or illegal publishing operation originating elsewhere. If judicial personnel from elsewhere came to investigate, the local government would tell them that "counterfeiting activities can only be dealt with at the production base and not during the sales process elsewhere." Likewise, local governments would not permit courts to try cases involving local enterprises that owed debts to creditors in other locations. Local governments would also protect economically powerful native criminals against legal action by judicial organs from outside the area. Most local courts also operate only in the local interest. Once a local court concludes that a lawsuit by an outsider is not favorable to its own people, it deliberately makes all kinds of trouble for the outsider, including accusations of perjury and forgery, seizure of property, freezing bank accounts, and even taking hostages, including ethnic Chinese with foreign passports.[18]

JUST HOW STRONG localism is became apparent in 1989. After the conservatives' victory in Beijing, they attempted, across the whole of the country, to revoke the most important reforms, such as the household responsibility system, the local fiscal contract responsibility system, the dual-track price structure, and the management contract system for state enterprises. The tug-of-war lasted more than a year, ending in a fiasco for the conservatives. In the spring of 1990, they abandoned their attempts to strangle the township and village enterprises and private companies by withholding raw materials and denying bank loans (the TVEs generated too large a share of national export revenues, which had now become all the more important since the Western "Tiananmen sanctions"—suspension of credits from the World Bank, intergovernmental loans, and other forms of assistance) if only to keep the debt service ratio at a level sufficient to pay off the increasing foreign debt.

Drastic attempts at recentralization would also have caused a severe recession, with political consequences much more serious than those caused by giving more power to local leaders. In March 1990 the TVEs were once again granted tax exemptions and bank credit. In late 1990 plans for the recollectivization of agriculture were revoked. The recentralization of fiscal revenues was also postponed, and in the spring of 1991 a new wave of reforms began. The reformists in Beijing used localists across the country to avert a leftist restoration.

Deng Xiaoping's whirlwind tour of the south in early 1992 demonstrated decisive support for local reformers against conservative centralism in Beijing. Support for blue instead of yellow, for the market instead of the plan. Considering there were no adequate national rules for the formation and functioning of the market, however, local authorities let the market function according to local needs. This led to unprecedented hypergrowth, in which the central government was less and less able to maintain macroeconomic stability and to preserve the balance between urban, rural, and inter-provincial interests. In mid-1993 the central government attempted to intervene with an "austerity and macroeconomic control program," whose main goal was to rein in the local "economic warlords" or "dukes."

In its attempts at fiscal recentralization, Beijing can count on the support of the poor provinces, which are aligned against the rich. The rich should not have to give anything up, but the poor should be better off. Within the framework of fiscal reforms, 1993 was the base year. If, in 1994, the income of the rich provinces dropped below 1993 levels, they would be refunded the difference from the state treasury. Beijing promised the poor provinces that if it reached its goal of increasing state revenues to 60 percent of the GNP, it would spend at least one-third doing away with interprovincial inequalities. The subsidies given to poor provinces had never been so low. Poor provinces in the northwest and the southwest formed blocks to squeeze more money out of Beijing, which in turn appealed to Guangdong. During the annual governors' conference in Beijing in July 1994, however, Guangdong refused to provide an extra 16 billion yuan, saying that it had been impoverished by the "tight money" policy of the austerity program, needed extra funds for poor counties within its own borders, and had been badly hit by floods. Shandong and Shanghai, on the other hand, were willing to cooperate, but a closer look revealed only limited altruism. They agreed only to transfer some of their old factories, complete with technicians, to poorer provinces for labor-intensive production.[19] The relocation of labor-intensive companies from the southeast to the inner regions has been going on since 1987, particularly from Shenzhen, which is under much closer control from the central government than Guangdong. More than thirteen hundred Shenzhen companies have moved to places as far as Xinjiang and Heilongjiang. Shandong, Jiangsu, and Shanghai have been major investors in the inland as well, more out of pragmatism and self-interest, however, than as a result of central government directives. Cheap labor and more space have guided coastal enterprises toward the interior.[20]

Guangdong is not in the forefront. The showdown in 1994 coincided with a third national conference for the development of Tibet. The rich provinces were asked to cough up 25 percent of the 2.4 billion yuan necessary for sixty-two development projects in Tibet. There are no laws or rules governing this kind of assistance, making it the subject of fierce, ad hoc infighting every year. Vice-premier Zhu Rongji wanted Guangdong to contribute many billions of yuan, also to be used in attaining other national goals. According to reports in the Hong Kong media, the tug-of-war between Zhu Rongji and Governor Zhu Senlin of Guangdong deteriorated into a shouting match.[21] In 1993 Guangdong paid only 7 billion yuan as compared with Shanghai's 13 billion. The state treasury was striving for an increase in income to 60 percent of the GNP within three years.

Rich provinces are often prepared to pay in exchange for noninterference. Sometimes Beijing simply takes the money from provincial accounts at the head office of the People's Bank. Poor provinces that are disproportionately dependent on the tax on consumer and luxury goods have become considerably worse off since the tax reforms. Yunnan and Guizhou, two provinces of national minorities in the southwest, specialize in tobacco and hard liquor, on which they levy high taxes for their own profit. According to the new regulations, however, 75 percent of these tax revenues must be sent to the state treasury. Subsidies and loans from the central government amounting to nearly a billion yuan have saved them from ruin.

When Vice-premier Zhu Rongji traveled in the spring of 1994 to Sichuan to announce that, owing to inflation, economic growth would have to be curbed and decentralization reversed, he was given the brush-off by Governor Xiao Yang. Sichuan has 110 million inhabitants and economically is only just above the level of the poorest provinces. The necessity for high growth often outweighs the need to fight inflation.

There have been various battles between central and provincial leaders, but things have not yet escalated to the point of open confrontations that could endanger the nation's integrity, as was the case in the Soviet Union before its disintegration. The will of the central authorities has thus far prevailed, its most effective instrument being the power to appoint and dismiss governors, party secretaries, and regional army commanders. Governors have increasingly become advocates of local interests, but when Beijing throws its weight around at decisive moments, then they become agents of central authority, striving for promotion to party secretary, minister, or vice-premier, or hoping to become vice-chairman of the National People's Congress or the Political Advisory Conference when they reach the mandatory retirement age for governors of sixty-five. They therefore cannot afford to indulge in insubordination. Beijing has always been able to replace recalcitrant regional leaders but is not always completely successful in getting its way in controversial matters of policy.

There are mixed views on the reasons for Li Peng's hesitation in imposing his will on the provinces in 1990. One analyst thinks that, owing to the economic-political tumult in 1988–89 and the upheavals in Eastern Europe, the regime lacked the self-confidence necessary to implement far-reaching, risky changes. Furthermore, because of the austerity program started in 1988, there was a sharp drop in growth, causing such a decline in revenues collected by the lower authorities that they had nothing extra to give to Beijing.[22] Another analyst provides a different, more speculative, but nonetheless very provocative interpretation, conjecturing that Li Peng was hesitant to act brusquely toward provincial leaders because he was thinking of his own position in the power struggle to be Deng Xiaoping's successor.[23]

During the fiscal tug-of-war in 1993, Zhu Rongji conducted private talks with local bosses to avoid having to face a coalition of "warlords."

CAN CHINA SURVIVE as a unitary state with a strong central government that is capable of pursuing an effective monetary and fiscal policy as well as handling matters of defense and foreign policy? Can it find a balance between the need for administrative fiscal and monetary centralism and economic decentralization? Or is China doomed to a permanent nonsystem of central-local rivalry over fiscal revenues and investment decisions, in which all balance is lacking between central administrative interests and regional economic concerns? The best solution seems to be to give the provinces, by means of constitutional procedures, far-reaching legislative autonomy and to give the inland provinces the same rights as the coastal provinces. This means, however, further fragmentation of central state power and a revolutionary change in traditional central-local relations, neither of which tallies with Chinese political thinking. Federalism, liberalism, and local self-government are suspect terms without historical precedents and for that reason are still unacceptable.

In the 1920s a debate raged over federalism (*liansheng zizhi*), but the political chaos of the moment turned it into a synonym for "warlordism."[24] None of the warlord regimes declared its independence, however, claiming instead to be a temporary national government for the duration of national division. Even the Nationalist government on Taiwan has not yet formally broken away from China and still wrestles with this constitutional dilemma.

The Communists reject federalism as a recipe for feudalism and national disintegration, which, according to official propaganda, is exactly what the West wants: a federal, polycentric, weak China that can be manipulated by Western governments and multinationals. Federalism is something for countries with great economic, ethnic, religious, and linguistic variety, "and that is not the case in China[!]. The Chinese people are fundamentally united." According to dominant political thought, only a strong, centralized, authoritarian, one-party state has the power and cohesion to keep China together.

In the leftist upsurge of 1996–97, the ideologues have fully linked the future of economic-fiscal and central-local relations to the political issues of the survival of the socialist system, the public-ownership economy, and the consolidation of the power of the Communist party.[25] This could result in renewed efforts at reinforcement of central controls, which is the last thing the regions are waiting for. This fragile equilibrium is expected to continue until a general crisis unfolds or until the time is ripe for constitutional reform.

CHAPTER 13

Guangdong: The Fifth Tiger Within China's "Cage"?

In the 1980s Guangdong was "Hong Kongized." Now it is our goal to "Cantonize" the rest of the interior, thereby transforming all of China into a market economy. But we'll still need at least ten years to do this.

JIN JIAN,
Cantonese economist, 1991

THE PEARL RIVER DELTA, the triangle formed by Macau, Guangzhou, and Hong Kong in China's southern Guangdong Province, is well on its way to becoming the largest megalopolis and industrial zone in the world. In 1984 Deng Xiaoping issued his antiegalitarian edict and encouraged those parts of the country with conditions favorable to development to get rich first. The delta met that requirement, thanks to an enormous reservoir of cheap labor and the proximity of capital, management, and modern infrastructure in the international cities of Hong Kong and Macau.

The delta was at that time still an area of unspoiled nature: muddy backwaters with ferryboats, marshes, tidal forest, and islands with reed lands and rice paddies. Now it's an unbroken chain of new cities, suburbs, and industrial zones. The hotel in Zhuhai, to the north of Macau, where I stayed in the spring of 1995, was called Bu Bu Gao (High Leaps Forward). A matter of taste—every available square meter has been covered with concrete, creating an industrial desert full of new multilane highways, bridges over the numerous arms of the river, and new harbors. Three brand-new airports are located within 50 kilometers of each other: Macau, Zhuhai, and Shenzhen, which will be competing in a few years with Hong Kong's new superairport. A six-lane tollway 123 kilometers long on high, massive concrete pillars, built by the Hong Kong magnate Gordon Wu, winds through and over the villages and fish and duck ponds.

At the time, Chinese leaders said that in their rush to catch up with the rest of the world, they would not make the same mistake that the established industrial powers had made, which was to pollute first and try to do something about it later. Here there is only unscrupulous polluting going on and nothing at all is being done about it, at least not in the short term. For miles and miles on both sides of the highway, there is nothing but a succession of factories producing plastics, chemicals, rubber, toys, and textiles. They are without exception ugly, unsafe concrete cubes where peasants' sons and daughters from all parts of the country work around the clock seven days a week. Trees are not green here: every leaf is covered with a layer of dust or industrial waste. Even on Sunday, trucks spouting clouds of black diesel smoke come and go with their container transports. Little old women wait at the roadside in desperation until someone shepherds them to the other side. Where the main estuary of the Pearl River is the narrowest, between Shunde and Dongguan, a bridge 8 kilometers long is under construction— partly on pillars, partly suspended from cables—which will link up the highways on the two sides. But this is child's play compared with the plans of the ambitious mayor of Zhuhai, Liang Guangda, who wants to build a bridge from Zhuhai, north of Macau, to Hong Kong just where the delta is at its widest (50 to 60 kilometers). Only in this way will the containers for export, which increase every year by 25 percent, be able to leave the country via Hong Kong's ports. Building new harbors on the western shores of the delta, where the water is shallow, would take much too long.

The Pearl River delta is an area covering 47,000 square kilometers with a population of 21 million people, one-third of the entire province. By the beginning of the next century, the delta will have three cities with populations of more than 5 million: Hong Kong, Guangzhou, and Shenzhen; five cities with more than a million inhabitants: Zhuhai, Huizhou, Foshan, Zhongshan, and Dongguan; and a number of cities each with approximately half a million: Macau, Zhaoqing, Shunde, Panyu, and Nanhai.

During his much-discussed trip to South China in early 1992, which breathed new life into economic reforms after three years of ideological regression, Deng Xiaoping announced a new variation on his antiegalitarian edict of 1984. He exhorted Guangdong—by then the richest province in China—together with the delta in the vanguard, to become "the fifth tiger of Asia."[1] The southernmost coastal province was encouraged to look to external capitalist economies such as Hong Kong, Taiwan, Singapore, and South Korea for examples of further internationalization. The implications of this were far-reaching. Should Guangdong integrate itself northward with the rest of China, or should it turn into a transnational border region, integrated with Hong Kong and Southeast Asia? The Pearl River delta, also known as Greater Hong Kong, is a model region-state, according to Ken Ohmae's definition: approximately 20 million inhabitants, compact, homogeneous, and prosperous. In 1993 the per capita income was $12,000 in Hong Kong, $5,695 in Shenzhen, $2,033 in Zhuhai, and $1,510 in Guangzhou. In contrast, the national average for all of China was $319.[2]

FOR RADICAL REFORMERS and internationalists in South China, Deng's imprimatur was fresh stimulus to distance themselves even further from the "yellow" Chinese hinterland and to orient themselves even more toward the "blue" ocean of trade and the world economy. But where was the limit? Within the great Han Chinese culture, Guangdong formed a unique regional subculture and even had its own languages: Cantonese, spoken by the great majority, and Hakka and Chaozhou in the north and northeast. It had its own popular religions, an exclusive culinary culture, and the longest history as an international trading center and treaty port. The Cantonese were despised by northern Mandarins and militarists as commercial barbarians. Commercially and financially, the province was completely interlinked with Hong Kong, Macau, and Southeast Asia. Beijing was two thousand kilometers to the north.

Not only was the Pearl River delta an industrial zone stage-managed by Hong Kong, but some of its cities, such as Taishan and Jiangmen, had closer ties to their overseas Chinese kinsfolk in the Chinatowns of California and Southeast Asia than with neighboring municipalities. The province had a history of particularism and separatism, most recently during the twilight years of the empire and the turbulent period of "warlordism" in the 1920s and 1930s. Guangdong even had its own Communist party, quite separate from that of Mao Zedong. In the 1920s the political activist Ou Qujia published *Xin Guangdong,* which, insisting that love of one's own province is greater than one's love for the immense nation as a whole, proposed greater provincial autonomy for Guangdong within a Chinese federation, to be followed by independence, after which the people of Guangdong would be their own master. Independence for Guangdong would be the prelude to "independence for all of China," i.e., fragmentation into competing states in a system resembling that of Europe.[3]

After the establishment of the Communist regime, the native-born marshall Ye Jianying became the ruler of Guangdong, although he collaborated with the indigenous, independent Communist movement. He was accused of regionalism in 1952 and was replaced by a "northern" regime headed by Tao Zhu and Zhao Ziyang, which broke the strength of the network of local cadres. In 1971 Marshall Lin Biao—Mao's close comrade-in-arms and a crown prince, who had suddenly turned against Mao—considered setting up an opposition government in Guangzhou, together with local kindred spirits, including Huang Yongsheng. In 1972 Zhao Ziyang returned to Guangdong as party secretary and governor. After Zhao was transferred to Sichuan in 1975, power was gradually resumed by local leaders, who were indispensable in opening up relations with Cantonese-speaking Hong Kong, which in the new strategy had assumed the role of financier of the modernization of South China. Of the current twenty-six top-level officials—governor, six vice-governors, chairman and vice-chairman of the people's congress and other commissions—nineteen are Cantonese.[4]

DURING THE MAO ERA, Guangdong was marginalized because it was a merchants' zone and vulnerable to imperialist aggression. As part of his strategy to counteract the effects of the Korean War, the American blockade, and the proximity of Taiwan, Mao had transferred the process of industrialization to the interior. As a result, Guangdong received practically no investment money from the central government. Growth in Guangdong averaged 5.1 percent annually between 1953 and 1978, 1 percent less than the national average. Since the beginning of reform in 1979 until the present day, however, its average rate of growth has been more than 3 percent higher than the national average of more than 9 percent. In 1978 Guangdong still gave Beijing 31 percent of its revenues, but in 1979 it entered into a very advantageous fiscal contract with the central government for a period of five years, which stipulated the annual payment of a lump sum of 1.2 billion yuan to the central government. It was also given an extraordinarily favorable contract regarding foreign trade: it was allowed to keep all hard currency above a certain amount. Fujian was given similar preferential treatment and assurances from the central authorities that Guangdong and Fujian would pioneer the experiments in economic reform and be exempt from the restrictions of the first austerity program proclaimed in mid-1979.

The architect of the preferential treatment received by the southeast coast was the new premier, Zhao Ziyang. His simple rationalization was that, because of Hong Kong and the overseas Chinese, Guangdong and Fujian needed little or no help from the central government and were therefore not a burden on the state treasury. In 1981 Guangdong and Fujian were exempted from import duties on raw materials and spare parts for the production of goods for export, and the Guangdong branch of the People's Bank was given greater freedom to extend loans. The central government issued taxation guidelines, but the two southeastern coastal provinces were free to implement them as they saw fit and to grant their own exemptions. These two provinces therefore had so many extra privileges and financial advantages that they naturally had a head start on the rest of China and could afford to spend more on subsidies to support the price reforms. In 1984 Guangdong transferred only 3 percent of its total revenues to the central government, in sharp contrast to Shanghai, which handed over 81 percent of its revenues to Beijing.[5]

In 1984, during an inspection tour of the four special economic zones, three of which were located in Guangdong Province, Deng Xiaoping not only demonstrated his support for the zones but extended similar privileges to fourteen "Open Coastal Cities," two of which, Guangzhou and Zhanjiang, were also located in Guangdong. Shanghai was also one of the fourteen and was given more favorable conditions for attracting foreign investments, but not a more tolerable fiscal regime.

In 1985 a new central government document extended the general privileges for all of Guangdong and Fujian for another five years. They were given the authority to use their own resources or foreign capital to finance construction projects costing less than 200 million yuan. The economies of the two provinces had doubled in size in five years, but their fiscal obligations to the central government were not increased. They were allowed to keep 30 percent of their income from foreign currency, 5 percent more than other provinces. Two serious incidents—the foreign currency crisis resulting from overexpenditure (see Chapter 1) and the big Hainan scandal (see Chapter 7)—put the radical reformers on the defensive, but they refused to back down and the privileges enjoyed by Guangdong and Fujian remained intact.

The fall from power of party leader Hu Yaobang in January 1987 also meant a weakening of the pro-Cantonese coalition, but Hu's interim successor, Zhao Ziyang, succeeded, with the support of Deng Xiaoping and despite escalating conservative opposition, in making Guangdong the trendsetter in his export-oriented coastal strategy. Guangdong's new status and strategic tasks were specified in the "Correspondence of the State Council 25" in 1988:

- extension of financial authority, such as credit policy and the setting up of financial markets;

- raising the ceiling to $30 million for the amount of foreign investment allowed without government approval;
- far-reaching autonomy in price reform and management;
- autonomy in wage policy and an experimental system of social security;
- maintenance of the annual fiscal "lump-sum transfer" to the central government, but with an annual increase of 9 percent;
- taking the lead nationally in reforming companies, propagating the shares system in state enterprises, and selling small state enterprises at auction;
- education reform, such as commercialization of scientific and technological research;
- privatization of housing and development of the real estate market;
- autonomy in planning with the emphasis on flexible, instead of binding, guidelines;
- small steps toward political reform, democratization of the policy-making process, the creation of a modern civil service (instead of the party cadre), administrative appeal procedures, and more consultation between government and the people.[6]

GUANGDONG WAS SKEPTICAL but otherwise powerless to do anything about the declaration of martial law and the military suppression of the protest movement in 1989. It was afraid of negative repercussions for trade and investment and feared complications resulting from the dismissal of the very pro-Cantonese Zhao Ziyang in the form of a general purge of his network in Guangdong and Shenzhen.

The crisis of 1988–89 put the whole of the new scenario for readjustment of central-provincial relations on a loose footing. After stabilization of the situation in 1990–91, another political wind from Beijing began to blow in the direction of Shanghai. Until the beginning of 1991, there had been the threat of a neo-Stalinist renaissance under the leadership of Premier Li Peng and his conservative economic mentor, Vice-premier Yao Yilin. They advocated restoring privileges to state enterprises instead of accelerated development of the coastal areas. The new pro-Shanghai top leadership in Beijing showed such a sympathetic response to the resentment felt by Shanghai and other provinces toward the more-than-special treatment received by Guangdong that a new blueprint was produced.

Guangdong was forced to pay the piper: it lost its status as chosen model for the country and had to curb growth and investments and relinquish part of its far-reaching economic autonomy. Owing to the austerity program and the tightening of macroeconomic controls, the national market had shrunk greatly, and Guangdong's light industry had taken the brunt of this contraction. The hawks in Beijing were incensed most at Guangdong's special ties to Hong Kong. China's highest representative in Hong Kong, Xu Jiatun, had demonstrated so much sympathy with the democratization movement in Beijing and the massive support shown in Hong Kong that he had fled to the United States for fear of the wrath of Li Peng, where he was taken under the wing of a Buddhist abbot from Taiwan. The hawks branded Hong Kong a subversive stronghold for the undermining of socialism in China. The Cantonese on the other side of the border were seen as the accomplices of the Hong Kong Cantonese. With the fall of Zhao Ziyang came the discrediting of his policy directed at the south. A new model had to be found, and it was Pudong, on the eastern shore of the Huangpu River in Shanghai.

IN 1989–90 Guangdong had a well-entrenched, native, crown-prince-like governor, Ye Xuanping, the son of the late marshall Ye Jianying. Marshall Ye had been the equal of Deng Xiaoping, making Ye's son, in semifeudal Chinese terms, at least the equal of Li Peng. The central government, however, wanted to dethrone Ye junior and once again place the wayward Cantonese under a northern agent of the central authorities.

In the summer of 1990, the north sent up a trial balloon announcing that the new governor would be Yuan Mu, Premier Li Peng's discredited spokesman and an exponent of the Great Lie after the crackdown in Beijing. This sparked the resistance that was only part of a much broader rebellion of a number of provinces against Beijing's efforts at recentralization. In the theoretical party organ Qiushi (Search for Facts), party secretary Lin Ruo defended the special policy guidelines and reminded the central government that most of the investment in Guangdong had come from Guangdong itself and not from the central government. In 1979 Guangdong received 80 percent of investment funds from Beijing; in 1992 this had dropped to 2 percent. Guangdong's funds came from international capital markets, from its own overseas Chinese, and especially from Hong Kong. This gave the province a degree of financial independence that was unknown elsewhere in China.

A national discussion followed, in which various ex-governors of Guangdong called upon the central government to take the "special policy guidelines" approved in 1988 seriously. At a national governors' conference

in the Jingxi Hotel in Beijing in September 1990, this reportedly resulted in
a showdown, in which Governor Ye Xuanping took the lead. A compromise
was reached by which the central government would continue to implement
completely the special policy guidelines but would brook no interference in
its right to appoint and dismiss provincial party secretaries and governors.
In January 1991 Lin Ruo was replaced by Xie Fei, also a Cantonese. Ye Xuanping, who had several times provided assurances that he would not leave
Guangdong, accepted a new post in March 1991 as vice-chairman of the People's Advisory Conference. According to insiders, he asked for two conditions, however: that the province be allowed to choose his successor freely,
and that he only be required to spend a minimum amount of time in Beijing. In May 1991 Zhu Senlin, a former mayor of Canton, was appointed as
Ye's successor. It appeared that Beijing had not been able to change the
brand of Cantonese politics that was all its own but had at least been successful in replacing a "southern stadholder."[7]

DENG XIAOPING'S SOUTHERN TOUR in 1992 heralded a breakthrough
in the central-provincial détente, in which he actually mobilized the provinces in order to derail conservative opposition in Beijing. His encouragement to catch up with the "four tigers" within twenty years boiled down to
a carte blanche to take the world economy as its guide and not decrees from
Beijing. At the Fourteenth Party Congress in October 1992, Xie Fei was appointed to the Politburo, the first time since 1949 that an incumbent governor of Guangdong received this honor. Seven officials from Guangdong
were also chosen to serve in the Party Central Committee. But the inconsistent, zigzag policies of Beijing quickly turned against Guangdong. By 1993
the cyclic boom-bust rhythm of the Chinese economy called for a new austerity and cooling-off program, this time led by the new economic tsar,
Vice-premier Zhu Rongji. Guangdong paid lip service to it at least, and Governor Zhu Senlin called upon all officials to implement Beijing's decrees. He
canceled no large-scale projects, however, and stuck to the long-term strategy of 13-plus percent economic growth and 17 percent growth in exports.
An inspection team from the People's Bank in Beijing was nevertheless sent
to Canton to curb the generous credit policies of the local banks, as some of
the banks had made sizable speculative investments in the real estate sector.

In January 1994 the fiscal contract responsibility system was replaced by
a new national two-stage tax system, which again led to skirmishing between Beijing and Guangdong. In 1988 the annual lump sum that Guangdong was forced to pay to the central government had been raised to

1.4 billion yuan, with an annual increase of 9 percent for three years. Between 1980 and 1989 Guangdong had contributed a total of 19.2 billion yuan to specific funds—state energy, transportation, construction, budget, and settlement funds. The dire straits the state finances were in, however, required more of Guangdong, and in 1990 alone it paid 5 billion yuan to the central government, 40 percent of the total revenues of the provincial government. The central government also wanted a larger share of customs, bank, and insurance revenues, larger contributions by centrally managed state enterprises, and more of Guangdong's foreign currency reserves. At the beginning of reforms, state enterprises in Guangdong paid in 440 million yuan, in 1990 alone nearly 11 billion yuan. By the beginning of the 1990s, Guangdong was paying in as much to the state treasury as Shanghai.[8]

The central government, on the other hand, transferred more financial obligations to the province, which did not accept them without a struggle. In 1991 Guangdong still had a much more favorable fiscal regime than Shanghai, but in the following years Guangdong's head start on the rest of the country came to an end.

THE NEW LEADERS, Xie Fei and Zhu Senlin, were more cooperative in toeing the central party line, especially in public relations. In 1993 Guangdong reported an increase in government revenues of 56.4 percent (34.6 billion yuan) and was able to pay the annual increase of 9 percent on its contributions to Beijing.[9] During the National People's Congress in 1994, Governor Zhu Senlin dismissed suggestions that the new national tax system be explained as recentralization of the financial power that had formerly been delegated to the provinces. At the same time, however, Guangdong refused to institute the VAT on real estate, because this would scare away investors, especially those from Hong Kong and Taiwan. The mayor of Canton, Li Ziliu, argued for postponing the VAT on land for two years, "considering it is a local tax category and it is undesirable to impose uniformity on the various places." In the summer of 1994 Guangdong also refused to pay the sum of 16 billion yuan demanded by Vice-premier Zhu Rongji as an extra contribution to the poorer provinces, giving as an excuse that it had been hard hit by floods and, unlike other provinces, had not received any aid from the central government. Guangdong said it was also badly in need of its own resources to combat poverty in its own mountainous northern counties. Research done by Hu Angang, the national authority on regional inequality, showed that Guangdong's richest city, Zhuhai, was thirty-four times richer than its poorest county, Heping.[10]

Zeng Bingsheng, director of finances of the Guangdong provincial government, announced at the opening of the Provincial People's Congress in February 1995 that Beijing was to receive 75 percent of the newly introduced value-added tax and the provincial treasury 25 percent. The provinces would be given a still-to-be-determined reduction in the amount of VAT handed over to the central government as compensation for the loss of other tax revenues.

As Guangdong loses its fiscal privileges and Shanghai's new superzone Pudong steals the show as the national model for accelerated economic growth, Guangdong, like Shenzhen, continues to search for new forms and definitions of uniqueness. The new priority is convergence with Hong Kong, not only in infrastructure but also in ideas. The Pearl River delta including Hong Kong is the model region-state. Ken Ohmae described the whole of Guangdong with Hong Kong, plus 20 million overseas Chinese who hail from the province, as the equivalent of the largest European economy, unified Germany.[11]

Provincial administrators clearly stress the head start, not only in economic terms, that Guangdong has over the rest of the country, emphasizing the better opportunities it has for integration with the outside world. At a conference of social scientists in the summer of 1994, the first vice-governor, Lu Ruihua (now governor) said in his paper entitled "Theories of Deng Xiaoping Regarding Opening Up to the Outside World" that the province had reached a new era in its socioeconomic development. Lu promised to lead Guangdong into the "postmodern" and "posturban" world. Along with other countries, the province will open up sectors like technology, culture, and social services. He called for the formation of "a new generation of modern people." Their main task is the development of services and the capital-intensive sector, and the relocation farther inland of labor-intensive industries. Cultural exchange should lead to a "moral face-lift" of society. Guangdong must shake off its past and enter the age of information. "Prosperity doesn't mean that we've become part of the international community. . . . As far as our system and ideas are concerned, we still have a long way to go."[12]

Political reforms are a reality in Guangdong. The People's Congress is now open to some groups of citizens, including private entrepreneurs. Guangdong has a Supervision Law, whereas this is still a bone of contention at the national level. The Supervision Law regulates citizens' surveillance of provincial and municipal governments, the courts, and public prosecutors. Provincial and municipal people's congresses can summon senior officials for questioning in cases of policy "malpractice." Shortly after this law took effect, Lu told the Provincial People's Congress that Guangdong needs $190 billion in foreign investments in the coming twenty years in order to realize his ambition of its becoming the "fifth tiger" of Asia.

THAT GUANGDONG IS RICHER than the rest of China is obvious, but whether or not it is ready socially and culturally for Governor Lu's "postmodern" world is another question altogether. A study of the social status of professionals in Guangzhou demonstrated that the Cantonese in Guangzhou are much more money-hungry that those in Hong Kong. The younger generation is driven by money and power, displaying more and more contempt for traditional professions like medicine. One's educational level is no longer a factor in professional prestige, whereas in Hong Kong one's educational standard plays an important role, and the social status of doctors is high. The results of the study made the lawless, corrupt nature of Chinese society abundantly clear. In Hong Kong one's income is determined to a large extent by one's level of education; in China by connections and power, which obviously leads to rampant corruption.[13] The study is in fact a devastating refutation of the Communist propaganda cliché that materialism and greed are capitalist vices that were brought to China from Hong Kong.

In the cultural and educational realm, Guangdong is decidedly below the national norm. According to the census of 1990, the proportion of Chinese in Guangdong who had completed their studies at institutions of higher learning was only 1,338 in 100,000.[14] The national average is 1,422. This confirms the northern prejudice that Guangdong, with its potential for a much higher budget for education, is actually a cultural desert.

In the realm of business reform, Guangdong is admittedly a trendsetter, though its efforts have only been partially successful. According to the national plan of November 1993, in the pioneering city of Guangzhou two-thirds of the nine hundred state enterprises should have been "corporatized," but owing to a conflict of interests, this has occurred in only seventy cases. After relinquishing their status as state property and issuing shares, the companies are supposed to lose their tax privileges, which has considerably dampened their will to reform. In Guangdong the state sector still comprises only about one-third of all industry (the national average is 43 percent). Even in Guangdong, further reforms in the state-owned sector have stagnated, owing to resistance from workers who do not want to lose their "iron rice bowl." During my visit to Guangzhou in January 1995, Professor Chen Chi, deputy director of the provincial Commission for the Reform of the Economic System, said that the bankruptcy of large companies is politically and socially impossible. The most faithful followers of the Communist party are the workers, whose mottoes are "Follow the Communist Party! No Bankruptcy! Iron Rice Bowl! Socialism Is Superior!"

Guangdong is nevertheless the national leader in the field of social security. At the Provincial People's Congress in February 1995, Governor Zhu Senlin said that 40 percent of the state enterprises in Guangdong are losstaking and that 50 percent of all business debts to banks are uncollectible. The solution must increasingly be sought in gradually laying off workers with the help of unemployment benefits and an early pension fund. In 1994, 5 million workers across the entire province became members of the unemployment fund and 7.7 million became members of the pension fund. Workers have a personal account in the fund, which is managed by the government. The pioneer was Guangzhou, where 90 percent of the workers became members of the unemployment fund, giving them the right to unemployment benefits of 45 to 50 percent of their wages for a period of two years.

THE QUESTION IS to what extent Guangdong's recent steps in the direction of economic globalization mean proportionate disengagement from the rest of China. The answer is probably fifty-fifty. In 1991 only 3 percent of investments in Guangdong came from Beijing, and this figure has since fallen. Guangdong attracts record-high investment from Hong Kong, amounting in 1994 to $11.5 billion, more than one-third of the national total. An unspecified amount, however, is Chinese money from the mainland which is first shunted through Hong Kong through gray channels and then invested in China as foreign capital, enabling it to profit from extra fiscal advantages. Huge sums from poor, inland provinces also flow into Guangdong, with the aim to rake in quick profits through real estate speculation. Approximately one-third of Guangdong's industrial products are destined for the Chinese domestic market. Of Guangdong's exports, 84 percent go to Hong Kong, where 72 percent of its imports originate. Raw materials and energy, especially cotton and steel, come in large part from the Chinese hinterland.

Although economic interaction between Guangdong and Hong Kong is greater than that between Guangdong and the mainland, it cannot be considered a centrifugal, transnational force. Hong Kong is, after all, historically a part of Guangdong and will in mid-1997 become a part of China. Tension between Guangdong and Beijing is largely creative, however, certainly not destructive. The trial of strength in 1990 was not brought to a head, it did not lead to a (constitutional) crisis—as was repeatedly the case between the Soviet government and its Union republics—and it ended in 1993 in compromise.

THE PRIORITY of provincial leaders in Guangdong is not yet South Chinese regionalism or autonomy but maintenance of their position as economic trendsetters for the whole country. Shanghai is threatening to take over this role, however. President Jiang Zemin, also general secretary of the party, has turned the Politburo into a stronghold of Shanghainese (four ex-mayors or party secretaries and two native Shanghainese are currently members, as opposed to only one Cantonese). At the top of the state hierarchy there is not even one Cantonese. The perception in Guangzhou is not yet that Guangdong is being treated unfairly, but with the conservative, leftist climate in Beijing, relations between the northern Beijing-Shanghai block and Guangdong have become more antagonistic. If Jiang Zemin succeeds in consolidating his position of power, he will undoubtedly strengthen Shanghai's already privileged position, not only because of political patronage from Beijing but simply because Shanghai has a broader industrial base with both heavy and light industry, as well as the best scientific and technological base. Liang Lingguang, who was governor of Guangdong in the early 1980s, said in this context: "Compared with Shanghai, our heavy industry has lagged behind, but our light industry has taken the lead. Our science, technology, and education are underdeveloped, but our information and trade are more advanced. We do not have Shanghai's advantage of being situated on the Yangtze River, but we have the advantage of the proximity of the financial center of Hong Kong [and Macau]. Our rich experience in reform and opening up has helped us in the last ten years to build a solid base, and this province will play a greater role and make wiser moves."[15] Will it be a big trial of strength between two coalitions, a northern one of Beijing-cum-Shanghai against a southern one of Guangdong-cum-Hong-Kong, with like-minded provinces joining them—Shandong joining the northern coalition and Sichuan the southern, for example? If it does become a trial of strength, Guangdong will always be at a disadvantage because the means of power wielded by Beijing are inexhaustible.

Until now, no hostile words have been exchanged in public. When two new vice-premiers were chosen at the National People's Congress in March 1995—one from Shanghai and the other from Shandong—Zhu Senlin, when asked if his province felt wronged, answered that the heavy workload of the senior vice-premier, Zhu Rongji, should be lightened.[16] During a visit to Guangzhou in January 1995, I put a series of questions on southern grievances to Vice-mayor Dai Zhiguo, but his set answer was "Guangdong has become what it is thanks to the special policy guidelines of the central government, and we are grateful. Our prosperity has advantages for the central government. We pay more taxes. We are Guangdong, but we are China's Guangdong."[17]

Local pride and resistance to the north are largely folk myths. There is no cohesive movement for political autonomy, let alone secession. Since 1982 Guangdong has been governed by Cantonese, and since 1989 they have succeeded in resisting transfer. The more Beijing tries to reduce the privileges enjoyed by Guangdong and the special economic zones, the more tension increases, strengthening Beijing's resolve to transfer Guangdong's governors to posts in poorer territories and to subject Guangdong once again to the authority of northerners.

After much speculation that a northerner would succeed Zhu Senlin as governor, another Cantonese, Lu Ruihua, got the job in 1996, although most of his current deputies are from elsewhere. Lu tells VIP visitors that it is very difficult being the governor of Guangdong, because if you are too obedient to Beijing, you get in trouble with your Cantonese subjects, and if you consider local interests too much, Beijing will be distrustful of you. The golden mean is the name of the game.

CHAPTER 14

Shanghai: Bastion of Central Control

Shanghai was once an international banking center. It is necessary to resume this practice. China's hopes of attaining an international financial position must be pinned on Shanghai.

DENG XIAOPING

The 1980s were the decade of Guangdong, the 1990s that of Shanghai.

XU KUANGDI,
mayor of Shanghai

DENG XIAOPING EXERCISED self-criticism at various times in his seventy-five-year-long political career. Twice, in 1973 and 1977, it amounted only to ritual confessions designed to help him recover his lost power. This made his admission in 1992—during his last major political initiative, his "southern sojourn"—all the more remarkable, when he said that one of his biggest mistakes was his failure to open up Shanghai to development earlier. He literally said, "In retrospect, one of my biggest mistakes was leaving out Shanghai when we launched the four special economic zones. If Shanghai had been included, the situation with regard to reform and opening in the Yangtze delta, the entire Yangtze River valley, and, indeed, the whole country would be quite different."[1] The development of Shanghai, or, better put, the renaissance of the city, did not begin until the early 1990s, ten years later than that of the southern coast.

"The 1980s were the decade of Guangdong, the 1990s that of Shanghai," runs the motto of the new city fathers of Shanghai. In this context, it is not insignificant that the most powerful central leaders in the 1980s had strong ties to South (and Southwest) China, and those of the 1990s to Shanghai.[2] Before and after the Cultural Revolution, Zhao Ziyang, premier from 1980 to 1988, had served two terms as governor and party secretary of Guangdong, and he was the one—with Deng Xiaoping's blessing—who most promoted the accelerated development of the south. The special conditions encouraging this were the increasing investments from nearby Hong Kong and the fact that, because of these investments, Guangdong received hardly any money from the central government and also paid extremely little into the central coffers. Shanghai, on the other hand, was the most important contributor of tax funds to the state treasury and could not yet be reformed for that reason. A variation on the label offered by Ezra Vogel for Guangdong, "one step ahead in China," would characterize Shanghai during the whole of the 1980s as "several steps behind."

Paradoxically, before the "liberation" in 1949, Shanghai was a century ahead of the rest of China. As a treaty port, Shanghai, under the dual administration (*dyarchy*) of the British extraterritorial International Settlement and the French Concession, was in the 1920s one of the most cosmopolitan cities in the world, and the one with the fastest-growing economy. The city could only be described in hyperboles, comparable to the flamboyant development of Hong Kong in the 1980s and 1990s.

"THE PARIS OF THE EAST" and "a paradise for adventurers" were the most popular epithets for Shanghai. The river boulevard, the Bund,* an eclectic variation on the embankment of the river Thames or the Seine, was Shanghai's most outstanding qualification for the title of world city. The International Settlement was governed by a mixed municipal council of British, Americans, and Japanese, and also three Chinese. The police—bearded, awe-inspiring Sikhs—were recruited in the Punjab in British India. The French Concession, with its palatial villas and country estates, was administered by the French consul general. Not one of the governments—British, Chinese, or French—exercised authority effectively. It was an "anarcho-plutocracy" with British bankers and *taipans* (business tycoons) at the top of the social ladder, but also extremely wealthy Westernized Chinese,

---

* There is a widespread and mistaken impression that "Bund" is German in origin, but it is a colonial Anglo-Indian word derived from *banda* meaning city or citadel.

who had begun as compradors (agents) for foreigners and without whose collaboration the foreigners were helpless. One of the most famous was Charles Jones Soong, the reluctant father-in-law of Sun Yat-sen and Chiang Kai-shek.* In spite of colonial relationships, Shanghai was a tremendously creative symbiosis of East and West, where Western and Chinese business-men made enormous fortunes side by side, where Chinese writers, journal-ists, and filmmakers were free from the censorship and restrictions of feudal China, and where Communists and liberals were safe from the secret police of the Kuomintang. As such, Shanghai had an innovating effect on China, the extent of which has been a matter of renewed study only in recent years.

The perception of race relations in Old Shanghai was determined for nearly the whole of the twentieth century both inside and outside China by a myth, namely, that at the entrance to the park on the Bund there was a sign with the inordinately racist and humiliating warning "Chinese and Dogs Not Admitted." Serious Chinese and Western historians have never been able to find proof of the existence of this sign, only an endless number of idle reports and banal reiterations in the media, travel guides, political pam-phlets, and textbooks. Reginald Johnston, the revered mentor of Pu Yi, the last emperor of China, wrote in a pamphlet in 1927: "It is the kind of slander which takes a lot of killing, and survives even the most authoritative de-nials."³ It is true that, according to an ordinance passed by the Municipal Council in 1885, Chinese were not allowed in public parks, but it is ab-solutely untrue that this was posted in terms so crass, even by the standards of that time. Over the years, there have been four official versions of the text, which all stipulated in the first clause that the gardens were for the exclusive use of the foreign community, with the fourth or fifth restriction being that dogs and bicycles were also forbidden. In 1928 these restrictions were lifted completely and anyone was admitted to the park upon payment of an en-trance fee, but the myth that the imperialists put Chinese on the same level as dogs was so indelibly fixed in the Chinese psyche, passed on by word of mouth as well as by Nationalist and Communist writings, that it continues to play a disturbing role in China's still-volatile relations with the West.

---

* A telling, though somewhat offhand, description of the compradors in Shanghai is given by Sterling Seagrave in his *chronique scandaleuse* of Chiang Kai-shek and his in-laws: "This role of *comprador* lies at the heart of the hatreds that fired the revolutionary up-heavals of the twentieth century. It was a complex role—somewhere between pimp and patrician—that linked the separate economic classes in the Orient and provided the lu-brication between East and West. Shanghai was a city of *compradors* (*The Soong Dynasty* [New York, 1985], p. 66).

By the time the "no admittance to the parks" ordinance was lifted in 1928, society in the International Settlement had become multiracial, with Japanese, other Asians, and Russians exerting a new influence. There were also numerous Sephardic Jews from the Middle East who had climbed to the top, including the Kadoories and Hardoons. During Hitler's persecution of the Jews, Shanghai became a refuge for European Jews as well. After the Japanese occupation of Manchuria in 1931, White Russians, who had previously fled to Harbin to escape the Bolsheviks and among whom were many members of the nobility, also came to Shanghai. Russian counts and barons became porters and waiters, and some of the countesses took up prostitution. The memoirs and travel literature on this short but legendary episode in Shanghai's eventful history are inexhaustible.

For people with a social conscience, Old Shanghai was a time bomb that exploded only after waves of hyperinflation dealt the death blow to the Kuomintang government in 1948. "If God let Shanghai endure, He owes an apology to Sodom and Gomorrah," Christian missionaries said at the time. It was not God who put an end to Old Shanghai but the Communists. International capitalism was not given the chance to stay under new conditions but was driven out lock, stock, and barrel. Poor, primitive invaders from the countryside seized power from the cosmopolitan, Westernized Chinese. Class struggle saw to the introduction of a new, socialist model order.

Everything that was modern disappeared. Part of the Chinese entrepreneurial class and the international business community left for Hong Kong, and the administrative apparatus moved to Taiwan. Communist party units moved into the elegant, imposing bank buildings on the Bund. For more than thirty years, almost nothing was built in Shanghai except factories and concrete apartment blocks.

Seen through the ideological prism of the Communists, Shanghai's past was nothing if not shameful. It had been a "parasitical" center of speculative, sinister commercial activities in the opportunistic service of imperialism and international capitalism, upholding a decadent lifestyle and "forcing Chinese girls into prostitution." The "whore of imperialism" was forced to undergo radical moral catharsis and make amends for its mistakes. Shanghai was meant to become a spartan center of production and to finance the modernization of the rest of China.

SHANGHAI CONTRIBUTED much more to the central coffers in the way of taxes than it received in the form of investments. From 1950 to 1983 investments made by the central government in Shanghai amounted to 14,781 billion yuan. In 1983 alone, Shanghai paid 18,195 billion yuan in taxes to the central government, paying in one year more than it had received in twenty-three years.[4] Until 1980 Shanghai was responsible for one-eighth of total industrial production nationally and more than one-sixth (17 percent) of total state revenues (representing 86.8 percent of its own revenues). This accounts for the fact that for thirty to thirty-five years there was no money for urban renewal, improvements in the infrastructure, water purification, and the environment in general. A Shanghainese historian, Betty Wei Peh-t'i, who returned to Shanghai in 1980 for the first time since the 1940s, verified this: "Nothing had changed, except that the city had not been cleaned up for thirty-five years."[5]

Shanghai's finances were completely controlled by Beijing and its system of central planning. The city became the trendsetting bastion of state industry when the central government transferred a large number of state enterprises to the city of Shanghai during the Great Leap Forward. This meant that 480 of the 536 centrally run state enterprises were now situated in Shanghai, accounting for a rise in municipal income from 1.5 to 17.5 percent of the nation's total, although the surplus quickly disappeared into the central state treasury.[6]

During the Cultural Revolution, Shanghai became the opposite of its prewar image of capitalist extravagance; it was turned into a battlefield of destructive leftist fanaticism. Chairman Mao had lost his grip on the central bureaucracy in Beijing and together with the Gang of Four, led by his fierce wife, Jiang Qing, launched in Shanghai an ideological crusade to regain control over the nation. After Mao's death in 1976, Shanghai had to pay the price for its close ties to the Gang. When revision of the arbitrary, secretive fiscal relations between central and local authorities began in 1979, Shanghai missed its chance of receiving a more favorable tax regime. In the early 1980s the city, unlike Guangdong, had no influential advocates in Beijing. Mayor Wang Daohan was not even a member of the party's Central Committee, let alone the Politburo.

The continuing tide of reforms meant an accompanying drop in the profitability of state enterprises, which accounted for 91.7 percent of Shanghai's revenues. Of course, this had negative repercussions for Shanghai's payments to Beijing, and the financial perils were so serious that the central government finally began to devote special attention to Shanghai. In the summer and fall of 1983, party leader Hu Yaobang and Premier Zhao Ziyang both paid inspection visits to Shanghai, and several months later the financial relations between Beijing and Shanghai were finally given a new basis. For a period of six years the city would be allowed to keep 23.5 instead of 13.2

percent of its local revenues, and it would receive 1.5 billion yuan extra annually in order to renovate the city and to assist it in its bid to recover its position as an international center of finance and trade.

It seemed like a good beginning, but the losses incurred by state enterprises increased so rapidly that by 1988 city revenues had dropped to less than half their 1983 level. The only solution was a drastic increase in subsidies which exhausted the city's finances to such an extent that in 1987 the new municipal government led by Jiang Zemin appealed for policy changes that would permit the city to become more international and market-oriented.

In February 1988 Beijing issued Document No. 27, which gave Shanghai a fiscal contract responsibility system similar to that adopted by Guangdong ten years earlier. Until 1990 Shanghai would pay to Beijing a round sum of 10.5 billion yuan per year, after which this sum would increase annually. This amount was considerably higher than that paid by Guangdong, whose 65 million inhabitants got off the hook with only 1.5 billion yuan per year. Candid city officials said quite plainly that Beijing was still "pulling a fast one on Shanghai."[7]

The solution was more resourcefulness and creativity. For the first time, the city began to look for other-than-fiscal sources of income: foreign investments and credit, bonds, and the leasing of land were applied toward improvements in the infrastructure, such as two bridges over the Huangpu River, the subway, and water purification projects. But even structural corrections and new methods brought no general improvement. During the 1980s the national growth rate averaged 9 percent per year, whereas in Shanghai it was only 5 percent. The net economic growth in the years 1985–91 was 62.8 percent for the whole of China, while in Shanghai it was only 3.3 percent. When examining statistics for Shanghai, however, one must take into consideration the dialectics of progress, as the per capita income in Shanghai was and still is one of the highest in the country—$1,202 in 1992, two and a half times the national average. After several devaluations of the renminbi, it was still $670 in 1996, well above the national average.

THE DEFINITE TURNING POINT for Shanghai came in 1990–92, and Deng Xiaoping's voice was the deciding factor. Only then did the complete determination to join all of Shanghai's unique qualities—its location on the center of China's eastern seaboard and at the mouth of the Yangtze River, its industrial potential, its pool of brainpower, and especially its controversial prewar past—gather momentum and transform it from the national economy's milk cow into its locomotive and model. In the mythical metaphors of

Chinese, the Yangtze River was "China's dragon," of which Shanghai was the "head." Shanghai still had to become a special economic zone, not directed by Hong Kong capitalists, however, but by Beijing bureaucrats.

Shanghai's territory of expansion lay on the east bank of the Huangpu River (Pudong = east of the river), across from the historic international city (Puxi = western). On 18 April Premier Li Peng announced that Pudong would be opened up for large-scale development and international investment. At that time, conservative ideologues dominated the political arena, and Deng Xiaoping had faded into the background since his resignation as chairman of the Central Military Commission in November 1989. After his return to public life in the spring of 1992, and especially after the publication of the third volume of his selected works in November 1993, Deng claimed that he had been the driving force behind Pudong. After an inspection visit to Shanghai in early 1990, Deng told the leaders of the Politburo that although he had withdrawn from public life, he wanted to remind them of the importance of developing Pudong. In April the Party Central Committee and the State Council declared Pudong the focal point of national opening-up and development projects. Deng also said, "Shanghai was once an international banking center. . . . It is necessary to resume this practice. China's hopes of attaining an international financial position must be pinned on Shanghai."[8]

This point is important because Pudong had initially been portrayed as the purely socialist opposite of the special economic zones in the south, the brainchildren of Deng and Zhao Ziyang which had meanwhile turned into enclaves of uncurbed capitalism. Pudong, on the other hand, was meant to become a state zone with a high level of state investments under the direct management of Beijing. Considering that the Pudong project was launched at a time when Deng Xiaoping seemed to have lost the initiative in the national policy agenda and orthodox Marxists were working hard to bring about a Stalinist renaissance, the impression that people had for a long time was that Pudong was the work not of chief architect Deng Xiaoping but of his Stalinist competitors. Deng's confession in 1992 that one of his biggest mistakes was not to have opened up Shanghai earlier, and the fact that a serious start was made in Pudong only after his confession, are confirmations that Deng's imprimatur was of overriding importance.

A number of other preferential policies were also not announced until after Deng's trip, such as expanded powers to approve foreign investments, tax exemptions, and tax cuts from 55 to 33 percent, the lease of land for seventy years, share issues, dealing in stocks and shares from other cities, and the go-ahead for foreign banks and other financial institutions, as well as department stores and supermarkets, to open up branches in Shanghai.

Deng encouraged Shanghai to become a pioneering model for the rest of the country, just like Guangdong, in fact giving it permission to sidestep central bureaucratic restrictions. The new measures led to a considerable increase in available funds in Shanghai. In 1992 alone, for example, Shanghai accumulated more than 20 billion yuan in funds by issuing shares and bonds for local projects, a sum that far exceeded its fiscal revenues that year. The second "liberation" of Shanghai had spectacular results: from 1992 through 1994 the city's economy grew at an average annual rate of 17 percent, 4 percent higher than the national average. In 1996 the GDP rose by 13 percent, still 3 percent above the national average.

SHANGHAI'S RENEWED SPECIAL STATUS and its ambition to become an international center of trade and finance brought about a radical revisionism regarding its prewar history. After decades of execrating prewar Shanghai as a national disgrace, the Shanghainese, including its Communist cadres, began in 1992 to reinterpret that period as its "golden age." In a series of articles appearing in the national media in the summer of 1994, historians also shed new light on the myth of the sign "Chinese and Dogs Not Admitted." The bimonthly magazine *Shiji* (Century) printed an article in April 1994 revealing that the sign had in fact existed, but that it had been a forgery, produced in 1950 by the curator of the new, Soviet-style Museum of the History and Construction of Shanghai. When a new museum was opened in 1983, the Shanghai Exhibition Hall for Historical and Cultural Relics, staff members who knew that it was a forgery threw the sign away, against the will of propaganda ideologues.[9]

During the marathon debate that arose in 1994, the hawks accused the revisionists of "not understanding the history of China's national humiliation, and of making light of the deep national humiliation with their skepticism. This is very dangerous."[10] Even the central government continues to maintain that the iconographic, symbolic value of the sign is more important than historical truth. In a white paper concerning human rights published in 1991, the Chinese State Council fulminated on the episode of the sign, implying that the West had no right to talk about human rights. The sign remains an indispensable, inexhaustible source of inspiration for China's hard-line, xenophobic foreign policy.

WITHIN THE FRAMEWORK of historical reinternationalization, the harbor boulevard, which had been rebaptized after the revolution as Sun Yat-sen Road East, was given back its old Chinese name, Wai-tan (Outer Quay), and bilingual street signs reappeared with "The Bund." A museum was even opened in 1995 dedicated to the history of the Bund, which houses a five-meter-long photograph displaying the intense cosmopolitan activity of the 1920s. The Bund became the symbol of Shanghai's renaissance, pointing not only to its former allure but also to the promise of future megabucks. Unbridled speculation in real estate has driven prices up to stratospheric levels in only a couple of years, while the quality of services and the infrastructure remain at Third World levels. Foreigners are often forced to pay rents of $10,000 a month for two-room apartments, while the Chinese live in flats costing $1 or $2 a month.

The municipal government has asked the top international real estate agents Brooke Hillier Parker Ltd. to assess the once-magnificent buildings on the Bund in order to sell them back to the eager banks from whom they were expropriated just after "liberation" in 1949. In a recent interview, Mayor Xu Kuangdi dropped the remark that prices in Shanghai probably weren't any higher than those in Hong Kong, Tokyo, and Paris, the world's three most expensive cities. The Dutch ABN-AMRO Bank was the first to sign a ten-year lease in the summer of 1994 and to move back into its old offices on the Bund. The offices are located on the ground floor and mezzanine of the Peace Hotel, formerly the stately Cathay Hotel.

Bangkok Bank followed a year later and signed a thirty-year lease on the former office building of the Commercial Bank of China, which was completely renovated by Thai architects with Thai motifs. Bangkok Bank is run by a Thai family of Chinese origin. The local Communist party and the municipal government—who, after "liberation," set up their main headquarters in the crown jewel of the Bund, the Hong Kong & Shanghai Bank building, bastion of the British empire in China—have already removed the red star from the impressive dome and have meanwhile moved into new headquarters on the People's Square. The Hong Kong & Shanghai Bank—which, owing to the imminent lowering of the Union Jack in Hong Kong next July, has bought the British Midland Bank and transferred its legal domicile to London in the form of a holding, the Hong Kong & Shanghai Banking Corporation Group—has been deliberating whether or not to spend hundreds of millions of pounds to buy back, lease, and renovate its former building. The bank's proposal to reacquire the building on the condition that it be permitted to build a twenty-story office tower behind it—to recover its cost in rent—was rejected by the municipal government, and HSBC opted out of further negotiations. Banque Indo-Suez has also given up on plans to repossess its former headquarters. In 1996 only obscure Chinese banks were moving into the Bund buildings for special domestic rates, thereby crushing hopes that the Bund would again become the shining, prime financial hub.

There are 110 historic bank buildings in Shanghai, 37 of which the city government wants to make available once again to foreign banks. Historically, international banks are generally tied to the Bund and the International Settlement, but according to the plan, Shanghai's new Wall Street will be located in Pudong, right across from the Bund in the Lujiazui Finance and Trade Zone, China's new Manhattan. The two big new bridges over the Huangpu River, however, are quite a distance away, the only direct connection being a two-lane tunnel that is difficult to reach. A second tunnel and a second subway line will not be finished until 1998, helping to strengthen the strong preference for the Bund and the old city, but doing nothing to alleviate the uncomfortable feeling that the financial center of the city will be moved to the east bank anyway in a few years. Foreign bankers who now have their offices on the west bank do not expect the move to happen for at least another five years.

THE TALK ABOUT SHANGHAI becoming a new international financial center that will compete with Hong Kong and Tokyo has so far been centered on its hardware. Shanghai's high-rises, telecommunications systems, computers, and English-speaking Chinese continue to proliferate, but what is missing is a financial system. Little heed is paid to international rules and regulations, with most things happening in the Chinese way—ad hoc, speculative, opportunistic, lawless, and secretive.

The stock exchange, still housed in the *petit opéra* theater in the nineteenth-century hotel Astor House, is a national gambling hall. There is an A-share market for domestic buyers and a B-share market for foreigners. Two-thirds of its daily turnover consists of shares being bought and sold back and forth by 5 million small punters, 80 percent of whom are unemployed workers with half-bankrupt state enterprises, housewives, pensioned professors, and so on. In 1993–94 they lost three-quarters of their savings on the stock market. Professional speculators are protected by insider knowledge of how things will progress, concentrating on a couple of blue-chip shares, which they sell and buy back every few days. Insider trading is completely normal in China as well as in other parts of Asia, where success in business is determined not so much by talent and luck as by political connections. Real information on companies and stocks is not available. All the printed news is bullish good news; there are no bears.

The stock exchange is an instrument of the government for reorganizing the state sector of the economy. The government decides which companies will be considered for a listing and issues quotas. The market is determined not by supply and demand but by the erratic policies of the government.

Spreading false rumors in order to manipulate the market is a disease that has affected nearly all Chinese. More than one investor has committed suicide during a stock-market dip.

After the stock market dropped by 77 percent in early 1993, speculative investment moved to the sphere of bank deposits and government bonds. For a few months it was feared that the stock exchange would be closed; it had only been opened in 1990 on an experimental basis because of ideological misgivings. At the end of July 1994, the government decided to intervene and prevent the market from collapsing completely. The Central Securities Regulation Commission (CSRC) announced a moratorium on new share issues, pumped 3 billion yuan into the half-dried-up bourse, and hinted that later this year international institutional investors would be admitted to the A-shares market. The B-shares market with its twenty-eight funds is too limited. Shortly after this announcement, the A-index shot up by 100 percent for a short time but then spiraled downward again and continues fitfully to have ups and downs. Offering a variation on the two great historical symbols of stock markets, the bull and the bear, one Shanghai professor described the local market as a "monkey market," continuously jumping up and down.

Another peculiarity is that China continues to bar foreigners from its A-shares market but wants Chinese firms to be listed on foreign stock exchanges, especially in Hong Kong and New York. The restrictions on foreign banks, which are not allowed to do business in local currency, are being relaxed only very slowly. Mao Yingliang, president of the People's Bank of China in Shanghai, nevertheless says that within five years his city will surpass Hong Kong, and within ten years will overtake New York, as a world financial center.[11] It is only a question of having faith in state voluntarism and propaganda. International bankers, though, reckon it will take at least twenty-five years.

Another prominent Shanghainese is somewhat more skeptical. Bao Youde, president of the Shanghai International Trust and Investment Corporation, had the following to say: "We will not become an international financial center simply by proclaiming it ourselves. We must be accepted as such by investors worldwide."[12] Wei Wenyuan, the thirty-nine-year-old chairman of the stock exchange, said at the Euromoney Conference in the fall of 1994, "We need a stable law governing the stock market instead of dependence on personal opinions and personal ideas."

At the same time as the collapse of the British bank Barings in March 1995, Shanghai experienced the biggest financial scandal in the five-year history of its stock exchange. Shanghai's biggest stockbroker, Shanghai International Securities Company (SISCO), foundered because of its practice of gambling in derivatives in China's burgeoning futures market. The economic tsar, Vice-premier Zhu Rongji, struck with maximum overkill. Trading in futures was forbidden and the two child prodigies of Shanghai's stock exchange, Chairman Wei Wenyuan and the president of SISCO, Guan Jinsheng, fell from grace.

AS REGARDS PUDONG, Chinese and foreigners perceive it in widely varying ways. According to municipal officials, it will take fifteen years for Pudong to become a "new Manhattan," but international architects, planners, and bankers reckon it will take thirty years. Pudong occupies an area of 520 square kilometers, nearly as large as Singapore, and comprises six special zones: the Lujiazui Finance and Trade Zone, the Jingqiao Export Processing Zone, the Waigaoqiao Free Trade Zone, the Zhangjiang High Tech Park, and the Sun Qiao Agricultural and Food Processing Zone. Its showpiece is Lujiazui with its 468-meter-high Orient Pearl Television Tower, the highest in Asia. Since 1990 the central government has invested 25 billion yuan ($3 billion) in buildings and infrastructure. Shanghai's city fathers say that this is a belated reward for the high contributions paid by the city for decades to the state treasury.

For the new Central Business District (CBD), plans were drawn up by four world-renowned architects, including Sir Richard Rodgers of Great Britain, Dominique Perrault of France, Massimiliano Fuxas of Italy, and Toyo Ito of Japan. It looks as though the Chinese will make their own final blueprint utilizing elements of each design. Another 80 billion yuan will be invested in the second phase: the new outer harbor, the new international airport, and improved telecommunications.

The occasional visitor to Pudong gazes in wonder at the scale and tempo of the developments there. First Pacific Davies, a real estate company from Hong Kong, calculated in the summer of 1995 that in just three years Shanghai had built 4.7 million square meters of office space in prime locations, as much as Hong Kong had built in thirty-three years. There is little doubt that during the first quarter of the next century, Shanghai will become the world's largest city and Pudong the "mother of all special zones."

The majority of investments in Pudong still come from the state, which prompted Milton Friedman to say that the city was not a manifestation of the market economy but a "state monument for an [almost] dead pharaoh [Deng Xiaoping], just like the pyramids." Nevertheless, forty-four multinationals have invested in Pudong, and twenty-six hundred projects are currently financed by foreign investments—including those from Hong Kong and Taiwan—of which 170 are already in production. Total foreign capital invested amounts to $2 billion, and agreements have been signed for another $10 billion, although much of it is in speculative real estate development and will remain unused until the great influx of companies starts. Pudong's new international airport (cost: $10 billion) will be a joint venture with 49 percent of its capital coming from foreign investors of different countries.

Shanghai is now the most popular destination for foreign investors, and according to the newspaper *Shanghai Star*, 95 percent of the companies with foreign investments are profit-making.

The central government is determined to turn Shanghai into an international, trendsetting stronghold of heavy industry (steel, automobiles, power plants, petrochemicals), and light and high-tech industry (telecommunications, white goods, computers, medicine) under state domination. Shanghai Volkswagen, one of China's most successful joint ventures, was making 160,000 automobiles per year in the mid-1990s and will expand production to 300,000 per year by 1997.

Dozens of conglomerates with annual turnovers of between 5 billion and 10 billion yuan will be formed in the coming years, and they are expected to bring fifty brand-name products onto the market before the year 2000. "The municipal government will not interfere with their growth," said Mayor Xu Kuangdi. In mid-1995 the Municipal Commission for Science and Technology introduced accelerated programs to enable them to reach the top of international high-tech development by the year 2010. The commission said that Shanghai was fifteen years behind the times as far as research and development was concerned, and twenty years behind in production technology.

Policy makers have identified the service sector as the leader, which will contribute 75 percent to the GNP by the year 2010, accounting for 30 to 40 percent of all employment opportunities. Shanghai is meant to compensate for the capitalist merger of light industries in Guangdong and Hong Kong, which the central government has little control over.

In the long term, Shanghai's stock exchange is potentially much stronger than those of Hong Kong and Shenzhen together, because Shanghai has a much broader industrial base and powerful backing from Beijing. Hong Kong's capital market is largely powered by real estate. The "blue chips" in Hong Kong are speculative project development companies; the "red chips" in Shanghai are to an increasing degree large state enterprises, expected to become big multinationals in the future. The former chairman of Daimler-Benz, Edzard Reuter, said in 1994 that his company wants a listing on a stock exchange in Asia, but probably in Shanghai, not in Hong Kong. "Hong Kong is still number one, but in 2010 the situation will most probably be quite different," said Reuter.

ACCORDING TO ONE futuristic description of Shanghai, it is destined to become Deng Xiaoping's model city, "not Mao's Marxist utopia but Deng's commercial utopia," a megacity where people get rich without challenging the political status quo, a city that is unquestioningly loyal to the central government in Beijing, and a cobastion for domination of the whole country. Whether or not this will come to pass is another question, because "for every new foreign bank branch that opens in Shanghai, a new group of dissidents will spring up," wrote dissident Yang Zhou in 1994 in a manifesto. The dissidents' goal is not to take immediate action but to lay the basis for large-scale, effective action in the future.

Preventive repression is draconian. Potential sources of social protest are the ruthless eviction of people from the old international city center and the messy situation on the stock exchange. Whole parts of the old city look like Berlin at the end of the Second World War. Old people who have spent their whole lives there in admittedly ramshackle dwellings are being forced to move to high-rises in Pudong or other new developments without shops or schools. This routinely gives rise to heartrending scenes that the dissidents try to take advantage of. The overly hasty "reinternationalization" of Shanghai and its redevelopment into a metropolis of the twenty-first century will require considerable sacrifices from the average Shanghainese.

The majority seem to be delighted by the return of the "golden age." Born-again, prewar chauvinism is stronger than ever. Mayor Xu has warned the Shanghainese again and again on television talk shows and in the newspapers not to display such arrogance toward outsiders who don't speak Shanghainese. Before the war, the Shanghainese derived an inborn feeling of superiority from the international status of their city and looked down on Chinese from elsewhere as bumpkins, which caused the other Chinese to disparage the Shanghainese as "imitation foreigners" (*jia yangguizi*). During the Mao era, the Cantonese and Shanghainese were both the dupes of extreme egalitarianism, but when the Cantonese were ostentatiously given preferential treatment at the beginning of Deng Xiaoping's reforms, the Shanghainese felt slighted indeed.

The Cantonese have become the best businessmen in China and look down their noses at the Shanghainese, who admittedly have better manners but live packed together like sardines. In early 1995 Vice-mayor Dai Zhiguo of Guangzhou said with pride that the average Cantonese has 9.2 square meters of living space, as compared with a mere 6 square meters for the average Shanghainese. In the summer of 1995, the city government of Shanghai unveiled a plan for general urban development that "promises the 40 million registered Chinese . . . 10 square meters of living space by the year 2000, and private toilets and kitchens in 70 percent of the new housing."[13] A large part of the population will therefore have to make do with communal kitchens and toilets and go without bathrooms for a long time to come. And in the old districts, the *matong*, that portable convenience that has to be emptied in the early hours of the morning into the dung cart and subsequently into the street drain, will continue to be of service. The gulf between the poor housing developments and the gleaming skyscrapers, superdeluxe hotels, villas, and pricey restaurants is just as wide as before the war. But that is less of a problem in the present "get-rich-quick society" than it was during the war or the turmoil of the Mao era.

One phenomenon for which Shanghai was renowned before the war was its nightlife, which is once again in full swing, but with special characteristics: "No sex please, only money." Of course, there is sex as well, but unusually invisible, and the prices are probably the highest in the world. Shanghai's main streets and back alleys, new chic districts and old slums all teem with flamboyantly lit nightclubs, dance halls, and karaoke bars, some of which are owned by the police or the army. The philosophy behind this is that it yields extrabudgetary funds and in this way remains "disciplined." There are routine "antivice campaigns," during which the police storm in and check whether or not the girls have proper residence permits. If not, then they are deported to their hometowns. In the nightclubs you can sit for hours with one or more of these girls under the glaring lights or in a dark "fondling corner," for which the charge is about $30 an hour. Every fifteen minutes she orders an XO cognac, which costs about $18. In the karaoke rooms you can sing songs with the girls upon payment of drinks, singing fees, and room rental, spending a couple of hundred dollars in a couple of hours without any progress being made in the direction hoped for by most of the customers. Finally, upon payment of a huge tip and an advance, the girl promises to phone your hotel room the following morning, because at night surveillance is too strict.

In this context, a former party secretary of Shanghai, Wu Bangguo, now a member of the Politburo and vice-premier, said in an interview for the Communist newspaper *Ta Kung Pao* of Hong Kong: "Some things are forbidden in Shanghai because we consider ourselves responsible for foreigners and for the 13 million citizens of Shanghai. We permit no harm to come of normal social practices. In the past, Shanghai was a paradise for adventurers. Everything good and evil was to be found here . . . including the underworld, kidnapping, and prostitution. We will not permit burned cinders to become glowing embers. We also cannot permit such things as horse racing, casinos, and gambling. Some well-intentioned friends from Hong Kong and Macau have written to me to point out the good aspects of these things, but after careful consideration we have decided against them. We will have no thinly disguised pornography and no beauty contests."[14]

THE SHANGHAINESE used to say that for years their leaders accepted unfavorable treatment by Beijing because traditionally they have always cherished the ambition of becoming central government leaders. This restrains them from going too far in their financial showdowns with Beijing. If this is conscious policy, then it has proved to be very effective. Shanghai was eventually rewarded for its financial sacrifices and faithfulness, first with investments in the billions for the Pudong New Area, China's most advanced special zone of the 1990s, and subsequently with an endless series of appointments.

There are now four ex-mayors/party secretaries of Shanghai in the Politburo: president and party leader Jiang Zemin, vice-premiers Zhu Rongji and Wu Bangguo, and the present party secretary, Huang Ju. The vice-president of the state, the non-Communist Rong Yiren, also comes from Shanghai. Two members of the Politburo who are also vice-premiers, Qian Qichen and Zou Jiahua, were also born in Shanghai, although they've spent the greater part of their careers elsewhere. Qiao Shi, one of the most powerful men in the seven-member Standing Committee of the Politburo, also has strong ties to Shanghai, though he is not necessarily a patron of what is called the "new Shanghai gang" or "clique" (following the precedent set by the ultraleft Gang of Four during the Cultural Revolution, whose power base was also Shanghai).

Since late 1992 the Shanghainese have seen so many of their former colleagues transferred from Shanghai to Beijing that jokes are made about Shanghainese having replaced Mandarin as the language of power in Zhongnanhai, the Chinese Kremlin. Wu Bangguo commented dryly, "I speak the Beijing dialect, but I understand Shanghainese." The present mayor, Xu Kuangdi, said in turn, "You have to speak Mandarin well, but not forget your Shanghainese."

If the burgeoning Shanghainese domination of the central party and government leadership manages to consolidate itself after the definitive end of the Deng era, this will only be more favorable to the current breathtaking developments in the city. But even if a leadership emerges whose regional origins are more diverse, it will hardly be able to damage Shanghai, even if it should wish to do so. Through its location, its history, and its resourceful, innovative, compliant population, Shanghai is destined by nature to become number one in China, both economically and commercially. Chronologically, Guangdong was the first to be singled out for a head start, but now it is the turn of Shanghai and the whole east coast. At the same time, the focal point of accelerated development is shifting to the whole Yangtze River basin—China's dragon—stretching to Wuhan and Chongqing, two thousand kilometers inland. This will occur, however, under the auspices of Shanghai, the dragon's head. Guangdong was the brainchild of Zhao Ziyang, Shanghai is the brainchild of the current regime, which wants to prove that it is better. Shanghai must therefore be more socialist and less wildly capitalist, as well as more orderly and harmonious. Actually, this does not conflict with Deng Xiaoping's strategic goal of making Guangdong, with the help of Hong Kong, the "fifth tiger" of Asia, just as integrated with the world economy as with the rest of China. Shanghai, on the other hand, remains primarily a national center, which must continue to serve as a locomotive for the entire country, subsequently becoming a world center of finance and commerce à la Hong Kong.

Pessimists in Hong Kong are fearful that the present ruling clique is determined to undermine Hong Kong's superiority and transfer its functions to Shanghai. A longtime observer thinks that the leadership wants a purely Chinese financial center, and not one infected with British administration.[15] In other words, Hong Kong will be punished and purged of its past, just as Shanghai was after 1949. After the hopeless trial of strength with Governor Chris Patten, it is obvious that Hong Kong will be kept on a short leash politically after 1997, but whether it will be thwarted in its further blossoming as a financial center, and whether political restrictions will automatically undermine its position, are questions that must wait to be answered. Singapore is the ideal combination of an authoritarian political system, including censorship, and an efficient international financial center.

Chinese leaders see no contradiction whatever between Hong Kong's status quo and Shanghai's potential position. In this context, Chen Yuan, vice-governor of the People's Bank, said that Shanghai would not replace Hong Kong in the short term, or as long as the Chinese currency, the renminbi, is not fully convertible. "In the long term, Shanghai, with the support of Hong Kong, will become a financial center, supported by the mainland market and with renminbi trade as its main activity."

Mayor Xu Kuangdi was more exuberant: "The two cities are like two motors of one airplane, two lead actors in the same play, or two eyes of one gigantic dragon. Shanghai tries to regain its glory as a financial center in the Far East with strong backing from the central government, while Hong Kong is an established center of financial services in the region. . . . Hong Kong's financial industry and foreign trade are more directed at internationalization, while Shanghai serves as a bridge that links China and the world market."[16]

CHAPTER 15

Northeast China and the Greater Northeast Asian Economic Sphere

We suffer here from the "Northeast Complex": the inability to emancipate ourselves from orthodox Communist thinking, industrial decay, the absence of the spirit of competition, and progressive pauperization. . . . Soviet influence was here first.

NORTHEAST CHINESE OFFICIALS

NORTHEAST CHINA and surrounding Northeast Asia is a geopolitical melting pot where every imaginable historical phantom wanders around unpredictably. For centuries the "Northeastern wilderness" was steppeland, scantly populated by Manchus, Mongolians, and Tungusic tribes. It was not until the beginning of the twentieth century that the imperial government, by that time in an advanced state of decline, opened up the area to Chinese immigrants, after which it grew into a Chinese Canada or Siberia. The aim of immigration was to offer more effective resistance to the Russian and Japanese advance into the region. Through a treaty signed in 1896, the Russians had exacted a sphere of influence in Manchuria, actually in order to build a railway to Vladivostok along a much shorter route than the northern one around the border rivers. After the epochal defeat of the Russians by the Japanese in the battle in the Tsushima Strait in 1905, the Japanese advance into Northeast China began in earnest, culminating in 1932 in the proclamation of the Japanese vassal state of Manchukuo, with Pu Yi as puppet emperor. After the Japanese capitulation in 1945, it again became a territory of special Russian interests until 1954.

Since the mid-1980s there has been a resumption of Japanese economic influence in former (South) Manchuria. Since the late 1980s the term used is the Greater Northeast Asian Economic Sphere. But if this time around it is not dominated by the Japanese, who does have the upper hand? Moreover, there is Chinese irredentism regarding the unnatural, unjust border dictated by the Russians in 1858–60; an increasing Russian demographic deficit, turning the Russian Far East into the sick man of the region; the legacy of the Cold War, which ensures that the Korean peninsula remains one of the most acute threats to world peace; Korean "transnationalism," which includes not just North and South Korea but also the Korean minorities in the former Soviet Union and in the Chinese province of Jilin; and finally a certain "pan-Mongolism," which seeks to do away with the porous border between Chinese Inner Mongolia and independent Outer Mongolia, and, as a result, potential resumption of Chinese irredentism regarding Outer Mongolia.

INDUSTRIALLY, Northeast China was once the most advanced part of the country. The Japanese quickly saw to the industrialization of their puppet state Manchukuo, and by the time of the Japanese capitulation in 1945, one-third of Chinese industry was located there. Six days before the end of the Second World War, Stalin declared war against Japan, hoping to place himself in a good position to accept the Japanese surrender and haul in the booty. The Soviets subsequently plundered the entire region, taking not only industrial equipment but also gold, foodstuffs, and other supplies.

Northeast China was the first area on which the Stalinist economic model was imposed. The legacy of the past is ponderous indeed. Centers of heavy industry are stubbornly trying to wrestle free from the influence of central planning. State enterprises still account for 80 percent of all industrial production in Heilongjiang—the highest percentage in the country— while township and village enterprises (TVEs) account for only 14.4 percent. Governors, mayors, and party secretaries talk in speeches and interviews about the Northeast Complex: the inability to emancipate themselves from "orthodox Communist thinking, industrial decay, the absence of the spirit of competition, and progressive pauperization."

During an inspection visit by Vice-premier Zhu Rongji in the summer of 1994, there was a large-scale cleanup among the top leadership in Heilongjiang, because in 1993 the province's rate of economic growth had been

8.6 percent below the national average of 13.5 percent. Hinting at unprofitable investments and subsequent bank loans necessary to keep businesses afloat, the new party secretary, Yue Qifeng, spoke of a "vicious circle of investment/stagnation/blood transfusion." Immediate diversification and "new concepts" were the only solution. The new motto became "Opening the Second Front," meaning the establishment of hundreds of special zones for township and village enterprises receiving investment money from Hong Kong, Macau, and Taiwan, and the conversion of one hundred large state enterprises into joint ventures. The second front was meant to help the first front with recovery, building up its strength further and accelerating the transition to a market economy. "The two fronts gradually infiltrate each other and intermingle until they eventually form a strong socialist market power with public ownership as the main element," said Yue.[1]

Another problem Heilongjiang had to contend with was a brain drain of top talent going south. More than 80 percent of all experts worked on the first front and had no chance to demonstrate their abilities, resulting after several years in the flight of scientific and technical personnel to the south, taking their expertise and achievements with them.

Yue pleaded for a policy of preferential treatment for Heilongjiang, to attract funds, technology, and talent from the southern coastal provinces in order to develop export products designed to reach the whole world via Hong Kong and Taiwan. "After a period of hard work, when the technological level of our products is higher and our export economy has expanded, our power to open up to the whole world will be much stronger, and the bad image of the products we now trade on the border with the Russian Far East will change."[2] Another recurrent theme of Party Secretary Yue was "competition in changing ideas," by which he meant that those who are not willing or able to change their ideas should be eliminated.[3]

By mid-1995 provincial authorities were claiming that the new, drastic measures were showing results. In 1995 Heilongjiang experienced its highest rate of growth in ten years: 8.9 percent, only 1.4 percent below the national average. The growth of nonstate enterprises was spectacular (36.7 percent), particularly the growth of the township and village enterprises (91.1 percent).[4]

LIAONING, the territory between China proper and the real "wilderness," has 1,278 large state enterprises, one-tenth of all large enterprises run by the central government (steel, heavy machinery, petrochemicals). It is the oldest concentration of heavy industry and also the largest "rust belt" of blast furnaces in all of China. In the old, centrally planned economy, Liaoning was the largest industrial center in the country, after Shanghai. But during the "second revolution"—the era of market reforms—it has sunk to fifth or sixth place. In 1994 it experienced industrial contraction of 12.6 percent. Many companies no longer offer their workers work and wages, giving them instead goods to peddle on the street. If they refuse these ersatz wages, they are given an extended leave of absence (*qing changjia*) and an allowance of about $9 a month. In the provincial capital, Shenyang, unemployment, social unrest, and crime are more prevalent than anywhere else in the country. A great many factory chimneys are no longer smoking in Shenyang—a relief for the lungs, perhaps, but not necessarily for the stomach. Strikes are a daily occurrence. Workers also demonstrate against the luxury cars of party functionaries that are parked in front of fancy restaurants by shouting "They live like this and we go hungry."

At the National People's Congress in 1995, Governor Wen Shizhen of Liaoning said that 18 percent of the state enterprises are insolvent and another 49 percent are "unstable and making no profits."⁵ In late 1994 the New China News Agency reported that unemployment had reached 18 percent (not counting redundant workers on extended leaves of absence, still receiving at least ersatz wages). Several years ago, Shenyang was a national experimental center for bankruptcy procedures. Already in August 1986 the Shenyang Explosion-Proof Apparatus Factory was declared bankrupt, with fifty-four other factories following suit. Twelve of these were state enterprises and the rest collectives. Their debts amounted to 220 million yuan and the average debt ratio was 200 percent. Ninety percent of the ten thousand workers fired have found new jobs. Seven thousand retired workers now receive pensions from local insurance companies. In 1995 the province declared bankruptcy in five more cases of medium-sized and small state enterprises that were hopelessly in debt, but the large enterprises are "untouchable" owing to political protection and fear of social upheaval. Industry officials increasingly admit, though not in public, that reorganization of the state sector is impossible without systematic revision of ownership rights and sales of assets, making capital available to finance unemployment benefits. Nevertheless, President Jiang Zemin has sworn to bring about a renaissance of the state sector. "This is a life-or-death struggle for the survival of socialism," he affirms. But without help from capitalism, the state enterprises are doomed.

The provincial government of Liaoning has unfolded a six-year "pioneer plan" with the motto "Marry and Link Up" to reform eight hundred large state enterprises, two-thirds of the total, into joint ventures by the year 2000. In the case of over two hundred companies, the goal is to attract more than

$20 million in foreign investments from Japan, Germany, South Korea, Hong Kong, Taiwan, and Australia.

Anshan, seat of the largest steel complex in the country with more than 200,000 employees, produces 50 million tons of steel annually, half of the national volume of production. It is also in the red, however. The current therapy for ailing state enterprises is to put former managers who were promoted to government positions back in charge of the enterprises, resulting in figures being fudged and statistics being blurred by bureaucratic tricks.

No matter which old methods and mottoes are dressed up to look new, the state sector is irretrievably lost, not only in a decrepit Stalinist reserve like Liaoning but in the whole of the country. State enterprises are increasingly being overrun by the 25 million township and village enterprises, joint ventures, public limited-liability companies, and private enterprises. Privatization is still taboo, but flamboyant private entrepreneurs with good connections prey like "raiders" on weak state enterprises, buying them up for a song and merging them with conglomerates with opaque systems of management. A good example is the Dalian Baolu Enterprise Group, a group of seventeen private, collective, and joint-venture firms which even runs a new development zone in Dalian. There are 900,000 people living in the four-thousand-square-kilometer zone of Zhuanghe, which plans to build a harbor, a railway, a power plant, and an automobile factory, all to be in private hands.

IN SPITE of the stagnant state sector in the northeastern interior, the coastal city of Dalian boasts one of the most internationalized economies in China. At the beginning of the twentieth century, the city, formerly known as Dairen, Lüda, and Lüshun (Port Arthur), was a Russian Hong Kong, subsequently under Japanese rule for forty years. The special rights exacted by Stalin after 1945 were not abolished until 1953. When fourteen coastal cities were opened up to foreign investment in late 1984, Dalian was the first to build an "economic technological development zone," one of the most successful thus far. The forward-looking mayor, Bo Xilai, son of the revolutionary veteran Bo Yibo, spoke again in 1995 of a northern Hong Kong, although Dalian is way behind Shanghai and even Guangzhou in attracting financial institutions.

Dalian is the port of entry to the northeast, and its harbor—the second largest in China (63 million tons annually)—ships more tonnage in foreign trade than Shanghai. The city is the focal point of what is probably the third most important region-state of China after Hong Kong–Guangdong and the Shanghai region. It houses 3,689 companies with foreign investments, most of them from Hong Kong and Taiwan, but the technological vanguard consists of 800 Japanese companies. Japan has shifted its investment strategy from North America and Europe back to Asia, and since Emperor Akihito's state visit to China in 1992, it is relocating its sphere of investment from Southeast to Northeast Asia. One-third of all Japanese investments in China are now concentrated in the area around Dalian. Ken Ohmae comments: "It is only natural that people in Dalian now feel that prosperity is created from without, not from the national center."[6]

This contrasts sharply with Shenyang, the provincial capital, which is linked to Dalian by a 375-kilometer-long freeway, the longest in China. Shenyang has a population of 6.5 million and a total foreign investment volume of $9.38 billion ($1.45 billion in 1996 alone). Dalian, with 5.2 million people, has foreign investments of $14.84 billion ($4.25 billion in 1996). Shenyang's volume of exports in 1996 was $682 million compared with Dalian's $2.63 billion. Liaoning is therefore tailor-made for the formula "one province–two systems."

Dalian is an ideal spot for the Japanese. A relatively large number of people speak Japanese and it is close to home, only a four-hour flight from Japan. A Japanese manager said that Dalian is to Japan what Mexico is to the United States, "a cheap industrial zone near the main office." The quality of the workforce equals that of Japan and sometimes even surpasses it, according to some Japanese managers. The cost of leasing one square meter of industrial land is one-fourth to one-third that in Shanghai. Wages are half those in Shenzhen or Shanghai and approximately one-twentieth of those in Japan. More than 100,000 highly trained workers are employed in Japanese high-tech joint ventures, and 2,125 Japanese managers live in Dalian. Mabuchi Motor has a factory there with 7,500 workers making micromotors for cameras and car mirrors. Canon has its largest production unit for laser printer cartridges; Matsushita makes mechanisms for video recorders, employing 490 robots. Toshiba makes printed circuit boards and Marubeni chopsticks.[7]

Mayor Bo says that Dalian, together with Shanghai, is one of the economic pillars of China. Bo calls his city of 2.4 million inhabitants in the greater urban area (5.2 million in the whole municipality) medium-sized. He hopes to prevent overexpansion into a megacity. "Big family, big problems!" Bo wants Dalian to become the best city in China, a beautiful city, with a superior investment climate and the highest standard of living in the country.[8]

. . .

THE REGION-STATE Dalian is part of a greater supraregional whole, the Bohai region, the coastal area of Bohai Bay with its surrounding territory. The erratic coastline, comparable to the Baltic Sea in Europe, offers an omnidirectional opening from North, Northeast, and Northwest China to the sea and forms the central part of the Northeast Asian Economic Zone. One day this will all become an interdependent "natural economic territory" (NET), led by Japanese and perhaps also South Korean investments. The region has four large existing ports—Dalian, Qinhuangdao, Tianjin, and Qingdao—and intends to build four new ones—Yingkou, Jingxi, Huanghua, and Tangshan. In 1992 the Bohai region was the third to be declared a macroregion in the national development plan, after the deltas of the Pearl River and the Yangtze River. As far as high tech is concerned, however, it will certainly surpass the Pearl River delta in importance. The Bohai Rim covers 1.12 million square kilometers and comprises parts of the provinces of Shandong, Liaoning, Hebei, Shanxi, the Inner Mongolia Autonomous Region, and the two megacities Beijing and Tianjin. Its subsoil contains 40 percent of the nation's coal, oil, and iron ore reserves, and together the region handles 40 percent of all cargo shipped out of China. It has 240 million inhabitants, one-fifth of the population of the whole country.

A grandiose plan exists to build a 134-kilometer-long link consisting of bridges, dams, and tunnels under the Bohai Bay, running from Dalian to Penglai in Shandong, a project many times larger than the European Channel Tunnel or the Japanese interisland bridges. Mayor Bo Xilai dismisses the plan as sheer megalomania. There is intensive ferry traffic, however, not only between Liaoning and Shandong but also to South Korea. The busiest line is the one between Weihai, the historical headquarters of the Chinese "North Sea Fleet," and Inchon, the Korean coastal city where General MacArthur made his famous marine landing during the Korean War. Since 1992 Korea has been an important newcomer to the investment scene, but it is still only number four or five after Hong Kong, Taiwan, Japan, and the United States. Korean restaurants and businessmen are legion in the cities of Shandong, and the waitresses come from the Korean minority in China's Jilin Province. In the summer of 1994, one of these girls told me how happy she was to be able to enjoy the freedom in China. "China is already too free," she said. "You should look at North Korea. There it's just like it was during the Cultural Revolution. Who would ever have dreamed that I would be able to leave my poor village in Jilin and come here to work in Qingdao in a luxurious Korean restaurant catering to rich South Korean businessmen?"

It is sometimes speculated that the South Korean presence on the Shandong Peninsula will become just as big and influential as that of the Chinese from Hong Kong and Taiwan in South China. According to the mayor of Qingdao, Yu Zhengsheng, this is impossible because "the people from Hong Kong and Taiwan are Chinese. Koreans are foreigners." The fraternization of the South Koreans and the Chinese Koreans is not without its problems. In Yantai and Qingdao city officials complain about the drinking and womanizing engaged in by South Korean businessmen. In the Northeast, Korean tourism, cultural exchanges, and investments are earmarked for political purposes. The first Korean Cultural Festival held in Harbin in the summer of 1995 turned into a debacle when, at the last minute, the local authorities forbade six South Korean artists to perform. According to the South Korean media, the audience of thirty-five thousand Chinese Koreans protested wildly, but the police would not relent. The South Korean media reported that China was systematically attempting to prevent all contact between South Koreans and Chinese Koreans out of a concern for "national splittism."[9] Giving in to pressure from China, South Korea subsequently decided not to invite Chinese Koreans to a Cultural Festival in Seoul.

Korean businessmen certainly do not always try to conceal their expansionist ambitions in Manchuria, which they claim is historically part of Korea. A Korean institute, *Damul* (Claim), organizes paramilitary excursions of Korean managers to Manchuria to fill them with patriotic fervor and induce them to reconquer the area through investment.[10] China is left with a life-size dilemma: it has its eye on investments, but ethnic-political movements fill it with extreme paranoia.

Historical Japanese-Korean antagonism is also an obstacle to developing Bohai and the Northeast into a transnational natural economic territory.

As though seized by fits of grumpiness, the Chinese media still periodically launch exaggerated tirades against the crimes of Western imperialism, while once again treating the Russians as friends (in need?). The traces of Western encroachments on China's integrity are, however, mixed, if not positive, as in the case of Hong Kong and Taiwan and their role as investment dynamos for the Chinese economy. One of the most negative and most enduring legacies of Russia's historical aggression against China is its cutting off of two northeastern Chinese provinces from the sea, thereby hindering the development of this territory until the present day.

In 1858–60 tsarist Russia forced the Manchu empire to relinquish 1 million square kilometers of territory in East Manchuria, redrawing the border with the decrepit Chinese empire in such a way as to cut off the two northeastern provinces of Jilin and Heilongjiang from an outlet to the sea, compelling them to import and export their goods via overburdened Dalian, 1,000 kilometers to the south.[11]

The border municipality of Hunchun in the northeast of Jilin Province is cut off from the Sea of Japan by a 15-kilometer-wide strip of Russian territory. Owing to tense Sino-Soviet relations lasting until the mid-1980s, China's international navigation rights through the Tumen River to the Sea of Japan were not restored until the Sino-Soviet summit between Mikhail Gorbachev and Deng Xiaoping in 1989. The river, though 800 meters wide, is only 5 to 6 meters deep, and without large-scale dredging unnavigable for ships of more than 400 tons. "Our strategic and historical goal of acquiring an outlet to the sea is nearing the stage of realization," said Jin Minxiong, the mayor of Hunchun. "This will put us in a position to become a northern Hong Kong or an eastern Rotterdam."[12]

THE "ROTTERDAM OF ASIA" is not an existing port that wants to expand, but rather the undeveloped area around the Tumen River shared by China, North Korea, and the Russian Far East. If the grandiose plans become a reality, $30 billion will be invested in the coming twenty years under the auspices of the United Nations Development Program (UNDP), turning the territory into a new "Golden Triangle," a Northeast Asian trading block with a population of 350 million around the Sea of Japan. The component parts of this block will consist of the neglected raw materials of Siberia, the Russian Far East, and Mongolia; the cheap labor of the three Northeast Chinese provinces and North Korea; and the financial and technological prowess of South Korea and Japan.

A ride along the Chinese shore of the Tumen River illustrated its potential for development. From the city of Tumen, which was given a rail link in 1993, all the way to Fangchuan in the southern appendix of the municipality, there lies on the Chinese side a 100-kilometer-long strip of meadow and woodlands. Green hills stretch into the distance on the North Korean side. A bus trip includes countless hindrances: in every village farmers have dug irrigation ditches in the gravel road which require an all-out effort, including help from the local mayor and municipal secretary, to fill up with stones so the bus can pass. At the point where the three borders—Russia, China, and North Korea—meet, there is a definite Cold War atmosphere. Soldiers manning the guard post on the hill got so worked up about one Russian and two South Korean television crews that it seemed as if war would break out any minute. Behind double barbed-wire barriers lies the Russian border town of Khasan, where wide Russian railway cars are shoved onto smaller undercarriages, with the railway bridge from Russia to North Korea in the foreground. It is a huge green void. There is no sign of life whatever, especially on the North Korean side. More than enough room exists here for new cities and vast industrial parks. When asked whether China had to force North Korea into cooperating, Vice-mayor Song Xuexian answered, "Who influences whom? Nowadays every country wants development. North Korea sees that we and the Russians are getting access to international finance and they don't want to be left out."

The framework for the unique collaboration in store between post-Communist Russia, semi-Communist China, and orthodox Communist North Korea is a multilateral project between five countries—six, including Japan—called the Tumen River Area Development Program (TRADP). Another distant participant has just been added, Outer Mongolia, which is also rich in raw materials though poor in population and capital. Tumen will also give Mongolia much easier access to the sea than the existing trade routes via the much more southern Chinese port cities of Dalian and Tianjin. In the year 2001 a new, albeit not ice-free, port—Fangchuan, with a capacity of 5 million tons—will be completed at the southern extremity of the Chinese Tumen shore.

You have to have a limitless imagination to envision all of this turning into a new Rotterdam. According to Mayor Jin, the comparison applies to a whole series of harbors in all three coastal states which will be integrated into a regional transportation system. In the nearby coastal region Russia has new, natural ocean ports that are more or less ice-free, and North Korea has antiquated harbors that are completely ice-free. "The local governments of the three states have already reached an agreement on the use of one another's ports. The key elements of the system will be the new rail link between the Chinese city of Hunchun and the Russian city of Zarubino, a new international ocean port 150 kilometers south of Vladivostok." It is an irony of fate, the nemesis of history, that this time it will be a Chinese railway on Russian territory.

On the Russian side there is also the coal harbor of Posyet at a distance of 40 kilometers from Hunchun, and on the North Korean side there are two ports, Najin and Chongjin, waiting like oysters to be opened up. Mayor Jin says that in the multilateral context of the UNDP, North Korea would be the willing recipient of foreign investment, especially from South Korea. Meanwhile, the Moonies, the sect led by Sun Myung Moon, have their eye on investment projects as well.

The Russians are rather cool about the whole project, partly for envi-

ronmental reasons, but more so because they prefer to give priority to reha-
bilitating and modernizing the ports at Vladivostok and Nakhodka instead
of building new ports in their own territory which will chiefly serve China.
Nevertheless, during the third Tumen conference in Pyongyang in May 1993,
the three coastal states agreed in principle on four critical legal and organizational questions:

1. The three riparian states will lease land with new and existing facilities and installations to a multinational company, which will
   manage the infrastructure, industry and trade, services, housing,
   and so on in the Tumen River Economic Zone.
2. The shore states will form a Tumen River Development Coordinating Committee that will become the highest organ of policy
   making in the territory.
3. An independent Tumen River Area Development Corporation
   will be formed with a board of directors consisting of representatives of the riparian states and foreign investors; the corporation
   will be subject to international management—from Singapore or
   the West, for example—to win the confidence of international
   investors.
4. An intergovernmental coordinating and advisory commission
   will be formed, composed of government representatives from the
   riparian states and other interested countries, with representatives
   of international organizations and multilateral development
   banks as observers.

The documents formalizing these important legal moves were supposed to
have been signed in the fall of 1993 in Vladivostok, but in the summer of that
year the director of the Pacific Center of Economic Development and Cooperation of the Russian Academy of Science in Vladivostok, Viktor Savaley,
said that China would benefit most from the project and that North Korea
and Russia were not yet ready for it. According to Savaley, the area south of
Vladivostok is a unique region of forests and woodland that should not be
spoiled by industry. In fact, Russia has no need to develop this area, as only
2.3 million Russians live in this region, compared with 100 million Chinese
in the three northeastern provinces, 66 million Koreans in North and South
Korea, and 125 million Japanese. Russian developmental priorities in this
area are the privatization and conversion of military and other large state industries, and these are not included in the Tumen project. "The only benefit to Primorski Krai—the Russian maritime territory—is the port of
Zarubino, for which we will receive only port dues from the Chinese. China

receives new, large-scale infrastructure, new industries, and better access to the Japanese market. Japan will have not only better access to the Chinese market, but through the new intercontinental railway to be developed, it will have a connection to Europe that is 1,700 kilometers shorter than the old one. South Korea will acquire cheap North Korean labor. The North Koreans don't yet know what they want. They don't want to create any diffi-
· culties, but they're against the internationalization of their coastal area. China stands to benefit most from it; there should be more balance of benefits," said Savaley.

Owing to Russian doubts and the North Korean nuclear and succession crises, and also to the Chinese austerity program begun in 1993, the project has been at a standstill for nearly two years. In May 1995, however, it was resuscitated with the signing of three new accords by China, Russia, Mongolia, and North and South Korea, by which North Korea would set up the Rajin-Sonbong Free Economic and Trade Zone, guaranteeing visa-free entry for parties to the project from other countries. They also reached an agreement on a Coordinating Committee and an Advisory Commission for regional cooperation in all of Northeast Asia, but could not agree on the location of the secretariat. After much wrangling, the intergovernmental coordination commission of the Tumen River Area Development Project (TRADP) convened in Beijing in April 1996 and decided to have its secretariat in Beijing, Seoul, and Vladivostok in turns. Even North Korea showed new willingness to join in and held an investment forum for the Rajin-Sonbong Free Economic and Trade Zone in September 1996. For at least another three years, the project will concentrate on a range of trade and investment promotion activities.

HUNCHUN HAS BECOME just as much of a boomtown as Shenzhen—the special economic zone on the border with Hong Kong 3,000 kilometers to the south—was ten years ago. This is borne out by figures presented by Mayor Jin: since 1991 the population has tripled from 80,000 to 250,000 and 386 central, provincial, and municipal government organizations from all over the country, as well as 1,900 firms, have opened up offices there to get in on the action at ground level. The influx of foreign investors has also started—96 to date, from South Korea, Hong Kong, Taiwan, Japan, Russia, and Australia. The state has invested 1.5 billion yuan ($180 million) in 468 infrastructure projects, and 4 million square meters of real estate is currently being developed. The railway to Zarubino should have been completed in the fall of 1994, but this has been delayed for various reasons. At first the Chinese and Russian governments could not agree on border-crossing procedures. In November 1996 it was announced that the railway itself was finished but that there were new delays because the facilities for switching the wheels on the Chinese boxcars to fit the wider-gauge rails in Russia were inadequate.

Real development cannot get off the ground until there is a minimum of infrastructure.[13] The question is whether international investors will actually come up with the $30 billion required during the next twenty years, in an area afflicted with great political insecurity. North Korea has opened its door on the northeast border only a crack, and for one project only; the future of this unstable, bankrupt country, which unilaterally disavows its debts, remains unpredictable.

HARBIN IS THE MOST Russian-looking city in China.[14] Here lies the heart of Russia's historical sphere of influence, where countless Chinese speak basic or at least broken Russian and even uphold Russian culinary traditions.

Until 1960 the Russians here were "Big Brother": nowhere were there so many as in Harbin, which in fact had originally been a tsarist Russian railway center and started becoming a Chinese city only after the revolution in 1917. It began swarming with Russians again about four years ago, but now the roles are reversed. The Russians are no longer the rulers or party bosses, but shabby peddlers, and the Russian women work as waitresses, nightclub dancers, and even prostitutes. "*Skolko?*" (How much?) and "*Kharasho*" (Okay) are heard in the international street markets just as frequently as the Chinese equivalents, "*Duoshao?*" and "*Hao-de.*" It is usually the Chinese merchants, however, who know the Russian terms, while the flood of traders from all parts of the former Soviet Union stick to Russian.

Until recently, two-way border traffic was completely visa-free. During the last four or five years, the whole border area has gradually changed from a military no-man's-land into a lawless trading and smuggling belt. At first there was only a continuous stream of trucks coming and going, arriving in the summer on ferryboats and driving in the winter over the frozen rivers. The Russians brought trucks, jeeps, helicopters, machines, cement, fertilizer, timber, and minerals, taking only textiles and food back with them. Two-thirds of the $7.7 billion in bilateral trade in 1993 crossed the border in Heilongjiang Province, and the rest went through Inner Mongolia. The infrastructure is completely inadequate, and a modern import-export regime is also lacking. The most incalculable component is so-called "people-to-people" trade. From a walk around the Nan Kang International People's Market, a grand name for your run-of-the-mill flea market, it is obvious that the type of trade going on here is even more unbalanced than state trade. What do the Russians carry into the country in their bags and suitcases? Military binoculars and infrared night glasses that are so heavy you can hardly lift them, as well as things like magnifying glasses, chronometers, and curvometers, all of them antiquated models such as you might inherit from your grandfather. There are also Yeltsin matreshka dolls, old tsarist coins, and other curios that are otherwise useless. The Russians have started to come more and more frequently with empty pockets, meaning without goods, in order to buy great quantities of Chinese textiles with American dollars that they buy at home on the black market and exchange for Chinese yuan. There is still no exchange rate between the ruble and the yuan. A group of Russians from the border city of Ussuriysk said that they make the trip once a week and earn $1,000 each time. Those who live farther away in Siberia come once every two weeks. They bring about $4,000 with them and load two enormous polyester bags with Chinese textiles. Besides travel and freight charges they also have to pay wages to Chinese coolies, who bring the goods to the station or the airport, bribes to Russian customs officials, and protection money to the mafia. Back home they sell their goods on the street at a 200 percent profit, and after deducting all their expenses, they still have $1,000 left. They admit that it is risky work, their biggest fear being the extortion practices of the mafia. "If you refuse to pay, you run the risk of being killed," said one Armenian. The first goal of most of the traders is to buy a second-hand Toyota and then, after they have managed to accumulate some capital, to switch over to more normal forms of trade.

Zhao, a functionary in the propaganda department of Heilongjiang Province, said that at the peak of activity in 1993 an average of two thousand Russians per day came to Harbin, including official delegations, casual traders, and single women. Zhao does not try to hide his dislike of the Russians. "Their fathers raped our women. In the 1950s, during the period of so-called 'socialist brotherhood,' no one dared to protest. Now that they're bankrupt, they come here to earn money. They stuff themselves in restaurants and then walk away without paying."

Most Russians display a deep racist condescension toward the Chinese, and the Chinese eagerly reciprocate, although their brand of racism seems generally to be less extreme and more pragmatic. Simple Russians swear at the Chinese as a natural reflex; the Chinese do not swear at people from whom they hope to earn money. The Chinese, after all, profit doubly from the situation. They earn foreign currency while managing to get rid of cheap junk that no one else wants to buy. The Russians enjoy more dubious benefits.

· · ·

THE RUSSIAN LEGACY is a ubiquitous feature of Harbin's cityscape. The old Russian city center, Pristan (in Chinese, Daoli), is an outdoor museum of prewar Russian architecture in all European neostyles, especially neo-Baroque, neoclassical, and art deco. Remarkably, the buildings are in a better state of repair than their counterparts in Vladivostok. Until the mid-1980s the Chinese gave precious little thought to architectural aesthetics, but now that their economic level has improved so much, more care is being taken to restore old (meaning eighty- to one-hundred-year-old) Russian and European buildings. The façades of all the buildings on the main street of Daoli have been replastered and repainted. The two best restaurants in the center offer Russian cuisine. One of them—called, strangely enough, "Hua-Mei" (Chinese-American)—boasts an interior in classical palatial style, and until 1952 had a Russian Jewish owner named Zuckermann. The other is called "Ha-Ha" and is a joint venture with the neighboring Russian city of Khabarovsk, the first syllable of which is also pronounced in Chinese as "ha," as in "Ha-er-bin," which explains "Ha-Ha." Both restaurants offer a variety and quality that, according to connoisseurs, are available in Russia only in hidden nomenklatura restaurants. Red caviar with vodka, borscht, cabbage rolls, and chicken shashlik sell for $6. What was missing in restaurant Ha-Ha were the Russian waitresses. The boss said that they had left two days earlier, when their contracts expired. The new crew was supposed to arrive shortly. But Sergei, an old Russian who had been stranded in Harbin during the war, said in Chinese that there were always problems with those girls and that they usually fled before their contracts were up. The trouble begins when they find out that they earn less than Chinese waitresses, but they are driven to the breaking point by the rough treatment they receive from China's nouveaux riches. Sergei said that the Chinese still have vivid memories of the way the Russians treated their women in the 1950s. The height of ecstasy for the newly rich Chinese is to live it up with a young Russian blonde and then, feeling superior, to rub it in.

The historical cycle has come full circle in more than one respect. For the second time in this century, Russians are seen as second-class whites. The first time was in the 1920s and 1930s, when great numbers of White Russians, including down-and-out members of the nobility, fled to Harbin and Shanghai, the men to take up positions as riding instructors or bodyguards, the women to work as "night owls." The question is whether the Russians will be saddled with the image they have in China for a long time to come. Ding Biao, export manager of a machine factory based in Shenyang, was convinced of the opposite. He said that the Russians have only just learned how to do business. Some of their products are good, others not. "Their prices are okay, but they've never heard of after-sales service. In five to ten years they will be competitors, however." Asked if China, as a future superpower and Big Brother, will try to bully them, he answered, "Oh no. We Chinese aren't really interested in bossing people around. We want to do business and get rich. China doesn't want to shoulder responsibility for world politics. Moreover, in another five to ten years Russia will be strong again, because Russian science and technology are still superior to ours."

ON THE SINO-RUSSIAN BORDER between Suifenhe and Pogranichnaya, 500 kilometers east of Harbin, an endless column of Russian trucks, brand name Kamaz, droned past, which in the summer of 1993 still bore the designation SU. They transported everything under the sun: bulldozers, excavation equipment, tractors, steel beams, steel plates, steel wire, automobile tires, and especially the trunks of birch trees, in such quantities that the Chinese had no room to store it all and much of it stood or lay next to the road, rusting or rotting away.

Suifenhe is the most important of the eighteen border crossings on the 3,040-kilometer-long border between Heilongjiang Province and the Russian Far East. It is 200 kilometers from Vladivostok and is called the terminus of China's Wild East. Suifenhe is also the only railway crossing in Heilongjiang Province, with its 35 million inhabitants. The closest border station is 1,600 kilometers to the northwest in Manzhouli in Inner Mongolia. There is still no bridge at all from Russia to China, none over the Ussuri and none over the Amur. In Heihe, 1,000 kilometers to the northwest, plans have been on the drawing board for years for a new railway and the first bridge over the Amur, but the first pile has yet to be driven into the ground for lack of funds on both sides. Suifenhe is therefore a gigantic, overcrowded bottleneck.

Five years ago, Suifenhe was still a sleepy, grimy hole with thirty thousand inhabitants. A few years after the signing of the border agreement in 1991, that number has risen to seventy thousand, and every day trading firms from all of the Chinese provinces open up offices there—in the short run for trade with Russia, but in the long run to cash in on Suifenhe's becoming one of Northeast China's two most important approaches to the Pacific Ocean, leading to Japan, Korea, and the whole world. As a result of Russia's expansionist policy in the nineteenth century, Heilongjiang, just like neighboring Jilin Province, has no access to the sea. The Tumen project will put an end to its isolation, however. Suifenhe nevertheless has a head start on Tumen because it is situated on the Eastern Railway, a branch of the

Trans-Siberian Railway crossing China to Vladivostok. Whereas most Chinese cities are filled with black-haired Chinese, here there are Russian blonds everywhere. On Sundays especially, they come by the trainload. In an enormous shed with 560 stalls covering 4,000 square meters, called the "Azure Clouds Market," the Chinese buy Russian furs, hats, and army clothing, especially overcoats, but also full-dress uniforms. Valuable furs, such as silver fox, are bartered here for Japanese electronic equipment, which is imported "tax-free" by smuggling syndicates. Through the muddy main street, where building materials lie in the puddles, Russians drag their heavy bags to the station. Here and there they rest along the wayside—unsavory characters, most of them—with a bottle of beer or vodka. Stout women who cannot manage to drag their loads sit on top of them, waiting for a Chinese with a pedicab or a donkey cart to do it for them. The station presents a scene of even greater chaos, partly because of the two differing rail gauges. At each platform are two tracks with a difference in width of 14.5 centimeters. Around the turn of the century, when the Russians insisted on building the railway through Manchuria as the shortest way to Vladivostok, they wanted to build it according to Russian specifications. According to Mayor Chen Lijie, the Chinese viceroy Li Hongzhang exacted a promise from his Russian counterpart—the finance minister Count Sergei Witte—to build the railway according to international specifications, but the Russians went ahead and did as they wished. It was not until thirty years later that the Japanese adjusted to the differing width, linking the line with the Chinese national rail network. At the station there are also a couple of cossacks, complete with rifles and astrakhan hats. They form a private security service that traders can hire to protect themselves from the mafia. The Ussuri cossacks have traditionally been very influential in the Far East and were the first colonists in Khabarovsk and Vladivostok 130 years ago.

Mayor Chen wants Suifenhe to become the largest inland port in Northeast China and hopes to increase the present volume of 1.3 million tons of cargo shipped each year to 10 million tons in the year 2000. At the border he wants to open a free auction-mart where Chinese and Russians can trade goods tax-free and duty-free, paying with either money or bartered goods.[15]

THE RUSSIANS are not enamored of this idea. "Trade is very much to our disadvantage. We supply strategic goods such as raw materials, wood, cement, and fertilizer, and in return we get mountains of cheap textiles, foodstuffs, and other junk from the Chinese," Valeri K. Lozovoi, the commissioner for International Trade and Foreign Affairs of Primorski Krai, the Russian maritime territory, said at his office in Belidom, the White House of Vladivostok.[16] Chinese-Russian relations have never been normal, and therefore there is no reason to assume that the situation is now stable. Trade reached a peak of $7.7 billion in 1993, but sank in 1993 by 30 percent to $5.1 billion, largely owing to the sharp drop in border trade, which was the result of Russian restrictions on the free entry of Chinese street vendors. "If the Chinese influx continues, we will have a situation like that under Genghis Khan. If we don't take effective action quickly, in twenty years' time it will no longer be clear what is China and what is Russia," lamented Lozovoi.[17] The restrictive measures implemented in 1994 resulted from fears of what the Russian government calls "the peaceful loss of territory." In retaliation, China detained Russian traders on grounds of violation of Chinese immigration laws.[18]

The illegal exodus of Chinese to the Russian Far East and Siberia could lead to a conflict between the two giants. According to Russian newspapers, there are already 2 million to 5 million Chinese in Russia, and demographers say that in the first half of the twenty-first century the Chinese will become the second-largest minority in the Russian Federation.[19] Russian officials dismiss these figures as grossly exaggerated, but admit there is a serious problem. Many Chinese are being arrested for poaching in the taiga and at sea. A Russian television station reported that every day at least ten Chinese with forged passports are sent back from the border post of Grodekovo alone, although the Russian border guards do not doubt for a minute that the same Chinese return in no time with "clean" passports.[20] On 12 April 1995 Chinese gangsters murdered the commander of a Russian border station in the eastern sector. Russian politicians are campaigning for the repeal of the border agreement of 1991.[21] In the run-up to President Yeltsin's second visit to China in April 1996, the governor of the maritime territory, Yevgeny Nazdratenko, refused to transfer back to China 1,500 hectares of disputed land under the Soviet-Chinese Treaty of 1991. The land was to be handed over on the orders of President Yeltsin as part of the process of finalizing the demarcation of the disputed eastern sector of the Russian-Chinese border.[22]

Concern about the Yellow Peril and the uncertainty about the border is greatest among sinologists and historians. At the beginning of the last wave of tsarist expansion in 1860, Vladivostok was founded literally to rule (*vladi*) over the East (*vostok*). At that time, the area had no Chinese population and was inhabited by paleo-Asian tribes, although it belonged to the domain of the Manchu-Chinese emperors. Chinese historical atlases declare the area to be Chinese and include the following description: "the territory that tsarist Russia stole from China by means of unequal treaties" (see note 11). After

1949 the Chinese Communists made no specific claims to the area, but Anna Khamatova, head of the department of sinology at the University of Vladivostok, is convinced that this is just a matter of time, because too many Chinese believe that the Russian Far East and most of eastern Siberia are an inalienable part of China, just like Hong Kong, Taiwan, and even Outer Mongolia. Khamatova could not substantiate this with new, concrete Chinese evidence, but it is her firm Russian conviction.[23] Valeri Podsousjnie, lecturer in the department of international relations, fears a Chinese annexation in twenty to thirty years. "Understand well that the British have been in Hong Kong longer than we have been here," he said. "And the British are leaving Hong Kong this year." The historical publicist Alexei Buyakov is a true crusader against the Chinese advance. He sees a systematic plan for Chinese expansion in three phases:

1. developing trade, which was initially barter, and is now the import of raw materials in exchange for the export of cheap Chinese goods of low quality;
2. encouraging the export of labor in the construction and agricultural sectors;
3. deepening demographic penetration, promoting the establishment of new industries, and strengthening Chinese domination of the economy.

Buyakov thought that the Chinese were so eager to restore old, historic buildings because they were determined to move into them in the future. Talks with Chinese on building sites do not confirm a cunning Chinese master plan of this nature, but nevertheless shed new light on the subject. In one of the depressing streets in the city center, dozens of Chinese are busy restoring the fin de siècle Versailles Hotel. It is a Russian-Japanese joint venture; the Japanese partner hired the Chinese because they were cheap and work seven days a week. The supervisor, Liao, says that they come from Dalian, the former Russian treaty port known as Port Arthur. "Russians don't like to do this work and they aren't any good at it. They would rather sell vodka on the street corner. They're good at spending money but have no idea how to earn it." He added that his grandfather had lived in Vladivostok before the war.

Buyakov confirmed that the Chinese had indeed played an important role in the prerevolutionary boom in Vladivostok. In 1907 the city had 65,000 inhabitants, of whom half were Chinese. In 1937, after the Japanese created the puppet empire of Manchukuo, Stalin ordered the deportation of all Chinese and 31,000 of them were expelled from the country with the loss of all their possessions, 2,500 were arrested, and 800 were executed. Buyakov and Lozovoi both admit that this makes for a potential legal and political problem if only a couple of individual claims to property rights are renewed. Buyakov stressed that he was devoting all his intellectual energies to disseminating a negative image of the Chinese and other Asians, by means of articles in the journal *Otchizna* (Motherland) and elsewhere. "We must strengthen our awareness of the prospect of a Chinese takeover. We don't want to become a Russian Nagorny-Karabakh in the midst of a Chinese sea. We have to prepare ourselves for a partisan war."

Dr. Michael Shinkovski, formerly head of propaganda of the local Communist party and now dean of the School of Journalism at the local university, illustrates the dramatic side of all this with his favorite formula for action: "If you're an optimist, you study English; if you're a pessimist, you study Chinese; if you're a realist, you learn how to handle a kalashnikov."

CHAPTER 16

Xinjiang and the Islamic World

Xinjiang has been an inalienable part of the Chinese motherland since ancient times.

Standard Chinese propaganda

The record of the Chinese in Central Asia is by no means continuous; in fact their effective control has been estimated at only about 425 out of about 2,000 years, divided into a number of periods, of which the present Chinese rule in the province of Sinkiang is the fifth major period.

OWEN LATTIMORE,
authority on Chinese frontier history

BEFORE MY THIRD VISIT to Xinjiang in July 1994, I read the following description in the new *Cadogan Guide to Central Asia*: "After the paralyzing shortages and inflation of the CIS, Ürümqi feels like New York."[1] This hyperbolic one-liner lends new shades of meaning to the theory of relativity, as well as being a literal "Invitation to the Dance." In 1992 I spent a week in Alma-Ata, the capital of Kazakhstan, and three weeks in Tashkent, Samarkand, Bukhara, and Khiva, the large, historical cities of Uzbekistan. Though amazingly interesting from a political and cultural standpoint, the hardship was overwhelming. It was more civilized and aesthetic than the ugly, messy Chinese cities, but that's where favorable comparisons ended. There were only outrageously expensive, substandard hotels, bad and monotonous food, no beer or wine, no service, demoralized people, empty stores, and a ghastly, gray, dark atmosphere.

Astonishingly, Ürümqi is in every respect the opposite. At that time, the newest, most cosmopolitan addition to its rapidly changing cityscape was a twenty-four-story Holiday Inn opened in May 1992. Ürümqi has become the most bustling boomtown in the country, after the great metropolises on the east coast of China. Because of the distance to Beijing—three thousand kilometers—a restive, free-booting border culture prevails in this extravagantly colorful melting pot.

Ürümqi is essentially a Han Chinese settler town, 80 percent of whose population of 1.3 million consists of Han Chinese.* The city has a dominant Islamic ambience, however. The older parts of the city are full of late-nineteenth-century Russian, ocher-colored buildings, Stalinist concrete complexes, crumbling mud huts, and factories. In recent years, though, hundreds of attractive examples of modern high-rise buildings have appeared along the wide, shady boulevards, all with Islamic characteristics: turban-shaped roofs, minaret-like turrets, and arched and onion-shaped ornaments and arabesques on the façades. All advertisements and signs are in two languages, with Uighur on top in the Arabic letters reintroduced in 1979.

The Uighurs are the largest indigenous group and make up 47 percent of the population of the whole region (16.3 million) and 15 percent of that of Ürümqi. Although in percentages the Chinese are in the minority with their 37.7 percent, they are absolutely dominant in terms of power. They have nevertheless made tangible cosmetic concessions to the local culture. At the time of the dissolution of the Soviet Union in 1991, only one mosque was in use in Alma-Ata and Tashkent. Except during the most extreme phase of the Cultural Revolution, there have always been hundreds of mosques open in Ürümqi.

In spite of these concessions to Islam, vulgar commerce and decadence run rampant. There is a surfeit of good restaurants—providing all regional Chinese cuisines, as well as Islamic, Western, and Russian—and also locally brewed beer and local wines of good quality, such as Loulan and Silk Road. Xinjiang has always been famous for its grapes, green grapes in particular.

Bright neon lights go on early in the evening and the numerous dance halls, karaoke bars, girlie bars, and thinly disguised brothels open up. At the large hotels, customers are actively solicited by prostitutes, mostly teenage drifters from Sichuan, China's largest inland province, one thou-

---

* Every citizen of China, whether a Mongol, a Tibetan, or an Uighur, is in national terms a Chinese (*Zhongguoren*). The ethnic Chinese majority (93 percent) is called Han Chinese or Han in this context.

sand kilometers to the southeast. Bazaars and stores are open till late at night, including the Rebiya Kadir Complex, which was opened in 1992, a six-story department store that is owned by Rebiya Kadir, a forty-nine-year-old Uighur woman who is the mother of eleven children. She first made her fortune by street peddling and smuggling goods from the former Soviet Union and Turkey and is now the head of a multinational trading conglomerate of eight firms that trade in everything from steel to textiles and jewelry and have assets of more than a billion yuan ($125 million).

The educational choices Rebiya Kadir has made for her children illustrate the practical problems plaguing the nouveaux riches in China's Wild West. Mrs. Kadir sent her oldest son, Kahar, not to a business school but to the police academy. He is now head of the private security service protecting her business empire from the mafia and parasitic government officials. After a stay of four days in Ürümqi, the most pressing question is just how representative the capital actually is of the whole region.

KASHGAR, fifteen hundred kilometers to the southwest, belongs to another time and place altogether. This is the ancient Middle East of China's Far West. Kashgar is the traditional spiritual and cultural capital of the Uighur people, and through its geographic isolation, it has retained its medieval character almost completely. More than 90 percent of the population is Uighur, around 2 percent are Kirghiz, and even fewer are Han Chinese. The high mountains of the Tian Shan cut the city off from Kyrgyzstan, the Pamir Mountains cut if off from Tajikistan and Afghanistan, the Karakoram Mountains from Pakistan, and the feared Taklimakan Desert from China. With its 280,000 inhabitants, Kashgar is the largest of the oasis cities fed by glaciers on the southern edge of the desert and has a legendary, two-thousand-year-old history in which silk caravans, Buddhist and Nestorian Christian priests, Marco Polo, and British and Russian spies figure prominently. Genghis Khan once conquered the city and Timur Lenk (Tamerlane) almost did.

While the Uighurs in Ürümqi and other northern cities such as Yining, Turpan, and Hami are partly sinified, speak Chinese reasonably well, and wear Chinese versions of Western clothing, the southerners have been left almost completely untouched by Chinese domination. Kashgar is the medieval Hong Kong of Central Asia. Whereas Hong Kong is a large shopping mall and banking center, Kashgar is a big bazaar and black market for currency, where everything is sold from camels and goats to Japanese electronic goods, which are brought in by bus, truck, and plane from every direction, including Afghanistan and Pakistan. One street in the shopping district specializes in fur hats, another in spices, yet another in tobacco. Ottoman dinars, tsarist rubles, money from the neighboring emirates and khanates conquered by the Russians in the nineteenth century—everything is for sale. The men wear half-length tunics and, over these, long striped overcoats, even in the summer, and Turkish trousers and high boots protected from the sand by rubber overshoes. The women wear knee-length skirts with thick, long stockings and long underwear underneath. On their heads they wear dark brown veils that are almost as thick as chain mail. Over everything hangs the penetrating smell of shish kebab—lamb meat on skewers—and hot red peppers, which offer protection against diarrhea and other illnesses. And everywhere is the clip-clop of donkey carts with tinkling bells, which transport goods as well as people.[2]

APARTHEID IS PRACTICED nearly everywhere. Whereas a workable coexistence is the rule in northern Xinjiang, the south is afflicted with deep-seated tension. Outbreaks of violence and bomb attacks are regular occurrences. Nonetheless, the Chinese Communist propaganda machine pretends that a natural and harmonious symbiosis has developed over the centuries. "Xinjiang has been an inalienable part of the Chinese motherland since ancient times" is the standard phrase, which, however, stretches the historical truth to the breaking point. Owen Lattimore, the éminence grise of Chinese frontier studies, writes in his standard work, *Inner Asian Frontiers of China,* that during the last two millennia there have only been about 425 years of Chinese control in Central Asia and that the present Chinese rule in Xinjiang is the fifth episode.[3] During the Han dynasty (221 B.C.–A.D. 220), military expeditions were launched against the Huns in 60 B.C., and a Chinese viceroy installed himself in Xinjiang, paving the way for the silk trade with the Eastern Roman empire. As in Europe, where nomadic invasions swept the Western Roman empire, Chinese rule over present-day Xinjiang was undermined by Kushans, Huns, Turkic, and Mongol tribes starting in A.D. 140. The Chinese were not able to reestablish their authority over the area until the Tang dynasty (618–906), but the grandiose plan of the Tang emperors to subjugate all of Central Asia was thwarted by the Arab victory on the Talas River in 751, one of the most important turning points in world history. Chinese domination in Central Asia then collapsed and the strong cultural ties were broken. The Buddhist kingdoms disappeared for good, except in Tibet, and Islam became the dominant cultural force. The Tibetans and Uighurs were once again the master in their own house. The

Chinese—or, more precisely, the Manchu—did not come back for a thousand years.

Genghis Khan conquered Kashgar in 1206, and Han-chauvinistic Chinese historians offer this as proof of the continuity of Chinese administration, because "Genghis Khan was the leader of an important Chinese national minority."

At the end of the seventeenth century, renewed attempts by the Mongols under Galdan Khan to reunite and found a new Greater Mongolian empire based on Genghis Khan's precedent forced the Chinese Manchu emperors to dispatch new military expeditions, first to Outer Mongolia under Emperor Kang Xi (K'ang Hsi) in 1696, and subsequently to Eastern Turkistan under Emperor Qian Long (Ch'ien Lung) in 1755–59. Qian Long established indirect rule, appointing a governor-general in Kuldja (Yining) and vice-governors in Tihua (Ürümqi) and Kashgar/Yarkand with the objective of guaranteeing Manchu influence without incorporating the territory into the Chinese provincial structure. Uighur peasants from southern Xinjiang were encouraged to settle down in the Ili Valley north of the Tian Shan in order to weaken the influence of Kazakh and Mongol nomads.

Order and prosperity increased, but Manchu authority began to decline in the first half of the nineteenth century. The new, double threat came from tsarist Russian expansion and from independence-seeking Uighurs. Between 1860 and 1864 the Russians annexed 440,000 square kilometers of land, thus pushing the border of the tsarist empire 250 to 600 kilometers eastward. In 1865 Yakub Beg—an adventurer from the khanate of Kokand, at that time just conquered by the Russians—became, with help from the Ottoman empire and British India, the ruler of a newly proclaimed state, Kashgaria. Prominent Manchu statesmen were divided on the limited advantages and immense disadvantages that Eastern Turkistan presented to the empire. Viceroy Li Hung-chang (Li Hongzhang) thought the expense prohibitive and wanted to abandon the idea. Imperial Grand Secretary Tso Tsung-t'ang (Zuo Zongtang) won the debate, however, and launched a military expedition in 1876 which destroyed Yakub Beg's kingdom in 1877.

In 1871 the Russians had occupied the Ili Valley, but the Chinese won it back in 1881 through diplomacy and indemnity payments. Only now did the Chinese feel compelled to give up indirect rule, incorporating Eastern Turkistan as the Chinese province of Sinkiang (New Domains or New Border) into the Manchu-Chinese imperial structure (the Western transliteration was changed in 1979 to Xinjiang). Chinese authority remained very fragile, however. During the last decades of the empire and the first four decades of the Republican period (1911–41), Sinkiang was a Russian sphere of influence under semi-independent "warlords." The Russians opened the oldest oil field in Karamay. Twice, in 1933 and 1944, the independent republic of Eastern Turkistan was proclaimed, the first time inspired by Muslim fanatics, the second time supported by Stalin.[4]

After the victory of the Chinese Communists over the Kuomintang, Xinjiang remained under Soviet influence for another four or five years, with a Russian satellite army and joint Russian-Chinese state enterprises. Everything was controlled from three huge Soviet consulates in Kuldja, Ürümqi, and Kashgar. At that time, Xinjiang had a total population of about 4 million, 75 percent Uighur, 10 percent Kazakh, 5 percent Mongol, and only 5 percent Han Chinese.

In 1959 the new Communist warlord, General Wang Zhen, established the Xinjiang Construction and Production Corps, popularly called "the Corps," consisting of Wang's own army, Kuomintang soldiers who had surrendered, and "volunteers," young intellectuals and technicians who had transmigrated from Shanghai, Tianjin, and other large coastal cities. The Corps laid the basis for the big, organized influx of Han Chinese. The Corps's motto was "A rifle over one shoulder and a shovel over the other"— appropriate indeed for these twentieth-century cowboys in China's Wild West. They defended the border against Russian penetration, cultivated wild land, dug irrigation ditches, looked after the enormous amount of livestock, and built up the infrastructure. In spite of the hardship, the 1950s were the "golden decade" in Xinjiang.

AFTER THE DEATH of Stalin in 1953, the whole special Sino-Soviet relationship was renegotiated, and in 1955 the Chinese proclaimed the Xinjiang Uighur Autonomous Region, a new euphemism for a modified form of Chinese Communist dominance. The chairmen of the regional people's government have always been Uighurs—Seypidin Azizi (Saifudin), Ismail Aymat, Tomur Dawamat, and now Abdulahat Amudurashid (sinified form: Abulaiti Amudurexiti)—but the real power lay in the hands of the Communist party secretaries, and these were Chinese generals: Wang Zhen, Wang Enmao, and Wang Feng. Wang III (Wang Feng) was succeeded by civilian Song Hanliang in 1985. In 1995 Wang IV, Wang Lequan, became acting party secretary.

The first big crisis was caused by the Great Leap Forward. As a result of the famine caused by the forced collectivization campaigns, eighty thousand Kazakhs and Uighurs fled in 1962 to Soviet Kazakhstan. Before the Cultural Revolution, Wang II, Wang Enmao, was the most important Chinese in Xinjiang. As party secretary, he pursued a policy of tolerance and cooperation with the elite of the native minorities. Under the influence of extremists who had come over from China, cultural autonomy, especially religious freedom, was trampled on during the Cultural Revolution. Mosques were closed or destroyed and elderly Muslims were forced to parade around the streets with pigs' heads tied around their necks. Many Muslims were even forced to breed pigs, and applicants for membership in the Communist party had to eat pork. A modified Latin alphabet was introduced for transcription of the minority languages, and the Arabic script was banned. Offenders were punished with a ban on prayer and forced labor on Fridays. In the midst of this intolerance, Wang Enmao faded into the background.

The denigration and vilification of Islam, the omnipotence of the army, and the nuclear tests carried out since the early 1960s in the Taklimakan Desert near Lop Nor had sorely tried relations with the native population. Mixed marriages were legion in the 1950s, but after the Cultural Revolution they were a rare occurrence. Aside from Han Chinese misconduct, there was one simple reason: the life of a Han Chinese is unthinkable without pork, which is anathema to an Uighur.

During the aftermath of the Cultural Revolution, a new crisis developed in 1980 as a result of the forced migration of Red Guards and other educated youth to Xinjiang and their vociferous demands to be allowed to return to their native provinces in East China. Large numbers of exiled young people wanted to return home, and because both local and central rulers had come to the conclusion that they were not doing any productive work on the state farms anyway, they were allowed to go. But their hometowns, especially Shanghai, could offer them neither work nor housing and did not want them back. This resulted in demonstrations and hunger strikes by Han Chinese youth in Xinjiang—who wanted to return home but were prevented from doing so by the central government—and they were supported by the sympathetic local Chinese garrison. The central government reacted by sending in other loyal troops from neighboring provinces, at which point the native minorities who wanted to be rid of the Han Chinese went into action.[5]

At the same time, in May 1980, the liberal party leader Hu Yaobang paid a visit to Tibet, acknowledged the failure there of the Han Chinese administration, and announced a policy of "Tibetization"—a systematic withdrawal of Han Chinese personnel. The Uighurs and other minorities demanded the same for Xinjiang, and in this tense atmosphere small incidents quickly took on exaggerated proportions. Wang I (Wang Zhen), the old warlord from the early days of Communism and a ruthless hawk, visited

Xinjiang three times during this period, followed by Deng Xiaoping himself. There was a period of massive rioting that was suppressed by the army. Wang III—Wang Feng, party secretary since 1978—was dismissed, and Wang II was recalled because of his tolerant service record before the Cultural Revolution. Details of what really happened were not made known until years later.

During my first visit to Xinjiang in 1986, I rented a Daihatsu Rocky jeep for the three-day trip from Ürümqi to Kashgar through the Tian Shan Mountains and the Taklimakan Desert. Two Uighur drivers were assigned to me, Musa Tomur and Hudaberdi. On the way, we talked at length about troubled Han-Uighur relations and what had happened in 1980. Hudaberdi came from Aksu and had this to say: "The Han Chinese killed one of *our* people. The Han police and soldiers did nothing. Our people then proceeded with massive reprisals. Hundreds of Han Chinese were beaten and their stores and factories destroyed. I don't know how many Han died, but it must have been hundreds." And things got much worse in Kashgar a couple of months later. Tomur related: "An army truck mindlessly ran over one of our people and killed him. The government and the courts in Kashgar consist largely of Uighurs. They sentenced the Han soldier to death, but the Chinese police corps refused to carry out the sentence. The garrison threatened to mutiny if their comrade wasn't released. Tensions escalated to the point where Deng Xiaoping himself came to Xinjiang to settle the matter. The Han soldier was released."[6]

As the wind screamed past us and the jeep was showered with sand and pebbles by the feared *Karaburan,* the black sandstorm, I continued to discuss race relations with Tomur and Hudaberdi. They asked if there were Chinese and Muslims living in the Netherlands and how they got along with each other. I answered that they were just two groups of foreigners who had no contact with each other. "Just like here," sniggered Hudaberdi. Tomur, the smarter of the two, asked what kind of Muslims we had in Holland. I explained that they were Moroccan and Turkish immigrant workers, and some Indonesians. "Oh yes, Indonesia was once ruled by the Dutch," he said. "But there the relations between Muslims and Chinese are bad, aren't they?" I affirmed that anti-Chinese unrest breaks out every once in a while, and that it always lasts a day or longer and results in some deaths before the police intervene. Tomur beamed. "Hudaberdi, did you hear that? Indonesia sounds like a nice place. There a Muslim can beat the hell out of a Chinese and the police don't do anything about it!"

In Kashgar the next day, I met a journalist from the *China Science and Technology Review* who was there on a family visit. She confirmed that it had been terrible for the Han Chinese in Xinjiang in 1980–81: "There was a massive exodus. Only those Chinese who could not possibly obtain work permits for the interior [China proper] stayed here." Typically, she added, "The Uighurs treat us as though we were foreign invaders. They don't realize that we come here to help them." This is simple colonial logic at its most banal. "Don't you understand that all peoples prefer their own government to better or more modern government by foreigners?" I asked. Han Chinese can be incurably chauvinistic, ethnocentric, racist, and just plain stupid when it comes to interethnic relations.

AS PART OF THE DEMILITARIZATION of life, the Xinjiang Construction and Production Corps was disbanded in 1975. But after the ethnic tension and frequent visits by the seventy-five-year-old founding father, General Wang Zhen, it was reestablished in 1982, supposedly as the unswerving bastion of Han Chinese power in a fundamentally unstable region that was not yet fully integrated into China.

An American author, in an account published in 1993 of his travels around Xinjiang five years earlier, wrote that the Corps had been demilitarized and given a civilian name. In 1990, however, the New China News Agency was still portraying the Corps in paramilitary terms and calling it by its original name.[7] When a new struggle against national secessionism and illegal religious activities was launched in May 1996, the leadership called to "vigorously strengthen the building of the Xinjiang Construction and Production Corps—under its commander Jin Yunhui—as well as the People's Liberation Army units stationed in Xinjiang in an all-around way."[8] The local party newspaper described the important tasks of the Corps "in the new historical period as . . . to safeguard Xinjiang's stability and construction . . . combine work with military training, open up wasteland, and garrison the frontiers."[9] In 1990 the Corps had a turnover of 9 billion yuan in economic, scientific, and technological activities, nearly 15 percent of the regional GNP of 63.2 billion yuan. The Corps had 100,000 members, 172 state farms with 1.5 million hectares of land, and 1,306 industrial enterprises, including coal mines and factories producing cement, chemicals, fertilizer, textiles, paper, and foodstuffs. The Corps was responsible for 20.3 percent of all industrial production in Xinjiang and 46.2 percent of all exports. It is a Han Chinese state in a multiethnic state with enormous power and doesn't want to have anything to do with economic reforms. The collective economy is limited in scope, and the private sector and foreign investments are minimal. The Corps reflected a conservative, antireformist, military influence on a large part of Xinjiang's economy.

POLITICALLY, Xinjiang has been besieged since the late 1980s by "enemy forces from abroad." The Han Chinese rulers probably exaggerate this to justify a high level of preventive repression, but warnings of external threats are amazingly frequent, as are outbreaks of violence. These problems are partly the result of the region's increasing opening up.

In 1986 the Karakoram Highway to Pakistan was completed, in 1988 direct air links between Istanbul and Ürümqi were started up, and 1990 saw the completion of the section of railway between Ürümqi and Alma-Ata—the last missing link of the so-called "Eurasian Intercontinental Land Bridge," the railway line between the east coast of China and Rotterdam. This transformed Xinjiang from the "back door of the Far East to the front door to the West" and reduced Xinjiang's inaccessibility as "the region farthest from the sea in the whole world." Moreover, dozens of border crossings were opened up for trade. In 1996 Xinjiang was linked to the outside world by twenty-six bus lines and forty-one international and domestic air routes.

The main cause of the region's instability is the natural disharmony of its interethnic relations, whereby a dictatorial, atheistic regime suppresses a traditional religious society—although the Han Chinese do not want to admit this. They always lay the blame first on the foreigners, not only Westerners but in this case especially the Turks. Since the beginning of this century, approximately 1 million Uighurs, Kazakhs, and Kyrgyz have emigrated to Turkey, inspired by pan-Turkism and "Turanism," the ethnic-Turkish equivalent of Zionism.[10] Nationalist, anti-Communist groups in Turkey have not yet given up their goal of freeing their brothers living under Communism. In October 1988 the chairman of the Regional People's Political Consultative Conference of Xinjiang, Ismail Yashenof, named seven separatist movements located outside China which have been trying to stir up tension between the Han Chinese and minorities, including the Committee for the Salvation of Eastern Turkistan, the Democratic Revolutionary Front for the Liberation of Eastern Turkistan, the Benevolent Foundation for Eastern Turkistan, the Kazakh-Turk Benevolent Union, and the Alliance for a Free Eastern Turkistan, Mongolia, Manchuria, and Tibet. Yashenof supplied no details of the base of these movements, but he said that the "Aisa clique" was the most active. Aisa Yusuf Alptekim was secretary-general of the last Kuomintang regime in Xinjiang and has lived in exile in Turkey since 1949. "The organizations publish and distribute magazines and finance schools to teach the Koran. They've established an anti-Communist party for Eastern Turkistan, bribe people to go on pilgrimages to Mecca, and send around agents to stir up negative opinions and hatred among the people."[11]

In 1990 there was an armed, counterrevolutionary rebellion in the village of Baren in the Kyrgyz Autonomous District not far from Kashgar, in which the official media reported twenty-two dead, but local sources many more. The government said that the revolt was started by a fanatical imam and its goal was the "reestablishment of the Islamic Republic of Eastern Turkistan."

In July 1991 the magazine *Cheng Ming* in Hong Kong reported that there had been armed revolts in the cities of Tacheng and Bole in the "Ili-Kazakh Autonomous Prefecture." In Tacheng the Kazakh minority supposedly demanded annexation to Kazakhstan, and 140 rebels were allegedly killed or wounded in armed fighting. In Bole the Kazakhs had demanded the right to set up an ethnic political party that would then participate in democratic elections for a new city government. Gunshots were exchanged between Han cadres and demonstrators, the army intervened, and rumor had it that five hundred people had been killed or wounded. In 1992 there were various bombings and riots in Ürümqi, killing a number of Han Chinese. In the summer of 1993, a devastating bomb attack on a government building in Kashgar was connected with the offer of its Han Chinese rulers to receive 100,000 Han Chinese migrants from Sichuan, who have to be evacuated because of the construction of the Three Gorges Dam on the Yangtze River. This plan has since been called off.

On 29 September 1993 an anonymous senior army officer confirmed on Radio Ürümqi the occurrence of the bombings without giving further details and admitted that there is often unrest, though it is "not so serious as the foreign media maintain." In the same interview, the general said that many Uighurs who had fled to Kazakhstan in 1962 now wanted to return.

In 1995 a Hong Kong journal again reported major unrest in six cities—Zhaosu, Tekes, Gongliu, Xinyuan, Nilka, and Qapgal—all in the Ili-Kazakh Autonomous Prefecture. More than 100,000 Kazakhs and Uighurs reportedly held antigovernment rallies, demanding a new Kazakh state, a merger with Kazakhstan, or a new state, Uighuristan. Two hundred twenty people were reported killed or injured. According to the authorities, the turmoil and armed rebellion were masterminded and instigated by forces outside the borders.[12] A few months before, regional party secretary Wang Lequan asserted in an interview with a Hong Kong television station that Wu'er Kaixi (Uerkesh Daolet), the flamboyant Uighur leader of the student rebellion in 1989, had also set up a separatist organization abroad.[13]

CONTRARY TO EXPECTATIONS, the dissolution of the Soviet Union in December 1991 did not cause an immediate crisis in Xinjiang, but the formation of five new independent states has created a new situation for China and Xinjiang, the long-term results of which are incalculable.

One month later, at the end of January 1992, I visited Ürümqi, Kashgar, and Yining and traveled overland to Alma-Ata. Increased military activity was not in evidence anywhere. The leaders' warnings against conspiracies led by native and foreign pan-Islamists and "splittists" sounded much more urgent, however. The foreigners include Pakistanis, Afghans, Kashmiris, Iranians, Turks, and Arabs who enter Xinjiang overland, distributing Korans and Islamic schoolbooks and apparently giving large donations to separatist movements. Internal ethnic tensions had escalated because increasing numbers of Han Chinese were arriving to exploit the rich mineral resources, the uranium deposits, the huge natural gas reserves, and especially the vast oil reserves under the Taklimakan Desert.

One Uighur, Ruzehaji, told me his favorite Chinese joke. An American, a Japanese, and an Uighur are sitting together at a kiosk in a park in Ürümqi. The American opens his pack of Marlboros, lights up one cigarette, and throws away the pack with the remaining nineteen. "How can you do such a thing?" asks the Uighur in surprise. "Too many cigarettes in America." The Japanese is listening to a tape, and when it's finished he throws away his Sony Walkman, with the tape still in it. "Too many Walkmans in Japan." Then a Han Chinese tries to sit down at the table next to them. The Uighur stands up, grabs him, and throws him over the railing into the street. "Too many Chinese here."[14]

Since 1975 the percentage of Chinese in the total population has hovered around 38 percent, but if current trends continue, within ten years the Chinese will be in the majority. The only consolation for the minorities is that they are exempt from the "one-child rule." In the cities they are allowed to have two and in the countryside three or four children.

ALL THE PEOPLE I spoke to had thought long and hard about independence. Enver, a raucous bazaar trader from Aksu, said: "Independence is naturally our ideal. But the Chinese will never let us go. Do you know what they do to appease us and keep us in China? They give us freedoms the Han Chinese have never even dreamed of. We can do anything we want." Besides being allowed to have more children, the Uighurs are above the law in many other respects. For the average Han Chinese, the word Uighur is synonymous with smuggler, black marketeer, illegal money changer, and worse.

For one Kazakh I met, Murad Batur, independence meant "Back to Kazakhstan. The Uighurs are a minority in China. We're a minority of a minority. It is the ideal of all peoples to have a country of their own." He was not afraid that Kazakhstan would long be dominated by the sizable Russian minority (38 percent). "The explicit policy of the government of Kazakhstan is to woo back the Kazakhs living abroad, and the implicit policy of the Kazakh people is gradually to edge out the Russians," Murad said.

The paradox is that many of Xinjiang's smaller minorities—the Mongols, Kazakhs, Kyrgyz, and Tajiks—have a neighboring country that they regard as their homeland. The Uighurs are a nation without a country. A minority regard Turkey as their abstract, ethnic *Heimat,* although it is three thousand kilometers away. Jilil, a trader whom I met on an airplane, spoke openly of "our Uighuristan." Jilil was aware that for the Kazakhs, Uzbeks, Kyrgyz, and Tajiks, independence simply fell into their lap with the collapse of central Soviet authority. "We Uighurs will have to fight for it, and that is problematic because there are too many traitors. Ninety percent of the people want independence and 10 percent are traitors." I told him they had no chance of achieving independence now and probably never would, because China, with its overwhelming supremacy in numbers (93 percent of 1.2 billion), is in a much better position to subdue its minorities than the former Soviet Union, where the Russians accounted for less than 50 percent of the population. He was aware of the arguments against independence but persisted in his view that it must be attempted anyway.

One big gap in the national identity of the Uighurs is their lack of symbols and heroes, except those of Islam. The Mongols have Genghis Khan and the Uzbeks Timur Lenk. Uighur history is a banned subject. The Chinese recognize only the eleventh-century linguist Muhammad al-Kashgarry as a famous, historical Uighur. When I asked Jilil whether Yakub Beg, the nineteenth-century founder of Kashgaria, could serve as a national hero, he said that he didn't even know about the epic events connected with him. In 1991 an intense campaign was launched against a new *History of the Uighur People* in three volumes, because it was "deceptive and promoted 'splittism.'" There are also severe restrictions on Chinese Muslims pursuing higher Islamic studies, especially abroad.

Jilil went on to say that he can no longer identify with China. "I've learned enough Chinese to be able to communicate, but more and more young Uighurs don't pursue the subject after taking the compulsory classes in Chinese in elementary school. They learn Urdu, Persian, and Arabic to use when trading with 'the new silk route.'"[15]

IN THE REVISED LIST of priorities of the Han Chinese authorities in Xinjiang, next to the old obsession with internal stability two new problems now dominate: the gap between Xinjiang and the rest of China, and relations with the new, independent neighboring countries. Already in 1992 Party Secretary Song Hanliang said that he was "agonized" at the gap between Xinjiang and the coastal areas.[16]

In a detailed article in *Xinjiang Ribao* published in late 1993, Song wrote that separatism had become the biggest menace in the region, at the same time criticizing the Chinese national pricing policy that discriminates against territories producing raw materials. The prices of the raw materials supplied by Xinjiang to the rest of China are artificially depressed by the state, whereas Xinjiang has to pay market prices that are continually driven higher by inflation for the consumer goods it imports from the coastal provinces. This only widens the gap between the ethnic territories and the coastal provinces.

Song said that Xinjiang's unity is not yet at stake for the reason that while it is poorer than China's Han provinces, it is still better off than its neighboring countries. "However, we should realize that most of our neighboring countries have better economic and technological foundations and their peoples are of better quality. Once they get over the difficult period, they will probably develop faster than us." Here Song cited the oft-repeated idea that Russia and the CIS are undergoing a temporary transitional crisis and that when this period is over they will once again be formidable, superior rivals. The new states do have more tolerant and more flexible political systems, with the possible exception of Uzbekistan. If China develops in the same direction, the Uighurs will probably seize upon democratization to achieve their aim of independence.

Song also called for a comprehensive plan to bridge the developmental gap between the eastern and western parts of the country. The prices of Xinjiang's most important products—cotton, sugar, silkworm cocoons, petroleum, natural gas, and coal—are still not liberalized and remain unreasonably low. This prevents the flow of capital to Xinjiang and induces skilled labor to leave. If this situation does not change radically, the territories of national minorities will be doomed to permanent underdevelopment.[17]

The socioeconomic gap between coastal China and inland China of the interior is daunting indeed. In 1994 economic growth in Xinjiang was 9.9 percent, slightly lower than the national average, and in 1995 it was 10.3 percent, exactly the national average. The per capita income of city dwellers was 3,170 yuan in 1994 and 4,163 yuan in 1995, both slightly below the national averages. But the gulf between urban and rural areas is especially big. The average annual income of a peasant family was only 935 yuan in 1994 and 1,135 yuan in 1995, or less than $135 a year.[18]

The three new areas with the largest growth potential are foreign investment, foreign trade, and petroleum extraction in the Tarim Basin, which is thought to contain a third of the national oil reserves.

The foreign trade volume amounted in 1995 to only $1.17 billion. Trade between China and the new CIS states in Central Asia was still negligible in 1993, but the share of border trade as a part of Xinjiang's total foreign trade increased from 20 percent in 1991 to 42.7 percent in 1992 to 63.6 percent in 1993. In 1992, 170 Xinjiang-Kazakh and 76 Xinjiang-Kyrgyz joint ventures were signed, in which firms from Xinjiang had a majority share. Foreign investment was only $196 million in 1994 and $188 million in 1995, but in 1996 contracted foreign investment in Xinjiang jumped to $1.4 billion. The CIS countries still conduct 70 percent of their trade with Russia, but it took only a couple of years for China to become their number two trading partner. Sino-Kazakh trade doubled between 1994 and 1995 to reach $350 million, and Sino-Kyrgyz trade reached $230 million in 1995, also more than double that of the previous year.

After years of waiting to hear whether China would open up the Tarim oil fields to international oil companies, in 1990 the truth came out that 93,000 square kilometers would be opened to foreign companies. The oil reserves in the Tarim Basin are estimated to be 18 billion tons and those of all of Xinjiang 20.86 billion tons. Modern oil stations have been built in the desert's barren landscape and twenty thousand Chinese from across the country have begun their lucrative prospecting. Minorities aren't given a chance here, though, because according to a spokesman from the China National Petroleum Corporation, "They aren't good enough. Training them takes too long and costs too much." The Uighurs, on the other hand, say openly to foreigners that it is their "Islamic oil" that the Chinese are now appropriating for their own use. Foreign participation in this project is still modest. The first foreign firm to sign a contract in 1991 was the Japan National Oil Corporation. China announced the first round of tenders in 1993, and in the meantime Exxon, Sumitomo, Indonesia Petroleum Ltd., Agip, and Texaco have signed contracts for blocks amounting to 25,000 square kilometers together.

China is in a hurry: in 1995 it became a net importer of oil for the first time. Xinjiang pumped 12 million tons of crude in 1995, accounting for 9 percent of the country's total figure. The Tarim bonanza is only in its beginning phase, and if it wants to reach maturity, a 3,500-kilometer pipeline will have to be laid, requiring investments of $8 billion. The pipeline will contribute to Xinjiang's infrastructural integration with the rest of China, but whether this will also further political and ethnic integration remains uncertain.

. . .

THE FUTURE OF XINJIANG will be determined just as much by the new Central Asian states as by the internal balance in China itself. Kazakhstan, with its large Russian minority, is in a class by itself, and Tajikistan, with cultural leanings toward Iran, is torn by civil strife, just as Afghanistan and Kashmir are. Of overriding importance is the emergence of four predominantly Islamic, ethnic-Turkic nation-states that are potential role models for the Uighurs. The question is whether the new states will be successful, as the Han Chinese party secretary of Xinjiang fears, or whether they will go the way of Tajikistan. A Chinese political analyst said, "In both cases we lose. If the Central Asian states collapse, the chaos will spread to Xinjiang. If they stabilize, the Chinese minorities will say: 'Look, it works there. Why can't we have our own country too?'"[19] During his visit to four of the five republics (and Mongolia) in April 1994, Premier Li Peng wanted to have included in the communiqués that their governments supported Chinese unity and would not tolerate any ethnic movements with objectives across the Chinese border. The power of those governments to curb transnational religious and nationalist groups is far from complete, however. These are classical dilemmas: open borders lead to more trade and prosperity, but the price is more uncontrollable cross-border activity, separatism, and sabotage.

On 26 April 1996 China scored a major diplomatic coup when the presidents of five neighboring countries in Central Asia—China, Russia, Kazakhstan, Kyrgyzstan, and Tajikistan—met in Shanghai and signed an "agreement on confidence-building measures" in the military field in border areas. The agreement effectively froze the status quo at the unstable borders. It benefited China more than any of the other countries because the three newly independent states took it upon themselves to oppose secessionist activities of any kind in their respective countries, meaning that they would oppose ethnic Kazakhs, Uighurs, Kyrgyz, and Tajiks engaging in separatist acts from their territories aimed at Xinjiang. It dashed the hopes of Uighur independence activists, both in Xinjiang and in exile in Kazakhstan, who had expected the new independent border states to support their cause. Demonstrations of the 200,000-strong Uighur exile community in Kazakhstan in front of the Chinese embassy in Alma-Ata had previously been tolerated, but from now on these would be banned.

The agreement had a clear message for the United States as well. Russian defense minister Pavel Grachev casually remarked: "If NATO goes East, Russia will go East as well." Chinese commentators added that the agreement was China's answer to the "U.S.-Japan Joint Security Declaration" signed nine days before, which "attempts to establish a security system in the Asia-Pacific Region with the United States and Japan jointly seeking hegemony." Three months after the signing of the agreement, President Jiang Zemin visited Uzbekistan, Kazakhstan, and Kyrgyzstan, and in the communiqués that concluded his state visits it was reiterated that both sides would not permit any organization or force to engage in separatist activities in their respective countries against the other side and that they were against inciting discord between countries, ethnic groups, and religions.

Coinciding with the signing of the "Shanghai Communiqué," the Chinese media launched a new antiseparatist campaign, the fiercest ever. It is unclear what came first: the chicken of an escalation in terrorism and assassinations, or the egg of the crackdown. Coinciding with a nationwide one-hundred-day "Strike Hard" campaign against common crime, the central leadership in Beijing ordered Xinjiang (and Tibet!) to clamp down on separatism and unlawful religious activity, as it had been "scientifically proven" that these were the key problems endangering both ethnic regions' stability. The launching of the campaign on Ürümqi Television on 6 May took aim not only at "an extremely small number" of separatists and party village branches that were still dominated by religious forces, but also at armed robbers, drug traffickers, abductors of women and children, and other archcriminals.

"The tree may appear calm, but the wind will not subside," wrote the *Xinjiang Ribao* of 7 May 1996, suggesting that there was a permanent undercurrent of secessionist and religious dissent. A whole series of articles lambasted leading cadres, who continue to be devout religious believers, despite repeated education. "They discriminate against nonbelievers, denounce them as 'pagans,' publicize the 'history of the holy war,' and engage in various kinds of religious fanaticism." The *Xinjiang Ribao* of 14 May 1996 pointed at "explosions, assassinations, and other violent terrorist activities of a political hue, involving party members and cadres," but the paper did not mention any specific cases. By late May, Hong Kong's *Ming Pao* reported that on 12 May a failed attempt had been made on the life of Aronghanaji, the seventy-three-year-old chief imam of Kashgar, who had been accused of pursuing a pro-China policy. In the city of Kuqa, nine separatists armed with guns and bombs smuggled in from neighboring states were killed in a pitched battle with police on 29 April. On 21 May, Urup Khaji, another imam, was assassinated in Kashgar for pursuing a pro-China policy. Uighur exile leader Yusupbek Mukhlissi said from Alma-Ata that by the end of May, forty-seven hundred Uighurs had been arrested in Xinjiang. The Chinese propaganda machine employed the "mass line" and Cultural Revolution–style hate jargon to corner the separatists. "We must fully mobilize the masses so that the enemy will be drowned in a vast ocean, and a small number of national splittists, and serious criminal offenders will become rats on the streets, chased by the people," wrote the *Xinjiang Ribao* of 30 May 1996. On 4 July, during the state visit of Jiang Zemin to Kazakhstan, Mukhlissi announced from Alma-Ata that separatists had killed twenty Chinese border guards in an attack in the Kundjerab Pass on the Sino-Pakistani border. Radio Australia quoted Mukhlissi on 25 August as claiming that about fifty bomb attacks had been carried out by his people since July. Chinese authorities claimed that twenty people had been arrested in connection with this. The *Xinjiang Fazhi Bao* (Legal News) reported on 16 August that nineteen schools in the Hotan area had been closed down for illegal religious activity and ninety-eight people had been arrested.[20]

By the fall of 1996, the campaign had lost steam or at least the intense publicity had faded, which raises the question of whether there actually was a significant escalation of secessionist violence and religious fundamentalism or whether the upsurge was magnified by the propaganda apparatus. Perhaps the regime chose to create a smoke screen of escalating terrorist violence because it suited the general political climate of leftism, class struggle, anti-American nationalism, and China's harsh way of dealing with common criminals. By blurring the distinction between Han Chinese political dissent, minority secessionist and religious dissent, and serious crime, the regime could create a climate in which it could strike indiscriminately at any perceived wrongdoing regardless of the seriousness of the offense.

China's policy in Xinjiang is at a crossroads. The Communist rulers in Beijing seem to be convinced that only a policy of harsh and permanent repression can guarantee continued Chinese rule in Xinjiang. If it relaxes its hard-line stand and introduces real autonomy, secessionist agitation and religious dissent will almost certainly spin out of control, but if it heightens repression further, things may polarize, making them equally uncontrollable.

Another Catch-22 situation.

PART FIVE

The Search for a New System

CHAPTER 17

The Dawn of the Post-Deng Era

If a man leaves his house, his tea won't stay warm long.

Chinese saying

THE MOST IMPORTANT domestic news event in 1996 in China, according to the Xinhua state news agency, was the "Sixth Plenary Session of the Fourteenth Central Committee of the Communist Party of China" in October, which adopted a "Decision Regarding Important Questions on Promoting Socialist Ethical and Cultural Progress." The decision is a lengthy mishmash of Marxism and Maoist moralism, geared at promoting "socialist spiritual civilization as a vital part of the grand cross-century blueprint of China's socialist cause." It concludes that ideological education and spiritual civilization have been neglected for a long time and that as a result "standards of moral conduct have been lowered and the practices of worshiping money, seeking pleasure, and [pursuing] individualism have grown; feudal superstitions and social vices like pornography, gambling, and drug abuse have resurfaced; the production of shoddy and imitation goods and fraud have become a social scourge; the cultural cause has been seriously affected by negative factors; corruption has been spreading . . . and a number of people have a weak concept of the state, and doubt and waver in the future of socialism." No attentive observer would question that social and moral decay is perhaps the most serious problem in China today, although one could argue with the remedies prescribed by the "Decision." These are strict adherence to Marxism-Leninism, Mao Zedong Thought, and Deng Xiaoping's Theory of Building Socialism with Chinese Characteristics "to train socialist citizens with lofty ideals, moral integrity, a good education, and a strong sense of discipline. . . . Comrades working in the ideological, cultural, and educational fields should all be *engineers of the human soul.*" The decision also calls for education in patriotism, "which has always been a banner for the struggles for unity of the Chinese people. . . . In modern China, patriotism and socialism have been organically integrated with the great practice of building socialism with Chinese characteristics, which serves as a strong driving force to encourage people across the country to strive for national revitalization." The mass media, films, television, major historical events, national flag-raising ceremonies, and singing of the national anthem should vigorously promote patriotism. Measures should be taken to tap fully the role of the Communist Youth League and the Young Pioneers (the Chinese Boy Scouts). Finally, the decision states that right has to be distinguished from wrong on such major issues as Marxism versus anti-Marxism, dialectical and historical materialism versus idealism and metaphysics, public ownership versus privatization, socialist democracy versus Western parliamentary democracy, and socialist ideology versus feudal and corrupt capitalist ideology and culture.[1]

The fact that the Communist party gives top billing to such a turgid document—ahead of the soft landing in the economy and the sustained victory over inflation, the selection of a chief executive for Hong Kong and the military maneuvers around Taiwan—really shows that the regime has reached the bottom of the barrel of ideas. To move forward, China needs more reform: economic reform and particularly reform of the political system. Key economic reform of state enterprises is at a standstill, and political reform is anathema because it will inevitably lead to political pluralism, the demise of Communism, and thence to the unknown.

To preserve Communism in its current half-reformed, corrupt, and repressive form, the party must revive ideology. If the real world is too ugly to face and you cannot change it, you create an illusory world of ideology, with engineers of the soul. Paradoxically, it was Deng Xiaoping, the great architect of reform, who provoked this leftist ideological renaissance with his final, renewed call for radical reform during his southern trip in 1992. The orthodox Marxist ideologues, never resigned to their defeat in 1987 (see Chapter 10) and their renewed sidelining in 1991–92, have been scheming and agitating since 1994 for a rehabilitation of Marxist ideology. The codification of all these efforts was an anonymous document entitled "Several Factors Affecting China's State Security," which was attributed to ultraleftist commissar Deng Liqun and his team of scribes. Starting in early 1995, it circulated internally and was then disseminated from Beijing to the provinces.

It was first published without authorization in July 1995 by the *Economic Work* monthly in Guizhou Province and was reprinted for the first time outside China in January 1996 in the Hong Kong weekly *Yazhou Zhoukan* (Asia Weekly). It became known as the "Ten-Thousand Character Statement."[2] It is an all-out attack on Deng Xiaoping's legacy of economic reform and a warning to the party that a new bourgeoisie may seize power if orthodox Marxist practices such as class struggle are not resumed.

The essence of the document is that the state-owned proportion of the national economy has declined to an intolerably low level: it is expected to be approximately one-quarter by the year 2000. The drain on state assets, estimated at 100 billion yuan a year, and the privatization trend will undermine the solidity of the socialist economic foundation and menace the consolidation of the proletarian dictatorship. The writers compare the current efforts by China's new entrepreneurs to "pay taxes in exchange for 'public goods' from the state such as the legal system, public order, national defense, and democracy" to the way the European bourgeoisie won political power from the absolute monarchies. Large numbers of entrepreneurs have become people's deputies, above-county-level officials, local officials, and mayors. "The embryo of a bureaucrat-bourgeoisie and a comprador-bourgeoisie has emerged. . . . There are now [semi-independent] newspapers, including the *Nongovernmental Entrepreneurs Daily* and the *Factory and Managers Daily,* which directly reflect their interests and demands. . . . It is estimated that when the situation permits, these people will not need much time to openly form a bourgeois political party." The writers quote Wan Runnan, computer tycoon and head of the Stone Group in Beijing, who financed part of the protest movement in 1989 and fled abroad after it was crushed. Wan said: "On the one hand, the middle class hates this system; on the other hand, they have to cooperate with this government in order to make money. Herein lies their interest. They use money and materials to corrupt the government and promote change in the society from the negative side. . . . As a result the CCP regime becomes irremediably corrupt. The more corrupt the regime is, the greater the possibility of a change in society."

The writers believe that the bourgeois liberals both inside and outside the party have systematic and definite views of the future; they think that the only realistic option for China, and the only feasible way for the CCP to save the party and the nation, is to start from nonideology in the propaganda and ideological field. This means diluting Marxism, gradually giving up the Four Cardinal Principles (uphold the leadership of the Communist party, the dictatorship of the proletariat, the socialist road, and Marxism-Leninism and Mao Zedong Thought), changing the economy to a free-market economy of private ownership, changing politically to a multiparty parliamentary democracy, and steadily bringing about, step-by-step, a "peaceful evolution" to capitalism through reform. The writers lament the drop in the quality of cadres, which has occurred despite improved education because they are competent only in their special fields, like science, engineering, and agriculture, and almost nobody specializes in Marxist theory anymore. This vacuum will hamper the party in its ability to correctly understand and handle classes, class contradictions, and class struggle, perhaps resulting in the loss of state power. The writers expect that China's bourgeois liberals, with the support of "hostile" foreign forces, will make an all-out bid in the next few years to bring about a reversal of the verdict on the 1989 democracy movement, i.e., a revision of the earlier official "Big Lie" that maintained it was a "counterrevolutionary rebellion" staged by a handful of conspirators. "When a political storm does come and we find ourselves in an unfavorable situation, it may be too late to change the situation," the document concludes.

The "Decision on Ethical Progress" is obviously one of the answers to the many questions that were raised in behind-the-scenes debates on the "Ten-Thousand Character Statement." Though less extreme leftist than the latter, the "Decision" also represents a strong veer to the left. Socialist ethics and spiritual civilization figure prominently on the political agenda of President Jiang Zemin, who has certainly lived up to the promise he made in his first press conference after the Tiananmen turmoil, in which he said that his two predecessors Hu Yaobang and Zhao Ziyang had lost their jobs because they had promoted reform too much and had neglected the struggle against bourgeois liberalization. He vowed not to make the same mistake. Ever since, Jiang has alternated Mao suits and Western attire and has used new recipes to rehash Mao speeches, such as his speech "On the Ten Major Relationships" or his talk "On the Correct Handling of Contradictions Among the People." Like Deng Xiaoping, he has performed a left-right balancing act, the important difference being that Deng Xiaoping's basic instinct was reformist and that in the end he always came out in favor of reform. Jiang is the opposite of his deposed predecessors: he has neglected reform and catered too much to leftist ideologues.

Jiang Zemin has been general secretary for eight years, chairman of the Central Military Commission for over seven, and state president for four. Never before have all these posts been held by one and the same person, not even by Mao Zedong. Jiang is up for reelection as general secretary at the Party Congress in the fall of 1997; his first term of office as president expires in the spring of 1998, and he is entitled to a second five-year term. It is generally assumed that Jiang is maneuvering to revive the party chairmanship, which is a much more elevated position that that of general secretary. Holding no top posts in the formal hierarchy himself, Deng Xiaoping saw to it that the chairmanship—the title symbolizing the personality cult and excesses of Mao Zedong—was abolished in 1980. He installed his protégé Hu Yaobang as general secretary (*Zong Shuji*), to be distinguished from the loftier-sounding secretary-general (*Mishuzhang*). "Imperial fathers" and other octogenarian gerontocrats have almost become extinct in China, and Jiang Zemin, himself seventy-one, wants to be his own "emperor," with the title of chairman of the party, the state, and the military commission. If all goes according to plan, Premier Li Peng—who will have to resign the premiership in early 1998 after serving two terms—and Congress chairman Qiao Shi should become the two vice-chairmen of the party. Whether Jiang's design will work remains to be seen, but his accumulation of titles is just one way of compensating for his lack of prestige and achievements. Jiang's record of service for the past seven years displays a reactive, zigzag policy of ideological nostalgia, go-slow on economic reforms, repression of any dissent, and a complete lack of innovative initiative and vision for the future.

At the time of the 1996 American presidential election, I attended a dinner for senior military officials and sat next to a woman colonel, the daughter of a general. During the animated conversation, I asked her whom she would vote for if China were to have free, direct presidential elections. She had no opinion whatever and had never given any thought to the matter. I urged her to think about it and to let me know what she decided. During dessert, she said, "I know. I'd vote for Jiang Zemin." Surprised, I asked, "Why? What are his merits?" She answered, "He has no merit, but there is peace and stability and that's the most important thing. A new strongman is not desirable now."

Compared with Russia and also India, there is indeed relative peace and stability in China, but those two countries have a high degree of transparency, elections, and an institutionalized mechanism for succession. These are lacking in China, making unpredictability and power struggles inevitable.

IT IS TRUE that since 1989 open power struggles and purges have been limited in China, but their unexpected eruption during 1995 was vehement. The suicide of a vice-mayor of Beijing, Wang Baosen, was the starting signal for a purge that claimed as its victim one of China's most powerful men, Chen Xitong, the party secretary of the capital. The immediate cause of Wang's suicide was an anticorruption investigation. China has conducted anticorruption campaigns since 1983. Most of them were rituals, not really intended to change things but rather to assuage the people's indignation. Petty thieves were rounded up, but the big swindlers were left in peace.

Popular anger at large-scale corruption was the main theme of the student protests in 1989. Eight years later, corruption is more of a problem than it ever was. It is, in fact, the Achilles' heel of Deng Xiaoping, blemishing his record and tarnishing his reputation. Deng has been responsible for unparalleled economic growth, but the flip side of the coin has been rampant corruption at all levels.

President and party leader Jiang Zemin has apparently chosen anticorruption as a means of strengthening his position and establishing his popularity with the people. Traditionally, new Chinese emperors have immediately distanced themselves from their predecessors. It is very easy indeed to exploit resentment of Deng Xiaoping's reforms. Chinese who voiced their respect and admiration for Deng Xiaoping before 1989 now express their indifference or animosity in one word only: "unfair" (*bu gongping*), referring to the social inequality that his regime has generated. From the classical philosopher Mencius to Mao Zedong, a guiding principle in China has been "Poverty is acceptable, but not inequality."

Jiang Zemin is taking a big gamble. In February 1995 he ordered the arrest of the first Communist prince, Zhou Beifang. Zhou is the son of Zhou Guanwu, chairman of Capital Steel, the largest diversified steel and financial conglomerate in China. The old Zhou, Deng Xiaoping's personal friend, was forced into retirement at the age of seventy-seven. One of Deng Xiaoping's sons was a business partner of the young Zhou, and for months an investigation was carried out into the dealings of this young Deng, Deng Zhifang, until he was finally cleared as a gesture of respect to the Deng family.

The suicide of the vice-mayor occurred in the middle of this, followed by the dismissal and arrest of Party Secretary Chen Xitong. The official reason for purging Chen Xitong was his responsibility for the scandal surrounding Wang Baosen, "who had misappropriated funds on a large scale and led a life of debauchery." Chen Xitong was undoubtedly corrupt through and through, but the main cause of his downfall was a deep-seated power struggle between Jiang Zemin and his allies in the party's top leadership on the one hand, and the coarse, arrogant rulers of the capital city on the other, who ran Beijing like an independent kingdom and no longer took orders from the central authorities.

This conflict dates from 26 June 1989, the day that Jiang Zemin, then party secretary of Shanghai, was called to Beijing during the aftermath of the military crackdown on the prodemocracy protests to succeed dismissed party leader Zhao Ziyang. Chen Xitong was one of the chief instigators of the bloody repression. As mayor of Beijing he willfully allowed the situation to escalate, along with Premier Li Peng and Party Secretary Li Ximing, reporting selectively to Deng Xiaoping with an eye to persuading the old man to seek a military solution to the crisis. Afterward all three expected to be rewarded with the highest office, but to their chagrin, an upstart from Shanghai received the post. Moreover, Li Ruihuan, party secretary of China's third city, Tianjin, was promoted to membership in the then six-member Standing Committee of the Politburo. Li Ximing and Chen Xitong received nothing for their efforts. On the contrary, three years later Li Ximing lost his seat in the Politburo as well as his post of party secretary. In October 1992 Chen Xitong became his successor. That was scant reward for such an ambitious man, who thought that he and Li Peng had saved Communism in 1989.

With the increase over the next three years in the number of Shanghainese in the Politburo, Chen Xitong's insubordination toward Jiang Zemin escalated still further. There were problems nationwide with wayward local rulers. The central government concluded that settling accounts with Chen Xitong would serve as a national demonstration of the consolidation of central authority.[3] Wang Baosen's suicide offered them an unexpected opportunity to conduct a large-scale cleanup operation in the municipality of Beijing, and this was Jiang Zemin's first chance to demonstrate how ruthless he could be. In mid-1996, however, Jiang met intense opposition when he tried to slap a heavy sentence on Chen for his "corruption and dissolute lifestyle." The conclusion of the Chen case has been postponed indefinitely.

MUNICIPAL SOURCES in Beijing had revealed earlier that Chen had been feverishly engaged in whitewashing Beijing's city finances in anticipation of the approaching inspection by Moody's Credit Rating Agency. There was general disgust with Beijing's sinister city government, and the citizens of Beijing discreetly expressed the hope that they would be given a cleaner, more civilized ruling clique, comparable to that of Shanghai.

It was feared, however, that no one could get a grip on the situation. At the height of their power, Mao Zedong and Deng Xiaoping had no hold on the hermetically sealed bastion of the municipality of Beijing, and both of them had had to turn to Shanghai to launch campaigns to win back their lost initiative in national politics: Mao Zedong in 1965 at the beginning of the Cultural Revolution, and Deng Xiaoping in 1992 to launch a new and final wave of reforms.

Then the unbelievable happened. Jiang Zemin, a leader generally held to be weak and mediocre, succeeded in breaking the back of the Beijing mafia. Jiang introduced a new style of government that was essentially different from that of Deng Xiaoping. Deng owed his power to his decade-long revolutionary record of service, as well as to his seniority in the three realms of power: party, state, and army. He preserved stability by maintaining a balance between factions, but in times of crisis he always hit the right harder than the left, a natural law that is always safe to observe in Chinese Communist politics. Jiang Zemin, who has no national power base of his own, has fallen back on Shanghai and is frantically engaged in bringing the Shanghai faction to the top of the national power pagoda.

Jiang worked in Shanghai as mayor and party secretary from 1983 to 1989, at which time he was hastily promoted to national party leader during the Tiananmen crisis. Since then, he has succeeded in bringing to the Politburo all his successors as mayor and party secretary of Shanghai, four in total. The state's vice-president, prewar capitalist Rong Yiren, also comes from Shanghai.

There is clearly a Shanghai faction that is machinating to dominate the national leadership with Jiang Zemin as *capo di tutti capi*. This put him in a position to fire the first shot at the capital city's bastion of power, although no more shots have followed. Many more were expected, however, not only in Beijing but across the whole country. Jiang lacked the necessary sources of power, however, and shrank back from further action. Anticorruption campaigns are risky, because they have a political and not a legal basis. You hunt down your corrupt enemies, such as Chen Xitong, but not your corrupt friends, such as Jiang Chunyun. Such campaigns quickly deteriorate into vendettas that can easily get out of hand.

The result of eliminating Chen Xitong has been to foster talk of a coalition between the Shanghai-dominated central government in Beijing, the city of Beijing led by the new party secretary Wei Jianxing, the city of Shanghai, and, as the fourth partner, the powerful northern coastal province of Shandong with its 82 million inhabitants. In 1994 Jiang Zemin promoted the corrupt, unpopular former party secretary of this province, Jiang Chunyun, to the Politburo and in March 1995 made him vice-premier responsible for agriculture, in spite of the fact that a record number of members of the National People's Congress voted against him, partly because of his involvement in the Tai-an corruption scandal in Shandong. This coalition is characterized by its leanings toward state socialism and away from a market orientation. Beijing is the national center of bureaucratic control; Shanghai is an obedient, loyal bastion of the central government and has always contributed the largest part of its revenues to Beijing. Shandong has the reputation of having acquired a prominent position in the national economy, based not on foreign investments but on its own agricultural surpluses. This reflects the orientation of the new regime: recentralization and resumption of state control after all the decentralization, wild capitalism, and lawless commerce of the Deng era. But it will not work, because the underlying social and economic dynamics across the country are moving in opposite directions.

THE DICHOTOMY between the statist, bureaucratic, more xenophobic north and the cosmopolitan, commercial, privatized south will be one of the major political contradictions in the early years of the post-Deng era. Shanghai has also made a start in resuming its cosmopolitan tradition, although under central control.

To preserve the privileges of the 1980s, a southern coalition has also taken shape between Guangdong plus Hong Kong, Hainan, Fujian, and, farther inland, Sichuan. The economic orientation of prosperous Guangdong–Hong Kong, Hainan, and Fujian is more toward Southeast Asia and the world economy than toward the rest of China. The poor province of Sichuan, with its 100 million people, hopes to become the next frontier for investments from Hong Kong and Guangdong as the only means of lifting up such a large mass of people from the depths of poverty. Sichuan is the biggest supplier of migrant labor, drifting around the country in search of work. The downfall of all the imperial dynasties was caused by the forces of the *liu-min* (the "floating population"). Which of the two now poses the biggest threat to China's stability—the floating peasant population or the threat of massive unemployment in the old centers of state industry—is difficult to guess and varies from region to region.

The potentially explosive social repercussions of the reforms in the state sector have been causing the party's leadership to zigzag back and forth. The so-called corporatization—not privatization—of the state sector, decided on by the Party Central Committee in November 1993 in its "Decision on Certain Questions Concerning the Establishment of a Socialist Market Economic Structure," has stagnated. Exactly one year later, the committee decided to intensify democratic centralism, i.e., dictatorship by acclamation, by reestablishing party cells at the grassroots level in the rural areas. The leadership was flirting for a while with Maoist ideas, to enable it to impose once again bondage-like controls on the restive peasants, tens of millions of whom are drifting around the country looking for jobs in the cities.

A CONTROVERSIAL BOOK, *China Seen with a Third Eye*, played an important role in the formulation of these regressive policies. This book was published in early 1994 and was attributed to a fictitious author, the "German sinologist Luo Yi Ning Ge Er" (Leuninger). The "translator," Wang Shan, a former Red Guard, later admitted that he was the author and had chosen to write under a pseudonym to give the appearance of having the freedom of expression of a foreigner and a claim to greater objectivity.[4] It is actually shocking that a Chinese intellectual thinks he has to pretend to be a foreigner in order to be taken seriously.

China Seen with a Third Eye is an unrealistic, incoherent work full of internal contradictions between the extremes of blind nostalgia for Mao and exaggerated criticism of the present situation. Chapter 1 is an ultranationalistic diatribe against "Western interference" in China, the last occurrence of which backfired in 1989. The author calls interference in the realm of human rights a "stupid crime."

He draws favorable comparisons between the misunderstood Mao and Deng Xiaoping. Mao knew how to deal with the peasants. His priority was hasty industrialization, for which he needed capital accumulated by the peasants, the most efficient way to do this being to shut them up in communes.

In 1978–79 Deng Xiaoping freed the peasants, primarily to combat famine. This created—selectively—new wealth, but also had all kinds of negative side effects, such as the loss of economies of scale, a decline in technology, the neglect of irrigation systems and agricultural equipment, deforestation resulting in floods, and especially the flow of peasants to the cities. The peasants no longer have any kind of relationship with the government and are an active volcano waiting to erupt. The author wants to solve this problem by repeating Mao's biggest success: chaining the peasants once again to the land. Otherwise they will cause a catastrophe in the cities. Degrading peasants to the level of a simple struggle for a full stomach is much safer than letting them earn money and become entrepreneurs.

Policy makers have mistakenly thought that growth leads to peace and stability, but this is a deceptive trap. A newly evolving social stratification has created a deep mental unbalance because for so long people were used to egalitarianism. The nouveaux riches have accumulated 2 trillion yuan in nongovernmental capital, twice the value of state assets. This capital will change into class capital. The reforms have turned into a runaway horse that no one can stop anymore. Socialism will ultimately collapse and capitalism will be reestablished. The coming class struggle in China will be cruel indeed.[5] The situation in China is such that dramatic developments will be unavoidable. The transitional society is very fragile and the potential crisis very deep. Everywhere regions are either asking for changes in policy or already implementing new policies illegally, or else they no longer have any policies at all. Macroregulation will backfire because the balance of power has essentially shifted. The government has nothing to offer to the new special interest groups. Each measure taken amounts to "cutting a piece of one's own flesh and giving it to one's opponent to eat."[6]

The party still has one weapon—ideological persuasion—but if this is to be successful, cadres have to have integrity and politics must be honest and open. China is still a long way from reaching this point and is obsessed with state secrets. What China needs now is an idol or symbol to believe in so that it can win back its self-confidence. Deng Xiaoping has always refused to allow a Mao-like personality cult to be created around himself. That chance has been missed, but a new idol must nevertheless be created (Jiang Zemin!) to take Mao's place.[7] China is not at all ready for such Western theories as human rights, democracy, and checks and balances. What is the solution? Back to Mao! But how? The author does not explain how the peasants are to be made into serfs again, how growth must be curbed, how the new capitalists are to be reined in, and how state enterprises can be transformed into profit-making businesses. He urges the government to employ extreme methods to take the initiative. The new "totalitarian temptation," Chinese-style.

Shortly after its publication, the book was praised by President Jiang Zemin and seemed to be part of the conservative, antireformist climate that has again been dominant since the spring of 1994. Later on, Jiang distanced himself from it, however, for fear that it would damage his image among intellectuals both inside and outside China. The scenario put forward in the book has been labeled pure fascism by liberal intellectuals such as Xu Liangying, China's leading historian of science.

The creative reformist solution for the landownership dilemma is to keep the peasants on the land by giving them complete ownership rights to it, paying free-market prices for all agricultural products, and importing grain. The éminence grise of China's agronomists, eighty-two-year-old professor Zhang Beigang, director of the Research Center of Economic Development at the Central Chinese University for Science and Technology in Wuhan, said in a daring speech at an international agricultural conference in Hong Kong in the fall of 1995 that peasants leave the land because they do not own it and have no permanent rights to it. Since decollectivization in the early 1980s, peasants have been given fifteen-year leases, later extended to thirty and now up to fifty years. "As long as the peasants have no ownership rights or permanent right to use the land, they will remain shortsighted and will not be prepared to invest their money in it. . . . The first step must be to give the peasants permanent rights, and if the leaders are sensible, they will privatize the land. Then there will no longer be any risk of peasant revolts," said Professor Zhang.[8]

The political will and drive to reform ownership rights of the land are still lacking, and the same applies to the state enterprises. According to the State Commission for Restructuring the Economy, by 1995 sixteen thousand businesses had entered into mergers and nine thousand had become public limited-liability companies, but in the case of "only a couple of small state firms had the ownership rights been transferred or the firms sold at auction," according to Hong Hu, vice-minister of the commission. There was no question of privatization on a somewhat larger scale. The most important reason is political, but there are financial reasons as well. The healthy state enterprises—about 40 percent of the total—must continue to serve as a source of state revenues. The rest are buried in debt to the tune of 1.7 trillion yuan ($205 billion).[9] In the fall of 1995, an international economist made a trip to the northeast of China (Manchuria) and, after talking with various local leaders, concluded that they understood that the only way to solve the massive debt problem of the state enterprises was the large-scale sale of state assets—in other words, reform of ownership rights and privatization. With these funds and the help of international insurance companies, provisions for social security would have to be made as the only way to ensure a successful transition to the market economy.

EVEN ZHU RONGJI, the economic tsar who was praised in 1992 as the new champion of radical reforms, has had a genuine change of heart and moved closer to the conservative camp. He now delivers speeches on the necessity of "socialist spiritual civilization," denouncing the worship of money, ultraindividualism, and decadent lifestyles. In a recent speech, Zhu defended recentralization as follows: "Don't be afraid of being criticized for moving backwards; don't be afraid of being blamed for introducing central planning again." The Shanghai clique in Beijing is now unanimous on this subject.

Not everyone agrees with them, however, not in Beijing and not in other regions. One of the three most powerful men in China is Qiao Shi. He is already seventy-three—not old by Chinese standards—and is chairman of the National People's Congress. His portfolio in the Politburo is Security. He is a somewhat mysterious man who tends to be absent at critical moments, such as in 1989, when he abstained from voting on the use of force to repress the prodemocracy movement. He is a legalist, and since becoming chairman of the National People's Congress in 1993 has greatly stepped up the legislative pace and supervisory power of the People's Congress. Two other influential members of the Politburo are counted among his supporters—Tian Jiyun, sixty-six, the first vice-chairman of the Congress, and Li Ruihuan, one of the top seven in the Politburo. Li, a sixty-two-year-old former carpenter, holds the portfolio of Culture and Ideology and is also chairman of the People's Political Consultative Conference, a sort of toothless upper house of mainly non-Communist intellectuals. In the spring of 1995 all three gave important speeches that deviated drastically from Jiang Zemin's conservatism. All three expressed scarcely concealed support of Guangdong in its resistance to Beijing's centralism.

Qiao Shi traveled to Guangdong and gave a speech in which he subtly objected to the plenum decision of November 1994. The theme of that plenum had been recentralization and strengthening of the power of Shanghai. Qiao said, "In implementing the guidelines of the fourth plenum of the Fourteenth Party Central Committee it is especially necessary to take local realities into consideration." Qiao went on to criticize the hazy ideological generalizations of Jiang Zemin and argued for accelerating reforms and taking more risks. These words echoed Deng Xiaoping's political testament of 1992. Tian Jiyun lashed out mercilessly at the passivity of the National People's Congress when he addressed the representatives of Guangdong Province. His now-famous speech (see Chapter 19) had the immediate effect of causing 36 percent of the representatives to vote against one of Jiang Zemin's candidates for the vice-premiership. At the same time, Li Ruihuan gave a witty speech to the Hong Kong delegates to the People's Political Consultative Conference in which he admitted that China had made mistakes regarding Hong Kong. He called the upcoming takeover an "unusually complicated process," in which China had no experience. "To govern Hong Kong and to keep it in good condition is no simple task, in spite of the fact that it is so small in size. . . . If you don't understand a valuable possession, you can't keep it intact for long," said Li. It was an overt attack on the simplistic, often primitive volleys of official propaganda fired at the British and Hong Kong governments which have the blessing of Jiang Zemin and Li Peng.

If this was not the sign of a power struggle, in any case it pointed to big differences of insight into the direction in which China should be developing and the complete lack of any reformist vision for the future on the part of top leader Jiang Zemin.

THE REGIONAL POWER BASE of the "reformists" lies principally in the south. There are continual reports in the Hong Kong media that they are touring the southern and southwestern provinces, especially Sichuan, to consolidate their power bloc. Their efforts are directed at keeping the power that was delegated to the provinces during the Deng era. Their slogan is "If we don't go on pushing for reforms, there will be retrogression." The reforms are stuck in Beijing but are advancing at provincial, municipal, and lower levels, where the generational transition has already taken place.

The two opposing visions of China's future are, on the one hand, a further opening of the door and acceleration of China's integration into the world economy, and, on the other hand, ideologically motivated mercantilism, protectionism, and a slowdown in market reforms under increasing state control. Just what the specific alternative agenda of these reformists is can only be guessed at, but there is no doubt that they want to speed up the pace of further economic reforms, start long-overdue political reforms, and promote national, moral reconstruction, not through renewed ideological dictatorship but through strengthening the rule of law, the supervisory powers of representative organs, and the freedom of the press to expose corruption and abuse of power by party and government organs.

The neoconservatives, led by Jiang Zemin, are very wary about this, fearing that accelerated economic reforms will destabilize the country and that further decentralization will endanger national cohesion and unity. China must remain a highly centralized unitary state with strict state control along reinvigorated Marxist-Leninist lines.

The outbreak of an open power struggle is unlikely, but it seems certain that a breakthrough will have to wait until several years after the death of Deng Xiaoping. A partial reshuffle of the leadership will occur at the upcoming Party Congress to be held in the fall of 1997. Li Peng's second term as premier expires at the beginning of 1998, and according to Article 87 of the constitution, he can only serve two consecutive five-year terms. He will then be only seventy years old, much too young to make his exit from the political arena. It would be logical to promote him to head of state, but for that to happen Jiang Zemin would have to relinquish the post and be content with his party and military duties. Jiang is adamant about keeping the presidency because it is the vehicle he uses to pose as an international statesman, equal to the president of the United States.

Jiang wants an expanded role for himself, not a reduced one. Apart from the three top posts in the party, state, and military realms, Jiang's supreme ambition is to become the "Great Teacher" of the Chinese people—in European terms, a "philosopher king," or in premodern times, a ruler who was emperor and pope at the same time.

In the first few weeks of 1997, Chinese television broadcast a twelve-part documentary on the life of Deng Xiaoping which was dominated by all the revolutionary veterans of the first generation and in which only one figure in the current leadership figured prominently: Jiang Zemin. Premier Li Peng, on the other hand, was shown only once. Jiang went to great lengths to portray himself as a titanic figure, the equal of Mao and Deng. As Deng was one of Mao's most prominent victims for about twelve years, Mao was shown lavishing praise on Deng, and the latter is shown in a warm handshake with Mao. The director of the *People's Daily*, leftist ideologue Shao Huazi, explained that the great historical merit of Deng Xiaoping was that he did not negate Mao, as Khrushchev did Stalin. He merely criticized some of Mao's mistakes, thus protecting the historical position of the late chairman, as well as that of the party and himself. Deng praised Jiang, and the message was clear: Jiang will protect Deng's legacy, albeit his own interpretation of that legacy. Deng was the great promotor of China's materialistic development and Jiang will be the great apostle of "spiritual civilization," issuing "encyclical decrees" on ideological, i.e., moral, causes. The problem with ideology, however, is that it is not informed by reality, but by a mixture of distortions, illusions, and lies. The Deng documentary is a case in point. Two major historical figures, Hu Yaobang and Zhao Ziyang, were ignored completely. Hu was not shown or mentioned even once, and Zhao was briefly visible only during the signing of the Hong Kong reversal agreement in 1984. Neither was anything said about Deng Xiaoping's two failed attempts during the 1980s to reform the political system.

If things go Jiang Zemin's way, there will be a lot of ideological education, not much economic reform, and even less political reform or none at all in the years ahead. The propaganda apparatus will resurrect the old selfless saints, from Lei Feng, Mao's model soldier of the 1950s, to Kong Fansen, the heroic Chinese cadre who sacrificed his life for the poor Tibetans in the 1990s, creating a whole new series of saints for the Chinese people to emulate. Whereas Mao Zedong had Dazhai—his ideological model commune—to teach peasants how to use muscle power, and Deng Xiaoping had Daqiuzhuang—a greedy nouveau riche village where peasants could learn how to get rich quickly—Jiang Zemin has Zhangjiagang, a model town of civilized citizens near Shanghai. It is China's mini-Singapore, where people do not smoke, spit, or litter, where there is no crime, not even cheating, and where citizens compete for trophies like the "Doubly Civilized Unit Cup" and the "Perfect Citizen Cup." Many Chinese agree that this is what they need after the dehumanizing political struggles of the Mao era and the corrupt, primitive capitalism of Deng's final years.

But will this alone make China a modern country? Probably not. Politically, China will remain a conservative gerontocracy for an indefinite period, because by the time the reshuffles of the 1997 Party Congress and the 1998 National People's Congress have been completed, Jiang Zemin will be seventy-two, Li Peng seventy, Qiao Shi seventy-four, Zhu Rongji seventy, and Qian Qichen seventy. They may very well want to stay in power for another ten years. The leaders of the next generation will be well into their sixties or over seventy when it is finally their turn to rule. Li Lanqing is now sixty-five, Li Ruihuan sixty-two, Ding Guangen sixty-eight, Li Tieying sixty-two, Huang Ju fifty-nine, Wen Jiabao fifty-five, Hu Jintao fifty-five, and Wang Zhaoguo fifty-six.

China will continue to enjoy high economic growth and will become more modern and prosperous, but politically it will most probably remain as conservative, secretive, and repressive as ever.

CHAPTER 18

The Three Neo's: Neonationalism, Neo-Confucianism, Neoauthoritarianism

In China Communism and nationalism are naturally blended. The metamorphosis from Communism back to nationalism is rather easy to make.

HUANG YASHENG,
Chinese political scientist

FOR MOST OF THE twentieth century, China has suffered from a negative nationalism that has rejected in militant terms its more than twenty-five-hundred-year-old, great national tradition of Confucianism. The progressive, nationalist May Fourth Movement of 1919 was the beginning of modern Chinese nationalism, discrediting the old sage with the motto "Down with the shop of Confucius," who roughly represented for the East what the Greek philosophers, Jesus of Nazareth, and Thomas Aquinas together had been for Western culture. Young pioneers and students declared that the age of Mr. S. (Science) and Mr. D. (Democracy)* had dawned. Western science, technology, culture, and democracy were called upon to re-

---

* Transliterations of the Chinese characters used for the first syllables of these Western words.

place the Confucian doctrine of ethical, hierarchical rites and rules that had brought centuries of static conservatism to China. In the general cataclysm into which twentieth-century China was plunged, such pure creations of Western culture as Mr. S. and Mr. D. were pitted in the battle for national "reconstruction" against the Western heretics Mr. Ma (Marx) and Mr. Lie (Lenin). During the Mao era, the influence of Ma and Lie seemed to be so irreversibly entrenched that during my first visit to China in 1975, a Communist functionary rejected my criticism that China, in spite of all its xenophobia and autarky, had nevertheless imported a foreign ideology, countering, "Marx and Lenin belong not to the history of Europe but to that of all mankind." Alongside Mao Zedong, four mustachioed and bearded semi-Europeans—Marx, Engels, Lenin, and Stalin—completely dominated the iconography of China's new, rough-hewn pseudoreligion until the end of the 1980s. At the same time, within the framework of the campaign for national reunification with Taiwan, there was a cautious rediscovery of pre-Communist roots, and the father of the first Chinese revolution of 1911, Sun Yat-sen, was restored to his place in the pantheon.

The reconstruction of national Confucianist tradition had begun discreetly in the 1980s among academics behind the scenes. It was still highly controversial politically, especially after the suppression of the student rebellion and the collapse of Communism in Eastern Europe and the Soviet Union, when China's gerontocrats suffered a one- to two-year bout of Stalinist orthodoxy. Since the official proclamation in 1992 of the transformation to the market economy, Marxism has become even more irrelevant, and Leninism continues to exist only as a rationalization for the repressive one-party state. The worship of money, ultraindividualism, and nihilism became the biggest evils of the chaotic transitional flux. China had once again become "a pile of loose sand" without cohesion. The search for new values, ideas, theories, and systems that could restore order and morality became more urgent every day.

Campaigns to encourage the emulation of simple heroes and the introduction of patriotic (nationalist) education were a first step. The "Program for Patriotic Education," launched in 1994, maintains that patriotism is the same thing as socialism: "Ideological education in patriotism, collectivism, and socialism is a trinity and is organically integrated with the great practice of building socialism with Chinese characteristics."[1]

Lei Feng, a self-sacrificing hero created by Mao Zedong in the early 1960s, has been largely forgotten. Now there is a new Lei Feng for the 1990s, Kong Fansen. His inventors are the same poison pens who incited schoolchildren to commit murder and manslaughter and to rebel against their parents during the Cultural Revolution. Xu Weicheng—the ghostwriter for Mao's widow, Jiang Qing—has survived all the about-faces to become executive deputy director of the Central Propaganda Directorate and hence chief strategist of the campaign for patriotic education.

Kong Fansen is an idealized party member from coastal Shandong Province who sacrificed ten years of his life to make heroic contributions to the construction, development, and stability of Tibet, which earned him the distinction of being proclaimed the "Lei Feng of modern times." He became party secretary of the county of Ngari, "the roof of the roof of the world." "The colder the frozen and snow-capped mountaintops, the greater his dedication and enthusiasm. He adopted two Tibetan orphans, donated blood, and gave the money he received for it to needy Tibetan brothers. His selfless service to the people filled the eyes of the Tibetans with tears. For Kong Fansen, the highest form of love was love for the people, and that was no abstract generalization, but a deep, fundamental feeling that was given expression in the suffering of many hardships. . . . He was a true member of the Communist party. He was truly worthy of being called a party member. . . . People used to say that members of the Communist party were made of special stuff. The moving deeds and noble character of Comrade Kong Fansen have again shown this to be true. . . . Comrade Jiang Zemin has called upon us to carry on the pioneering spirit of Kong Fansen. The most fundamental reason why Kong Fansen is the way he is, is because he still studies Marxism-Leninism and Mao Zedong Thought, as well as Deng Xiaoping's theory of building socialism with Chinese characteristics."[2]

The cynical reaction of the people to this maudlin glorification of Kong Fansen is encapsulated in the question: Who is the real model Communist? Kong Fansen or Wang Baosen, the corrupt, decadent vice-mayor of Beijing, who committed suicide at the height of the Kong Fansen glorification campaign.

A patriotic book campaign is also under way with books tailor-made for students at elementary and secondary schools. No effort is being made to appeal to students at the university level. Not that it has more effect on younger children, but the books, at any rate, are printed in huge editions and delivered to the schools. None of the children of my Chinese friends or acquaintances have read even one of these books, however, partly because their parents and teachers do not encourage them to do so. "Patriotism must begin among children of elementary and secondary school age. In order to stimulate national self-respect, self-confidence, and dignity among the members of the younger generation, it is necessary to tell them how beautiful our mountains and lakes are, how old our history is, what a magnificent and glorious cultural heritage we have, and how many heroic people with high ideals we've had."³ Leading the top hundred for all age groups are the life stories of Mao Zedong and Liu Shaoqi, but how can you explain to children that Mao intentionally had Liu Shaoqi killed? You can't, so you keep quiet about it. This kind of patriotism doesn't rely on truth, only on empty slogans.

Simplistic, all-encompassing, but meaningless clichés cannot solve the deep identity crisis faced by China. During this period of transition, this "changing of dynasties," people are busily "rectifying terms," the "reevaluation of all values." Something else is needed, but what?

PATRIOTISM MEANS love of China, but not necessarily for the People's Republic and certainly not for the current corrupt, repressive Communist regime. The regime tries to strengthen its legitimacy and durability with anti-Western phraseology, but the Opium Wars are just about the only thing that can stir up anti-British—not necessarily anti-Western—feelings in the average Chinese. In their outward behavior as well as in numerous other respects, the Chinese are the most Westernized people of Asia, not only in Hong Kong and Taiwan, but also on the mainland. Other great Asian peoples—such as the Indians, Japanese, and Indonesians—still wear traditional Eastern attire at least part of the time, greet each other in an Eastern way—bowing, with folded hands—whereas the Chinese use the Western handshake and, since the mid-1980s, wear only Western clothing: suits and ties, T-shirts, miniskirts, jeans. Young people know nothing about their traditional culture, never watch a Peking opera, and are completely absorbed in Western pop culture and Western literature, which is channeled into China via Hong Kong and Taiwan. Their idols are Western soccer players and movie stars, and their ideal is to emigrate to the West.

A Chinese researcher at a think tank offered an apt summary of all these dilemmas: "China is no longer Eastern, not yet Western, and also not Marxist. Therefore it's nothing! That sounds very nihilistic, but is less hopeless than it seems, because it is actually a mixture of everything, although it doesn't know itself yet and doesn't know how consciously to use the various aspects of its identity to make itself whole, to give the youth a purpose, to mobilize the people better for the development of the country and for integration with the world. The party has decided that we must become a market economy, but they cannot adopt the norms and values of a market economy that have been developed in the West, both because they don't want to and because they don't know how it can be done. They want to remain Marxist, but run into big problems because Marxism has never had anything positive to say about the market economy. Ingenious interim definitions offered by transition ideologues are the 'early stages of socialism' or even 'early stages of capitalism' with all its crude, inhuman practices. While the economy is growing, enormous new problems are springing up. The huge ideological and cultural vacuum is threatening to plunge the country into chaos again."

ONE SOLUTION that is often put forward is total Westernization, but that is anathema for ideological and nationalistic reasons. Then there is partial Westernization, which was already urged more than a hundred years ago along the lines of the "*ti yong* concept" (literally, body and function), meaning maintenance of the Chinese essence, i.e., the cultural system, combined with the introduction of Western functions, i.e., Western science and technology (but not its culture). In the meantime, Western science and technology have found broad acceptance in China, but the endless series of upheavals has also stood Chinese culture on its head. In the 1980s Chinese liberals both in and outside the party were arguing for a new, partial transplantation from the West—the adoption of Western humanism—although since 1989 this has been totally unacceptable because Western human rights and democracy are part of it.

In recent years the conclusion has been drawn that "reinvention and modernization of its own tradition" must be the ultimate panacea. Emperors of all dynasties understood that they could not rule without Confucianism, adapting it to fit the needs of their era accordingly. Even the present-day Communists, after all their iconoclasm and destruction, have realized that political tides, classes, and dynasties come and go, but that Confucius remains. The needs of the present era are order, discipline, morality, and education, all of which are basic themes of Confucianism. The Communists hold tenaciously to their Marxism but tacitly accept the rebirth of Confucianism. The debates are no longer academic but are now carried on in official party organs. This culminated in the fall of 1994 in a series of articles in the media on the superiority of Confucianism. An article in the *People's Daily*, printed on 19 September 1994, stated that "in the twenty-first century superior Confucianism [will] replace Western culture." The author, Ma Zhenduo of the Philosophical Research Institute of the Chinese Academy of Social Sciences, wrote that "Western culture, . . . due to these two major components [Christianity and science], has dual functions: seeking truth while advising the people to do good works; actively exploring the external world while showing concern for the values of life and advancing and regulating society. Over a rather long period it has been the world's most complete and advanced culture."

Ma went on to say that Western culture is now undergoing a crisis because science and religion are no longer compatible. "If Westerners' morals and values were based on another humanism rather than on Christianity, the above contradiction would not arise. The right solution is Confucianism, because it is a nonreligious humanism that can provide a basis for morals and the values of life; the culture resulting from combining it with science will also have dual functions—seeking truth while advising the people to do good works."

Ma concluded that in East Asia a culture combining science and secular humanism has taken shape. Because this new culture is free of the contradictions plaguing Western culture, it is therefore better. This culture will put East Asian countries in a position to modernize at a much quicker pace while avoiding the defects of the West. "As this culture better suits the needs of the future, it will thrive particularly well in the next century and will replace modern and contemporary Western culture."[4]

In the fall of 1994, on the occasion of a conference honoring the 2,545th birthday of Confucius, various top leaders, including Jiang Zemin, Li Ruihuan, and Li Lanqing, subsequently praised Confucianism as the main pillar of traditional Chinese culture and the pride of the Chinese nation. "The Chinese people have the responsibility to systematize it scientifically, making it serve the contemporary needs of everyday life."[5]

Vice-premier Li Lanqing, the official keynote speaker at the conference, stressed the special significance of Confucius in teaching morals. "Under the present social conditions in a developing market economy with increased commodity production, Confucianism provides rich material for the fostering of a new, idealistic, moral, and disciplined generation. . . . The twenty-first century should be a period of the mutual development of material and spiritual civilization.

"The Confucius of China's traditional culture will shine with new life in the new century and make new contributions to the continuing development of human society."

The Mao era and the Deng era up to 1989 were dominated by the dogma of the superiority of socialism. Now, with astounding ease, the superiority of Confucianism has been proclaimed the new sinocentric dogma, the basis of the inborn superiority of the Chinese and their predestination to dominate the world in the following century.

. . .

IT IS A BEWILDERING PARADOX that the Chinese Communists, who spent the greater part of this century maligning Confucius whenever they got the chance, now see the ancient sage and not Karl Marx or Mao as one of the pillars, even the main one, of twenty-first-century world civilization. Two European cosmopolites, Gottfried Wilhelm Leibniz (1646–1716) and Voltaire (1694–1778), were already convinced in their time of the superiority of Confucianism. In his book *Neues China* (New China), published in 1697, Leibniz concluded that China had surpassed Europe in political ethics and practical philosophy, while Europe excelled in metaphysics, mathematics, and astronomy. Leibniz thanked God for the opportunity of having been exposed to a non-European secular civilization that, he was convinced, could be combined with European civilization to create a world civilization for all of mankind. He wanted to bring Chinese missionaries to Europe and was able to interest the Russian tsar Peter the Great and also King Frederick the Great of Prussia in the project, which, however, never got off the ground.

Voltaire was deeply impressed by the secular character of Confucianism. Here for once was no prophet, let alone someone claiming to have been sent by a supernatural supreme being, but rather a wise magistrate who instructed people in ancient laws, preaching a doctrine of virtue that had nothing to do with belief or mysteries.[6]

The Communists saw the matter quite differently at first and spent a long time hesitating before finally getting around to parroting the words of Leibniz and Voltaire in 1994. After the foundation of the People's Republic, Confucianism was criticized as a superstructure of feudalism, and the modern nationalism of the Kuomintang was rejected as a bourgeois ideology. In their place sprang up a brand of patriotism based on myths inspired by Mao Zedong from the caves of Yanan, which combined primitive, atavistic elements like the spirit of the Yellow River, resistance to the Japanese invader, class struggle, and the yearning for a utopian world.

During the Mao era, Confucianism gradually crumbled into oblivion until 1966, when the greatest "iconoclastic fury" in the history of China, the Great Proletarian Cultural Revolution, again brought the teachings of Confucius into the limelight, although this time in a negative sense. Inpired by the revolutionary spirit of Chairman Mao, Red Guards descended on Qufu, the birthplace of the Master in the eastern province of Shandong, which for them meant the "resting place of the stinking corpse of Confucius." Within Chinese culture, Qufu combined the functions of Athens, Nazareth, and Rome. Mao's storm troopers destroyed every commemorative column, statue, and piece of furniture that was not too large or massive for their hammers, crowbars, and battering rams, laying waste to temple interiors and palaces alike.[7]

In 1973 another cryptic campaign was launched with Mao's blessing, aimed at two widely contrasting targets: the venerable sage Confucius and the radical marshall Lin Biao, once designated as Mao's successor. It was the equivalent of a campaign in Europe against Jesus Christ and Hitler's *Reichsmarschall* Hermann Göring. *Pi Lin, Pi Kong** (Criticize Lin Biao and Confucius) was a veiled attack on then premier Zhou Enlai and his "restorationists" (among whom was Deng Xiaoping), who were trying to restore order and stability after the chaos of the Cultural Revolution.

Zhang Huimin, a veteran Chinese journalist, once told of a friend of his named Zunkong (Respect Confucius) who was forced during the campaign to change his name to Pikong (Criticize Confucius). Chinese diplomats even transferred the battlefield to the headquarters of the United Nations in New York, where on 17 September 1974 a calligraphy made by Sun Yat-sen bearing a quote from the Old Master describing a world society of mutual trust and abundance had to be removed.

Ashamed of the vandalism and desecration and tired of all the revolutionary fanaticism, Chinese intellectuals started searching for an alternative to Maoism in 1977 and put forward a selective, limited reevaluation of Confucius. After decades of having its social and family relationships poisoned by class struggle and extreme political-ideological campaigns, there was a need for something that would bring peace and harmony instead of discord and hatred.

In the late 1970s a new international vision of Confucianism arose which certainly contributed to the rehabilitation of his teachings within China. The pioneer was the American futurologist Herman Kahn of the Hudson Institute in New York, who suggested in his book *World Economic Development: 1979 and Beyond* that Confucianism was for East Asia what the Protestant ethic had been for Western Europe.[8] Just as, according to Max Weber, the spirit of capitalism arose in Europe from Protestantism, the rise of industrial capitalism in the four tigers of East Asia—South Korea, Taiwan, Hong Kong, and Singapore—had been driven by their common Confucian heritage. The overseas Chinese family business is the main pillar of East Asian capitalism (outside Japan) and, with the exception of Hong Kong, Taiwan, and Singapore, has generated considerable surplus value in all of the Southeast Asian economies. Discipline, hard work, frugality, respect for authority, and a passion for learning—all within the family—form the main elements of the neo-Confucian work ethic.[9] Weber's notion about religion in China— that Confucian society suffocated capitalist activity and had no ethic that

---

* Confucius is the Latinization of the Chinese Kong Fu Zi.

promoted commerce—was given a new twist in the Chinese diaspora: "aggressive Confucianism, Samurai Confucianism, post-Confucianism, once appearing in an Adam Smith tie."[10]

The least successful heirs of Confucius, however, were the Chinese on the mainland, for many reasons. Family businesses had been eradicated during the Mao era. China had turned its back not only on Confucius but on the whole world. Until the late 1980s Chinese economists and social scientists continued to view the policy of autarky as the main reason for China's backwardness. On the other hand, they attributed the success of New Industrial Asia not at all to the positive aspects of Confucianism but rather to Western aid, economic incentives created by the wars in Korea and Vietnam, the world market, and cultural Westernization. In 1988 a standard answer was given to the question as to why China, the cradle of Confucianist culture, had failed where the little tigers with the same cultural tradition had succeeded. In an interview in the newspaper for intellectuals, *Guangming Ribao,* Zhan Xiaohong, a researcher at the Chinese Academy of Social Sciences, offered the following ingenious ideological construction: "I think the blame lies in the Chinese worship of and blind belief in things foreign, so much so that they ignore some of the superior traditions of their own culture. In spite of the tradition of the golden mean and moderation, China has had the tendency to do things to extremes: in the 1950s it blindly followed the Soviet example and now [in 1988] again Western ideas are the rage." Zhan urged taking the experiences of East Asia as an example and not those of the West or the Soviet Union.[11] The East Asian countries have demonstrated just how important Confucianism has been for their modernization.

DURING THE 1980S a very gradual and guarded reassessment of Confucius took place. In an article appearing in 1981 in the Shanghainese newspaper *Wen Hui Bao,* the sociologist Yan Beiming of the Chinese Academy of Social Sciences was the first to write that Confucius had not been an ultrareactionary demon at all and should be rehabilitated. Of course, one was allowed to criticize him, but did this mean that memorials should be destroyed and his name cursed? "Confucius was not the boss of the antique shop. The shop was kept running by the feudal system that ignored the progressive, reformist aspects of Confucianism and upheld its backward aspects," said Yan.[12]

During the party leadership of the liberal Hu Yaobang (1981–87), the margins of the debate were gradually broadened in support of Deng

Xiaoping's rational, pragmatic reform policies, which contained various Confucian elements, such as the following:

- respect for intellectuals, teachers, and good education, which had been destroyed by Mao;
- a hierarchically organized society, which had been turned upside down by the rebellious spirit of the Mao era.

Certain ideas of Confucius' sound like pure Maoist thought: "Not scarcity, but unequal distribution, not poverty, but dissatisfaction should be feared." Confucius also pleaded for extending education to the lower classes in order to mobilize all existing talent.

In 1983 a symposium was held on the topic of whether Confucius was an idealist or a materialist. One of the conclusions was that he was the initiator of the Chinese tradition of "naïve materialism," which was characterized by an emphasis on human affairs. Some said that Confucius was a materialist, owing to his skepticism about religion, while others said that his emphasis on ethics made him an idealist. At any rate, his teachings contained dialectical elements and it had been these contrasting ideas that had caused various schools to develop among his disciples.[13]

The main characteristic of Confucianism is a practical, humanistic rationalism that excludes mysticism and fanaticism. It rejects both asceticism and hedonism/sexual permissiveness as two extremes and guides human feelings and desires toward moderation, rejects nihilism and egoism, and seeks a balance between humanism and the cultivation of the individual. In short, fairness, moderation, and the golden mean.

Different eras of Chinese history have created their own image of Confucius: a tolerant Confucius; an orthodox and religious, almost theocratic, Confucius; a sage; a mythological figure; and a wizard.[14] He was subject to so many interpretations that the great Chinese historian Gu Jiegang once said, "If you talk about Confucius, don't talk about all of them at once." During the Song dynasty, Confucianism was reformed by Chu Hsi (1130–1200) into an orthodox scholastic philosophy that, mixed with Buddhist and Taoist elements, took on all the aspects of a medieval religion, including antirationalism, obscurantism, and clericalism. The Confucianist religion was inimical to new ideas and fatal to the development of production technology and scientific discovery in China. Starting with the Ming dynasty, Chinese science, which had led the world until then, fell behind.[15] The reformulation of Confucianism into a religion was given its trappings approximately three-quarters of a century before Thomas Aquinas (1224–1274) systematized classical Christian theology in his *Summa Theologica*. In Western civilization, however, there followed the Renaissance, the Reformation, the Enlightenment, and the industrial revolution. In Chinese culture, there were no more innovations until the twentieth century.

THE CONFUCIANISM that post-Communist ideologues are now praising is of course the secular ethic needed to restore the function, if not the essence, of religion after the moral havoc wreaked by nearly half a century of Communism. It is a comprehensive system of rules serving as the basis for interpersonal relations and authority.

Confucianism combined with autocratic politics must guide China through the next fitful stage of reforms, serving a number of stabilizing aims:

- adoption of a conservative ideology that does not cast doubt on the mythical, organic state;
- acceptance without protest of the post-Communist hierarchy;
- provision of rules for family and social relations which guarantee harmony and stability: the son follows the father, the woman the man (at least the majority of them), the student the teacher, the younger their elders, the worker the manager, and so on;
- support for Jiang Zemin's fight against corruption; Confucius' central idea of the "great man," who first sets a good example and then invites others to follow it, serves this purpose perfectly: "If you have honest magistrates instead of corrupt ones, the people will be obedient. If you have corrupt magistrates instead of honest ones, the people will be restless," said Confucius in the *Analects*.

Confucianism can also serve to cement together Greater China, an obvious bridge between the authoritarian political culture on the mainland and the liberal one on Taiwan.

But there are also risks involved in using Confucianism to legitimize Communism. Confucius opposed oppression and pleaded for love of one's fellow man, lessons that the Communists have not taken to heart. Confucianism also dictates the duty of a morally righteous government to be accountable for its actions. Confucius' most important epigone, Mencius, taught that the people had the right, even the duty, to bring about the downfall of a degenerate ruler. Communists have preventive medicine for this contingency. They make mistakes and cause catastrophes, but "the party is great and cannot be toppled, because it corrects its own mistakes."

During the leftist tide of 1996, Confucianism was again criticized as "un-scientific, feudal, and conservative," and neo-Confucianism was declared unfit to play a role in the campaign for spiritual civilization, which could only be guided by Marxism.[16]

IN SINGAPORE, Southeast Asia's overwhelmingly ethnic Chinese city-state, Confucianism has become the antidote to Western evangelism, which attempts to impose liberal democracy and human rights as a universal political philosophy. Because of its large corps of eloquent, English-speaking politicians, educated in the West and hardened by patriarch Lee Kuan Yew, Singapore has taken the lead in the regional campaign for Asian (Confucianist) values and against decadent Western values. Articles appear regularly in the *International Herald Tribune* and academic magazines written by ethnic-Chinese and ethnic-Indian Singaporeans who confidently present the West, especially the United States, with a series of warnings to put their own house in order before sending American government officials to Asia's capitals with a long list of demands, telling them how to run their countries.

China is fighting the same battle in the diplomatic-political arena that Singapore is fighting in the press, using Confucianist phraseology such as order, discipline, and the prevalence of the collective good over individual good in order to reject Western interference in domestic affairs and Western universalism in the field of human rights. Considering the lyricism with which Chinese leaders and intellectuals have sung the praises of superior Confucianism as the ideal, universal, nonreligious humanism that will replace Western culture in the twenty-first century as the dominant world culture, it is quite possible that, in a few decades, China will claim the leadership of an East Asian Confucianist coalition that will include Korea, Taiwan, Malaysia, Singapore, the overseas Chinese, and perhaps Vietnam as well. George Yeo, Singapore's minister of information and culture, spoke of "the rebirth of a common East Asian consciousness" and predicted that with the economic growth of the region, it would become a "cultural renaissance of historical significance."

It is still an open question whether this new East Asian culture will have any real content and whether neo-Confucianism will be more than just rituals and slogans for neonationalist, neoauthoritarian propaganda. Skeptics consider the region too diverse to project coherent political and social values.

It is even more doubtful whether the much-discussed scenario of the American political scientist Samuel Huntington—a "Confucian-Islamic connection that will challenge Western interests, values, and power"[17]—will become a reality (see Chapter 1). The network of military supplier-client relations between China on the one hand and Iran, Iraq, Libya, Algeria, and Pakistan on the other is too opportunistic and ad hoc, and Islam too divided internally, to constitute a strategic threat to the West. China does not share the militant, religiously motivated hatred of the West harbored by many Muslim groups. After all the humiliations it has suffered since the middle of the nineteenth century, the Chinese regime is only frustrated that it is still not taken seriously, especially by the United States, as a new, equal superpower.

DURING THE SUMMER and fall of 1996, China experienced its most sustained outburst of anti-Americanism since the "anti-imperialist" mass rallies of the Mao era. The immediate cause was President Clinton's dispatch of two naval battle groups to the seas around Taiwan to stabilize the confidence crisis resulting from the relentless Chinese military maneuvers around the island. Many Chinese perceived the arrival of the two aircraft carriers to be the culmination of a series of orchestrated maneuvers on the part of the United States to frustrate China's rise as a great power. The first was the U.S. congressional resolution in 1993 opposing China's bid to host the Olympic Games in the year 2000. This was followed by heightened U.S. interference in human rights issues, particularly in Tibet; its continuing arms sales to Taiwan; the U.S.-led campaign to impose strict conditions on China's entry into the World Trade Organization; and the strengthening of security ties with Japan and other countries in the region, which was seen as a budding "anti-China club."

Amid this furor, a whole series of anti-American books were published during the summer of 1996, virulently attacking the United States' hegemonistic policies around the world, as well as Japan's economic imperialism and its inability to come to terms with its criminal war past.[18] Most inflammatory of all was China's warning to the United States that if it entered into one more confrontation on the Taiwan issue, another wall would have to be built in Washington, higher and wider than the one built for the dead of the Vietnam War, with many more names engraved on it of those young Americans who perished in the Taiwan Strait. "We deeply believe this Great Wall will be the graveyard of America's soul," wrote Song Qiang in the best-selling polemic *China Can Say No*.[19] He warned the American military that China is not Iraq. In an interview with a Singapore newspaper, the authors said that they had been inspired by Russia's erratic ultranationalist Vladimir

Zhirinovsky. The book was described in most of the American media as the high noon of China's rabid new nationalism, though this assessment was based not on a reading of it but on brief interviews with the authors. On close examination, however, it was more of a counterattack on American China bashing than a manifestation of Chinese nationalist assertiveness. If Chinese nationalism exists, it is warped, negative, and defensive. There is nothing of the militant, messianic nationalism, based on racial superiority, that gripped Germany and Japan before the world wars. The book's central theme as printed on the blurb is that when the Chinese say "No," they are not courting confrontation, but are seeking dialogue in an atmosphere of greater equality.

The authors stridently attack the U.S. administration for its insensitivity toward China in general and CIA plots in particular. They even say that the CIA was behind the Mao-debunking book written by the personal physician to the late chairman, Dr. Li Zhisui, and the undercover operations of Chinese-American dissident Harry Wu.

At the same time, they lambaste the fawning attitude toward the United States of many young Chinese who have an inferiority complex and no national self-respect, such as "girls who as children were so good at singing patriotic songs and twenty years later dashed to the embrace of the American white man after smelling his wealth." They also mention a young Chinese husband, studying in the United States, writing to his pregnant wife in China advising her to abort the child, join him happily in America, get pregnant again there, and give birth to an American citizen.[20] The authors themselves were also infatuated with the United States and demonstrated for democracy in 1989, but changed their minds in the course of their studies after learning more about American imperialist bullying, one example being its policy toward Palestine.

They show their respect for the French who burn Hollywood movies, taking that as an inspiration to end "cultural murder" and develop their own Chinese culture.[21] They express their contempt for the Japanese, because their "renaissance" was not self-made but delivered by the sword and armed force of General Douglas MacArthur.[22] Japan is a clone of the United States, alienated from Asia. China has a deep yearning to reinvent its own identity and fully determine its own future.

The book is an anthology of simple, immature polemics and sound bites, with one-liners such as "We don't want MFN!" and "Once we are strong, we will teach you a lesson!" This is grist for the mill of those in the West, Japan, and Southeast Asia who have been propagating the theory of a new Yellow Peril for the last few years.

China Can Say No was obviously endorsed by the regime, although it is unclear at what level. When it made its appearance in the bookstores in June, it was—not surprisingly—praised by the state news agency Xinhua as "fully reflecting popular opinion" on the deep malaise in Sino-American relations, which were not yet on the mend. The process of "putting relations back on track" gained momentum during the fall of 1996, and as this proceeded and Chinese newspapers increasingly criticized the book, the leadership distanced itself from it. Foreign minister Qian Qichen told the French newspaper *Le Figaro* in September that the book's success demonstrated deep popular resistance to pressure from the United States on a range of issues, adding that the youthful authors were "inexperienced in foreign affairs."

In November the Hong Kong daily *Ming Pao* reported that the Central Propaganda Department and the State Press and Publications Administration had criticized the concepts set forth in the book as being "irresponsible," arousing certain "ideological confusion" among readers at home and abroad, and "resulting in negative effects such as interference and impact" on implementation of the foreign policy of the state. According to *Ming Pao,* the book has misled overseas readers, giving the outside world the impression that the nationalist ideological trend in China has grown to the point of fanatic irrationality, which in turn has lead to diplomatic pressure on China, running counter to the authorities' diplomatic strategy of exerting efforts to fight for a peaceful international environment.[23] What the whole episode has shown is that elements in the regime at first toyed with the idea of mobilizing the people to put extra pressure on the United States. When this had unwelcome side effects, it deflected this pressure for a while to Japan, criticizing its reluctance to come to terms with its war past and the rekindling of the dispute over the Diao Yu (Senkaku) Islands by Japanese ultranationalists. As both controversies died down, China's nationalist rage subsided, having revealed itself as largely "man- or regime-made."

A consistent, long-lasting, anti-Western nationalism is difficult to imagine among the apolitical, pragmatic Chinese. It is a reactive mood, not systematic nationalistic thinking, springing from the memories of a century of national humiliation and shame. After the "self-reliance" of the Mao era, the Chinese do not want to be cut off again from Western information, capital, and technology. Their memory of Mao is very selective in this respect, though. For most Chinese, Mao was not the man who isolated China but the one who had the courage to stand up, first to America and then to Russia, and this still fills the Chinese with a deep, primordial pride.

Now that Confucianism is, for the time being, out of favor again and nationalism is considered "a tiger hard to dismount once you ride it,"[24] the most likely scenario is that the top leadership will continue to propagate a cocktail of Marxism, patriotism, and authoritarianism and that the people—if left alone—will practice pragmatism, combined with Confucianism, Western and native religion, and superstition.

CHAPTER 19

Democracy with Chinese Characteristics?

In our country, all the powers belong to the people. This is something that countries in the West can hardly match. We have every reason to state proudly that, compared with Western countries' "tripartite" political system, China's NPC system is much more democratic and superior.

JIANG ZEMIN,
president of China, June 1996

One of the distinctions between democracy and other forms of government is that while democracy is messy on the surface, other forms of government are messy underneath.

DANIEL BOORSTIN,
American historian

IN 1991, shortly after the collapse of the East European Communist regimes in 1989–90 and the dissolution of the Soviet Union, the American scholar Francis Fukuyama presented his neo-Hegelian theory on "the end of history and the last man." He again posed the question that has preoccupied great philosophers for centuries: whether world history has an unequivocal direction, and if so, what its final destination is. His cautious conclusion—following Hegel's example—is that after centuries of slavery, feudalism, theocracy, aristocracy, monarchic despotism, and the great aberrations of Fascism and Communism, the final destination of ideological evolution is liberal democracy, and that a consensus has arisen worldwide that liberal democracy is the most rational political system for humanity. Marx's criticism of Hegel—that his liberal democracy was not capable of resolving class differences—has been rendered obsolete by the monumental failure of Marxism to serve as a basis for humane societies. There are no principles or forms of social and political organization that are superior to liberal democracy. It is the highest synthesis of everything that has gone before and therefore the end of historical dialectics. The statistics are convincing: there were five liberal democracies in the world in 1848, thirteen in 1900, thirty-six in 1960, and sixty-one in 1990.[1] Freedom House, an organization based in New York that has fought for political and civil rights worldwide since 1941, wrote in its annual report in 1993 that there are seventy-five free countries, twenty more than ten years previously. Only 31 percent of the world's population still lived under repressive regimes (two-thirds of whom live in China), 44 percent less than ten years before.

Formerly Communist states in Eastern Europe have again joined the democratic world, post-Communist Russia is in a difficult transitional period, and formerly authoritarian states in East Asia, such as South Korea, Taiwan, and even the oldest satellite of the former Soviet Union, Mongolia, have also become multiparty democracies.

After the suppression of the student rebellion in China in June 1989, numerous Western and Chinese optimists, including the exiled leaders of the rebellion, predicted that the death throes of the Chinese regime were a question of two years at the most, and that then the worldwide democratic tide would also engulf China.[2] Now, eight years after "Tiananmen," the Chinese Communist regime is still—or again—firmly in the saddle and there is no sign that things are going to change in the near future.

During the aftermath of the suppressed "counterrevolution," everything has been attempted—an orthodox-Stalinist restoration in 1989–90, an accelerated breakthrough to the socialist market economy in 1992–93, and, since 1994, slowing down and returning to a conservative, zigzagging policy of ideological sloganeering, repression, and cautious economic reforms. The durable element in all this has been the integration in the region and the world economy, following the so-called East Asian model of economic development, which had been held up as the blueprint before 1989 under the leadership of Premier Zhao Ziyang. The result was the resumption and further increase in high growth, reaching levels of 12 to 13 percent in 1992–94, by which the discredited regime acquired new power and legitimacy.

. . .

MUCH HAS BEEN WRITTEN about the East Asian model that enabled Japan to transform itself within thirty years from a defeated, devastated war zone into an economic superpower and that guided the four tigers—South Korea, Taiwan, Hong Kong, and Singapore—on their path to becoming new industrial countries. What are the most important contrasts now between the four tigers on the one hand and China on the other?

According to authoritative economists, China is approximately twenty years behind the four tigers. China had the disadvantage of its immense size, but the four tigers also had to battle enormous problems at the beginning. Korea was at war until 1953. Taiwan and Hong Kong each had to absorb more than 2 million refugees from Communism. Under the soft authoritarian hand of a British governor, Hong Kong was alone in following the laissez-faire principle of "the best government in the field of economics is the one that does the least." South Korea, Taiwan, and Singapore were rigorously anti-Communist but followed economic policies that were actually socialist in a number of respects, with land reform, large state enterprises, active regulation by the government of income disparities, high rates of saving, far-reaching government protection, support and dirigisme—even in the private sector—as well as a shielded home market. But in contrast to socialist countries and countries with import substitution and political patronage (such as in Latin America), businesses were punished with the loss of government support if they did not become efficient and competitive in the short term on the international market. Foreign (American) aid in the early stages followed by investments from the whole world increased the technological level of the economy, which produced an ever-broader and higher-quality assortment of export products, as well as trade surpluses and currency reserves for imports according to the principles of free trade. For more than twenty years, these four countries achieved annual growth rates of 9 to 10 percent, owing in part to an educational policy that gave the highest priority to training top technocrats.

In China the opposite was the case. First it followed the Soviet model, which, thanks to a high level of state investment, initially achieved high annual growth rates of 7 to 8 percent, allowing the country in a short time to enter the coal and steel age. These growth rates could not be maintained, however, because of low productivity and the increase in population. Instead of improving productivity by means of income differentiation, Mao sought refuge in more state control, egalitarianism, and repression. In 1955 there followed the complete socialization of the economy and everything, except the smallest street vendors, was taken over by the state. Monopoly was considered superior to competition. In 1958 agriculture was completely collectivized into inefficient people's communes. This was followed by Mao's insane, messianic experiments with mass mobilization, the so-called Great Leap Forward, which led to the immense wastage of resources and manpower and ended in famine, killing tens of millions of people. The next stage was a power struggle between neo-Stalinists, including Deng Xiaoping and the utopian Maoists, who advocated complete autarky and even wanted to reinvent the lightbulb themselves instead of importing it. Until Mao's death in 1976, a destructive political battle raged, economic policy—especially regarding investments—swayed back and forth, and education was neglected to a shocking extent. Nevertheless, from the beginning of the Cultural Revolution until Mao's death, there were annual growth rates of 4 to 5 percent. The economy had become increasingly inefficient, however, and the standard of living and level of consumption had not improved.

The big change began within a year after Mao's death. In the summer of 1977, the plain truth finally came out: antiegalitarianism was the name of the new game. Material incentives, such as higher wages for more and better work, were permitted. This immediately led to an increase in growth to between 8 and 9 percent. Gradually the attitude toward foreign trade and investment changed completely. China became a member of the International Monetary Fund (IMF) and the World Bank and, following the example set by the four tigers, opened up special export zones, and foreign trade suddenly grew by more than 20 percent annually. Already in 1985 Harvard economist Dwight H. Perkins had concluded that in 1977 China was at the level where Taiwan and South Korea had stood at the beginning of the 1950s, that the politically dramatic change in course had brought the country closer to the East Asian model, and that, under certain circumstances, there was every reason to expect that China would undergo a socioeconomic transformation that would resemble in a number of respects the change undergone by other East Asian countries.[3] Eight years later (1993), the American banker William Overholt went a step further: "Contemporary China is not another Soviet Union nor the totalitarian state it was in 1966, but rather a gigantic, vintage 1972 South Korea."[4]

Of even more importance for the East Asian model is that with the exception of colonial Hong Kong, the other three small tigers all had dictatorial regimes during their takeoff and high-growth phases—just as China still has today—regimes that admittedly tolerated a number of civil, religious, and especially economic freedoms, but that were very restrictive and repressive with regard to political freedoms, such as the right of association and assembly, or freedom of speech. Until the second half of the 1980s, South Korea and Taiwan had undemocratic, authoritarian regimes. With the increase in prosperity, the increase in per capita income to about $4,000, and the establishment of a well-educated middle class, political pluralism and the formation of a multiparty system could no longer be blocked. Now that it is following many aspects of the strategy for economic development of the three tigers, will China also follow their political scenario and become a politically pluralistic society in twenty to twenty-five years? In short, will China develop according to Hegel's universal law, recently reformulated by Fukuyama, and celebrate "the end of history" as a liberal democracy and not as a Communist utopia?

There is a whole range of reasons to assume that China will ultimately develop one variation or another on Western democracy, but there are perhaps even more factors that will impede that process, keeping China for an indefinite period at the stage of authoritarianism. An authoritarianism that can be very flexible economically, but that in the political realm will at best alternate cycles of (selective) tolerance with repression.

In three of the four tigers, general elections have already been held for years, albeit with mixed rules and results. Owing to the unique colonial situation in Hong Kong and the initially invisible but now highly visible hand of China, the development of the political system there has been blocked. Twice already in South Korea, direct presidential elections have been held which have ousted the ruling party. In Taiwan the first high-profile, direct presidential election was held in the spring of 1996, and parliamentary elections have led to the continual shrinking of the majority of the ruling Kuomintang—to such an extent, in fact, that a changing of the guard by the opposition is no longer unimaginable.

IN SINGAPORE the longtime patriarch Lee Kuan Yew resigned as prime minister in 1991, but he still wields a great deal of power behind the scenes like a new Deng Xiaoping, Singapore style. The democratic and electoral systems are organized in such a way that the ruling People's Action party will never lose its overwhelming majority in the eighty-one-member parliament. The opposition has never even won more than four seats. Singapore is the best example among the tigers of another Huntington theory, that of the "dominant party system," in which one party is permanently in power. South Korea was the first to give up this system, followed by Japan, and in Taiwan the system has begun to falter. Singapore is essentially a meritocracy, in which the power of capable bureaucrats is legitimized by electoral means, without the existence of complete democratic freedoms. It is paternalistic, hierarchical, and authoritarian. Order and discipline prevail over individual freedom. In essence it is a one-party state, but Singapore differs from China in that it is modern, efficient, and not corrupt—ideals that are still far from being realized in China.

The political culture in China is in many respects a protoversion of Singapore. But considering that Singapore is, quantitatively speaking, only the equivalent of a medium-sized Chinese city, it is questionable whether the Singapore model is relevant for a continental country like China. Zhao Baojiang, mayor of the Chinese city of Wuhan with 7 million people, once spoke to me with tears in his eyes about the order, discipline, and hygiene in Singapore. "That city is run better than American or even German cities," said Zhao. A Chinese banker once referred in a conversation with me to his rejection of South Korea as a model. "That means instability and periodic battles in the streets. Since the one big battle in 1989, China has no longer experienced that." The Chinese media—just like their counterparts in Singapore—also refer with sarcasm and contempt to Taiwan's democracy with its mafia influence, money politics, vote buying, and routine fistfights in parliament. In short, Hong Kong is a colonial antimodel that never reached maturity, and South Korea and Taiwan are chaotic copies of the West. Singapore seems like an ideal combination of liberal economic policies and paternalistic authoritarianism, not in a transitional phase on its way to liberal democracy, but a model and end in itself and, as such, a rival to liberal democracy.[5]

The Singapore government's agenda—strict political control; far-reaching censorship; efficient and honest government; extremely severe but open administration of justice; the state as guardian of morals and family values, using legislative measures to force children to support their aging parents and to keep divorce, illegitimate children, and crime to a minimum; and, above all, a self-conscious and unwavering rejection of Western, and especially American, hectoring—is an advanced version of what Chinese leaders and perhaps a majority of the people see as the best blueprint for the future.[6]

A Chinese magazine, *Liaowang* (Outlook), presented Singapore's war with the Western media as an example for China. The magazine wrote approvingly about the antilibel suits and other sanctions taken by the government of Singapore against the *International Herald Tribune* and others and recommended that China deal with the BBC in the same way because of its documentary—in cooperation with the Chinese-American dissident Harry Wu—about China's commercial transplantation of the organs of executed criminals.[7]

It is very much a question whether the next generation of leaders and citizens of Singapore will continue to see paternalistic authoritarianism as the ultimate goal, or whether they will also prefer a more flexible form of political-social postmodernism. A much more important question is whether the perfectionism that works on the miniature scale of Singapore can be successfully magnified five hundred times to the scale required by China.

THERE ARE MANY ARGUMENTS against democratization in China, some of them subjective arguments put forward by its rulers, who want to preserve the status quo at all costs, some of them objective arguments expounded by foreigners. To begin with, the Communist party has spasmodically clung to Marxism-Leninism and ideological sloganeering, utopianism, or ideals, but it is purely and simply a closed system of power monopolized by a privileged oligarchy that cannot afford to democratize because this would mean losing its privileges. The Chinese ruling class is, furthermore, inherently and fundamentally antidemocratic. It will never permit the masses to make the wrong choice. Sun Yat-sen argued that the educational level of poor Chinese was too low for democracy and that they must first be placed under the tutelage of strong leaders who would then educate them in democracy. Even the Communist party takes the position that it is the vanguard that has been chosen to rule. The party says that the people lack a civic consciousness, which they blame on the people, not on themselves. The party says it will prepare the people for socialist democracy. The party also rejects the arguments of intellectuals that the rise of a middle class can form the social basis of a democratic system. Private entrepreneurs cannot be considered a middle class.

Under no circumstances does Chinese political culture accept the idea of a loyal opposition. Referring to Wei Jingsheng, Deng Xiaoping said that a loyal opposition does not exist. Opposition means the power to sabotage. A multiparty system would undermine the country's unity. In such a system, the country's power cannot join forces. If the absolute power of the Communist party is not accepted by everyone, China will sink back into discord and chaos. Supervision is not necessary. The party has made serious mistakes, but it has always corrected them itself. Since 1989 the party has become completely obsessed with the idea that any political change will destabilize the country. In 1994 the practice of democratic centralism, which had been out of use since 1987, was reinstated. It is defined as "the integration of centralism based on democracy with democracy under the guidance of centralism. . . . Centralism means the concentration of the will and wisdom of the whole party and its concerted action . . . , so that there is discipline and freedom, unity of purpose, personal peace of mind, and vitality."[8] In practice, it all boils down to dictatorship by acclamation.

Deng Xiaoping permitted the limited liberalization of 1984–88 under Hu Yaobang (and Zhao Ziyang) not as an in-between stage toward democratization, but in order to promote economic growth, thereby strengthening the absolute power of the party. Deng Xiaoping believed that a combination of growth in prosperity and repression would bring long-term stability to China.

Other arguments insist that the alternative structures necessary for the transition to democracy are completely lacking in China. There are no alternative centers of power in China, such as the church and labor unions in Eastern Europe. All (weak) independent and private organizations and firms were completely eliminated during the Mao era. The dissident movement is weak and divided, and has been decimated by constant waves of repression. Since 1989 most of the quasi-independent institutions that came into being during the "liberal" 1980s have been disbanded, such as think tanks of private businesses and independent intellectuals.

Overly hasty democratization in China would also be dangerous, perhaps plunging the country into total chaos, and, according to an apocalyptic vision Deng Xiaoping had in 1990, would cause an exodus of hundreds of millions of refugees, which would threaten the stability of the entire region and even the whole world. Democratization and national elections would furthermore lead to the independence of Tibet and Xinjiang, perhaps to be followed by further disintegration of the multiethnic continental empire. Moreover, elections are no guarantee that democracy will be the result. In times of social unrest, growing inequality, and political uncertainty, it could be the enemies of democracy that climb to power.

Another aspect unique to China is that democracy is still the aspiration of only a minority of intellectuals and up-and-coming businessmen. There is still no mass demand for it. A democratic culture or climate scarcely exists. The large majority of Chinese still accept as natural the "mandate of heaven," the Chinese version of the Western divine right, on the basis of which the king has the right to rule and the subjects have the duty to obey. The silent majority of Chinese are passive, docile, and bend like bamboo in the wind. The liberalization of the mid-1980s was a gift from magnanimous leaders, not a codified right.[9] Historically, there is no democratic precedent. Chinese tradition is despotic and proto-totalitarian. The political reformer Liang Qichao wrote in 1903, "The Chinese possess not one of the qualifications necessary for the citizens of a republic."[10] Since then, things have changed somewhat, but neither the Kuomintang regime (1928–49) nor the Communists (1949 to the present) have done much to promote the civic consciousness of the population. The Chinese do not know and have never known what Alexis de Tocqueville called *l'art de l'association,* from the bottom up."

It is, moreover, a question whether China has the economic conditions that will culminate in a modern political "neoauthoritarian alternative" that will usher in the transition to democracy. The essential difference between China and the small tigers is that a partial market economy has come into being only recently and that it is based not on a free market but on post-Communist networks of political connections. The four tigers owed their earlier high rates of growth to market-friendly policies, excellent macro-economic management that ensured stability for private investments, and a highly educated technocratic elite. In China all this is still fragile and inconsistent, there is no competitive climate for private enterprises, the private sector is much too small, and the modern class of professionals trained in the market economy is still negligible."

Prompting change from the outside is very problematic in China's case, considering its size and unwieldiness. Several wars, military defeats, and Euro-American occupations were necessary to transplant democracy to capitalist Germany and Japan. It is doubtful whether China will become democratic and modern as a result of internal, more or less peaceful capitalist development. American engagement and pressure have had a stimulating effect on the process of democratization in South Korea and Taiwan. More so than his predecessors, President Bill Clinton has made the expansion of democracy and human rights the cornerstone of American foreign policy, but in the case of China it has so far backfired. Former prime minister Lee Kuan Yew of Singapore, who regularly acts as China's international advocate, said, "The customs and values of four thousand years of Chinese statecraft cannot be swept away just like that by outsiders, and certainly not by resolutions passed by the American Congress."

In conclusion, numerous East Asians are not convinced that America's extremely polarized democracy is the best political system in the world or even that is has any universal value at all. For decades high economic growth under authoritarian regimes has proved that democracy is not a basic condition for this, just as it is not a prerequisite for a market economy. American democratic evangelism often has a counterproductive effect, strengthening not the democratic forces but, in the case of China, negative nationalism and repression.

THE LIST OF ARGUMENTS against democratization is not complete and could be expanded with more abstract and historical substantiation. The series of arguments in favor of democratization is partly the mirror image of the arguments against it, though much harder and more specific. The process of substantiating these arguments is creeping along or else overtly under way.

Deng Xiaoping was the last emperor of China. He was less powerful than Mao, but his instructions carried the weight of imperial decrees, based on his personal authority, which was the twentieth-century version of the "mandate of heaven." Many Chinese intellectuals think that if the Tiananmen debacle of 1989 had not occurred, then Deng himself, like President Chiang Ching-kuo of Taiwan, would have initiated political liberalization before his death. Since Deng's death, in the absence of a new strongman, a pattern of collective, pluralist authority has arisen. Its power is no longer due to a great revolutionary personality, but to consensus, increasing constitutionalism, and proceduralism. This will not lead to liberalization or democratization immediately, but to a shift away from "rule by men" and toward the rule of law (*fazhi daiti renzhi*). At the same time, China will remain a repressive, politically unreformed one-party state, but economic developments outside the old state system (*tizhi-wai de jingji-fazhan*) have drastically weakened the power of the party over society, while considerably strengthening the autonomy of the individual, the family, business, and local authorities. A majority of top leaders are in favor of more economic reforms, which will continue to generate impulses for further liberalization. Political liberalization from the bottom up is in full swing and is more important for people than democratization and the right to vote. Economic and administrative power has been decentralized to such an extent and the fight for jurisdiction between higher and lower levels of government is such that the chance of high-handedness has been reduced across the board. Legal protection of the individual is still woefully inadequate, but a series of libel suits against well-known people, such as the ex-minister of culture Wang Meng and the dissident journalist Dai Qing, has done much to improve the legal consciousness of the average citizen and has reminded the state to be more cautious.[13]

The new middle class of free entrepreneurs, more highly educated employees of foreign firms, independent intellectuals, and civil society are on the upswing. For the time being, the middle class is satisfied with its material share of high economic growth, but sooner or later it will demand better education, more information, and the freedom to establish its own political party. The regime can try to suppress this, but only at the cost of economic growth and progress. China is trying by means of high tariffs to limit access to the Internet and has blocked a number of Web sites, but many Chinese have found ways around this. The censors have not been successful in limiting the number of satellite dishes either.

For the next five or ten years, the command posts of the Chinese government will still be manned by "Soviet alumni," such as Jiang Zemin and Li Peng, who were trained in Moscow in the early 1950s. But at the same time, as in Taiwan and South Korea in the 1980s, a younger generation, many with doctorates from American universities, will begin to occupy positions of economic and political power, which will cause the political system to open further.

FOR SEVERAL YEARS ALREADY, Western sinologists have been debating whether the radically altered Chinese society is already a civil society, defined in sociological terms as the emergence of an autonomous sphere of voluntary associations, capable of organizing the interests of emergent socioeconomic groups and counterbalancing the hitherto unchallenged dominance of the Marxist-Leninist state.[14] Until the twilight years of the last imperial dynasty, China had a tradition of state omnipotence (*quan-neng zhu-yi*), and it was only at the beginning of the twentieth century that autonomous social and cultural organizations began to spring up. These were so weak, however, that they did not survive the state of emergency during the war against Japan. After "liberation" in 1949, the remnants of feudal state omnipotence expanded into rigorous, modern totalitarianism. The minimum amount of civil society that did exist was completely usurped by the totalitarian one-party state. The dividing line between society and the state disappeared entirely. During the Deng era, the rise of economic pluralism has created the conditions for the rebirth of a civil society. The ever greater diversity of tasks in the more complex society geared toward the market economy is too much for the manpower and financial resources of the government, and more and more has to be entrusted to private firms in the service sector and nongovernmental organizations (NGOs) working on behalf of the environment, consumers, women, mental health, private schools, and so on. The NGOs remain hybrid semisatellite organizations of the state, however, even though they operate in a gray zone of increasing state indifference. The government has its own environmental protection organ, but nonetheless permitted the independent organization Friends of Nature to be formed in 1994. Intellectuals view the group as a "discussion salon for 'subpolitical' problems." In 1994 the well-known dissident Dai Qing received an American prize for her activism against the Three Gorges Dam on the Yangtze River and spent the money on a piece of land, a "special environmental zone," where children are urged to plant trees. Environmental activists try to work internationally, but joining Greenpeace is problematic, as witnessed by the suppression of the recent Greenpeace demonstration in Tiananmen Square against Chinese nuclear tests.

In the publishing world, there are also the first signs of autonomy. State publishing companies are deep in the red because there is no market for the many titles they publish. Independent agents are hired by writers to employ dubious methods to buy state registration numbers (like ISBN numbers), enabling them, through their own gray channels of distribution, to bring books to market which are instantly sold out before they can be censored. In this way, the book *Bloody Snow* came on the market, which tells a much bloodier version of the Communist campaigns in the 1940s than the story recounted by party historians.

Existing state religious organizations are trying to extricate themselves from the state's yoke. The Catholic Patriotic Association employs passive resistance toward bishops who are imposed on them by the state and works more and more with the underground, pro-Vatican church. In the summer of 1993, the bishop of Yichang in the central province of Hubei said that the regime is deeply concerned about the powerful attraction of the church. Since the restoration of limited religious tolerance in 1978, only seven of the sixty churches have been restored to his diocese. The regime is acutely worried that if it were to allow the reopening of more, if not all, churches, the church would become uncontrollable.[15] Estimates of the growth of the Christian churches are very difficult to make, but according to the international Christian organizations "China Ministries International" and "Church in China Research" in Hong Kong, there are at least 50 million Protestants of various denominations. Caritas Hong Kong estimates the number of Catholics to be 20 million. That is considerably higher than the membership of the Communist party, and among party members only a small number are "practicing" Communists! Buddhist and Taoist temples, qigong (natural healing) societies, and secret societies play an increasingly important role in social work and mutual aid.

Hot lines for everyday marriage problems and help desks for computer quandaries fill an enormous gap in society that the government cannot begin to deal with. There are more than three hundred of these hot lines in the whole country, and some of them receive foreign aid, from the American Ford Foundation as well as others. Tony Saich, representative of the Ford Foundation in China, said in the fall of 1995 that legislation was pending which would no longer require unofficial organizations to be an appendix of an official state organ (*gua-gou dan-wei*), but in the resurrected leftist climate of 1996, there has been continuous backtracking and strict controls have been reimposed.[16]

One of the most sensitive organizations is the Committee for Japanese Reparations, which since 1990 has formed a network on a nationwide scale to underline its demands for compensation for personal losses sustained during the war, by means of demonstrations in front of the Japanese embassy and other methods. The government is deeply troubled by this, not only because it is adamantly opposed to demonstrations no matter what the cause, but also because in diplomatic accords with Japan it has renounced all claims to reparations in exchange for bilateral help for the state. The committee is becoming increasingly assertive and, after much government obstruction, has already sent a delegation of fifteen war victims to Japan to submit claims worth 200 million yen. The government must proceed with the utmost caution, because thwarting citizens in their attempts to right Japanese war crimes is anathema to a regime that has declared itself the savior of the Chinese nation. The government is all the more nervous because the committee is an organization with broad objectives and is trying to use Japan's past war record as a tactic to promote its strategic goal of democracy.

SYSTEMATIC DEBATES on reforming the political structure at the national level have not been held in Chinese political circles, academic forums, or the media since 1986. The need for political reform continues to be underlined periodically, but specific proposals have been only partial and fragmentary. Before the suppression of the student rebellion in 1989, there had already been repeated suggestions by members of the National People's Congress to reduce the membership (currently 2,900) drastically, to hold more than one annual plenary session lasting two to three weeks, and to permit the members to devote more time to their work—in other words, evolution in the direction of a professional parliament in the Western sense, one that supervises, investigates, corrects, and takes initiatives.

In 1991 the elderly but reformist chairman of the National People's Congress, Wan Li, suggested the drafting of a Supervision Law that would give the People's Congress well-defined authority to supervise the State Council, or cabinet. The bill was stillborn, however, because it was reportedly vetoed by party leader Jiang Zemin. The harangue delivered by Jiang stated that China should not practice Western-style division of powers and that there would be no question about it as long as he was in office.[17]

Arguments in favor persisted, however, especially in semi-independent newspapers in Guangdong. Commentaries and newspaper articles by well-known, non-Communist politicians, professors of social science, and economists demanded not only that a system of supervision be introduced within the Communist party, but also that an independent system outside it be established, to monitor the National People's Congress (NPC), the Chinese People's Political Consultative Conference (CPPCC), and the media. "Otherwise corruption would never be curtailed."[18] The party, however, still mindful of 1989, was in no mood to give in, because it was afraid that everyone now asking for supervision would try at a later stage to shunt the party to the sidelines. Jiang Zemin nevertheless stressed yet more strongly that "anticorruption campaigns must remain the party's internal affair . . . , because the Western powers have never abandoned their strategy of peaceful evolution and are trying to confuse us and to undermine the construction of our socialism. We must therefore press ahead in our fight against peaceful evolution and against *liang-hua* [literally, twice *hua*] means, *xi-hua* [a code word for total Westernization], and *fen-hua* [the splitting of the country]."[19]

At the same time, the CPPCC, the umbrella organization of the eight so-called "democratic" (satellite) parties (see Chapter 1), was striving to strengthen its supervisory and monitoring influence under the leadership of the Communist party. The assertiveness of the NPC and the CPPCC has been most strongly expressed since 1989 by their opposition to the construction of the controversial Three Gorges Dam on the Yangtze River. Prominent professors who were members of the CPPCC introduced amendments in 1990 that delayed the plan for two years, and when it was finally accepted in 1992, 177 members of the NPC voted against it and 664 abstained. In 1995 this record was beaten when only 1,746 of the 2,752 representatives approved the candidacy of Jiang Chunyun for the vice-premiership. Many from his own province of Shandong let it be known that as governor and party secretary he had neglected provincial interests to ingratiate himself with the central government. Others said that he had too little education and intellect and that he was too old—he was sixty-four years old at the time—to take on responsibility for the nation's agriculture. A third reason was that there were already three vice-premiers from the central bureaucracy, one from Shanghai and now another one from Shanghai, Wu Bangguo. Guangdong and the inland provinces claimed the two extra vice-premierships but received nothing. Large numbers of them therefore got even by voting against Jiang Chunyun. It was a result that any politician in a parliamentary democracy would have been satisfied with, but in the immature Chinese political culture of docile acceptance, unanimity, and acclamation, it was disgraceful. After the vote, the new vice-premier, Jiang Chunyun, was a damaged, shaken man.

. . .

No one criticized the political "child psychology" of the Chinese people's representatives more sharply than the first vice-chairman of the People's Congress, Tian Jiyun. He did this during the 1995 session in a speech to the representatives of Guangdong Province, who are the most freewheeling in the country. "The comrades in the National People's Congress have no guts. They're afraid of stepping on people's toes.... Usually we're wild about toadyism or else deaf to criticism." Tian complained that the Supervision Law had been pending for years but that no one dared to cut the knot. "If the law becomes as slippery as an eel instead of as sharp as a knife, then it won't help us at all.... If we ratify a Supervision Law, it should be an effective one." Tian also lamented the opposition to voting for officials from among a range of candidates vying for one seat or post. "We Chinese find this unacceptable.... If there are five candidates for four posts as vice-governor, then one of them must lose. The defeated candidate is then so ashamed that he never shows his face again. Chinese provinces, with their populations of tens of millions of people, are the equivalent of big countries. In foreign countries there is also competition at elections, with several candidates competing for the jobs of president and vice-president. Only one can win. The defeated candidate still thinks it was an honor to be allowed to compete. This must become the trend [in China]."

Tian proceeded to criticize the elderly, and to do this you have to be sure of yourself. This has, after all, cost a number of young leaders their heads, or more recently, their jobs. Tian himself is sixty-six and therefore still young! He said that many retired ministers, ambassadors, governors, and other senior officials automatically become vice-chairman, committee chairman, or a member of the Standing Committee of the National People's Congress or the Political Consultative Conference. "But we have to get younger people on the Standing Committee instead of filling all the posts with elders. All you see is a lot of light shining on all those bald heads if you sit on one of the back benches and look at all the people. We have to put people with black hair among them," said Tian. (One typical aberration in Chinese political culture is that many leaders dye their hair black, mostly with dye of very bad quality. If you see President Jiang Zemin or the foreign minister Qian Qichen, it looks as though they sprinkle a pot of ink over their heads every day.) Lastly, Tian also recommended making bills available months ahead of time instead of at the beginning of the session. "To tell you the truth, considering our cultural level, we can't identify problems by leafing through a bill once or twice, unprepared. It is not only a question of cultural level, but also of procedures. We must set deadlines for research and consultation. If we do that consistently, set up a supervision mechanism, and promulgate the Supervision Law, then the role of the People's Congress with flourish."

For years newspaper readers have been used to experienced, critical foreign journalists reporting on the sessions of Congress in this way, but to hear such a story coming from the mouth of the senior vice-chairman of the Congress itself gives one hope. This speech was not published in the Chinese domestic media, however, only in the pro-Communist *Wen Wei Po* in Hong Kong.[20] The effect of Tian Jiyun's performance was what you could call "creating a democratic climate," such as existed from 1985 to 1987 under Hu Yaobang and Zhao Ziyang. Admittedly, it is not institutionalized and can therefore easily be swept away, but it is nevertheless a good sign. Tian Jiyun used to be a close colleague of Zhao Ziyang's and has a consistent service record as a reformer. He is also known for his forceful speeches. In 1991, when the to-do about a Stalinist restoration was at its height, he suggested creating a "special leftist zone" for ideological cave dwellers, where, waving their Little Red Books, they could once again pursue class struggle, turn one another in, work in a centrally planned economy, and stand in line with ration coupons for scarce goods of bad quality. The relatively young Tian seems to be the right man to succeed the current colorless, but nonetheless reformist, chairman of the Congress, the seventy-one-year-old Qiao Shi, and to speed up the legislative process in a liberal direction.

The session of the National People's Congress of March 1996 was completely overshadowed by the saber rattling in the Taiwan Strait and by nationalist outbursts against the American dispatch of aircraft carriers. Tian Jiyun's "democratic climate" had completely subsided. One Congress delegate discreetly expressed her worries that Tian will never succeed the current low-key chairman, Qiao Shi, because Jiang Zemin considers him far too liberal.

THE FACTOR that perhaps offers the best prospects for democracy in China in the distant or not-so-distant future is the systematic way in which democratization is now taking place at the lowest level in the countryside. In November 1987 the "Organization Law of the People's Republic of China for Villagers' Committees" was adopted, and since 1988 the population of the two lowest administrative levels, the hamlet (*zhen*) and the village (*xiang* = small rural municipality), have been voting directly on an experimental basis for committees of villagers (*cunmin weiyuanhui*) and village chiefs (*cun-zhang*). Above this level there are indirect elections. The committees elect rural county councils (*xian*). These councils elect Municipal People's Congresses, the Municipal People's Congresses elect the Provincial People's Congress, and they in turn elect the National People's Congress. The Communist party plays an influential but not always dominant role in who does or does not get elected. Wang Zhenyao, the young deputy director of the department of basic administration in the ministry of civil affairs, said at a seminar in the spring of 1995 that around the year 2000 there would be general village democracy in China. Wang went on to say that between 1988 and 1994 at least one election had taken place in all of China's more than 1 million villages—1,004,349 to be precise—although standardized procedures do not yet exist. In the places where there were several candidates for village chief, in the case of reelections, 20 percent of the incumbent potentates were voted out of office. In several provinces, 50 percent of the chairmen chosen by the village committees were non-Communists: in the prefecture of Zaozhuang in Shandong, 50.7 percent of the 3,049; in all of Fujian, 51.2 percent of the 11,913 villages. Ten percent of the elected village heads are independent entrepreneurs who have the skills necessary to preserve a balance between the competing interest groups in a pluralist economy. The average age of the committee members elected was forty, and 70 percent of the members had more than nine years of education. According to the Organization Law, the Villagers' Committee, which usually has seven members, should have at least one woman among them. Turnout is generally above 80 percent and in some places even as high as 100 percent.[21]

Wang Zhenyao explained that basic self-government must have priority in the strategy to develop democracy in China. "Basic democracy has to do with interest relations, not with liberal slogans. Democracy that is unconnected to the interests of villagers will not lead to a healthy democratic system."[22] Wang Zhenyao believes in the power of village democracy because both the state and the party have little power in the rural areas. During the Mao era, the party secretaries in the villages—which at that time were called production teams—were small emperors who ruled over every aspect of life. But since the rise of a pluralist economy, there has been less and less for them to do—so little, in fact, that they have become entrepreneurs themselves. Moreover, village democracy has been well received only in developed areas, where the first signs of a differentiation in class structure already exist.

Especially in the richer villages on the coast, party organizations continue to exist only in name. During a visit to three villages in the former county (now promoted to city) of Zhaoyuan in the coastal province of Shandong, I was told in the summer of 1994 that the party committees still have only three tasks: keeping tabs on the one-child rule, determining the grain quota that peasants are required to sell to the state, and resolving conflicts between villagers.

Of great significance in this context is the decision made by the Party Central Committee at its plenary session in November 1994—"Decision Regarding Some Important Questions Concerning the Strengthening of Party Construction"—by which the party tried to take away with one hand what it had just given with the other. Although the party realized its own inadequacy and permitted elections to take place at the grassroots level, it strove fiercely to rebuild the power it had lost. One year earlier, party leader Jiang Zemin had said at a National Agricultural Conference in October 1993, "Most of the cadres at the base are good, but some party organizations are incompetent, lax, or half-paralyzed; some regions take more from the peasants than they give, and relations between the cadres and the masses are tense. If we don't change this situation quickly, the rural economy will not be able to develop. Moreover, it will endanger stability and cause the foundation of our state and party in the countryside to become shaky."

The party plenum in October 1994 announced the decision to rebuild party cells at the grassroots level, but Chinese intellectuals say that it is a lost battle. Family clans, the mafia, and other secret and religious societies have taken the place of the party in large areas of the countryside. The vice-minister of civil affairs, Yan Mingfu, sketched the situation very aptly in the fall of 1995 when he accidentally mentioned to an international economist that the party ranks in the countryside consisted only of "three old men with five teeth."

During the annual session of the National People's Congress in 1995, the Electoral and Organization Law was ratified, which provides for elections in rural municipalities and at the county level, one level higher than that regulated in 1988–94. The director of the Legislative Commission of the NPC, Qiao Xiaoyang, said a few months later that the people's congresses should not compete with the Communist party, considering that the supreme position of the party had been laid down in the constitution. This means that the people's congresses and village chiefs will indeed become more influential, but that the party secretaries will remain number one.

The trend has been set for the gradual introduction of elections at higher levels (city, prefecture, and province). In a briefing before the international media, Wang Zhenyao repeated the vision of Deng Xiaoping, pronounced in 1987, that within fifty years [!] general elections would be held in China.[23]

. . .

THERE IS, HOWEVER, a fundamental counterforce to large-scale democratization, which is formulated differently from "the third eye" but boils down to the same thing: peasant phobia. The April 1992 number of *China Spring,* a monthly put out by exiled dissidents in New York, published an article by Hua Sheng, adviser-in-exile to deposed party leader Zhao Ziyang: "In China's present circumstances the principle of democracy means that the peasants will have the ultimate decision-making power. But this is unacceptable to China's existing interest structure, i.e., the urban intellectual elite." Peasant dynamism (township and village enterprises) is a decisive factor in China's high economic growth and threatens not only the urban bureaucrats but also the urban intellectual aristocracy. For this reason, a new layer of leadership must be created made up of urban and rural intellectuals. While some intellectuals will perhaps switch allegiance to the privileged classes to maintain the status quo, others will undoubtedly support the peasant class. Large numbers of well-educated rural youth will become active leaders who will use their talent and entrepreneurial abilities to bring about democratic changes. The peasant class has many conservative, negative qualities, such as cultural underdevelopment, superstition, and secret societies, which could become important obstacles to social reconstruction. The rise of such phenomena, however, also means the weakening of the Communist dictatorship. If secret societies begin to operate openly, there will no longer be any effective way to prevent other political groups from organizing themselves and taking action. Village elections will probably lead sooner rather than later to the formation of political groups or parties, for example, the Peasant Entrepreneurs party, the Peasant Veterans of the People's Liberation Army, the Transmigrants, and similar groups. They will represent real political power.

The fact that urbanites are apprehensive about this makes the whole spectrum of democratization much more complex, less readily acceptable, and certainly less urgent. The conclusion is that the Communist party is not the only obstacle to democratization. Its silent partner is the class of urban intellectuals who prefer to wait until the fragile, incomplete transitional society has become more balanced and real political reforms can begin.

Afterword to the Vintage Edition

CATHARSIS

THE YEAR 1997 was a momentous and cathartic one for China. Lingering fixations on long-awaited landmark events ended when retired patriarch Deng Xiaoping's oft-reported death finally occurred on February 19 and when the Hong Kong handover was completed on July 1. Both events compelled the country to reflect anew on how to deal with rapidly changing situations, both domestically and globally. The Fifteenth Congress of the Communist Party in September enabled President and General Secretary Jiang Zemin to step out of the long shadow cast by Deng, ushering in a new era and wave of Dengist economic reforms. U.S.–China relations, after seven troubled years since the Tiananmen crackdown of 1989, has stabilized and continued to improve, but whether a new strategic partnership will take shape in the aftermath of Jiang Zemin's U.S. visit remains to be seen.

The death of Deng Xiaoping was a non-event in political terms. Deng's role as a semiretired "imperial father" behind the scenes had virtually ended in 1992 when his "Southern Whirlwind Tour" had rekindled economic reform, culminating in an unprecedented bout of rapid economic growth. Having already vanished almost completely from the scene, his physical demise merely marked the continuation of Dengism without Deng. Continuity was the watchword.

One of the most telling episodes during this period was a speech by the director of the *People's Daily,* who expounded that Deng Xiaoping's greatest merit was that he didn't drag down Mao Zedong the way Khrushchev had with Stalin, but had only criticized the mistakes of Mao. He thus had saved the historical position of the extravagant late chairman, the regime, and himself. The message was clear: Jiang Zemin extolled Deng Xiaoping to the sky and would preserve his legacy—but would redefine Dengism in light of new circumstances. These required more attention to the struggle against corruption and how the growing gap between the nouveau riche and the poor should be bridged.

THE CORE

SINCE HE WAS CALLED to national leadership from his post as municipal party secretary in Shanghai during the turbulent spring of 1989, Jiang Zemin has had eight years to consolidate his position. The widely held notion of the early 1990s that he was merely a transitional figure had become outdated by 1995 when he showed his mettle by having his main rival—the tough, powerful party secretary of Beijing, Chen Xitong—ousted from the top leadership and arrested for corruption and a "dissolute lifestyle." Jiang Zemin, whose standard honorific is "core of the third-generation leadership," has been the first formal party leader to preside over two party congresses since Mao Zedong.

In a new hidden struggle behind the scenes, the number three man in the hierarchy, the mysterious Qiao Shi, chairman of the National People's Congress, also considered a rival of Jiang's, spectacularly lost his seat on the standing committee of the Politburo and Central Committee during the congress in September 1997. No explanation whatsoever was given, illustrating how far the party is still removed from transparency and accountability. The Chinese media hinted that Qiao is too old, but at seventy-three he is only two years older than Jiang himself. Few Chinese regret the departure of Qiao Shi for policy or personal reasons, but the abrupt, secretive way in which he was forced out is considered a setback for the cause of political reform that has slowly returned as a topic for debate on the national agenda.

ECONOMIC BREAKTHROUGH

THE LACK OF PROGRESS in the political field at the Party Congress was amply compensated for by a new breakthrough in the economic field in 1997. Key economic reforms of state-owned enterprises (SOEs) and banks had been lagging during 1994–1996, mainly because of concerns over massive layoffs as a result of bankruptcies and mergers. According to the blueprint for the transformation to the socialist market economy, announced in 1993, state-owned enterprises were to become "modern corporations" with the state continuing its ownership role and assuming a new role as a majority share-holder, leaving the rest of the shares for trading in stock exchanges. "Corpo-ratization" (*gongsihua* in Chinese) meant partial de facto privatization but not de jure: Public ownership would put the socialist system in jeopardy, so shareholders would acquire de facto property rights without being able to exercise them. During the last few years, in any case, only limited progress has been made with corporatization due to strong leftist ideological oppo-sition, vested interests, lack of clarity about property rights, and concerns about social unrest.

Although 1995 was meant to be the critical year for reform of the state sector, it turned out to be a year of slowing down rather than breakthrough. Since SOEs had more dramatic losses in 1996, the State Commission for Re-structuring the Economy decided to extend the length of the 1996 "trial pe-riod" for the corporatization until the end of 1997. More than 80 percent of the one thousand enterprises selected to test the modern enterprise system preferred the old system of full state ownership with the state as single shareholder and the chairman of the board of directors doubling as general manager.

This, of course, is hardly surprising. Most factory managers in China are Soviet-style engineers without expertise in modern financial management, which explains their reluctance to have a board of directors and outside shareholders in a superior position. Under the old system, they had a soft budget and could use their connections to plug the leaks; guarantee supplies of raw materials, energy, and credit; cover up fraud and theft; use state funds for luxurious meals, travel, and entertainment; and manipulate financial re-ports and falsify statistics to ensure their promotion. Many if not most of them would prefer to keep it that way.

Progress has therefore remained slow. Only 5 percent of large SOEs had been corporatized by 1996. SOEs still account for one-third of industrial output, two-thirds of urban employment, and more than half of invest-ments in fixed assets. In 1996, about 50 percent of them were loss making, their losses being propped up by subsidies and cheap credits from state banks. Bank loans account for 80 percent of the assets of state enterprises and 95 percent of their working capital. The net value of the four major state commercial banks is negative, and it is getting worse because they still face the requirement of lending to numerous projects selected by the State Planning Commission, instead of according to commercial criteria. Major bank insolvency in China is looking more and more likely.

DENG XIAOPING THEORY

BY THE END OF 1996 and into early 1997, economic reform was at an impasse and international economists wondered whether the regime would have the political will and energy to break it. Deng Xiaoping's reformist legacy was under systematic attack by leftist ideologues and orthodox Marxist economists.

During 1996, many observers still perceived Jiang Zemin as sympathetic to leftists. After Deng's death, however, Jiang redefined his role as the defender of the Deng reforms. On May 29, 1997, Jiang delivered a startling speech at a graduation ceremony for senior cadres at the Central Party School. It was entitled "Upholding the Great Banner of Deng Xiaoping's Theory on Building Socialism with Chinese Characteristics, Seizing Current Opportunities, and Making Bold Explorations to Advance Our Cause to the Twenty-first Century." It advocated exactly the opposite of what the leftists had fought for, short of all out privatization, which remained anathema. The speech set the path for the important party congress in September during which Jiang announced a new reformist breakthrough.

What appears to have swayed Jiang was realism and a sense of increasing urgency. In the preamble of his congress speech he said,

> As the new century approaches, we are faced with severe challenges and even more with unprecedented favorable conditions and excellent opportunities. We must soberly realize that international competition has become increasingly fierce and that our gap behind developed countries . . . is putting great pressure on us. . . . We must fully realize that peace and development have become the main theme in the contemporary world. . . .'

The congress established Deng Xiaoping theory as its guiding ideology by explicitly stipulating in the party constitution that the Chinese Communist Party takes Marxism-Leninism, Mao Zedong thought, and Deng Xiaoping theory as its guide to action. Jiang described Deng Xiaoping theory as "the Marxism of present-day China . . . a scientific system of building socialism with Chinese characteristics" of which the "three benefits" are the basic criteria—that is, benefiting the productive forces of the socialist society, augmenting the overall strength of the socialist state, and improving the living standard.' Deng Xiaoping's most famous aphorism of the early

1960s—"It doesn't matter whether the cat is black or white, as long as it catches mice"—had now been redefined by communist reformists and entrepreneurs alike as: "It doesn't matter whether the state is socialist or capitalist as long as it is strong!"

Jiang also revived the old ideological concept that China remained "in the primary stage of socialism." First introduced by his predecessor, Zhao Ziyang, in 1987 to overcome leftist opposition, this notion holds that Chinese socialism had emerged from the womb of a semi-colonial, semi-feudal society, with the productive forces lagging far behind those of developed capitalist countries. Capitalist practices should therefore be allowed during a very long primary stage before proceeding to real socialism. During the primary stage of socialism economies of diverse ownership should develop simultaneously, with public ownership nonetheless remaining as the main component.

In using the concept, Jiang showed surprising flexibility and ambiguity on the way public assets should dominate: "Dominance should feature in quantitative terms, but more so in terms of improved quality." Jiang accepted that the state could no longer dominate a broad assortment of industries and was satisfied as long as the state-owned sector was in a dominant position in major industries and key areas that concern the lifeblood of the national economy (such as steel, oil, mining, and grain).

> On the premise that China keeps public ownership in the dominant position, that the state controls the lifeblood of the national economy and that the state-owned sector has stronger control power and is more competitive, even if the state-owned sector accounts for a smaller proportion of the economy, this will not affect the socialist nature of our country.[3]

Jiang expressed support for "a large number of diverse forms of joint stock partnerships in the urban and rural areas," noting that China would set up highly competitive large enterprise groups with transregional, cross-ownership, and transnational operations. It would also accelerate the pace in relaxing control over small SOEs and invigorating them through reorganization, association, merger, leasing, contract operation, joint stock partnership, or sell-off. Structural readjustment, personnel mobility, and layoffs would be inevitable but this would be, fundamentally speaking, good for economic development and the long-term interests of the working class.

Jiang's words sound powerful, but talk is cheap. Given the very limited progress in reform since the watershed corporatization blueprint of 1993, skeptics will understandably ask, why should we expect more this time? In fact, several reasons exist for taking Jiang at his word.

One misconception about the 50 percent losses in the state sector, for example, is that most of these losses are incurred by the old big behemoths. In fact, 90 percent of these losses are suffered by small SOEs managed by local governments; nobody wants to buy them at auctions. The new breakthrough plan is now that the bulk of these 300,000-odd small enterprises will introduce shareholding, not at stock exchanges but to employees—and this so-called "stock cooperative system" (*gufen hezuo zhi*) is the most popular of all the reform models. It is flexible and, because it is implemented locally, it can be varied according to local circumstances and local vested interests. It amounts to privatization, but to use that name would be to provoke leftist attacks on the whole scope of reforms.

Interestingly, the Chinese word for privatization—*siyouhua*—carries negative connotations of promoting egoism and greed. The issue is therefore not only ideological but also cultural. Even in Taiwan where many state enterprises have been privatized, it is called *minyinghua*, or "civilianize." In China other obfuscating terms are preferred such as "diversification of property rights" and "ownership reform."

On the other hand, one very significant difference between Chinese-style privatization and the so-called real privatization in the former Soviet Union and Eastern Europe will make the practice more viable in China. In Eastern Europe, workers got vouchers and became co-owners of enterprises without contributing anything but their labor. In China, there are huge private savings—4 trillion yuan in the hands of individuals, including workers—and workers pay for their shares with cash over the counter. This massive pool of savings will inject new capital into the small firms as they are sold, thus enhancing their viability. Workers are not eager to buy shares in loss-making enterprises, but they do it nevertheless for the sake of employment. They basically invest in keeping their jobs, because if the enterprise doesn't get a new capital injection, it will go bankrupt and they will lose their jobs. In some places people have a long discussion to clarify their rights, e.g., the right to kick out old managers, the right to full autonomy. The government often yields, and in that case, things go smoothly. But when it is conducted as a mass campaign with deadlines, there are conflicts. So far it is manageable. In most cases people don't buy the shares unless the government withdraws completely from the enterprise. A lot of enterprises have started setting additional requirements for this kind of privatization, e.g., that the managers take 10% of the shares. Then they have personal stakes in the company. One of the biggest problems with state enterprises was that the managerial establishment didn't have a stake. They had a soft budget and if they suffered losses, they just went to the bank for a policy loan. This is now history, at least in most places.

Fan Gang, a prominent young Chinese economist, said that the reformists don't believe in workers' shares in the long run, but only as a transitional measure. The idea is that workers start trading shares and help to spark a concentration of shares into the hands of some entrepreneurial individuals. The consensus view of economists is that this is the most feasible, acceptable way to change the ownership structure and will keep things permanently changing while avoiding obstruction and conflict.

Ultimately, practices such as stock cooperative systems will lead to full privatization, but this should take enough time that it will not challenge the socialist system in a counterproductive way. Even if all small enterprises get fully privatized, this will encompass slightly more than half of the state sector. The number of small state enterprises is very large, more than 99 percent of the total, but their assets only represent 55 percent of the total, their tax payments 51 percent, and their profits 47 percent. In the meantime, the transformation of large state enterprises into shareholding corporations will continue, but without a clear strategy. The magic formula to accelerate this, adopted during the party congress in September 1997, was to step up mergers and acquisitions. Strong enterprises had to "marry and adopt" weak ones and form conglomerates that, by the year 2000, would enter the world market and compete with Fortune 500 companies. During autumn, when the financial and currency crisis was spreading from Thailand to the rest of East Asia, "merger mania" was taking hold of China like an epidemic. Delegations of managers from all over China made trips to South Korea to study the *chaebol* model. By October the magnitude of the failure of Korea's state-sponsored conglomerates, based on a cozy, illicit relationship between politicians, corporations, and banks, exploded in a spectacular way. Chinese leaders and economists got the message and are now questioning the wisdom of so called "conglomeratization." Fortunately, most of the mergers were still in the planning stage and they have been quietly shelved. Mergers usually involved good and bad companies. The good one would have to help out one or more bad ones. The good one resisted, now has more excuses for its resistance, and is now happy that the policy has been reconsidered.

Skeptical Chinese economists mocked the conglomeratization with a telling metaphor. They say that those who have no notion of a market economy think that if you weld a bunch of sampans and junks together, you get an aircraft carrier—but they very soon discover that the world is more complicated. Reform of the large state enterprises will from now on be carried out in an eclectic way. Chinese economists think that it will zigzag for another five to ten years before there is a comprehensive policy. The conglomerate model has not been rejected outright, but the way it had been financed, particularly in South Korea, has now highlighted the overriding priority of a radical and complete overhaul of the Chinese banking system. In the meantime, experimentation with small enterprises at the local level will be enhanced, and small- and medium-sized companies will play an increasingly important role in the Chinese economy. They will receive better treatment in terms of raw materials and energy supply and qualify for bank loans, which they could not have gotten before.

This pattern of local experimentation as the foundation for reform and change is also evident in politics. Political reform—the other forbidden P-word—at a national scale is considered too risky, too difficult, and too divisive, but at the basic level of villages, experiments with direct elections for village chiefs and councils have been conducted for years and in many respects successfully. Beijing is now giving thought to extending these elections one or two echelons higher, to the rural township (*xiang*) and county (*xian*) levels. The employee cooperative shareholding system in small, local state enterprises is the economic dimension of village democracy, and these two processes will change China—slowly but fundamentally—from the bottom up.

For his part, Jiang Zemin did speak about political reform in his report, but he mostly rehashed old cliches about "expanding socialist democracy" and "perfecting the socialist legal system by the year 2010." Nevertheless, the shift to undiluted post-ideological pragmatism and rapidly expanding social and economic pluralism in China has now progressed to such an extent that it is bound to culminate in political reform—sooner rather than later. Intellectuals in think tanks take the view that the debate on political reform, abruptly aborted in 1989, will resume within two to three years and that the subject will dominate the agenda of the next party congress in 2002.

CONVERGENCE

DURING THE SINO–BRITISH BICKERING over political reform, Beijing demanded, starting from the late 1980s, that Hong Kong "converge" with China. With the new wave of reforms one can say that China is now converging with Hong Kong and the world in the economic sense. Hong Kong will enter a new phase as the financial center for the new wave of economic reforms in China although this process will be slowed by the current turmoil in regional financial markets. In the bargain, the prospects for "convergence" of the two systems within one country will likely improve in the political sense.

Although it is premature to anticipate long-term developments, the situation in the Hong Kong Special Administrative Region (SAR) half a year after the handover is more favorable than most would have expected. Even the Clinton administration expressed a "largely positive" view of the transition during the official visit of the chief executive of the Hong Kong SAR, Tung Chee-hwa, to Washington in September 1997, and Hong Kong Democratic Party leader Martin Lee has complimented China and Tung as well. Business is in a way better than usual, because the bitter acrimony between former British governor Chris Patten and the Chinese propaganda machine is a thing of the past and because a harmonious atmosphere exists now between the Chinese and SAR governments. There hasn't been a single case of media censorship, restrictions on the freedom to demonstrate (even against premier Li Peng), or high-handed behavior by Chinese officialdom, military or civilian, thus far. A recent report by the New York-based "Committee to Protect Journalists" alleged that self-censorship was growing, but there is only anecdotal evidence for this, such as an opinion poll in September 1997 in which 68 percent of respondents expressed the belief that the media would prefer not to criticize the Chinese government.

Some foreign journalists, very critical of China and working for Hong Kong English-language media, anticipated in recent years that they would have to leave Hong Kong after the handover. They have now realized that there is no such pressure and have stayed on and operate as before. The popular, outspoken, anti-Beijing Chinese language *Apple Daily*, owned by flamboyant tycoon Jimmy Lai, has been denied accreditation for news coverage on the mainland but has yet to meet with any reprisal in Hong Kong. Even the Chinese-language monthly *Cheng Ming*, which has been assailed in China's official commentaries for rumormongering and slander, continues to publish. One researcher in a government institute in Beijing jocularly said that it would be shortsighted to close down these journals because they are a motley source of uncensored information for Chinese officialdom.

Politically, democracy in Hong Kong has sustained a major blow, but not a mortal one. The Provisional Legislative Council, selected by pro-China committees, is now making new, complex electoral arrangements that will be more favorable to the pro-China camp than to the British "first past the post" system. Yet although this represents a step backward, it isn't as bad as the Hong Kong Democrats and the international media make it look.

The cliche about the upcoming elections in May 1998 is that 2.7 million people will be disenfranchised compared to Patten's elections in 1995; the fact is that the disenfranchisement only applies to nine of the thirty functional constituencies in the Legislative Council. When Patten designed his electoral reform package in 1992, his predecessor, Lord Wilson, after consultation with China, had established only twenty-one of the thirty functional constituencies. They included the medical and legal professions, banking and educational institutions, trade unions, and so on. Patten reserved the remaining nine seats for members of the working class, which amounted to a second vote for a large segment of the population, altogether 2.7 million people. The new SAR government has now reintroduced corporate voting for these nine constituencies, cutting the size of the electorate to about ten thousand.

It is commonly forgotten, though, that altogether only about one million people (35.8 percent of the electorate) used their right to vote in 1995. To say now that 2.7 million people have been disenfranchised without further qualification is misleading. The figure is theoretical and applies only to nine of the sixty seats.

The ten seats that were indirectly elected by the (elected) district boards will be decided next year by an eight-hundred-member election committee that will be dominated by pro-China businessmen, professionals, and social groups. Only twenty seats will be decided by direct popular elections in a system of proportional representation, in which the electorate will be split in five large districts with multiple seats, rather than by the British single-seat, plurality system in geographical constituencies, used in the past.

In any event, the public will have the final say on election day in May 1998. If voters consider the arrangements unfair, they may elect a majority from the Democratic Party in the twenty seats open to direct elections, and a few democrats may win seats in some of the functional constituencies. According to all political observers, and also Martin Lee himself, the democrats and their allies will return as a significant, but not a dominant force in Hong Kong politics.

JUST AND HONORABLE DIPLOMACY

THE HONG KONG HANDOVER has major implications for the future of relations across the Taiwan Straits. Taiwan's most painful trauma is its diplomatic isolation. China has now started portraying Tung Chee-hwa as an example of how Taiwan's foreign relations between the two sides could evolve after reunification. Since the handover, Tung has visited many foreign countries (Malaysia, Singapore, the United States, Belgium, the United Kingdom, Japan, and Canada) and he was received everywhere as a de facto head of state. China's news agency for Hong Kong, *Zhongguo Tongxun She,* commented tellingly:

Tung Chee-hwa, chief executive of the Hong Kong SAR, has proceeded with his overseas tours justly and honorably, and returned openly and legally. . . . In comparison to this, Lee Teng-hui's foreign tours proceeded in the manner of so-called "vacation diplomacy" or "alumni diplomacy," leaving the impression that he was surreptitiously visiting foreign countries. . . . Comparing the Hong Kong and Taiwan leaders' foreign tours, we can draw this conclusion: only by returning to the motherland's embrace can Taiwan procure a broader arena for its activities.

Cross Straits relations still have not recovered from the military tension and mutual recrimination following President Lee Teng-hui's controversial visit to his alma mater, Cornell University, in Ithaca, New York, in June 1995. The institutionalized dialogue between the two government-sponsored "unofficial" bodies, the Taiwan Straits Exchange Foundation (SEF) and the mainland Association for Relations Across the Taiwan Straits (ARATS), was broken off after Lee's U.S. visit, and only occasionally has contact taken place since, and never higher than at the deputy secretary general level. China is unshakable in its demand that meaningful talks can resume only if Taiwan returns to the "one China" principle. In 1992, SEF and ARATS agreed to disagree about this, and both stuck to their own definition of "one China." Beijing obviously insists that "one China" is identical to the People's Republic of China, but for Taipei it means a reformed, post-communist democratic China in the (distant?) future. Since Lee Teng-hui moved to enlarge Taiwan's diplomatic arena in 1995, China is more vehement than ever in branding Taiwan's unrelenting diplomatic struggle to buy recognition from impoverished third world countries as a plot to create "two Chinas." A new "two China" scheme in Beijing's perception is Taiwan's gradual elimination of its provincial government. Taiwan has two governments, whose responsibilities partly overlap. One is the national or central government of the Republic of China, residing in the "temporary" capital of Taipei and theoretically still claiming jurisdiction over all of the Chinese mainland, including internationally recognized (Outer) Mongolia. The other is the government of Taiwan Province in the provincial capital of Taichung. During Chiang Kai-shek's lifetime, the idea was that the national government would reconquer the mainland, return to its mainland capital of Nanking, and the provincial government would then be in place to take over Taiwan province. During the National Development Conference in December 1996, President Lee Teng-hui submitted proposals to freeze provincial elections and progressively eliminate the province, because it was a huge waste of money. The elected governor, second generation mainlander James Soong, and Beijing are equally opposed to the impending moves: Soong because he is losing his elected office, and Beijing because the moves remove a powerful symbol of Taiwan's status as a province of China.

In one odd development, President Jiang Zemin surprised Taiwan in March 1997 with the "generous" offer of a new job for a Taiwanese leader: to become vice president of the People's Republic of China. Taiwanese intellectuals were shocked because Jiang's offer amounted to crude negation of Taiwan's proudest achievement, democracy. In present-day Taiwan, no one can assume a leadership post without being elected, while in China, posts are still handed down—and withdrawn—by imperial decree.

Yet China and Taiwan have continued to draw a bit closer even amid the bluster. Shipping links across the Straits were finally established in April 1997, in anticipation of the termination of Hong Kong as an avenue for indirect mainland–Taiwan interaction. The new trade link is limited to the major Taiwanese port of Kaohsiung and the two secondary mainland port cities of Fuzhou and Xiamen in Fujian Province. Taiwan maintains that the link is legally still "indirect," because mainland cargos will not be allowed to go through Taiwanese customs but will be processed through what is called an "offshore transshipment center." Even now, most outbound cargo from Taiwan to the mainland continues to pass through Hong Kong, which has been designated a "special area" of China by a new Taiwanese law, the Hong Kong and Macau Relations Act. The act formalizes the "one country–two systems" concept for China, Hong Kong, and Macau, thus ensuring maintenance of the status quo—trade, finance, investment, transport, and cultural links with the SAR and indirectly with China.

The first wave of Taiwanese investments in the mainland started in 1988 and amounted to the relocation of Taiwan's low-grade, labor-intensive industries—shoes, textiles, plastics, and toys—to the mainland's southeastern coastal provinces. Larger companies who made higher-grade investments in all of eastern and northern China undertook the second wave. Concerned that Taiwan would become too dependent on the mainland, the Taipei government tightened restrictions on trade and investment in 1994, encouraging diversification of investment targets to Southeast Asia and, more recently, to countries where Taiwan still has diplomatic representation, such as Central America, the Caribbean, and Paraguay. This policy disregards market forces, and has managed to reduce investment on the mainland by a paltry 2 percent. It failed to bring down trade, still largely indirect, through Hong Kong: Taiwan's trade with China and Hong Kong grew by 6 percent during the first nine months of this year and now accounts for 23 percent of Taiwan's exports.

Now, Taiwanese businessmen are eager to launch a third wave of investments on the mainland, this time in high-tech areas, but their own government is trying to block their way as much as it can. The Taipei government is deeply worried that Taiwanese high-tech companies are averse to making strategic investments in the small home market, preferring the enormous promise of the mainland.

Taiwan's biggest conglomerate, the Formosa Plastics Group, which canceled a $7 billion petrochemical project in Fujian Province in 1993 at the instigation of the Taipei government, has recently yielded to government pressure again and postponed a $3.2 billion thermal power plant project in Fujian. The newest government regulations prohibit investments on the mainland in thirteen sectors, including railways, roads, ports, airports, irrigation, water supply, power generation, and development of industrial zones. The chairman of Formosa Plastics, Wang Yung-ch'ing, is so fed up with government interference that he is rumored to be pursuing his power project in Fujian in secret, with financing from his U.S. subsidiaries. The local authorities in Fujian confirm this covert investment; Wang in Taipei denies it. In 1988, the motto of Taiwanese investors was "Move all your obsolete machinery to the mainland and keep the quotas and orders from the international market." Now it is "Bureaucrats think up a thousand restrictions and we a thousand-and-one ways to sidestep them."

In September 1997, Wang launched his own proposal to break the political deadlock between China and Taiwan. The essence of the stalemate is China's insistence that Taiwan accept the "one country–two systems" formula as a basis for reunification. Taipei adamantly rejects this as suicide and downgrading to a provincial or local authority. It has lowered its bottom line from "one country–two governments" or "one country–two regions" to "one country–two (sovereign) entities," and doesn't want to yield any further. Wang Yung-ch'ing emphasized in a recent newspaper interview that the differences between the mainland and Taiwan in all aspects are so vast that their immediate integration is impossible. As a compromise, he proposed the establishment of a "confederation" grouping Taiwan, Hong Kong, and the mainland in which the three entities would keep their cultural links and cooperate and compete well into the next century. It is an old idea, favored among many political scientists and constitutional lawyers since the early 1980s. The fact that a senior business leader who has the ear of Beijing has now embraced it may give it some more weight, not only in academic but also in political debates.

Perhaps the most promising move in Taipei toward a new accommodation with the mainland is the replacement of ineffective Taiwan premier

Lien Chan by energetic technocrat Vincent Siew. During his farewell press conference in August, Lien expressed regret that he had not been able to improve relations with the mainland. Vincent Siew (Hsiao Wan-chang) appears to have the best credentials to achieve a new pragmatic breakthrough with Beijing: as chairman of the Council of Economic Planning and Development, Siew criticized ideologues who in 1993 tried to slow down Taiwan's "Great Leap" toward the mainland. He dismissed the idea that Taiwan would become overly dependent on the mainland market. "Restrictions will hurt us first and them afterwards," he said at the time.

Since President Lee Teng-hui was banned from attending summits, Siew went in his place and met Presidents Jiang Zemin and Clinton at the APEC summit in Seattle in 1993. In 1994, Siew hatched the idea of making Taiwan an "Asia Pacific Regional Operation Center" along the lines of Hong Kong—an argument for which direct shipping and aviation links with the mainland were essential. For a short time he chaired the Mainland Affairs Council and in that capacity drafted a plan to circumvent political and legal obstacles and open shipping links with the mainland. In winning a seat in the Legislative Yuan, Siew defeated incumbent Trong R. Chai, a heavyweight in the Democratic Progressive Party and an outspoken advocate of Taiwan's independence. This did not go unnoticed in Beijing, where Chai, a former leader of the "World United Formosans for Independence" in the United States, was high on the black list.

Whether Siew can be successful in bringing about quick détente with the mainland will depend on the room for maneuver that President Lee gives him and on needed gestures of flexibility and magnanimity by Beijing. The mainland should return to the broader "one China" definition and resume a dialogue on economic and nonpolitical issues without preconditions.

However, the dynamics of Taiwan's democratic politics may soon render China's monolithic, axiomatic approach to the problem outdated and inadequate. In December 1997 elections for Taiwan's twenty-three city mayors and county chiefs, the Democratic Progressive Party (DPP) won twelve local posts, leaving the Kuomintang with only eight (the remaining three went to independents). This shocking loss bodes ill for the Kuomintang's continued grip on national power; the party's defeat in parliamentary elections in 1998 and presidential elections in 2000 is now a distinct possibility. China will then have to deal with the DPP, which is about as committed to the "one China" concept as the Communist Party is to Marxist dogma—which is to say, not at all. DPP leaders continue to advocate self determination and a referendum on Taiwan independence, but in the wake of their electoral victory they have assured the people of Taiwan and the United States that they will not set the island on a collision course with the mainland.

THE ASIAN FINANCIAL CRISIS

ONE UNEXPECTED EXTERNAL FACTOR that is likely to draw the three Chinese economies closer together is the East Asian financial crisis. Since the three Chinas—and also Singapore, which is ethnically Chinese to a predominant degree—have more balanced economic structures than the other Asian countries (thanks primarily to their high domestic savings rates, low debts, and huge reserves), they weathered the storm much better than non-Chinese Asia. The Chinese and Taiwanese currencies are not convertible on the capital account, which made them invulnerable to attacks by hedge funds and currency speculators. Nor did the Hong Kong dollar fall at first, because the SAR government showed strong determination to maintain its peg to the American dollar, a connection that remains an article of faith for Hong Kong's monetary autonomy. The most important external condition for the maintenance of this connection is the unwavering support of the Chinese government, which pledged the backing of its massive foreign exchange reserves in case of any attack on the Hong Kong currency.

The price for Hong Kong's fixed exchange rate is a high interest rate. Combined with a substantial appreciation of the Hong Kong dollar against the Southeast Asian currencies, this will result in a drastic slowdown of Hong Kong's tourism and domestic exports (as opposed to exports from China). Taiwan's exports will also suffer, unless it attempts competitive devaluation of the New Taiwan dollar. For its part, China has pledged it will not devalue its renminbi—a decision that will likely reduce Chinese exports during 1998 by 5 to 10 percent. Before the crisis, worldwide foreign investment in China, as well as investment from Taiwan, was already on the wane; in the wake of the crisis, the downward trend in investments from Southeast Asia, South Korea, and Japan will further accelerate.

The Asian crisis, by pushing non-Chinese Asia into recession, will have the by-product of drawing the three Chinas closer together—during the next few years, they will depend more on each other for alternative markets. China will need Hong Kong more for new listings on its stock market, and Taiwan for foreign direct investment, than in the recent past.

This stimulus will not necessarily lead to full-scale direct links in the near future, not to speak of negotiations on political reunification. But it will join other positive factors encouraging some degree of mainland–Taiwan accommodation. Perhaps the preeminent factor is the stabilization of Sino-American relations since President Jiang Zemin's state visit to the United States. As long as the United States does not expand its level of support for Taiwan as it appeared to do in 1995, the issue may very well fade as the most divisive one in Sino-American relations. President Lee Teng-hui, reviled by Beijing, will have departed from the scene in the year 2000. A new leader, possibly from the DPP, will not necessarily be easier to tackle, but a new leaf can be turned and a new relationship with the Chinese leadership could emerge. These developments might coincide with the slow but irresistible trend towards political liberalization on the mainland. A Chinese admission that any reunification deal should be acceptable to the people of democratic Taiwan could then pave the way for peaceful reunification in the distant future on the basis of a new formula, acceptable to both sides. In the meantime, the China–Hong Kong–Taiwan economic "triangle" will emerge as a more unified voice in the region in the near future.

Willem van Kemenade
Beijing, February 1998

NOTE ON THE SPELLING
OF CHINESE NAMES

The pinyin system of romanizing Chinese, introduced in 1979, has generally been used throughout this book for personal and geographical names, as well as for other terms current in the People's Republic of China. Exceptions have been made for names that are universally known in their old Wade-Giles spelling, such as Chiang Kai-shek.

Pinyin is generally considered to be an improvement over the Wade-Giles system, which is still in use in Taiwan. For the most part, the pinyin system is pronounced as it looks, although native speakers of English should take note of the following exceptions:

Pinyin	English	Example	Pronunciation
c	ts	cang	tsang
q	ch'	qiao	ch'iao
x	ss	xi	she
z	dz	zang	dzang
zh	dj	zhong	djong

The "i" is often pronounced as in the English word "sanity."

The Wade-Giles system has been used for Taiwanese names, and Hong Kong names have been rendered in the locally used transliteration of the South Chinese Cantonese dialect.

In Chinese names, the family name comes first, e.g., President Jiang Zemin is not Mr. Zemin, but Mr. Jiang. Chinese who come into daily contact with Westerners often choose a Western first name, such as Joe Zhang. Chinese living in the West who do not use a Western first name often put their Chinese given names first, one example being the political scientist Huang Yasheng, who calls himself Yasheng Huang in the United States.

NOTES

CHAPTER 1

1. *World Bank Atlas 1996*; World Bank, *Global Economic Prospects and the Developing Countries*, Washington, D.C., 1993; World Bank, "*Poverty in China: What Do the Numbers Say?*", Washington, D.C., 1996.

2. From *Selected Works of Deng Xiaoping, 1982–1992*, vol. 3 (Beijing, 1994), pp. 110ff.

3. "The Market Economy and Morality," *China News Analysis*, no. 1509, Hong Kong, 1 May 1994.

4. Xinhua News Agency, 15 July 1995.

5. Hong Kong newspapers constantly write in shocking detail about the criminalization of Chinese society. See, for instance, *Ming Pao Yue Kan* (Ming Pao Monthly), no. 8, Hong Kong, August 1992; *Cheng Ming*, Hong Kong, 1 May 1992.

6. *Zhongguo Jijian Jiancha Bao* (China Discipline Inspection and Supervision Daily), 12 March 1996.

7. Willem van Kemenade, "Hu Yaobang was tot zijn dood populair: Gevallen leider noemde zich man van vlees en bloed" (Hu Yaobang Remained Popular Until His Death: Fallen Leader Called Himself a Man of Flesh and Blood), *NRC Handelsblad*, 17 April 1989.

8. Andrew Wedeman, "Corruption and Politics," *China Review*, 1996, Chinese University Press, Hong Kong.

9. *Zhongguo Gongshang Shibao* (China Business Times), 6 April 1994.

10. *Guangming Ribao*, 20 October 1993.

11. Political and Economic Risk Consultancy Ltd., Hong Kong, April 1994, *Transparency International Corruption Index 1995*, Göttingen, Germany.

12. Willem van Kemenade, *Asia, Inc.*, Hong Kong, November 1993.

13. "Decision on Certain Questions Concerning the Establishment of a Socialist Market Economy," 14 November 1993, by the third plenum of the Fourteenth Central Committee of the Communist Party of China.

14. *China Review*, 1996, p. 275.

15. Joseph Kahn, "Officialdom May Thwart China's Bankruptcy Law," *Asian Wall Street Journal*, 15 September 1994.

16. "State Council First Half-Year Economic Report Criticized: National People's Congress Demands to Read Central Government Account That Reflects the Truth," *Ming Pao*, Hong Kong, 31 August 1996.

17. China News Agency, 7 August 1996, in *Summary of World Broadcasts*, 15 August 1996, FE/2691 S1/5.

18. "Wu Bangguo Opposes Simply Freezing the Debts of State-Owned Enterprises," *Ming Pao*, Hong Kong, 10 August 1996, p. A14.

19. Wu Shuqing, "Maintain Public Ownership as the Main Body," *Renmin Ribao* (People's Daily), 12 September 1996.

20. Interview with the author, September 1996.

21. "China's Economic Development and Its Implications for Asia and the World Economy," *Nomura Asia Focus*, December 1994/January 1995.

22. Peter D. Sutherland, "Trade with Developing Countries Is Good Business," *International Herald Tribune*, 21 December 1994.

23. Wu Yi, minister of foreign trade and economic cooperation, "Objective Appraisal of the Balance of Sino-U.S. Trade," *Renmin Ribao*, 21 May 1996.

24. *South China Morning Post*, Hong Kong, 3 November 1994.

25. Willem van Kemenade, "Interview with Wei Jingsheng," *NRC Handelsblad*, 4 March 1994.

26. "Li Peng Warns US over Trade," *Financial Times*, 11 June 1996.

27. *Zhongguo de Renquan Zhuangkuang* (China's Human Rights Situation), Information Office of the State Council, Beijing, November 1991.

28. Samual P. Huntington, "The Clash of Civilizations," *Foreign Affairs*, Summer 1993.

29. John W. Lewis, Hua Di, and Xue Litai, "Beijing's Defense Establishment: Solving the Export Enigma," *International Security*, Spring 1991, p. 96.

30. Richard A. Bitzinger, "Arms to Go: Chinese Arms Sales to the Third World," *International Security*, Fall 1992, pp. 105–6; François Godement, "China's Arms Sales: Trends and Evaluation" and "China's Economic Reform: The Impact on Security Policy," IISS/CAPS conference, Hong Kong, 8–10 July 1994, p. 18.

31. Paul H. B. Goodwin, "PLA Incorporated: Estimating China's Military Expenditure," IISS/CAPS conference, p. 26.

32. Ibid., passim.

33. David Shambaugh, "Wealth in Search of Power: The Chinese Military Budget and Revenue Base," IISS/CAPS conference, pp. 32–33.

34. IISS, discussion paper on Chinese military expenditure for IISS/CAPS conference.

35. One of several anti-American books that appeared in China in 1996, *A Depiction of Trials of Strength Between China and the United States,* disclosed—it claims for the first time—that the former U.S. ambassador to China, James Lilley, masterminded Lee Tenghui's visit to the United States. *Summary of World Broadcasts*, 15 July 1996, FE/2664 G/1.

36. *Renmin Ribao*, 10 June 1995.

37. *Ta Kung Pao*, Hong Kong, 16 February 1996.

38. *International Herald Tribune*, 15 April 1996.

39. Speech given by Secretary of State Warren Christopher at a meeting jointly sponsored by the Asia Society, the Council on Foreign Relations, and the National Committee on U.S.-China Relations, New York, 17 May 1996.

40. "Christopher, in Shanghai, Ducks Partnership Issue," *International Herald Tribune*, 22 November 1996.

CHAPTER 2

1. According to the *World Bank Atlas 1996*, the per capita income in Hong Kong in 1994 was $21,650; in England $18,410; and in China $530. In PPP dollars, it was Hong Kong $23,080; England $18,170; and China $2,510.

2. Hugh D. R. Baker, "Life in the Cities: The Emergence of Hong Kong Man," *China Quarterly,* no. 95, September 1983.

3. Interview with the author, October 1992.

4. The most recent and complete version is to be found in Frank Welsh, *A History of Hong Kong* (London, 1993).

5. Ibid., p. 443.

6. Steve Yui-Sang Tsang, *Democracy Shelved: Great Britain, China and Attempts at Constitutional Reform in Hong Kong, 1945–1952* (Hong Kong, 1988); Robert Cottrell, *The End of Hong Kong: The Secret Diplomacy of Imperial Retreat* (London, 1993), p. 27.

7. This account of the Sino-British negotiations is based on my own reports in the *NRC Handelsblad,* supplemented by Cottrell, *Hong Kong,* passim.

8. Ibid., p. 102.

9. Ibid., pp. 124–28.

10. Willem van Kemenade, *NRC Handelsblad,* 27 September 1984.

11. Willem van Kemenade, "Hongkong was eens een oase van rust, nu volop polarisatie" (Hong Kong Was Once an Oasis of Peace, Now It's Completely Polarized), *NRC Handelsblad,* 30 November 1987.

12. This remark was made in an interview with the author. See Willem van Kemenade, "Jaar van de Draak moet Hongkong meer Geluk brengen" (The Year of the Dragon Should Bring More Luck to Hong Kong), *NRC Handelsblad,* 19 February 1988.

13. Willem van Kemenade, "Chris Patten tart China" (Chris Patten Taunts China), *NRC Handelsblad,* 11 November 1992.

14. Jardine Matheson was once again the target of Chinese vengeance because the company had lobbied for the removal of Governor Wilson and had supported Governor Patten's reforms.

15. Recorded in an interview with the author, September 1995.

16. *Far Eastern Economic Review,* 22 June 1995.

17. *South China Morning Post,* Hong Kong, 26 July 1995.

18. Ibid.

19. *Wen Wei Po,* 4 October 1995.

20. Xinhua News Agency, 15 April 1996.

21. *Wen Wei Po,* 16 April 1996.

22. "Does Britain Want to Rule Hong Kong for Another 50 Years?", *Ta Kung Pao,* 9 May 1996.

23. Xinhua News Agency, Beijing, broadcast in Chinese for Hong Kong, 10 August 1996.

24. Martin Lee, "We Have to Be True to Our Principles," *South China Morning Post,* 18 August 1996.

25. "Support for Selection Process: Democrats Urged to Join In as Public Backs Preparatory Committee to Ensure Fair Play," *South China Morning Post,* 26 August 1996.

26. "How C. H. Tung Caught China's Eye: A Financial Debacle Sharpened His Skills and Won Him Contacts," *Asian Wall Street Journal,* Hong Kong 28–29 June 1996.

27. Vice-premier and foreign minister Qian Qichen indicated in an interview with the *Asian Wall Street Journal* that there would be limits to free speech. Personal attacks on Chinese leaders and political activities that directly interfere in the affairs of the mainland, such as commemorations of the bloody 4 June 1989 crackdown, would be banned. *Asian Wall Street Journal,* Hong Kong, 16 October 1996.

28. "Lu Ping Says He Hasn't Heard about Selection Committee Members Going to Beijing to 'Lodge Complaints,'" *Ming Pao,* 27 November 1996.

29. Tung Chee-hwa, speech to the Joint Chambers of Commerce, 17 December 1996.

CHAPTER 3

1. These fifteen countries represent half of the approximately thirty countries that still maintain diplomatic relations with Taiwan: Nicaragua, Swaziland, Costa Rica, Grenada, Niger, Panama, the Dominican Republic, Dominica, the Solomon Islands, Guatemala, St. Lucia, St. Vincent and the Grenadines, Burkina Faso, Guinea-Bissau, and the Central African Republic. Central News Agency, Taipei, 21 July 1995.

2. The People's Republic of China has never exercised sovereignty over Taiwan, and this was hardly ever the case with the regimes preceding it. From 1622 until 1661 a Dutch colonial regime ruled the island—then known by its Portuguese name, Formosa—after which it became loosely attached to the Chinese empire. It did not become a province of China until 1885. From 1895 until 1945 Taiwan was a Japanese colony, and was handed over to the Republic of China after the Japanese capitulation. The formal transfer of sovereignty from Japan to the Republic of China was not sealed until the signing of the peace treaty with Japan in 1952.

3. Tibet and Outer Mongolia declared their independence after the fall of the Chinese empire in 1911. Tibet's independence has never been recognized by any other country, but Mongolia was successful in consolidating its independence in 1924 as the first "Soviet satellite." The weak Chinese governments did not accept this, however, and as a result the status of Mongolia dominated the negotiations in July 1945 between Stalin, T. V. Soong (Chiang Kai-shek's brother-in-law and minister of foreign affairs), and Chiang Ching-kuo (Chiang Kai-shek's son) concerning a (Nationalist) Chinese-Russian friendship treaty. Chiang demanded the restoration of Chinese rule in Mongolia, but Stalin would not relinquish his satellite out of fear for the security of Siberia. Chiang asked for and received a promise from Stalin that, immediately after the Japanese capitulation, Soviet troops would help China to restore its authority in Manchuria, and that Stalin would also help in bringing the Chinese Communist armies under the authority of the Nationalist Chinese government. In exchange for this, Chiang recognized Mongolia's independence. Stalin kept his troops stationed in Manchuria until May 1946, however, which gave the Chinese Communists the opportunity to take control of the area. This was a violation of the treaty, which gave Chiang reason enough to repeal it. In this way, Mongolia reverted "cartographically" to China, and is still indicated as a Chinese territory on all the maps in Taiwan. See Tang Tsou, *America's Failure in China, 1941–1950* (Chicago, 1963), pp. 270–327.

4. Willem van Kemenade, "Taiwan: Onafhankelijk of Chinees" (Taiwan: Independent or Chinese), *NRC Handelsblad,* 21 December 1991.

5. The Taiwan Relations Act was initiated by the American Congress and passed in spite of opposition by President Carter. The law stipulates: "It is the policy of the United States to maintain the capacity of the United States to resist any resort to force or other forms of coercion that would jeopardize the security, or the social or economic system, of the people of Taiwan." United States Code Annotated, Public Law 96–98, 10 April 1979.

6. "Ye Jianying on Policy for Peaceful Reunification," *The Taiwan Issue: Its History and Resolution,* Beijing Review Publications, 1987, pp. 98–99.

7. *Questions and Answers on the "Guidelines for National Unification,"* Government Information Office, Taipei, August 1993.

8. One of the reasons why Taiwan did not make more use of the Tiananmen massacre of 1989 for propaganda purposes has to do with a public discussion still raging in Taiwan itself over a bloodbath on a much larger scale that took place on 28 February 1947. It was perpetrated by troops sent by Chiang Kai-shek from his mainland capital of Nanking, who massacred a great number of indigenous inhabitants of the island during demonstrations against the year-and-a-half-old misrule by the Kuomintang. George Kerr, the American consul in Taipei at the time of the "2-28" massacre, estimated the number of dead at "some 10,000" (*Formosa Betrayed* [London, 1966]). The blood bath was the mainspring of the movement for Taiwanese independence. Until Lee Teng-hui took office, the people were "terrorized" into silence by this immense drama. Only in 1991 did the president finally order a committee of historians to conduct independent research on the matter. They presented their report at the end of February 1992, in which they concluded that, during the suppression of the disturbances and the period of "white terror" that followed, between 18,000 and 28,000 citizens were massacred or executed without benefit of trial. Critics maintain that the report tells only half the story. The government has steadfastly refused to offer an apology but has meanwhile raised the compensation paid to the relatives of the victims to nearly $250,000 per family. If "2-28" gives any indication of the settlement to be expected for "6-4" (the bloodbath in Beijing on 4 June 1989), then decades might pass before the truth of that drama is known. Julian Baum, "Unfinished Business: KMT Still Evasive over Role in 1947 Massacre," *Far Eastern Economic Review,* 19 March 1992; "KMT Won't Apologize for Massacre," *South China Morning Post,* 15 June 1994.

9. Chong-pin Lin, "Beijing and Taipei: Dialectics in Post-Tiananmen Interactions," *China Quarterly,* no. 136, December 1993, p. 779.

10. "Refusal to Rule Out the Use of Force Against Taiwan—A Cross Section of Position Statements from Peking," Mainland Affairs Council R.o.C., Taipei, 1992.

11. Jason Hu, "The Case for Taipei's UN Representation—'The Virtuous Will Not Be Alone' [Confucius]," Speech at the Atlantic Council, Washington, D.C., 17 September 1993.

12. *Renmin Ribao (People's Daily),* Overseas Edition, 22 June 1994.

13. Taiwan MAC statement on PRC White Paper, *Summary of World Broadcasts,* 16 October 1993, FE/1821 F/1.

14. The best discussion of the various viewpoints on Taiwan's campaign for UN representation is to be found in Ross H. Munro, "Giving Taipei a Place at the Table," *Foreign Affairs,* November/December 1994.

15. In 1993 the Chinese mainland absorbed 66.5 percent of all Taiwanese foreign investments. This was thought to be dangerously high and measures should be taken to bring it down to a reasonable level ("BBC Monitoring," *Far East Weekly,* March 1994, 0323 WF/19). Wen C. Ko, president of the WK Technology Fund, one of Taiwan's leading investment consultancies, said that Taiwan, in order to effect a qualitative improvement of its economy, should continue to integrate itself for 70 to 80 percent with the economies of OECD countries, reducing its level of investment on the mainland to 20 to 25 percent. "If we plunge in completely, we'll drown" (*NRC Handelsblad,* 1 February 1994).

16. Central News Agency, Taipei, 5 October 1993, in *Summary of World Broadcasts,* 5 October 1993, FE 1813 F/1, 7.

17. Annette Lu Hsiu Lien, *Tzu Li Wan Pao,* in *Summary of World Broadcasts,* 16 June 1994, FE/2030 F/2, and 20 June 1994, FE/2026.

18. "White Paper on Cross-Strait Relations," Government Information Office, Taipei, 5 July 1994.

19. *Lien Ho Pao,* Taipei/Hong Kong, 16 October and 23 December 1994.

20. Cheng Lang-ping, *1995 Jun Pa-yue: Chung Kung Wu Li Fan Tai Shih Chi Ta Yu Yen* (August 1995: Great Prediction of the Communist Chinese Invasion of Taiwan, English subtitle: *T-Day, The Warning of Taiwan Strait War*), Taipei, 1995.

21. Michael Swaine, "Arms Races and Threats Across the Taiwan Straits," IISS/CAPS conference, Hong Kong, 8–10 July 1995.

22. Jiang Zemin, "Continue to Promote the Reunification of the Motherland," *China Daily,* 2 February 1995.

23. Chu-cheng Ming, "Political Interactions Across the Taiwan Straits," *China Review,* 1996, Chinese University Press, Hong Kong.

24. Radio Beijing reported on 4 September that Lee paid more than $100 million to buy his way into the United States (*Summary of World Broadcasts,* 9 September 1995, FE/2404 G/8). See also *Liaowang* (Outlook), June 1995; *China Daily,* 12 June 1995; Robert S. Greenberger, "Waving the Flag, Taiwan Lobbyists Reach Deep into the Heart of U.S.," *Asian Wall Street Journal,* May 1995; William Overholt, "Noisy Taiwan Backers Threaten a Virtuous Circle," *International Herald Tribune,* 21 July 1995.

25. This information was supplied to the author by Dutch officials.

26. Four commentaries by the Xinhua News Agency and the *People's Daily,* 23–26 July 1995: 1. "A Self-Vindication of Advocacy for Splitting the Motherland"; 2. "Political Hallucinogen for Taiwan Independence"; 3. "Absolutely No Space for the Existence of the Independence of Taiwan"; 4. "Lee Teng-hui Continues to Damage Ties across Straits."

27. Xinhua News Agency, 2 August 1995.

28. *Wen Wei Po,* Hong Kong, 13 August 1995.

29. Central News Agency, 22 August 1995.

30. One presidential adviser, now a minister without portfolio, told me just before the election that there was evidence that General Hau was part of a Beijing plot to undermine Lee Teng-hui and was receiving money from the Communists. The evidence could not yet be produced, however.

CHAPTER 4

1. Lucian W. Pye, "China: Erratic State, Frustrated Society," *Foreign Affairs,* Fall 1990.

2. Ou Qujia, a Cantonese pamphleteer, argued in the 1920s for the independence of Guangdong (see Chapter 13). Jin Guantao, one of the writers of the script for *He Shang* (see Chapter 10), is of the opinion that an early division of China into smaller states would have brought progress at an earlier stage. Yan Jiaqi, a leading political scientist in the 1980s, now argues for the federalization of China.

3. Li Dun Jen *The Ageless Chinese: A History* (New York, 1965).

4. At an international conference, a Dutch specialist on this period, Leonard Blusse, said, "It can be stated, without too much exaggeration, that Taiwan is a Chinese province because of the politics of the Dutch East India Company." Taiwan's leading specialist in this field, the historian Tsao Yung-ho, agreed with the essence of this, saying that the structural economic reforms of the Dutch had laid the basis for the later mass emigration from China. ～e also Willem van Kemenade, "Taiwan: Made in Holland. Schipperen in den Vreemde van

VOC to RSV" (Navigating the Unknown from the Dutch East India Company to the RSV), *NRC Handelsblad*, 27 November 1982.

5. *China and the Question of Taiwan: Documents and Analysis,* ed. Hungdah Chiu (New York, 1973), pp. 195–206.

6. Edgar Snow, *Red Star over China* (New York, 1938), p. 96.

7. Frank Kierman, *The Fluke That Saved Formosa* (Cambridge, Mass., 1954).

8. For more details on this episode, see my M.A. thesis, "Peking's Liberation of Taiwan; Sino-American Relations in the 1950s," University of Amsterdam, 1977, pp. 51–65.

9. Ibid., pp. 65–81.

10. In 1980 the mother and daughter of a political prisoner, Lin Yi-hsiung, were murdered in their home while Lin's wife was visiting him in prison. In 1981 Chen Wen-cheng, a professor at an American university who was visiting his family in Taipei, was murdered after being interrogated by the Garrison Command on a university campus in Taipei. Neither murder was ever solved. In 1984 gangsters acting under orders from the Taiwanese military intelligence agency murdered Henry Liu in a suburb of San Francisco. Liu was the author of a critical biography of President Chiang Ching-kuo. The murderers and the person who had given them orders were given long prison sentences but have meanwhile been released.

11. "The Present Situation and the Tasks Before Us," in *Selected Works of Deng Xiaoping* (Beijing, 1984), pp. 224–59.

12. Lin Chong-pin, "Return of the Native Students," *South China Morning Post,* Hong Kong, 13 February 1995.

CHAPTER 5

1. "The Present Situation and the Tasks Before Us," in *Selected Works of Deng Xiaoping* (Beijing, 1984), pp. 224–59.

2. *Wen Wei Po,* Hong Kong, 28 September 1990.

3. A systematic, encyclopedic, but rather uninspiring treatment of the coastal cities is to be found in Yue-man Yeung and Xu-wei Hu, *China's Coastal Cities: Catalysts for Development* (Honolulu, 1992).

4. Quoted from a brochure handed out at the Investment Symposium on China's Fourteen Open Cities, Hong Kong, November 1994, cited in "Veertien vrijgestelde steden" (Fourteen Open Cities), *NRC Handelsblad,* 21 November 1994.

5. *Special Economic Zones: Construction and Development* (Beijing, 1991), p. 55.

6. Willem van Kemenade, "Grootneuzen en de invloed van de Communistische Partij" (Big Noses and the Interference of the Communist party), *NRC Handelsblad,* 7 June 1988.

CHAPTER 6

1. "We Should Draw on the Experience of Other Countries," in *Selected Works of Deng Xiaoping, 1982–1992,* vol. 3 (Beijing, 1994), p. 262.

2. Yuki Kimura, Shigeto Suda, and Yasuo Sone, *Hong Kong: Entering a New Phase,* Nomura Research Institute Hong Kong Ltd., December 1991.

3. Ezra Vogel, *One Step Ahead in China: Guangdong Under Reform* (New York, 1990).

4. Harvard Business School study, quoted by Mike M. Murad, in "Ignore the Skeptics; Hong Kong Will Prosper," *International Herald Tribune,* 13–14 July 1996. The World Trade Organization lists Hong Kong as the ninth-largest export economy and the seventh-largest import economy.

5. Xinhua News Agency, 22 May 1995.

6. Interview with the author at Shenzhen University, 11 January 1995.

7. Ibid., 9 January 1995.

8. Ibid., 10 January 1995.

9. "Shenzhen Comes Back Fighting; Exchange Shakes Up Rival," *China Business Review* (*South China Morning Post*), 11 July 1996.

10. "Shenzhen Revisited," *China News Analysis,* no. 1552, 15 January 1996.

11. The *Shenzhen Special Zone Daily* called Hu an "academic rascal" (*liu-mang*); *Ming Pao,* 21 August 1995; *South China Morning Post,* 15 September 1995.

12. "Chinese Premier Speaks on Role of Special Economic Zones," Xinhua News Agency (in Chinese), 4 April 1996, in *Summary of World Broadcasts* (special supplement), FE/2581 S1/5.

CHAPTER 7

1. Willem van Kemenade, "Arm Chinees eiland plotseling in de ban van modernisering" (Poor Chinese Island Suddenly in Thrall to Modernization), *NRC Handelsblad,* 29 July 1992.

2. Lynn Pan, *The New Chinese Revolution* (London, 1987), p. 98.

3. Willem van Kemenade, "Hainan wil Hongkong en Taiwan overschaduwen" (Hainan Wants to Outshine Hong Kong and Taiwan), *NRC Handelsblad,* 30 July 1992.

4. Willem van Kemenade, "Hainan: The Newest Post-Marxist Business Frontier," *Asia, Inc.,* Hong Kong, November 1992, pp. 30–37.

5. Kari Huus, "How Special Is Special?", *China Trade Report* (*Far Eastern Economic Review*), Hong Kong, May 1994.

6. *South China Morning Post,* Hong Kong, 13 July 1994.

7. During the regional forum of the Association of South East Asian Nations (ASEAN) in Brunei in August 1995, the Chinese foreign minister announced that China was prepared to accept the Convention of Maritime Law of 1982 as a basis for settling the dispute.

8. Barry Wain, "Beijing and Hanoi Play with Fire in the South China Sea," *Asian Wall Street Journal,* 20 July 1994.

CHAPTER 8

1. *Special Economic Zones: Construction and Development* (Beijing, 1991), p. 50.

2. "Harvest Time at Xiamen," *China News Analysis,* no. 1413, Hong Kong, 1 July 1990, pp. 7–9.

3. Qi Luo and Christopher Howe, "Direct Investment and Economic Integration in the Asia Pacific: The Case of Taiwanese Investment in Xiamen," *China Quarterly,* no. 136, December 1993; special issue, "Greater China," p. 754.

4. Willem van Kemenade, "China: Taiwans natuurlijke groeimarkt" (China: Taiwan's Natural Growth Market), *NRC Handelsblad,* 12 February 1988.

5. Willem van Kemenade, "Taiwan en Fujian overwinnen tweedracht" (Taiwan and Fujian Overcome Discord), *NRC Handelsblad*, 3 June 1988.

6. Julian Baum, "Taking the Plunge, Formosa Plastics Confirms Huge Petrochemicals Plan," *Far Eastern Economic Review*, 22 April 1993, p. 75.

7. More than 90 percent of the Taiwanese and other foreign companies in Xiamen never give their workers contracts. At one Taiwanese company in Xiamen, there were forty-three cases reported of mutilated arms, hands, and fingers. Most accidents are never reported to the authorities, however. *Liaowang* (Outlook), 31 January 1994.

8. Interview with the author at the Taiwan Affairs Office, Xiamen, 13 January 1995.

9. *Free China Journal*, Taipei, 18 September 1992, p. 3.

10. Jeremy Mark, "Taiwan's Ardor for China Cools as Many Companies Hit Snags," *Asian Wall Street Journal*, 13/14 May 1994.

11. Interview with the author in the Haicang zone, Xiamen, 14 January 1995.

12. Shiau uttered these words in January 1995. Several weeks later, President Jiang Zemin gave a very temperate speech, but after President Lee Teng-hui's trip to the United States in June, a real crisis erupted with a great display of military might.

13. Interview with the author at the Xiamen Keentech Composite Technology Company Ltd., 14 January 1995.

14. Willem van Kemenade, "Taiwan: zelfgemaakte Chinese democratie" (Taiwan: Self-Made Chinese Democracy), *NRC Handelsblad*, 1 February 1994.

15. Interview with Zhu Yayan, deputy mayor of Xiamen, 13 January 1995.

16. Dong Ruisheng, "Zengchuang xin youshi, Tequ hai neng 'te'" (Create New Superiority; the Special Zone Can Still Be Special), *Liaowang* (Outlook), 19 December 1994.

CHAPTER 9

1. The Four Cardinal Principles required adherence to and upholding of 1. the socialist path; 2. the dictatorship of the proletariat; 3. the leadership of the Communist party; 4. Marxism-Leninism and Mao Zedong Thought.

2. "Uphold the Four Cardinal Principles" (30 March 1979), in *Selected Works of Deng Xiaoping, 1975–1982*, vol. 2, (Beijing, 1984), pp. 166–92.

3. Ibid., p. 181.

4. Speech delivered by Marshall Ye Jianying on the occasion of the thirtieth anniversary of the People's Republic on 1 October 1979.

5. At the launching of the Great Leap Forward in 1958, Mao Zedong boasted that it would take only fifteen years to catch up with the West.

6. "On the Reform of the System of Party and State Leadership" (18 August 1980), in *Selected Works of Deng Xiaoping, 1975–1982*, vol. 2, (Beijing, 1984), pp. 302–25.

7. Merle Goldman, *Sowing the Seeds of Democracy in China: Political Reform in the Deng Xiaoping Era* (Cambridge, Mass., 1994), Chapter 4 ("The Campaign Against Bai Hua and Other Writers"), pp. 89ff.

8. "Help the People Understand the Importance of the Rule of Law," in *Selected Works of Deng Xiaoping, 1982–1992*, vol. 3, (Beijing, 1994), pp. 166–67.

9. "On Reform of the Political Structure," in ibid., pp. 178–83.

10. Willem van Kemenade, "Brandpunt van hervormingsproces in China verschuift naar politiek: De pogingen van 'sterke man' Deng Xiaoping om de almacht van de partij in te tomen stranden op sabotage van hoge en lage partijbonzen" (The Focus of the Reform

Process Shifts to the Political Arena: The Attempts of "Strongman" Deng Xiaoping to Curb the Omnipotence of the Party Are Sabotaged by Party Bosses Great and Small), *NRC Handelsblad,* 30 August 1986.

11. Willem van Kemenade, "Peking gaat bij-effecten hervormingen aanpakken: Central Comité komt met 'leidende principes voor socialistische ethica'" (Beijing Tackles the Side-Effects of Reforms: The Central Committee Issues "Guiding Principles for a Socialist Ethic"), *NRC Handelsblad,* 29 September 1986.

12. Willem van Kemenade, "De Chinese Boemerang: Averechtse effecten van de studentenprotesten" (The Chinese Boomerang: Student Protests Backfire), *NRC Handelsblad,* 17 January 1987.

13. See my obituary of Hu Yaobang in the *NRC Handelsblad,* 17 April 1989.

CHAPTER 10

1. Deng Xiaoping, "Take a Clear-Cut Stand Against Bourgeois Liberalization," in *Fundamental Issues in Present-Day China* (Beijing and New York, 1987), pp. 161–66.

2. Merle Goldman, *Sowing the Seeds of Democracy in China: Political Reform in the Deng Xiaoping Era* (Cambridge, Mass., 1994), p. 226.

3. Willem van Kemenade, "Deng sluit zijn compromissen aan de bridgetafel in Beidaihe. Voorhoedegevechten voor komende partijcongres worden geleverd in China's meest luxueuze badplaats" (Advance Guard of Upcoming Party Congress Skirmish in China's Most Luxurious Resort), *NRC Handelsblad,* 8 August 1987.

4. Mao's ideas are not considered to be an "ism." The term "Maoism" refers to the ultra-left derailment of Mao's teachings, such as was practiced during the Cultural Revolution by the Gang of Four.

5. Zhao Ziyang, "Advance Along the Road of Socialism with Chinese Characteristics," report delivered at the Thirteenth National Congress of the Communist Party of China on 25 October 1987.

6. Willem van Kemenade, "Chinese partijleider verliest controle economie" (Chinese Party Leaders Lose Control of the Economy), *NRC Handelsblad,* 10 September 1988.

7. President Li Xiannian had resigned at the age of eighty-one in March 1988 on account of old age and was succeeded by another eighty-one-year-old, General Yang Shangkun.

8. Author's interview in November 1988 with Jin Guantao, one of the writers of the series, for the Dutch radio program *Het Gebouw* (The Building).

9. Willem van Kemenade, "China in de ban van een opruiende tv-serie" (China Under the Spell of Subversive Television Series), *NRC Handelsblad,* 17 September 1988.

10. "Neo-authoritarianism: Debates on China's Political Structure," in Michel Oksenberg et al., eds., *Beijing Spring 1989: Confrontation and Conflict. The Basic Documents* (New York, 1990).

CHAPTER 11

1. The hybrid name Wu'er Kaixi is the Chinese version of his original Turkic Uighur name, Uerkesh Daolet.

2. "It Is Necessary to Take a Clear-cut Stand Against Disturbances," editorial in *Renmin*

Ribao (People's Daily), 26 April 1989, included in Michel Oksenberg et al., eds., *Beijing Spring 1989: Confrontation and Conflict. The Basic Documents* (New York, 1990), pp. 206–8.

3. Chen Xitong, "Report on Checking the Turmoil and Quelling the Counterrevolutionary Rebellion" (30 June 1989), Xinhua News Agency, 6 July 1989. For inexplicable reasons, this was not included in *Beijing Spring*.

4. Jane Macartney, "The Students: Heroes, Pawns or Power Brokers," in George Hicks, ed., *The Broken Mirror: China After Tiananmen* (Hong Kong, 1990); Merle Goldman, *Sowing the Seeds of Democracy in China: Political Reform in the Deng Xiaoping Era* (Cambridge, Mass., 1994), Chapter 12 ("A New Kind of Intellectual Activist"), pp. 338–60.

5. "Text" of Zhao Ziyang's 1989 self-criticism: "It is more than unreasonable to put blame for the escalation of turmoil on me." In *Summary of World Broadcasts*, 9 June 1994, FE/2018 S1/1; translated from *Hsin Pao*, Hong Kong, 4 June 1994, p. S1/1.

6. Ibid., p. S1/4.

7. Orville Schell, *Mandate of Heaven: In China, a New Generation of Entrepreneurs, Dissidents, Bohemians, and Technocrats Grasps for Its Country's Power* (New York, 1994), p. 113.

8. Deng Xiaoping, "June 9 Speech to Martial Law Units," quoted in Oksenberg, *Beijing Spring*, pp. 376–81.

CHAPTER 12

1. Cited in Joseph Kahn, "Beijing Struggles to Stem Slide in Taxation Power," *Asian Wall Street Journal*, 24 July 1995.

2. Chongqing was elevated to the status of a self-governing city, directly under the central government, at the National People's Congress in March 1997. Two neighboring cities and another prefecture were added to Chongqing Municipality, making it China's largest conurbation by far, with 30 million inhabitants. Thus, the population of Sichuan Province was reduced from 110 million to 80 million people.

3. Kenichi Ohmae, *The End of the Nation-State, the Rise of Regional Economics: How New Engines of Prosperity Are Reshaping Global Markets* (New York, 1995).

4. "Regional Economic Zones in National Development Programme Detailed," Xinhua News Agency, 11 March 1996.

5. Interview with Hu Angang, *Ming Pao*, Hong Kong, 21 August 1995.

6. Ibid.

7. Ibid.

8. Concerning the central-local relationship before economic reform, I have relied on Zhao Shuisheng, "China's Central-Local Relationship: A Historical Perspective," in *Changing Central-Local Relations in China: Reform and State Capacity*, ed. Jia Hao and Li Zhimin (Boulder, Colo., 1994), as well as Luo Xiaoping, "Rural Reform and the Rise of Localism," in the same book.

9. Luo, p. 122.

10. Wang Shaoguang (Yale University) and Hu Angang (Chinese Academy of Social Sciences), *Guoqing Baogao: Jiaqiang Zhongyang Zhengfu zai Shiqiang Jingji Zhuanxingzhongde Zhudao Zuoyong; Guanyu Zhongguo Guojia Nengli de Yanjiu Baogao* (Report on the State of the Nation: Strengthening the Leading Role of the Central Government During the Transition to the Market Economy; Research Report Concerning the Extractive Capacity of the State), (Beijing/New Haven, Conn., 1993), pp. 21–25.

11. "Decision on Certain Questions Concerning the Establishment of a Socialist Market Economy," 14 November 1993.

12. *International Herald Tribune,* 14 July 1995.

13. Quoted in Joseph Kahn, "Beijing Struggles to Stem Slide in Taxation Power," *Asian Wall Street Journal,* 24 July 1995.

14. "Historic Tax Gain Reported," *China Daily,* 10 January 1997.

15. Wang and Hu, *Guoging Baogao,* pp. 107–8.

16. Willem van Kemenade, "Succes Chinese provincies in hun campagne tegen Peking" (Success of the Chinese Provinces in their Battle Against Beijing), *NRC Handelsblad,* 11 December 1990.

17. "China's Feuding Regions," *Economist,* 20 April 1996.

18. "Oppose Local and Departmental Protectionism! The Central Political and Legal Group Convenes Conference to Discuss How to Prevent Legal Corruption from Interfering with Law Enforcement," *Fazhi Ribao* (Legal Daily), 31 August 1996, pp. 1–2.

19. "Fighting Regional Disparities. Help from the East," *China News Analysis* no. 1567, 1 September 1996, pp. 8–10.

20. *South China Morning Post,* 21 July 1994.

21. Ibid., 30 July 1994.

22. Dali L. Yang, "Reform and the Restructuring of Central-Local Relations," in *China Deconstructs: Politics, Trade and Regionalism,* ed. David G. Goodman and Gerald Segal (London, 1994), pp. 75–78.

23. Susan Shirk, *The Political Logic of Economic Reform in China* (Berkeley, 1993), p. 191.

24. Stephen Fitzgerald, "The History of the Death of China," in *China Deconstructs: Politics, Trade, and Regionalism,* ed. David G. Goodman and Gerald Segal (London, 1994) p. 40.

25. "Revealing New Connotation on Correctly Handling Relations Between Central and Local Authorities: Thoughts on Studying Comrade Jiang Zemin's 'On Correctly Handling Several Major Relationships in Socialist Modernization,'" *Renmin Ribao* (People's Daily), 2 May 1996, in *Summary of World Broadcasts,* 23 May 1996, FE/2619 G/9–13.

CHAPTER 13

1. "Talks in Wuchang, Shenzhen, Zhuhai and Shanghai," in *Selected Works of Deng Xiaoping, 1982–1992,* vol. 3 (Beijing, 1994), p. 363.

2. Kenichi Ohmae, *The End of the Nation-State, the Rise of Regional Economies: How New Engines of Prosperity Are Reshaping Global Markets* (New York, 1995).

3. Ou Qujia, *Xin Guangdong* (New Guangdong), cited in Prasenjit Duara, "Deconstructing the Chinese Nation," *Australian Journal of Chinese Affairs,* no. 30, July 1993.

4. David G. Goodman and Feng Chongyi, "Guangdong, Greater Hong Kong, and the New Regionalist Future," in *China Deconstructs: Politics, Trade and Regionalism,* ed. David G. Goodman and Gerald Segal (London, 1994), p. 182.

5. Concerning fiscal relations between Beijing and Guangdong in the 1980s, I have drawn in part on Peter Tsan-yin Cheung, "The Case of Guangdong in Central-Provincial Relations," in *Changing Central-Local Relations in China: Reform and State Capacity,* ed. Jia Hao and Lin Zhimin (Boulder, Colo., 1994), pp. 205–37.

6. Ibid., pp. 218–19.

7. Willem van Kemenade, "Grote Sprong Terug blijkt in Kanton onuitvoerbaar" (Great Leap Backward Apparently Unfeasible in Canton), *NRC Handelsblad*, 12 February 1991.

8. Dali L. Yang, "Reform and Restructuring of Central-Local Relations," in *China Deconstructs*, ed. Goodman and Segal; pp. 86–87.

9. *South China Morning Post*, Hong Kong, 20 February 1994.

10. Ibid., 21 July 1994; *Zhongguo Xinwenshe* (China News Agency), 15 February 1995, in *Summary of World Broadcasts*, 25 February 1995, FE/2237 S1/5.

11. Ohmae, *End of the Nation-State*, p. 102.

12. *South China Morning Post*, 16 June 1994.

13. Quinton Chan, "Money-mad Guangzhou Beats Hong Kong in the Greed Stakes," *Sunday Morning Post*, Hong Kong, 15 January 1995.

14. Goodman and Chongyi, "Guangdong," p. 188.

15. *Zhongguo Gongshang Ribao* (China Business Times), 8 October 1994.

16. *South China Morning Post*, 20 February 1995.

17. Interview with Vice-mayor Dai Zhiguo of Guangzhou, 11 January 1995.

CHAPTER 14

1. Deng Xiaoping, *Selected Works of Diang Xiaoping, 1982-1992*, vol. 3, (Beijing, 1994), p. 376.

2. The powerful top-level leaders and Politburo members who initiated the preferential treatment received by Guangdong in the 1980s included Premier Zhao Ziyang, governor and party secretary of Guangdong from 1957 to 1967 and from 1971 to 1975; Marshall Ye Jianying, native-born governor of Guangdong; Marshall Yang Shangkun, mayor of Canton from 1977 to 1981; and Xi Zhongxun, governor of Guangdong in 1982. In 1995 there was only one Cantonese left in the Politburo, party secretary Xie Fei. In contrast, there were by then four ex-mayors and party secretaries of Shanghai in the Politburo: Jiang Zemin, Zhu Rongji, Wu Bangguo, and Huang Ju.

3. British Committee on Information, *A Mischievous Slander* (Tientsin, 1927), cited in Robert A. Bickers and Jeffrey N. Wasserstrom, "Shanghai's 'Dogs and Chinese Not Admitted' Sign: Legend, History and Contemporary Symbol," *China Quarterly*, no. 142, June 1995, p. 447.

4. J. Bruce Jacobs and Lijian Hong, "Shanghai and the Lower Yangzi Valley," in *China Deconstructs: Politics, Trade and Regionalism*, ed. David G. Goodman and Gerald Segal (London, 1994), pp. 229–30.

5. Betty Wei Peh-t'i, *Shanghai: Crucible of Modern China*; interview with Ms. Wei in the *Asian Wall Street Journal* (Shanghai Special, sec. 2), 22 November 1994, p. S9.

6. Lin Zhimin, "Reform and Shanghai: Changing Central-Local Fiscal Relations," in *Changing Central-Local Relations in China: Reform and State Capacity*, ed. Jia Hao and Lin Zhimin (Boulder, Colo., 1994), pp. 240–41.

7. Interviews with the author in May 1987.

8. "Opening Up Pudong Area Was Deng's Brainchild," *China Daily*, 15 January 1994.

9. "Jiekai 'Huaren yu gou bude runei' liuchuan zhi mi" (Revelations Concerning the Puzzle of the "Chinese and Dogs Not Admitted" Sign), *Shiji* (Century), no. 2, 1994.

10. Ye Qing, "Guanyu 'Huaren yu gou bude runei' de yixie shishi" (Some Facts Concerning the "Chinese and Dogs Not Admitted" Sign), *Guangming Ribao*, 13 June 1994. For

the whole history and debate surrounding this sign, see Bickers and Wasserstrom, "Shanghai's 'Dogs . . . ,'" pp. 444–66.

11. Joseph Kahn, "Beijing Holds the Cards; SHANGHAI: China's Financial Capital?", *Asian Wall Street Journal* (special supplement), 22 November 1994, p. S3.

12. Jesse Wong, "Long Way to Go (Can Shanghai Ever Catch Up with Hong Kong? The Answer, Coming from Many Hong Kong Financial Professionals, Is a Qualified Yes—on a Time Scale that Stretches Far into the Future)," *Asian Wall Street Journal* (special supplement), 22 November 1994, p. S4.

13. Chen Qide, "Urban Area Will Get a New Look," *Shanghai Star,* 28 July 1995.

14. *Ta Kung Pao,* Hong Kong, 15 January 1994.

15. Robert Elegant, "Their Confidence in a New Hong Kong Is Misplaced," *International Herald Tribune,* 7 April 1994.

16. *Shanghai Star,* 24 March 1995.

CHAPTER 15

1. Yue Qifeng, secretary of the Provincial Party Committee, "Research on Heilongjiang's Economic Development," *Heilongjiang Ribao,* 1 November 1994.

2. Ibid.

3. Heilongjiang People's Broadcasting Station, Harbin, 6 April 1995.

4. *China Daily Business Weekly,* 30 July–5 August 1995.

5. Press conference with Governor Wen during the National People's Congress, March 1995.

6. Kenichi Ohmae, *The End of the Nation-State, the Rise of Regional Economies: How New Engines of Prosperity Are Reshaping Global Markets* (New York, 1995), p. 85.

7. Emily Thornton, "Opportunity Knocks: Dalian Has Become a Haven for Japanese Companies," *Far Eastern Economic Review,* 8 December 1994.

8. Tony Walker, "Building a New Hong Kong in the North: Mayor Bo of Dalian Outlines His Visions of the Chinese Port City's Bustling Future," *Financial Times,* 8 April 1995.

9. *Chungang Ilbo,* Seoul, 3 June 1995; Yonhap News Agency, Seoul, 3 June 1995, in *Summary of World Broadcasts,* 5 June 1995, FE 2321 D/9.

10. Steve Glain, "White-Collar Armies Target Manchuria, Crusading Guide Leads Korean Executives on Rigorous Study Tours," *Asian Wall Street Journal,* 10 October 1995.

11. "Sha E lueduo Zhongguo lingtu (Dongbei Bufen)" (The Territory That Tsarist Russia Stole from China by Means of Unequal Treaties), *Zhongguo Jindai Shi Gao Dituji* (Atlas of Contemporary Chinese History), 1983.

12. Willem van Kemenade, "Burgemeester Jin Minxiong van Hunchun voorziet 'Rotterdam van Azië.' Mirakel aan de Tumen-rivier" (Mayor Jin Minxiong of Hunchun Predicts "Rotterdam of Asia." Miracle on the Tumen River), *NRC Handelsblad,* 10 August 1993.

13. Interview with Mayor Jin Minxiong of Hunchun, 28 August 1995.

14. Willem van Kemenade, "Voor de Chinezen in Harbin stinken alle Russen" (The Chinese in Harbin Think all Russians Stink), *NRC Handelsblad,* 21 July 1995.

15. Willem van Kemenade, "Alles mag aan de oostgrens tussen China en Rusland" (Anything Goes on the Eastern Border Between China and Russia), *NRC Handelsblad,* 23 July 1995.

16. Willem van Kemenade, "Vladivostok wil het Hongkong van de toekomst zijn" (Vladivostok Wants to Be the Hong Kong of the Future), *NRC Handelsblad,* 9 July 1995.

17. Ibid.

18. Paul J. Smith, "East Asia's Immigration Crisis Demands Careful Choices," *International Herald Tribune*, 22 May 1995.

19. Alexei D. Vokressenski, "Russia's China Challenge," *Far Eastern Economic Review*, 22 June 1995.

20. "Russian Far East Border Troops Commander Describes Chinese Border Situation," TV channel "Russia," Moscow, 2 February 1995, in *Summary of World Broadcasts*, FE/2219, G/3.

21. Interfax News Agency, Moscow, 30 April 1995.

22. 14 March 1996. Nazdratenko, the most unruly of the semi-independent regional warlords in the Russian Federation, sticks to his noncompliance up to the present day. He taunts Moscow bureaucrats, saying that if they want to return territory to China, they should hand over their dachas around Moscow. How would Beijing view this insubordination? "The Chinese are patient and understand our problems," a senior Russian official added.

23. Interview with the author, July 1995.

CHAPTER 16

1. Giles Whittell, *Central Asia: The Practical Handbook (Turkmenistan * Uzbekistan * Tajikistan * Kyrgyzistan * Kazakhstan * The Karakoram Highway * Western China)* (London, 1993), p. 299.

2. Willem van Kemenade, "Kashgar hoopt op herleving van de oude zijderoute" (Kashgar Hopes for a Revival of the Old Silk Route), *NRC Handelsblad*, 1 November 1986; "In Kashgar gaat het straatleven ook 's winters tot middernacht door" (Kashgar's Street Life Goes on Till Midnight Even in the Winter); and idem, "Onafhankelijkheid voor ons Oeigoeristan" (Independence for Our Uyguristan), *NRC Handelsblad*, 12 February 1992.

3. Owen Lattimore, *Inner Asian Frontiers of China* (Oxford, 1988), p. 171.

4. Regarding the earlier history of the area, see Gavin Hambly et al., *Central Asia* (London, 1969). For twentieth-century history, see Andrew D. W. Forbes, *Warlords and Muslims in Chinese Central Asia: A Political History of Republican Sinkiang, 1911–1949* (Cambridge, 1986).

5. June Teufel Dreyer, "The Xinjiang Uygur Autonomous Region at Thirty: A Report Card," *Asian Survey*, vol. 27, no. 7, 1986.

6. Willem van Kemenade, "In Xinjiang leven de Oeigoeren naast, niet met de Han-Chinezen" (In Xinjiang the Uighurs Live Alongside, Not with, the Han Chinese), *NRC Handelsblad*, 23 October 1986.

7. A. Doak Barnett, *China's Far West: Four Decades of Change* (Boulder, Colo., 1993), pp. 398–401; Xinhua News Agency, 31 October 1990.

8. Xinjiang Television, Ürümqi, in standard Chinese, 6 May 1996, in *Summary of World Broadcasts*, 13 May 1996, FE/2610 G 9–10.

9. *Xinjiang Ribao* (Xinjiang Daily), Ürümqi, 7 May 1996, in *Summary of World Broadcasts*, 23 May 1996, FE/2619 G/4–7.

10. Pan-Turkism is an expansionist movement that seeks to bring together all Turkic peoples from the Balkans to Mongolia in one state. "Turanism" is a romantic movement aimed at returning to Turan, the symbolic birthplace of all those of Turkic origin in North-central Asia. See Frans van Hasselt, "Er zal een machtige Turkse wereld verrijzen" (A Mighty

Turkic World Will Rise Up), *NRC Handelsblad,* 27 January 1990; Willem van Kemenade, "China en zijn Turkse 'buren.' Nog altijd zijn er volks-verhuizingen langs de zijderoute" (China and Its Turkic "Neighbors." There Are Still Migrations of Peoples Along the Silk Route), *NRC Handelsblad,* 4 November 1986.

11. Willem van Kemenade, "Peking beschuldigt Turken van onrust in westen China" (Beijing Blames Turks for Unrest in the West of China), *NRC Handelsblad,* 27 October 1988.

12. *Tung Hsiang* (The Trend), no. 118, 15 June 1995, in *Summary of World Broadcasts,* 22 June 1995, FE/2236 G/5–6.

13. Television Broadcasts Ltd., Hong Kong, 9 March 1995, in *Summary of World Broadcasts,* 11 March 1995, FE/2249 G/5–6.

14. Willem van Kemenade, "Het gist aan de rand van China" (Ferment on the Edge of China), *NRC Handelsblad,* 8 February 1992.

15. Willem van Kemenade, "Onafhankelijkheid voor ons Oeigoeristan" (Independence for Our Uighuristan), *NRC Handelsblad,* 12 February 1992.

16. Party Secretary Song Hanliang quoted by New China News Agency, 17 October 1992.

17. Song Hanliang, "Work Hard for Xinjiang's Stability and Development: Thoughts after Studying Volume 3 of the *Selected Works of Deng Xiaoping*," *Xinjiang Ribao* (Xinjiang Daily), 11 December 1993, published in *Summary of World Broadcasts,* 4 January 1994, FE/1886 G/8.

18. "Xinjiang 1994 Economic and Social Development Statistical Communiqué," in *Summary of World Broadcasts,* 5 April 1995, FE/0378 WS1/14.

19. Lillian Craig Harris, "Xinjiang, Central Asia and the Implications for China's Policy in the Islamic World," *China Quarterly,* no. 135, September 1993, p. 125.

20. The quotes from *Xinjiang Ribao* (Xinjiang Daily) are all from the *Summary of World Broadcasts,* Far East, passim.

CHAPTER 17

1. Decision Regarding Committee on Important Questions on Promoting Socialist Ethical and Cultural Progress, Xinhua News Agency, Domestic Service in Chinese, 13 October 1996, in *Summary of World Broadcasts,* 16 October 1996, FE/2744 S2/1–13.

2. "Several Factors Affecting China's State Security," in *Summary of World Broadcasts,* 16 September 1996, FE/2718 S1/1–9.

3. Jen Hui-wen, "A Perspective on the Nature of the Chen Xitong Affair," *Hsin Pao* (Hong Kong Economic Journal), 12 May 1995.

4. Luo Yi Ning Ge Er, *Di san zhi yanjing kan Zhongguo,* trans. Wang Shan (Shanxi Renmin Chubanshe), 1994. The specialist magazine *China News Analysis* provides the plausible but uncorroborated theory that *China Seen with a Third Eye* is the work of a team of writers led by Pan Yue, the son-in-law of the neoconservative general Liu Huaqing, one of the leading members of the Politburo. Pan Yue was also the editor of the hard-line documents in which China's policy answer to the collapse of the Soviet Union was revealed: maintenance of the status quo by means of radical repression. *China News Analysis,* no. 1528, Taipei, 1 February 1995, p. 5.

5. Ibid., p. 201.

6. Ibid., p. 193.

7. Ibid., p. 214.

8. Agnes Cheung, "Call for Land Rights," *South China Morning Post,* 28 August 1995.

9. Fu Jian, "State Must Tackle Firms' Debt," *China Daily,* 6 April 1995.

CHAPTER 18

1. Xinhua News Agency, 4 September 1994.

2. Ibid., 6 April 1995; *Renmin Ribao* (People's Daily), 8, 9, 10, and 11 April 1995.

3. *Renmin Ribao* (People's Daily), 24 May 1995.

4. Ibid., 19 September 1994.

5. Xinhua News Agency, 5 October 1994.

6. Colin Mackerras, *Western Images of China* (Hong Kong, 1989), pp. 37, 95.

7. Willem van Kemenade, "Report of a Visit to Qufu," *NRC Handelsblad,* September 1985.

8. Lynn Pan, "Playing Fast and Loose with Confucian Values," *Far Eastern Economic Review,* 19 May 1988, p. 46.

9. Gordon Redding, *The Spirit of Chinese Capitalism* (Berlin and New York, 1990), pp. 43–50.

10. Meredith Woo-Cummings, "The 'New Authoritarianism' in East Asia," *Current History,* September 1994, pp. 413–16.

11. *China Daily,* 30 September 1988.

12. "Record of Contending and Blooming: Confucius Shop Must Be Destroyed, Confucius Must Be Rehabilitated," *Wen Hui Bao,* 2 March 1981.

13. "Scholars Probe Confucius World Outlook: A Hundred Schools Contend," *Xinhua Digest,* 23 April 1983.

14. Li Zehou, "A Reevaluation of Confucius," *Social Sciences in China,* no. 2 (Beijing, 1980), pp. 99–127.

15. During the Song dynasty, a rigorous centralization of the empire took place accompanied by a recognition of the need for a uniform, orthodox ideology. This became the "scholastic philosophy of neo-Confucianism." The next step was to give this ideology the sacred blessing of a spiritual authority, and in this way Confucianism was transformed into a religion. During the Wei and Jin dynasties, it was mixed with Buddhism and Taoism and the three were used complementarily or alternatively, according to the preference of the ruler. The architect of neo-Confucianism during the Song dynasty, the idealist Zhu Xi (Chu Hsi), was even more deeply preoccupied with Taoism, and the materialist-reformer Wang Anshi (1021–1086) was a Buddhist. The Song materialists found no contradiction whatever between Confucianism and Buddhism and thought the two were in perfect harmony: teaching people to embrace virtue and shun evil. During the Song dynasty, the "deification" of Confucianism, a process that had been going on for centuries, was completed. One critic wrote, "The Confucians did not have all the characteristics of most religions, but they did have all the most important elements: clericalism; asceticism; the concept of original sin; obscurantism; worship of idols; an introspective, contemplative, religious method of self-cultivation; a hostile attitude towards science; disdain for productive labor—all these backward attitudes of medieval scholasticism can be found in the Confucianist religion" (quoted from Ren Jiyu, "Confucianism as a Religion," *Social Sciences in China,* pp. 128–52).

16. Lu Mingzhuo, "Scientific Appraisal of Confucianism," *Renmin Ribao* (People's Daily), 27 July 1996.

17. Samuel P. Huntington, "The Clash of Civilizations," *Foreign Affairs,* Summer 1993.

18. A trailblazer and sensational best-seller among these books was *Zhongguo Keyi Shuo Bu* (China Can Say No) by Song Qiang, Zhang Zangzang, Qiao Bian, et al. The same authors wrote a second book, *Zhongguo haishi keyi shuo Bu* (China Can Still Say No), as well as others, including *Demonizing China* (a critique of the American media's China coverage), *Atlas of Shame* (detailing China's humiliation at the hand of world powers over the past century), and *A Depiction of Trials of Strength Between China and the United States.*

19. *China Can Say No,* p. 42.

20. Ibid., pp. 22–23.

21. Ibid., p. 133.

22. Ibid., p. 29.

23. "Chinese Authorities Criticize Book *China Can Say No,*" *Ming Pao,* Hong Kong, 10 December 1996.

24. James R. Lilley, "Beijing Should Beware of the Nationalism Tiger," *International Herald Tribune,* 25 October 1996.

CHAPTER 19

1. Francis Fukuyama, *The End of History and the Last Man* (London, 1992), pp. 49–50.

2. Liu Binyan predicted in an interview with the *NRC Handelsblad* in Hong Kong (23 June 1989) that the "reactionary cabal of the cruel, devious, merciless, old-man junta of Deng Xiaoping [would] not last longer than two more years." Yan Jiaqi also declared in an interview from Paris with the *NRC Handelsblad* that within two years he would be able to return to a freer, post-Deng China (*NRC Handelsblad,* September 1989).

3. Dwight H. Perkins, "Is China Following the East Asian Pattern?", in *China, Asia's Next Economic Giant* (Seattle, 1986).

4. William Overholt, *China: The Next Economic Superpower* (London, 1993); Robert Wade, "The Visible Hand: The State and East Asia's Economic Growth," *Current History,* December 1993.

5. Fukuyama, *End of History,* p. 241.

6. Go Chok Tong, "Social Values, Singapore Style," *Current History,* December 1994.

7. *Liaowang* (Outlook), Beijing, 12 September 1995.

8. Deng Xiaoping, "Uphold the Four Cardinal Principles" (30 March 1979), in *Selected Works of Deng Xiaoping, 1975–1982,* vol. 2, (Beijing, 1984), pp. 166–92.

9. A good illustration of this is the attitude of Wan Li (born in 1916), the ex-chairman of the National People's Congress. This relatively liberal old gentleman routinely takes to the road with reformist speeches. During the first wave of student demonstrations in late 1986, he traveled to Hefei, the capital of Anhui Province, where he had once been governor, to warn Vice-rector Fang Lizhi to keep the students off the streets. "I've already given you enough freedom and democracy," he said, to which Fang Lizhi supposedly answered, "Democracy is not given by individuals" (quoted in Merle Goldman, *Sowing the Seeds of Democracy in China: Political Reform in the Deng Xiaoping Era* [Cambridge, Mass., 1994], p. 200).

Even more remarkable is a statement made by ex-president Yang Shangkun to a group of visiting Taiwanese academics. Yang asked three times in a row why the Kuomintang could not elect General Chiang Wei-kuo, the youngest son of Chiang Kai-shek, to the presidency.

In other words, in Chinese politics anything can be arranged behind the scenes. *Far Eastern Economic Review Yearbook 1991*, Hong Kong 1991, p. 220.

10. Andrew J. Nathan, *Chinese Democracy* (New York, 1985), p. 132.

11. Fukuyama, *End of History*, p. 218.

12. World Bank, *The East Asian Miracle: Economic Growth and Public Policy. A World Bank Policy Research Report* (Oxford, 1993), p. 10.

13. William P. Alford, "Double-Edged Swords Cut Both Ways: Law and Legitimacy in the People's Republic of China," in *China in Transformation*, ed. Tu Wei-ming (Cambridge, Mass., 1994), pp. 45–71; previously published in *Daedalus*, Spring 1993.

14. Gordon White, Jude Howell, and Shang Xiaoyuan, *In Search of Civil Society: Market Reform and Social Change in Contemporary China* (Oxford, 1996).

15. Author's interview with Bishop Francis Xu of Yichang, June 1993.

16. Author's interviews with Tony Saich, October 1995 and January 1997.

17. *Ming Pao*, Hong Kong, 6 August 1993.

18. *Chinese Business Times*, Guangdong Province, 20 August 1993.

19. *Renmin Ribao* (People's Daily), 21 August 1993.

20. *Wen Wei Po*, Hong Kong, 16 March 1995.

21. China Rural Villagers' Self-Government Research Group, *Zhongguo Nongcun Cunmin Weiyuanhui huanjie Xuanju Zhidu* (Study on the Election of Villagers' Committees in Rural China), China Research Society of Basic-Level Government, 1 December 1993; Gang Bai, "Villagers' Autonomy: Political Participation of Chinese Peasants," *Journal of International Cooperation Studies*, vol. 3, no. 2, December 1995.

22. Speech given by Wang Zhenyao, February 1995.

23. Ibid.

AFTERWORD TO THE VINTAGE EDITION

1. Jiang Zemin, "Political Report to the Fifteenth National Congress of the Chinese Communist Party," Chinese Central Television, September 12, 1997.

2. Ibid., BBC version, *BBC Monitoring Summary of World Broadcasts*, "Far East," S1, pp. 4–5.

3. Ibid., S1, pp. 9–10.

BIBLIOGRAPHY

Amnesty International. *Political Imprisonment in the People's Republic of China*. London, 1978.

Asia Watch. *Detained in China and Tibet*. New York, 1994.

Barme, Geremie, and Linda Jaivin. *New Ghosts, Old Dreams: Chinese Rebel Voices*. New York, 1992.

Barnett, A. Doak. *Communist China: The Early Years, 1949–1955*. New York, 1964.

———. *China's Far West: Four Decades of Change*. Boulder, Colo., 1993.

Becker, Jasper. *Hungry Ghosts: China's Secret Famine*. London, 1996.

Black, George, and Robin Munro. *Black Hands of Beijing*. New York, 1993.

Brosseau, Maurice, and Kuan Hsin-chi, eds. *China Review*, 1991, 1992, 1993, 1994, 1995, 1996. Chinese University Press, Hong Kong.

Brzezinski, Zbigniew. *The Grand Failure: The Birth and Death of Communism During the Twentieth Century*. New York, 1989.

———. *Out of Control, Global Turmoil on the Eve of the Twenty-first Century*. New York, 1993.

Byron, John, and Robert Pack. *Claws of the Dragon: Kang Sheng, the Evil Genius Behind Mao and His Legacy of Terror in People's China*. New York, 1992.

Cabestan, Jean-Pierre. *Taiwan-Chine populaire: l'impossible reunification*. Paris, 1996.

Cheng, Lang-ping. *1995 Jun Pa-yue: Chung Kung Wu Li Fan Tai Shih Chi Ta Yu Yen* (English subtitle: *T-Day: The Warning of Taiwan Strait War*). Taipei, 1995.

Chiu, Hungdah, ed. *China and the Question of Taiwan: Documents and Analysis*. New York, 1973.

Ci, Jiwei. *Dialectic of the Chinese Revolution: From Utopianism to Hedonism*. Stanford, 1994.

Cottrell, Robert. *The End of Hong Kong: The Secret Diplomacy of Imperial Retreat*. London, 1993.

Cradock, Percy. *Experiences of China*. London, 1994.

Crozier, Brian. *Chiang Kai-shek: The Man Who Lost China*. New York, 1976.

Dai, Qing. *Wode Ruyu* (My Imprisonment). Beijing, 1991.

Deng Xiaoping. *Selected Works of Deng Xiaoping*. 3 vols., Beijing, 1984–93.

Dittmer, Lowell, and Samuel S. Kim, eds. *China's Quest for National Identity*. Ithaca, 1993.

Esherick, Joseph W., ed. *Lost Chance in China: The World War II Despatches of John S. Service*. New York, 1974.

Forbes, Andrew D. W. *Warlords and Muslims in Chinese Central Asia: A Political History of Republican Sinkiang, 1911–1949*. Cambridge, 1986.

Franz, Uli. *Deng Xiaoping*. Boston, 1988.

Fukuyama, Francis. *The End of History and the Last Man*. London, 1992.

Goldman, Merle. *Sowing the Seeds of Democracy in China: Political Reform in the Deng Xiaoping Era.* Cambridge, Mass., 1994.

Goodman, David G., and Gerald Segal, eds. *China Deconstructs: Politics, Trade and Regionalism.* London, 1994.

Hambly, Gavin, et al. *Central Asia.* London, 1969.

Harding, Harry. *A Fragile Relationship: The United States and China Since 1972.* Washington, D.C., 1993.

Hicks, George, ed. *The Broken Mirror: China After Tiananmen.* Hong Kong, 1990.

Hopkirk, Peter. *The Great Game: On Secret Service in High Asia.* London, 1990.

Howe, Christopher, ed. *Shanghai: Revolution and Development in an Asian Metropolis.* Cambridge, 1981.

Huntington, Samuel P. *Political Order in Changing Societies.* New Haven, 1968.

Jenner, W. J. F. *The Tyranny of History: The Roots of China's Crisis.* London, 1992.

Jia Hao and Li Zhimin, eds. *Changing Central-Local Relations in China: Reform and State Capacity.* Boulder, Colo., 1994.

Kalicki, J. H. *The Pattern of Sino-American Crises: Political-Military Interactions in the 1950s.* Cambridge, 1975.

Kemenade, Willem van. *Peking's Liberation of Taiwan: Sino-American Relations in the 1950s.* Amsterdam, 1977.

Kennedy, Paul. *Preparing for the Twenty-first Century.* London, 1993.

Kerr, George. *Formosa Betrayed.* London, 1966.

Kierman, Frank. *The Fluke That Saved Formosa.* Cambridge, Mass., 1954.

Lai, Tse-han, Ramon H. Myers, and Wei Wou. *A Tragic Beginning: The Taiwan Uprising of February 28, 1947.* Stanford, 1991.

Lam, Willy Wo-Lap. *China After Deng Xiaoping: The Power Struggle in Beijing Since Tiananmen.* Singapore and New York, 1995.

Lattimore, Owen. *Inner Asian Frontiers of China.* Oxford, 1988.

Lau, Siu-kai. *Society and Politics in Hong Kong.* Hong Kong, 1993.

Li, Dun Jen. *The Ageless Chinese: A History.* New York, 1965.

Lieberthal, Kenneth, and Michel Oksenberg. *Policy Making in China: Leaders, Structures and Processes.* Princeton, 1988.

——. *Governing China: From Revolution Through Reform.* New York, 1995.

Liu, Binyan. *People and Monsters and Other Stories and Reportage from China After Mao.* Bloomington, Ind., 1992.

Luo Yi Ning Ge Er. *Di san zhi yanjing kan Zhongguo (China Seen with a Third Eye).* Translated by Wang Shan. Shanxi Renmin Chubanshe, 1994.

Mackerras, Colin. *Western Images of China.* Hong Kong, 1989.

Myers, Ramon H. *Two Societies in Opposition: The Republic of China and the People's Republic of China, After Forty Years.* Stanford, 1991.

Naisbitt, John. *Megatrends Asia.* London, 1995.

Nathan, Andrew J. *Chinese Democracy.* New York, 1985.

Ohmae, Kenichi. *The End of the Nation-State, the Rise of Regional Economies: How New Engines of Prosperity Are Reshaping Global Markets.* New York, 1995.

Oksenberg, Michel, Lawrence Sullivan, and Marc Lambert, eds. With an introduction by Melanie Manion. *Beijing Spring 1989: Confrontation and Conflict. The Basic Documents.* New York, 1990.

Overholt, William. *China: The Next Economic Superpower.* London, 1993.

Pan, Lynn. *The New Chinese Revolution.* London, 1987.

———. *Sons of the Yellow Emperor: The Story of the Overseas Chinese.* London, 1991.

Perkins, Dwight H. *China, Asia's Next Economic Giant.* Seattle, 1986.

Peyrefitte, Alain. *The Collision of Two Civilizations: The British Expedition to China, 1792–1794.* London, 1993.

Redding, Gordon. *The Spirit of Chinese Capitalism.* Berlin and New York, 1990.

Roberti, Mark. *The Fall of Hong Kong: China's Triumph and Britain's Betrayal.* New York, 1994.

Ruan, Ming. *Deng Xiaoping: Chronicle of an Empire.* Boulder, Colo., 1994.

Schell, Orville. *To Get Rich Is Glorious: China in the 1980s.* New York, 1985.

———. *Discos and Democracy.* New York, 1988.

———. *Mandate of Heaven: In China, a New Generation of Entrepreneurs, Dissidents, Bohemians, and Technocrats Grasps for Its Country's Power.* New York and London, 1994.

Seagrave, Sterling. *The Soong Dynasty.* New York, 1985.

Shambaugh, David. *The Making of a Premier: Zhao Ziyang's Provincial Career.* Boulder, Colo., 1984.

Shirk, Susan L. *The Political Logic of Economic Reform in China.* Berkeley, 1993.

Smil, Vaclav. *China's Environmental Crisis: An Inquiry into the Limits of National Development.* New York, 1993.

Snow, Edgar. *Red Star over China.* New York, 1938.

Song, Shun-ching. *Voltaire et la Chine.* Aix-en-Provence, 1989.

Tsang, Steve Yui-Sang. *Democracy Shelved: Great Britain, China and Attempts at Constitutional Reform in Hong Kong, 1945–1952.* Hong Kong, 1988.

Tsou, Tang. *America's Failure in China, 1941–1950.* Chicago, 1963.

Tu Wei-ming, ed. *China in Transformation.* Cambridge, Mass., 1994.

Vogel, Ezra F. *One Step Ahead in China: Guangdong Under Reform.* New York, 1990.

———. *The Four Little Dragons: The Spread of Industrialization in East Asia.* Cambridge, Mass., 1991.

Wang Shaoguang (Yale University) and Hu Angang (Chinese Academy of Social Sciences). *Guoqing Baogao: Jiaqiang Zhongyang Zhengfu zai Shiqiang Jingji Zhuanxingzhongde Zhudao Zuoyong; Guanyu Zhongguo Guojia Nengli de Yanjiu Baogao* (Report on the Condition of the Country: Strengthening the Leading Role of the Central Government During the Transition to a Market Economy; Research Report Regarding the Extractive Capacity of the State). 1993.

Wei Peh-t'i, Betty. *Shanghai: Crucible of Modern China.* Hong Kong, 1987.

Welsh, Frank. *A History of Hong Kong.* London, 1993.

Whittell, Giles. *Central Asia: The Practical Handbook (Turkmenistan * Uzbekistan * Tajikistan * Kyrgyzistan * Kazakhstan * The Karakoram Highway * Western China).* 1993.

Wilson, Dick. *China—The Big Tiger: A Nation Awakes.* London, 1996.

World Bank. *China: Between Plan and Market.* Washington, D.C., 1990.

———. *Revenue Mobilization and Tax Policy.* Washington, D.C., 1990.

———. *Global Economic Prospects and the Developing Countries.* Washington, D.C., 1993.

———. *The East Asian Miracle.* Washington, D.C., 1994.

Yan Jiaqi. *Towards a Democratic China: The Intellectual Biography of Yan Jiaqi.* Hong Kong, 1989.

———. *Lianbang Zhongguo Gouxiang* (Conception of a Federal China). Hong Kong, 1992.

Yeung, Yue-man, and Xu-wei Hu. *China's Coastal Cities: Catalysts for Development.* Honolulu, 1992.

Zhongguo Nongcun Cunmin Weiyuanhui huanjie Xuanju Zhidu (Study on the Election of Villagers' Committees in Rural China). China Rural Villagers' Self-Government Research Group, China Research Society of Basic-Level Government, 1 December 1993.

ACKNOWLEDGMENTS

It is common practice among journalists who have been posted to a foreign capital for quite some time to write a book. In my case this was made possible by the Dutch newspaper *NRC Handelsblad*, which generously accorded me the privileges of a Communist functionary: a lifelong tenure at the posting of my choice. Thus, after two years of study in Taiwan in 1975 and 1976, I spent the next twenty years in Hong Kong and Beijing, interrupted by extended stays in Taipei and Jakarta. I thank the editors of the *NRC Handelsblad* for this long and special assignment, in particular Ben Knapen, editor from 1990 to 1996, and his deputy, Joost van der Vaart, for their generosity in relieving me of my reporting duties, first to enable me to write my Dutch book and subsequently to work on the American edition.

I also owe many thanks to the numerous Chinese who have shepherded me through the arcane world of Chinese politics and have hosted me during my frequent visits to twenty-seven of China's thirty provinces. I would like especially to mention Shi Huiye, the Dutch-speaking guide on my first trip to China in 1975, who became a good friend and intellectual sparring partner. I also thank my research assistants Liang Jingdong and Song Gang, as well as Du Gangjian, a professor of law at the People's University.

Many thanks also to Pieter Bottelier, chief of the World Bank Mission in Beijing, and to E. C. Hwa, its senior economist, for their counseling on the Chinese economy. Tony Saich, senior representative of the Ford Foundation, Brigadier General Michael T. Byrnes of the United States embassy, and Konstantin Vnoukov, senior counselor at the Russian embassy, offered bountiful expertise. I am also indebted to my colleagues Zorana Bakovic and Graham Hutchings for their frequent and challenging brainstorming.

In Taiwan I am very grateful to my friend Antonio Chiang, editor and publisher, who has guided me through the intricacies of Taiwanese politics since 1975; Chin Chung of the Chung Hua Institution for Economic Research; Su Chi, formerly of the Mainland Affairs Council and now with the Government Information Office; Andrew Yang of the Council for Advanced Policy Studies; Jean-Pierre Cabestan, director of the French Research Center on Contemporary China; and Julian Baum of the *Far Eastern Economic Review*.

In Hong Kong I owe special thanks to Professor Byron Weng of the Chinese University and Professor John Burns of the University of Hong Kong; Richard Margolis of Merrill Lynch; Christine Loh of the now disbanded elected Legislative Council; and Anthony Chan of James Capel.

Finally, abundant thanks to my wife, Phoenix, and my son, Alexander, for coping with the quirks of a moody author for so long.

INDEX

coal, 271–2, 338, 385
coastal vs. interior China, 260–1, 274, 276, 343
Cold War, 40, 145, 311; end of, 76, 117
colonialism, x, 4, 17, 18, 62, 68, 143, 233, 293–4, 334; British, in Hong Kong, x, 4, 17, 37, 55 and *n.*, 56, 58–70, 150–1, 158, 300, 328, 386–7; Dutch, 143; treaty ports, 161–2, 293
Commonwealth Immigration Act, 73
Commonwealth of Independent States (CIS), 260, 344, 345
Communism, 143; Chinese erosion of, 151, 265; Chinese history of, 4–12, 32, 46, 55, 58–60, 146, 265–6; post-Deng era, 351–66; world collapse of, 6, 13–14, 76, 104, 117, 127, 210, 368, 383; *see also* Chinese Communist Party (CCP)
Company Law, 27
computer industry, 34, 35, 199, 392
Confucianism, 40, 105, 233, 367–8, 371, 373; neo-Confucianism, xiii, 368–78, 381
construction, 15–16, 37, 259, 328; corruption, 22; Hong Kong, 56–8, 61, 64, 74–6, 79–80, 82; special economic zone, 163–7, 175, 178, 187–90, 278–9, 282; *see also* infrastructure
"containment" policy, 47, 48, 59, 145
copyrights and patents, pirating of, xi, 16–17, 34–5, 46, 51
corruption, x, 10, 18–25, 46, 171, 185, 195, 288, 356, 377; Communist Party, 20–5, 212–13, 223–8, 240, 352–9, 370, 396–8; economic, 10, 15–16, 34–6; government, 15–25, 111, 212–13, 223–8, 240, 272–3, 353–9, 370, 396–8; Hong Kong, 176; IPR violations, xi, 16–17, 34–6, 46, 51; legal system, 18–25, 35, 122–3, 176, 272–3; military, 43–4; national anticorruption campaigns, 20–5, 34, 176, 355–6; scandals, 20–5; special economic zone, 171, 176, 186–7; Taiwan, 194–8; trade, xi, 16–17, 34–6, 186
cotton, 16, 289, 343
counterfeit products, xi, 16–17, 34–6, 46, 51
Court of Final Appeal (Hong Kong), 80–2
Cradock, Sir Percy, 75
Crestone Energy Corporation, 192
crime, 18–25, 171, 185, 313, 346, 388; mafia, 18–20, 22, 323, 326, 332, 358, 388, 400; Taiwanese, 194–5, 198
Cultural Revolution, 5, 14, 60, 111, 153–5, 174–5, 210, 211, 244, 263, 293, 296, 307, 331, 335–6, 358, 369, 373–4, 386
culture, 287, 371; Confucianism, 368–78; Guangdong, 287, 288–9; pop, 151, 153–7, 215, 225, 370; reforms, 213–23, 230–4; *River Elegy* documentary, 230–4
Czech Republic, 131

Daily News, 176
Daimler-Benz, 38, 304
Dai Qing, 246, 392, 393

Dalian, 165, 166, 314–16, 319, 328
decentralization, xi–xii, 9–10, 235, 257–77; of economy, 257–77, 364; of government, 261–77; history of, 262–5; of taxation, 264–9, 271–3, 275; of trade, 264, 269–73
defense budget, 43–5
defense industry, 259
Democracy Wall Movement (1978), 8, 210–11
Democratic Alliance for the Betterment of Hong Kong (DAB), 82–4, 98
Democratic League, 10*n.*, 219
"democratic parties," 10 and *n.*, 213, 219, 396
Democratic party (Hong Kong), 82–4, 89–90, 99–101
Democratic Progressive party (DPP), 106, 109, 110, 117, 124, 126, 128, 133, 135, 136
democratization, x, xii, 8–9, 11, 235, 367, 383–4; in China, 209–23, 224–36, 237–53, 261–77, 284, 354, 383–401; in Eastern Europe, 6–8, 13–14, 117, 210, 212, 224, 275, 368, 383, 384; in Hong Kong, 56, 58, 70–2, 76–91, 97–101, 151, 158–9, 209, 387; neoauthoritarianism and, 234–6; in Taiwan, 104, 105–37, 151, 153, 158–9, 387, 391; Tiananmen demonstration (1989), 237–53; village, 398–401; *see also* political reforms
Deng Bin, 21
Deng Liqun, 32, 215, 226, 227, 352
Deng Xiaoping, xii, 6, 21, 41, 105, 121, 127, 150, 154, 237, 262, 318, 374; death of, ix, 29, 181, 392, 403; documentary (1997), 364–5; economic and political reforms, 4, 6–14, 31–2, 210–23, 224–36, 261–8, 273, 278–80, 285, 287, 352–60, 365, 375–6, 386, 389–90, 400; Hong Kong policy, 61–9, 71, 73, 150; ideological about-face, 210–13; political style, 8–9, 210–11, 240, 358, 392, 404, 406; Shanghai policy, 292–3, 297–9, 305; Sino-American relations under, 53; South China trip (1992), 279–80, 285; on special economic zones, 164, 167, 169–70, 174, 181, 182, 185, 187, 279–80, 282, 308; "Speech for the Ten Thousand Cadres," 160–1; on student demonstrations, 222, 237–53; on Taiwan issue, 148, 150–2, 160–1; Xinjiang policy, 337
Deng Yingchao, 217
Deng Zhifang, 21, 356
Ding Shisun, 30
discos, 43–4, 153–6, 157, 225, 306
dissidents, 36–9, 47, 52, 109, 114, 305, 388, 390, 401; Tiananmen crisis (1989), ix, 12–13, 36, 41, 72–8, 114, 156, 170, 195–6, 237–53
"dominant party system," 387
dual-track price structure, 12, 182, 229, 273
Dulles, John Foster, 145, 147
Dutch colonialism, 143
dynastic China, 58, 218, 232, 233, 262, 333–4, 376, 393

285–9, 290; Hong Kong, 32–4, 36, 61, 68, 84–5, 125, 163, 166, 169–83, 193–4, 197, 198, 202, 279, 304, 308–9, 385; imports, 33–6, 37, 172, 186, 188, 265, 270, 289, 344; interprovincial, 271–3, 274; maritime lack of, 232–3; MFN status for China, 37–40; MOFERT monopoly, 269–70; Northeast China, 314–15, 317–29; Shanghai, 297, 299, 303; "Sino-Sino-foreign joint ventures," 171–4, 179–80, 193–205; special economic zones (SEZs), 160–205, 278–80; Taiwanese, xi, 32, 33, 112–14, 116–17, 120–1, 124, 125, 128, 158, 161–2, 173, 179, 193–205, 304, 385; Taiwanese investments in Xiamen, 193–205; treaty ports, 160–1, 165–7; WTO membership issue, 35–6, 48, 379; Xinjiang, 332–3, 339, 344, 345
trade unions, 36, 83, 180, 213
transnationalism, xii, 311
transportation, 203–4, 259, 263; Northeast China, 318–21, 325–6; Xinjiang, 339
treaty ports, 160–1, 293; reopening of, 165–7
triangular loans, 26–7
Trong B. Chai, 416
Truman, Harry, 58, 59; China policy, 144
Tsang Yok-sing, 84
Tu-Elliott, Elsie, 98
Tumen River Area Development Program (TRADP), 318–21, 325
Tung Chee-hwa, 91–7, 98, 101, 411, 412, 413
Turkey, 332, 339, 342

Uighuristan, 340
Uighurs, 330–47
unemployment, 26, 28, 31, 289, 313, 359
unification, 141–3
United Daily News, 126
United Nations, 49, 67, 85, 103, 374; Security Council, 144; Taiwan membership, 103, 104, 117–19, 124, 131
United Nations Development Program (UNDP), 318, 319
United Nations Industrial Development Organization (UNIDO), 162
United States, 6, 42, 43, 45, 73, 107, 203, 345, 391; anti-Chinese sentiments in, 47–8; arms sales to Taiwan, 37, 51–2, 78, 104, 113, 127–8, 147–9, 379; business interests in China, 37–40, 51–2, 164, 167–8, 171, 174, 192, 200; Chinese students in, 153; economy, 7, 194; media, 45, 47, 378, 388; military power, 41, 42, 50–1, 59; protectionism, 194; Soviet relations with, 147, 149; Taiwanese relations with, x–xi, 4, 9, 37, 45–53, 59, 104, 111–12, 127, 130–7, 144–9, 161, 379; Taiwanese students in, 153; *see also* U.S.-Chinese relations
U.S. Air Force, 59
U.S.-Chinese relations, ix, xii, 36–53, 210; anti-American sentiments, 38, 39, 47, 52, 130, 160,

379–81; anti-Chinese economic sanctions, 35, 37–40, 51–2, 114, 115, 171, 196, 273, 379; Bush era, 37, 49, 238–9; Carter era, 9, 49, 147–9; Chinese arms sales to American adversaries, 40–7; Clinton era, ix, 36–9, 49–53, 134–6, 379, 391; "containment" policy, 47, 48, 59, 145; economic issues, 33–8, 51–2, 114, 171, 196, 273, 379; Eisenhower era, 146–7; hegemonism, 160, 379–80; human rights issues, 36–40, 46, 48, 51–2, 114, 171, 196, 238–9, 273, 379, 391; MFN issue, 37–40; military relations, 40–53, 128, 147–8; Nixon era, 46, 48, 49, 53, 111; nuclear threat, 37, 42–3, 46, 47, 51, 147–8; Olympic Games of 2000, 38, 48, 118, 379; post-World War II, 58–60, 144–9; Reagan era, 49, 149; Taiwan question, x–xi, 37, 45–53, 59, 111–12, 128–37, 144–9, 379; Taiwan Strait crisis (1996), ix, 49–52, 134–6, 379; trade issues and sanctions, 33–6, 51–2, 114, 115, 171, 196, 273, 379, 391; Truman era, 144; U.S. arms sales to Taiwan, 37, 51–2, 78, 104, 113, 127–8, 147–9, 379; U.S. business interests in China, 37–40, 51–2, 164, 167–8, 171, 174, 192, 200; WTO membership issue, 35–6, 48, 379
U.S. Congress, 40, 46–7, 53, 80, 115, 127, 130; Taiwan Relations Act, 148–9
U.S. Navy, 59, 104, 144, 147; in Taiwan Strait crisis (1996), 50–1, 134–5
U.S. State Department, 46–7
Universal Declaration of Human Rights, 39
Ürümqi, 330–2, 334–40, 341, 346
Uzbekistan, 330, 342, 343, 346

value-added tax (VAT), 268–9
Vietnam, 35, 41, 59, 120, 145, 189, 192, 202, 378
Vietnam War, 46, 50, 58, 111, 375
village democracy, 398–401
Vladivostok, 319, 320, 324–9
Vogel, Ezra, *One Step Ahead in China: Guangdong Under Reform*, 173
Voltaire, 373

wages, 179–80, 289, 313, 386
Wah, Szeto, 77, 99
Wang, Y. C., 196–7, 199–200
Wang Baosen, 22, 355–7, 369
Wang Dan, 52, 241–2, 246, 247
Wang Daohan, 116, 121, 131, 296
Wang Enmao, 335–6, 337
Wang Feng, 335, 337
Wang Kun-lun, 152
Wang Lequan, 335, 340
Wang Meng, 217, 392
Wang Ruowang, 221, 222
Wang Shan, 360
Wang Shaoguang, 267
Wang Yung-ch'ing, 415